**Principles, Practices, and Creative Tensions in Progressive Higher Education**

# Principles, Practices, and Creative Tensions in Progressive Higher Education

*One Institution's Struggle to Sustain a Vision*

*Edited by*

**Katherine Jelly and Alan Mandell**

SENSE PUBLISHERS
ROTTERDAM/BOSTON/TAIPEI

A C.I.P. record for this book is available from the Library of Congress.

ISBN: 978-94-6300-882-2 (paperback)
ISBN: 978-94-6300-883-9 (hardback)
ISBN: 978-94-6300-884-6 (e-book)

Published by: Sense Publishers,
P.O. Box 21858,
3001 AW Rotterdam,
The Netherlands
https://www.sensepublishers.com/

Cover image: *If the Shoe Fits*, Joan Mellon, 2013; oil on paper, 7 × 10.25 inches

*Printed on acid-free paper*

All Rights Reserved © 2017 Sense Publishers

No part of this work may be reproduced, stored in a retrieval system, or transmitted in any form or by any means, electronic, mechanical, photocopying, microfilming, recording or otherwise, without written permission from the Publisher, with the exception of any material supplied specifically for the purpose of being entered and executed on a computer system, for exclusive use by the purchaser of the work.

# TABLE OF CONTENTS

Acknowledgements ... ix

Introduction: Creative Tensions in Progressive Higher Education: Theories and Practices in a Changing Context ... 1
*Katherine Jelly and Alan Mandell*

**Section I: Underlying Principles, Ideas and Values: Perennial Questions**

1. Empire State College and the Conflicted Legacy of Progressive Higher Education ... 29
   *Wayne Carr Willis*

2. Conflict, Change, and Continuity: ESC's Goddard College and British Open University Connections ... 43
   *Richard F. Bonnabeau*

3. John Dewey, Constructed Knowing, and Faculty Practice at Empire State College ... 65
   *Xenia Coulter*

**Section II: Student-Centered Pedagogy: The Mentoring Model and What It Has Meant**

4. Is the Authority in the Dialogue? A Memorandum ... 93
   *Lee Herman*

5. Educational Planning at Empire State College: Fluidity vs. Structure, Process vs. Product ... 111
   *Susan Oaks*

6. Interdisciplinary Education at Empire State College: Many Opportunities, Ongoing Challenges ... 133
   *Lorraine Lander*

7. The Cipher and Empire: Teaching and Mentoring through Hip-Hop ... 149
   *Himanee Gupta-Carlson*

**Section III: Let 1,000 Flowers Bloom: Our Students and the Programs and Procedures That Support Them**

8. "I Don't Write, I Work": Writing and Reading with Trade Union Apprentices ... 167
   *Rebecca Fraser and Sophia Mavrogiannis*

TABLE OF CONTENTS

9. A Progressive Institution Takes on Academic Support, 21st Century Style    183
   *Seana Logsdon and Linda Guyette*

10. On the Leading Edge: International Programs and Mentoring in Transnational Settings    201
    *David Starr-Glass*

11. Inherent Tensions within the Practices of Prior Learning Assessment at SUNY Empire State College    215
    *Nan Travers*

**Section IV: Organizational Frameworks: Infrastructure, Culture, and Change**

12. Organizational Complexity in a Progressive Educational Environment    243
    *Lynne M. Wiley*

13. Technology Meets the Local: One Mentor's Reflections on Autonomy and Connection in a Dispersed Institution    255
    *Chris Rounds*

14. Family Feuds, Shotgun Weddings and a Dash of Couples Therapy: The Center for Distance Learning/Metropolitan Center Blended Learning Initiative    273
    *Sarah Hertz, Cathy Leaker, Rebecca Bonanno and Thalia MacMillan*

15. Growth and Its Discontents: Organizational Challenges to a Radical Vision    295
    *Cindy Conaway and Christopher Whann*

16. At a Crossroad: The Shifting Landscape of Graduate Education    313
    *Barry Eisenberg*

**Section V: Empire State College in a Broader Context: The Impacts of External Forces**

17. Empire State College: Exceptionalism and Organizational Change in the SUNY System    339
    *Edward Warzala*

18. Current Technologies and Their Uses at Empire State College: Benefits, Costs, and Possibilities    357
    *Betty Hurley*

19. Implications of Emergent Content, Experimentation, and Resources
    for Outcomes Assessment at Empire State College    375
    *Joyce E. Elliott*

Afterword: Living the Questions to Sustain the Vision    393
    *Alan Mandell and Katherine Jelly*

About the Contributors    399

Index    407

# ACKNOWLEDGEMENTS

Many people contributed to this project. We thank them all very, very much: to Bob Carey, Morris Fiddler and Connie Krosney, for their helpful input at the early stages of organizing this book; to Karen LaBarge, for her genuinely helpful and meticulous attention to detail and for her thoughtful questions at every turn; to Terri Hilton, for her support in helping us to keep track of early correspondence; and to the authors of these chapters, for their ideas and insight, their interest in and careful attention to the themes of this volume, and for their patience with the process of bringing it all together. We would also like to thank our colleagues at SUNY Empire State College for their tireless commitment to our students and for their efforts to sustain, renew, and work imaginatively with the creative tensions that confront us all every single day. We sincerely hope this book supports all of us – at ESC and beyond – in doing that.

KATHERINE JELLY AND ALAN MANDELL

# INTRODUCTION

*Creative Tensions in Progressive Higher Education:*
*Theories and Practices in a Changing Context*

HIGHER EDUCATION TODAY: OUR CURRENT CONTEXT

There is a crisis today in postsecondary education. Institutions of higher education are grappling with significant challenges as they strive both to fulfill their historical mission of offering liberal and professional education, and to adapt to dramatic changes in their contexts. These challenges and changes are both multifaceted and related. First, the explosion of new technologies serves not only to allow for remote access to education but also to alter profoundly the teaching and learning that occur, whether at a distance or "on campus." Second, the demand for vocational and professional education and for the credentials attesting to that preparation for the workplace has increased markedly, and has resulted in a commensurate decrease in demand for liberal studies. Third, the demographics of students attending college also have changed significantly, with increasing numbers of adults and part-time students attending. Another powerful change has occurred with the globalization of education, which has spawned both dispersed organizational structures in postsecondary institutions and more and more cross-cultural interaction and exchange. Fifth, with heightened demand for the accountability of colleges and universities – accountability to the public and to the workplace – have come increased emphases on assessment of student learning and on standardization of program and curricular offerings. In addition, a decrease in public funding and changing funding models have forced institutions to reassess not only their organizational processes and systems but even their pedagogical approaches. And finally, in a context of exponential growth in knowledge and of widely disparate cultures and perspectives, the contesting of curriculum is ongoing, with questions about what constitutes knowledge, as well as whose knowledge has any legitimacy at all, raised at every turn.

Any of these challenges to the place, role and purposes of postsecondary education would be sufficient to command careful attention on the part of colleges and universities. Taken together, they signify a time of rapid, unprecedented and genuinely disruptive change, change that requires of each institution focused analysis of the issues at hand, rigorous examination of the institution's purposes and practices, and strenuous assessment of its particular capacities and strengths. And, in light of this examination and assessment, institutions of higher education must not only undertake thoughtful and deliberate innovation to accommodate a shifting context; they must also use this context to strengthen and enhance what they do. For some – the elite, the financially secure, the minority of institutions – these kinds of shifts in the landscape can present opportunity for creative response and revitalizing change. But for many – the more precariously positioned, the less financially secure, the majority of institutions of higher education – it is not so much their ability to thrive and improve but their very survival that is at stake.

Among those colleges and universities that are especially challenged in these turbulent times are what we are calling nontraditional institutions, schools such as, among many, Goddard College, Union Institute & University, and Walden University, that embrace a progressive approach (about which more below) emphasizing individualized, student-centered pedagogy; interdisciplinary and/or problem-focused study; and attention to community, diversity and social justice. These progressive colleges and universities are facing particular challenges to their academic and organizational models. When funding is drastically cut, there is pressure to grow, which is challenging for educational models employing mentored, highly individualized study – models that prize the faculty-student relationship. When accountability and assessment are the order of the day, standardization follows – another external pressure directly undercutting individualization. When various technologies fuel a parlance of "instructional design" and of "delivering content" in a sequence of modules, the potential for student-initiated, student-designed study is lessened. And when these same technologies enable access from a distance, community as well – a key dimension in most progressive pedagogy – can be undermined. Thus the very tenets of these organizations' distinctive academic programs are among the most threatened in the landscape of higher education today.

One such institution, Empire State College (ESC), a nontraditional college within the State University of New York (SUNY), is the focus of this book. ESC was founded in 1971 to offer greater access to students in all contexts, including working adults; to give students opportunities to work closely with a faculty mentor to design studies in relation to their particular interests; and to allow students to integrate their academic, professional and personal goals throughout their course of study at the College. Thus ESC's history and current challenges provide an illuminating example of some of the pressures that nontraditional institutions of higher education are confronting and the ways in which they may be struggling to sustain their progressive vision and approaches.

Throughout this edited volume, contributing authors write about what we are terming *creative tensions*, that is, the ongoing and generative interplay between what are in some ways competing emphases and values. These tensions reflect complex issues in education. Identifying them and the issues they raise can, in our view, allow us to address them more thoughtfully and purposefully, to develop more creative, effective approaches to our mentoring and teaching, and to create and/or sustain more supportive, capacious organizational structures and processes. But, as noted above, and as is evident throughout these chapters, we are mindful as well of the possibly compromising pressures at work – both external and internal – on our institutions. So, just as we need to identify and examine *creative* tensions that are inherent in the work that we do, we need also to analyze possibly undermining pressures and demands and their impact if we are to address these both innovatively and intentionally and to sustain and strengthen our progressive pedagogies and identity.

## WHY THIS BOOK?

We see this book as part of that effort. A close look at Empire State College, which has been devoted for almost a half-century to progressive adult higher education, will help us to see more clearly and to examine critically the changes, challenges and multiple creative tensions that are currently at play in contemporary American higher education and, we would argue, across the world. At its core, then, the purpose of this book is to use an examination of a single progressive, alternative public institution of higher education to help educators and students of education grapple with the complexities of issues in higher education and the challenges of trying to sustain a progressive vision in the face of internal and external pressures undermining that vision.

Using a case study approach such as this examination of Empire State College will allow us to delve into the forces at work, the problems and questions arising, the interplay of educational theory and practice and, too, the fact of and need for constant change in order to meet the challenges of the day. Can we make sense of the tensions and the changing context? Can we pinpoint the challenges we face? Can we understand what is at stake? And can we chart a course that both accommodates change and sustains a vision and the values and principles on which that vision rests? While this volume focuses on one institution, in our view it is this careful and multifaceted look at one organization that will shed light on these questions and have resonance and significance well beyond one college.

## THE HOW OF IT: A CASE STUDY IN CHANGE

To undertake this investigation, we have looked at myriad aspects of the institution, including: its principles and values, the various mentoring and teaching practices occurring across the College, its diverse students and multiple programs, and the institutional frameworks, i.e., the organization and infrastructure, within which teaching and learning at ESC take place. And we have included many voices, people in different roles and contexts across the College, and thus a range of perspectives and interpretive stances – all, in our view, essential to surfacing and gaining insight into the many issues and conundra at hand.

We are both delighted and honored that in this edited volume, 25 Empire State College colleagues have offered their ideas, their points of view, their angles of entry – their distinctive ways of thinking about this college and the challenges it is facing. We hope that, as a result of their contributions, the crisis in higher education that we experience today can be more helpfully and hopefully understood as a series of tensions, of creative tensions, that can, with our efforts, maintain their vitality and keep an alternative, progressive vision of adult higher education alive.

## PROGRESSIVE AND ADULT HIGHER EDUCATION: THEORETICAL UNDERPINNINGS

### *Progressive Education*

To begin, then, with key theoretical underpinnings of Empire State College's academic programs and pedagogical models, we should note here some basic tenets, first of progressive education, grounded in the thinking of John Dewey (1938) and William Heard Kilpatrick (1951), and then of adult education more broadly, which draws on the work of Eduard Lindeman (1926), Malcolm Knowles (1973), Paulo Freire (1970), Jack Mezirow (1991), Stephen Brookfield (1986), and others. Progressive education, reflecting not just the generally understood connotation of forward thinking, but rather referring more specifically to the particular ideas and perspective of the progressive school of thought in philosophy, has drawn heavily on Dewey's ideas of working from and toward the student's purposes; of integrating a learner's experience – prior, current, and future – into education; of engaging in ongoing experimentation – both in education and in society; and, importantly, of working toward social change and reconstruction.

Fundamentally, progressive education is student-centered, by which we mean not simply – as it is often used in today's parlance – doing what is best *for* the student, but working *from* the student's very particular experience and *toward* the student's own unique goals. Honoring and drawing on the student's context and working toward the student's purposes, progressive education is typically highly individualized. In consultation with faculty, students at schools such as those mentioned above and, for example, Antioch College, Fielding Graduate University, the School for New Learning at DePaul University, and Empire State College literally create their own degree programs and design their own studies, both identifying the content needed and framing the learning activities – all toward their own articulated questions and learning goals. And thus studies such as these are often focused, for example, on a particular problem or issue that the student wishes to explore rather than on a given academic discipline. In this model, a student may bring any number of disciplines to bear on the question at hand, integrating these as they inform the issue. And intrinsic to this Deweyan, genuinely student-centered model is an emphasis on working with the student as a "whole" person, which includes acknowledging his/her life context and the relationship among and between a student's academic, professional and personal goals, and supporting the student in integrating these facets of his/her studies.

In addition, the student may draw not only on prior experience and study but also on his/her current context, integrating ideas and experience and using each to inform and examine the other. Related to this process of the integration of theory and practice is a fundamental tenet of Dewey's thought, an emphasis on experimentation, on innovation, not for innovation's sake but for improvement, for gaining insight and efficacy as new approaches to teaching and learning (and in ESC's model, mentoring) and to addressing social problems are tried. As will be discussed below, ESC has been and continues to be an experimenting institution as it strives to serve students and to support their learning in ever more effective, meaningful, and generative ways.

In Dewey's progressive thought, democracy – what contributes to and shapes it, what it yields, how it can be supported by education – is central. As such, in some progressive institutions, participatory decision-making and nonhierarchical models of both management and governance prevail. In others, a more collaborative relationship between faculty and student is essential to the pedagogical model. When working toward the student's goals and sharing the learning enterprise, the relationship between teacher and student becomes dialogical. Similarly, in a context of shared authority, evaluation of a student's work may be undertaken jointly, with the student's self-evaluation contributing as much as the faculty's judgment to a shared evaluation of learning in any given study. And in many progressive models, an emphasis on community – again, on what contributes to and supports its development and on what it yields – is key. Thus attention is paid to respectful and productive group processes and to shared decision-making in group contexts. Famously saying that education should not be merely preparation for life, that education *is* life, Dewey (1893) believed that students – of all ages – must experience some degree of democracy in their learning. Whether meeting individually with a mentor or participating in a group study or class, in Dewey's view students must learn by doing, must, therefore, gain a sense of what it means to live in or contribute to a democratic society. In progressive education, an underlying commitment to constructive participation is accented at every turn.

Closely related, in progressive thought, to ideas about and educational practice toward supporting democracy are strong emphases on broadening access to education, honoring diversity, and working toward social justice. In Dewey's thought, social reconstruction, related to his ideas regarding both experimentation and democracy, is necessary to and should be an outcome of effective education. Thus the aims of education for Dewey were both individual and social; education must contribute to the development of both. And as progressive education has developed along with its changing context, this multipronged idea of social reconstruction has placed more and more emphasis on drawing on, learning from, and celebrating our increasingly diverse society.

*Adult Higher Education*

Turning to adult education, we can see not only strong echoes of each of these tenets of progressive education – the centrality of the student and of the student's knowledge, experience and context; the integration of theory and practice; the importance of ongoing experimentation; the emphasis on a dialogical, collaborative relationship between teacher and learner; and social reconstruction and change. We also find further development of these ideas, as adult educators have continued to examine, for example, the role of experience in learning, have theorized about the processes involved in making new meaning and constructing knowledge, and have probed the intimate connections between transformation and learning. They have as well placed considerable emphasis on critical reflection, have analyzed the place of such reflection in effecting change, and have considered what it would mean for education to be emancipatory.

Like progressive educators, in keeping the student at the center of the process, theorists and practitioners of adult education have placed major emphasis on the rich knowledge that their adult students bring to their studies and on mining that knowledge for how it can inform next questions. Similarly, just as progressive theory treats a multilayered conceptualization of experience as central, so does adult learning theory. Acknowledging students' prior experience, supporting reflection on – in order to learn more from – that experience, and integrating current experience into the learning enterprise, adult educators are echoing the progressive view. And like critical theorists, about whom more below, adult educators are encouraging delving into one's experience in order to surface the questions and possible contradictions arising and to consider new ways of seeing.

In Mezirow's (1991) conceptualization, we all have "meaning perspectives" that filter how we perceive the world; that is, we organize and represent the events and ideas that we encounter, the experiences we have, into certain schema, schema of which, often, we are unaware. And it is through examination of these meaning perspectives that we may become more aware of the structures of meaning that shape our consciousness and our lives and may develop more advanced perspectives. Thus, in Mezirow's thought, through a process of critical reflection, through questioning and discovering contradictions, adult students can – and do – make new meaning. Key here, and consistent with progressive education theory, is the notion of the student as the author of meaning, as a constructor of knowledge. Rather than the teacher being understood to be the sole keeper of sacred, given understandings, "delivering" that knowledge to the student, the student too brings rich, significant experience, knowledge, and insight to any given study. In this way, the learning enterprise is necessarily dialogical and collaborative, as the mentor seeks to support the student in his/her quest and as both are learning through this process. Yet while both student and teacher are learning through shared inquiry, the emphasis is on the student, who, in consultation with the teacher or mentor, not only gains understanding, but also makes new meaning, constructs new ideas, imagines new possibilities, and develops his/her capacities for action in and on the world. Thus, just as is the case in progressive theories of education, in much adult education theory, it is the student, and not the "teacher" (or advisor or mentor), who is central.

Closely related to the idea of each individual student making meaning of the world, many adult education theorists (Mezirow, 1991; Cranton, 1994; Freire, 1970) argue that learning can be genuinely transformative, as a student may alter profoundly his/her perspective on and sense of that world. And through such learning experiences, in transformative learning theory it may be not only the individual student who is transformed; the world too, through the student's ability to act on that world, may be changed – not just ideationally, but in particular and concrete ways.

And related to each of these ideas – of the student as an author of meaning, of the importance of integrating theory and practice, and of learning as potentially transformative – the notion of critical reflection is key. Having been extensively explored and variously defined, critical reflection has been widely embraced by educators of all stripes. Examining one's experience (and/or one's action), one may "theorize" that experience; one may develop innovative ideas or frame new meanings; and one may conceive new possibilities, may try different approaches. Harkening back to Dewey's emphases on the importance of integrating theory and practice, of experimentation, and of social reconstruction, this kind of critical reflection asks of us – whether as learners or teachers or citizens – that we probe our experience, inquire into the results of our and others' actions, and that we constantly experiment and evaluate; it suggests an ongoing cycle of action, observation, analysis, evaluation, and innovation – whether in our studies, our work world, or, indeed, our personal lives. In Paulo Freire's (1970) conceptualization, this critical reflection constitutes *praxis*. In Donald Schön's schema (1984), reflection in and on and for action is essential to constructive change; in his view such reflection necessarily makes a "revolutionary demand" (p. 338).

So, whether viewed in the strictly educational context of teaching and learning or in an organizational context or in the adult "life-world," the concept of critical reflection speaks not just to thoughtful examination but also to constructive change. And in this respect, several aspects of critical theory have significantly informed progressive models of adult education as, in keeping with Freire's advocacy for conscientization and Schön's "revolutionary demand," many adult education theorists (Brookfield, 2005; Welton, 1995; Ohliger, 1974; Cunningham, 1998) have emphasized looking closely both at students' particular contexts, and more broadly as well, at the oppressive structures and systems that reign over that context. Thus, while some transformative learning theorists have tended to emphasize individual development and change, other adult educators, while seeking to honor the widely varying identities and individual perspectives of their students, have also argued that careful examination and questioning of the systemic political, social, and economic structures of domination, within which both "teacher" and "learner" function, is essential – both to the individual learning process and to any education purporting to contribute to a just society. Through examining one's context critically, developing a more critical consciousness of the world, and, as Freire (1970) puts it, "naming the world" newly, one can "re-create that world" (p. 78). Clearly akin to transformative learning theory, and harkening back as well to Dewey's framing of social reconstruction, this is a distinctly more political view. But the point shared by all – progressive and adult educators and critical theorists – is the centrality of the student's critical questioning, which not only can foster individual development and change but also can lead to envisioning and working toward social change, toward a more just and life-supporting society.

Clearly, adult education theory and practice draw heavily on progressive education. Both attempt genuinely student-centered education; both emphasize that a broad and deep conceptualization of experience is central to teaching and learning; both honor and support meanings the *student* makes, capacities the *student* brings to learning and to acting on the world; both strive to recognize, to work within, and to examine the student's context; both reexamine authority – whether that of the "teacher" or that of the social, political, and economic systems within which we live – acknowledging and supporting *students'* authority; and both argue that education must contribute to ongoing social reconstruction and change. Similarly, adult educators are informed by critical theory, as, in addition to these tenets shared with progressive thought, many adult educators have brought in a more emphatically political perspective, as they work to support their students' analyses and questioning of dominant, and often oppressive, structures and systems at work, not just in their own lives but across the globe. Thus, while Dewey and other progressive theorists emphasized social reconstruction and ongoing societal change through experimentation, adult educators who have drawn on critical theory have added a distinctly leftist thrust to this reconstruction.

There are, of course, many alternatives to so-called traditional education. But we wanted to offer a brief introduction to some of the ideas, the theoretical context, informing many so-called nontraditional or alternative institutions of higher education for adults. Some institutions may emphasize, for example, the integration of theory and practice, through giving attention to incorporating the professional and academic realms through action research; others may focus more on participatory decision-making toward developing a "just community" within a school; in other settings, the emphasis is on reflective practice, through which students examine critically their work and the context within which they carry out that work. Yet each of these institutions stands on a body of ideas emphasizing the need to honor and work in relation to the student's experience, context, needs, and goals, and thus to open new avenues to both the individual student's and our society's development. Like other nontraditional programs and institutions for adults, Empire State College was founded on these ideas and has continued to develop academic programs and pedagogical models in keeping with them.

## INTRODUCTION

### PROGRESSIVE ADULT EDUCATION AT EMPIRE STATE COLLEGE: BRINGING IDEAS TO ACTION

From the call for its creation as set out by then SUNY Chancellor Ernest L. Boyer in 1970, to the earliest years of its deliberate construction as an innovative public institution within the State University of New York system, Empire State College embraced the tenets of progressive education as summarized above. That is, in the very structure of the institution, in its core values and its institutional mission, and in the pedagogical ways that established it as a significant alternative to conventional higher education, Empire State College proclaimed itself to be a college that championed, at least in spirit, Dewey's vision of teaching and learning.

It is important to note that, just as the social, political, economic and ideological realities of our current context have a direct impact on ESC and higher education, the historical context within which Empire State College was established played a central role in shaping the College. The early 1970s was a time of deep questioning of the institutional arrangements of American society and of what was understood by some as a military-industrial-educational complex in which the American university played a key role in reproducing a society of inequity, war and alienation. That is, far from the image of an "ivory tower" set apart from the ruckus of oppression, institutions of higher education were seen by many as complicit in a system of division, hierarchy, conformity and anonymity. ESC's creation was, in this sense, part of a broader social movement – one that included the civil rights movement, the women's movement, and the anti-war movement – that set out both to question and to reimagine the basic foundations of society. As noted above, while surely borrowing from a rich tradition of educational experimentation (for example, Alverno College, The Evergreen State College, Warren Wilson College and Black Mountain College, along with others previously mentioned), Empire State College (in some ways like its United Kingdom counterpart, the British Open University, which also welcomed its first students in 1971) was to be a new kind of college.

At the heart of ESC, echoing the progressive mindset, were what might be thought of as four calls: the call to individualization, the call to innovation and experimentation, the call to access, and the call to democratic social change.

Championing a student-centered approach to teaching and learning at every turn, the College deliberately created policies, stipulated processes and invited practices that focused attention on the student and on neither some sacred body of knowledge nor the assumed authority of faculty experts. While sometimes stormy debates about the possibilities and limitations of a truly student-centered approach have shadowed the College throughout its history, a focus on the individual and his/her academic, professional and personal goals was understood as an antidote to the systematic inattention of the contemporary university to the student's unique purposes and experiences, indeed to the self. In the spirit of progressivism, Empire State College seemed to be asking: How can the individual student take charge of his/her own learning?

Four elements of such student-centeredness became the hallmark of ESC: the shared development of the learning contract, which situates faculty and student in a dialogical relationship; prior learning assessment, which acknowledges a student's past experiential learning; the individualized degree program, which reflects directly a student's purposes; and the role of the faculty member as mentor who facilitates and supports students' study as opposed to asserting professorial authority.

The learning contract was established in the earliest years of the College as a template, a distinctive educational architecture, that called on students and their faculty mentors (their educational guides, the facilitators of their learning) to create ever-new learning opportunities, and that could serve as a guide for and record of this individualized study. As opposed to the fixity of the course and the omnipresence of the course catalog that defined most institutions' claims about what-is-to-be-learned, both constructed well outside of any student's realm of control (early in ESC's history, the word "course" was, to many, anathema; the word "catalog" was avoided at all costs), the learning contract – focused on the individual student's questions, interests, goals, and statements of individual purpose – was developed to support the student as a self-directed learner. And the learning contract could serve as the space for experimenting with learning activities as well as with learning purposes.

This same emphasis on the student-as-active-knower, not as receiver of all that should be known, was reflected in the College's early embrace of "prior learning" and of providing opportunities for students to identify, describe, document, and earn credit for college-level learning gained outside of any university. In so doing, Empire State College policy not only acknowledged what might be thought of as progressivism's faith in the underlying curiosity and ongoing learning of individuals (which Dewey saw in learners of all ages), but its belief in the richness of experience itself, of the importance of learning from experience, and of the responsibility of any institution devoted to learning to take such so-called "informal" learning seriously. Here again, the centrality of the individual and the hearty embrace of the distinct possibility that significant knowledge could be gained in areas not previously framed as a university's predefined course of study drove the inclusion of prior learning assessment (PLA) as a significant feature of this new institution.

The student-drivenness of individual studies as reflected in the learning contract and the possibility of truly individualized learning captured through prior learning assessment gained even greater centrality in ESC's progressive ways through the expectation that each student create his/her own "curriculum" – an individualized program of study or, in ESC parlance, degree program plan. Two ideas vital to the progressive tradition stand out here: the notion that knowledge itself is provisional and that established bodies of knowledge as framed in college curricula are constructed; and the idea that students, the learners themselves, should participate in developing a plan of study relevant to them. The ideal of each student being actively engaged in the research regarding and the articulation of a rationale for his/her college program directly situates students at the center of their educational journey. And the academic legitimacy of the completed program results from a multilayered approval process and reflects ESC's best efforts to support the student's creation of an individualized college-level curriculum that is responsive to his/her personal, academic, and professional goals.

Perhaps at the heart of these experimenting pedagogical practices at ESC was the fashioning of a new faculty role – the role of the mentor. Although mentoring practices have a long tradition in and outside of the academy, Empire State College embraced a particular faculty-as-mentor role in order to accent three progressive tenets: the student's role as an active learner who needed regular support and careful guidance, but whose individual questions and directions would animate the learning; the critique of the role of the faculty member as an all-knowing expert (the image of the professorial sage); and the ideal of learning-as-dialogue – as the ongoing grappling with and development of ideas formed in a process of inquiry shared by student and mentor. What better way for a student to gain practice as a participant in an activity relevant to his/her life? What better way for the faculty to gain practice working in a more nonhierarchical structure unlike those of more conventional institutions? What more effective way than in dialogue for students and mentors to learn about what might be understood as democratic practice: the common engagement in serious work about topics introduced by those who want to learn and understand and be guided by those who can help to facilitate that learning?

Intimately interconnected with the College's focus on individualization was a second call – the call to innovation and experimentation. To focus on the personal, academic and professional interests and needs of the individual; to craft individual studies and whole curricula that were responsive to a particular student; to pull and shape college-level learning from a person's repository of life experiences, and to reimagine the faculty role as one of facilitator and guide – all of these elements of ESC pedagogy embraced innovation and championed pedagogical experimentation.

This kind of purposeful instability meant that discussions about how to teach and what to learn and how to judge the adequacy of any particular version of a "college education" became significant to a college culture of ongoing debate. Thus, educational traditions that might adroitly steer more established institutions, at ESC became contested terrain, as faculty and administrators sought to craft policies, define processes, and model practices that reflected the mission and core values of this new institution. The very vocabulary of traditional academe was regularly challenged. Indeed, as earlier noted, terms such as "learning contract," "degree program (or educational) plan," and even "mentor" were politically charged and used as both symbolic and substantive reminders of the experimenting nature of this institution and of its turn away from more accepted practices.

Three examples could be instructive: Significant time was (and has been) spent thinking about the limitations of a word like "class" and the distinctions between a class and a "study group" or "group study." If, for example, individualization, an experiment in itself, was at the heart of the College, was there any room for experimenting with what could be gained in a group – a locus of learning so central to the adult education tradition? Not only did ESC's Harry Van Arsdale Jr. Center for

Labor Studies offer "classes" (which they conceived of as different from traditional classes) from the start but, over time, faculty around the College have tried out different approaches to group learning, that now include group residencies and other forms of blended learning (blending face-to-face and online learning modes), innovative unto themselves, and that take advantage of students learning from one another.

Second, efforts to question the vocabulary and thus the very structures of the educationally conventional were also reflected in the decision to organize the curriculum and the faculty according to rather loose and voluntaristic "areas of study," as distinct from more disciplinary-based academic departments. Wouldn't more innovation be encouraged, more ideas about what and how to teach unleashed, if faculty were freed from departmental hierarchies and strictures and if students were freed from the boundaries of traditional disciplines? The melding of ideas, cutting across more conventional fields of study, and, of course, responding to what students wanted to learn could, it was argued, benefit from broader "areas of study" such as "Cultural Studies," "Community and Human Services," and "Business, Management and Economics." Disciplinary silos were thrown open to question, even while, over these more than 40 years, some faculty wondered about, even yearned for, a way to support and advance their own academic (and often disciplinary) agendas.

Thirdly, for some, innovation and experimentation have taken the form of distance learning. From the start, the face-to-face student/mentor dialogue was at the very core of the institution. Such encounters were, for many, its heart and soul. And yet, now for decades, along with the image of the student and mentor sitting side-by-side at a table were the radical possibilities of students breaking barriers of distance by communicating with faculty initially through traditional means of "correspondence," and more recently through online study. Typically enrolled in courses (a structure, as noted, which was contested in itself) and taking advantage of the new technologies, these students were offered access to vast and rich resources that ranged well beyond the imaginative grasp of most of ESC's founders. We have seen where innovation – possible not only as a result of dramatic technological changes over the last half-century, but as a result of the call to change in the very ways we teach and learn – could take us.

It thus makes sense that the call to access, another key principle of both adult education and the progressive tradition, has spurred reflection and innovation throughout ESC's history. Why should higher education, that is, serious learning attentive to the individual, be available only to a tiny number of 18- to 22-year-olds? Why can't what is considered the best of education be available to anyone regardless of background, degree of preparation, age or gender, and, too, why not in a public institution? Here was the bold claim: Student-centeredness and individualized learning should not be solely the prerogative of an elite who attend small, selective, private colleges. Such a mission should be part of a large public university system as well.

This call to access has manifested itself in several ways, the core of which was the establishment of a highly decentralized institution with 35 locations across the state of New York. A public university, then SUNY Chancellor Ernest Boyer argued, had to be available to all the citizens of the state, whether one lived in a major urban center (e.g., New York City or Buffalo), or in a less populous and more remote area (e.g., Auburn or Plattsburgh). In keeping with the strong adult education tradition of bringing educational opportunities to the people rather than expecting them to take up residence in some semi-cloistered environment far from their communities, and, too, in the spirit of other experimenting efforts of the time to create vibrant universities "without walls," Empire State College sought a statewide footprint – with some offices as small as a single mentor and one support person, whether in an office building or on the campus of a community college – thus offering students a chance to earn a four-year degree at a public institution not far from home.

Interestingly in regard to ESC's goal of broadening access, Empire State College was not designed as a college for adults; indeed, during a time of significant campus protests and of students leaving colleges because of what were perceived as their multiple rigidities, ESC was seen by some as a true alternative, as a place in which traditional-age college students could create their own program for learning and have access to those who would devote themselves to guiding them. But older students, working adults with families and often deep community ties, were also at the door, and ESC (with most of its students still, today, in their mid-30s) became an institution that was welcoming, reasonably inexpensive, encouraging to those who had been educationally bypassed, and willing to accommodate both the student who had not found a comfortable match in traditional higher education and the professional, whether in business or human services, who needed some new expertise and a credential. Although never, at least on paper, a fully "open admissions" institution, ESC embraced as much openness and inclusivity as possible. And doing so it has been regularly pushed to find ways to respond to the personal, academic and work needs of a widely varied student body, including academically underprepared students, adults for whom college seemed alien territory, women and men with significant accomplishments in the community but little experience of college study, and students returning to higher education after having had previous academic success and now seeking degree completion.

Perhaps this call to access, along with the previously described calls to innovation/experimentation and to individualization should be understood within the context of the fourth call: the call to democratic social change. Public institutions across the United States – such as Empire State College, the Vermont State Colleges, Metropolitan State University (Minnesota); "external degree programs" that were created at existing universities, such as The University of Alabama; and the "university without walls" movement, such as the one at the University of Massachusetts – developed alongside experimenting private institutions, such as the School of New Resources at The College of New Rochelle (New York) and the School for New Learning at DePaul University (Illinois). All of these institutions were part of a movement for educational change that recognized the potentially powerful transformative role that a more progressive higher education system could have on the broader society. As noted earlier, these kinds of experimenting institutions saw change at the core of their mission: traditional institutional ways could give way to modes of teaching and learning that were more responsive to the individual student; curricula could be reimagined to cross disciplines, and create alternative ways to identify and shape the knowledge that could be gained; the faculty role itself could be rethought; and the entire university system could become a more inclusive one, breaking down barriers and welcoming those who had previously been excluded.

Three dimensions of change are relevant here: In the first, institutions like Empire State College sought to change the internal fixtures of the university – questioning structures (for example, at ESC, the taken-for-grantedness of the entire departmental edifice) and roles (for example, the hierarchies, activities and expectations of the faculty). Second, this movement of educational change claimed that higher education had, to date, failed to respond meaningfully to the social, cultural, technological and economic changes – and to the conflicts – taking place across the globe. It was incumbent upon the university not to defend and try to bolster its old ways but to name and try out new ways in which higher education could play a constructive role in what was perceived to be a society-in-transformation. And finally, change meant the responsibility to educate women and men who, as more engaged and responsible participants in their own education, were gaining new critical awareness and important experience as future citizens who could play a vital, constructive role in their society. As the progressive movement continued to remind us, society needed its educational institutions to contribute to the creation and sustenance of a more just and equitable world.

## IMPLICATIONS FOR PRACTICE: MANY MODELS

These guiding principles and calls to develop a certain kind of college have resulted in the development of a wide variety of programs and models for mentoring, teaching, and learning at ESC. As noted above, in order to meet students' need for access, widely dispersed regional centers and satellite units across the state were developed. As Empire State College grew and technologies evolved and were tried to accommodate students outside the state, ESC later developed the Center for Distance Learning (CDL), which involved experiments in technologically-mediated study. While some regional centers' preponderant modes of study have been individualized, with students meeting one-on-one and face-to-face with their study mentor, other centers offer more group studies; and some offer studies that include both a residency and online study. The Harry Van Arsdale Jr. Center for Labor Studies offers a classroom model but with curriculum developed in direct response to the particular context of its students. The Center for Distance Learning offers all study online, some of which is highly individualized and shaped by the student and some of which is faculty-designed; indeed, even within CDL, there is a wide range of practice on a spectrum from student-driven study allowing for emergent curriculum on one end to structured, program driven, preset curriculum on the other. And the

# INTRODUCTION

College's graduate programs vary significantly, as some, in professional studies such as the Master of Arts in Teaching program offer pre-structured sequences of study that enable students to meet requirements for licensure, while others such as the Master of Arts in Liberal Studies provide for individual students' design of their unique program of study. Many locations across the College are now supporting blended study, i.e., study which integrates face-to-face and online work, whether with a group or individual student. And the College has continued to experiment through the development not just of new academic programs and pedagogies but also of administrative structures and procedures, which just recently have entailed altering what has been, from the start, a center-based system.

Experimentation with such a multiplicity of modes has both supported adult learners in working within the mode best suited to their needs and context, and provided greater access to more students whose schedule and location may not allow for traditional schedules for attendance. And what has been a history of ongoing experimentation has resulted in the proliferation both of widely varying modes of study and of new areas of inquiry. ESC's School for Graduate Studies, for example, responding to changing times, has added programs in health care administration, emergency management, and emerging technologies. Mindful not only of responding to students' changing context but also of having impact on that context, these graduate programs strive to engender students' critical and creative capacities so that they can make significant contributions to their chosen field. Whether working with undergraduate students in the liberal arts or graduate students in professional fields, ESC faculty continue to emphasize attention to students' developing critical understanding of their world, their place in it, and what constructive – indeed "reconstructive" – impact they might have. Yet, though undergirded by shared values and commitments, this dispersed and varied development of the College has resulted in no single practice, in no one way of doing things, in not even one culture.

## ISSUES AND QUESTIONS ARISING: THE CREATIVE TENSIONS

About these many different embodiments of ESC's core values and of its roots in the progressive and adult education traditions, it should be no surprise that all along the way there has been vigorous debate, as new ideas have been contested and innovative approaches tried. With each rethinking, each suggestion, questions have been raised. Beginning with the very founding of the institution, when faculty debated what became known as the (Arthur) Chickering model for individualized study and the (Loren) Baritz model for faculty-designed courses open to all, faculty raised concerns about the development of a wholly online program and its implications for individualized learning and community; later questioned the development of graduate studies, most of which have been more professional in their emphases; and, currently, are discussing questions related to moving to more centralized administrative structures and processes. All of these developments have raised hotly contested issues and deep, long and difficult discussions, which touch not just on the direction of the College but on its very mission, its core, on what many in the College hold sacred. And discussions of this kind, often contentious, have gone on throughout the history of the College.

Within these varied and evolving practices and the questions raised about them, what we are calling creative tensions have emerged. We say "creative" because the tensions we see – sometimes within a given practice, sometimes across quite different approaches – actually *are* creative. That is, these tensions reflect longstanding, rich questions in education; they inform our thinking; whether implicitly or explicitly, they animate our institutional and pedagogical ways; and they help us to examine, experiment with, and improve our practice. We say "tensions" because the questions they raise reflect an interplay of values, principles, and approaches along a spectrum, and because, though often a particular balance is struck, this relationship, typically between seemingly opposing elements, is rarely static. Yet it is precisely in the opposition, in the ongoing dance between divergent ideas, that the creative potential resides. Rather like Rainer Maria Rilke's counsel to "live the questions," in our view it is our awareness of and willingness to live these tensions that deepens our insight and our practice. Far from some single-minded schema, which serves to narrow our scope and stunt our ideas, such tensions allow our thinking, our practice, to grow. So, whether arising within a collegial conversation regarding the pedagogical merits of a given practice or emerging from deep differences across, for example, different programs of study, these discussions, as they reflect the genuinely creative tensions involved, will continue not just to shape our dialog but also to inform our work.

We have chosen to place these creative tensions and the issues they raise into five categories, related to:

1. philosophy (philosophical principles and core values);
2. students (who they are; what they bring; what they need);
3. pedagogy (pedagogical models; mentoring and teaching practice);
4. the institution (internal structures and policy; external demands and constraints);
5. broader context (the social and global context within which our institution functions).

The essays included in this volume explore these areas of tension in the context of specific policies, procedures, and pedagogical models, as well as through the lived experience of ESC over time of faculty, students, administrators, and staff. Here, we will provide just a brief preview of what these tensions entail and the kinds of questions they raise, not just at Empire State College but in higher education generally.

*Creative Tensions: Underlying Philosophical Principles*

In regard to questions of education philosophy, for example, when one talks of genuinely student-centered pedagogy, i.e., of approaches to mentoring and teaching in which the student sets the agenda and the faculty member works to support the student's study, questions immediately arise: How does a mentor respond to the student's stated goals while also sharing his/her own knowledge and expertise that could be helpful to pursuing those goals? How does a mentor offer guidance without "taking over" the direction of the study? Just what is the appropriate balance in the locus of authority shared between student and mentor? While these kinds of dilemmas arise even within a given study, they also play out *across* various practices in the institution. In ESC's varied programs – some grounded in student-designed study, others based on faculty-designed curriculum – the balance can look very different.

Another question in the realm of education philosophy, which plays out both across and within institutions of higher education, concerns the longstanding tension between the goals of equity of access and quality. Can the College continue both to broaden access and to provide to students highly individualized study and significant time with faculty? Can we continue to increase faculty student load while admitting students needing extra support? In some ways, the very mission of the College is at stake in how we respond to these questions.

Other issues arising – again, both in higher education generally and at ESC in particular – relate to education as a reproductive system and education as a force for reconstruction, an age-old question about the proper role of education in society. At ESC, as emphasized above, faculty support students' critical questioning of the systems, structures, and ideas undergirding our society while also helping students to gain the knowledge and skill to work *within* that society (a goal that often propels students' coming to ESC in the first place). And, again, the balance we strike plays out both within a given study and across programs having very different priorities and emphases. Similarly, longstanding questions related to the relative emphases on individual and community, supporting the development of each while attending to the interplay as well, are completely embedded in any teaching – whether in negotiating the goals of a given study, setting the content, or designing the learning activities.

So, too, must we walk a tightrope between treating knowledge as given and treating knowledge as constructed. It would be easy to reduce this juxtaposition to an historical claim that, for example, traditionally knowledge, accepted as given, was there to be "passed down" or that content, identified by faculty, was there to be "delivered," while from a more progressive and/or constructivist perspective, knowledge, sought through faculty/student collaboration, is constructed, as new meanings are made together. Yet such a characterization would be utterly simplistic. As with other genuinely creative tensions, there is a complex interplay here; dilemmas arise; the balance struck will vary; the context within which inquiry occurs matters.

*Creative Tensions: Students*

In addition, an array of tensions animate ESC's understanding of and response to students: who they are, what they bring with them to their college studies, and what they need from the institution. Five issues are especially salient.

Perhaps the most central creative tension in regard to students concerns assumptions about an adult student's so-called "independence." In keeping with a significant body of work by adult and progressive educators about the autonomy of the adult learner, ESC principles and practices have emphasized that the adult student's independence must be honored. That is, the role of the institution and the responsibility of the mentor are not to constrict, not to prejudge nor even to give direction, but to provide the terrain for and facilitate the carrying out of studies and entire degrees inspired by an independent learner who knows his/her own interests and goals. Can the autonomy of the adult learner be honored even as the institution or the individual faculty mentor recognizes the student's need for guidance, oversight, and for supervision in carrying out his/her plan? Is it ever possible to draw a clear line between supporting independence and giving direction?

A second creative tension concerns the College's (and the mentor's) awareness of the complex lives of adults, who are often juggling personal, professional and community responsibilities and obligations, and the dictates of the institution's academic structure. What creative tensions exist between, on the one hand, specific college policies regarding a student's "satisfactory academic progress" and, on the other hand, our acknowledgment of a student's need for flexibility and the faculty's need for the ability to improvise (e.g., to change the details of a study to respond to a student's changing interests or a personal or job crisis)? Can a faculty mentor acknowledge the context of an individual adult student's life and, at the same time, represent and carry out an institution's rules and requirements that could be at odds with such a student-centered spirit?

Within a relatively open-access institution such as ESC, a third creative tension which occurs frequently concerns the widely varied levels of readiness that adult students bring to their college studies. How is it possible for a progressive institution to carefully, fairly and systematically respond to such lack of college-study preparedness and still function within a student-directed model? What is the responsibility of the College? Or, put in yet another way, what does responsiveness to the individual who is deemed un- or underprepared mean in an institution that embraces student-designed study?

Fourth, students often bring to ESC years of rich professional activity, or community work, or knowledge gained as a result of personal inquiry. One could argue that at the heart of any progressive college, and particularly one like ESC that prides itself on offering students credit for what has been learned outside of a formal institutional framework, is the honoring of student experience. But how does that body of learning mesh (or not) with the deep traditions of the academy? How does a faculty member walk the tightrope of helping a student identify and describe what she knows without taking over that process? How can, for example, new and imaginative academic questions and areas of study be explored that begin with honoring the distinctive experiences of the students whom the institution is seeking to serve?

Fifth and finally, there are creative tensions arising in relation to the acknowledgement of and respect for a great range of diversities among ESC students (whether those diversities are defined by gender, age, race, class, culture, learning styles, tastes and values, and/or personal histories) and the more generic – and perhaps narrow – expectations of performance to which the institution adheres. How can a progressive institution claim to be fair, to be transparent, to provide equal treatment, if, at the same time, it takes pride in shaping its evaluative criteria (whether these are judgments made of an individual study or of an entire degree) to the particulars of an individual or of any group of students?

*Creative Tensions: Pedagogy*

And these tensions related to underlying philosophy and to the students we serve are mirrored directly in the various models of pedagogy occurring at ESC. Put simply, theory and practice inform one another; and creative tensions arising in underlying theory and in relation to the students we serve are evident in practice as well. Thus, for example, when mentor and student begin to identify and clarify that student's interests and goals, as mentioned above, careful attention must be paid not only to the student's own purposes and passions but also to any relevant external expectations or requirements – whether of the institution, the workplace, graduate programs, or accrediting bodies. While a given study might be individualized to respond to a student's driving interests, if the student's study or preparation is to have credibility, so too must it accommodate shared expectations of knowledge in the field. Not unrelated, as noted in relation to philosophical underpinnings, there is always the delicate interplay between a dialogical, collaborative approach in which student and faculty work together, and a more didactic model in which the teacher provides expertise. At what point, in what ways, and to what extent should the mentor share particular knowledge so as not to foreclose or eclipse the student's exploration or discovery? How does the mentor both support the potential for new questions, new ways of seeing, and impart currently accepted understandings?

In study at ESC, often curriculum is emergent: As understanding is deepened, new questions arise; next steps may shift from what had been planned. How does one walk this tightrope between carrying out a well-conceived plan and staying open to new, possibly fruitful, directions? What is the optimal balance between emphasis on mastery of particular content and emphasis on attention to the learning process itself? And in regard to assessment of student work, while criteria may need to be carefully attuned to the content and learning activities of a highly individualized study, how can we also find the shared criteria for evaluating learning outcomes and for what constitutes quality?

Another creative tension in our pedagogy – which occurs both in higher education generally and at ESC, and which, at ESC, is addressed differently across programs – is the relative emphasis given to the liberal arts and sciences and to professional education. Even from one concentration to another, from one study to another, from one level to another, this balance may be differently struck. How do we incorporate into studies both critical questioning and skill development? Where, when and how should the emphasis between liberal and professional study shift – whether within a given study, within a concentration, or over the course of preparing for a career?

Lastly in regard to our pedagogical choices, we must pay attention to students' need for connection – with the institution, their mentor, and their fellow students. At the same time that we want to honor and support our adult students' relative autonomy in their studies, we must not allow that independence to drift into isolation. Our uses of electronic media, for example, while seeking to provide for access and connection across distance, without careful attention, can also present barriers to "contact," can result in increased feelings of both isolation and anonymity. Even working face-to-face with a mentor in an independent study can have isolating effects as the student may not have interaction with other students or the vibrant exchange of a group. Reflecting directly the theoretical tension between individual and community, how, more concretely, do we establish an appropriate balance between relatively independent, autonomous study and the stimulation and support of a group?

*Creative Tensions: The Institution*

It is impossible to understand the myriad ways in which creative tensions display themselves and ripple through the College without paying attention to Empire State College as an organization – to ESC as a macro-environment in which teaching and learning take place in very particular ways. A number of creative tensions stand out.

As a distributed institution with offices across the state of New York, the founders of Empire State College purposefully chose a nonresidential form in order to offer greater access to those for whom higher education was otherwise unavailable. As noted earlier, in effect, the College was constructed as an assemblage of "learning centers," some in urban and others in more rural areas. While such an institutional architecture has provided significant flexibility and ease of access, it has also meant, over time, that faculty and staff at particular locations have developed cultures of practice responding to their often distinctive student bodies. But the beauty of such diversity – the opportunity, for example, for faculty to find their own styles, mores and procedures, and, physically distant from the College's main administrative office in Saratoga Springs, their own interpretations of College policy – has also meant that there is no single ESC "student experience." And this inconsistency of policy implementation and of favoring certain teaching/mentoring forms over others has, at times, created a rather bumpy institutional terrain. In effect, decentralization has opened the way to significant degrees of academic freedom and experimentation and, at the same time, to challenges and complications in identifying and sustaining the institution's core, its shared identity.

And how can such a decentralized multi-centric institution ever be governed and managed? Here again, one can see creative tensions at work surrounding the pull of more conventional hierarchical academic ways and the benefits (given both the College's philosophy and the realities of its dispersed presence) of a more participatory model of decision-making. How can faculty, who on a day-to-day basis feel their authority as decision-makers in their location, share governance with collegewide administrators, some of whom do not know particular local cultures and who are making decisions for "the College"? Who decides, and how can even a complexly layered local and collegewide committee structure (taking up everything from the faculty review process to proposing and vetting academic policies across the state), relying on those at the local level to participate actively in multiple facets of institutional life, ensure that policy mandates move forward and effectively reflect institutional expectations? On the one hand, if the College is founded on the principle of student participation in their most important educational decisions, shouldn't such an academic ethic be mirrored in the faculty's role in major college decisions? On the other hand, when does local decision-making, innovation, and implementation give way to a lack of clarity and/or to organizational instability?

But there also has been an even larger context. ESC, itself a decentralized institution, is part of a much larger, also decentralized institution. Critical to the very existence of Empire State College has been the fact that it is a public institution which is a part of the country's largest state university system: The State University of New York. To what extent could (or should) ESC exist in relative autonomy, able to develop its own distinctive and alternative institutional and pedagogical ways without having its policies and procedures scrutinized by SUNY at every turn? To what extent does that scrutiny help the College as it may support both the College's quality and legitimacy? In what specific ways has the College's embeddedness in a huge SUNY bureaucracy and its complex budgetary systems (which themselves are tied to the erratic politics of the New York legislature) been detrimental to this nontraditional institution? With no residence halls, library buildings and sports facilities, how can ESC's distinctive budgetary needs be understood by the SUNY system? It has been beneficial to students to be able to earn a SUNY degree and to pay state university tuition while at an unconventional institution in which they can create their own unique studies and academic programs, programs of study that would not have been possible at other SUNY institutions. But how far can ESC bend to accommodate SUNY policies and procedures without losing its distinctiveness? Is it possible for an experimenting institution to sustain its nontraditional character and still answer not only to traditional educational bureaucracies such as SUNY but also to powerful external accrediting bodies such as the Middle States Association of Colleges and Schools?

*Creative Tensions: The Broader Context*

While our outline of creative tensions that have been evident at Empire State College from its earliest days has focused thus far mainly on its own internal dynamics, ESC has also been influenced by the broader social, economic, political and cultural milieu in which it is embedded. That is, while the College can be seen as a complex micro-world, it must also be understood as part of a macro-world that has influenced not just ESC but higher education generally at every turn.

One way in which the power of the larger social context has touched the College has been the weight of market realities. When public funding has been dramatically diminished and yet the demand for more affordable higher education is increasing, how can an institution with a mission of access and (what today might be called) educational personalization maintain itself? And further, what are the ramifications for ESC of a highly competitive market for so-called adult students not only among public institutions and within the SUNY system itself, but among private institutions and the for-profit sector? How can ESC both respond to these market realities and sustain its distinctive mission and identity?

With significant reductions in the state's direct financial contribution to SUNY and with tuition dollars thus becoming that much more critical to the basic workings of the College, ESC has been under increasing pressure to grow. How, with more students (some, younger in age without years of experiential learning; some, needing additional levels of academic support), can we sustain our highly individualized model? While for some such growth is in keeping with a larger social access mission, still the question remains, from what other source can operating expenses come besides tuition dollars? In the terms of the day, is Empire State College "scalable"?

A third tension opened up by a changing macro-world concerns new technologies that are continuously developing and omnipresent. Many of these technologies have created real and potential connections between faculty and students – across New York state, nationally and internationally. While in the College's early days individualization took the form of face-to-face student-mentor contact, now, most ESC students are formally engaged, whether using an array of electronic media to work with faculty or enrolled in a formal distance learning course, in some kind of internet-based academic work. Yet rather than being a leader in electronically mediated teaching and learning, ESC is actually struggling to stay abreast of change. With ESC and more and more of higher education turning to online learning, how can the College both take advantage of new technologies and sustain the values informing its unique pedagogies? How can we ensure choosing and making the best use of new technological innovations while maintaining attention to the individual learner and to the kinds of academic flexibilities that have been the trademark of Empire State College?

Finally, and linked to all of the creative tensions around ESC as only one institution in a much larger context, there remains a basic question: Can ESC sustain the essential elements of its pedagogical model, can it provide high quality public education for a widely diverse group of adult learners, in a world in which its progressive core runs counter to current trends, including standardization, accountability, and vocationalization, in higher education? If survival means something other than falling back on romantic educational visions of a bygone era, how can Empire State College remain a progressive institution and, at the same time, meet the demands of this society and the realities of students' lives and their personal, academic and professional needs today?

INTRODUCTION

For any of these tensions related to theoretical underpinnings, students, approaches to teaching and learning, organization, and the current context within which higher education operates, the issues that arise allow us to probe our intentions, to examine our methods, to be more conscious of the choices we make and of our rationale for those choices. And while these tensions occur in any educational enterprise, in institutions of all stripes, it is the ways we choose to answer them, the balance we determine, that sets one organization apart from another and that gives an institution its identity. That is why we want to surface these tensions: to understand more deeply what we at ESC intend and achieve as a progressive institution, who we are as educators, and what will have the most significant, positive impact on our students, our society, and, indeed, our globe.

## OVERVIEW: THE STRUCTURE OF THE BOOK

Contributing authors to this volume will be exploring these creative tensions more fully and concretely as they examine the many facets of this complex institution. Looking at such creative tensions from various angles and perspectives, these current and former Empire State College colleagues examine the College as it has evolved over time, as it currently functions, and as it grapples with ongoing questions, the answers to which will profoundly affect its future. We hope that our organizing of authors' essays directly in relation to the specific creative tensions we have identified will serve to illuminate the questions and issues at hand.

In the first section of the book, "Underlying Principles, Ideas, and Values: Perennial Questions," W. Willis' chapter "Empire State College and the Conflicted Legacy of Progressive Higher Education" first lays out three central tenets of progressive education and then examines ways in which growth, increasing emphasis on vocationalism, and standards and accountability have undermined both individualization of study and the goal of social reconstruction. In Chapter 2, "Conflict, Change, and Continuity: ESC's Goddard College and British Open University Connections," R. Bonnabeau presents the original and continuing debate between those supporting the value of broad access to well-designed courses and those advocating for highly individualized study design. And in Chapter 3, "John Dewey, Constructed Knowing, and Faculty Practice at Empire State College," X. Coulter looks more closely at Dewey's philosophy of progressive education in order to examine the degree to which ESC has developed pedagogical models and an organization that reflect these principles, and the extent to which we have been or could be such an institution.

The second section of the book takes up "Student-Centered Pedagogy: The Mentoring Model and What It Has Meant" for the learners who come to Empire State College. L. Herman's contribution (Chapter 4) focuses on the role of dialogue in ESC teaching practices and on the abiding tensions between the goals of transmitting knowledge and sustaining dialogue. In Chapter 5, "Educational Planning at Empire State College," S. Oaks examines the ways in which the calls for students to develop their own academic plans open up ongoing tensions between "fluidity and structure" and between "process and product." In her discussion of interdisciplinary education at ESC, in Chapter 6, L. Lander discusses the ways in which the term *interdisciplinary* has been used at ESC – the opportunities it has offered and the challenges it continues to present. And in Chapter 7, "The Cipher and Empire: Teaching and Mentoring Through Hip-Hop," H. Gupta-Carlson explores the fascinating parallels between an experimenting academic institution and pedagogy grounded in an inventive artistic practice, both of which were created in the early 1970s.

In the third section of the book, "Let 1,000 Flowers Bloom," which contributes further to the emerging profile of our students and the programs that serve them, authors take up questions arising in widely varying programs serving a diverse student body. Beginning with a portrait of their students at the Harry Van Arsdale Jr. Center for Labor Studies, in Chapter 8, "'I Don't Write, I Work': Writing and Reading with Trade Union Apprentices," R. Fraser and S. Mavrogiannis discuss the rich tensions involved when faculty and students whose contexts are so different from one another are learning together. Chapter 9, by S. Logsdon and L. Guyette, explores some of the creative tensions inherent in academic support of underprepared students in a progressive individualized program model. In Chapter 10, focused on ESC's International Program, D. Starr-Glass discusses the challenges, contradictions, and benefits involved in employing a fundamentally student-centered model when working with students of a different culture and with profoundly different experiences and expectations of schooling and higher education. And, talking about ESC's prior learning assessment program, in Chapter 11, N. Travers digs into some of the creative tensions involved in recognizing a student's learning gained outside of academe and locating that knowledge within a university curriculum.

The fourth section of the book focuses on the tensions related to the organization of the College – to its basic architecture and infrastructure. In Chapter 12, L. Wiley examines the complexities of this "new kind of college" (Ernest Boyer's phrase) that has struggled to build systems around student learning and that is so widely dispersed, both geographically and administratively. Then C. Rounds (Chapter 13) reflects on "autonomy and connection" in such a physically dispersed, statewide institution. In Chapter 14, "Family Feuds, Shotgun Weddings, and a Dash of Couples Therapy," S. Hertz, C. Leaker, R. Bonanno, and T. MacMillan uncover some of the struggles involved in developing studies that bridge disparate cultures and pedagogies and that may either complement or live in critical tension with one another. C. Conaway and C. Whann take up another facet of these tensions in Chapter 15 by pointing to the organizational challenges that come with the institution's uneven growth. And in Chapter 16, B. Eisenberg uses the example of changes in the health care industry to point to tensions surrounding standardization and individualization in the creation of ESC's graduate programs.

The fifth section, in which authors focus on impacts of the broader context on institutions of higher education today, begins in Chapter 17 with E. Warzala's examination of the myriad tensions that have existed between an alternative college, ESC, and its institutional home, the State University of New York, a large, public bureaucracy. In Chapter 18, B. Hurley discusses ESC's responses to and development and uses of changing technologies and their implications for the institution and for mentoring, teaching, and learning at the College. And in Chapter 19, concerning assessment at ESC, J. Elliott looks at the questions, challenges and creative tensions arising when a progressive institution, which offers nontraditional and interdisciplinary areas of study and means of evaluation, must address external demands for accountability and assessment.

It is our sincere hope that the 19 essays that follow, organized in relation to the creative tensions that we have identified, will shed light on the complex challenges and demands that higher education is facing today and that nontraditional institutions in particular are experiencing so acutely. We hope that what we intend as both a close and broad look at one nontraditional, public institution will be of direct relevance to institutions of higher education, whether public or private, traditional or alternative. Through such a case study, we want to identify the issues, surface the tensions, and frame the questions we must address if we are to make thoughtful, intentional choices about the organizational structures and pedagogical practices that, in the midst of extraordinary pressures and rapid change, will allow us to sustain our progressive vision and best serve our students and society.

## REFERENCES

Brookfield, S. D. (1986). *Understanding and facilitating adult learning*. San Francisco, CA: Jossey-Bass.

Brookfield, S. D. (2005). *The power of critical theory: Liberating adult learning and teaching*. San Francisco, CA: Jossey-Bass.

Cranton, P. (1994). *Understanding and promoting transformative learning*. San Francisco, CA: Jossey-Bass.

Cunningham, P. M. (1998). The social dimension of transformative learning. *PAACE Journal of Lifelong Learning, 7*(1998), 15–28.

Dewey, J. (1893). Self-realization as the moral ideal. *The Philosophical Review, 2*(2), 652–664.

Dewey, J. (1938). *Experience and education*. New York, NY: Collier.

Freire, P. (1970). *Pedagogy of the oppressed*. New York, NY: Seabury.

Kilpatrick, W. H. (1951). *Philosophy of education*. New York, NY: Macmillan.

Knowles, M. S. (1973). *The adult learner: A neglected species*. Houston, TX: Gulf.

Lindeman, E. C. (1926). *The meaning of adult education*. New York, NY: New Republic.

Mezirow, J. (1991). *Transformative dimensions of adult learning*. San Francisco, CA: Jossey-Bass.

Ohliger, J. D. (1974). Is lifelong adult education a guarantee of permanent inadequacy? *Convergence, 7*(2), 47–58.

Schön, D. A. (1984). *The reflective practitioner: How professionals think in action*. New York, NY: Basic Books.

Welton, M. R. (Ed.). (1995). *In defense of the lifeworld: Critical perspectives on adult learning*. Albany, NY: State University of New York Press.

SECTION I

# UNDERLYING PRINCIPLES, IDEAS AND VALUES: PERENNIAL QUESTIONS

In Section I, three essays take up issues and creative tensions arising in a progressive institution, as they examine ideas underlying Empire State College's founding, history and current practice. In Chapter 1, "Empire State College and the Conflicted Legacy of Progressive Higher Education," W. Willis first situates ESC's founding in a brief history of progressive education and then outlines three key progressive ideas that have informed the College's development: greater access to education; student-centered, individualized study; and education as a force for social reform. Considering "certain tensions and oppositions" inherent in progressivism, he looks at how ESC has confronted such tensions over time. In Chapter 2, "Conflict, Change, and Continuity: ESC's Goddard College and British Open University Connections," R. Bonnabeau provides a history of this "conflicted legacy" as he presents the original debate at the College between the value, on the one hand, of highly individualized, student-designed study (in the tradition of Goddard College) and, on the other hand, of broad access to faculty-designed courses offered to students at a distance (modeled after the British Open University). He then examines the ways in which that debate, and the creative tensions informing it, continue to this day. In Chapter 3, "John Dewey, Constructed Knowing, and Faculty Practice at Empire State College," while noting the strong connection between Dewey's ideas and those of ESC's founders, X. Coulter asks if greater appreciation of the philosophical underpinnings of faculty practice would have helped them to stem the "drift" toward conventional approaches, and to more intentionally sustain a progressive vision.

WAYNE CARR WILLIS

# 1. EMPIRE STATE COLLEGE AND THE CONFLICTED LEGACY OF PROGRESSIVE HIGHER EDUCATION

At its founding in 1971, Empire State College (ESC) entered an American scene bustling with new schools and programs in revolt against the *status quo* at all levels of education. Identifying their institutions variously as experimenting, alternative, innovative, free, open, or nontraditional, dissenting educators infrequently chose to call their ventures "progressive." This term, dating from the political and social reform movements of the early 20th century, was no longer in vogue and, indeed, had fallen into disrepute during the Cold War era. This was particularly true in the world of education, where critics frequently attributed the mediocrity of so many schools to the influence of John Dewey and other progressive theorists. However, as Lawrence Cremin wrote presciently in 1961, "the authentic progressive vision remained strangely pertinent to the problems of mid-century America. Perhaps it only awaited the reformulation and resuscitation that would ultimately derive from a larger resurgence of reform in American life and thought" (p. 353). This is precisely what would happen in the 1960s and '70s. Although advocates for sweeping educational change preferred to emphasize the originality of their ideas, the rising scholastic counterculture embraced some of the old progressives' fundamental goals, concepts, and methods. It also inherited certain tensions and oppositions that had surfaced within the earlier movement. We can gain a clearer understanding of the difficulties that Empire State College has faced in forming and implementing a coherent educational vision if we place its struggle within the larger history of progressive education's internal conflicts.

I.

As Cremin (1961) showed in his classic *The Transformation of the School*, there can be no "capsule definition of progressive education" because those who called themselves progressive (and eventually organized in 1919 as the Progressive Education Association) were a loose collection of thinkers and practitioners whose specific initiatives were too diverse to constitute an integrated, consistent program of reforms. Progressivism also went through several historical phases that reflected changes in the political and economic climate of the nation and in the views of intellectuals. Thus, "the movement was marked from the very beginning by a pluralistic, frequently contradictory character" wherein "progressive education meant different things to different people" (p. x). Still, there are some persistent themes within the progressive critique of American education from the elementary to the collegiate level that provided rationales for many of the reforms advanced during progressivism's early 20th century heyday and in the later revival period that brought forth ESC.

First, progressives argued that America's educational institutions excluded or poorly served too many people who could potentially benefit from them. Access needed to be greatly expanded to better serve children, youth, and adults across the full spectrum of the population, whether the student was urban or rural, native or immigrant, male or female, and regardless of religion, ethnicity, race, or economic standing. From the late 1800s onward, progressives campaigned for improved rural schools, vocational training, health education, student counseling, the creation of adult education programs offered by a vast array of voluntary associations, and the evolution of the high school into an institution of mass public education. Within higher education, progressives championed the growth of state university systems and two-year public colleges, university extension programs for adults, and new educational opportunities for women either in sex-segregated or coeducational colleges. After World War II, the GI Bill extended this egalitarian thrust to veterans, community colleges grew dramatically in the 1960s, and by the 1970s optimists were forecasting the arrival of a "learning society" based upon universal higher education and continuous learning throughout the life cycle (Cremin, 1961; Kett, 1994, pp. 257–292, 403–448). In 1928 the progressive president of the University of Minnesota, Lotus D. Coffman, had written, "The state universities and the public schools from the beginning have been maintained to provide freedom of opportunity," recognizing that "genius and talent do not belong to any class because of wealth or social position." For Coffman, however, this commitment to educational opportunity meant that the student of "less talent" should also "be permitted to progress as rapidly as his abilities will permit to the approximate limits of his attainment. The student of few talents will not be denied his opportunity while the student of many talents is given his" (as cited in Cremin, 1961, pp. 314–315). A similar vision of open access became one of the foundation stones for ESC. Empire State College's (1971–1972) first bulletin declared, "For the last hundred years the United States has made a little education universally available and a lot of education available for the few. Now a lot of education must be available for many" (p. 10).

Second, progressives contended that most existing schools failed to connect with the genuine learning interests, needs, and goals of many students due to curricular and pedagogical rigidities rooted in outworn academic traditions or the self-interest of inflexible faculty and school administrators. This lack of "child-centeredness" (or "student-centeredness" as it was named at the college level) stifled the learner's natural curiosity and made it unlikely that a conventionally educated student would develop the independent intellectual spirit and skills of inquiry needed for what Dewey (1900) called "effective self-direction" of one's own journey through life. Dewey was certainly not the only progressive theorist to argue that education should begin with "the immediate instincts and activities of the child" (pp. 44, 51). But Dewey became by far the movement's most widely known and respected thinker. His Laboratory School at the University of Chicago was commonly cited as a model of best progressive practice. (Likewise, Dewey was the most visible target for the ridicule of critics who claimed that other learner-centric schools typically descended into anarchy.)

The concept of child- or student-centered education has often been stretched to cover practices that are far from what Dewey and his allies had in mind. However, research has generally shown that only a few public school systems converted to individualized learning rooted in students' self-generated interests and questions, while this form of progressivism exerted a powerful influence on the founding and development of many small, private, elementary and secondary schools (Ravitch, 2000; Cuban, 1993; Zilversmit, 1993). These places shaped, for better and worse, the ambivalent reputation of the progressive school as a refuge for "free spirits." From the 1920s to the '40s, a handful of new, private colleges, such as Bennington and Sarah Lawrence, carried this philosophy into higher education. Here "functional curriculums" were tailored "to each individual student" on the premise that educational coherence "is something to be sought in the individual student, not in the curriculum" (Brubacher & Rudy, 1997, pp. 276–277).

During the big wave of reform that swept through American education from the mid-1960s through the early '70s, the surviving progressive colleges of the earlier period were joined by hundreds of others, either brand new institutions or experimental divisions within existing colleges and universities. Many of these newcomers tried to give their students a personalized and "liberating" educational experience by reducing or rejecting core curriculum and distribution requirements, empowering students to take a large measure of responsibility for designing their own academic programs and individualized learning projects, facilitating off-campus experiential learning activity in the community or workplace, replacing letter grades with narrative evaluations, encouraging teaching and learning across disciplinary boundaries, and fostering more egalitarian relations among all members of the academic community (Kliewer, 1999). For the most part, these "innovations" were actually adoptions on a wider scale of long established practices in progressive schools and colleges. This is what made it possible for so much seemingly new thinking to be put in play so rapidly during the '60s and '70s. When ESC declared that it would place its focus on the individual student and embraced all of the student-friendly features described above, it was being bold but not especially original. (As I will discuss, ESC was more distinctive in its combining of various elements from progressive thought and practice to serve a student body composed mostly of part-time adult learners.)

Along with the need for more access and student-centeredness, a third theme in the progressives' critique of America's schools was that they did not sufficiently prepare students to address contemporary social problems. Many progressives believed that a primary goal of education was to equip students to become intelligent, informed, and caring citizens of a democratic, forward-looking society – people who could work together effectively to improve life in the United States and around the world. In his book *Dynamic Sociology,* Lester Frank Ward (1883) claimed that education was the "great panacea" for society's ills (p. 698). Dewey echoed this opinion. "Education," he wrote, "is the fundamental method of social progress and freedom." Teachers "engaged not simply in the training of individuals, but in the formation of the proper social life." For modern Americans this must mean education for democracy, which was "more than a form of government; it is primarily a mode of associated living." Moreover, Dewey was convinced that "the growth of mind" in the individual depends upon "participation in conjoint activities having a common purpose." Therefore, his Laboratory School had been set up "to discover ... how a school could become a cooperative community while developing in individuals their own capacities and satisfying their own needs." Dewey hoped that in progressive schools students would develop a "spirit of service" to be carried forward to adult life (as cited in Cremin, 1961, pp. 100, 118, 120, 122, 136).

Progressive educators often tried to live up to their ideal of enlightened civic activism, taking positions that were usually toward the left on many public issues. During the late 1920s and '30s, Dewey became the most prestigious American intellectual to make the case for a "new liberalism" that approximated democratic socialism (Dewey, 1935). George Counts and other radicalized progressives of the Depression era called upon the schools to help "build a new social order" based upon "the administration for the common good of the means of production and the wide adoption of the principles of social and economic planning." In order to be genuinely progressive, Counts maintained, educators needed to teach from a politically progressive perspective that reflected their authentic social insight and not be stifled by "the bogeys of *imposition* and *indoctrination*" (as cited in Cremin, 1961, pp. 259, 263).

The relationship of educational reform to the nurturance of social consciousness and social action again became a pressing concern during the tumultuous '60s and '70s. Within higher education was it enough to widen access and design institutions that were highly responsive to the perceived interests and needs of individual students? Or did dissenting academics have a responsibility to guide their students toward a heightened awareness of social issues, or even a particular vision of society, its problems and their possible solutions, that derived from the faculty's own study of these matters? At ESC, faculty were invested with little authority to require students to address great social questions or to teach any "correct" analysis of them. But the 1971–1972 *Empire State College Bulletin* proclaimed that the future survival of humanity would require "sound judgments and wise priorities," lest a "new human nature" develop "combining the animal irrationality of primitive man with the materialistic greed and lust of industrial man, and powered by the destructive forces available from modern technology." The bulletin's rhetoric virtually threatens students with the urgent need to think together with their faculty mentors about how their education might help the world avoid calamity and achieve "expansion of human satisfactions and potentials" (p. 11).

Viewed from certain angles the progressive goals of general access, student-centered learning, and education for democratic social reform appear quite compatible with each other. In the progressive vision, educational opportunities of many kinds would become much more broadly available. All learners would be treated as individuals with their own interests, objectives, needs, and circumstances taken into account to achieve appropriately personalized educational outcomes. Since individuals must cooperate with one another to sustain and improve any functioning society, schools at all levels would also enable students to acquire the knowledge, skills, and disposition needed to confront and resolve social problems in a democratic manner.

Yet this progressive vision was far more harmonious in the abstract than it was when put to the test of practice. Serving large and ever growing numbers of students did not easily go hand in hand with meticulous attention to the learning interests of individuals, let alone the coordination of those interests to explore some Deweyan "common purpose" through "conjoint activities." This is one reason why student-centered learning never took hold as well in most public schools and colleges as it did in small, private, alternative institutions. Nor did commitment to free individual self-expression and development blend smoothly with the desire to raise students' social and political consciousness and activism, particularly when faculty and administrators had strong views of their own about what positions on public issues a well-educated person should hold. In practice, student-centeredness, expanded access, and education for social change often became competing goods that struggled for institutional supremacy. A paramount drive to construct an ideologically "correct" academic community placed inherent limits on the number of students who would feel comfortable within that community and upon the individual student's sense of intellectual freedom. An overriding commitment to self-directed, individualized learning could limit a school to serving a select group of highly introspective (and perhaps overly self-absorbed) students. A predominant concern for continuous expansion might cause an institution to find ways to serve more and more people, but in a mass production mode, that did little to stimulate the unique potential of individuals or thoughtful engagement with social issues.

In short, there was, as Cremin (1961) said, an "authentic progressive vision" for the future of education, but it was one that conveyed a conflicted legacy to new generations of educational reformers who were, in effect, challenged either to choose among competing goals and values, or to try to find ways to bring them into acceptable balance. This became the challenge for Empire State as a college in the progressive tradition.

II.

ESC's founders committed the College to the paired goals of greatly expanded access and highly student-centered education, viewing these objectives as fundamentally consistent with each other. The State University of New York's

(SUNY) Chancellor Ernest Boyer stated that this new college was created "in response to an urgent need ... to serve more students of all ages" while "keeping the individual student constantly in mind and tailoring education to his requirements" (Empire State College, 1971–1972, p. 5). In his investiture address, the first president, James W. Hall, said that ESC would seek to "demonstrate that individual learning and mass education need not be contradictory." Hall thought that a "focus on the individual student" could improve the overall quality of American higher education (Hall, 1991, pp. 128–129). ESC would enable each student not just to obtain a college degree, but to achieve an education that was better for him or her than it might have been had the student gone elsewhere. If, as Hall later said, traditional institutions felt "threatened" by ESC (Empire State College, 2006, p. 10) it was perhaps less due to the College's pledge to serve largely ignored groups, such as adult and part-time and place bound students, than to Empire's assertion that personalized degree planning, individual learning contracts developed in collaboration with faculty mentors, and many other of the College's features "should help people learn better, not merely differently ... to improve *what* is learned as well as how it is learned" (Empire State College, 1972–1973, p. 5). If this was true, then maybe *all students* who attended more traditional institutions were among the "underserved." In 2013 ESC's new president, Merodie Hancock, welcomed students by stating that the College was founded "to allow students to earn a college degree without taking classes at a set time and place" in order to "fit the lives" of "adult learners" (Empire State College, 2013–2014, p. 1). But in its early years ESC did not present itself mainly as a second chance school or a college of last resort for adults who found it difficult to attend at a fixed time and place. Indeed, the idea that ESC and other institutions with similar progressive characteristics could produce *superior* educational outcomes led some within the College to argue that a new model was being generated that should be adopted throughout higher education.

Open admission to a system of guided independent study did mesh well with an individualized approach to student-centered education when it made it possible for students who wanted to study unusual subject matter, or combine subjects in an unusual way, or approach them using unusual methods, to do so by designing customized degree programs and learning contracts. Even when ESC students chose to organize their programs around entirely traditional academic fields and topics, individualized learning contracts could take into account the particular interests, goals, questions, experiences, life situation, and learning style that the student brought to the study. (Let a thousand variations on Introduction to Psychology bloom!) Under the influence of Arthur Chickering, its first vice president for academic affairs, a belief became deeply embedded within Empire's early culture that it was best for all students to pursue their intellectual and affective development by placing a unique personal stamp on their education, both through the design of the degree plan and the execution of the studies within it. To ensure academic integrity, this was to be done under the guidance and ultimate authority of the faculty, and in accord with several broad cognitive and developmental objectives defined by the College (Bonnabeau, 1996, pp. 22–26, 41–42; Empire State College, 1972–73, pp. 45–55).

This "Chickeringesque" concept of self-initiated, collaboratively constructed learning was often claimed to be Empire State College's educational ideal, and it continues to appeal to a number of veteran faculty hired during the 1970s and '80s, as well as some newer colleagues. However, it was never an uncontested vision within the College, nor ever the entire reality of daily practice. In order to provide effective access for students who "desire a more structured and predictable educational experience," as the 1972 annual report put it, President Hall supported the creation of pre-structured independent study course materials (Empire State College, 1972, p. 7). This initiative took several forms, but by the end of the 1970s brought the Center for Distance Learning (CDL) into being, offering a substantial number of tightly constructed courses that could be delivered by a changing core of adjunct instructors in addition to CDL's full-time coordinating faculty. At first these courses were commonly regarded outside CDL as a substitute for the true Empire experience, but useful for students whose geographic location or personal circumstances made it too difficult to come to the College's regional learning centers and units for one-to-one study with mentors. However, when CDL grew in the online era to become ESC's largest single program, it appeared a bit ludicrous to say any longer that it was not the "real thing."

Additionally, a very large majority of students attracted to ESC turned out unexpectedly to be adults with jobs and families who chiefly appreciated the opportunity to attend college without the obstacle of a fixed classroom schedule. Many of them were more than content to let their faculty mentors assume the lion's share of responsibility for setting their learning objectives, selecting their text materials, choosing their writing topics, and planning other details of their studies. One might say that these students were escaping from the freedom extended to them by Empire's educational principles and policies, but the connotations of student-centeredness were elastic enough to allow this shift to be defended as an appropriate response to students' needs or desires. Looking back from 2006 on his long tenure as president, Hall distinguished between "individualization and responding to the individual." "For me," he said, "responding to each student as an individual always seemed less limiting, less coercive, less of a new orthodoxy than individualization" (Empire State College, 2006, p. 12).

If many students made no demands to be treated as individuals with regard to the academic content of their studies or how their performance in them would be assessed, this freed faculty with large numbers of students studying the same subject to create generic learning contracts for continuous reuse. (Let one version of Introduction to Psychology bloom!) A growing student body composed mainly of part-time students imposed heavy workloads on faculty, moving them increasingly to look for ways to reduce individualization, as a special committee on faculty roles frankly phrased it in 1994. The committee asked the College to consider some major changes: creating "pre-established curricula" for students "wishing a specific disciplinary education," which would "eliminate the need for degree program planning"; directing students "into less 'individualized' learning arrangements for a part of their program," such as CDL courses and group studies; making the registration system similar to a traditional college by replacing individualized enrollment cycles with several "fixed terms"; and "the use of grades rather than narrative evaluations" to record and assess a student's performance at the end of a study (Altes, Coughlan, Gerardi, & Muzio, 1994, pp. 13–14).

As a number of these changes, and other standardizing measures, were eventually put in place, gaining momentum since the early 2000s during the presidencies of Joseph Moore and Alan Davis, there was much conversation about whether the College was losing its sense of itself as an alternative and progressive institution (Willis, 2007). ESC might be serving ever more students, and perhaps doing it more efficiently, but was it also becoming primarily an alternative "delivery system" for a conventional and impersonal education? President Hall had surely been right to worry that individualization could become a constricting "new orthodoxy," limiting the College's ability to work with a large and diverse population of potential students who were not attuned to this way of thinking about education. However, Empire's original claim to provide its students with better, more authentic learning than they had (or would have) experienced at more traditional institutions was based principally on individualization, as is quite evident in the language of the College's early publications, often written by Chickering. The sense of professional purpose and pride of many faculty stemmed from the belief that as mentors they were helping their students achieve something of special value in their lives that went beyond a degree or a career boost or a typical package of collegiate knowledge and skills, but reached deeper levels of self-discovery and personal growth. Recognizing that most students probably did not arrive at ESC with this expectation, it was still disheartening to think that as an institution ESC was losing interest in moving students toward what some faculty called a "transformative" educational experience.

In order to preserve this vision of educational possibility, it seemed necessary to nurture "the quality of the mentor and student relationship," which "largely determines the quality of the student's education," according to the College's first formulation of its Core Values in 1993 (as cited in Altes et al., 1994, p. 3). Since then, efforts to sustain, revitalize, and better comprehend the activity of mentoring have been made by the ESC Mentoring Institute and its successor, the Center for Mentoring and Learning. Many articles in the College's journal *All About Mentoring* have been devoted to the challenge and promise of academic mentoring, as is the book *From Teaching to Mentoring* by Lee Herman and Alan Mandell (2004) based on their work with students at ESC. The Center for Distance Learning's pre-structured group course model was long seen as the College's greatest deviation from the path of individualized education. But in recent years some faculty have developed online distance offerings that provide individual students with quite rich opportunities to define and pursue their personal interests within the very broad framework of the course (Ball, 2009; Ball, 2010; Vander Valk, 2010).

Nevertheless, more than a few might agree with the mentor who argued that ESC is no longer "a school built around individualized study," if it ever really was, and that few of its students or faculty now "are prepared to teach or learn through individualized methods." To face up to these alleged realities, this mentor proposed that a special program be established to "invite inventive degrees" and devise individualized studies for those who want them. The much larger portion of ESC could then happily drop any pretense to individualization (Wunsch, 2011, p. 46). The complete elimination of narrative evaluations of students' learning in 2012 and their replacement by transcripts consisting entirely of letter grades was one of the College's most striking departures from the individualized practices long advocated by progressive educators. Composing written evaluations of each student's learning in each of their studies had always been a time consuming, burdensome part of the faculty's work life. But the College had consistently maintained that narrative evaluation was "central to its educational program" and "an integral part of the learning process," enhancing the students' "learning and understanding" of their own personal "strengths, weakness, abilities and accomplishments" (Empire State College, 2011–2012, p. 20). The divisive debates within governance bodies that preceded the abandonment of narratives showed that, while many current faculty supported grades as a work reduction measure, they also no longer believed that narratives were an especially valuable or necessary method for expressing the content and outcomes of a student's learning endeavor. If grades, written comments on papers, and feedback in student conferences were sufficient at most other institutions, why not at ESC? Instead of priding itself on its differences from the academic mainstream, as it had in earlier years, the College appeared increasingly willing to let that mainstream set the standards by which it judged itself. Faculty now frequently describe themselves as "teachers" or "instructors," rather than as "mentors," to their students, and they carefully list their own degrees, faculty rank, and subject area specializations in their internal communications with students and colleagues.

Highly individualized learning is unlikely to disappear completely at ESC. Still, in a recent interview, former president Moore urged ESC to recognize that "the core of any higher education enterprise now is enrollment ... The key is enrollment growth" to meet the need for increased revenue (Warzala, 2013, p. 53). ESC's continuing drive to serve greater numbers, adding structured degree programs and certificates targeted at specific "cohorts" of prospective undergraduate and graduate students does not place individualization at the forefront of the College's approach to learning. Nor does the Academic Assessment Plan drafted in 2013 stipulating every individual learning contract study be designed with "clearly articulated," predetermined learning outcomes that will also be in "alignment" with a new set of collegewide learning goals approved in 2012, *and* with outcomes statements *and* rubrics developed by the faculty for concentrations in each of ESC's "areas of study" *and* for each of the subject categories required by SUNY's undergraduate general education policy. As the plan states, "a critical component of alignment will be the linkage of course/contract outcomes to goals at the program/concentration, general education, and college learning goal levels." The formulation of this multilayered plan is ESC's response to pressures upon America's colleges and universities today to demonstrate their "ongoing, continued assessment of student learning and institutional effectiveness" to skeptical external accrediting and funding organizations (Empire State College, 2013). But it is easy to imagine the spirit of free, individual inquiry being crushed under the weight of all these prescribed outcomes. As one mentor put it at the point of his retirement, the College "has moved in ever tightening circles toward greater structure and accountability" that conflict with the "pristine model of open-ended collaboration" between learner and mentor upon which his own 30-year career at ESC had been based (Lewis, 2013, p. 67). The current ESC bulletin (which now, inauspiciously, calls itself the "undergraduate catalog") no longer assumes that students will do *any* individualized studies in their programs. It does say that the College "strongly encourages students to create individualized studies that move you closer to your goals" (Empire State College, 2013–2014, p. 38). Might that sentence eventually be revised to read, "Students may attempt to create individualized studies that are appropriate to their programs," and be relegated to a footnote in small print?

And what of progressive education's third theme, democratic social reform? Although its first bulletin had rather stridently called students' attention to the grave dangers facing the late 20th century world, ESC has always prioritized access and student-centeredness over education with a progressive political agenda. The College's early publications conveyed an impression that many students were looking to forge lives and careers outside the corporate world, as teachers, social workers, labor union officials, public administrators, writers and artists. Within some corners of the College, this atmosphere survived beyond ESC's formative period. But from the profiles of students and their interdisciplinary liberal arts degree programs featured in the 1972–1973 bulletin, one would not guess that Business, Management, and Economics quickly became the most popular area of study and has stayed on top decade after decade (Empire State College, 1972–1973, pp. 9–28). Be that as it may, ESC's adult students have thick connections to society. They often are heavily engaged in a variety of community activities when they enter the College, sometimes to the point where they need to cut back on these involvements in order to find time for study. Those who concentrate in Community and Human Services or Public Affairs often connect their prior experiential learning to new theoretical and applied studies in social and behavioral science. A far smaller number of students have chosen to develop concentrations in the area of Social Theory, Social Structure, and Change where fundamental questions about the organization and direction of society are perhaps most likely to be raised and explored in depth. (The renaming of this area of study as simply "Social Science" in 2014 might signify to some a declining interest in the use of social research to spark major social change.)

Over the years, faculty have repeatedly expressed concern about the narrowly careerist content of many students' self-designed programs and occasionally argued that perhaps all should be required to address a few topics of critical social importance, such as cultural diversity or the world environmental crisis. Proposals of this sort never really took hold. The honoring of the individual student's self-declared learning interests and objectives had sunk deeper roots in ESC's institutional culture. "We are not social reformers," said Herman and Mandell in *From Teaching to Mentoring* (2004, p. 10). But in its increasingly prescriptive mode, ESC now defines "Social Responsibility" as one of the new "learning goals" in which *all* graduates are to "demonstrate competence," including ability to "engage in ethical reasoning, and reflect on issues such as democratic citizenship, diversity, social justice and environmental sustainability, both locally and globally" (Empire State College, 2013–2014, p. 17). Whether this ostensible requirement will stimulate a vibrant climate of social concern and activism among students and their mentors remains to be seen. Like other core curricular requirements throughout higher education, it might be predicted that this one (if it is actually enforced) will be embraced by some, resented by others, and passively endured by many more.

At the institutional level ESC's sense of its own social responsibility has always been connected to its commitment to educational access. Might a dramatic expansion of access itself be a vehicle of social transformation? The 1971 SUNY *Prospectus* for ESC went so far as to claim that "An intelligent person from the ghetto or urban area or isolated community who is currently at a disadvantage in learning the predominant cultural symbols system in our society will not be excluded because he cannot communicate within that symbol system or reflect its cultural expectations. He will learn for his own purposes and at his own pace within a community of his own choosing" (as cited in State University of New York, 2003, p. 9). ESC has never actually attempted to construct such a radically "Open Community of Learning," although it has accepted most applicants with a high school diploma or its equivalent, and struggled with the resulting problems of students who are underprepared for college-level learning as it is usually conceived. Exactly because it appears to set aside conventional academic standards in order to serve the very most nontraditional of learners, the *Prospectus* remains, over 40 years later, the College's most provocative, if forgotten, gesture toward the *societally* transformative possibilities of education.

III.

There are many reasons why alternative colleges of one sort or another gradually revert to more conventional thought and practice, if they even survive long enough to do so. Jencks and Riesman observed in 1968 that at "offbeat" colleges, "True believers feel obliged to testify to their faith both in and out of season, and such an atmosphere makes daily life more strenuous than most people can stand for ten or twenty years. This is one reason why almost every experimental college has eventually redefined its goals, or at least the distinctive manner by which it initially pursued them, in such a way as to bring it closer to the academic mainstream"

(p. 502). Moreover, with the passage of time, successful alternative colleges start "to attract prospective faculty and students only partially committed to the original revolutionary vision." Applying this analysis to ESC, it is true that by the 1990s, if not well before, senior faculty were caught between their lingering "faith" in the ideal of individualized education and their weariness at trying to live out that ideal in their work with large numbers of students who were themselves not committed to it. These senior mentors were steadily joined by new colleagues who often admired the College's ideals and values, but wanted a more traditionally balanced professional life that left them with time and energy to devote to scholarly or artistic projects not directly tied to their work with students (Rounds, 2009).

Perhaps ESC could have accommodated mounting external demands for accountability and the desire of its faculty for a more manageable and balanced work life without shedding so many of its old ways, if it had been able to operate like a small, private, liberal arts institution in the progressive tradition with full-time students selected (and self-selected) to fit its educational philosophy. But ESC was not created to be a public equivalent of Hampshire or Sarah Lawrence or Goddard, challenging though that would have been. Rather, ESC was intended to serve a large, growing, heterogeneous, unselective body of students only a small fraction of whom were consciously seeking a Goddard- or Hampshire-like learning environment. Throughout the 20th century, progressive schools devoted to expanding access had usually provided a far more standardized type of education than progressive schools that were born to assist the self-educational quests of individual students (Ravitch, 2000, p. 59). Few institutions that serve over 20,000 students per year, as ESC now does, are known for their ability to provide a highly personalized educational experience. By seeking to become both a large, open access institution and a place for intensively individualized learning, Empire State from the outset internalized tensions that made it very difficult to form an intellectually cohesive community of faculty, administrators, and students who were genuinely dedicated to common principles and practices.

This incoherence continues to buffet and beleaguer those who work and study at ESC today. Students shuttle confusedly between highly pre-structured courses or one-size-fits-all learning contracts supervised by faculty who may grant them little personal agency, and individualized tutorials, small study groups, weekend residencies, and online learning opportunities with mentors who expect them to take a very active role in shaping, and even evaluating, their learning. Is the student to regard herself mainly as the fortunate beneficiary of the faculty's instructional moves, or as a learner increasingly adept in the art of intellectual self-direction? How far should a mentor go in acceding to the preference of a student who appreciates being told "exactly what to do" and says that other ESC "courses" have provided him with this explicit and expert guidance? ESC may be as far away as it has ever been from being able to respond to such questions in a consistent and credible manner that unites principle with practice.

It must be noted that none of this has prevented the College from establishing itself as a very successful institution by measures such as growth, student satisfaction surveys, and excellent accreditation reviews. Collegewide meetings and any issue of *All About Mentoring* reveal a lively atmosphere of academic debate and experimentation, although some "fresh ideas" within the ESC context (such as rubrics and grading standards) reinvent the College as a more traditional and formal institution. For better or worse, the ESC professional community now appears to be tolerating the College's inconsistencies in a rising spirit of live and let live that defers to the reality of our condition, however unsatisfying this may be to anyone who hungers for a coherent college culture and a consistently applied philosophy of education. This may be Empire State College's organizational destiny – an educational eclecticism that is conceptually rather cloudy but pragmatically sufficient to the day as the College seeks to survive and thrive while managing the inherently conflicting tendencies within the legacy of progressive education.

## REFERENCES

Altes, J., Coughlan, R., Gerardi, J., & Muzio, L. (1994). *The mentor role report*. Saratoga Springs, NY: Empire State College.
Ball, E. L. (2009). A tale of freedom and temptation, part 1. *All About Mentoring, 36*, 41–51.
Ball, E. L. (2010). A tale of freedom and temptation, part 2. *All About Mentoring, 37*, 4–19.
Bonnabeau, R. (1996). *The promise continues: Empire State College – The first twenty-five years*. Virginia Beach, VA: The Donning Company Publishers.
Brubacher, J. S., & Rudy, W. (1997). *Higher education in transition: A history of American colleges and universities* (4th ed.). New Brunswick, NJ: Transaction Publishers.
Cremin, L. A. (1961). *The transformation of the school: Progressivism in American education, 1876–1957*. New York, NY: Alfred A. Knopf.
Cuban, L. (1993). *How teachers taught*. New York, NY: Teacher's College Press.
Dewey, J. (1900). *The school and society*. Chicago, IL: University of Chicago Press.
Dewey, J. (1935). *Liberalism and social action*. New York, NY: G. P. Putnam's Sons.
Empire State College. (1971–1972). *Empire State College bulletin*. Saratoga Springs, NY: Author.
Empire State College. (1972). *Seeking alternatives*. Saratoga Springs, NY: Author.
Empire State College. (1972–1973). *Empire State College bulletin*. Saratoga Springs, NY: Author.
Empire State College. (2006, March 23). *Convocation for James W. Hall*. Saratoga Springs, NY: Author.
Empire State College. (2011–2012). *Empire State College undergraduate catalog*. Saratoga Springs, NY: Author.
Empire State College. (2013, January 7). *Empire State College academic assessment plan, revised draft*. Saratoga Springs, NY: Author.
Empire State College. (2013–2014). *Empire State College undergraduate catalog*. Saratoga Springs, NY: Author.
Hall, J. W. (1991). *Access through innovation: New colleges for new students*. New York, NY: Macmillan Publishing Company.
Herman, L., & Mandell, A. (2004). *From teaching to mentoring*. New York, NY: Routledge.
Jencks, C., & Riesman, D. (1968). *The academic revolution*. New York, NY: Doubleday and Company.
Kett, J. F. (1994). *The pursuit of knowledge under difficulties: From self-improvement to adult education in America, 1750–1990*. Stanford, CA: Stanford University Press.
Kliewer, J. R. (1999). *The innovative campus*. Phoenix, AZ: American Council on Education/Oryx Press.
Lewis, S. (2013). One last narrative evaluation. *All About Mentoring, 43*, 67–68.
State University of New York. (2003). Prospectus for a new university college: Objectives, process, structure and establishment, 1971. *All About Mentoring, 26*, 9.
Ravitch, D. (2000). *Left back: A century of failed school reforms*. New York, NY: Simon and Schuster.
Rounds, C. (2009). A sustainable model for mentoring. *All About Mentoring, 36*, 4–7.

Vander Valk, F. (2010). Fugitives, freedom, and the mentoring moment. *All About Mentoring, 38*, 41–44.
Ward, L. F. (1883). *Dynamic sociology, or applied social science, as based upon statical sociology and the less complex sciences* (Vol. 1). New York, NY: D. Appleton and Company.
Warzala, E. (2013). A conversation with Joseph B. Moore, part one. *All About Mentoring, 43*, 50–55.
Willis, W. (2007). "Killing the spirit"? Empire State College in the 21st century. *All About Mentoring, 32*, 4–8.
Wunsch, J. (2011). Old Socrates and a new beginning. *All About Mentoring, 40*, 45–46.
Zilversmit, A. (1993). *Changing schools: Progressive education theory and practice, 1930–1960*. Chicago, IL: University of Chicago Press.

RICHARD F. BONNABEAU

# 2. CONFLICT, CHANGE, AND CONTINUITY

*ESC's Goddard College and British Open University Connections*

> When the history of Empire State College is written … notice will of course be taken of the wide range of sources of ideas and practices which fed into the unusual institutional context which became Empire State College. …
>
> Forest K. Davis

The State University of New York's Empire State College (SUNY ESC) came into being in 1971. It was planned the year before by a task force of top SUNY System administrators gathered by Chancellor Ernest L. Boyer. Boyer, a progressive educator, was a colleague and friend of Royce "Tim" Pitkin, the founder of Goddard College. Pitkin was a staunch follower of John Dewey and William Heard Kilpatrick – the latter a proponent of Dewey's educational philosophy and subsequently a faculty colleague at Columbia University's Teachers College.

Boyer's task force included James W. Hall, SUNY's assistant vice chancellor for policy and planning, who was subsequently appointed ESC's first president. Hall served in that capacity for 27 years. During his first years as president, he worked to strengthen connections between Empire State College and the British Open University.

THE EMPIRE STATE COLLEGE GENOME: TWO HEREDITARY STREAMS

Two hereditary streams dominated Empire State College's evolution, and they were radically different from one another. One flowed from the progressive educational philosophy of John Dewey, elaborated by William Heard Kilpatrick, as well as other reformist educators. It was brought to Empire State College from Goddard College by Arthur W. Chickering, ESC's founding vice president for academic affairs. This progressive philosophy emphasized individualized study springing from the student's purposes and co-designed by students and faculty. It placed the student's learning at the center of the educational dialog and recognized learning wherever it might have been gained. The second stream, whose emphasis was on access, was correspondence study, whose American lineage stretched back in time to the 1800s. It was considered both inferior to classroom-based education and, like the revolutionary advent of online education in the latter part of the 20th century, a threat to traditional classroom-based education. Despite subsequent advances in audio and

*K. Jelly & A. Mandell (Eds.), Principles, Practices, and Creative Tensions in Progressive Higher Education, 43–64.*
*© 2017 Sense Publishers. All rights reserved.*

televisual technology in the 1950s and 1960s, it remained a less well-respected segment of American higher education. But Empire State College, in keeping with its founding charter, tested various innovative approaches to structured independent study, including materials and technology, to provide alternatives to individualized contract learning.

Key to some of ESC's early success was the creation of the British Open University (BOU) in 1969, formally known as "The Open University." It was established by Prime Minister Harold Wilson and his Labour Party as an alternative to the elitist universities of the United Kingdom. The BOU's brand of correspondence study, combined with supplemental course materials produced by the British Broadcasting Company (BBC), rocketed the university to stratospheric heights of acceptability and worldwide acclaim. Soon the dominance of the classroom-mode of delivery in the United Kingdom was upended by a nationwide distribution system of independent study guides for adult learners, supported by study centers as well as by BBC radio and weekly television broadcasts, which were boosted by the allied technologies of audio and video tape players for their further distribution and asynchronous utility.

Eventually, Empire State College joined the growing number of American colleges and universities that became avid consumers of BOU print and mediated course materials to serve the growing market of adult learners. These institutions, including ESC, wanted to make the most of correspondence course materials and technology to bridge distance and increase access. But they also, as part of a nationwide effort, wanted to respond to critics, including disaffected youth, who at a time when higher education was implicated in much that seemed wrong with a society embattled by the civil rights movement and an unpopular war in Southeast Asia, were demanding more accountability from American higher education. ESC hopped on to the bandwagon after having invested heavily and failing in the first few years of its existence to promote among its pioneer faculty the use of learning modules, a unique brand of flexible and often interdisciplinary independent study guides – some produced by notable scholars.

## GODDARD COLLEGE: ROYCE "TIM" PITKIN AND ARTHUR W. CHICKERING

It would however be the progressive stream championed by Arthur Chickering that initially dominated ESC's academic program, a development that created deep ideological discord among faculty and administrators, some of whom were advocating for a more comprehensive approach than just individualized learning rooted in student purposes. Chickering had joined Goddard in 1959. He had a bachelor's degree in comparative literature from Wesleyan University, a master's degree in teaching English from Harvard, a Ph.D. from Columbia University's Graduate School of Education, and a background in teaching at the secondary and college levels. Both Pitkin and Chickering were New Englanders – as was Dewey; both were strong willed and compassionate; both had a deep commitment to the sanctity of the individual learner and the progressive principles of democratizing education in an era when curricular rigidity was the norm; and both had followed similar paths in their doctoral dissertations at Columbia by signaling an independence of mind and a desire to break new ground.

Goddard College was Pitkin's creation. He joined Goddard in 1935 when it was a Universalist seminary. These were troubled times. Vermont was in the depths of the Great Depression and plummeting enrollments threatened Goddard's existence. Under Pitkin's leadership, Goddard evolved from being a seminary to being a junior college that connected the last two years of high school and the first two years of college; and in 1938 it became a four-year liberal arts college. Pitkin revolutionized the curriculum, drawing heavily on Dewey's *Art as Experience* to provide guidance "about teaching and learning, and to help ... develop an educational theory" (Benson & Adams, 1987, p. 32). His thinking was "greatly influenced at the outset by Bennington [College, which both Dewey and Kilpatrick had an instrumental role in founding], by Sarah Lawrence, and to some extent by Antioch [University's] off-campus work idea" (Benson & Adams, 1987, p. 207). Under Pitkin's leadership, Goddard became a college without prescribed curricula and without exams and grades. In their stead, students charted their own pathways in declaring their purposes and goals with the guidance of faculty counselors. Notably, grades were replaced by thoughtful narrative evaluations composed by both faculty and their students.

Pitkin had a deep-seated belief that students should educate themselves. Of course, Goddard students did not start off with independent study. The first two years, called the junior division, were devoted to courses on large topics akin to the British Open University's foundation courses: They were broad in thematic scope, but radically different in not focusing on a lockstep progression – unlike the BOU – through rigidly defined content. This approach allowed for individualized independent study forays driven by student interest as opposed to the prescribed curricula. This was learning that was made palpable by the dialectical thrust and parry of discussions with fellow students as well as faculty – a methodology highly prized by Pitkin that he had experienced as Kilpatrick's graduate student at Columbia University. Within two years, Goddard students were ready to enter the senior division, which focused on independent studies and senior theses, but not before presenting convincing rationales for their readiness to do so.

There was more to Goddard than just providing an intense learner-centered environment. In keeping with Dewey's philosophy, the College aimed at the education of the whole person and at education for democracy. Guided independent study was not enough. Students had to become engaged with other students – individually, cooperatively, and democratically – in the operation and maintenance of Goddard's buildings and grounds, including the scrubbing of floors, cleaning bathrooms, sharing in cafeteria duties, tapping maple trees, participating in student government, and becoming a voice in the affairs of the community beyond the campus. In this way, they "would see life as a whole, rather than as a collection of parts" (Benson & Adams, 1987, p. 20). Goddard was in a sense an educational commune, but for some neighboring Vermonters and even educators afar, it smacked of communism with a capital C. If there was anything totalitarian about Pitkin's commonwealth, it was the insistence communicated by Pitkin and reinforced by senior faculty that newcomers, especially those fresh from graduate school, not import the repressive practices of conventional education. As Pitkin put it, "Faculty should not stay and teach at a college if they disagree with the school's basic philosophy" (Benson & Adams, 1987, p. 41).

This was the environment that most shaped Chickering's thinking as an educator. In regard to Pitkin's influence and that of other Goddard colleagues, he observed that Pitkin "was far and away my number one mentor. My whole career has been built on what I learned from him, George Beecher, Forest Davis and my immersion in the Goddard experience" (Chickering, 2012b).

### BONDS OF UNION: ROYCE S. PITKIN, ERNEST L. BOYER, AND SAMUEL B. GOULD

Pitkin had not lost sight of Goddard's potential role in promoting adult education opportunities, and he did so brilliantly. By 1954, Goddard had offered

> sixteen years of conferences, workshops, and undergraduate education. Goddard led the nation in developing programs that responded to the need for adult education in a society of growing complexity and declining job hours. ... It was a pioneering institution dedicated to teaching, to creating an environment in which people could educate themselves. It breathed the spirit of freedom. (Benson & Adams, 1987, p. 134)

Pitkin became a prime mover in the creation of a national consortium called the Union for Experimenting Colleges and Universities (the Union), which begat the Union Graduate School and fostered the University Without Walls movement in the United States and beyond. Both the principles and practices of this movement were based on Goddard's Adult Degree Program, though Antioch got "credit for an idea that originated with Goddard" (Benson & Adams, 1987, p. 209).

Pitkin and his Union associates offered Ernest Boyer the position of executive officer. At the time, Boyer was the director for the Center for Coordinated Education at the University of California, Santa Barbara. He had been hired by Samuel Gould, who had developed close ties with Boyer through Goddard during his tenure as Antioch's president (1954–1959). As Forest Davis noted,

> [Gould] used to come to Goddard, as they all did, and Ernest [Boyer] did. They were all in and out of each other's projects quite a bit. Once in a while Royce Pitkin would get up a group of six or eight of us and take us some place to a conference. They would show up. (Davis, 1991, p. 7)

Gould had vacated his presidency of Antioch College to assume the post of chancellor for the University of California at Santa Barbara, which he held until 1964 when he was hired as SUNY's new chancellor. Boyer turned down Pitkin's offer to join the

Union in order to follow Gould and serve as SUNY's executive university dean, and to play a key role in Gould's strategy to integrate the campus fiefdoms into an integrated state university system, a process continued by Boyer and energized by Chancellor Nancy Zimpher, the current SUNY chancellor (Benson & Adams, 1987, p. 208).

Boyer's appointment as SUNY's first executive dean for universitywide services was the beginning of his meteoric ascent to become one of America's most prominent educators in the last quarter of the 20th century. In 1970, Boyer succeeded Gould as chancellor, a position he held until 1977, when he was appointed U.S. commissioner of education by President Jimmy Carter. In 1979, Boyer began his tenure as president of the Carnegie Foundation for Education, for which he relocated from Washington, D.C., to Princeton, New Jersey.

Pitkin had known Boyer since the mid-1950s, when Boyer was the dean at Upland College, a Brethren in Christ College in California. Boyer worked with Pitkin as a member of the Council for the Advancement of Small Colleges (CASC). He stated emphatically in 1981 in an address presented at Evergreen College, that "It was [due to] the influence of Tim Pitkin that I urged the Trustees of the State University of New York to start Empire State College ..." (Boyer, 1981, p. 2). Notably, in 1968 Boyer had discussed with SUNY Chancellor Gould the possibility of introducing various progressive alternatives to SUNY campuses, among them experimental units analogous to the University Without Walls. But Boyer became "convinced that what SUNY really needed was a new, free-standing college – a non-campus institution with an integrity and identity of its own. Chancellor Gould agreed." SUNY campuses, however, were "under siege" by rebellious students protesting the war in Vietnam, which delayed implementation. Yet, continued Boyer, the launching of the British Open University "kept the spark alive" (Boyer, 1990, pp. 2–3).

## ESC'S FOUNDING CHARTER, *A PROSPECTUS FOR A NEW UNIVERSITY COLLEGE*

Boyer's task force began its work in 1970, the year that he was appointed chancellor and the year that the Kent State massacre ignited massive nationwide student protests. By February 1971, the task force plan, called *A Prospectus for a New University College* (Boyer, 1971), was ready for review. Boyer included Arthur Chickering on its panel of distinguished American educators. His selection made good and perfect sense. Chickering had gained national prominence through his award-winning 1969 book, *Education and Identity*, and his long association with Boyer through Goddard College made his contribution potentially invaluable. Chickering found much to like in a document resounding with the progressive language of learner centeredness and access:

> It will be a commitment to the people that the educational process shall serve the variety of individuals of all ages, throughout society, according to their

own life styles and educational needs. It will seek to transcend conventional academic structure which imposes required courses, set periods of time, and residential constraints of place upon the individual student. ... This emphasis will place the central focus upon the individual student learning at his own pace with the guidance and counseling of master teachers. (Boyer, 1971, p. 4)

Of particular note was the emergent definition of the mentor role, which became so central to the spirit of ESC's pedagogy, whose genealogy, if not nomenclature, would be shared with the unique advisement role of faculty created by Pitkin during the very first year of Goddard's existence.

The ESC equivalent of faculty counselors became known as "mentors" – a term first used by James Hall in his *All Hallows' Eve Reflections*, penned in 1970, and part of a one-page statement of how a tutor/mentor model might work. Deputy Chancellor Merton Ertell, the chief planning officer for Boyer's task force, included Hall's reflections with three proposed models presented to Boyer that November:

Ertell liked the tutor/mentor model, a more flexible program than the Brockport or the British model. In addition, the program could be 'centrally administered through a network of collegiate tutorial centers, many of which might be located on a [SUNY] campus ... [and] easily extended to adults.' (Bonnabeau, 1996, p. 17)

In fact, the word "mentor" with grammatical variations is mentioned often in the *Prospectus* and figures prominently in the proposed staffing of a model regional learning center. A center would serve 400 students with three full-time mentors positioned at the apex of a silo of part-time instructional staff, including 20 study tutors and 16 correspondence tutors (Boyer, 1971, p. 27). The mentor was a key figure in various curricular modes of study, including a "more open program individually designed" and "tutorially guided"; and, in the interdisciplinary mode, the learning resource is identified as a "[c]oncept of a 'contract' of study" (p. 17). Through the interceding decades, the word "mentor" – in its popular usage – has earned a prominent position in the American lexicon.

Other elements shared with Goddard included placing "the responsibility of learning on the student in return for his freedom to pursue his education according to his individual needs and interests," having "learning ... related to his experience in the external world and ... problem solving activities which are real, as opposed to artificial abstractions," undertaking a "sustained task over time, to explore, where possible, without penalty of mistake" and being "enabled to see and understand his own emotions ..." (Boyer, 1971, pp. 5–9).

## THE *PROSPECTUS* AND THE BRITISH OPEN UNIVERSITY

While Goddard was not mentioned specifically in the *Prospectus*, the British Open University was. But it was quickly dismissed for not having relevance to the needs of the "New University College," neither as exemplar, nor as potential provider of course materials, because the BOU "requires each student to go through the same general structure of learning" (Boyer, 1971, p. 6). As Walter Perry, subsequently Lord Perry of Walton and the founding chief executive officer of the BOU, put it, the Open University could "only offer a limited choice to students on a take it or leave it basis ..." (Empire State College, 1982, p. 5).

The task force dismissal of the BOU was a rather curious aside. Chancellor Boyer had sent a number of members of his task force to the BOU to discover what they might find of value. Boyer even asked Arthur Chickering – no advocate for norm-referenced learning – to investigate. Boyer and Chickering "were good friends" (Chickering, 2011, p. 4). The BOU visit "reinforced ... [Chickering's] belief that such an approach would not serve diverse adults ... well" (Chickering, 2012a). For Hall, however, who was appointed by Boyer "to bring this unusual institution to life" (Empire State College, 1972, p. 22) the visit to the British Open University and meeting with Walter Perry would make a lasting impression.

## THE ADVENT OF ARTHUR W. CHICKERING: "THE ANVIL OF CONFLICT"

Boyer and Hall offered Chickering a top administrative post in the new College as vice president for academic affairs. Hall endorsed Boyer's choice enthusiastically and had even recommended Chickering for the presidency. For Chickering, being vice president for academic affairs was an opportunity to create in the public sphere a college based on the progressive principles practiced at Goddard but on a vast and monumental scale. With the *Prospectus* forecasting enrollments – almost as bold as the BOU's first cohort of 25,000 – reaching 10,000 students within three years and possibly 40,000 by 1975–1976, it was not difficult to imagine such an outcome (Boyer, 1971, p. 12). The potential was electrifying but the challenge, given Chickering's strongly-held values, would be putting into practice progressive principles to a magnitude never imagined by Pitkin. Though Pitkin had a major impact on American higher education, he kept Goddard numbers low (250 being the ideal), believing that small numbers provided for the low student-faculty ratio necessary to progressive education and to a democratic, vibrant and cohesive community of learners. So growth had to be organic; a mitotic process of replication to propagate new communities that adhered to these basic principles.

Chickering did not immediately accept Boyer's offer, conveyed by Hall. In fact, he had two dreams, two nights in a row that accurately foretold that troubled times lay ahead (Chickering, 2011, p. 15). He accepted Boyer's offer but they soon had vehement confrontations, defined as "maelstroms" by Chickering, about deeply-held fundamental principles with Loren Baritz, provost and vice president for learning resources: "Usually one of Loren's favorite strategies [at administrative council meetings] was to find some particular learning contract that was suspect and show it to Jim [President Hall], who would go ballistic" (Chickering, 2011, p. 9). Baritz was a scholar and a faculty member in SUNY Albany's (now known as the University at

Albany) Department of History, where Hall held a joint appointment when he was SUNY's assistant vice chancellor for policy and planning. Baritz, a very popular teacher, favored pre-established curricula as opposed to Chickering, who believed in the supremacy of student-driven purposes.

Chickering, as recounted by Hall, was

> '... very concerned with education as the central tool of human development and growth,' and recognized the opportunity 'to take this idea, this very personal individual approach ... [and] ... thereby improve the quality of education.' He did not want a 'pre-established curriculum,' believing that 'once you define a curriculum, no matter how creative it is, that becomes the driving force and the individual must be subordinate to it. ... The individual approach to designing a curriculum was truly revolutionary.'

For Baritz,

> 'responding to students as individuals did not mean going beyond meeting their intellectual needs,' nor did it mean 'constructing individualized curricula.' Although Baritz shared with Chickering the mission of creating student-centered alternatives to traditional education, he questioned the readiness of most students to pursue individualized study. Baritz disagreed with Chickering that 'every curriculum had to be individually constructed through a contract with an individual student.' As Baritz noted, he 'didn't know ... how the student was going to get a general education and not just follow his nose.'

As only Baritz could express it in his special brand of sardonic humor,

He brought this concern to overseeing the first 'learning contracts that were coming out of the various centers and scribbling little notes to people [mentors] about why they were criminals—doing a bad job,' Baritz believed, therefore, that structured independent study modules, often interdisciplinary in organization and designed by 'some of the most high-powered intellectuals in the country' was the best approach. (Bonnabeau, 1996, p. 24)

Chickering, though admiring Baritz for being "very creative and very original" about the content of learning modules, observed that

> [Baritz] thought faculty should be the primary determinant of what was taught and what was learned. I [Chickering] was certainly pushing the boundaries of having all the learning anchored in the students' purposes and motives and recognizing their background through assessing prior learning for work-life experiences. So, he and I were really two ends of a team. It was unfortunate in a way because content is clearly important, and he was socially and politically liberal. He and I were very much on the same page with these attitudes and

values, and, in so many ways, we were very similar but we were tangled up in this educational battle. (Chickering, 2011, p. 8)

## FORGING THE ACADEMIC PROGRAM

As vice president for academic affairs, Chickering moved quickly to give shape to the academic program. This included incorporating practices common to Goddard, such as contract learning – connected with the mentor role in the *Prospectus* – though not called as such at Goddard but emphasizing the primacy of student purposes. ESC students were expected to eventually write their own contracts and to join mentors in evaluating their own work, another Goddard-inspired practice (which in time gave way to the pressures on ESC mentors to keep up with mountains of paperwork and draconian deadlines). In regard to Chickering's academic legacy, as Forest Davis, a close colleague at Goddard and then founding associate dean at what was known as the Long Island Regional Learning Center, observed:

> Chickering represented – what shall I say – a kind of pouring of the concrete into certain molds of ways of doing things which he conceived of as being educationally worth doing, and which, no doubt, he also had learned partly at Goddard and partly from other sources because he was much more traveled, and much more institutionally exposed than the rest of us were, who had simply been at Goddard for a long time and might have been at one or two institutions in between. Chickering was always a guy who went everywhere and talked with people about everything and who knew people who did the same kinds of things. A professional consultant is a different kind of animal. And I often thought that, in those early days, Chickering did the college a great service to the extent that he fixed rather firmly certain ways of conducting educational processes largely from the administrative standpoint so that even when the college began to be shaken up constantly as it was in the middle '70s ... those ways of doing things pretty much endured. (Davis, 1991, p. 4)

In February 1972, to create greater consistency in practice across the College – just halfway through ESC's first year of existence – Chickering assembled two task force committees composed of faculty and administrators focused on academic practices. One was on contracts, records, and transcripts, and the other on assessment of prior (learning) experience. He chaired both committees. Also, Chickering further consolidated his position by having a major hand in hiring faculty recruited mostly from small colleges and "heavily invested in teaching and learning and sophisticated about those issues. They liked working one-on-one with students and the mentor role'" and Chickering believed that he "had very broad support among the faculty and among most of the learning center deans with a couple of exceptions" (Chickering, 2011, p. 10). Baritz, in contrast, saw his role in the hiring practice as "looking for bright people – who were driven to do research, who had done it all, and who were very dubious about the institution – hoping that they would drive it in the right direction" (Baritz, 1990, p. 10).

While Baritz hammered away at Chickering, he was unable to win much support for his learning modules program. In fact, Baritz had first run into strident opposition to the modules at the inaugural workshop to prepare faculty to work with students. It was the first All College Meeting (today, known as the All College Conference), held at the Institute on Man and Science in Rensselaerville, New York, from September 18 to 21, 1971. The presentation of learning modules, though they were innovative and ready resources, was seen as an intrusion by the faculty, "especially the younger ones"; and so they were quite vocal about not wanting "experts" coming down from Saratoga and interfering with their role in developing the academic program (Bonnabeau, 1996, p. 31). Chickering issued a statement shortly after the workshop: "Materials disseminated from the Learning Resources Center are simply additional resources for use by mentors and students. They are not prescriptive" (p. 32). In a convoluted way, this was a strange concession on Chickering's part in a bitterly fought battle between two highly principled individuals who would not yield in the slightest way to one another's strongly held convictions.

According to John Jacobson, who succeeded Chickering as the academic vice president, this was the beginning of a deeply-embedded conflict:

> The regional center faculty thought of themselves as being locked in mortal combat with the Development Faculty. So the Development Faculty weren't going to get anywhere with doing any programs that didn't conform to the mentoring center model. (Jacobson, 1993, p. 12)

The tension between the two groups of faculty was exacerbated by Baritz's expectation, which was voiced in the *Prospectus,* that his development faculty were to serve, in effect, "like department chairs and the mentors in the various regional centers were to be responsible not only to their regional deans but also to the person in their areas [of study] … in Saratoga" (Jacobson, 1993, p. 4).

In this struggle for control over the academic program – between the mildly prescriptive curricula of the modules and student purpose-driven learning – Baritz continued generating modules against the rushing tide of individualized contracts, though by 1976, only just under nine percent of learning contracts used them. The modules were at times inspiring, offering new and flexible pathways of learning and covering every area of study offered by the College, including business and human services. Some were supplemented by various media to bolster independent study, while others were narrow esoteric forays into the liberal arts and intellectually out of reach for the average student. The modules were written in welcoming narratives of conversation – similar to the BOU's courses that were tutorials in print rather than the lectures of traditional correspondence courses – but with opportunities for focusing on what the student might find of interest; and, at times, they connected the student to other modules. But the modules were prescriptive, assuming what students might want to learn, and called upon mentors to locate tutors to guide the student through the study – perhaps the greatest obstacle in securing their popularity.

Baritz observed, "Part of the difficulty was that their use depended not on the development faculty but upon the mentors" (Baritz, 1990, p. 19). Also, the divide between the Learning Resources faculty and the mentors of the regional learning centers widened as the latter carried what many perceived to be intolerable workloads compared to their colleagues at the Learning Resources Center.

By July 1974, the Learning Resources Center offered over 100 modules in its catalog – some of them launched with media-orchestrated fanfare in Saratoga. Despite not igniting faculty enthusiasm, the modules were an effective means of demonstrating to the world of higher education, including adversarial colleagues at SUNY campuses, Empire's commitment to academic excellence. In fact, the following year, the New York State Education Department urged their further integration into the academic program, suggesting ways to improve them, and even emphasized the program's importance as expressed by students who used them. And this praise for learning modules was contrasted with remarks about the shortcomings of individualized contracts (Carr, 1975, p. 35).

The learning modules kept before the College community Hall's intention of creating alternatives, as anticipated by the framers of the *Prospectus*, for those students who desired more structure and more direction, and less introspection and self-discovery in planning programs of study. And they served as well the need to create ways to identify and distribute educational resources throughout the College. The *Prospectus* had clearly articulated a full spectrum of learning alternatives and even anticipated that "Any individual student's program would probably be a blending of both options," combining "completely unstructured" and "fully structured" learning resources while recognizing at the same time that a student could "complete the entire requirement by following one or the other extreme" in its entirety (Boyer, 1971, p. 16).

In taking the long view of ESC's evolution, Hall concluded that

> one of the things that explains the depth and complexity of Empire State is that there were these different major viewpoints which we tried to pull together into one institution – for the benefit of the student – so that we weren't a single mode institution. We weren't a monomodal craft that would have to fly on that wing. (Hall, 1990, p. 5)

Hall held firm to maintaining this flexibility, which he believed was essential not only for serving the needs of students but for the long-term survival of the College. The founding *Prospectus* had envisioned a flexible model that would serve widely diverse students across a broad range of academic specialties, serving, as noted earlier, as many as 40,000 students. He believed that the mentors, already under considerable pressure to identify the supporting resources, tutors and learning materials for each student, would find it difficult to sustain such workloads in the years ahead. He also recognized that external regulators would eventually require greater clarity regarding the content, level of study and qualifications of the faculty.

Chickering's tenure as vice president for academic affairs was followed in early 1974 by his appointment as ESC's vice president for policy and analysis. The next year, Baritz resigned his post to serve as executive director of SUNY's Commission on Purposes and Priorities. Chickering remained with the College until 1977. During that time, he secured a number of major grants, including one from the Danforth Foundation to create the Center for Individualized Education (CIE). The latter was a key to sustaining the momentum of developing the mentor role. Chickering recruited F. Thomas Clark, the dean of the Albany Center, to direct the program. He became in the absence of Chickering "a very important instrument in the development of the academic program of the College" (Jacobson, 1993, p. 14). Also, Chickering and Hall worked with Alden Dunham, the lead grants officer for higher education issues at The Carnegie Corporation, to secure a grant to support PLA (prior learning assessment). This evolved into Morris Keaton inviting ESC to join what became CAEL (Council for Adult and Experiential Learning), a small consortium of new institutions.

## NEW DIRECTIONS: THE BRITISH OPEN UNIVERSITY AND THE CENTER FOR DISTANCE LEARNING

John Jacobson, the dean at the Genesee Valley Learning Center, succeeded Chickering as vice president for academic affairs in early 1974. In the fall of the following year, the administration launched Extended Programs, developed by mentors George Bragle and Richard Bonnabeau under the supervision of William R. Dodge, the dean for Statewide Programs and former SUNY System acting university dean for continuing education, which at its peak served 6,000 students. Dodge was the architect of using distance learning resources to create alternatives to the regional center model. In 1972 he created Statewide Programs, a series of satellites with one or two full-time mentors who served students who were out of reach of the regional learning centers.

Extended Programs was a pilot unit created with the intention of being the nucleus of a center designed to serve students at a distance. It focused on offering entire degree programs built upon SUNY Independent Study courses and a number of popular learning modules, as well as individualized learning contracts when these were necessary to close gaps in the student's program. Also, the program included outreach through independent studies to specialized populations such as disabled individuals and others who could not meet face-to-face with mentors at the regional learning centers or their satellites. Among these were students located in other states or overseas, and students who wanted a mode of study based on well-defined degree programs and independent study materials, including inmates at New York state correctional facilities. The programs also offered group studies for employees at nearby developmental centers of the New York Department of Mental Hygiene.

Extended Programs was ESC's first programmatic effort – perhaps the first in the United States – to offer associate and baccalaureate degrees at a distance through primarily distance learning resources.

By 1976, connecting Empire State College to the British Open University became an important objective. As noted earlier, the New York State Education Department's review of ESC's academic program, though laudatory, focused on what needed improvement. The reviewers raised concern about learning modules not becoming an integral part of ESC's academic program and concern about inconsistencies in the quality of learning contracts, as well as the insufficiency of liberal arts in programs of study. And ESC had to find less labor-intensive ways for mentors to accommodate growing enrollments. In Hall's and Jacobson's thinking, given the quality of BOU courses – universally praised in the world of higher education – it made sense to make them available to ESC students. And by this time, American students by the thousands were taking BOU courses adapted for use by their colleges and universities. Following in this path, therefore, was a significant means of being responsive to the need voiced in the *Prospectus* for providing structured learning alternatives. Moreover, ESC's association with the British Open University was sure to enhance the College's standing among SUNY campuses. And it did.

In the spring of 1976, Jacobson convened a conference attended by Barry Shorthouse of the BOU's North American Office in Manhattan, New York, as well as representatives from the State University of New York's system administration and SUNY campuses, and from Empire State College. The conference generated positive momentum leading to the creation of ESC's Open University Review Panel. The panel, composed of ESC faculty and administrators, including Dean Dodge, met in May, July, October, and December and laid the groundwork for a major field test of BOU courses launched in January of 1977. The courses were evaluated jointly by ESC's Office of Research and Evaluation and the Office of Academic Affairs. The report was massive in size, 363 pages, and a monumental testament to the administration's determination to infuse ESC's academic program with independent study courses of exceptional quality (Lehmann & Thorsland, 1977).

Early that year, Robert Hassenger, acting dean and former associate dean at the Niagara Frontier Regional Learning Center, came to Saratoga to begin adapting BOU courses for statewide use as the director of the Independent Study Program, which offered students two instructional options: study at a distance by phone and mail or face-to-face group studies; the latter program assuming that there would be sufficient enrollments at the regional learning centers. In effect, there were now two programs headquartered in Saratoga Springs offering directed independent study: Extended Programs, demonstrating the feasibility of providing degrees earned through study at a distance, including students located overseas, by employing a variety of structured learning resources; and Hassenger's Independent Study Program, which consisted primarily of correspondence courses – essentially lectures in print with assignments, which had been transferred from SUNY to ESC in 1971. Though not offering degrees, Hassenger's program had great success converting huge blocks of BOU courses, equivalent to 16 and 32 credits, into 4- and 8-credit courses. These courses were also offered to students throughout the SUNY network of campuses as well as to any prospective ESC student seeking independent study options. Hassenger was assisted in this effort by BOU administrator, sociologist and course developer Vincent Worth who joined him that March for three months. In freeing Worth to assist Hassenger, BOU's Sir Walter Perry wanted ESC to know that it was a "sign of the special affection they have for us" (Orill, 1977).

By February 1978, the ESC administration decided to merge Extended Programs and the Independent Study Program into a full-fledged center – the Center for Independent Study. It was a risky proposal because it could easily be viewed as an unwelcomed attempt to recreate Baritz's Learning Resources Center. Almost a year later, Hall and other ESC representatives made a presentation at SUNY System Administration headquarters. SUNY Vice Chancellor for Academic Programs, Policy and Planning James Perdue was very pleased with the progress of the new center, making specific references to the use of BOU courses, and praised Empire for its "plans to revitalize the independent study thrust of [ESC's] campus mission" (Perdue, 1979). This remarkable endorsement that ESC was on the right track was followed by Hall quickly investing more resources in the new center and by changing its name to the Center for Distance Learning – following the suggestion of Vincent Worth. This name change strengthened ESC's association with the British Open University.

The creation of the Center for Distance Learning (CDL), infused with more resources, was not immediately welcomed across the College. At a time of contracting state revenues, the new center – so different from the other centers in form, function, and mission – was viewed as a threat to the regional center model. Candace Zort, an ESC consultant who assisted CDL in the early planning stages, accurately foretold that, "One day, the Center for Distance Learning would be the tail wagging the dog." She viewed this center in terms of its potential importance for the College, though for the center deans it was another matter. These deans loudly protested the creation of the center while clamoring for more resources.

The protests were politely considered by President Hall and then dismissed. But faculty enamored of the progressive spirit of individualized learning would have to be won over by CDL's efforts to incorporate progressive elements in its distance learning pedagogy and by demonstrating the Center's practical potential for easing the heavy burden of student workloads carried by mentors around the College through the cross-registration of their students in CDL courses. The latter dimension began immediately as the "Mentor Workload Reduction Program," boldly inscribed in its announcement for the fall 1979 term (Bonnabeau, 1996, p. 86).

To dampen the tensions between the proponents of pedagogy driven by student purposes as advocated by Chickering and those of norm-referenced learning advocated by Baritz and supported programmatically by Dodge, the administration strategically created an entity that, at least on the surface, was unlike the defunct

Learning Resources Center and much more like regional learning centers. First, the Center for Distance Learning would have its own students, an astute political maneuver that was quite a departure from the Learning Resources Center whose primary mission was to generate and identify learning resources for the rest of the College. Second, the CDL faculty served as mentors (though "advisors" was the official term) to their own students, which put them on an equal footing with faculty at the regional learning centers. Third, students had the option to do 16 credits of individualized learning contracts in their programs of study.

Moreover, CDL faculty from the get-go had to be working more like mentors in the regional centers, slogging it out in the trenches to serve students. The faculty of the new center taught courses and mentored students doing learning contracts at a distance; they oversaw discrete portions of the curricula according to specific areas of study expertise; they hired, trained, and supervised instructors; and they worked diligently at course creation, acquisition, adaptation, and maintenance. Moreover, having their own students to mentor, which the Extended Programs faculty had managed statewide, nationally, and globally on a small scale, meant that the faculty were motivated to examine closely how well distance learning courses served their own students and the students of mentors around the College.

Though CDL students taking faculty-designed, structured courses did not have learning contracts, they, like other students in the College, received narrative evaluations of their coursework, but with far less detail than the individualized evaluations produced at the regional learning centers. And all CDL matriculated students prepared – under the guidance of their advisors – degree programs that included rationale essays explaining their design in relation to their educational purposes. Instead of face-to-face meetings, CDL advisors and instructors employed the telephone and mail as the primary modes of communication for advisement and instruction, while the learning activities for structured courses were designed as much as possible to relate to student interests and experience, a point often made in various College forums by Daniel Granger, a subsequent CDL director. This individualized thrust was highly applauded by BOU colleagues.

Though CDL was not exactly a wolf in sheep's clothing, it was still viewed by progressive mentors – and would be for a long time – as a resurrection of the defunct Learning Resources Center that was harboring an enclave of reactionaries cheered on by the administration. In fact, CDL Director Scheffel Pierce noted the enmity of colleagues in his report that detailed preparations for CDL's first term. Pierce stated, referring to the center's national and international standing among institutions promoting distance learning, "*I believe we are well known and generally looked upon beneficently – except among our own Empire State College colleagues*" [emphasis added] (Pierce, 1979a, p. 2). Initially, as might be expected, the Center for Distance Learning drew heavily upon British Open University courses. They were decidedly difficult, foreign, and dependent on expensive course materials shipped from England. Pedagogically, CDL confessed to their being "a regression toward the traditional mode to reach other adult learners" as noted in the fall 1979 term announcement, which also included two nationally-acclaimed telecourses (Pierce, 1979b, p. 3).

To connect the importance of the British Open University's relation to the Center for Distance Learning and to Empire State College, a collegewide convocation was held in 1982, awarding Lord Perry of Walton an honorary Doctor of Humane Letters degree. Jacobson, in his introductory remarks, observed, "Our Center for Distance Learning is avowedly modeled on the Open University" (Empire State College, 1982, p. 4). Though Jewish faculty colleagues mirthfully remarked that the event was also the Center's bar mitzvah, no one could doubt that CDL – three years after its creation – was rapidly reaching its majority and set on a path of rapid expansion to become an integral part of the College. Today, CDL courses account for nearly half of the total credits generated at the college (J. King, personal communication, June 2, 2016).

## THE ADVENT OF THE PERSONAL COMPUTER AND ONLINE LEARNING

The use of technology to support directed independent study had figured prominently in the *Prospectus*. ESC had inherited the SUNY Independent Study Program from the SUNY System, which included supplemental electronically-mediated materials, and the resources produced by the defunct SUNY of the Air. So there was much momentum to sustain the commitment to technologically-supported learning. CDL's interest was focused mostly on utilizing materials produced by the BOU, the Maryland Open University, and various national consortia, including telecourses produced by and/or transmitted by the Public Broadcasting Service (PBS).

Once connected to the internet, the personal computer established a pathway that would revolutionize distance learning pedagogy. Notably, the pedagogical chasm between CDL and its sister centers would begin to narrow in the late 1980s with the advent of online learning – first promoted by CDL Director Daniel Granger and mentor Lowell Roberts. They valued the cognitive and socializing dimensions of computer conferencing for students interacting asynchronously with their peers. This interactive dimension was completely absent in the delivery of print-based courses and courses relying heavily on other technology to deliver content. For that matter, it was mostly absent in ESC's individualized contract learning, though regional centers began to offer more and more group studies after Chickering's departure. Meg Benke, a CDL director and subsequent dean, brought online learning to fruition during the 1990s and the following decade through the continued cooperation of what was then the College's Center for Instructional Technology, under the direction of Patricia Lefor, vice president for educational technology. Moreover, through efforts funded by the Alfred P. Sloan Foundation, ESC "became part of a national community supporting the development of online programs across the country ..." (Benke, 2016). ESC's connection with SUNY community colleges, participating in what was known as the Sloan Consortium (Sloan-C; now the Online Learning Consortium [OLC]), became the basis of the SUNY Learning Network. Before the advent of the personal computer and the internet, students in CDL were connected to their advisors and mentors by phone and by mail. But the impossibility of face-to-face meetings, so prized by faculty colleagues at regional learning centers and their satellites, continued to raise nagging questions about quality assurance.

With time, online learning became more powerful and sophisticated with advances in technology and by a growing professional regard for online distance learning pedagogy. Moreover, regional center faculty became enamored of the computer as an administrative device and educational tool to mentor their own students, thus eliminating the pressure of frequent face-to-face meetings; and, over time, regional mentors began more and more to utilize CDL courses for their students, especially mentors who were coordinators of or faculty in regional learning center satellites in remote parts of New York state or in units overseas. The technology also made it possible for regional center mentors to also serve as CDL instructors and, at times, as course developers.

The chasm between regional and CDL faculty was narrowing, though there remained faculty proponents of individualized learning who were skeptical about the quality of instruction and the looming threat, which remains with us today, raised by new technologies. These mentors were offended and threatened by the draft of the ESC technology plan, "Prelude to the 21st Century," which questioned the academic efficacy of intensive and costly individualized mentoring and tutoring, while it celebrated the economies-of-scale provided by computer-mediated instruction for the many. Its authors predicted that ESC would become steadily marginalized in the world of higher education by ignoring "the efficacies of technology and continu[ing] our primary instructional modalities unchanged" (Perilli & Roberts, 1994, p. 5). Almost two decades later, we were reminded by the Open SUNY proposal (Davis, 2012) of this same issue about the fundamental principles of pedagogy inherent in the mandate to provide access, which goes back to the first days of the College's existence. But both in the *Prospectus* and in the aftermath of the clashes between Chickering and Baritz, it was the particular needs of the student that determined the outcome. We were not to take – using President Hall's injunction – a "monomodal" approach to student learning (Hall, 1990, p. 5). In fact, and as noted earlier, the original *Prospectus* anticipated individual student programs being a mix of an entire spectrum of modalities.

Over the years, the Center for Distance Learning has evolved more in line with the rest of the College. Online courses, which have completely replaced print-based courses since the presidency of Joseph Moore (2001–2007), have moved students more to the center of attention, as both progressive principles and advances in technology have infused distance learning pedagogy. In effect, as once observed in 1845 by a newspaper reporter marveling about the miraculous potential of the telegraph to "annihilate space" (Blaszczyk & Scranton, 2006, p. 118), through online learning platforms, CDL has annihilated isolation – the last obstacle separating students from the immediacy of access to networks of other learners.

Notably,

> a distinctive model somewhat different from the BOU evolved. This included a more intensive approach to adjunct faculty development and engagement. Rather than investing in highly mediated and structured courses like those at the BOU, ESC relied more heavily on promoting student centered teaching through a highly integrated adjunct community. This included not only an orientation to teaching at a distance, but also to the philosophies of mentoring embraced by the rest of the college. (Benke, 2016)

Students are now engaged with their peers, sometimes intensively, and with their instructors in ongoing course discussions – the very dialectical method exalted by Royce Pitkin. They have regular opportunities to work collaboratively with peers in online learning communities through presentations, shared projects, and other group-based activities, just as students do at the regional learning centers and their satellite units, where they participate in face-to-face seminars, workshops, and group studies. The first step into the co-agency dimensions of online learning begins with the "ice breaker" component of CDL courses. It is an informal but "incredibly powerful opportunity to validate and build upon the experience and interests of the individual student that establishes a path for discovery in a highly collaborative learning environment" (T. Mackey, personal communication, August 20, 2012).

Center for Distance Learning faculty have become skilled practitioners of distance learning. They have scholarly regard for, and commitment to improving their craft; are well-versed in various progressive pedagogies as they relate to adult learning theory and practice; embrace the application of new advances in technology; are ready to test new approaches to course delivery – MOOCs (massive open online courses) being the most recent; are respected presenters on distance learning pedagogy at professional conferences; have impressive records of scholarship in their own fields; and have an important voice in College governance.

In an extraordinary turn of events, which was impossible even to begin to imagine at CDL's inception in 1979, its faculty have been welcomed as resident mentors by their colleagues at other locations in the College, a role that serves many important purposes. In institutional terms, it represents the integration of CDL into the rest of the College, a center that was perceived in 1979, to paraphrase the BOU's Vincent Worth, as an epistemological betrayal (Worth, 1979, p. 3).

While it could be argued that CDL has not reached the exalted realm of progressive education as practiced at Pitkin's Goddard, its commitment to such ideals is embedded in a huge array of discrete courses – more than 400 in number. This development is admirable for fusing two opposing viewpoints, which at least on the surface once appeared to be forever pedagogically immiscible. Over time, the Center for Distance Learning, as we have seen, has made sincere and successful efforts to align its program with the rest of the College – to have both the progressive and distance learning streams share the same conduit, if not converge entirely. These two hereditary streams of educational philosophy, brought together in a single institution, dramatically changed the character and quality of adult, continuing, and distance education as witnessed by its contributions to SUNY's systemwide development of online learning.

## OPEN SUNY

Today, as a result of a proposal crafted in 2012 by now former ESC President Alan Davis (2012), Empire State College is a key part of Open SUNY – as it was in the creation of its predecessor, the SUNY Learning Network. The proposal was drawn up in consultation with Meg Benke, then vice president for academic affairs, ESC faculty, other administrators, professionals, and support staff as well as in consultation with key SUNY System representatives. The Open SUNY proposal was a response to Chancellor Nancy Zimpher's call for "systemness" and is now a SUNY-wide effort designed to integrate and maximize the resources of the largest university system in the United States.

The plan for Open SUNY aimed to focus the dispersed resources of the State University devoted to online learning in a unified system of collaborating campuses. It has great potential to energize Empire State College. It brings to the forefront decades of ESC's experience in distance learning, while sharing with and building upon the accomplishments of SUNY campuses through the SUNY Learning Network – a program essentially spawned by ESC under President Hall's leadership during his two-year appointment (1993–1995) as SUNY's vice chancellor for educational technology while serving as ESC's president. The proposal called for a bold initiative:

> SUNY has the capability of collectively offering the most extensive array of online courses and programs in the country. Open SUNY Online would build on the achievements of the SUNY Learning Network, which, in this proposal, would form the core of Open SUNY Online, and expand to include all of SUNY's online offerings, and be enhanced by the other dimensions of Open SUNY. In other words, to support the next generation of online teaching and learning. (Davis, 2012, p. 5)

Two years later, in 2014, Chancellor Zimpher launched Open SUNY. In her *2016 State of the University Address*, the chancellor credited the synergy of "systemness" behind the creation of the "world's largest consortium for online learning ... comprising ... 472 online programs and 20,000 course sections ... extending access to limitless numbers of people, anywhere in the world" (Zimpher, 2016, III. Accomplishments through Systemness: Open SUNY section, para. 1). Since 2014, Open SUNY has enrolled over 250,000 students and continues to grow, and has every expectation of accommodating the continued extraordinary growth in enrollment of online learners, including adults seeking professional and personal enrichment opportunities. In the process, the challenges Open SUNY faces – massive student enrollments and maintenance of distance-learning pedagogy – are substantial.

Empire State College, as it has for the past two decades of cooperation with the other campuses, will continue to address these system challenges. In this respect, "Empire State continues to experiment with educational technologies. Funded by the Gates and Lumina foundations, experimentation is underway with adaptive learning and competency-based education. But these experiences are still grounded in the philosophies of putting the student at the center, and making sure that the technology is driven by connecting faculty and students where most appropriate" (Benke, 2016). Open SUNY campuses share with Empire State College the recognition that learning outcomes are directly related to bringing students and their instructors together into learning communities (course sections) of manageable size and to supporting students' cognitive and affective development. This pathway will promote the two pedagogical streams that support effective mentoring. Open SUNY will continue to promote systemwide campus cooperation and collaboration that began with Empire State College and a small nucleus of SUNY campuses.

Mentoring individuals or groups of students, either face-to-face or at a distance, is still virtually unique to ESC. It embraces the principle that student purposes govern how ESC utilizes educational resources and their delivery. Empire State College's practices and educational philosophy stem from core values first articulated by *A Prospectus for a New University College* (Boyer, 1971). As SUNY prepares to accommodate the anticipated many more thousands of students in online courses, it must find a reasonable balance between costs and maintaining high quality services if Open SUNY is to be important in the current highly competitive environment for recruitment and retention.

## QUESTIONS AND CONCLUSIONS

Therefore, important questions remain: In this era of soaring higher education costs, will ESC and SUNY succumb to the call of the economies-of-scale inherent in some approaches to online learning? Considerable numbers of institutions, public, independent, and for-profit, are using technology to forge a self-paced, lock-step, interchangeable course system – a reborn industrial model that minimizes interaction with other students and faculty, cutting costs deeply. From this perspective, such a low cost, often profitable strategy, might surrender the powerful educational character that has separated Empire State College and Open SUNY from these rigid approaches to higher learning.

From this concern arise derivative questions: There is little doubt that traditional faculty roles will change, but a reborn industrial model could adversely transform the faculty role. Is there a tipping point in serving large numbers of students where effective teaching and the incentive to enter such a role could so alter the excitement and satisfactions of teaching and learning as to render it irretrievable? Will student essays, term papers, team presentations, vibrant asynchronous exchanges among students, direct communications from their instructors, and other modes of interaction that personalize student experience succumb to standardized competency-based methods of instruction and evaluation? Ultimately, for good or for ill, the social and psychological dimensions of the educational journey students take with their peers and instructors is as important as the subject matter picked up along the way. It is essential for the survival of the concept of a university, that we find ways to lift up and perpetuate the human experience of being a student in an engaged community of learners.

As a SUNY-wide effort by Chancellor Nancy Zimpher to integrate the resources of the largest university system in the United States, Open SUNY brings to full circle, as encapsulated by the term "systemness," the pioneering efforts by Chancellors Samuel B. Gould and Ernest L. Boyer – both inspired by the promise of technology – to keep the State University of New York steadfast on a path of innovation. In this regard, Empire State College continues to share its experience in supporting innovation with other campuses in the SUNY System, thereby fulfilling the original SUNY mandate for its creation.

## REFERENCES

Baritz, L. (1990, March 20). *Interview by R. Bonnabeau* [Transcript of tape recording]. Oral History Project. Empire State College Archives, Saratoga Springs, NY. [Note: This transcript in accord with Dr. Baritz's instructions is not available to other researchers.]

Benke, M. (2016, April 3). *Email to R. Bonnabeau*. Empire State College Archives, Saratoga Springs, NY.

Benson, A., & Adams, F. (1987*). To know for real: Royce S. Pitkin and Goddard College*. Adamant, VT: Adamant Press.

Blaszczyk, R. L., & Scranton, P. B. (2006). Baltimore Patriot supports government regulation of telegraphy, 1845. In R. L. Blaszczyk & P. B. Scranton (Eds.), *Major problems in American business history* (pp. 118–119). Belmont, CA: Wadsworth Cengage Learning.

Bonnabeau, R. F. (1996). *The promise continues: Empire State College – The first twenty-five years*. Virginia Beach, VA: The Donning Company Publishers.

Boyer, E. L. (1971, February 8). *A prospectus for a new university college: Objectives, process, structure, and establishment. Draft*. Albany, NY: State University of New York.

Boyer, E. L. (1981, July 8). *Draft: The experimental college: Its heritage, its future*. Address at Evergreen College, Olympia, WA. Retrieved from http://boyerarchives.messiah.edu/files/Documents1/1000%20 0000%200791ocr.pdf

Boyer, E. L. (1990, August 31). *Interview by R. Bonnabeau* [Transcript of tape recording]. Oral History Project. Empire State College Archives, Saratoga Springs, NY.

Carr, E. (1975, March 24). *Memorandum to J. Hall: Report of the New York State Education Department (NYSED) Evaluation Team*. Empire State College Archives, Saratoga Springs, NY.

Chickering, A. (1969). *Education and identity*. San Francisco, CA: Jossey-Bass.

Chickering, A. (2011, June 27). *Interview by R. Bonnabeau* [Transcript of videotape recording]. Oral History Project. Empire State College Archives, Saratoga Springs, NY.

Chickering, A. (2012a, July 23). *Email to R. Bonnabeau*. Empire State College Archives, Saratoga Springs, NY.

Chickering, A. (2012b, August 8). *Email to R. Bonnabeau*. Empire State College Archives, Saratoga Springs, NY.

Davis, A. (2012, April). *Proposal: Open SUNY*. Empire State College Archives, Saratoga Springs, NY.

Davis, F. (1991, March 16). *Interview by R. Bonnabeau* [Transcript of tape recording]. Oral History Project. Empire State College Archives, Saratoga Springs, NY.

Davis, F. (1996). *Things were different in Royce's day: Royce S. Pitkin as progressive educator: A perspective from Goddard College, 1950 – 1967.* Adamant, VT: Adamant Press.

Empire State College. (1972). *Empire State College annual report: Seeking alternatives I.* Saratoga Springs, NY: Author.

Empire State College. (1982, Summer). *Empire State College news.* Saratoga Springs, NY: Author.

Hall, J. (1990, June 13). *Interview by R. Bonnabeau* [Transcript of tape recording]. Oral History Project. Empire State College Archives, Saratoga Springs, NY.

Jacobson, J. (1993, August 4). *Interview by R. Bonnabeau* [Transcript of tape recording]. Oral History Project. Empire State College Archives, Saratoga Springs, NY.

Lehmann, T., & Thorsland, M. (1977, December). *Joint Report of ESC's Office of Research and Evaluation and the Office of Academic Development: Empire State College Field Test of British Open University Courses.* Empire State College Archives, Saratoga Springs, NY.

Orill, R. (1977, February 2). *Memorandum to John Jacobson.* Empire State College Archives, Saratoga Springs, NY.

Perdue, J. (1979, June–July). *Memorandum to James H. Hall.* Empire State College Archives, Saratoga Springs, NY.

Pierce, S. (1979a, June–July). *Report: Review and prospectus.* Empire State College Archives, Saratoga Springs, NY.

Pierce, S. (1979b, August). *Center for distance learning fall term announcement: Workload reduction plan.* Empire State College Archives, Saratoga Springs, NY.

Perilli, R., & Roberts, L. (1994, November). *Draft #3. Technology plan: Prelude to the 21st century.* Center for Learning and Technology. Empire State College Archives, Saratoga Springs, NY.

Worth, V. (1979, January 3). *Memorandum to William R. Dodge.* Empire State College Archives, Saratoga Springs, NY.

Zimpher, N. L. (2016, January 11). *2016 State of the university address.* Retrieved from https://www.suny.edu/about/leadership/chancellor-nancy-zimpher/speeches/2016-sou/

XENIA COULTER

# 3. JOHN DEWEY, CONSTRUCTED KNOWING, AND FACULTY PRACTICE AT EMPIRE STATE COLLEGE

A prospective student sits down across my desk.

"Is it really true that at Empire State College I don't have to go to class and I can study whatever I want?" he asks. "I mean, like, do I have to take math to graduate?" I smile at this common concern.

"Yep, you're correct on both counts," I tell him. "You'll meet your instructors in individual appointments, and you'll create a degree program (with some help from your mentor, of course) that meets your needs and interests. If math isn't something you need or want, then you won't have to take it."

"Are you kidding?" he exclaims. "I can really skip the classroom bit and only take courses that interest me?"

I nod. "What *are* you interested in?" I ask.

In response, he tells me that he's been in the police department for more than 15 years. He was involved in computerizing the department and has now become, more or less, the department's technology person. But he'll be able to retire soon, he explains, and while he never did that well in community college, what he does enjoy – and indeed does even now in his spare time – is to study history.

"So I really could spend my time reading history books, and still get a college degree without wasting a lot of time on stuff I'm not interested in?" he asks, still not quite believing that higher education might be more rewarding than he anticipated.

FINDING DEWEY

This little vignette, written some 20 years ago, was intended as an opening for a book that would explore how a very simple change in procedure – periodic face-to-face meetings with students individually rather than regularly scheduled classes – could radically transform higher education. Although the idea was recently revisited (Coulter & Mandell, 2013), the book itself was never written. Indeed, as the College moves increasingly toward standardized online instruction, such conversations are increasingly rare. Yet, it remains a striking reminder of what Empire State College originally sought to achieve. And today, since most Empire State College adult students are as busy and as capable of self-direction as in the past, the idea of maximal flexibility, even if only in terms of time and place (as is mostly the case today), is still very attractive to them.

K. Jelly & A. Mandell (Eds.), *Principles, Practices, and Creative Tensions in Progressive Higher Education*, 65–90.
© 2017 Sense Publishers. All rights reserved.

What is notable about the imagined conversation – and indeed the proposed book – was its focus upon procedure. In retrospect, one might say that the faculty who would have authored this book thought about education from the inside out – a "connected" way of knowing that according to Belenky, Clinchy, Goldberger, and Tarule (1986) "comes from personal experience rather than the pronouncements of authorities" (p. 112). It is probably not surprising that faculty who saw themselves as mentors – that is, academic agents who help students progress along their own educational journeys[1] – would be totally absorbed in those practices of the College that promote deep engagement by students in their studies and keep them focused upon their academic goals.

Yet, faculty, who also see themselves as scholars, might have been expected to be equally comfortable promoting a more theoretical perspective – a view Belenky et al. (1986) referred to as a "separate" way of knowing, which emphasizes objective analysis and critical reasoning. That they were not could be because all faculty – no matter what their disposition – tend to apply their most abstract thinking not to teaching, but to their particular scholarly disciplines. *All About Mentoring*, a publication of Empire State College faculty writings, illustrates this rather well: Articles by faculty about their own fields of study tend to present reasoned arguments; articles about teaching or mentoring experiences tend to offer case studies.[2] A similar avoidance of theory or philosophy is also evident in Bonnabeau's (1996) account of the College's early history. While the founders were clearly caught up in the prevailing progressive movement, their initial developmental activities focused primarily on implementing and propagating new ways of practice.[3]

Belenky et al. (1986) claimed that the pinnacle of true understanding is "constructed" knowing, which integrates both connected and separate perspectives. It becomes an interesting question to ask whether such an integration might have made a difference at Empire State College as it struggled to establish itself as a unique college for adults. Would those struggles have been lessened by a greater familiarity with – and perhaps a stronger adherence to – a philosophically-based rationale for the procedures the College so eagerly embraced? Would faculty and administrators have better appreciated the broader significance of these nontraditional procedures had they taken ownership of "authoritative" writings as much as they did the practice of mentoring? Indeed, would a more intentional appreciation of philosophy have provided us with a better anchor with which to weather the many storms of the 21st century that have increasingly challenged our original sense of good practice?

Arguably America's most important and prolific authority on education, specifically progressive education, is John Dewey. A philosopher, Dewey certainly embraced the analytical approach so prized by Western scholars; however, his thinking was also very much tempered by his intimate knowledge of everyday practical issues. Unique in the world of philosophers, Dewey, for a number of years, actively tested and further developed his ideas by creating and administering a real school – a "laboratory" in which numerous approaches to helping students learn were worked out and seasoned with actual learners. While Dewey's sometimes long-winded and old-fashioned style of writing has been misunderstood by some scholars,[4] a careful study of The Dewey School (Mayhew & Edwards, 1936/1965/2007) rewards the reader with unmistakably clear illustrations of how Dewey intended many of his well-known theoretical arguments about education (e.g., Dewey, 1897/1959; 1897/1964; 1899/1959; 1902/1990; 1910; 1916; 1938) to be played out in reality.

But given his preoccupation with elementary and secondary school children, why would Dewey's writings on education, practical or otherwise, have any authority relevant to a college specializing in adult learners? Why, indeed, are his ideas so extensively cited in the adult learning literature? Peter Jarvis (1987/1991), for example, presented Dewey as one of the 13 most influential scholars from the last century in the field of adult education. Kolb (1984), Houle (1984), and even Mezirow (1991), all important theorists in the field of adult education, made frequent reference to Dewey, and in their book, *Philosophical Foundations of Adult Education*, Elias and Merriam (2005) cited Dewey more often than any other writer (with only Malcolm Knowles running a fairly close second).

Not only did Dewey write almost entirely about children's education; he also focused exclusively upon the classroom as the appropriate setting for learning. In considering the social construction of knowledge and the importance of peer-to-peer discussion, some writers even regard Dewey as an important early proponent of learning in groups (e.g., Rogoff, 1995). While traditional colleges may take classroom discussions as a given, peer-to-peer classroom conversations are strikingly at odds with Empire State College's early reliance upon individual teacher-learner mentoring relationships and independent study. Would not this difference alone raise serious questions about the relevance of Dewey's writings to the original goals and purposes of our College?

For a number of reasons, the answer to this question is no. Dewey was not wedded to any particular practice – the thrust of his writings on education was to develop and champion educational experiences that fully engaged the learner regardless of age. Dewey had originally taught in high school and no doubt must have struggled with the difficulties of captivating adolescents in a prescribed curriculum with traditional rote methods.[5] That he also began to think seriously about education at the same time that he began his own family[6] was probably not a coincidence (e.g., Simpson, 2005, p. 3). It was clear to him that students did not enjoy school: The learning activities were physically unpleasant, and the subject matter did not connect to their own lives or interests in any meaningful way. Still, he also understood that an education that would prepare them for an ever-changing and increasingly complex world was crucially important – not only for the children but society as well.[7] In essence, the problem he addressed had to do with student motivation. He described the alacrity with which children in their own homes learn useful household or important farm chores. He then argued that the essential components of this simple home-bound model should and could be transplanted into the public school. If presented within the context of universal human concerns, education might then consist of the kinds of naturalistic experiences children seek to engage with enthusiasm (Dewey, 1899/1959, pp. 36–39).

Without question, children naturally enjoy group activities. That enjoyment, however, comes from what they do together, not the bare fact of close proximity. In other words, for students who are together but forced to sit unmoving in uncomfortable chairs reciting lessons, the group experience is not natural, appealing, or particularly meaningful. Nor is it an effective way of learning. Noting that children will spontaneously work together happily solving myriad problems in less formal situations, Dewey argued that a solution to student motivation would be to present school lessons as learning problems that children could most easily solve together.[8] Taking an inherent characteristic of human behavior – sociability – and instead of inhibiting it as is the case in most classrooms, Dewey embedded it into the learning process. Group learning thus was indeed an important part of his philosophy – not as an end in itself, but as a means of more effectively helping students learn.[9]

Empire State College faculty have also been concerned with trying to promote learning with students uncomfortable in formal classrooms. Many adult students are former college dropouts,[10] often returning to school reluctantly, still bearing scars from their earlier "failures." In addition, almost all are fully occupied elsewhere – with their families, work, and community – and in many cases view the classroom experience *per se* as a waste of time, boring, and expendable. Unlike children, adults are already situated in numerous group situations where they work on real-life problems,[11] so that the artificiality of class meetings is not particularly attractive. On the other hand, individual attention, personal guidance, and the opportunity to engage in intellectual conversation freed from the distractions of home or work are very appealing, and arguably a more "natural" adult activity than sitting in a classroom. If we then take Dewey's focus on motivation – and the importance of creating an educational environment that is maximally likely to interest children and stimulate learning – the case can be made that the creation of a one-on-one mentoring relationship for adult students meets the same purpose as Dewey sought to achieve when promoting group activities for children.

The societal situation faced by Dewey was also very much the same as what we face today – a daunting need for universal education. One hundred years ago, high school was deemed essential for everyone; today, for both political and economic reasons, this need extends to college. Within that context, differences between children and adults may not be ideologically important but simply concrete circumstances that demand different approaches. In essence, then, what Dewey and public colleges such as ours share is a common mission: to make education attractively accessible to as many learners as possible. While we have tended to see this goal in terms of *physical* accessibility, Dewey makes abundantly clear that *intellectual* accessibility is every bit as important. Thus, particularly in relation to Empire State College's key (and perhaps most publicized) aim of access, Dewey's philosophy of education does appear to be explicitly relevant.

Dewey, of course, had considerably more to say about his philosophy as he continually worked out the implications of a form of education we now call "student-centered." There was no detail that he was not willing to consider, as illustrated throughout his very long, very prolific career. While it is impossible to systematically review this corpus of writings in one short chapter,[12] we can still explore how his writings might (or might not) have provided theoretical support for certain Empire State College educational practices. In particular, we can ask to what extent the ways faculty have dealt with such constantly arising concerns as adult life experience, student self-direction, subject matter, faculty control, and intellectual skill development are compatible with Dewey's vision.

## APPLYING DEWEY

### Adult Experience

Perhaps the most radical – and controversial – practice at Empire State College has been its enthusiastic willingness to award students college credit for what they may have learned at work, at home, or as community volunteers without requiring that this knowledge be tied to traditional course offerings. Put more broadly, College policy recognizes that significant college-level learning can indeed emerge from extracurricular experience. And arguably, this belief was also at the heart of Dewey's educational philosophy, much of it summarized in his late-written brief retrospective, *Experience and Education* (Dewey, 1938). A more concrete example of Dewey's thinking on the matter of experience and education, however, is illustrated in the following passage from *The Dewey School* (Mayhew & Edwards, 1936/1965/2007):

> Little did the experimenting child realize that he was studying physics as he boiled down his cane or maple syrup, watching the crystallization process, the effects of heat on water, and of both on the various grains used for food. ...The teacher knew, although he did not, that he was studying the chemistry of combustion as he figured out why fire burned, or weighed, burned, and weighed again the ashes from the different woods or coal and compared results. ... From the teacher's standpoint, this was geology and geography or biology as the children examined the seed, their distribution, and use of food or the life of the birds and animals in the open fields. From the child's standpoint, however, these ideas were interesting facts or skills as he went about his various occupations; they were reflected, as it were, in the series of activities through which he passed in becoming conscious of the basis of social life. (p. 33)

The parallel between this passage and the ways adult students describe their work experiences and then struggle to characterize what they have learned by, for example, managing a food processing plant, is somewhat uncanny.[13] Even the College requirement that this knowledge must also be clearly articulated was similarly reflected at Dewey's school:

> Opportunity was constantly given for expression in various mediums. By means of crayon, pencil, color, and scissors, as well as through the spoken and written word, the children were encouraged to record the memories of a walk, the apples they had gathered, the story they had heard, or the process they had imagined or carried through. ... (p. 51)

However, a key difference for Dewey, his staff, and volunteer subject-matter experts,[14] is that with children, these learning experiences were very carefully planned and tested to make sure they successfully guided the students toward the kind of educationally relevant knowledge they were expected to acquire. What mature Empire State College students learned outside of school from work or other worldly experiences was of their own choosing – or at least not selected by academics. Considerable after-the-fact attention, therefore, has been focused on whether this knowledge, whatever it might be, was truly "college-level." Nonetheless, adults' learning processes themselves are often the kind of natural experience Dewey sought to reproduce in his school.

Ironically, when it came to learning under the auspices of the College, however, the use of experience as the appropriate medium was not particularly widespread. Not surprisingly, a tradition of "book learning" was not only strong, but attractively simple to plan and carry out. Moreover, there was no body of available methods faculty could easily draw upon for generating traditional forms of academic knowledge through hands-on activities. And, because students studied on their own, unlike what occurred at the Dewey school, the process of such learning, had it taken place, would have been outside instructor purview. Thus, it depended significantly upon the imagination and energy of individual faculty and the students themselves as to whether a course of study was developed around work, home, or community experiences. Learning activities could consist of interviews, observations, or reflections-in-action (e.g., Schön, 1984); and materials for evaluation *might* include videos, formal proposals, work-based manuals, and artworks. Where needed, students could also cross-register at traditional colleges for supervised research or equipment-dependent activities, or undertake internships supervised by experts in the field. But the fact remained that many of the studies carried out at the College consisted of learning activities that involved acquisition of knowledge through print media, periodic discussions with the mentor about these materials, and a demonstration of what was learned through the writing of essays and reports.

In retrospect, it may just be that "experience," as defined by Dewey for children as hands-on, engaging, and meaningful activity from which learning emerges, may not be, just as with peer-to-peer classroom discussions, as motivating or necessary with more mature learners. Adults' daily lives are already crammed with such activities as they fulfill their roles as parents, workers, homeowners, sports enthusiasts, hobbyists, arts supporters, community activists, and so forth. Indeed, for many to have the opportunity to engage in solely "mental" activity may in itself be attractive and valuable. The experience of talking about intellectual issues with an interested mentor, and even the process of studying alone in what pockets of solitude students are able to find – in their offices after hours, at the dining room table late at night, or at the local library on weekends – may have been welcomed and rare opportunities for serious thinking. While book reading, abstract fact ingestion, and paper writing can be seen as relatively unnatural activities for children, the same is not necessarily true for adults.

*Self-Directed Study*

As a crucial part of making education meaningful to children, Dewey always made certain that his young students were involved in deciding what they should learn.[15] Just how the collective interests of 9-year-olds were determined is described in Mayhew and Edwards (1936/1965/2007) as follows:

> The starting point grew out of discussion. As was customary in their first meetings, the general possibilities for study reverted to last year's work, and a quick review was made. ... [In considering what they already knew about local history and geography], [t]he group decided they would like to know more about the United States and how it began, and finally agreed that the place where they lived [Chicago] would be a good place to start. ... This had been the teacher's objective; but because it was obtained by means of a group process, the children regarded the plan as their own. (p. 145)

At Empire State College, the individual student-mentor meeting made it relatively easy to carry out a comparable process, one that often began with simple questions about the student's interests and concerns. While the learners may have been at first somewhat surprised at being given the freedom to decide what they wanted to study, they caught on quickly. Choices were certainly not infinite, especially given the constraints imposed by what they already knew and what they needed to show evidence of knowing for a particular job, further education, or the College expectations of "breadth."[16] But very few students had difficulty in identifying and articulating particular problems, concerns, or interests, or in choosing methods of tackling them that they found attractive. "Why does my organization get in the way of meeting its own goals?" "How can I better deal with my adolescent daughter?" "Where can I find information about my Native American heritage, which I really want to better understand?" "Is the Islamic way of punishing crime really effective?" "Can you help me learn more about robotics and its role at work?" Herman and Mandell (2004) offered from their work at Empire State College very detailed descriptions of this process and its powerful impact upon the learner, as did Daloz (1999) from his work with adult undergraduates in rural Vermont.

Given that Dewey's students worked together on a topic of common interest, some scholars have questioned whether he would have seen as appropriate such an emphasis upon individualization (e.g., see Willis's response in Coulter, Mandell, Shaw, Willis, & Winner, 2008, p. 10). Because the learning in both situations was stimulated by student interest and guided by critical inquiry, there is little reason to suppose that Dewey would have cared whether students learned together in a group or by themselves. Indeed, there is some direct evidence that Dewey explicitly supported individualized student inquiry. In evaluating the use of "projects" or "problems" as a way of organizing and directing student learning (Dewey, 1931/1964),[17] he described as acceptable a process that very closely approximates the College's inquiry-based or guided independent studies. His concern was only that the inquiry itself be "educative," the criteria for which he identified as follows: (a) the ensuing investigation must pose new questions and create a demand for new knowledge, (b) the organization of the study must grow out of the question asked, and (c) the project itself should exact both intellectual and overt activity (pp. 423–424). And, as amply documented in Daloz (1999), Herman and Mandell (2004), and indeed, any issue of *All About Mentoring*, student/mentor-initiated studies easily match those criteria.

However, such studies produce another result that Dewey did not have to explicitly address: highly individualized learning outcomes. In principle, of course, even identical experiences cannot be expected to produce the same learning – neither in substance nor quantity. Nonetheless the public expects students to acquire a core of common understandings that can be readily identified by title. While student interest at the Dewey school provided a flexible lens through which students could investigate any area of study, children were still guided, however gently, toward a pre-determined body of acceptable knowledge. A particular adult inquiry, however, while also guided toward relevant existing bodies of knowledge, often produces learning outcomes derived from unique, possibly even idiosyncratic, combinations of information from sometimes highly diverse sources. For example, a student seeking to understand why the human mind is different from that of a chimpanzee might acquire some unique combination of knowledge from neuroscience, primate behavior, philosophy, and cognitive psychology, but with none of these areas being studied in their own right. Therefore, unlike children at the Dewey school, Empire State College students could (and did) graduate without having any courses of study in common. Yet, even though the College assured the coherence and academic quality of individual degree programs[18] by requiring that each one be vetted by a faculty committee, some mentors and many administrators were concerned about a lack of equity and the need for standardization.

How might Dewey have responded to that concern? Given that his primary educational goal was to perpetually engage students in authentic questions about human experience, he could not have deemed any study stimulated by genuine student concern, and certainly a whole program of such studies, as anything but a fully worthwhile educational experience. As he put it (Dewey, 1931/1964):

> If a student does not take into subsequent life an enduring concern for ... knowledge and art, ... schooling for him has been a failure, no matter how good a "student" he was. The failure is again due, I believe, to segregation of subjects. A pupil can say he has "had" a subject, because the subject has been treated as if it were complete in itself, beginning and terminating within limits fixed in advance. A reorganization of subject matter which takes account of outleadings into the wide world of nature and man, of knowledge and of social interests and uses cannot fail, save in the most callous and intellectually obdurate, to awaken some permanent interest and curiosity. (p. 425)

Standardization and equity in the sense of "equal" or "in common" were not of concern. As Dewey (1916) explained in *Democracy and Education*, "... one is mentally an individual only as he has his own purpose and problem, and does his own thinking. The phrase 'think for one's self' is a pleonasm [redundancy]. Unless one does it for one's self, it isn't thinking" (pp. 302–303). Thus, he concluded, "when [human] variations are suppressed in the alleged interests of uniformity," it ultimately destroys such characteristics as originality, self-confidence, and intellectual independence that are essential for a flourishing democracy (p. 303).

*Subject Matter*

Thus, so long as the student is the main agent of inquiry, it could be argued that the actual subject matter of formal education should not matter. Clearly a few progressive educators did hold that point of view, which Dewey (1938) sought to deal with in *Experience and Education* as he contemplated schools where in his name, children were given complete freedom to pursue whatever they wished. At every turn in his school, however, students took up traditional subjects such as history, art, music, mathematics, literature, and science, whether they were so identified or not. Similarly, at Empire State College, as student-centered as it might be, student inquiries still ended up incorporating whatever knowledge any relevant discipline might have to offer. While it is understandable that a university scholar might then decide that the disciplines are the ultimate source of what "every educated person should know," Dewey's point was that the disciplines are the *result*, not the cause, of human experience and should certainly be taken up, but only secondarily. The direct study of the disciplines is for trained scholars, not the appropriate starting place for students grappling with meaningful questions about their own experiences. Mayhew and Edwards (1936/1965/2007) illustrated how the disciplines were made subordinate at his school:

> Thus, for the learners at Dewey's school, the day was not divided into separate periods devoted to different disciplines; rather, the curriculum evolved organically around basic human motives. Starting at the bottom of Maslow's hierarchy, the youngest learners began their studies by taking up the most fundamental need – safety and security, along with such related topics

as hunting, food production, housing, and clothing. In considering issues of housing, for example, it was inevitable that at some point the need for warmth would eventually surface as students wondered how indeed, were people able to stay warm in their primitive caves. Fire would immediately come to mind, of course, which then raised such questions as where does fire come from, how is it initiated, why does it produce warmth, how is heat distributed by a fireplace, and so forth. Today's parents would be horrified to learn that students in Dewey's school learned to actually start fires, first by rubbing stones and sticks and later by using matches, and they then learned about how heat was generated inside a dwelling by physically building together their own fireplace. (p. 321)

This way of selecting subject matter strongly parallels what the mentor-student instructional model makes possible for adult students at Empire State College. While they do not necessarily build fireplaces (although they might receive credit for the knowledge needed to do so), adult learners are easily able to design studies organized around what Lindeman (1926) some 90 years ago referred to as "situations," as distinct from "subjects" (pp. 7–8). Thus, instead of acquiring a quantity of disciplinary knowledge to be available "just-in-case" an appropriate need arose in the future (Collins & Halverson, 2009, p. 48), our students can, just as did Dewey's pupils, learn what they need to know "just-in-time" (pp. 14–15) as they address the question at hand. Again, what matters only is that the initial inquiry relate in some way or another to authentic problems of living.

However, educators, throughout history, have been highly reluctant to accept such a broad and amorphous definition of what students must learn in school. Instead, they have continuously endorsed an organizing scheme created by the early Greeks and endorsed by the Romans in which subject matter is divided into two mutually exclusive categories – the so-called liberal and professional arts. Despite their questionable relevance in a world with infinitely more knowledge available today than 2,500 years ago, all courses are still routinely identified as belonging to one or the other category. As a result, Empire State College mentors have spent hours debating, for example, whether a study of "drafting" is liberal or professional. If one student's purpose is to learn the skill for a particular job whereas another's is to investigate various forms of visual communication, should the designation vary from professional in the first case to liberal in the second? Or should it be determined solely by whether drafting is taught by an architect or an engineer? Business Law is typically not considered a liberal arts study because both business and law are professions, unless the course is called The Legal Environment of Business in which case the word "environment" seems to promise a more abstract consideration of the subject matter. In this case, the study merits the "liberal" label because it (presumably) includes a reasoned discourse on the very nature of the topic, in contrast to a more worldly "professional" study that focuses on how that topic can be carried out. This abstract versus instrumental distinction, of course, does not satisfy those who prefer to distinguish these two categories of study by discipline.[19]

To Dewey (1916), however, the division of knowledge into just two categories was absurd. In addressing the idea of liberal versus professional as in culture versus vocation, he writes:

> No one is just an artist and nothing else, and in so far as one approximates that condition, he is so much the less developed human being: he is a kind of monstrosity. He must, at some period of his life, be a member of a family; he must have friends and companions; he must either support himself or be supported by others, and thus he has a business career. He is a member of some organized political unit, and so on. We naturally *name* his vocation from that one of the callings which distinguishes him, rather than from those he has in common with all others. But we should not allow ourselves to be so subject to words as to ignore and virtually deny his other callings when it comes to consideration of the vocation phases of education. (p. 307)

And in making a distinction between the intrinsic and the instrumental, he said:

> We must not ... divide the studies of the curriculum into the appreciative, those concerned with intrinsic value, and the instrumental, concerned with those which are of value or ends beyond themselves. ... Literature and the fine arts are of peculiar value because they represent appreciation at its best. ... But every subject at some phase of its development should possess, what is for the individual concerned with it, an aesthetic quality. (p. 249)

In looking at yet another way in which these two categories of learning have been distinguished – as being appropriate for leisure in contrast to labor – he had this to say:

> [This distinction is] ... embodied in a political theory of a permanent division of human beings into those capable of a life of reason and hence having their own ends, and those capable of only desire and work, and needing to have their ends provided by others. These two distinctions ... effected a division between a liberal education, having to do with the self-sufficing life of leisure devoted to knowing for its own sake, and a useful, practice training for mechanical occupations, devoid of intellectual and aesthetic content. (pp. 260–261)

Dewey then concluded: "The problem of education in a democratic society is to do away with the dualism and to construct a course of studies which makes *thought a guide of free practice for all* [emphasis added] and which makes leisure a reward of accepting responsibility for service, rather than a state of exemption from it" (p. 261). When learners do in fact use their own thoughts to guide their educational pursuits, pigeonholing the learning outcome into one or another category provides no insight or added value to the process.

Fortunately for Dewey's lab school, the liberal/professional distinction was (and continues to be) of little importance in primary and secondary education.[20] Unfortunately for Empire State College, the distinction carries considerable weight since it affects the kind of college degree students can obtain. The key measurement is a ratio of the number of liberal arts credits earned relative to professional credits. In particular, according to State University of New York (SUNY)[21] policy, a Bachelor of Arts (B.A.) degree requires a ratio of 75 liberal arts to 25 professional credits; a Bachelor of Science (B.S.) degree requires a 50–50 ratio; and a Bachelor of Professional Studies (B.P.S.), a ratio of 25-to-75. Thus, the dualism Dewey deplored is impossible for the College to reject. And truth be told, since Empire State College is identified as a liberal arts college, most faculty have internalized the bias that the degree designations associated with the ratio measurements imply. Because the more highly-valued liberal arts presumably represent the true essence of a college education, they are the benchmark against which all other studies are assessed; thus, the B.A. degree is clearly viewed as superior to the B.S., and certainly to the B.P.S. And thus, the passion with which ESC faculty seek to distinguish those studies that are liberal from those that are not seems to be driven by a very real fear of excessive "vocationalism" and the desire to guard the academic world against the incursion of too many studies that could be directly applied to the world of work. Although the practice of prior learning assessment has the potential to expose our tacit academic preference for learning "about" over learning "to do" (see, e.g., Herman & Coulter, 1998), the College policy that governs these assessments supports this bias for the liberal arts by demanding evidence of abstract understanding before a student's experiential knowledge can be deemed truly college-level.[22]

Here then we find a College practice clearly at odds with Dewey's philosophy of education. While his opposition to this subject matter duality was an integral part of his entire philosophy, Empire State College faculty have not seen this traditional division as a critical contradiction to the overall mission of the College. Given the duration, strength, and impact of this tradition, faculty have accepted, without much further thought, the elevated status of the liberal arts as an immutable, if not always rational, fact of life in the academic world. Ironically, however, they have also failed to note that the negative side of each of the dualities discussed by Dewey – culture versus vocation, intrinsic versus instrumental, and leisure versus labor – are the very concepts used to stereotype adult learner interests as compared to those presumed for traditional-aged college students. Thus, when the College community not only accepts the liberal/professional arts distinction but sees the liberal arts as the "better" option, it reveals an unacknowledged assumption that adult students' worldly interests are not as educationally valuable as the scholarly interests of the faculty. As a result, a seemingly small and occasionally annoying imposition from traditional practice covers up tacit beliefs by the faculty that contradict the very democratic goals of the adult education they explicitly espouse.

*Faculty Control*

Besides the imposed division between the liberal and professional arts, other forces in higher education have served to curb a full expression of student self-direction. One would be remiss not to acknowledge the explicit impact of the faculty themselves. Although nearly all those who joined the newly formed College in the early '70s were eager to overturn the deadening practices that seemed to define traditional education, particularly for nontraditional students, they did not recognize how strongly they had been shaped by those same practices. Those who had earned Ph.D.s in traditional academic disciplines embraced those disciplines as strongly as they did the importance and value of student-centeredness. They defined themselves not by their practical skills, but by their disciplinary expertise and their comfort with such academic values as theory, abstraction, circumscribed terminology, and structure. They were highly critical of the ways such values were imposed upon students unprepared to appreciate their importance; they felt strongly that education must be developed around the skills and dispositions that students bring with them to college; they understood that disciplinary studies may not always be the appropriate place to begin; but their sense of what it meant to be "college educated" – what the outcome of university study should be – was largely consonant with the mission statements of most traditional colleges. No wonder, perhaps, that the major focus of these early mentors was upon procedure.

At the outset, SUNY also demanded that individualized programs of study must fit within a particular pre-determined (and officially registered) "area of study" and meet an established list of faculty-determined knowledge requirements for that area. Faculty mentors felt comfortable tempering this attempt at control (particularly in disciplines not their own), by interpreting these requirements as "guidelines" and treating them with a good degree of flexibility. More insidiously, however, despite efforts to weaken the iron hand of the disciplines by subordinating them within areas of study, it was the continued identification of faculty with their particular discipline that made it almost impossible to allow unfettered student-initiated studies that did not eventually include what faculty themselves were expected to have learned as college graduates. Many mentors and tutors have felt compelled – almost with a sense of moral responsibility – to expose learners to all the important topics their own discipline encompasses. Such exposure is typically implemented through the use of standardized textbooks, convenient repositories of the major theories, issues, references, and conceptual organization that make up the very substance of a particular field – but, unfortunately, a resource that leaves no room for student input.

That such a clearly teacher-centered focus could so easily reside within a student-centered institution is often justified by the claim that the student has an interest in or need for such knowledge. Similar evidence of this type of study, along with a similar rationale, can also be found in *The Dewey School* (Mayhew & Edwards, 1936/1965/2007). Children were not forced to learn to read or to study mathematics, but the learning activities were so arranged that sooner or later even the most reluctant child would feel the need for these skills. And in that case – that is, when the child requested it – appropriate instruction with reliance upon traditional textbooks was provided. Similarly, older children preparing for, say, college entrance exams, could seek out conventional instruction in those areas in which they felt unprepared.

However, forND, an intentional study of a discipline for its own sake was acceptable *only if* the demand came directly from the student and arose out of an authentic and urgent need. A secondhand recommendation or systemic requirement was not a sufficient reason. When simply told to undertake a particular course, Dewey (1916) wrote, the student becomes merely "a spectator … like a man in a prison cell watching the rain out of the window." Only if the student has a real need for the actual knowledge involved does he become a true "agent or participant … like a man who has planned an outing for the next day which continuing rain will frustrate" (p. 124). In other words, Dewey took care to distinguish different meanings of the word, "interest." It is one thing, he argued, to know certain information of relative interest; it is quite another to need that information for reasons of one's own. That it will rain tomorrow is an interesting fact; that the rain will ruin one's plans gives that fact significant meaning.

For several reasons, however, Empire State College faculty have not made much of this distinction. First, interests have not been distinguished by purpose, but by their content and the topic of the study that they lead to. Second, because discipline-based studies are of great interest to them, most mentors or tutors believe that with sufficient exposure others will enjoy them as well; indeed faculty offices typically abound with a variety of intellectually accessible books or videos that can be used as initiating "hooks" with which to reel in student attention. And third, adult students – particularly in an institution of higher learning – are expected to know their own minds, and if they say they "need to take" some subject matter, faculty are not necessarily disposed to investigate the source and nature of that need.

In the early days of the College, teacher-controlled disciplinary studies were not the rule. Instead, by a strange twist in the history of the College, a major effort was directed toward developing a repository of teacher-designed *interdisciplinary* studies. Distinguished faculty from outside the College were invited to follow their own lines of inquiry in creating credit-bearing "learning modules" that the College published as small pamphlets that were made generally available to students (Bonnabeau, 1996, pp. 60–62). Because of their exciting intellectual content, these packaged studies were expected to stimulate student interest in college-level studies. But, just as Dewey would have predicted, such "spectator" courses had little appeal to students in comparison to the unique learning contracts mentor and student designed to address the student's own concerns.

Still, after expending considerable energy in creating these one-off studies, many mentors could not resist trying to interest other students in those same lines of inquiry. Thus, over time, numerous libraries of often idiosyncratic, always interdisciplinary, learning contracts accumulated in individual mentor offices where they were increasingly called upon when they seemed at least in some way relevant to some other learner's goals, purposes, or interests. In other words, one student's original inquiry was turned into a study that for another student was largely determined by the mentor. As a result, purely student-initiated, unique studies became less and less the norm as more and more "pre-used" or "canned" contracts were put into play.[23] The fact that student degree programs could still consist of some unique mix of student-initiated, disciplinary, and mentor-designed studies was taken, even to this day, as evidence for the College's attention to the individual needs of our adult learners.

One reason that this mixed outcome was not seen as a betrayal of the College's professed student-centered focus is that it emerged out of the College's core feature – the student-mentor relationship. That the outcome resulted from a shared social process is, interestingly enough, consistent with Dewey's analysis of necessary control. As he saw it, control imposed for reasons unrelated to those experiencing it is undesirable and quite different from control that is an inherent part of the experience itself (Dewey, 1938, pp. 51–56). Thus, structure and rules – in the educational situation, control over what to learn – are both necessary and acceptable as long as the participants working together are focused upon a common purpose. Freedom is important here, not because students have the right to do whatever they wish, but because it allows their real interests and concerns to be given room for full expression in working toward that purpose (p. 62).

As a result, the question of control becomes a matter of discussion. If only because of ordinary conversational etiquette, mentors interact in a friendly fashion with their mentees as social equals. Within that context, the conversation that ensues thus prevents the mentor from too easily relegating the mentee to the category of ignorant student and encourages a sense of collaboration that softens the lines of authority that would ordinarily allow a teacher simply to tell the student what to learn. Thus, the mentoring relationship itself, even if inadvertently, can provide some of the very conditions that Dewey saw as essential for actively engaging the student in the learning process and in helping her take ownership of what to learn no matter who initiated the actual content.

*Intellectual Skills*

Regardless of what students actually learn, the push for universal college accessibility is, if anything, stronger today than when the College first opened in 1971. If higher education is no longer to be restricted to an elite group of like-minded individuals being trained for leadership or a special guild of scholars being trained for research, James Hall's words (with Barbara Kevles) some years ago that "social imperatives … require the vast majority of educational institutions to serve multiple student constituencies with highly diverse curricular expectations" (Hall & Kevles, 1982, p. 15) are all the more cogent.[24] With a wider constituency in a world changing under our feet, he was echoing Dewey's position exactly. As a pragmatist who was profoundly influenced by the new discoveries the scientific approach made possible in his day, Dewey saw that the traditional philosophical search for absolute truth or certainty was wrongheaded (Boisvert, 1998). As an educator, he also saw that no extant knowledge should be exempt from skeptical review. Thus, he considered it imperative that, whatever the curriculum, students also acquire the intellectual skills needed to critically judge for themselves what is worth knowing. Therefore, in *How We Think*, Dewey (1910) analyzed the process of reflective thought, created a model of what we now call "critical thinking," and argued strongly for the importance of the intentional "training of thought":

> While it is not the business of education to prove every statement made, any more than to teach every possible item of information, it is its business to cultivate deep-seated and effective habits of discriminating tested beliefs from mere assertions, guesses, and opinions; to develop a lively, sincere, and open-minded preference for conclusions that are properly grounded, and to ingrain into the individual's working habits methods of inquiry and reasoning appropriate to the various problems that present themselves. (pp. 27–28)

In addition to thinking, the importance of numeracy, literacy, and communication skills was repeatedly emphasized in every grade of the Dewey school, regardless of the topic of study (Mayhew & Edwards, 1936/1965/2007). Without question, these skills are regarded as exceedingly important today. Intellectual strategies rather than specific bodies of knowledge are considered essential for navigating the huge amount of ever-growing unevaluated information on the internet. The scholarly challenge is no longer to *locate* information, but to sift through and *select* what is important and accurate. In today's business world, college graduates are valued for their intellectual nimbleness rather than for their mastery of facts, as employers look not for specific knowledge as much as for strong skills in communication, problem solving, and critical evaluation (e.g., Hart Research Associates, 2010). (Note how the extent to which the job world helps dictate what students need to learn in college is a clear illustration of Hall's point about the "social imperative," a theme that is also taken up in Dewey's [1916] *Democracy and Education* [particularly pp. 81–99].)

However, traditional college educators are not of one mind as to the best way these skills should be developed. Not everyone sees a flexible, provisional, and evolving curriculum as a particularly good context in which to strengthen student skills of inquiry, critique, and reflection. Having themselves acquired these skills successfully through disciplinary study, many faculty regard a fixed curriculum such as they experienced as the more appropriate venue. Donoghue (2008) offered particularly harsh words about the business world's pragmatic view of schooling as he scornfully cited Andrew Carnegie in claiming that when "Hebrew and Greek barbarians are models" and "Shakespeare or Homer is the reservoir from which they draw," traditionally-educated students are being "adapted for life on another planet" (p. 4). Blunt as Carnegie's statement might be, its sentiment is not inconsistent with Dewey's (1916) position when he wrote: "The study of past *products* will not help us understand the present" (p. 75). Yet, even just the *appearance* of questioning the value of Socrates and Shakespeare seems to undermine the very bedrock of a liberal education. Moreover, such questions inevitably also challenge the expertise of teachers, particularly of university professors whose claim to competence rests much more upon their knowledge of past products than their mastery of intellectual skills that transcend their disciplines.

Although its progressive roots encourage the College as an institution to welcome faculty comfortable with a flexible curriculum designed to help move students to higher cognitive levels (e.g., Kegan, 1994), it is also home to faculty like Donoghue (2008) who made strong arguments for certain fixed and revered courses of study.[25] Moreover, given how swiftly the demand for a particular skill can turn into a course requirement, the distinction between intellectual skills and received wisdom is not as clear-cut as it may first appear. Some years ago, William Perry (1981) offered evidence of intellectual development – specifically the growth of open-mindedness to multiple and conflicting beliefs – that occurred over four years of study at an elite liberal arts college. By his analysis this development took place in small incremental steps as students moved from one intellectual stage to another, and this growth was attributed to the entire college experience both in and out of class. Yet, 25 years later, Kronman (2007), a professor from another elite liberal arts college, argued that such intellectual tolerance can be attained only if students take specific courses in philosophy. Similar claims today are made for the importance of single courses designed to transform students into critical thinkers, environmental advocates, or promoters of human diversity.

The reasoning is simple: For every desired intellectual disposition, there should be an appropriate course, and all students should make sure such courses are represented in their transcripts. Yet evidence suggests that the development of new ways of thinking is a slow process that cannot be restricted within the space of a single 15-week course.[26] Further, such courses once developed begin immediately to look like studies of "past products." Courses in critical thinking or human diversity, delivered with textbooks, workbooks, and exams, clearly intended to impose an already fully developed viewpoint, are very unlikely to encourage students to strengthen or flex their own intellectual muscles.[27] The opposite is true when students actively engage studies built around their own concerns. To the extent that these concerns are embedded in contemporary life, questions related to human differences or sustainable practices, or that call for critical thinking, can hardly be avoided. Thus, by continuously embedding a need for such skills, and attention to their further development, within every learner-initiated inquiry, Empire State College makes it possible for its students gradually and naturally to acquire and strengthen those important dispositions just as Dewey encouraged such growth in his lab school.

That such an approach is possible, however, does not mean that it necessarily took place. That Dewey's vision could be put into practice through the flexible procedures available at Empire State College does not mean that faculty, much less students, were familiar with this vision. That faculty sought to create good learning experiences for their adult students does not mean that mentors explicitly promoted, much less agreed with, the progressive emphasis on student-centeredness. That adult students require physical accessibility does not mean they demanded, or even expected, a constructivist form of intellectual accessibility. We are left wondering, then, to what extent, if at all, did Dewey's ideas actually have an impact on the College?

## EVALUATING DEWEY'S IMPACT

Our close examination of certain key practices at Empire State College leaves little doubt that in most instances they are compatible, if not entirely consistent, with Dewey's thinking about education. Although no written record exists that ties these practices to Dewey, Richard Bonnabeau,[28] college historian, has shared that Ernest Boyer, the SUNY chancellor who was primarily responsible for the College's creation, was a student of William Kirkpatrick who, throughout his life as an educator, was a fervent supporter of Dewey and his lab school (Lounsbury, 2005). Thus, there is every reason to believe that the similarities between Dewey's vision and the original conception of our College were not accidental. A key question for this chapter, however, is whether faculty would have been better able to sustain those practices had they been as well informed about their philosophical underpinnings as they were aware of their practical advantages.

In addressing this question, it might be relevant, first, to ask how important close contact with Dewey himself was to the prominence of philosophy at his lab school. Empire State College is nearing the 50 year mark. In contrast, the Dewey school remained under his leadership for only about seven years. Concrete hints about the lab school's later years come from two mentors (see Coulter's and Winner's responses in Coulter et al., 2008), who were also once students at another Dewey-inspired school in Ann Arbor, Michigan[29] some 50 years after the start of the original school in Chicago. Neither mentor recalled learning experiences that even approximated what was described in The Dewey School (Mayhew & Edwards, 1936/1965/2007). They set no fires, took part in no daily cooking of breakfast (or any cooking at all), built no model towns, engaged in no serious investigations outside the classroom. No one was exempt from learning to read, write or do math (Coulter et al., 2008). A recent examination of faculty notes and correspondence during that period suggests that the Michigan school's main purpose as a "laboratory" was not to investigate how children best learn, but to provide human subjects for university graduate theses.[30] Dewey's grand vision had morphed to an almost astonishingly different end.[31] Empire State College is also a very different institution today than when it was first founded. Terms are now fixed, students receive grades, course catalogs are published, and increasingly students learn online in simulated classrooms. Teacher-designed studies are now the rule; independent study is engaged, not necessarily as an opportunity for self-directed inquiry, but because a student is required to take a particular course not otherwise offered during that term.

Is it reasonable to suppose that these changes in practice could be attributed to ignorance of or at least inattention to their philosophical base? When Dewey was at the helm of the lab school, faculty and staff met weekly, research findings were published regularly, and learning activities were continuously reviewed and revised (Mayhew & Edwards, 1936/1965/2007). Conceivably, when Dewey and his university colleagues were no longer involved, the excitement for and commitment to translating philosophy into practice slowly declined. In the beginning years of Empire State College, faculty and administrators similarly spent considerable time and energy discussing and justifying the kinds of methods that could make college study truly responsive to individual adult student needs and purposes. These conversations were not recorded, but it is reasonable to assume that early on, these new practices were supported by a broad swath of philosophical beliefs. Unfortunately, these discussions took place largely as part of the process of implementation rather than as an ongoing and permanent feature of the College. As college practices became routinized, such conversations were increasingly relegated to local faculty meetings where they were nearly always squeezed out by the need to talk about individual student issues, enrollment statistics, faculty workload, and other day-to-day practical problems. Thus, the pattern of change that occurred at both the original Dewey school and at Empire State College could indeed have been the result of a growing disconnection from their philosophical roots.

Why would such a disconnect have taken place? For one thing, both schools began to grow in size. When Dewey left, the original cohort was now finishing the elementary grades, so the school still had another five or six grades to add. Arthur G. Wirth, a Dewey scholar, indicated that it was "the pressure of an expanding education system" that prevented further consideration of Dewey's ideas (as cited in Jackson, 1990, p. xi). At Empire State College, after the first year or so, Bonnabeau (1996) reported that the school was bombarded by an unexpected onslaught of highly diverse adults eager for a new (and convenient) way of learning (p. 44). With a sudden demand for more time spent mentoring, time for regular open-ended collegial discussions rapidly dissipated.

It is also the case that the implementation of a college mission that appears to run counter to prevailing practice takes a lot of effort. In Dewey's case, Schwab concluded that "what teachers were required to do was simply too demanding" (as cited in Jackson, 1990, p. xii). While workload at Empire State College was not insurmountable, it was certainly burdensome enough that few faculty were willing to intentionally expand the mentoring process without a very strong reason. A mentor could comfortably cater to a student who did not want to study mathematics, as long as the mentor had the patience and belief that in time the learner would come to see the value of such knowledge and change his mind. However, when the mentor had no strong theoretical backing for this effort, the difference between waiting for students to choose this study by themselves and simply telling them up front that it was required, soon began to feel like a waste of precious time when the end point was ostensibly the same. And yet, for Dewey, the end points were not at all the same, representing, as they did, a seismic shift away from student agency back to teacher control.

That not all practices at the College were well aligned with Dewey's philosophy may also have played a role in downgrading the importance of a philosophical foundation. The ready acceptance of the liberal/professional division, for example, served, almost without notice, to promote the teaching of distinct and separate disciplines and to demote the value of student-initiated studies not hemmed in by those disciplines. As such discrepancies slowly undermined the original College mission, mentoring practices began to drift back to more conventional, and familiar, ways of teaching. That this "drift" was regarded by some, particularly those unfamiliar with the College's early history, as "a return to standards" certainly suggests that these changes did not reflect some new alternative vision. In addition, although the College promoted the idea that effective – accessible – education must begin with student interest, it failed to investigate in any detail the nature of "interest" in itself, whether all "interest" is good, and how to evaluate the worthiness of an educative experience that a particular interest might lead to.[32] The College did not recognize that different understandings of the role and meaning of "student interest" may well have been at the heart of the various academic conflicts that simmered throughout the College's history. Those who promoted generally available pre-constructed courses and those who advocated for unique individualized studies[33] did not see that it was the meaning of "student interest" that differentiated these forms of study. Instead, advocates on either side strongly defended the rightness of their own ways of instruction, and without a deeper investigation of the issue, it was the weight of tradition in education – that is, "how things have always been done" – that ultimately decided how that division would be resolved.

Some have regarded the devolution of the College away from its progressive beginnings as the result of a kind of epic battle between numerous mutually exclusive dualities: student versus teacher control, unique multi-disciplinary versus shared disciplinary studies, anticipated (future-oriented) intellectual skills versus received knowledge ("past products"), liberal reflections versus practical concerns – indeed, progressive versus traditional education. By that view, the current face of the College could be characterized as some combination of either uneasy truces or provisional winners and losers on either side of these various divides. Dewey, however, would not have accepted that kind of outcome. As he explained in *Experience and Education*, while "[m]ankind likes to think in terms of extreme opposites," neither end of the spectrum, he argued, can be wholly put into action (Dewey, 1938, p. 17). When the extremes reflect endpoints on some continuum, such as degree of student agency, the real situation is typically some position in between. When the extremes appear to represent different qualitative states, such as progressive versus traditional education, the resolution may require new perspectives and further inquiry. As Dewey also wrote, "… differences in abstract principles will not decide the way in which the moral and intellectual preference involved shall be worked out in practice" (p. 20). If all learning is said to occur as a result of some kind of experience, it is incumbent upon progressive educators to carefully examine and evaluate the nature of the experiences they promote as they are actually played out in practice:

> What is the place of and meaning of subject-matter and of organization *within* experience? How does subject-matter function? Is there anything inherent in experience which tends toward progressive organization of its contents? What results follow when the materials of experience are not progressively organized? (Dewey, 1938, p. 20)

Or, if adherence to authority or the imposition of external control is what differentiates traditional from progressive education, it is not necessarily true that a resolution would require a rejection of authority or the removal of control. It might well be, as Dewey (1938) argued, that one needs to search for "a more effective source of authority" or "factors of control inherent within experience" (p. 21). Such a form of analysis, if applied to the many opposing positions within the College, might have revealed them to be more apparent than real.

But we did not have Dewey's philosophy to guide us. Given our apparently irresolvable points of view, it is perhaps not surprising that in the end faculty clung to practice as the only available haven. Without any clear philosophical backing, however, these practices became revered ends-in-themselves – ideologies[34] – and, as new people entered the College, increasingly vulnerable to challenge. For Dewey, the fundamental goal of education was never to be "student-centered," or to encourage "independent study," or to promote "mentoring relationships," but to create a situation in which students take ownership of their own learning. At the College, it became all too easy over time to regard such critical practices simply as adult-friendly methods of getting learners to engage subject matter seen as important to their teachers. The outcome was to lose touch with what students might actually have wanted to learn for themselves, and in the end, to make Empire State College not that different from any college where good teachers go to great lengths to attract and maintain student interest in their courses.

In sum, it is clear that Dewey's philosophical writings not only could have easily served to justify the unique learning processes that the College embraced in its early years, but also could just as importantly have shown faculty ways of resolving the serious divisions that began to arise as the College matured. It is unlikely that the inability to stay the progressive course can be solely attributed to the failure by the originators of the College to provide a strong philosophical scaffolding. No doubt other factors were important too, for example, that progressive practices are difficult to adapt to economies of scale or that human psychology ultimately pushes people, no matter what their theoretical ideals, toward greater efficiency. Nonetheless, the result is that the College never attained Belenky et al.'s (1986) final stage of "constructed" knowing. One of the hallmarks of constructivists, they wrote, is "a high tolerance for internal contradiction and ambiguity" and a willingness to "abandon completely the either/or thinking so common to the previous [connected and separate] positions" (p. 137). Much of the movement in the College toward more traditional practices has been the direct result of an almost total absence of those characteristics.

Ironically, in the first quarter of the 21st century, considerable dissatisfaction is being expressed regarding the effectiveness and value of precisely those traditional practices that are increasingly a part of the College today. Various attempts have been made by many an academic to suggest new ways of thinking about how a college education ought to be implemented; so far, it is not yet common to hear calls for the kind of school that Dewey had in mind:

> … one in which old divisions and separations had been overcome or had otherwise disappeared. Gone were to be the barriers and artificial hindrances that long had separated school and society, the child and the curriculum. Gone too were to be the airtight compartments of work and place, thought and action, cognition and volition, and of all the other dichotomies we so commonly use to categorize and ultimately to isolate the polarities of human experience. (Jackson, 1990, p. xxxvi)

In its most flexible and creative form, Empire State College was able to realize much of Dewey's dream, and in so doing serve its students remarkably well. Perhaps in responding to current complaints, the next generation will find a way to take up this dream again. But, this time, the story of Empire State College's experiences may help these future educators ensure that the major stakeholders construct an institution that fully integrates both theory and practice, where a philosophical vision, not just new practices and procedures, guides student learning. With that kind of grounding, we can imagine that supporters of such an institution will be better able to effectively resolve those conflicts that threaten the sustainability of a vision that challenges customary practice. In so doing, they will find that the words and ideas of Dewey will certainly play an integral role.

## NOTES

[1] Mentoring appears to defy clear definition (see e.g., Jacobi, 1991, and Crisp & Cruz, 2009). However, following Daloz (1999), Empire State College's concept of a mentor who guides individuals during their own academic journey emanates from Homer, who described how Athena (in the guise of a man named Mentor) assisted Odysseus and, separately, his son Telemanche, on their various journeys.
[2] One exception relevant to this chapter is an article by Eric Zencey (2003), "Dewey's Process of Inquiry."
[3] On the back cover of Bonnabeau's book (1996), then-president James Hall described mentoring as a "*structural* [emphasis added] transformation in the way students and faculty teach and learn."
[4] How else to account for such publications as Edmondson's book (2006), John Dewey and the Decline of American Education: How the Patron Saint of Schools has Corrupted Teaching and Learning, or more recently a New York Times blog in which Dewey is criticized for (presumably) being opposed to the teaching of mathematical algorithms (Crary & Wilson, 2013).
[5] Westbrook (1991, p. 8) reported that Dewey did have "considerable problems with classroom discipline," which may be, at least in part, what propelled him back to college to pursue a more scholarly career.

⁶ The first of his six children was born in 1887, and the last in 1900. During this period, Dewey moved to Chicago in 1894, opened the University of Chicago laboratory school in 1896, and wrote "My Pedagogic Creed" and "Ethical Principles Underlying Education" in 1897, and "The School and Society" in 1899.

⁷ See Robinson (2010) for a modern-day expression of similar views.

⁸ An interesting contemporary demonstration of this argument made by Sugata Mitra (2010) shows young children finding computers (in a random "hole in the wall") and figuring out together how to manipulate them.

⁹ It was also a fitting way for children to learn and articulate the rules needed to promote effective problem-solving together – rules of group conduct that Dewey also considered an essential requirement in a democratic society.

¹⁰ Roughly 85 percent of adults enrolling at Empire State College have prior college records.

¹¹ And they are already fully conversant with the expected rules of conduct.

¹² Dewey wrote more than 700 books, articles, and other materials that make up the 37 volumes of his collected writings (Simpson, 2005). From Boydston (1970), we can roughly estimate that about 30 percent of these documents relate directly to schooling and the philosophy of education. If we include writings about the theory of knowledge and logic (topics taken up in Zencey [2003; see also footnote 1], the number exceeds 40 percent.

¹³ The author, along with Lee Herman, Tom Hodgson, Sylvain Nagler, and Irene Rivera de Royston (1994), participated in a year-long project, sponsored in part by the National Council on Adult Learning (NCAL), in which such conversations were videotaped. This description is a composite of several of these tapes.

¹⁴ Dewey made good use of his colleagues from the University of Chicago, of particular note, James Angel, George Mead, and James Tufts (Mayhew & Edwards, 1936/1965/2007, p. 4).

¹⁵ For example, staff meetings at his school always included student representatives.

¹⁶ Although early on the College imposed no specific course requirements, "breadth" and "depth" have always been seen as essential characteristics in any academically-defensible program. How these are achieved, however, was typically left to the mentor and student to determine and defend.

¹⁷ What is described in this article seems identical to what is now referred to as "problem-based learning" (Knowlton & Sharp, 2003).

¹⁸ A degree program at Empire State College is similar to the traditional transcript in that it lists every study and number of credits completed by a particular student in order to earn a specific degree.

¹⁹ The liberal arts studies are supposed to reside in the so-called arts and sciences (the humanities, arts, social and natural sciences, and mathematics); the professional arts are those originating in schools of business, engineering, law, agriculture, and so forth. Some see this as a distinction between disciplines that stress "knowing" and those that stress "doing." Kimball (1986), however, in tracking down the history of the term, "liberal arts," made a convincing argument for two different definitions that have existed side by side since the time of the early Greeks. For him, it is the distinction between the intellectual focus of the orator and philosopher that results in two different meanings: either the liberal arts are seen to represent a repository of "received wisdom" (as delivered by orators) or to represent those disciplines that stimulate new perspectives and deeper thought (as promoted by philosophers). With such a contradiction, no wonder it's difficult to decide what course or study merits the liberal arts title.

²⁰ There is no entry at all for "liberal arts" in the index of The Dewey School (Mayhew & Edwards, 1936/1965/2007).

²¹ Empire State College is one of 64 campuses that constitute SUNY, a state-wide system that oversees public higher education in the State of New York.

²² It also suggests that the College's embrace of experience as a source of learning has devolved, over time, from a considered position about the nature of knowledge, to the position taken by many adults who come initially to the College for the very practical reason that their experiential knowledge will accelerate the completion of their degree.

²³ Additionally, students could take advantage of pre-structured courses developed and offered by faculty at the Center for Distance Learning, a unit that was created for students unable to physically access the college or, as Bonnabeau (1996) described it, for "passive students or the intellectually insecure"

(p. 80). That Dewey believed it was just such a curriculum that made students passive or insecure was a source of considerable discomfort to the more progressively-oriented mentors. However, that these courses were available when requested – e.g., an accounting course seen as essential by a business student – was also seen as useful and in itself not necessarily inconsistent with a student-centered approach.

[24] James Hall was Empire State College's first president.

[25] Note how well this difference matches the liberal arts orator/philosopher distinction described by Kimball (see footnote 19).

[26] A report about the actual ability of recent college graduates to meet the intellectual standards of employer demands (Head, Van Hoeck, Eschler, & Fullerton, 2013) found post-graduate research skills be to be both "limited and limiting" (p. 86). In the words of an employer, "They do well as long as the what, when, why, and how is clear in advance. It's that their toolkit and their whole sense of searching is limited" (p. 86).

[27] Spector and Prendergast (2015) made a similar and excellent argument in their critique of character education.

[28] In private correspondence.

[29] While not well known, perhaps, Dewey spent the first 10 years of his academic life as a professor at the University of Michigan (Williams, 1998). The Ann Arbor lab school, which was opened in the late 1920s, was very conscious of its connection to the Chicago school and to Dewey.

[30] These materials were made available to the author and her colleague from Grand Valley State University, Barbara Roos (also a former student at the Ann Arbor lab school) by the University of Michigan Bentley Historical Library during the summer of 2011.

[31] As Jackson (1990) remarked, "Whatever else today's Laboratory Schools might be, they certainly are not the educational laboratory their founder envisioned" (p. xiii).

[32] It is ironic that such analyses did take place by mentors curious about the nature of what students learned from experiences outside the College. Unfortunately, these were mostly individual faculty efforts (e.g., Coulter, 2001, 2002), and their relevance to learning within the College was not readily apparent.

[33] Remember Dewey's distinction between being a spectator and an agent of action.

[34] Or, according to Mandell and Coulter (2016), "terms of endearment" (p. 35).

## REFERENCES

Belenky, M. F., Clinchy, B. M., Goldberger, N. R., & Tarule, J. M. (1986). *Women's ways of knowing: The development of self, voice, and mind*. New York, NY: Basic Books.

Boisvert, R. D. (1998). *John Dewey: Rethinking our time*. Albany, NY: SUNY Press.

Bonnabeau, R. F. (1996). *The promise continues: Empire State College – The first twenty-five years*. Virginia Beach, VA: The Donning Company Publishers.

Boydston, J. A. (Ed.). (1970). *Guide to the works of John Dewey*. Carbondale, IL: Southern Illinois University Press.

Collins, A., & Halverson, R. (2009). *Rethinking education in the age of technology: The digital revolution and schooling in America*. New York, NY: Teachers College Press.

Coulter, X. (2001). The hidden transformation of women through mothering. *All About Mentoring, 22*, 46–49.

Coulter, X. (2002). The role of conscious reflection in experiential learning. *All About Mentoring, 24*, 13–22.

Coulter, X., & Mandell, A. (2013). Can adult students transform our universities? In C. J. Boden-McGill & K. P. King (Eds.), *21st century adult learning in our complex world* (pp. 142–160). Charlotte, NC: Information Age Publishing.

Coulter, X., Herman, L., Hodgson, T., Nagler, S., & Rivera de Royston, I. (1994, September). *Assessing adults' experiential learning*. Paper [executive summary of results in research funded by NCAL] presented at the meeting of the National Center of Adult Learning, Saratoga Springs, NY.

Coulter, X., Mandell, A., Shaw, J., Willis, W., & Winner, L. (2008). Experiencing Dewey on experience: A conversation. *All About Mentoring, 34*, 9–14.
Crary, A., & Wilson, W. S. (2013, June 16). *The faulty logic of the 'math wars.'* Retrieved from http://mobile.nytimes.com/blogs/opinionator/2013/06/16/the-faulty-logic-of-the-math-wars
Crisp, G., & Cruz, I. (2009, September). Mentoring college students: A critical review of the literature between 1990 and 2007. *Research in Higher Education, 50*(6), 525–545.
Daloz, L. A. (1999). *Mentor: Guiding the journey of adult learners.* San Francisco, CA: Jossey-Bass.
Dewey, J. (1897/1959). My pedagogic creed. In M. S. Dworkin (Ed.), *Dewey on education: Selections* (pp. 19–32). New York, NY: Teachers College Press.
Dewey, J. (1897/1964). Ethical principles underlying education. In R. D. Archambault (Ed.), *John Dewey on education: Selected writings* (pp. 108–138). Chicago, IL: University of Chicago Press.
Dewey, J. (1899/1959). The school and society. In M. S. Dworkin (Ed.), *Dewey on education: Selections* (pp. 33–90). New York, NY: Teachers College Press.
Dewey, J. (1902/1990). *The child and the curriculum.* Chicago, IL: University of Chicago Press.
Dewey, J. (1910). *How we think.* Boston, MA: D.C. Heath.
Dewey, J. (1916). *Democracy and education.* New York, NY: Free Press.
Dewey, J. (1931/1964). The way out of educational confusion. In R. D. Archambault (Ed.), *John Dewey on education: Selected writings* (pp. 422–425). Chicago, IL: University of Chicago.
Dewey, J. (1938). *Experience and education.* New York, NY: Collier.
Donoghue, F. (2008). *The last professors: The corporate universities and the fate of the humanities.* New York, NY: Fordham University Press.
Edmonson III, H. T. (2006). *John Dewey and the decline of American education: How the patron saint of schools has corrupted teaching and learning.* Wilmington, DE: ISI Books.
Elias, J. L., & Merriam, J. B. (2005). *Philosophical foundations of adult education* (3rd ed.). Malabar, FL: Krieger.
Hall, J. W., & Kevles, B. L. (Eds.). (1982). *In opposition to core curriculum: Alternative models for undergraduate education, number 4.* Westport, CT: Greenwood Press.
Hart Research Associates. (2010). *Raising the bar: Employers' views on college learning in the wake of the economic downturn.* Retrieved from http://www.aacu.org/leap/documents/2009_EmployerSurvey.pdf
Head, A. J., Van Hoeck, M., Eschler, J., & Fullerton, S. (2013). What information competencies matter in today's workplace? *Library and Information Research, 37*(114), 74–104.
Herman, L., & Coulter, X. (1998). John and Maria: What mentors learn from experiential learning. *All About Mentoring, 15*, 21–25.
Herman, L., & Mandell, A. (2004). *From teaching to mentoring: Principle and practice, dialogue and life in adult education.* New York, NY: Routledge.
Houle, C. O. (1984). *Patterns of learning.* San Francisco, CA: Jossey Bass.
Jackson, P. W. (1990). Introduction. In J. Dewey (Ed.), *The school and society/The child and the curriculum* (pp. ix–xxxvii). Chicago, IL: University of Chicago Press.
Jacobi, M. (1991). Mentoring and undergraduate academic success: A literature review. *Review of Educational Research, 61*(4), 505–532.
Jarvis, P. (Ed.). (1987/1991). *Twentieth century thinkers in adult education.* London, UK: Routledge.
Kegan, R. (1994). *In over our heads: The mental demands of modern life.* Cambridge, MA: Harvard University Press.
Kimball, B. A. (1986). *Orators and philosophers: A history of the idea of liberal education.* New York, NY: Teachers College Press.
Knowlton, D. S., & Sharp, D. C. (Eds.). (2003). *Problem-based learning in the information age.* San Francisco, CA: Jossey Bass.
Kolb, D. A. (1984*). Experiential learning: Experience as the source of learning and development.* Englewood Cliffs, NJ: Prentice Hall.
Kronman, A. T. (2007). *Education's end: Why our colleges and universities have given up on the meaning of life.* New Haven, CT: Yale University.
Lindeman, E. (1926). *The meaning of adult education.* New York, NY: New Republic.

Lounsbury, J. H. (2005, February). *William Heard Kilpatrick*. Retrieved from http://web1.gcsu.edu/education/drwilliamheardkilpatrick.htm
Mandell, A., & Coulter, X. (2016). Academic mentoring as precarious practice. In K. Peno, E. M. Silva Mangiante, & R. A. Kenahan (Eds.), *Mentoring in formal and informal contexts* (pp. 23–42). Charlotte, NC: Information Age Publishing.
Mayhew, K. C., & Edwards, A. C. (1936/1965/2007). *The Dewey school: The laboratory school of the University of Chicago 1986–1903*. New Brunswick, NJ: Aldine Transaction.
Mezirow, J. (1991). *Transformative dimensions of adult learning*. San Francisco, CA: Jossey Bass.
Mitra, S. (2010, July). The child-driven education [Video file]. Retrieved from http://www.ted.com/talks/sugata_mitra_the_child_driven_education?language=en
Perry, W. (1981). Cognitive and ethical growth: The making of meaning. In A. W. Chickering & Associates (Eds.), *The modern American college: Responding to the new realities of diverse students and a changing society* (pp. 76–116). San Francisco, CA: Jossey-Bass.
Robinson, K. (2010, October 14). Changing education paradigms [Video file]. *RCA Animate*. Retrieved from http://www.youtube.com/watch?v=zDZFcDGpL4U
Rogoff, B. (1995). Observing sociocultural activity on three planes: Participatory appropriation, guided participation, and apprenticeship. In J. V. Wertsch, P. Del Rio, & M. Alvarez (Eds.), *Sociocultural studies of mind* (pp. 139–164). Cambridge, UK: Cambridge University Press.
Schön, D. A. (1984). *The reflective practitioner: How professionals think in action*. New York, NY: Basic Books.
Simpson, D. J. (2005). *John Dewey: Primer*. New York, NY: Peter Lang.
Spector, H., & Prendergast (2015, December 7). Thinking and thoughtlessness in character education. *Teachers College Record*, ID number: 18775. Retrieved from https://www.tcrecord.org/Content.asp?ContentID=18775
Westbrook, R. B. (1991). *John Dewey and American democracy*. Ithaca, NY: Cornell University Press.
Williams, B. A. (1998). *Thought and action: John Dewey at the University of Michigan*. Ann Arbor, MI: Bentley Historical Library.
Zencey, E. (2003). Dewey's process of inquiry. *All About Mentoring, 26*, 82–85.

SECTION II

# STUDENT-CENTERED PEDAGOGY

*The Mentoring Model and What it has Meant*

In Section II, four essays examine the ways in which the spirit and ideas underlying ESC's mentoring model have informed various aspects of teaching and learning practice at ESC. Through these different lenses on mentoring, teaching and learning, authors in this section highlight some of the creative tensions and questions arising as they probe their practice in relation to their core value claims and/or espoused theory.

In Chapter 4, "Is the Authority in the Dialogue? A Memorandum," L. Herman takes up the tensions between the ideals of a "dialogical learning process" and the realities of a traditional frame of reference in which knowledge is given and transmission is expected. In doing so, he makes visible the collaborative inquiry between mentor and student and beckons us to comprehend the tensions between "two contrary dispositions: to control and to free, to profess and to inquire." In Chapter 5, "Educational Planning at Empire State College: Fluidity vs. Structure, Process vs. Product," S. Oaks presents the history and significance of individualized degree design, and examines how the calls for "structure" and "product" have often collided with an emphasis on "fluidity" and "process." Chapter 6, by L. Lander, "Interdisciplinary Education at Empire State College: Many Opportunities, Ongoing Challenges" looks at the ways in which the promise of and freedom to create interdisciplinary learning opportunities at both the individual study and degree levels have lived in tension with the inclination by faculty and students to reproduce disciplinary traditions. And in Chapter 7, "The Cipher and Empire: Teaching and Mentoring Through Hip-Hop," H. Gupta-Carlson wonders about the historical and cultural parallels between hip-hop as a musical genre and way of being in the world, and the pedagogy and core values of an experimenting college trying, as hip-hop has, to offer critique and alternative practice.

LEE HERMAN

# 4. IS THE AUTHORITY IN THE DIALOGUE?
# A MEMORANDUM

And is this not the most debased ignorance, to think one knows what one does not? (Plato, *Apology*, 29b)[1]

Then, since we agree that it's our duty to seek after what one does not know, is it fitting that we try together to find out what virtue is? (Plato, *Meno,* 86c)

It's time for me to go now. But you go persuade Anytus, our fellow, of the things you have been persuaded of so far, that he might become gentler. If you can do this, you will do something good for the Athenians. (Plato, *Meno*, 100b)

Empire State College used to sponsor many discussions about mentoring – what it is, why, how to do it. Usually, these were inconclusive. We didn't decide, at least not with much detectable consequence in policy or practice, what mentoring is and isn't, why it's a good thing to do or not, and how to do it and how not to.

This was both delightful and frustrating. It was delightful because endless fields of educational exploration and creation opened before us. It was frustrating because of the indefiniteness: At best, it was hard to know if our efforts to learn had any consequence in policy and procedure; at worst, we habitually failed to act responsibly toward the educational discoveries we made, especially about the practice of mentoring itself. Forty-five years ago and now, we want to know what to do. And so do our students. They and we want to *know*. Otherwise, being here at ESC is pointless.

Yet, repeated, endless discussion – among ourselves and, as I learned, with our students – was somehow what the place was all about: dialogue. By "all about," I refer to the qualities that made Empire State College distinctive and wonderful. But those qualities have had to coexist with their near opposites: Then and now, students come here to get degrees, sooner rather than later, to get on with their lives, equipped with knowledge and certifications that qualify them to compete and thrive in an often brutal, changeable world. From the beginning then, the College comprehended a terrific tension between transmitting knowledge and sustaining dialogue. Gradually, and within the recent decade, more swiftly, it has poorly cared, at every level, for this complexity. Dialogue is less and less our currency and character. Increasingly, we fit Stanley Aronowitz's (2001) description of a "knowledge factory."

During one of those College discussions about mentoring, the small group I'd joined wrestled the question of who's in charge in the mentor-student relationship, especially when mentor and student disagree. We'd made our way to understanding that mentoring had much to do with equality, with collaboration, with sharing authority. We knew that mentors ought therefore surrender, set aside, let go of some of the authority teachers and professors customarily exercise over students. But, how much, how, when … and then what?

At a particularly intense moment during the discussion, the College provost and academic VP at the time, John Jacobson, walked by. He paused, listened, and then intoned: "Authority? The authority is in the dialogue."

Really? What does this mean? How does that meaning coexist with the basic obligation of professional educators, including ESC mentors, to help their students learn and to certify the learning they achieve? Whatever our delight in egalitarian, inconclusive dialogue, we are responsible for legitimating the learning of our students by naming, assessing, and grading it. How has this tension between the dialogical learning process and the assessable achievement of results played out in the history of ESC?

This chapter will explore answers to those questions. It will do so with frequent reference to a similarly puzzling history: the figure of Socrates.[2] He created dialogical education, but insisted that he was not a teacher. He considered the search for truth a duty, but never finally answered, in his view, any of the questions he asked. He claimed that self-examination through the dialogue was the best way for humans to care for themselves, but pointed to no evidence of good results. Indeed, many of his interlocutors came to no good at all. What therefore could such a person offer us, or we, inspired by him, offer our students?

To begin, what is "dialogue"? It has to do with talking, talking something through, talking something through in a reasonable way or reasoning something through in words. The word comes from the Greek, *dialegesthai*, a verb (Liddell & Scott, 1968). It means talking, reasoning, examining something through for oneself but usually with others. It's conversation-as-learning, both internal and social. The activity doesn't necessarily imply a beginning or an end, just as we do not necessarily attribute a beginning or an end to thinking. Both the social and internal forms of such conversation are not hierarchical. No one is really in charge. Everyone's ideas and questions are important. That's how we learn what we do not know. It's also how we treat our own and others' intellects with respect, as capable of learning. These political and ethical aspects of what might seem to be a simply cognitive or academic transaction are the essence of what Jürgen Habermas (2001) calls "communicative action."

This essential equality and openness of dialogue at ESC are very close to the dialogues in which Socrates engaged.

Even as shapely written representations of the real thing, Plato's Socratic dialogues have a "by the way" quality at the beginning, as though they'd spontaneously begun from matters the participants had been thinking about already. And nearly always they end with a reminder of inconclusiveness. There's more to say, more to ask, and much more to be understood: The knowledge the participants believe they have acquired remains provisional. Very good photographs have this quality. Something leads your eyes beyond the image; something makes you ask a question, wonder, what's going on beyond the image, which the thing before you cannot answer. You want to see more; you want to know more. Thus, a good photograph evokes wonder, as does a good conversation.

Perhaps most importantly, every participant's ideas and assertions, no matter how seemingly perverse, are examined. Why? Because any willing participant might have something to contribute to everyone's learning, even a cheeky question or a willful demand. In this way, dialogical inquiry is inherently democratic and egalitarian. No doubt, Socrates is conducting the show. And he's often accused of being "ironic," in the sense of saying the opposite of what he really means. Nonetheless, I've never been able to find any compelling evidence that Socrates isn't completely honest – however jestingly – when he claims "I do not know" and that every participant, no matter how hostile, is his "friend" or at worst his fellow human, a potential inquirer after wisdom.[3] Socrates never proffers himself as an authority on anything – except "love matters," which always take the lovers, especially of the intellectually questing kind, toward truths which are absolute, wondrous and indefinitely just beyond our complete and final grasp (Herman, 2004).

We also know that Socrates so cherishes dialogical inquiry that he's happy to die rather than give it up. In fact, supremely happy: There just might be an afterlife in which he gets to continue asking and seeking for all eternity:

> It would be the greatest thing, doing there just as here, searching out and questioning people, anyone who is wise and anyone who thinks so, but isn't. (*Apology*, 41b)

The inquiry goes on and on because human beings don't have the wisdom of gods, who know things absolutely. We continue to inquire – at least we ought to – because that's how we learn more, understand better. Ironically (yes, here, the word is right), human wisdom, the very best human knowledge, turns out be discovering one's ignorance (*Apology*, 21d–23c) and then continuing to search (*Meno*, 84a–d). Socrates believes that evoking such perplexing discoveries and the perpetual desire to learn in himself and others (80c–d) is very great service: It is the care of the soul (*Apology*, 29d–e). Moreover, he believes that engaging himself and others to such inquiries is a duty placed upon him by the gods (e.g., 23b). Ironically, this defendant against a capital charge of *im*piety believes that his disturbing inquiries are in fact *pious* acts.

We can never finish, can never justly say, "Now, at last, I am wise." And yet, paradoxically, Socrates insists that we can do nothing better than continue dialogical inquiry. By default, it would seem that the dialogue itself is the very best thing humans can do. It is caring for oneself and others, a duty. But participation in the dialogue, the activity itself, *is* the good life we seek, the happiness of perpetually provoked curiosity. It is the most fundamental liberal art of all, for it frees us from the self-abuse of thinking that we know what we do not (*Apology*, 29b). Who would deny the authority of living well?

Yet how remote this seems from Empire State College, let alone a conventional one! ESC's student-centered and adult-friendly ways hardly include preaching the care of the soul to our students. How odd and presumptuous it would be for ESC mentors to speak to their students as Socrates does to his fellow citizens:

> Are you not ashamed [Athenians], giving so much attention to things, money, status and honor – as much as you can get of them – that you do not attend to or think as much as possible of what is truest and of the very best in your soul? (*Apology*, 29d–e)

Forty-five years ago and now, students come to ESC for worldly, pragmatic reasons. From the very first *Empire State College Bulletin* (Empire State College, 1971–1972) on, we have asked students to define their own purposes or, as the Bulletin calls it, "objectives" (pp. 17ff). Learning contracts asked students to define their "General" and "Specific" purposes. Early degree program forms asked students to do the same. Defining one's own purposes is a major learning goal of the Educational Planning study and a necessary part of the degree program rationale every student is required to write. The name the College gave to the faculty role of engaging students in these discussions was "mentor" (Empire State College, 1971–1972, p. 32). When mentors ask students what they want to learn, we also ask them why. If the answer is something like "I just want to get a degree as soon as possible to get a better job," we do *not* criticize, let alone shame that. Indeed, although we faculty may go on a bit now and then about how valuable a liberal arts education is, we are proud that we can help our students fulfill *their* goals as *they* define them.

Not surprisingly, Socrates didn't work in a school. He didn't lecture, give quizzes or assign grades. He took no money for his service. He was poor. He produced no scholarship. And he insists that he doesn't teach anybody anything (even when it looks very much like he does exactly that in helping a young slave learn how to geometrically construct a square double the area of another (*Meno*, 82b-85c). If dialogical learning is about caring for the soul, and that necessarily means devaluing the pursuit of worldly good things, then that's not what we do at Empire State College.

Nonetheless. ...

Dialogical learning is exactly what ESC offered instead of fixed curricula, required and off-the-shelf courses, and a rigid academic calendar. We were not about transmitting our expertise to students, and requiring them to accommodate their educational purposes to what we believed we already knew and considered important. Following the old teaching cliché, we start from where the student's at – each and every one.

How do you do this?

You ask questions.

"What do you want to learn? Why? How? What do you think you know already? How did you learn it? What does it have to with what you want to learn now?"

(Herman & Mandell, 2004, pp. 44–67). We do this at orientation. We do this at the beginning of each enrollment, in beginning the design of an entire degree program, in collaborating with a student to design an individual study. We ask questions like these about what students read, hear, see and write. And, we take their answers seriously. Does this mean we take their answers as absolute, final truths? Certainly not. More questions follow. But it does mean the students' answers are at least as important to consider as carefully and thoroughly as we would our own. Their considered, thoroughly explored answers – yes, this requires time, often a lot of time – make their way onto reading lists; they form essay topics and revisions, and topics of entire studies. Their answers create the content of their degree programs, including the courses they transfer from other colleges, the experiential learnings they seek to be evaluated for academic credits, and the contents of the ESC studies, the new learnings, they choose to do.

Their answers help us learn what they are learning and how well. Their answers lead to the next reading or rereading, the next essay topic or revision. Their answers enable us to evaluate and grade the learning they have achieved. Their answers stimulate us to learn what next questions to ask and suggestions to offer. Our conversations with students are collaborations. And the results determine the content and process, in every aspect, of the State University of New York education our students achieve: "The authority is in the dialogue."

These questions, "What do you want to learn? Why?" and the rest, are not as apparently grand as the questions Socrates and his interlocutors take up: "What is justice? What is courage? Can virtue be taught? What is virtue? What is knowledge? What is love?" Our students do not very often come to ESC to study philosophy.

Yet if we simply let the dialogue flow, so many conversations with our students open philosophical questions, questions about the care of the self and others, and about a good life:

> You want to get a degree as soon as possible. Studies in what area will help you do that?
> Business.
> Why business?
> To get a better job.
> 'Better' means what to you?
> More money, for sure. Also, work I enjoy more.
> More money? …
> For me and my family to live well, of course!
> Living well. OK. And how about work that's more enjoyable?
> Just more interesting to do, not zombie work, and where I'm respected, not just a machine part.
> And what do you and your family enjoy, just, you know, for the enjoyment?
> Well, our kids of course, just loving whatever they do. And our home, being there and also going new places, just to see.

So more interesting and respected work and workplaces, and doing kid things and traveling around just for the pleasure of it? Are these things you'd like to learn more about too?

What do you mean?

In reality, a conversation like this might occur over weeks, months, even longer. Have we arrived at formal philosophical study and taken stock of the soul straight on? No. But meshed in with hard granules of everyday pragmatic living, there are strands of wonder about things for their own sake. Where do they lead? At the beginning, we students and mentors don't precisely know (Herman & Mandell, 2006). For some students, these ends-in-themselves may be the contentment and sheer fascination with the work they do: running a business, making things to sell, helping others, writing poetry, nurturing children. It may be a kind of recreation: bass fishing, coaching soccer, traveling, gardening, reading history. It may be the enjoying of simply being with one's family. Any or all of those things. We don't know; we inquire together, discover and decide. But "ends in themselves," construed in terms embraced, often generated by the student, are now on the table. Even though we don't at first know the exact names or the content, they become topics of learning. And through our collaborative conversation, they are legitimated by both of us: "The authority is in the dialogue."

And in another way, our students and we are not so far from Socrates. Both our questions and the students' uncertainty are honest and important. They are necessary conditions to begin the inquiry and to continue it. Our conversation about what is to be learned, why, what is already familiar and valued requires that we – students and mentors – are ready to acknowledge our ignorance. What a mentor presupposes might be the best answer to common student questions may turn out not to be for any particular student. And the answer that the student supposes might have been good enough may turn out to be not so clear, and not so reliable or satisfying as it first seemed to be. To learn better answers, both mentor and student need to be ready to recognize their ignorance. We become practitioners of Socrates' merely human wisdom: learning that we do not yet know what we'd believed we had.

Becoming absorbed in these conversations, we – students and mentors – are no longer entirely working in a knowledge factory, no longer entirely encased in a system of cognitive acquisition governed by money and power. Engaging in the dialogue, we do not presume that we know what is good for the student. We need them to tell us and, together, we find out more about it. We are line operators in a knowledge factory, a system of production governed by money and power. Instead, in the dialogue, we join our students in what Habermas and others call "the lifeworld" (Habermas, 1985; Mandell & Herman, 1999). This is the dimension of experience in which human beings live a life they have reasons to value for its own sake (see Sen, 1999). As a liberal arts college, Empire State did not offer a canon of the knowledge most worth having, the prescribed content of an institutional curriculum. Instead, we offered the experience of engaging in dialogical inquiry. The authority of the dialogue is that it is simply a good way to live.

The strange and difficult thing about ESC is that it offered this dialogical learning within a public academic institution: It was a complex, bureaucratic system of knowledge transmission organized to sustain and certify a means of learning that was also a way of living.

We said to students, "Come here. Tell us what degree you want and what you want to do with it. We will honor your purpose by conversing with you: We'll help you learn what you need to know, plan how to do that, and complete the degree as quickly as possible. All the along the way, from orientation through your final study, we'll ask you a lot of questions about what you think you have learned, what you need and want to learn, and why. We'll take your answers seriously by assessing and certifying the knowledge you already have, and by connecting you with the people and materials that will help you learn what you need. When you've completed your your plan, we'll give you a diploma publicly certifying your education."

Those conversations, comprising what we called the "mentor-student relationship," we offered as a necessary means to the ends students sought. But, that instrument – dialogical inquiry – engaged our students and us in an activity profoundly gratifying in its own right. The collaboration of mentor and student is pragmatically stimulated. It is undertaken to discover what is to be learned and why, as well as to recognize what is already learned and not learned – whether about the content of an entire degree plan or the meaning of a few pages in a statistics text, a few lines of an Emily Dickinson poem, or a few sentences in a student's essay. In this collaboration, mentor and student are both inquirers. In this way, they are equals. Further, in order to gain the benefit of each other's questions and understandings, they need to treat one another respectfully. The intellectual, ethical and political gratifications afforded by this activity become cherished. To simply follow the dialogue where it leads is to embrace a kind of freedom in giving up certainty about things and control over others. It means that learning is not bounded by degrees or expertise; it becomes lifelong. Bureaucracies exist to organize efforts to efficiently produce intelligibly consistent and tolerably uniform results. It is remarkable that ESC existed and flourished at all when its core activity was to nurture fruitful uncertainty.

Socrates pursued his dialogical inquiries outside any formal institution except the city-state itself. Plato's versions demonstrate how difficult they can be to sustain by themselves, and how readily such freewheeling, critical inquiry disturbs political sensitivities. We can then understand better how improbable it was that dialogue could be sustained at Empire State College.

For example, Meno, in Plato's dialogue of the same name, wants to know from Socrates if "virtue" is teachable. Meno's curiosity is pragmatic and very ambitious.

Socrates says he doesn't know if virtue is teachable, because he doesn't know what virtue is. Sensibly, he suggests that if he and Meno learn first what virtue really is, they can then find out if it's teachable. Grudgingly and unreliably, Meno agrees. The ensuing dialogue includes several failed attempts to define virtue and ascertain its teachability. Confusion and inconclusiveness abound.

In a famous passage (*Meno,* 80a-d), Meno complains that Socrates has paralyzed his mind as a cuttlefish paralyzes its prey. Socrates, however, thinks things are going very well. He shares Meno's perplexity. He doesn't know what virtue is either. He asks Meno to continue to collaborate with him in their dialogical search. And Meno responds with a "gotcha" paradox of his own:

> But how will you seek something, Socrates, which you absolutely don't know what it is? […] Or, even if you stumbled on the very thing, how will you know that it's what you didn't know? (80d)

Socrates says he thinks this is a trick argument. But, most remarkably, he takes up Meno's lead and they pursue the inquiry into how it might be possible for human beings to learn anything at all (pp. 81a ff).

In *Meno*, we travel quickly from practical pedagogy, to philosophical ethics, to metaphysics and epistemology. At the beginning, Socrates tries to cajole the curriculum: the move from "Is virtue teachable?" to "What is virtue?" But Meno's curiosity is persistent. The new topic – the nature of knowledge and learning – is not so far from what he really wants to know. Moreover, it's a topic, as the ensuing dialogue demonstrates, in which the two of them have a common interest. They are led to consider the immortality of soul, and the possibility that all learning is simply recollection, implying that there is really no such thing as "teaching" at all, except perhaps the teaching one does within oneself. Socrates tries to demonstrate his odd idea by helping an unschooled slave boy (Meno's servant) learn to use geometrical construction to double the area of any square. Socrates gently prompts and asks questions. He insists he's doing no teaching but merely stimulating the boy's recollection (*Meno*, 81a-c). With less metaphysical ambition, perhaps we can agree that good teachers are enablers: They help students teach themselves, an activity ESC calls "mentoring independent study."

Socrates' notion that learning is the immortal soul remembering what it's always known, is merely a provisional assertion. It's not relied on later in *Meno*, nor does it appear, without significant modification later in Plato. Nonetheless, provisionally held, it's an idea that Meno and Socrates can share for now. Having been refreshed with a break from being questioned and with the proffer of an idea that excites him, Meno is now eager to join the inquiry again.

What happens next is stunning, briefly leaving Socrates as confounded as Meno had complained Socrates had left him. Meno does agree it is necessary to try to learn what one has discovered one does not know. Socrates asks then, "Does it seem right that … we should try together to search for what virtue is?" Meno replies, "Absolutely!" And then, with barely a pause:

> But … Socrates, but really, the thing I first asked about, that's what *I* would really want to look into and hear about [i.e., whether virtue is teachable]. … (86c)

Socrates nearly loses it here: "Now Meno, if I controlled not only myself but you as well. …" Yet he continues, not without a little dig,

> Since you are not trying to control yourself – you so want your freedom – I will try, I will control myself, and I will give way and join you. (86d)

Socrates leaves go of where the logic of the inquiry has led in order to embrace the object of Meno's willful curiosity. In other words, sustaining the dialogue trumps a logical lesson plan. That's taking "the authority is in the dialogue" very far indeed. Imagine a whole college running this way.

But there's more. Socrates is not simply humoring Meno. Off they go, trying to find out if virtue is teachable. They return briefly to geometry. They review what geometers mean by "hypothesis," namely an assertion taken to be *provisionally* true in order to test if it really is so by the logical or empirical results that follow. Socrates proposes to test the hypothesis that virtue is teachable by looking for the results one would expect if it were so (86–87b). He and Meno agree on two results that would follow if virtue is teachable: If virtue is teachable then there should exist actual teachers of virtue; and, there should exist virtuous people who have actually learned virtue from others who already know what it is.

Neither result seems to be true. Adducing a number of instances, Socrates indicates that many Athenians renowned for their wisdom, raise children who are *not* virtuous (87c-94e). And, taking up a somewhat popular prejudice, he claims that the sophists (some of whom claim that they can teach anything, virtue included) turn out, upon examination, not to know what they say they know (95a-96e). No teachers of virtue, no students who've been taught it; therefore, virtue is not teachable.

But the inquiry continues. Socrates and Meno explore the distinction between knowledge and "right opinion" (97bff). The latter, while corresponding to the truth, does so by lucky accident rather than understanding. The conversation ends with a new hypothesis: Whatever apparently unteachable virtue itself really is, it might be something that comes to humans as a gift from the gods:

> In all this reasoning so far, if we have inquired and discussed well, virtue would be something that comes neither by nature nor teaching, but by divine fate, without understanding, to those for whom it might come. ... (100a)

Confusing, surprising? We know that this is not how Meno expected things to turn out. He's orated before, "hundreds of times" to "large audiences" about the nature of virtue (80b). For the sake of his business, he wants to believe that virtue is teachable. And Socrates? He insists throughout that he doesn't know what virtue is. So maybe it's just some incomprehensible thing that comes by divine grace. Maybe. Socrates reminds Meno at the very end of the dialogue that the nature of virtue remains to be discovered (100b). And we might be reminded to consider that if humans cannot *learn* virtue (perhaps an entirely separate matter from teachability?), Socrates' entire quest – to seek virtue through inquiry, his effort to care for his own soul and those of others through demanding intellectual activity – would be a waste of time, a fool's errand. Just as paradoxically, this conclusion would fly in the face of Socrates' own very persistent belief that this very task, dialogical inquiry, has been laid upon him by the gods themselves (*Apology* 23b).

Such is the delicate, intricate, bewildering play of dialogue. It offers provisional propositions, importunate and important questions that are seemingly unanswerable. Anyone can participate, but must do so freely: None can "govern" another; each is bound to speak honestly. Everyone's curiosity and ideas matter; none is immune from questions from another. Further, the dialogue requires the participants to believe, no matter how confused and uncertain they become, there are in fact truths governing the activity and drawing it onward. One of course can willfully avoid the dialogue, but not on the basis of the claim that nothing can be demonstrated to be either true or false. That would paralyze our minds even more thoroughly than Meno's cuttlefish: for of course such a claim, that there are no demonstrable truths, would have to include that very assertion. Dialogue offers the wonder of discovering new ideas and prospects and questions: the nature of teaching and learning, what makes one's life worth living, how shall one raise one's children or do justice to one's fellow humans. But it also inevitably yields somewhat maddening experience of realizing as we learn more and more, the absolute truth of the matters we most desire to fully understand remains persistently, seductively beyond our grasp. We never quite finally know the things we want to know the most. We are left to choose to live an examined life or a mindless one.

Consider an academic institution – awarding credits and degrees, employing professors, enrolling students – that placed this tempestuous, inclusive experience at its core. *Every* distinctively defining feature of Empire State College essentially requires dialogue. In the learning contract, we collaborate with our students to define a topic of learning, its purposes, means, and outcomes. Educational Planning – the one single course required of every ESC matriculant – is simply a meta-version of a learning contract: Mentor and student seek to discover what learning (prior, current and future) will serve the purposes of the individual student, helping to make a life she or he has reasons to value for its own sake. In prior learning assessment (PLA), student and mentor collaborate to identify what extra-academic learnings the student may have achieved and articulate those for academic evaluation. Throughout these distinguishing educational activities, the Socratic mentor engages each student, one at a time, in dialogue about what the student has learned and intends to learn, and why. The mentor does not presume to know what the student needs until that emerges from their dialogue. The students learn to tolerate and to use their discoveries of ignorance, to seek new learning. Importantly, they sometimes discover that they knew more than they'd realized; and often, they discover that they are more academically capable than they'd supposed. Dialogue, with all its disruptive, unpredictable potency, is the heart of the College. From the beginning, this is the venture ESC made.

And also from the beginning, precisely because it is an academic institution and not only an *agora* of profound conversation, ESC imposed policies and procedures, and tolerated customs that obstruct and smother dialogue.

## IS THE AUTHORITY IN THE DIALOGUE? A MEMORANDUM

One of the basic functions of the academy is deeply conservative: preserving and transmitting knowledge. This does not easily coexist with fostering inquiry. Faculty have to be scholars, experts who can make original but expertly accepted contributions to currently accepted knowledge. This is the traditional, intellectual basis of our authority with peers and over students. It is also the rationalization of our coercive authority: the power of the academy to control access, through admission and graduation, to other forms of social power beyond its gates and walls. Viewed cynically or not, no culture can function without canonical knowledge and without a recognized community of literates, almost exclusively authorized to possess and discretionarily transmit that knowledge. Such a community can hardly welcome the idea that the most important kind of knowing of all is discovering one's own ignorance.

Accordingly, students cannot be justly faulted for demanding the knowledge and expert professorial services they've worked hard and paid much to possess. They expect ESC to be like what they know, for better and worse, as "school." ESC, along with its growing number of competitors, markets its services as a necessary way to get ahead. We thus contribute to the commodification of learning; and we ought not be distressed if students are suspicious when we interminably respond to *their* questions with *our* questions and with murky advice like, "Well, it depends on what you decide. What do you think?"

From this unavoidable, institutional view, knowledge is a complete, certain and stable acquisition. In contrast to the provisional and flowing nature of dialogical learning, this academically canonical knowledge is particulate, firmly apprehensible. It can be acquired from texts, lectures, standardized curricula and courses, courseware, and learning objects. It can be consistently assessed and marketably certified through competency tests. Since the beginning, ESC has offered all of these kinds of things. They are far more familiar, easily recognized and convertible to academic and social capital than dialogue.

This particulated learning is delivered and managed by systems. These are the operational protocols of all large, complex, formal organizations, including Empire State College. Transcending the inherently idiosyncratic personhood of employees, students and other "stakeholders," organizations endure through repeatedly and uniformly applying impersonal policies and procedures controlling decisions, behaviors and resources. Simply, this is what it means to be "organized." An academic organization made of these features generates a budget, enrollment targets, curricula, and standard measures of scholarly and learning production. The legal and marketable legitimacy of Empire State College depends on those things. Without them, ESC would not exist, nor would the promise of dialogical education it has harbored within.

The institutional, systemic view is necessary but overweening. It is remarkably seductive. Precisely contrary to the egalitarian, democratic nature of the dialogical inquiry it houses, the College, as part of the State University of New York, is entirely hierarchical in governance and formal organization (see State University of

New York, 2009). Alexis de Tocqueville (1988), who coined the word "bureaucracy," predicted that large democracies would founder on bureaucratic despotism (pp. 690–695). Max Weber (1958/2003) famously described bureaucratic rationalism as an "iron cage" without "spirit" or "heart" (p. 182). Nonetheless, this tremendous organizational instrument does offer power and control.

The human desire for power and control is strong and deep as curiosity and, as lust itself. Rather than control ourselves, as Socrates does in agreeing to follow Meno's lead (described above), we try to control whatever and whoever is around us. Finding nothing new to learn that matters to him, Goethe's (1951) Faust, a revered professor, retranslates the opening of the Gospel of John as, "In the beginning was the Deed" (*Faust*, I.5. 1224–1237). With not so very much help from Mephistopheles, he manages to kill or destroy nearly everything and everyone he loves; for in his absorption in power, he exorcises love itself. A century later, Freud speculated that behind the "compulsion to repeat," there lies the drive for control, the drive for the organism to so completely protect itself that by controlling stimuli impinging upon it, finally it blocks every stimulus, and therefore, dies (Freud as cited in Strachey, 1955, pp. 7–64). Knowledge-as-control, untempered with strong, dialogical doubt, becomes deadly. Seeing in the first test of the atomic bomb the inarguably awesome results of the massive applied science project he managed, Robert Oppenheimer recalled the words of the Bhagavad Gita, "I am become Death, the destroyer of worlds" (see Hijiya, 2000, p. 123). We should be skeptical of any scientific proclamation that we are on the verge of achieving a true and final "theory of everything" (e.g., Hawking & Mlodinow, 2010). Our skepticism might save the world we actually live in.

Some democratic institutions have a structural skepticism: voting and separation of powers. These constitutionally mandated and protected systems are costly and slow. Although they fail the economist's test of "utility," they do restrain the exercise of unchecked power. By making way for "other" voices, they interfere with office holders believing they know what is best, what is just, when in fact they do not. They preserve the possibility of Socratic wisdom. Classical Athens was a direct democracy and lacked the formal separation of powers with which we are familiar. However, most state offices were filled by lot rather than appointment or party-based electioneering. Moreover, all citizens had the constitutionally and divinely protected right of *parrhesia*, the capability of honestly speaking one's mind in public deliberations. The voice of the "other" was a necessary condition of justice. Sometimes, Socrates' interlocutors, frustrated by his logically confounding questioning, seek to humor and control him by simply telling him what they suppose he wants to hear (e.g., Thrasymachus). Socrates begs them not to, but rather to say what they really mean (*Republic* Book I, 350e). Discovering the truth, the care of the soul through the examined life, depends upon it.[4]

It is all the more remarkable then that the governance of Empire State College, home to academic dialogical inquiry, is constitutionally undemocratic, as required by the policies of the state university of which it is a part. Though customarily obliged to "consult" with others, the president exercises within the College nearly absolute power, checked only by the contracts of faculty and clerical unions and the wishes of the university's chancellor. This constitutional isolation from other voices, from *parrhesia*, is also, as of this writing (2015), geographically enhanced: The headquarter buildings of ESC are located on the east side of Saratoga Springs, New York. No faculty or students are to be found there in the daily course of business. A few poignantly distant miles away to the west, on the other side of town, ESC students and faculty engage in learning. It is perhaps not coincidental that no current senior administrators have any experience of educational mentoring.

One should not see this dangerous concentration of power as a labor versus management problem. It is reproduced by the geographical dispersion of the faculty and the circumstance in which we normally do our educational work. We are scattered in small clusters, about 35 of them, across the state, by and large physically invisible to supervision. And, we do our educational work with students, in person and online, in the isolation of our offices. There are no witnesses and no obligatory assembly in which other voices are welcomed. Moreover, despite the call for us to engage in dialogue with students, to genuinely collaborate and thus share authority with them, we are by formal education and appointment, "professors." Our Ph.D.s assure the students and us that we are experts. Our tenure, once achieved, protects us from all but the most egregious violations of our responsibilities. Those egregious violations do not include eschewing dialogue for pontification. In these circumstances, it is easy for us to anatomize and dispense knowledge in controllable, readily assessable bits.

However, it would be silly, impossible, and unjust to dispense with the particulate aspect of knowledge. It would be silly because then we'd all be wandering about – starving, diseased, unclothed and unhoused – during our brief miserable lives, just wondering. It would be impossible because most fundamentally, the particulate aspect of cognition enables us to recognize, apprehend anything at all: things, people, phenomena, language, and ideas. Without it, I'd not recognize my coffee mug, or myself, from one infinitesimal moment to the next – let alone understand a question or statement a student makes during our conversation. And it would be unjust to discard standardized knowledge. As Weber (1946) understands perfectly well, it is exactly the intelligible, depersonalized and routinized rules of bureaucracy that enable a peasant, a foreigner, or anyone "different" to cash a check at a bank without having to worry if the clerk happens to be benevolent. Bureaucratic rules enable innumerably diverse minorities to enter universities, and enact the principle of due process of law for all (pp. 224ff). We depend upon knowledge-as-power, those solid, bounded, persistent and measurable facts and crystalline ideas about things. Had Socrates not pursued his inquiries in an orderly if misguided *polis*, he'd likely have been simply murdered for being such a gadfly, for asking impertinent questions, as I'll describe below. That is why, when offered a safe chance to escape prison and the death penalty, he refuses to dishonor "the laws" (*Crito* 50a-53a).

To persist and thrive for 45 years, Empire State College needed to house these two reciprocating but contesting understandings of education: the dialogical inquiry and the acquisition of knowledge. With a growing enrollment, faculty, and administration – all powerfully drawn by the desire for certainty, operating in an ever more elaborate, hierarchical system, and, beset by demands for accountability, cultural literacy, productivity – it is not so hard to understand that it would be difficult to institutionally sustain and promote dialogical learning. The financial, political and academic "opportunity costs" are very high.

But so are the risks of failing, as ESC increasingly has, to pay them. Consider a consequence of Socrates refusing to try to control others, just so the dialogue might continue:

Following the winding and unmapped route of the dialogue, he and Meno arrive at the provisional and unsettling conclusion that virtue comes not from teaching but by divine gift. Along the way, they are temporarily joined by Anytus, a politically ambitious citizen of Athens. He joins when they are entertaining the strong possibility that virtue is not teachable because so many prominent men, reputed for wisdom, fail to raise virtuous sons. Anytus would like to be thought of as one of those prominent men. He's insulted by Socrates' impertinent, if provisional, conclusions. He leaves the conversation with this warning: "Socrates, you easily speak evilly of people. I would advise you, if you are willing to be persuaded by me, to beware" (94e). Socrates and Meno continue on.

But at the very end of dialogue, Socrates urges Meno:

> Go persuade Anytus, our companion, of the things you have been persuaded of so far, that he might become gentler. If you can do this, you will do something good for the Athenians. (*Meno*, 100b)

It's unknown if Meno ever tried. We do know that Anytus did not become gentler. Soon, in the trial of Socrates, he will be the lead plaintiff and prosecutor (the two being one and the same in the Athenian legal system). Giving authority to the dialogue means not trying to control others, fully engaging their questions and ideas. It risks losing one's grasp on ideas one cherishes, such as those enhancing one's self-importance. And, it risks offending others – citizens, politicians, professors and administrators, proudly dependent upon their certainty and power. Were it not for the laws of Athens, Anytus might have merely murdered Socrates in the streets. Such violence had occurred in Athens, just a few years prior to Socrates' trial in 399 B.C., during the Tyranny of the Thirty (Colaiaco, 2001, p. 163). But the laws, while necessary, are not sufficient for justice. One might regard Anytus' prosecution of Socrates as judicially initiated murder. For justice, in addition to laws, it is equally necessary to nurture the uncertainty and freedom of inquiring persons, engaged in dialogues of unpredictable outcomes. For justice, one must embrace the perpetually fluxing, flowing of ideas and words, within and between differing, restless minds. If this is "the Logos," the true life of the mind and world, it is as hard to seize, Heraclitus knew, as water, fire, or a lovely chord evoked from the vibrating strings of a lyre (Kirk & Raven, 1964).

In point of hard fact, the "deliverables," the easily grasped and tallied results of Socrates' work are not much to brag of. Anytus, as we've seen, does not become "gentler." And as we know from the exhaustive biographical catalog compiled by Debra Nails (2002), many of the historical figures populating conversations with Socrates did not seem to benefit much from the experience. To list a few: Meno himself is reputed to have become a cruel and traitorous military commander. Critias (in *Charmides* and in Plato's "Seventh Letter") is a leader of the junta that overthrew Athenian democracy in 404–3 B.C.E., the Thirty, infamous for their arbitrary violence. And most infamous of all, there is Alcibiades (*Symposium*). His rapturous love of Socrates seems not to affect his wild intemperance: drunkenness, promiscuity, vandalism, ostentation, and ambition so unrestrained that he'd offer his considerable rhetorical and military skills to whatever side seemed to be winning the catastrophic Peloponnesian War. The Persians, whom he both betrayed and served, finally had him assassinated (see Nails, 2002).

Of course, not all of Socrates' companions turn out badly, Plato himself being a pretty decent example. For that matter, Socrates himself comes across as so good-natured and contented, that he's not afraid or bitter about his death sentence. He is happy (Vlastos, 1991, pp. 233–235). But that's somewhat beside the point. Whatever good dialogical inquiry does, it's not to be found in the production of experts on virtue or anything else. It's not an educational technology. Be that as it may, the Athenians hold him responsible for what they took to be *his* results. He's put to death not only for impiety but also for corrupting the youth of Athens.

Even so, Socrates insists that engaging the dialogue makes us "better, more stalwart, and less useless" (*Meno* 86b-c). He hopes that re-engaging Anytus in the conversation will make him gentler (100b). But none of it can be coerced. We ought to control ourselves, not others.

When that is how the learning goes, then the virtues enabling us to value our lives are experienced in the dialogue itself. The four traditional Greek virtues are courage, temperance, justice and wisdom. All of them are necessarily immanent in the dialogue. And I'll venture to add another: magnanimity. To participate in the dialogue, you must say what you really mean, regardless of what you fear others might think of or do to you. This is courage. But you are required as well to follow ideas through to their logical consequences and abide by the conclusions, no matter how disagreeable and provisional. This is temperance. To learn beyond your own suppositions, you must take others' ideas as seriously as you do your own. This is doing justice, by respecting others as you do yourself. To come closer to what you most want to know – how to live well – you must repeatedly embrace the discovery of your own ignorance. This is wisdom. And to do all this living among others, thus to afford yourself the opportunity to learn from them what you do not know, you must help them care for themselves as you do yourself. This is magnanimity. To engage in the dialogue means to accept the authority of these virtues, and thus to live hopefully and well.

At ESC, we promised to engage students in this way. It is a delicate, difficult enterprise … all the more so because we and our students are unavoidably surrounded, pressed, obliged and tempted by the acquisition of knowledge for the sake of power and prosperity. An institution that offers both acquisitive and dialogical learning must comprehend and sustain two contrary dispositions: to control and to free, to profess and to inquire. That contrariness must be embodied in policy, procedure, and common custom, with all the confusing, inefficient consequences so subversive of the very idea of a well-organized institution. And it is just as difficult for students and faculty to achieve and sustain the breadth and agility of mind necessary to engage in these contrary ways of learning. One is routinized but familiar and reliable; the other is refreshing but alien to our received ideas of school and education. The questioning, challenging voice of the other can be annoying and felt to interfere with achieving the practical purposes that brought us to university in the first place, to strive to prosper in the world, including as academic professionals.

It is therefore not surprising that dialogical inquiry, the distinguishing vital spirit of ESC, has declined. The students arrive not knowing what it is and hear little about it when they are oriented. The faculty has little time and reward for actually practicing the "student-centered" education they'd heard the institution was about. And the administration has even less occasion and reason than the students to know about "the authority of the dialogue." Some administrators, including the most senior ones, seem to regard the student-mentor relationship as a costly "boutique enterprise," primarily valuable as a brand for marketing ESC in an ever more competitive world of adult higher education.

It's amazing, indeed quite magnificent, that ESC made as much room, and for so long as it did, for dialogical learning. It was an improbable thing to have occurred in the first place, and easy to neglect thereafter. One hopes, though, that some ideas, true and good, will be relearned, recollected. The authority of the dialogue is something to be remembered, hence this written memorandum.

## NOTES

[1] I've modified all English translations from the Greek in the Loeb Classical Library edition of each text. References are the traditional "Stephanus Numbers."

[2] I use the word "figure" to sidestep the abiding historical controversy about who that person really was and about what he, who wrote nothing, really believed. Taking this move further, in this chapter I refer only to the version of Socrates Plato gives us. Moreover, I refer almost exclusively to the character we encounter in *Apology* and *Meno*, which is to ignore yet another controversy about how very much the Socrates of the earlier dialogues differs, some say and others hotly deny, from the Socrates of the so called "Middle" and "Late" dialogues.

[3] For a different and very influential account of this much debated topic, see Vlastos, 1991.

[4] On *parrhesia* and the care of the soul, see Michel Foucault's (2011a; 2011b) final lectures, 1982–1984. On Socratic discourse and democracy, see Gerald Mara (1997), *Socrates' Discursive Democracy*.

## REFERENCES

Aronowitz, S. (2001). *The knowledge factory: Dismantling the university and creating true higher learning*. Boston, MA: Beacon.

Colaiaco, J. (2001). *Socrates against Athens: Philosophy on trial*. New York, NY: Routledge.

de Tocqueville, A. (1988). *Democracy in America* (G. Lawrence, Trans.). New York, NY: Harper Perennial Library. (Original work published 1848)
Empire State College. (1971–1972). *Empire State College bulletin.* Saratoga Springs, NY: Author.
Foucault, M. (2011a). *The government of self and others: Lectures at the College de France, 1982–1983* (G. Burchell, Trans.). New York, NY: Picador. (Original work published 2008)
Foucault, M. (2011b). *The courage of truth: Lectures at the College de France, 1983–1984* (G. Burchell, Trans.). New York, NY: Picador. (Original work published 2008)
Goethe, J. W. (1951). *Faust, Eine Tragödie* (R-M. Heffner, H. Rehder, & W. F. Twaddell, Eds.). Lexington, MA: DC Heath.
Habermas, J. (1985). *The theory of communicative action, volume 2: Lifeworld and system: A critique of functionalist reason* (T. McCarthy, Trans.). Boston, MA: Beacon Press.
Habermas, J. (2001). *Moral consciousness and communicative action* (C. Lenhardt & S. W. Nicholsen, Trans.). Cambridge, MA: The MIT Press.
Hawking, S., & Mlodinow, L. (2010). *The grand design.* New York, NY: Bantam Books.
Herman, L. (2004). Love talk: Educational planning at Empire State College, State University of New York. In E. Michelson & A. Mandell (Eds.), *Portfolio development and the assessment of prior learning* (pp. 100–120). Sterling, VA: Stylus.
Herman, L., & Mandell, A. (2004). *From teaching to mentoring: Principle and practice, dialogue and life in adult education.* London, UK: Routledge.
Herman, L., & Mandell, A. (2006). Wonderful bewilderment: In praise of knowing that one does not know. *Progressio: South African Journal of Open and Distance Learning Practice, 28*(1&2), 6–16.
Hijiya, J. (2000, June). The *Gita* of J. Robert Oppenheimer. *Proceedings of the American Philosophical Society, 144*(2), 123–167. Retrieved from http://www.amphilsoc.org/sites/default/files/proceedings/Hijiya.pdf
Kirk, G. S., & Raven, J. E. (1964). Heraclitus of Ephesus. In G. S. Kirk & J. E. Raven (Eds.), *The pre-Socratic philosophers: A critical history with a selection of texts* (pp. 182–215). London, UK: Cambridge University Press.
Liddell, H. G., & Scott, R. (1968). *A Greek-English lexicon.* Oxford, UK: Clarendon Press.
Mandell, A., & Herman, L. (1999). On access: Towards opening the lifeworld within adult higher educational systems. In A. Tait & R. Mills (Eds.), *The convergence of distance and conventional education: Patterns of flexibility for the individual learner* (pp. 17–38). London, UK: Routledge.
Mara, G. M. (1997). *Socrates' discursive democracy: "Logos" and "ergon" in political philosophy.* Albany, NY: State University of New York Press.
Nails, D. (2002). *The people of Plato: A prosopography of Plato and other Socratics.* Indianapolis, IN: Hackett Publishing.
Plato. (1962). *Meno* (W. R. M. Lamb, Trans.). The Loeb Classical Library. Cambridge, MA: Harvard University Press.
Plato. (1963). *Republic* (P. Shorey, Trans.). The Loeb Classical Library. Cambridge, MA: Harvard University Press.
Plato. (1966). *Apology and Crito* (H. N. Fowler, Trans.) The Loeb Classical Library. Cambridge, MA: Harvard University Press.
State University of New York. (2009). *The State University of New York: The policies of the board of trustees.* Retrieved from http://www.suny.edu/Board_of_Trustees/PDF/Policies.pdf
Sen, A. (1999). *Development as freedom.* New York, NY: Alfred A. Knopf.
Strachey, J. (1955). *The standard edition of the complete psychological works of Sigmund Freud, volume XVIII (1920–1922): Beyond the pleasure principle, group psychology and other works.* London, UK: The Hogarth Press and the Institute of Psychoanalysis.
Vlastos, G. (1991). *Ironist and moral philosopher.* Ithaca, NY: Cornell University Press.
Weber, M. (1946). Characteristics of bureaucracy. In H. H. Gerth & C. W. Mills (Eds.), *From Max Weber: Essays in sociology* (pp. 196–244). New York, NY: Oxford University Press.
Weber, M. (2003). *The protestant ethic and the spirit of capitalism* (T. Parsons, Trans.). Mineola, NY: Dover. (Original work published 1930)

SUSAN OAKS

# 5. EDUCATIONAL PLANNING AT EMPIRE STATE COLLEGE

*Fluidity vs. Structure, Process vs. Product*

INTRODUCTION

1986. Two of the first students I worked with, whom I'll call "Lola" and "Jason," came from very different backgrounds, were at very different stages of life, but had similar goals to use their degrees for professional advancement. Lola was just starting a college education in her late 40s. She had always worked with children and wanted an associate degree as a step toward pursuing certification to open her own day care center. She had limited college experience, a lot of work experience, and the desire to advance professionally, as well as to fulfill a personal goal by completing a college degree. Jason was in his 20s, a graduate of a technical school and an employee at a large corporation that dealt with technology. After a few years as a laborer, he had been chosen to enter the company's management program, which required that participants pursue a bachelor's degree. I worked with both students to fulfill Empire State College's 4-credit requirement for a course devoted to the planning of one's degree.[1] The one commonality in the course was that both students had to learn what was expected by Empire State College in terms of credits, broad areas of content, and degree design. Both students, in close consultation with the mentor, had to develop two common outcomes – a degree program (an individual curriculum plan), and "rationale essay" (written justification of the plan) – that blended the College's academic expectations with their own immediate and longer-term personal, academic, and professional goals.

Lola's individualized educational planning course focused on learning about required coursework for New York state certification in early childhood education. It also focused on skill development in writing, as that was a self-identified area in which she needed more competence in order to succeed with her college work. Jason's educational planning course focused on learning about the nature of a college education in the U.S., specifically the concept of breadth of study in a liberal arts degree, something that was very different from the focused technical study he completed previously. Both Lola and Jason gained new learning, not only about the details of degrees at Empire State College, but more importantly about areas germane to helping them develop as students. Lola and

Jason both approached their educational planning courses with some trepidation, in that these studies involved new kinds of reflection on their experiences and goals. Nonetheless, as the studies progressed, each saw more of the value and significance of these studies.

My own initial reaction to mentoring educational planning, though, bordered on outright fear. I had had multiple conversations with each student. But had I listened well in order to make suggestions about activities to be included in this study that would support them in pursuing their planning goals? I could diagnose writing and literature comprehension problems as an instructor, but my educational and work background was purely writing, literature, and teaching, and not academic counseling. Would I know enough to help guide degree development in the fields of educational studies and business? My own degrees were in English, with a minor in secondary education, and American literature. Educational concepts were not foreign to me, but accounting and economics surely were. Could I help these students identify the prior experiential learning that they might pursue for credit, which could inform their planning? Learning in an area such as "systems architecture," one of Jason's interests, was well outside my field. After the students completed their educational planning course, their degree programs and their rationale essays would be reviewed by an assessment committee of other faculty. These faculty would review these documents in regard to how students addressed the academic expectations of the College within the context of each student's goals. Would these degree designs "pass" and get committee approval? If not, how would these students continue to trust our working relationship? Even though college work functioned through dialogue, under the philosophy that students participate in building their own education, I was still in a position of responsibility. All of these fears, and more, were in play. How on earth could this educational planning process succeed?

As I learned more about educational planning through working with more students, talking with many faculty (including a coworker who functioned as my mentor), and participating in assessment committee reviews, I started to realize that the inherent nature of educational planning, as defined by Empire State College, resided in contrasts: fluidity versus structure, process versus product. The educational planning course content, created through dialogue between student and mentor that started far before the student enrolled for the actual course, was itself a way of structuring a more intense conversation leading to the concrete products of the degree plan, rationale essay, and the academic work resulting from individual investigations carried out by students in the educational planning course. The "trick" was, and remains, finding the right *balance* between fluidity and structure for each student in his or her own program of study. And the trick was, and remains, finding the right *emphasis* between fluidity and structure, process and product, for options within the educational planning course itself across the institution.

## PEDAGOGY AND HISTORY OF EDUCATIONAL PLANNING

Although educational planning courses at Empire State College result in a degree plan and rationale essay – two common, relatively straightforward, seemingly simple outcomes – developing those outcomes involves serious academic work on the part of the student, approached through the application of active learning techniques and one-to-one conversations with faculty mentors. Faculty mentors support the approach that Coll and Draves (2009) found to create student satisfaction, spending time "… discussing personal values with students and possible academic majors/concentrations" (p. 221). Faculty mentors also go further. They often ask leading questions about the student's practical goals for the degree and motivation for pursuing a degree. They help students investigate academic and professional fields. Through dialogue, student and faculty mentor formulate both questions to investigate and strategies to enact investigations. The academic work of educational planning involves research, evaluation and analysis of information, writing, and shared analysis of outcomes – all key academic skills.

Educational planning evolved from the College's basic philosophy based on the vision of Ernest Boyer and relevant to educational theories of Knowles, Mezirow, Daloz, and others. Boyer (1971), in *A Prospectus for a New University College*, stated that the College would "rely on a process, rather than a structure, of education. …This emphasis will place the focus upon the individual student learning at his [sic] own pace with the guidance and counseling of master teachers" (p. 2). "The rate and pace of learning may vary, the substantive content may be open, and the exciting possibility of creatively restructuring a future substantive area of study is likely" (p. 4).

Boyer's vision and the ways in which the College enacted this focus on process, as opposed to specified content, were supported in the literature related to learning theory published in the early 1980s. Malcolm Knowles' (1980) conceptualization of andragogy emphasized learning processes and looked at collaborative, real-world, problem-focused learning grounded in the student's experience. Jack Mezirow's evolving theory of transformative learning, according to Kitchenham (2008):

> … became more developed as he expanded the view of perspective transformation by relating the emancipatory process to self-directed learning to form three revised types of learning. The original three types of learning (technical, practical, and emancipatory), based on Habermas's (1971) work, became (a) instrumental, (b) dialogic, and (c) self-reflective (Mezirow, 1985). Simply stated, learners ask how they could best learn the information (instrumental), when and where this learning could best take place (dialogic), and why they are learning the information (self-reflective). (p. 109)

Knowles' and Meizrow's approaches lie at the heart of educational planning, the purposes of which include helping students to frame their own real goals, to build upon their experiences, to examine their reasons for undertaking the studies they have chosen, and to determine how best to carry out those studies.

Daloz's theories of the importance of mentoring in adult learning also informed the theory and practice of educational planning, with its focus on how to engage students in the process of considering their learning. In an interview published by Geoff Peruniak in *Aurora*, Daloz (1990) explained clearly his view of mentoring, first published in 1986 in *Effective Teaching and Mentoring*:

> Our job is to help students to integrate what they are learning in the academic world with how they process knowledge and how they are growing in an epistemological way. So mentorship is firmly grounded in an interactionist perspective. It is firmly grounded in the notion that we develop through the way in which we make use of knowledge in the environment and also through the way that is concerned with the growth in process and in the form of our thought. You can't simply separate process and content. (para. 10)

All of these theories underlie the creation of educational planning learning experiences with unique content that (1) relates directly to students' goals and life experiences, (2) supports our adult students in examining their purposes, and (3) involves them in planning and evaluating their learning experiences.

The philosophy behind educational planning approximates what Mascolo (2009) more currently called "guided participation," in which faculty help prompt new or deeper understandings in students by listening, reframing, and asking guiding questions to help students understand more fully a process of learning. Mascolo stated that:

> ... the idea that students must actively construct their skills and understandings *for themselves* is not the same as suggesting that [students] must actively construct their skills and understandings *by themselves*. Conceptions of faculty as mere 'facilitators' or 'coaches' whose function is to support a student's active attempts to discover or reconstruct knowledge through their own actions relinquishes the central role of teachers in the pedagogical process. This point can be illustrated with reference to Vygotsky's (1978) concept of the *zone of proximal development*. ... Learning occurs as less expert social partners appropriate and reconstruct higher-order knowledge and skills that have their origins in the [student's] participation in social interaction with others. (Rogoff, 1993, p. 7)

The College's educational planning policy itself emphasizes the process and collaborative orientation of educational planning:

> Within educational planning as a formal academic study, the primary mentor guides the student through substantive academic work, including reading, research and writing assignments that relate directly to the program design itself and to broader professional and intellectual issues. ... Ideally, learning

activities should respond to a particular student's interest and needs, and support a more reflective, transformative process. (Empire State College, 2009, Educational Planning Studies and Outcomes section, paras. 2–3)

Through the mentoring conversation, which occurs informally during the student's time with the College and formally in the educational planning course, students and faculty decide what might best help them plan their degree and/or enact those plans, exploring information that, in some way, will help them develop or hone a skill, research a profession, or investigate an academic discipline. All of these learning goals and activities for the educational planning study itself are in keeping with Dewey's (1938) concept of "learner participation," and Chickering and Gamson's (1987) principles of good practice, which include active and diverse types of learning. So although they must address ESC expectations to develop their degree plans and rationale essays, the rest of the academic content of each student's educational planning course may be very different, based on that particular student's goals, life experience, interests, and learning needs.

Educational planning initially existed as a process; it was not always a course. In the early days of the College, a credit-bearing educational planning study did not exist. Faculty and students were expected to work together to design their degrees, and degrees were expected to evolve as the student evolved, with the experience of one study leading to discussion and choice of the next, based on the student's developing academic interests and academic needs. As Richard Bonnabeau (2005), college historian, stated: "Student goals ... were paramount and served as the organizing framework of study, not prescribed curricula" (p. 8). But added factors came into play:

> ... the New York State Education Department, which gave the college time to flesh out its mission those first few years, began to seek more accountability about academic quality, as did the State University of New York (J. Jacobson, 11/10/14). Area of study guidelines, consequently, came into being as a response to mounting external pressure. A college without a curriculum needed to define itself in ways that connected with traditional higher education. (p. 8)

Bonnabeau (1990) delineated the creation and approval of guidelines for degrees, from the creation of nine areas of study for accredited degrees in 1973, to the creation of initial guidelines for each area in 1974, to the work during 1979–1981 to further specify the areas of knowledge and skill expected for degrees in each registered area of study.

The evolution of educational planning as a credit-bearing course (and, important to note, in the early years of the College, it was not credit-bearing) runs somewhat parallel with the evolution of area of study guidelines, moving from a very fluid dialogue to a more structured or formal study, albeit one that emerged from ongoing discussion and was based on individual student interests and needs. Educational planning as a credit-bearing course developed from certain external and practical pressures as well, such as the need to acknowledge and legitimize the real academic work and the time involved for both student and faculty mentor, and the need for students to fund all academic work through financial aid. Just as guidelines provided some structure of knowledge expected in degrees, without listing specific courses or requirements, the existence of an educational planning study requirement provided some structure in which students and faculty could plan their individualized degrees. While both students and faculty continued to grapple with the balance between structure and fluidity, product and process, they now had a formalized process within which to engage these creative tensions.

## EDUCATIONAL PLANNING INVESTIGATIONS: CONTENT AND PROCESS

By 1986, when the College had been in existence for 15 years, certain conventions regarding the content of educational planning courses had developed at some of the centers of the College. That is, degree planning throughout the College came to be codified in regard to academic areas of investigation that might be appropriate to students, depending on student interest and need. These broad areas of inquiry and the activities appropriate to them allowed for some regularity to coexist with the philosophy and practice of individualization, and typically included the following:

Broad Educational Focus:

- Researching/reading/reflecting/writing about some relevant aspect of higher education – e.g., the U.S. system, comparative higher education systems, educational philosophies, liberal learning, connected learning, progression of learning within a degree.
- Researching/reading/reflecting/writing about some relevant aspect of adult learning – e.g., learning stages, the importance of experience to adult learning, what constitutes learning and college-level learning.

Specific Educational Focus:

- Considering academic skills needed for success in higher education – identifying and then working on skills (including writing, math, and critical thinking) needed for academic and/or professional advancement.
- Learning how to learn – e.g., time management, learning styles, research skills, goal setting, notetaking, reading skills.
- Learning about critical, analytical thinking – e.g., how to read and write analytically, how to identify an issue, how to apply those skills to an investigation.

Broad or Specific Professional Focus:

- Researching/reading/reflecting/writing about the changing nature of work and workforce skills.
- Researching what it means to be a practitioner in a specific field – e.g., connecting with working professionals in that field, evaluating and using professional journals in the field.

- Researching specific professional requirements – e.g., for professional certifications, to change a profession, for a particular job advancement.

General:

- Researching/reading/reflecting/writing on a topic or issue relevant to the student's education, interests, and/or profession.

The fact that such an iteration of possible areas of focus existed and that certain academic content and investigations were suggested, highlights the basic creative challenge in planning individualized degrees. A broad investigation such as planning an academic degree needs some organization, some concrete suggestions in terms of process and content, in order to both start and proceed. What does not work is to say that "anything is possible" – whether within the educational planning study itself or within the degree plan as a whole. While much is possible, such a promise would be too vague or misleading for most students coming mostly from traditional educational backgrounds. A continual creative tension resides in deciding how many concrete examples to give to students, so that they understand educational planning's purpose and possibilities, but do not feel as though these examples are prescriptions. Some students who need more structure are uncomfortable with having any of their own input into this course, while others embrace it. Degree planning in its early stages of developing the course is an iterative process. Faculty need to proceed carefully, step-by-step, in the process of eliciting information and ideas from students and framing those ideas in terms of possible academic investigations, while avoiding telling students directly what to do. Faculty mentors eventually learn to deal with this creative tension and develop explanations and approaches to educational planning in their own ways, generalizing processes and approaches as they work with more and more students.

Through the years, my mentees have done a wide variety of investigations and academic work as part of their degree planning, work that resulted in new and valuable learning. Many students dealt with very individualized investigations related to their careers and interests. For example, one student who worked in a large New York state organization wanted to learn why people who were eligible for financial aid did or did not engage in higher education. We focused on how to create a survey and how to analyze results, skills that the student could then transfer to other academic and professional situations. Another student had a child with special needs. She wanted to learn how to write a proposal to the school system arguing that her child should be placed into mainstream classes. This student developed skills in analyzing, researching, and writing – skills that she could then transfer to other academic and professional situations. Yet another student wanted to start writing a personal narrative about her experiences with boxing and working with a famous trainer, as a prelude both to pursuing credit through prior learning assessment (a process through which students' learning outside the academy can be evaluated for credit), and to writing a more extended memoir. Current students are focusing on a study of learning styles in order to enhance effectiveness as a vocational instructor, and developing e-portfolio pages for personal, academic, and/or professional purposes. Other students emphasize more traditional academic investigations: what they need in their bachelor's degree in order to get into and succeed in graduate school; what courses they need in order to achieve professional certification in a field; what prior learning they have gained and what makes sense to translate into credit requests; what traditionally constitutes academic content in their field and how much they need to adhere to tradition given their personal, academic, and professional goals. In sum, there is tremendous variety in the kinds of activities students can undertake in their educational planning.

No matter what type of investigation, educational planning involves substantive academic content and new learning for students and, as such, it involves creative challenges for both students and mentors. Students participate in identifying academic investigations of interest and value to them; faculty aid in suggesting inquiry and study based on conversations with the student, and then need to confront their comfort level with supervising and evaluating a potentially wide variety of learning – a major challenge for a mentor who may be working with students outside her or his area of academic expertise.

This description, however, reflects how the content of the educational planning course was explained to me. Different structures developed and exist to this day, based not only on personal student and faculty inclination, but also on the location in which the faculty person works within our distributed College. No matter what its focus, the emphasis of the educational planning study is on developing new, relevant, transferable learning. Still, the content of the educational planning study was and still is debated: Should it be focused more narrowly on investigations related directly to the student's academic and professional field, for the purposes of planning the credits for the degree? Should it be focused more broadly on investigations that develop skills and/or deal with potentially widely-ranging content? Obviously, I was introduced to the latter, with more of a fluid/process orientation, but other faculty in other locations of the College were introduced to the former, with more of an academic field/product orientation. Collegewide orientations for new faculty, which occur twice a year, often take place alongside center-based orientation activities; so interpretation and implementation of the focus of the educational planning study can vary based on the particular cultures of practice that have developed across the College.

Resources available collegewide have been developed, though, again giving some structure to varied content and multiple processes. One resource example is the existence, by the early 1980s, of various publications to help students with educational planning in different fields (e.g., *Degree Program Planning in Health Related Studies* [Empire State College, 1981], revised 1985). Such publications took care to explain that, for example, students in health sciences would find many possibilities for study at the College. Yet the very existence of resources highlights many students' and mentors' basic needs for some structured content in a vague or fluid process. Since educational planning became a credit-bearing study, many individual faculty mentors' approaches to educational planning have evolved into sets of readings and activities that are often used with many students to structure a given student's investigations for the study.

The tensions between fluidity and structure, process and product, in the educational planning course are evident in the College's Center for Distance Learning's (CDL) archive of published educational planning courses from 1979 and beyond. Although the opportunity to do what might be considered a fully independent study in educational planning always existed, from the late 1970s to the late 1990s, it was felt that students working away from a physical location of the College needed more structure in order to be comfortable with learning at a distance. Thus early educational planning courses at CDL structured both content and process, while asking reflective questions to help personalize the learning, such as the following (Benson & Dehner, 1985):

1. In what specific ways do the studies outside the concentration lead to my ability to:
   - Make purposeful observations?
   - Engage in critical reading and recall?
   - Make critical analyses?
   - Engage in information synthesis and creative thought?
   - Identify and use primary and secondary information sources and do so in more than one area of study?
2. How do the studies I have selected prepare me to cope with unexpected changes in my future? What in this program prepares me for lifelong learning?
3. How do these studies prepare me to function in my community, including the global community, in ways other than through my job?
4. What benefits can I expect from the liberal arts requirement?

Based on changing student needs, at CDL, our distance educational planning courses evolved with various content and processes, focusing at different times on academic skills assessment (assess and reflect on critical reading, writing, math, time management, and information retrieval skills), or the qualities of an educated person and a liberal arts education in the U.S. By the late 1990s, in a now fully online environment at CDL, we tried to address the complexity of educational planning investigations by splitting educational planning credit into various courses. One course, Planning and Finalizing the Degree, structured a process to help students learn about (1) the overall nature of a college degree in the U.S., (2) the concept of "breadth of learning" via general education, (3) traditionally-expected learning given the student's degree focus, and (4) ESC conventions and detailed requirements. This course scaffolded this learning in order to support students in completing investigations that would help them create the degree plan and rationale essay. It currently exists in six different versions. Although each version of the course focuses on producing the same products, a degree plan and rationale essay, each course varies in its emphasis and structure, from an emphasis on reflection and self-assessment, to an emphasis on research related to one's profession, to an emphasis on ESC area of study guidelines and assessment of degree plans. These different versions exist as starting places for approximately 100 mentors who mentor online. Mentors can then customize or create their own version of the course, based on their sense of their students' needs and priorities. No matter what the academic focus of these educational planning courses, their real value resides in helping to formalize the ongoing student-mentor conversation and investigation of the student's goals, of broad and particular academic requirements, and of professional expectations for academic preparation.

Other courses have focused on more familiar content areas that many students have traditionally opted to investigate as part of their educational planning process. These 2-credit courses, that might complement the planning and finalizing course, include Effective Academic Writing, Introduction to Critical Thinking, Making Time: Time Management and the Sociocultural Construction of Time, Reflective Learning, Adults as Learners: Theories and Strategies, Learning Styles, Assessing Learning, 21st Century Careers, Exploring the Disciplines (Information Systems, Literature, Thinking Mathematically), and Exploring the Professions: Child Care Management. One or more of these possible courses is taken either in conjunction with or at a different time from the official degree planning course, as appropriate to each student, thus helping the student learn more about skills or careers, in addition to learning about broader expectations of U.S. higher education and the particulars of planning a degree.

It should be emphasized that the philosophy underlying all of these courses is that no one process or set of content fits all; there is choice of content and fluidity of process for both students and faculty. In addition to addressing the need for flexibility, this model has attempted to address the different types of learning outcomes within one course, some more internally-focused on understanding the concept of a degree and creating a degree plan and essay, and some that are more externally-focused on skills or academic or professional knowledge (e.g., writing, research, critical thinking, understanding academic content, understanding the nature of work in the 21st century). No matter the content of the course, each contains substantive reading, writing, and discussion assignments.

Yet the very existence of these courses exemplifies the tension between structure and fluidity. Courses themselves structure content and process, while the overall existence of multiple courses creates a fluid, adaptable process. However, it should be noted that this approach is nonetheless different from the organic conversation out of which a truly individualized course grows. Again, the question is how to balance fluidity and structure in some way that makes educational planning courses and overall educational planning processes understandable, manageable, clear, cost- and time-effective, and scalable.

Currently, I have been experimenting on a small scale with ways to increase fluidity in both content and process for students planning their degrees. In this new model of Planning and Finalizing the Degree, there is more student-controlled content and an open process structure. This educational planning course offers four broad areas of research (personal, academic, professional, degree details), and asks students to base their specific focus on individual answers to reflective journal questions. Students engage in whatever area of research with which they choose to start and proceed to other areas as they wish; the only structure is that they need to complete their different areas of research, their degree program and their rationale essay drafts by certain deadlines within the term.

For example, when students do the "academic content" investigation, they are asked to read the College's area of study guidelines for degrees in the area they are pursuing. Then they respond to the following journal questions (S. Oaks, Planning and Finalizing the Degree course, 2014):

1. What key concepts did you learn about expected academic content in degrees in your area of interest – things that you did not know before you did this research?
2. What, if anything, confused you about the content you read?
3. Did the guidelines you read relate fully to what you want to study/how you want to use your degree? If not, how are you starting to rethink or refocus some of the contents of your degree?
4. What do you need to research further in order to understand more fully what might be expected for a degree in your area of interest and focus?

Students are provided with sample scenarios to aid their thinking about further research that might be needed, and then are expected to follow through on that research. After they complete their individual research, they are then asked to answer closing journal questions, one of which requires them to apply the results of their research and identify what makes sense as a next step in moving forward in their own process of degree design (S. Oaks, Planning and Finalizing the Degree course, 2014):

1. From your research into academic content, identify two knowledge or skill areas that you were especially surprised to learn are expected in order to create an academically-sound degree in your field. Explain how you might address those concepts in concrete terms in your degree.
2. Based on what you learned from this research, identify at least one logical "next step" related to your academic work/planning your degree. How might you go about taking that step?

In effect, the intent was for students to structure their own process and content within broadly-defined areas, based on their interests and needs. An additional piece of new learning for most students in this version of the course deals with the value and process of reflective journaling.

Early experiments with this approach have been successful, with most students able to work through the course both straightforwardly and creatively. One student in particular embraced doing this course in an e-portfolio environment, creating pages that allowed her both to retain and to concretize the results of her research and degree design processes, and share her thoughts, learning, and products with others, both visually and verbally via her e-portfolio pages. Doing the planning course in a way that not only gives students some control over content and timing, but also allows them to structure the environment in which the course exists for them, has real potential for supporting active learning, as well as teaching 21st century skills.

Others in the College are experimenting similarly with different content and structures, using journals, e-portfolios, and a variety of audio and visual as well as written resources. At a time in which new technologies and the College's philosophy of individualization are merging, we have the potential for interesting, creative possibilities for educational planning courses.

## CURRENT CONTEXTS: FLUIDITY AND STRUCTURE

However, we are also situated at a time in which both internal and external realities run somewhat counter to ESC's intention in the educational planning process. Educational planning is expensive to the institution in terms of faculty time. Faculty traditionally have worked as generalist mentors, taking time to learn about many fields of inquiry and aspects of degree planning across these fields. Educational planning pedagogy and practice were developed at a time when both the organization and the students it served seemed to have the luxury of more time and money. Empire State College faculty definitely had more luxury in terms of numbers, serving far fewer than the 19,000 to 20,000 students we currently serve per year. Most mentors are working with many students at a time in educational planning (sometimes as many as 20 in the course itself and 50 to100 mentees total) and so need consistent, organized approaches. In addition, given this reality, approaches to educational planning courses and processes need to be scalable, that is, to be cost-effective, for the institution.

Educational planning is also expensive for students – in terms of both time and tuition. Tuition keeps rising, and the economy is weak. Many students do not immediately see the relevance of spending tuition on educational planning courses that, in their view, are unnecessary to their pursuit of a professional degree. Adult students who previously had some time and inclination to explore potential areas of study within a degree now often have more urgent professional goals and economic needs. Our adult students, with an average age in their mid-30s, exhibit characteristics of the millennial generation as identified in a Pew Research Center (2014) publication: They are "… linked by social media, burdened by debt" (para. 1) and see "educational attainment [as being] highly correlated with economic success" (Educational Hardships section, para. 5).

Many of our current students assume that educational planning courses will be like traditional college courses: relatively pre-structured with non-negotiable learning activities that they have to complete according to a specific timeline. The concept of exploratory, process-based learning seems to them somewhat more foreign than it did in 1971 or 1986 or even 2000. As a course, students assume that there will be contact not only with their mentor, but with other students as well. Even though they understand and embrace the concept of individualized degrees, many students assume that individualization occurs in their choice of courses rather than within the content and process of a given course. Non-completion rates for term-based educational planning courses are higher than the College would like, even though students who complete educational planning are more likely than others to move forward to complete their degrees. There may or may not be a correlation between completion rates and student expectations for educational planning courses. This is an issue that warrants further research.

Additionally, like some students, not all mentors are comfortable with the fluidity of course content and process; educational planning may not play to all faculty members' teaching interests or academic or personal strengths. Faculty may not be comfortable suggesting and/or responding to a potentially wide range of student investigations, and they are divided in wanting to be generalist mentors or subject specialists. The concept of every faculty person mentoring as a generalist mentor, which arose out of the educational philosophies of co-exploration and guided participation, is now being questioned at the College, as perhaps it should be. Informal student surveys show that while the mentor is the most important student link to the College, and a primary reason for student satisfaction, the mentor can also be the source of problems if there is a mismatch or a perceived lack of professional content expertise.

Internally, we are asking whether all faculty mentors should be expected to participate, just as all students are expected to participate, in educational planning courses and processes. Some faculty would rather focus on other academic tasks; should an institution that honors individualization honor it for faculty as well as students? What, then, becomes an equitable means of determining faculty work commitment? Because some faculty reject the idea of being generalists and want to advise students only in their own fields of study, should the College formalize what has been an informal process to date, and create a faculty role of academic expert consultant to play to faculty strengths and offer the opportunity for specialization (and, too, account transparently for workload)?

Outside pressures to standardize exist as well. Higher education in general is experiencing the trends that Bryan Alexander (2014) identified, including competition with noncollegiate educational resources and opportunities, and alternative certifications. Alexander sees a very results-oriented climate with increased emphasis on professional/vocational study and the addition of more structured academic programs, both part of an effort to attract more students and maintain college enrollment in a shifting and more competitive environment.

In an effort to standardize an academic structure, the State University of New York (n.d.) instituted general education guidelines for all 64 campuses (including ESC) in 1998, detailing 10 general education areas and specifying that students need to fulfill seven of 10. In the same vein, Empire State College is moving from offering only individualized degrees to offering some pre-structured concentrations. We are dealing, for example, with market pressures to be able to say we offer a degree in "Business Administration" or "Health Care Management," for example, as opposed to a degree in the general area of study of Business, Management, and Economics.

All of these contexts seem to be swinging the pendulum away from fluidity and toward structure, often a very traditional academic structure. Our creative and communal challenge is to reconsider our mission and values, relook at our current practices and contexts, and find some way to proceed. What faculty seem to agree on, as seen through the evolution of educational planning courses, is that change is necessary in order both to avoid stagnation and to maintain the relevance of the planning experience. It is the nature of the change that is under debate.

## EDUCATIONAL PLANNING FOR THE 21ST CENTURY: JUGGLING CONTEXTS AND PEDAGOGY

Changing contexts have produced interesting debates about the value, content, and processes of the educational planning course for students in 2015. Citing the need for equity, clarity, and quality of service to students, many current discussions focus on the concept of structuring the educational planning experience for students more fully. One thread of this discussion focuses on the critical relationship between student and faculty mentor. Should the individual and/or location-based structures that have evolved for educational planning be centralized and/or homogenized in some way? What is equitable for students? For faculty?

Another thread of the educational planning discussion involves clarity and consistency of information provided to students. Although the College provides general information about educational planning, practice can vary some across the College based on local cultures and even on individual mentor practices. Even if educational planning conversations and courses remain individualized, should we adopt a more robust, commonly held (across the College) set of definitions and resources that clearly explain the purpose, context, and possibilities of educational planning?

The College discussion about quality includes comments related to the need for commonly expected academic outcomes in all studies that use the phrase "educational planning" in their title. In addition to common products, such as the degree program and the rationale for it, in a climate of educational accountability, should all or some subset of expected educational planning learning outcomes be standardized?

The College community is also discussing other basic issues regarding educational planning processes and the educational planning study. One issue deals with student input and choice. If many, but not all, students find value in the process of planning their degrees, should the educational planning study be optional? Would some students who are planning more conventional concentrations benefit more from devoting the educational planning course credits to additional studies in their concentration or even to electives that could be of interest to them? Regarding the nature of educational planning as a credit-bearing study, should it be not a course, but instead a series of relevant learning experiences, chosen by the student in consultation with a mentor – experiences that the student would engage as questions and issues arose? If educational planning were not a credit-bearing course, what would that change indicate about the value placed on the process? At an even more fundamental level, what is the College's commitment to learner-centered, guided participation as a philosophy and methodology, epitomized through educational planning processes and studies?

What is interesting is that the pedagogy and educational theories upon which educational planning philosophy and processes were based have been confirmed by more current learning research. Jensen (2008) stated that:

> The more learning is generalized, contextualized, and reframed, the more the learner owns it. Deep learning requires usage and feedback. Over time, the meaning of the material expands, and eventually the learner develops a level of expertise. The new model of teaching, analogous to offering substance for the learner to fill his or her own container, reframes the teacher as more of a learning coach. (p. 102)

Zull (2002), in *The Art of Changing the Brain*, posed challenging questions based on research into learning processes:

> Why not say that all learning is experiential, school learning included? The structure of the brain does not change when we enter a school, so why should we think school learning is different? Aren't classes experiences? Won't students reflect on that experience? Won't they generate their own ideas about what the experience means? Won't their actions come from these ideas? In fact, isn't that the way it has always been? (p. 27)

The dialogic, mentoring approach taken in educational planning processes and courses ideally falls within this realm, with a mentor asking the student about his or her own experiences and goals, helping to reframe those within an academic and/ or professional context, and helping the student create his or her own learning path.

Current educational theorists such as George Siemens (2006) also support a focus on fluid process. Siemens' theory of connectivism offers the concept that learning resides in the ways in which learners reflect on and integrate various contents, learning experiences, and learning resources. Stephen Downes (2006) discussed an "ecosystem" approach to learning, which focuses on learning design that "characterize[s] the nature of the *connections* between the constituent entities" in an environment in which there is no predetermined structure (The 2.0 Architecture section, para. 7). There again is a focus on process and guiding learners through processes, with less emphasis on unique content. Crisp and Cruz (2009) exemplified this more contemporary emphasis on process via an extensive bibliography on the value of mentoring processes in higher education.

Along with evolving theory, there is also current interest in the application of theory to practice. At Harvard, Richard Light (2015) and others have instituted a new course with activities "… designed to help freshmen identify their goals and reflect systematically about various aspects of their personal lives, and to connect what they discover to what they actually do at college" (para. 5). Questions in Harvard's course deal with goals and commitments, choosing an academic field, breadth versus depth in academic work, and core values. Light reported that, "Three years later, when we check in with participants, nearly all report that the discussions had been valuable, a step toward turning college into the transformational experience it is meant to be" (para. 18). A focus on mentoring, formalized more fully during educational planning, essentially offers a similar focus on structuring leading questions, engaging in conversations that can be approached in many different ways, and reflecting on and integrating knowledge, thus highlighting the individual student's own processes for learning.

There's no easy resolution to retaining and/or redefining a focus on fluid, student-driven process within contexts that all seem to demand more structure. Yet there may be ways to address scalability, cost, student and faculty preference, and equity by reconsidering educational planning creatively within current contexts. The College engaged in a series of extensive discussions about educational planning in 2014, and is committed to both continuing the discussion and piloting emerging models in 2015 and beyond. Ideas that emerged from this series of collegewide discussions include: (1) a model in which mentors have different roles, some as generalists, some as consulting specialists, and/or some as discipline-specific mentors; (2) a model in which common learning outcomes, expected collegewide, are identified and linked to small, credit-bearing, academic components, which students pursue as appropriate (through either an individually chosen sequence or a preset sequence), in consultation with a mentor; and (3) a model in which students in very traditionally-structured programs do smaller-scale or even no academic work related to planning a degree. The year 2016 will be a time in which the College makes a first attempt to further specify and, on a small scale, operationalize at least one of these models in an attempt to create some commonly agreed to, scalable structure within which flexibility resides – an interesting balance.

## CONCLUSION: CREATIVE CHALLENGES

It is 2015. Two of my students, whom I'll call "Ben" and "Julie," come from very different backgrounds, are at very different stages of life, but have similar goals to use their degrees for professional advancement. Ben has a varied background related to the hospitality industry, ranging from cooking professionally to organic farming to teaching. His goal is to get a degree so that he can teach culinary arts at a vocational school. He comes to the College with some previously completed credit and the potential for a maximum amount of credit through prior learning assessment. His concerns are maximizing his credit – both to validate his prior learning and to keep tuition costs low – and organizing his varied, potential credit into a coherent degree. He comes to Empire State College with a good sense of his prior learning, an expectation to individualize and plan his degree, and a real readiness to engage in the planning process. In regard to the fluidity/structure and process/product spectrums discussed earlier, he falls on the fluidity/process end. Julie, on the other hand, falls on the structure/product end of the spectrum. Coming to the College with specific goals and a specific timeline, she wants to complete a bachelor's degree with a concentration in psychology, then a master's degree in counseling psychology, and then to pursue New York state licensure as a mental health counselor. She brings in substantial transcript credit, plus some potential prior learning credit, and her current goals are very clear, direct, well-researched, and well-thought-out. She is not interested in the process of degree planning because, in her view, she has already done the requisite research and her path is clear. She simply wants a mentor and the College's degree approval process to verify that her course choices are appropriate; she sees no immediate need to talk through her decisions more fully than that. She completed an educational planning course in her first term with the College, only because she needed to meet the requirement, and she needed approval of her degree plan; she wanted to be certain that she could follow her chosen path.

In 2015, there are many Bens and Julies, just as, in 1986, there were many Lolas and Jasons. Student situations themselves have not changed much through the years. Students are still coming to Empire State College to build on already-completed credits, pursue credit through prior learning assessment, and complete their degrees, most often with the purpose of using those degrees for professional advancement. The overall educational planning *process*, with student and mentor talking one-to-one throughout the student's time with the College, has not yet changed. What has changed, in my view, are the assumptions that both my students and I are making about the educational planning *course*, as well as the contexts in which the College is operating and in which students are pursuing their degrees.

As a faculty person, I gave up the assumption a long time ago that one method or approach (individualized, one-to-one) meets the needs of all students for educational planning. I talk with students about individual versus group learning experiences, and ask what situation for learning in the context of educational planning might work best for them. In regard to the content of their learning, I do not assume that each student will pursue unique content, following his or her own, unique process, but instead I have come to understand that each student will pursue some content uniquely. But even with more flexibility and choice of learning modes and courses, are we providing enough for student design of their degree programs and studies? While students are choosing from the multiple courses available to them to plan degrees, work on academic skills, and/or investigate careers, at least at CDL, and increasingly across the College as well, they are still essentially locked into taking courses. How can we offer comparable learning experiences in multiple ways, using multiple modes to link with students' individual learning styles? How can we continue to listen to student voice and preference in approaching educational planning, in a way that's student-centered and not mentor- or course-dependent? If there are multiple approaches, supporting many different types of content and individualized processes, how can we organize and explain those approaches? How can we develop some sort of transparent tracking system to help students and faculty know exactly what's been done, what some logical next steps are, and what yet needs to be done in terms of a degree? More importantly, how can we stay true to the College's core values and mentoring approach in educational planning, and still address both student and faculty mentor needs for some structure, as well as larger organizational needs for consistency and equity across the College?

One way, which would both represent a large shift in current processes and, at the same time, emphasize the College's initial philosophy, would be to *model* the individualized, student-directed, dialogic, and reflective processes of educational planning, as opposed simply to offering "Educational Planning" as one or two courses. Current technological tools make it possible to enact the original philosophy and practice of educational planning in a more scalable, integrated fashion. One could envision, for example, the following, which I offer drawing on ideas voiced in recent collegewide discussions.

*A Scenario*

A student comes to Empire State College. The orientation process walks the student through a simple series of questions about interests and learning, the answers to which an adaptive learning system uses to organize and offer ideas for students regarding their learning paths and multiple, appropriate investigations related to planning their degrees. Thus the process identifies some possible first steps in terms of learning and methods of learning.

Orientation occurs within an easy-to-use, individual electronic learning space – a personal learning environment for each student. Through the process of moving through orientation, students learn rudiments of navigating this environment. As this is the place to communicate with the student's mentor and to house and organize the student's academic work, there is a strong incentive to use this space. Those two things – conversations with a mentor and a place to house academic work – are the only two things expected of all ESC students within this space. However, there are models showing other ways in which this space might be used, and resources providing tutorials should the student want to use the space more fully, *a decision totally up to the student* in this student-controlled environment.

One of the first mentoring conversations is based on the ideas generated by the student's answers to the orientation questions, which provide a starting place for the student's conversation with his or her ongoing primary mentor.

In addition to a primary mentor, who is the student's constant touchstone with the College, there are well-organized and multiple resources available for the student to access as needed. Resources include not only static text and videos, but also mentors in particular academic and professional fields who serve as discipline experts; faculty and professionals expert in prior learning assessment content and processes; and other students and faculty in multiple and fluid content-, course-, and interest-related groups, both College-generated and student-generated. Should students choose, they can link to and/or house relevant learning resources in their learning spaces, thus adding to their personal learning environments.

Certain courses in which the student is enrolled, such as those required for general education, or key courses in certain fields, contain assignments that are automatically sent to the student's learning space, along with instructor comments. Student and mentor thus have an ever-expanding series of artifacts upon which to focus in their conversations about the student's learning, a conversation that informs educational planning.

Educational planning occurs as appropriate to each student, within a wider range of credit (e.g., 2 credits up to as many as needed), as a series of discrete learning activities and inquiries done over time. Educational planning can also occur as a formal course. The choice is up to the student, aided by adaptive learning technologies and mentor conversation, both of which can help the student decide on effective approaches for him or her. Decisions, therefore, about the content and processes of educational planning content and process are put much more into the hands of the learner.

Educational planning learning experiences/courses have the potential for becoming both organic and communal, growing out of the needs of groups of students and faculty with similar interests and/or approaches.

Toward the end of the student's time with the College, student and mentor review data in the student's learning space, and the student is asked to consider what he or she has learned, as a way of bringing closure to educational planning at ESC.

The most important thing is that this type of scenario would present educational planning as integral to the student's learning and to the usual academic work of the College; it would reframe the academic work of educational planning so that work is not perceived as the "other" course within the academic program, or as just another required course. Educational planning thus would exist as both a process, involving ongoing student-mentor conversation, and a community, involving broader communication with multiple individuals, groups, and drawing on a wide range of resources, with choices regarding engagement determined by the student. For students who wanted a course structure, educational planning would also exist as a formal course or courses, but a course consciously chosen by the student as a result of educational planning conversations and processes.

Such a scenario attempts to model Downes' (2006) ecosystem of learning and his discussion of personal learning environments (PLEs):

> In essence ... to learn is to immerse oneself in the network. It is to expose oneself to *actual* instances of the discipline being performed, where the practitioners of that discipline are (hopefully with some awareness) *modeling* good practice in that discipline. The student then, through a process of interaction with the practitioners, will begin to *practice* by replicating what has been modeled, with a process of *reflection* ... providing guidance and correction. (A Network Pedagogy section, para. 4)

Learning, in other words, occurs in communities, where the practice of learning is the participation in the community. A learning activity is, in essence, a *conversation* undertaken between the learner and other members of the community. This conversation, in the web 2.0 era, consists not only of words but of images, video, multimedia and more. This conversation forms a rich tapestry of resources, dynamic and interconnected, created not only by experts but by all members of the community, including learners. (A Network Pedagogy section, para. 5)

Graham Attwell writes, ... The 'pedagogy' behind the PLE – if it could be still called that – is that it offers a portal to the world, through which learners can explore and create, according to their own interests and directions, interacting at all times with their friends and community. 'New forms of learning are based on trying things and action, rather than on more abstract knowledge. "Learning becomes as much social as cognitive, as much concrete as abstract, and becomes intertwined with judgment and exploration."' (A Network Pedagogy section, paras. 11–12)

In the above scenario, educational planning could be scalable, even though individualized, because of the technological tracking that would enable mentors and students to have records of conversations, choices, academic activity, and learning results. However, there would be large start-up costs, first of all in terms of getting "buy-in" to the idea that the College's core belief in flexibility of both content and process can actually exist within an overall clarifying structure. There would also be large start-up costs in terms of time and money, to implement systems, train College personnel, and most importantly to work through adaptive learning strategies, all requiring substantial institutional and technical support along with very careful planning. Is a scenario like this even feasible, either wholly or in portions? There's no one, easy answer to these creative tensions and practical challenges.

So the basic questions remain. How can we clarify and create an institutional, scalable, time- and cost-effective structure for the fluid, individualized processes of educational planning? Should we even consider creating such a structure within current, more traditional academically-structured contexts? If so, how can we address both process and product within this structure? How can we ensure enough fluidity in process to address individual student, faculty, and institutional needs? These are the creative challenges that face us as student-centered teachers, faculty mentors, and an open, innovative institution as we move ahead.

## NOTE

[1] The only credits that all Empire State College students are required to take in common are 4–8 credits of "educational planning," some of which are devoted to planning their individual degrees. The current policy states that:

Individually planned degrees are a hallmark of Empire State College's academic program. The college was founded in 1971 as an experimenting institution, designed to pioneer innovative ways for adults to gain access to a college degree. Individualized degree planning is a key element of this mission for innovation and access, and reflects the college's commitment to empowering adults to define and pursue their own educational goals. (Empire State College, 2009, Individualized Degrees section, para. 1)

Educational planning is the core undergraduate degree requirement* at Empire State College, and students must complete from 4 to 8 college credits in this topic. The college recognizes a range of learning modes and activities, mentoring styles and student needs and preferences for educational planning. There are also varied enrollment models (e.g., 4 credit studies, 2+2 or 4+2 models, other more modular approaches).

*With the exception of a very few pre-structured programs. (Empire State College, 2009, Educational Planning Studies and Outcomes section, para. 1)

## REFERENCES

Alexander, B. (2014, June). *Future trends in technology and education, June 2014: A monthly futures report for higher education, compiled by Bryan Alexander.* Retrieved from http://pitweb.pitzer.edu/information-technology/wp-content/uploads/sites/31/2014/11/FTTE-2014-6.pdf

Benson, L., & Dehner, T. (1985). *Educational planning course guide.* Saratoga Springs, NY: Empire State College.

Bonnabeau, R. (2005, Spring). A piece of history: On the origins of areas of study. *All About Mentoring, 29,* 8–9. Retrieved from http://www.esc.edu/media/ocgr/publications-presentations/all-about-mentoring/2005-6/Issue-29-AAM-Spring-2005.pdf

Boyer, E. (1971, February 8). *A prospectus for a new university college.* Albany, NY: State University of New York.

Chickering, A., & Gamson, Z. F. (1987). *Seven principles for good practice in undergraduate education.* Retrieved from http://teaching.uncc.edu/learning-resources/articles-books/best-practice/education-philosophy/seven-principles

Coll, J. E., & Draves, P. (2009, Spring). Traditional age students: Worldviews and satisfaction with advising; A homogeneous study of student and advisors. *The College Student Affairs Journal, 27*(2), 215–223. Retrieved from http://files.eric.ed.gov/fulltext/EJ882664.pdf

Crisp, G., & Cruz, I. (2009). *Mentoring college students: A critical review of the literature between 1990 and 2007.* Retrieved from http://www.researchgate.net/profile/Gloria_Crisp/publication/225402519_Mentoring_College_Students_A_Critical_Review_of_the_Literature_Between_1990_and_2007/links/541c3b460cf241a65a0bcc85.pdf

Daloz, L. (1986). *Effective teaching and mentoring: Realizing the transformational power of adult learning experiences.* San Francisco, CA: Jossey-Bass Higher and Adult Education.

Daloz, L. (1990). *Helping adults learn: Mentoring and the definition of a good education* [Interview by G. Peruniak]. Retrieved from http://aurora.icaap.org/index.php/aurora/article/view/39/50

Dewey, J. (1938). *Experience and education.* New York, NY: Kappa Delta Pi.

Downes, S. (2006). *Learning networks and connective knowledge.* Retrieved from http://itforum.coe.uga.edu/paper92/paper92.html

Empire State College. (1981). *Degree program planning in health related studies.* Saratoga Springs, NY: Author.

Empire State College. (2009, July). *Advanced standing: Policies and procedures that govern the assessment of prior learning policy.* Retrieved from http://www.esc.edu/policies/?search=cid%3D40463

Jensen, E. (2008). *Brain-based learning: The new paradigm of teaching* (2nd ed.). Thousand Oaks, CA: Corwin Press.

Kitchenham, A. (2008, April). The evolution of John Mezirow's Transformative Learning Theory. *Journal of Transformative Education, 6*(2), 104–123. Retrieved from https://www.usm.maine.edu/olli/national/postConference/2012_confWorkshops/workshopMaterials/Jon%20Neidy/The%20Evolution%20of%20John%20Mezirow's%20Transformative%20Learning%20Theory.pdf

Knowles, M. S. (1980). *The modern practice of adult education: From pedagogy to andragogy.* New York, NY: Cambridge.

Light, R. J. (2015, July 31). How to live wisely. *The New York Times.* Retrieved from http://www.nytimes.com/2015/08/02/education/edlife/how-to-live-wisely.html?action=click&contentCollection=Pro%20Football&module=MostEmailed&version=Full&region=Marginalia&src=me&pgtype=article

Mascolo, M. F. (2009). Beyond student-centered and teacher-centered pedagogy: Teaching and learning as guided participation. *Pedagogy and the Human Services, 1*(1), 3–27. Retrieved from https://www.academia.edu/1027631/Beyond_student-centered_and_teacher-centered_pedagogy_Teaching_and_learning_as_guided_participation?auto=download

Pew Research Center. (2014, March 7). *Millennials in adulthood: Detached from institutions, networked with friends.* Retrieved from http://www.pewsocialtrends.org/2014/03/07/millennials-in-adulthood/

Siemens, G. (2006). *Knowing knowledge.* Retrieved from http://www.elearnspace.org/KnowingKnowledge_LowRes.pdf

State University of New York. (n.d.). *SUNY general education requirement* (SUNY-GER). Retrieved from http://system.suny.edu/academic-affairs/acaproplan/general-education/

Zull, J. E. (2002). *The art of changing the brain: Enriching the practice of teaching by exploring the biology of learning.* Sterling, VA: Stylus.

LORRAINE LANDER

# 6. INTERDISCIPLINARY EDUCATION AT EMPIRE STATE COLLEGE

*Many Opportunities, Ongoing Challenges*

Empire State College was created over 40 years ago as a nontraditional institution dedicated to the education of those students not adequately served by institutions of the State University of New York (SUNY), of which it is a part. Various processes and practices that differed from more conventional campus approaches were part of the initial design and continue to be utilized at the College to effectively serve its mainly adult student body. Individual interdisciplinary studies and entire interdisciplinary degrees – educational efforts that fall across more than one academic discipline or between academic fields – have been one defining feature of these efforts.

Historically and philosophically, the development of a college like ESC was well justified academically at the time it was created. On a practical level, with a distributed campus (currently 35 locations across New York state) and an independent study model that did not require classroom attendance, the design suited the needs of nontraditional students. ESC's creation was part of a larger expansion of public universities across the United States, all linked to the push to recognize the importance of greater access to higher education. Additionally, as a result of the civil rights and women's rights movements, campus protests and, overall, a more critical and experimenting approach to a wide range of social institutions, an individualized approach to learning fit the political and cultural thinking of the early 1970s, when differences were celebrated and gained status in diverse ways. Taken together, this was an environment that was supportive of the innovative work of a new SUNY institution that became Empire State College.

Design elements of ESC's educational work reflected ideas drawn from Dewey and Dewey's (1915) emphasis on active learning and from a long and rich tradition of adult education. In practice, this meant that students were encouraged to create their own academic majors ("concentrations" is the term used at ESC), contribute to the development of their individualized learning contracts for independent study, and focus their learning on activities relevant to their own experiences and personal, professional and academic goals. Thus, to consider interdisciplinary approaches at ESC, one needs to consider what an actual interdisciplinary concentration and degree will look like in practice when so many features considered to be interdisciplinary education (IE) at other institutions are already typical facets of study at Empire State College.

K. Jelly & A. Mandell (Eds.), *Principles, Practices, and Creative Tensions in Progressive Higher Education*, 133–147.
© 2017 Sense Publishers. All rights reserved.

Still, there is tension between the intent of the founders of ESC – including their creation of an effective adult education institution that includes key features of interdisciplinary approaches – and the current contexts and goals of higher education. Is ESC falling short in its efforts at interdisciplinary education? If so, why might this be, given the structural opportunities and basic philosophical commitment to such an interdisciplinary approach? And, in the context of 21st century higher education and the multiple goals of various stakeholders in higher education today, are interdisciplinary efforts at ESC serving current student needs? That is, can interdisciplinary efforts at the College continue to exist in spite of 21st century pressures and tensions? It is these kinds of questions that are the focus of this chapter.

## INTERDISCIPLINARY EDUCATION AT EMPIRE STATE: PHILOSOPHY AND POLICY

At its core, Empire State College was designed to foster interdisciplinarity. Historically, both Ernest Boyer and Arthur Chickering – two key figures in the early history of the College – were proponents of interdisciplinary academic study (Boyer, 1990, 1994; Chickering, 1977, 1983, 1984). In fact, the College was created with several structural components that facilitate interdisciplinarity, including the freedom to design course content without the need for a lengthy approval process, and a model of teaching and learning that could more easily support unique and creative interdisciplinary learning. Student-led design at both the degree and course levels allowed for the exploration of topics and content that easily crossed disciplinary barriers.

Boyer (1990) wrote passionately about the importance of connecting knowledge across academic fields in scholarship, as well as on the importance of integrating knowledge in general education. He believed that integration situated discoveries in larger contexts (Boyer, 1994) and that conversations across the disciplines promoted meaning-making as a result of processes of critical analysis and interpretation that would necessarily take place (Boyer, 1990). For Boyer, faculty and students benefit from these efforts.

Chickering (1977, 1983, 1984) also wrote persuasively on the benefits of integrating knowledge. In 1977, for example, he wrote about how higher education needed to change in response to the shift in this country from a production to a service economy. He proposed that interdisciplinary coursework is beneficial to students' educational development because it fosters the type of creative thinking and active learning necessary for the complexity of new professional careers. Further, Chickering believed in the importance of interdisciplinary education for promoting the transformation of ideas into action and theories into practice. For him, individual academic disciplines can make strong contributions to an integrated education. But as Chickering, as well as so many adult educators, had argued, given the interdisciplinary nature of life experiences that adult students draw from and are interested in working with and applying their knowledge to, celebrating interdisciplinary methods for an institution devoted to adult students made a great deal of sense.

It was in this philosophical context that Empire State College was founded on the idea of nontraditional students creating their own concentrations. "Areas of study" were designated as a way of organizing undergraduate concentrations and degrees into broader categories that roughly aligned with the academic disciplines. The areas of study include: The Arts; Business, Management and Economics; Community and Human Services; Cultural Studies; Educational Studies; Historical Studies; Human Development; Interdisciplinary Studies; Labor Studies; Public Affairs; Science, Mathematics and Technology; and Social Theory, Social Structure and Change (recently renamed Social Science). The inclusion of Interdisciplinary Studies as one of the College's 12 areas of study lends further support to the early efforts to encourage IE, but also raises the question: What does a degree designated as "interdisciplinary" do that others do not?

Each area of study has guidelines for student degrees designed within that field. According to the Area of Study Guidelines: Interdisciplinary Studies policy (Empire State College, 1995), an interdisciplinary degree at ESC must:

> ... bridge two or more program areas so as to connect or combine the different perspectives of those areas. ... (Statements section, para. 1)

> Some concentrations are interdisciplinary by nature and are already recognized and defined by the scholarly community. ... On the other hand, an interdisciplinary concentration also can be created from scratch to match a particular student's interest. As with all concentrations, it may be focused upon a theme, problem or profession, or on a topic that necessarily includes several disciplines. (Statements section, para. 2)

These guidelines form the official interpretation of interdisciplinarity at the program level. They state that an interdisciplinary concentration at ESC is a joining of one or more of the College's areas of study. However, those areas may also be interdisciplinary within themselves, suggesting that a degree designated as within the "Interdisciplinary Studies" area of study may be just one kind of interdisciplinary degree that "bridges" certain broad academic disciplines and that is not already reflected in other areas of study.

## INTERDISCIPLINARY EDUCATION: CURRENT DEFINITIONS AND TRENDS

As Klein (1990) pointed out, interdisciplinary learning is a process aimed at synthesis and integration of information, often starting with a problem, question, topic or issue. This definition aligns well with some of the educational planning approaches that exist at Empire State College. Deeper considerations of IE at the College must start with what this concept entails. The term "interdisciplinary" is a complex concept and various definitions exist starting with a narrow view that the term refers to knowledge that falls outside of or between other disciplines (Klein, 1990). Others (Angus, 2011; Strober, 2011) consider any academic learning that bridges more than one discipline as interdisciplinary. Although occasionally the term "multidisciplinary" has also been used in these cases, two or more academic fields appear to be the more common understanding in the literature.

Another term to describe these educational efforts is "integrated studies," which has been adopted by a variety of institutions of higher education to describe their efforts to bring together the knowledge of more than one academic discipline within a degree. While "integration" is a goal of IE, since we integrate schools, neighborhoods and many other aspects of our lives, the term "integrated" is used in many other contexts and has been criticized for having less descriptive value for this reason. In fact, Drake and Burns (2004) describe three approaches to interdisciplinary education with integration being one aspect (multidisciplinary and transdisciplinary are the other two). In addition, Klein (1990) emphasizes the importance of "interpretive synthesis" of information, as well (p. 188).

Interdisciplinary education is growing, suggesting increased interest and potential value to these offerings. From 1975 to the year 2000, IE programs and degrees in the United States grew by 250 percent (Brint, Turk-Bicakci, Proctor, & Murphy, 2009). The last several decades have also seen a movement away from undergraduate degrees that focus on academic disciplines to more professional degrees, which, not unusually, are often interdisciplinary in nature, although not often described using that label. In fact, at ESC, degrees in business and human services are the two most common concentrations, reflecting this trend toward more applied and often interdisciplinarily-focused degrees.

Given the unique structures of the College and original design, and with these trends in higher education, how has IE at ESC progressed? Over the last eight years, the ESC *Fact Book* (Empire State College, 2010–2011, 2014–2015) reveals that degrees that are specifically called interdisciplinary make up approximately nine percent of the degrees awarded at the College, although many of these are broadly based associate degrees (this data indicates that approximately 23 percent of associate degrees are termed "interdisciplinary" and approximately 5 percent of bachelor's degrees are considered to be within the Interdisciplinary Studies area of study). This number has held relatively steady throughout the last dozen years, indicating that those degrees officially designated as "interdisciplinary" are not growing in as great a number as they are at some other institutions.

## EXTERNAL PRESSURES AND INTERDISCIPLINARY EDUCATION

No institution of higher education exists without influence from the outside. While a nontraditional institution might feel less pressure to follow the pattern of other academic institutions, Empire State College also is part of the State University of New York system and is regionally accredited by the Middle States Commission on Higher Education. Both of these affiliations bring with them constraints. Some consideration of the current context for IE may be helpful in understanding ESC's efforts in this regard.

A variety of factors seem to be pushing higher education toward more interdisciplinary study, at least as manifested in more opportunities for applied project-based and problem-focused education. Students want degrees that are marketable and will guarantee jobs. The increased cost of higher education and mounting levels of student loan burden are making the usability of degrees a more prominent concern. Recognizing both the need for the more effective application of skills and the benefits of bringing together fields in interdisciplinary and multidisciplinary courses and degrees in order to strengthen the ability of students to apply their knowledge more effectively after graduation (Wood, 2012), the federal government has been urging institutions to strengthen integrated STEM (science, technology, engineering, and mathematics) education. The Executive Office of the President/President's Council of Advisors on Science and Technology (2012) has challenged higher education institutions in this country in a proposed "Engage to Excel" project to produce a million additional college graduates with STEM degrees.

In general, IE focuses on a problem, question, issue or target population (such as clients in business and human services) and thus lends itself to employment of knowledge for an applied purpose. These interdisciplinary approaches provide cognitive organization to the knowledge that is theorized in order to facilitate recall and applicability.[1] With employers seeking employees able to perform in a new context, higher education is being pushed from several directions to produce graduates able to find productive employment.

At the same time, while such factors push higher education toward a more interdisciplinary orientation, other pressures push against this direction. For example, there is a growing movement in higher education for the kind of standardization that mirrors that which is taking place at the K-12 level. Signs of this include the recent decision by SUNY to create a common course numbering system to provide for easier transfer of students from one SUNY institution to another. This numbering system will be tied to common learning outcomes. While these policies may benefit students who seek to transfer credits from one SUNY institution to another, they may potentially stifle innovation in more interdisciplinary courses.

The growing assessment movement as an approach to surveilling student learning outcomes is also influencing higher education in the same way that it has been influencing public K-12 schooling. Accrediting bodies such as the Middle States Commission are now expecting institutions to establish and systematize learning goals at various levels, from course to general education to degree. Assessment methods must be identified for each of these outcomes; so must a process for validating continual improvement through the analysis of these outcomes.

The pressures on interdisciplinary study are obvious. Assessment of content in standard academic fields is an easier approach than measuring learning in what are more complex interdisciplinary courses and degrees. Thus, externally mandated assessment expectations may discourage the creation of interdisciplinary courses at both the institutional and faculty levels, because of what is perceived as the extra burden of identifying learning outcomes and of designing and using appropriate assessment methods to satisfy these expectations. So too, the lack of specific professional development for faculty members who attempt interdisciplinary education without experience in curriculum and assessment design – an absence not only at more conventional institutions, but, not insignificantly, at Empire State College as well – may also contribute to reliance upon disciplinary rather than interdisciplinary approaches.

## OPPORTUNITIES AND CHALLENGES IN INTERDISCIPLINARY EDUCATION APPROACHES AT ESC

At the program level, the pressures described above mean that interdisciplinary education confronts a variety of challenges at many institutions. Some of these exist at ESC, but many do not. In terms of structure and policy, ESC's curricular processes make creation of interdisciplinary degrees easier. At most institutions, there are structural challenges for development and implementation of interdisciplinary programs that take months, if not years to design. These do not exist at ESC in terms of a student's freedom to design interdisciplinary and even unique degrees, at both the undergraduate and graduate level (for example, in the College's the Master of Art in Liberal Studies program). However, the design process is not without serious effort on the part of both student and faculty mentor. An internal approval process for all students' educational plans can lead to stress and delays in feedback about planned degrees. (Some of the specific challenges in this process experienced by students will be further discussed later.)

At the course level, about 27 percent of all ESC curriculum is delivered via independent study (Empire State College, 2010–2011), which allows for much flexibility and many possibilities for interdisciplinary study topics and degree designs. Such a guided independent study mode was at the heart of ESC's original model; yet as other forms of study – particularly online courses that tend to be more structured and disciplinary in approach – have become more typical, there are fewer of these opportunities. In terms of flexibility, tensions exist between the older model of student-driven learning goals (that could even be modified during a study) and the current need for learning outcomes to be identified at the start of a study and adhered to throughout the study period. The standardization and assessment movements described above may also have a significant impact on future student-mentor flexibility at ESC.

And there is another factor at work in the extent to which interdisciplinary study occurs at ESC. That factor is that while the legacy of Boyer, Chickering and others inspired the birth of an experimenting institution in which the spirit of interdisciplinarity was vital, it is unclear whether such interdisciplinary educational efforts at the College are a current focus of effort and innovation.

There is evidence in both directions. Signs of interest in the importance of IE at the undergraduate level are contained in the *2011–2015 Academic Plan* publication of the College (Empire State College, 2012), which supports and encourages interdisciplinarity through a framework of academic direction for the College around eight interdisciplinary themes, including: Initiatives in Human Services; Globalization; Environmental Sustainability; Communication, Media and The Arts; Business in the 21st Century; Initiatives in Health Care; Technology, Information and Society; Adult Learning and Education (p. 17, para. 4). Potentially, such themes stretch across all degrees at the College. According to this document, the College "... envisions a future rooted in the premise that the effectiveness of the college rests on maximizing the complementariness of the disciplines ..." (p. 17, para. 2). Sources of inspiration for these interdisciplinary themes reported in the document are: the educational and the professional needs of students, growth areas of the economy, and topics of social importance that would encourage the College to support its mission and commitments, and, at the same time, connect with faculty expertise (p. 17, para. 3). No doubt, as the College goes forward to explore and implement studies and degrees tied to these themes, there could be many opportunities for IE, as well as the potential for more innovative assessment of the effectiveness of interdisciplinary student learning.

Unfortunately, a few years after publication of that document, there are few visible signs that these themes are being used in any meaningful way to guide the College. In addition, the College is making no concerted effort to tout interdisciplinary study in order to attract prospective students for whom this opportunity could be meaningful but is often invisible.

One quite favorable structural feature of Empire State College that can support interdisciplinary work is its distributed organizational structure across New York state, which can provide more opportunities for collaborative and interdisciplinary work among the faculty. Many faculty members are located in interdisciplinary groupings around the state, allowing for far more contact and communication among faculty of different disciplines than occurs on traditional campuses. So too, governance and service work are conducted with a great mix of faculty from various academic fields and backgrounds. Even hiring and continuing appointment (tenure)/ promotion decisions are given an interdisciplinary basis. Within this review model, faculty members from different disciplines are brought together to function as a team in decision-making about the professional hiring and advancement of colleagues.

And finally, there is the value placed on IE in meeting the needs of students in a variety of ways (personal, intellectual, career, etc.), as well as in responding to societal needs (ethical, practical, cultural, etc.). Attending to these dimensions can be a complex matter, since it is possible that neither students nor society may perceive the value of interdisciplinary approaches. In fact, as institutions of higher education have come to be what they understand to be more consumer-responsive in their offerings, it is unclear how messages regarding the value of less traditional educational methods can be adequately communicated. Should institutions simply give students what they come into the doors wanting or thinking they need? Do institutions bear a responsibility to educate students about approaches and methods that may be less familiar to them, but that have significant educational and professional value? Does a progressive institution, such as ESC, have a responsibility to communicate alternative educational methods, such as IE, to its students? Importantly, but perhaps ironically, at Empire State College today, the two largest areas of study are Business, Management and Economics, and Community and Human Services, two professionally-oriented areas that offer the possibility of significantly interdisciplinary approaches. College degrees in these areas could gain value and deepen students' understanding if they were genuinely interdisciplinary and if they cultivated inquiry that encourage the disciplines to come together regarding the questions at hand.

## EMPIRE STATE COLLEGE STUDENTS, INTERDISCIPLINARY STUDY, AND STUDENT LEARNING

As described within this chapter and throughout this volume, Empire State College was created as a progressive institution where students have a wide variety of ways to engage in learning. This student-centered tradition has been upheld with a broad range of undergraduate learning opportunities today, including over 600 online courses, dozens of residency courses (online study with one mandatory weekend or days of physical attendance), numerous seminar-style study groups and, quite literally, thousands of undergraduate independent study opportunities. Several graduate programs also exist that employ interdisciplinary approaches. There are numerous examples of potential opportunities for interdisciplinary work taking place at ESC at both the degree level and the course level.

One of the core features of the College is offering assistance to students in reaching their self-identified goals. The educational planning course required of all ESC students typically begins with articulating such goals that then become the organizing principle for the students' studies. What kind of guidance is provided to students in the naming of their goals and in planning how to achieve them, thus becomes important. So, for example, tensions often exist regarding whether the faculty mentor should accept the student's initial goal(s), which sometimes invite a disciplinary framing, or should suggest other learning opportunities that may ultimately prove more helpful to the student in achieving his or her goals, such as interdisciplinary work with which the student might be much less familiar.

Studenthood and intellectual engagement at the College were built around intellectual explorations and curiosity, as much as around the attainment of a degree or the earning of a credential. However, students may have changed in important ways since the early 1970s. First, students seeking a bachelor's degree 40 years ago were likely considering the achievement of that undergraduate degree as their final education goal. Now educational expectations have risen and many students arrive at ESC to work on associate and bachelor's degrees while at least considering subsequent graduate school. They worry about acceptance in graduate programs and have concern that unique degree concentrations may hurt their graduate school admittance, as well as their employability. So, too, current students are often concerned with the practical aspects of their degree leading to a better career and opportunities for advancement.

Thus, if IE is not understood by students as an approach that can help them to pursue more focused and applied degrees, or to prepare for graduate school, or to develop thinking skills that span academic fields (making knowledge potentially more useable), then students – and faculty – may assume that interdisciplinary studies and interdisciplinary degrees are not beneficial or even relevant to the task at hand. That is, without some concerted effort to communicate to students the many professional and academic benefits of interdisciplinary approaches, such practices may languish at a progressive institution even as they are gaining a foothold at in more conventional ones.

Finally, there is the key issue of student learning. Within interdisciplinary study, there are clear examples of courses and entire degrees that most would agree are interdisciplinary. These feature explicit identification of the fields that are being integrated and synthesized with a thoughtful and dedicated approach to how that synthesis and integration will take place. In faculty-designed programs of interdisciplinary study, knowledge, theories and methods of thinking, as well as research, are brought into the course or degree in well-defined ways but with the result that the student may not be finding and working with the synthesis or integration. In student-designed programs of study, more typical at ESC, many of which are generated by a problem, issue or question determined by the student, there is more potential for students themselves to undertake the synthesis and integration.

Still, most of the work labeled as "interdisciplinary" at ESC does not meet the criterion of explicit attention to synthesis and integration. This is unfortunate, in that it robs the student of an important opportunity for metacognitive understanding and development of self-directed learning skills. While some interdisciplinary work at ESC may contain synthesis and integration, this usually occurs at the implicit level and typically comes about through investigation of an interdisciplinary topic. Or, in practice, so-called interdisciplinary study simply becomes a multidisciplinary collection of studies. When the latter becomes the rule, the student could lose many of the benefits of the learning that genuine interdisciplinarity can offer.

## INTERDISCIPLINARITY AND THE EMPIRE STATE COLLEGE FACULTY

At many higher education institutions, IE can be difficult to develop because of the battles over departmental funding and the model of reimbursing faculty by course, which, together, can discourage the kind of collaborative teaching that can foster IE. Challenges at Empire State College are somewhat different. Historically, funding at ESC has been based on a regional center (satellite campus) model and tied to course credits generated by students associated with that center.

Yet this lack of competition between departments has not helped the promotion of IE at the College. And as regional centers and the online division of the College (the Center for Distance Learning) have hired faculty to work with students, they have not systematically sought out and hired those faculty whose academic identity and scholarly activities have focused on interdisciplinary work. As a result, there are no faculty members dedicated to a "department" who could or would specifically champion its benefits. In addition, there is no departmental structure to promote this approach to students and other faculty, leaving little internal communication or academic leadership around interdisciplinary approaches.

And, also in regard to faculty, the broader context of higher education affects the realities of IE at Empire State College. Most Ph.D.s graduate with degrees in traditional academic topics and were hired by the College for their expertise in one of the areas of study (and in the disciplines of which these are made up) deemed central to the ESC program. Further, faculty members who stay active professionally attend conferences in academic fields, as well as conduct scholarship and publish in journals that typically are also aligned with more traditional academic disciplines. There are only a small number of conferences and publications that directly relate to interdisciplinarity and/or interdisciplinary areas of study. While ESC, as a teaching institution, has not typically held the kinds of scholarly expectations of more research-driven institutions, faculty members who receive continuing appointment (tenure) and promotion are expected to regularly engage in scholarly work. Thus, at least for some, without an institutional celebration of IE, a faculty member may conclude that becoming a proponent of interdisciplinarity may interfere with his or her professional success and development. For those who enter the College and later develop an interest in interdisciplinary education, it is unclear how the College would support the kind of professional development needed to move toward a fuller and deeper engagement in interdisciplinary teaching methods and/or resource development.

In addition, the realities of a demanding workload for faculty continue to be a major issue at the College, and given the labor-intensive and more individualized attention that interdisciplinary study design can demand, engagement in interdisciplinary mentoring and teaching can be a workload issue. At the concentration and degree design levels, and at the level of individual learning contract development, student-designed and faculty-mentored study provide rich opportunities for interdisciplinary inquiry and allow for many more academic combinations and approaches than exist at many other institutions. Still, even with the academic freedom provided that encourages innovative and interdisciplinary efforts, making room for such activity in an environment that calls on mentors to take on multiple responsibilities is an abiding challenge for the faculty.

## INTERDISCIPLINARY WORK AT ESC: EXAMPLES AND CHALLENGES

There are myriad examples of interdisciplinary work at Empire State College. As has been described throughout this chapter, colleagues from across the institution are, as a matter of course, engaged with students in various interdisciplinary projects and in the development of interdisciplinary educational plans. The goal of this section is to offer a glimpse into the kind of work that is taking place.

One of the most interesting examples of interdisciplinary work at ESC is the annual Keep-Mills Symposium on Ways of Knowing. This is a blended interdisciplinary study taught collegewide that features an online component and a weekend face-to-face residency, funded by a college endowment. Each year, the topic of the study changes with the requirement that the focus be something topical and approached from multiple disciplinary perspectives. Examples of past topics include: the meaning of freedom; forgiveness; powerlessness and empowerment; and love. Several faculty (typically four to five) volunteer to work as a team and, together, identify that year's core topic or theme. These individuals coordinate how to approach their multiple perspectives and pull them together into a coherent educational experience. Having been part of the faculty team three times, I can attest to the strong commitment of the faculty who organize and facilitate these studies, as well as to the enthusiastic response of students from around the state who participate. When asked about the value of this study, one student related to me how much he appreciated having faculty members involved in mediating and modeling the integration of the various disciplinary viewpoints being presented and discussed. Participation by the faculty is often intense and time-intensive. Thus, while faculty typically find the work that they do together enriching and see it as an important opportunity to learn about the ideas, approaches and perspectives of colleagues, as noted earlier, the workload consequences of this collaborative teaching project can be an issue. So too, and again noting some of the concerns introduced earlier in this chapter, while the Keep-Mills Symposium topic is always covered from different academic perspectives, the work on synthesis and integration that could be taken up, is often not explicitly addressed.

Another example of an interdisciplinary effort is a study group on civic engagement that was offered several years ago at one of the College's regional centers. Five faculty members and an administrator, from various disciplines, came together with five students to engage in a common reading and online discussion with an opening and closing in-person meeting. The study culminated with each student becoming civically engaged in a personally relevant way, and reflecting and reporting back on that experience. In regard to workload, the six colleagues involved, dividing among them the academic credits from working with five students, did the work that one faculty person might have done. So although this was an exciting and interesting interdisciplinary experience, and certainly worthwhile for the students involved as they reported so eloquently in their final meeting about their civic engagement project, questions about workload for this type of collaborative teaching continue to exist.

One type of study that I offer under the generic title, Sustainable Living, allows individual students to undertake projects in relation to their own goals and interests. And studies related to sustainability can thrive with an interdisciplinary approach. At the core of sustainability is a concern for a problem or issue, the systems related to that issue, or the context that these systems inhabit. A heavy emphasis on problem-solving, which is often, although not always, a key goal, is also important and best supported with a multidisciplinary or interdisciplinary approach. In routinely mentoring students in Sustainable Living, students and I start with discussing their particular interests. A basic textbook on the topic is often the beginning reading, but then students can delve more deeply into particular topics that align with their interests and academic goals, such as social-based marketing, an approach that connects businesses to sustainability; or students can acquire more knowledge of ecopsychology and/or ecotherapy, if they are interested in the human services or the social sciences. A final project for the study can bring together the various knowledge areas explored and can promote synthesis and integration. These final projects are again individually designed to support individual student's goals. Some students thrive with this kind of choice and independence, while others can be mystified about why they are not being "told what to do" in order to be successful, an attitude that may have served them well in school (and at previous colleges, too), but may not be so helpful at ESC. For those students who lack comfort with this flexibility, it may take more time for the faculty at ESC to support them in a study developed in this way.

In addition, entire undergraduate degree programs may be interdisciplinary and can range from options like combining technology with business to form a tech management degree, to those that are unique to a student and unlikely to be repeated. For example, a student who had been an artist and poet and whose goal was to teach elementary school-aged children chose to bring together her passions. She named her concentration within this interdisciplinary degree "Art and Literature in Educational Contexts." This student's studies combined inquiry into the field of education as well as into art for children and various forms of literature. One particular independent study created for this degree focused on bibliotherapy, the study of how reading stories can influence child development. By developing a degree that served her own real purposes, she more easily overcame the many obstacles our adult students face and found the time and energy needed to complete this degree while working full time. After completing this degree, the student went on to earn a master's degree in library science. The degree planning process for such an individualized interdisciplinary program of study can be a difficult, if not daunting, task for some students who may be inexperienced in developing curricula and even for some mentors who may feel less than expert in the disciplines involved. Both a high level of commitment on the part of the student and a willingness to consult with subject matter experts on the part of the mentor are essential to carrying out this process effectively and developing rich and coherent interdisciplinary degrees.

As mentioned earlier, Empire State College also has a thriving graduate program in liberal studies, where all students engage in interdisciplinary work. After three required foundational graduate courses, which are intended to prepare students to gain grounding in certain interdisciplinary topics and in interdisciplinarity itself, students design their own graduate degree around a problem, issue, or activity of interest that would benefit from examination from a variety of disciplines. Many of the College's full-time faculty are called on to assist with the wide variety of student programs and individual projects that are at the core of this graduate program. Again, as with some undergraduate degrees, the actual interdisciplinary nature of these degrees is often seen not so much in interdisciplinary coursework, but rather in the integration of disciplines across courses, with a final capstone project that unites the perspectives gained in the student's earlier studies.

In regard to degree program design, there are, however, challenges associated with crafting a unique interdisciplinary degree. At the broader curricular level, there are challenges associated with crafting a unique interdisciplinary degree. The College's "Area of Study Guidelines" must be satisfied by and successfully explained in writing by the student as he or she goes through the approval process for his or her individually-crafted degree plan. Given the intellectual demands of curriculum building, the expectation that undergraduate students who have not yet been fully educated in a field (or fields) of study relevant to their degree could engage in this type of design work and its accompanying explanation, may be unrealistic. We do know the degree approval process is stressful for many students. Sometimes weeks may go by before a degree receives final approval from a faculty committee, and evidence suggests that the heavy demands of this kind of student-generated plan of study degree may lead to retention issues.

No doubt, in pursuing the creation of an individualized interdisciplinary curriculum, the student must engage in work not asked of others whose degrees more easily follow (if not in detail, certainly in spirit) those of the academic disciplines. In addition, unique learning contracts shaped by student and mentor, such as a capstone that seeks to pull together the fields incorporated into an individualized degree plan, must be created and carried out. Here is part of the tension: Not all students are interested in this additional work and, too, not all faculty members may have the time, inclination or the expertise to work with such a student. Indeed, as noted earlier, it is unclear if the orientation of new ESC faculty members to the College is adequately educating these new mentors about the full range of possibilities for unique interdisciplinary degrees, or if the College is adequately supporting faculty in carrying out this interdisciplinary work.

## FINAL THOUGHTS: WHAT INTERDISCIPLINARY STUDY CAN OFFER AND WHAT IS NEEDED TO SUPPORT IT

There are wonderful opportunities for innovative, interdisciplinary work at Empire State College. The philosophy and structure of the institution invite this important academic work of faculty and students. However, the challenges and tensions involved are real. To see an increase in these efforts or, better, a leadership role for the institution in interdisciplinary teaching and learning, there will need to be some modification of current direction and efforts. More needs to be done from an administrative standpoint to assist in bringing to reality the interdisciplinary themes in the current academic plan in order for them to have a true impact on the academic practices of the institution. Professional development for interested faculty needs to be enhanced overall, and in particular, should focus on helping faculty to think carefully about paths to the synthesis and integration of ideas and lenses on inquiry, as well as to gain practice in effectively assessing these ongoing efforts. Faculty leaders will need to step forward to help with these efforts and work together with the administration to help students understand the benefits of these interdisciplinary approaches – in terms of knowledge, skills, intellectual development, employability and potential for graduate study. In the academically conservative world of many students, taking a chance on something different may seem too risky, and creating a study or an entire educational program with a concentration title that is not recognizable to others or is not seen as potentially marketable is uncomfortable.

Some may question the benefits of interdisciplinary education over an academic degree that follows a more conventional disciplinary direction, and each student must choose for him or herself what kind of degree will help to reach his or her goal. But the proponents of IE would argue that this approach is more than a possibly valuable choice; it is – as Boyer and Chickering argued many years ago – essential to all learning and to helping students bridge the gap between acquiring knowledge and being able to use it. In the 21st century, knowledge is easily accessible and constantly changing. What students of today need are guidance and practice in how to find information, think critically about it, and apply it to answer questions and solve problems. That ESC has the structure and the experimenting tradition to engage students in this way is, in itself, exemplary; but the future is unclear given the directions of public higher education today. The type of individualized approach that was such a core feature of Empire State College may now be seen by many as too difficult, too costly, and too cumbersome to prevail. However, interdisciplinary education is clearly an approach in line with the mission, commitments and values of Empire State College and has much to offer students, faculty and society in terms of the quality of graduates who engage in such work.

## NOTE

[1] See Ivanitskaya, Clark, Montgomery, and Primeau (2002) for a review of these perspectives.

## REFERENCES

Angus, I. (2011). The telos of the good life: Reflections on interdisciplinarity and models of knowledge. In R. Foshey (Ed.), *Valences of interdisciplinarity: Theory, practice, pedagogy* (pp. 47–72). Edmonton, Alberta, Canada: AU Press/Athabasca University.

Boyer, E. L. (1990). *Scholarship reconsidered: Priorities of the professoriate*. Princeton, NJ: Carnegie Foundation for the Advancement of Teaching.

Boyer, E. L. (1994). Scholarship reconsidered: Priorities for a new century. In National Commission on Education, & Council for Industry and Higher Education (Eds.), *Universities in the twenty-first century: A lecture series* (pp. 110–131). London, UK: Author. Retrieved from http://files.eric.ed.gov/fulltext/ED378898.pdf

Brint, S. G., Turk-Bicakci, L., Proctor, K., & Murphy, S. P. (2009, Winter). Expanding the social frame of knowledge: Interdisciplinary, degree-granting fields in American colleges and universities, 1975–2000. *The Review of Higher Education, 32*(2), 155–183. Retrieved from http://www.highered2000.ucr.edu/Publications/Brint%20et%20al%20%282008b%29.pdf

Chickering, A. W. (1977). *Experience and learning: An introduction to experiential learning.* New Rochelle, NY: Change Magazine Press.

Chickering, A. W. (1983, June). Education, work, and human development. *New Directions for Experiential Learning, 20,* 5–16.

Chickering, A. W. (1984). The modern American college: Integrating liberal education, work and human development. In J. N. Burstyn (Ed.), *Preparation for life? The paradox of education in the late twentieth century* (pp. 154–177). Philadelphia, PA: Falmer Press.

Dewey, J., & Dewey, E. (1915). *Schools of to-morrow.* New York, NY: E. P. Dutton & Co.

Drake, S. M., & Burns, R. C. (2004). *Meeting standards through integrated curriculum.* Alexandria, VA: Association for Supervision and Curriculum Development.

Empire State College. (1995, May 1). *Area of study guidelines: Interdisciplinary studies for students matriculated before Sept. 3, 2014 policy.* Retrieved from http://www.esc.edu/policies/?search=cid%3D38193

Empire State College. (2010–2011). *Fact book.* Saratoga Springs, NY: Author.

Empire State College. (2014–2015). *Fact book.* Saratoga Springs, NY: Author.

Empire State College. (2012). *2011–2015 Academic plan.* Retrieved from http://www.esc.edu/media/academic-affairs/Academic-Plan-1-11-2012.pdf

Executive Office of the President/President's Council of Advisors on Science and Technology. (2012, February). *Engage to excel: Producing one million additional college graduates with degrees in science, technology, engineering, and mathematics.* Retrieved from http://www.whitehouse.gov/sites/default/files/microsites/ostp/pcast-engage-to-excel-final_feb.pdf

Ivanitskaya, L., Clark, D., Montgomery, G., & Primeau, R. (2002, December). Interdisciplinary learning: Process and outcomes. *Innovative Higher Education, 27*(2), 95–111.

Klein, J. T. (1990). *Interdisciplinarity: History, theory, & practice.* Detroit, MI: Wayne State University Press.

Strober, M. H. (2011). *Interdisciplinary conversations: Challenging habits of thought.* Stanford, CA: Stanford University Press.

Wood, P. (2012, February 7). *Obama's higher education agenda.* Retrieved from http://chronicle.com/blogs/innovations/obamas-higher-education-agenda/31515

HIMANEE GUPTA-CARLSON

# 7. THE CIPHER AND EMPIRE

*Teaching and Mentoring through Hip-Hop*

INTRODUCTION

It is September 2009 and the start of a new semester. Students have gathered for the first meeting of my New Politics, New Possibilities class at Cornish College of the Arts in Seattle, Washington. We are seated around a table and are going through the syllabus. The readings include reports on hip-hop's emergence in the 1970s; America's conservative turn in the 1980s; and a recently-elected President Barack Obama's agenda for the early years of the 21st century. The schedule features hip-hop artists as guest speakers, and over the semester the students will work with hip-hop's artistic practices to examine local graffiti, write performance poetry, develop social change proposals, and produce the do-it-yourself, punk era-inspired graphic publications that are widely known as "zines."

I can hear students responding to what the syllabus promises: "This is going to be great!" "I'm going to love this class!" But one young man, who earlier had introduced himself as a music major specializing in percussion, seems skeptical. He approaches me after class. He tells me he's looking forward to the class but wants to ask me a question.

"What kind of hip-hop music do you listen to?" he asks. "Who do you follow?"

I stammer out an unconvincing response. "I like the music that I hear at live hip-hop shows. I'm not real good at identifying or following specific artists."

The true story behind my statement is that I don't know all that much about hip-hop music. I am studying the history of hip-hop as a post-civil rights cultural and political movement and have been interviewing young underground artists about their work as community builders and political activists. Modeling my teaching intentions on my graduate program where the credo was not to answer questions but to pose them as a way of eliciting more questions, and where my favorite professors had organized seminars around topics they themselves were just beginning to delve into, I had organized my class around the research questions I hoped to explore. In short, I didn't have answers. I just had questions.

The student standing beside me gave me a long, slow look. And then he smiled.

"Can I make you a tape of the hip-hop music I like?" he asked.

I remember sighing inwardly in relief, feeling as if I'd been let off the hook.

"Please do. Even though I'm teaching this class, I still have a lot to learn."

## BATTLING, CIPHERING AND BUILDING

Looking back at that moment, it seems that I indeed did have a lot to learn both about hip-hop as a cultural way of life and its applicability to teaching the kinds of adult learners in the student-driven, individualized learning way for which Empire State College came to be known from its start in 1971.

Hip-hop, like the College, also was birthed in the 1970s. It evolved out of creative activities in the inner city boroughs of New York City around 1973 as a collection of artistic practices that help its participants develop skills, which most of its earliest figures assert leads to the creation of knowledge. Working with this knowledge is a learning practice that hip-hop practitioners call the "Fifth Element." Although the actual origins of hip-hop are debatable, most documentarians point to dance parties that a then 28-year-old Jamaica-born resident of the South Bronx (Clive Campbell, better known as DJ Kool Herc) began holding with his sister (Cindy Campbell). "Herc," short for "Hercules" because of his muscular build, was a largely self-taught electronics technician who liked to serve as a party deejay. He had figured out that by playing music on two turntables at once and manipulating the record needles, he could prolong the beats of the reggae and funk songs that he favored. Teens – a mix of African-American, Afro-Caribbean and Chicano youth – loved dancing to the prolonged beats, and began making up moves that at times mimicked street fighting and martial arts. Gradually, graffiti-inspired artwork and a practice of speaking politically in poetic form were added to the mix. From this inventiveness, the four artistic practices that are considered the foundational elements of hip-hop developed: deejaying, emceeing (or rapping), graffiti writing, and break dancing (or "b-boying" and "b-girling"). Because hip-hop devotees often used their arts to promote alternatives to violence and to make political statements in ways that helped them understand while informing others of the socioeconomic conditions of their time, pioneering figures began to speak of the Fifth Element as a practice of self-growth through knowledge.

Four decades later, loyal practitioners view hip-hop as a cultural way of life. The dance moves, the artwork, the poetic lyrics of rap and the grassroots creation of beats are for them statements of self-sustainability, entrepreneurial inventiveness, and acts of economic and cultural survival against forces of violence, structural inequality, and racial and cultural xenophobia. Hip-hop also has come to be regarded as a philosophy of teaching and learning tied to critical pedagogy (the idea of helping students view their role in education as participation in both societal critique and collective struggle for a more egalitarian and just society) (Schapiro, 1999, p. 9). In the evolving understanding of what it means to be a hip-hop pedagogue, one can engage with education on one's own, or in partnership with a teacher or mentor, or in collaboration with a peer, or collectively in a classroom or comparable environment. These engagements parallel much of Empire State College's own approaches to adult learning, as other essays in this volume have discussed and as I shall also describe in more detail below.

What might be called "the pedagogy of hip-hop" contains two complementary modes of communication: the battle and the cipher.[1]

The battle can be viewed as a dialogue or debate waged with words, rhymes, and/or bodies (Schloss, 2009, pp. 3–4). Historically, it began as the dance moves and beats that youth organized into groups (now known as "crews") used to challenge youth groups from rival communities for control over neighborhood turfs. These battles with dance and with music offered nonviolent alternatives to the fists, chains, and knives deployed in gang fights. Today, battles often are staged performances or informal dialogues. They might begin with insults, challenges, or even simply a series of questions like the ones the student at Cornish College of the Arts presented to me. In this sense, battles are not so much about violence as they are about besting and boasting. They can be used to build relationships with others where the creation of knowledge through conversation in a process of first deconstructing and then reconstructing particular societal assumptions is the goal.

The cipher is a process through which a circle of people work with each other to create new knowledge (Pough, 2004, pp. 11–12), much like a classroom with chairs arranged in a circle or a discussion styled as a Socratic seminar. Sometimes characterized as safe spaces and sometimes as intimidating arenas, the cipher often is the space where battling ensues. In the artistic spaces where the foundational elements of hip-hop play out, the cipher consists of bodies that surround a performer, creating for that performer a safe space free of external distraction. At the same time, the safe space is a vulnerable space in that one must drop one's inhibitions to perform.

As a space where the Fifth Element is enacted, the cipher also consists of bodies – organized around a table in a face-to-face classroom or in a shared learning space such as an online discussion forum. After one speaker expresses a thought, another steps up to speak. These learning spaces also are both safe and vulnerable. If the cipher operates properly, all participants are expected to contribute to the creation of shared understandings and honest insights. In these spaces, it is understood that if you are not honest, the other cipher participants have a right to let you know that they perceive you as not being upfront with them and that you need to change your approach and start speaking your truth.

I opened my 2009 fall semester course at Cornish with activities grounded in a knowledgebase with which I felt comfortable: A panel of voters who had cast ballots in the 1980 election spoke with students about the mood of the country at the time and how they had perceived politics to have shifted in the course of their adult lives. Students viewed and discussed two documentaries on hip-hop history, discussed community-based hip-hop practices in Seattle with guest speakers, and completed an out-of-class visual project that captured graffiti in the city. But as the semester progressed, it became increasingly clear to my students that I was not being upfront with them about my knowledge of hip-hop, and my lack thereof. And, it was becoming clear to me that they were going to let me know eventually, not to be disrespectful, but because they felt they had a right to know what I knew and how that related to what they knew and might or might not be relevant to their lives.

Their comments in the midterm evaluations said it all: "How can this course engage with hip-hop if we're not listening to hip-hop?" "Why are we talking about hip-hop when we should be listening to hip-hop?" "The teacher is very knowledgeable about history and politics, but does she listen to hip-hop?"

Ciphers also rely on a method of call-and-response. After the students offered their statements on the midterm evaluations, it was my turn to respond. I set aside a half-hour of class time, and the students and I formed a circle around our seminar table. The circle – in hip-hop's language of the cipher – is said to equalize power relationships, lessening the distance between the instructor and students. In this de-hierarchizing space, I put on my hat as a then 47-year-old professor and confessed.

"Well, the reason we're not listening to hip-hop is that, well, I'm an old lady. ..."

"Na-na-nnaaaaa," intoned one student, a theater major, mimicking my demise.

"... and, well, yeah, that's no excuse. I don't listen to hip-hop music much."

The room was silent. I tried to take the pulse of the students.

"I don't understand hip-hop like you do," I added. "I see it as a community, as a culture, as a movement. I know it's also about music, but I don't know the music."

The silence continued.

"So, what are we going to do about that?"

One student, a graphic design major, spoke up. "Well, you know a lot about history and politics. Can we bring in the music we listen to and help you?"

And, thus, an agreement was struck. Every class session would open with one or two songs that students would bring. Students would describe the artist and their interest in the song. We would listen to the music; examine its beats, lyrics, mood and political messages; and look at how the music might converse with other course materials. In the process, the students and I would practice a third component of hip-hop, which is building. In the spirit of the Fifth Element, we would build knowledge together and create something new (Rob "Blue Black" Jackson, personal communication, July 2013).[2]

## THE CIPHER AND EMPIRE STATE COLLEGE

Just as the battle and cipher shaped my interactions with my Cornish students, both processes and the principles underlying them have come to inform how I teach at Empire State College and how I articulate my place within the history, mission, and core values that have come to comprise the College culture. Well before I understood what I was trying to articulate, I was convinced that battling, ciphering, and building contained a sense of pedagogy that resonated with Empire State College's mission of educating the adult learner. My move in 2010 from urban classrooms in Seattle to rural northeast New York resulted in a geographic relocation as well as a significant shift in my teaching life. I was removed from teaching in face-to-face classrooms on three separate campuses and placed instead in a mostly online teaching environment in which I rarely met face-to-face with students but was available to communicate with them in an ongoing electronic environment. I underwent these changes as the College itself was changing, and my work with hip-hop has continued to inform how I sort out these differences between face-to-face and online teaching.

This reflection leads me to suggest that hip-hop might provide other faculty and staff an opportunity to cipher in a way that both battles and builds upon the College's mission of helping older, "nontraditional" students better their lives through individualized learning, independent education, and growth through mentoring. Such an opportunity may help all of us consider how to be more effective educators at a time when Empire State College and other institutions of higher education are engaged in debates over whether education can or should become a commodity and if students should be treated in this vein as "customers."

As noted above, like hip-hop, Empire State College came of age in the early 1970s, celebrating its 40th anniversary in 2011. And, as the College developed, it came to be defined, also like hip-hop, as a set of localized entities where teaching and learning would take place not on a unified campus but in numerous regional centers loosely linked but strongly defined by their particular geographic characteristics and local affiliates. Such centers represented a radical departure from the conventional college or university campus in that the students were not asked to come to the college; the college would come to them.

Learning, like learning in hip-hop, was conceptualized as being a process of shared creative curricular development in which students would work one-on-one with mentors to design learning plans that worked for each student. In these mentor-mentee relationships, the hierarchical distance that a professor's credentials might command would be lessened and the prior learning – academic and experiential – that students brought to the educational process would play a part in the teaching and learning. Although not articulated as such, students in this framework were like hip-hop artists. They would engage creatively with topics that interested them and in the process would develop the skills that would produce the knowledge needed to make them stronger, more engaged civic participants. The mentors would facilitate students' growth, and through these relationships co-learning journeys would evolve. When I joined the College, I sensed that this learning process matched many of the practices I had tried to enact, sometimes covertly, in prior teaching experiences so I was delighted to come to a place that advocated such experimentation.[3]

Yet, one battle that exists in the ESC cipher is that the legacy of its past is a nonconsensual understanding of the College's history and of its present. Hence, how we as younger, newer teachers and mentors within the College articulate our roles does not necessarily find a comfortable fit with the perceptions of more longtime faculty. While I understand the mission to be alive and in conversation with my understanding of how one should teach and learn, others presume it is dead – or perhaps never was enacted at all.[4] Adding to this contested terrain is what was superimposed over the intricate network of regional sites, that is, the center with which I am affiliated, the Center for Distance Learning (CDL). Formed in 1979,

CDL is both the largest and least geographically-specific center site in the College. As a CDL mentor, I occupy an office in Saratoga Springs, New York, the small town where the College's administrative headquarters are based, but work with faculty and staff and teach and mentor students all over New York state, not to mention the world.

The global virtual community that CDL cultivates is similar to that of hip-hop. While artists affiliate with a local space – naming one's self in terms of one's "hood" is a time-honored hip-hop way of introducing and positioning one's self – they understand themselves to be a part of a hip-hop "nation" or "planet" that is global in scope. Like the members of the "imagined communities" concept that Benedict Anderson coined in the 1980s, participants in hip-hop may never meet one another face-to-face but still imagine themselves to be a community with a shared set of beliefs, values, and practices (Forman, 2012; Anderson, 1991). Hip-hop practitioners understand the origins of their artistic and knowledge-building practices to be closely associated with block parties that took place in such locales as the tenements in the South Bronx. There, African-American, Caribbean, and Latino musical beats and rhythms co-mingled in a tense post-civil rights era socio-economically marginalized space, whereas on the internet activities are defined by social media sites, and participants might be multimillionaire celebrities and entrepreneurs.

These relationships, local and global, both in hip-hop events and at Empire State College are, however, contentious. Community-based hip-hop artists and educators fight to preserve a sense of individual identity against a profit-oriented discourse of corporate capitalism that has defined many products of hip-hop – particularly rap music – as commodity items. And at Empire State College, some members of regional center and local unit affiliates characterize CDL as the online faceless behemoth that is going to obliterate the character of each center and each unit, as well as their relationships with one another.

There have been other similarities between the College and hip-hop, too. Related, for example, to the ideas of sampling and mixing, contributors to this volume have delved into and shared reflections on the early roots of ESC's mentoring practices and highlight a mixing of trial-and-error and an emphasis on process over the philosophy that informed foundational elements of the College's mission. These time-honored practices bear resemblance to practices in hip-hop like sampling, where artists pull together beats, rhythms, lyrics, dance moves, and thoughts from an array of historic and genre traditions, and then create what are referred to as mixtapes or remixes – blends of old and new. Sampling and mixing are artistic practices, which hip-hop artists honor as innovative and scholars in hip-hop studies point to as representing the artistry innate in those who are self-taught.[5] However, some critiques of ESC's practices liken the result to having created a foundation for a learning experiment with no philosophy. Because of this lack, the argument goes, the College is struggling to retain an identity as it approaches its 50th anniversary; and faculty, administrators, and professional staff are not in agreement over how the tenets of adult learning might – and should be – put into practice. In this environment, how might one learn as a faculty member to participate and contribute to the College's intellectual life?

From the lens of hip-hop, it seems that Empire State College did have more of a philosophical foundation than such critiques suggest. The practices of sampling (trial-and-error) and mixing (blending varieties of experiences to create individualized study plans for students) were built, like hip-hop, on a premise that knowledge was neither static nor inviolable. Yet, this understanding was not apparent as I entered the cipher. At the time that I arrived at the Center for Distance Learning, enrollments in the humanities in particular were falling, and discussions among my new colleagues hinted that the time-honored practice of customizing courses to meet student needs was endangered. Faculty at the Center for Distance Learning were debating whether to do away with individualized degree plans in favor of the more structured approaches associated with conventional colleges, as well as the merits of creating new classes and studies that might not find a robust market. Longtime faculty noted the growing prominence of CDL within the College and issues of overwork associated with an obligation to be online and available to students all of the time.

For me, the loss of a unique mission was a paramount concern. I believed in the idea of knowledge as conversation, and of learning as a co-creative experience that would allow students to share and exchange lived experiences and knowledge acquired outside of the classroom in a way that would enable all classroom participants to grow in their learning together. I liked how Empire State College placed the adult learner at the core of its mission and sought to tailor education to each student's need. I also liked the fact that Empire State College spoke of professors as generalists who could stretch disciplinary training in new directions. These reflections of the College's core values resembled the knowledge-building that hip-hop's Fifth Element encouraged via its ciphers.

At the same time, I did have questions about how the Center for Distance Learning's practice of developing predesigned courses in the asynchronous virtual world of the online learning environment meshed with the experiences of a cipher in a face-to-face classroom. Among the questions I asked were: How does learning take place in hip-hop? And, if hip-hop's past resembles Empire State College's past, but if I teach for CDL, how might I sample from both pasts to remix a course for the present?

## LEARNING IN A HIP-HOP CIPHER

It is February 2009, and I am at a coffee shop in Seattle interviewing Lee, a 23-year-old break dancer. Our conversation happens to take place a few days before a big community-based event, the anniversary of 206 Zulu, a chapter of the worldwide organization Universal Zulu Nation.[6] The culminating event is a break dancing battle in which dancers and crews from all over the nation will perform in a competition. Because Lee will be among the competitors, I ask her to tell me about battles and suggest that she do so by describing the upcoming event.

"The doors will open at 7 p.m.," she begins, "but the actual battle won't begin for at least two or three hours."

That introductory statement along with her continuing explanation illustrated how hip-hop's practices of teaching and learning are at work in all kinds of events. What matters is not so much the purpose of the event but the prior learning brought by participants and how they share what they know. The battle was to take place in a dance hall. As the space filled up, ciphers would form. While the battlers on stage would engage in learning as a sort of spectator sport in which the competitors interacted with one another while others observed, the cipher participants would do so more intimately in a way that might enable a dialogue to emerge among all those who were part of the circle creating the cipher. To battle formally, one needed an invitation, the ability to pay a registration fee, and a crew with which one could affiliate.[7] However, anyone could join the less formal ciphers. As Lee explained it, while the battles created a larger sense of community for the whole group in attendance, the ciphers were about building relationships and forming community among smaller circles within the larger group. They were a chance to practice dance moves and perhaps get some feedback about what was working and what could be improved. They also were a chance to show what you knew how to do and where you fell short. Even watching was a chance to learn further, she said, because you could see what someone else was trying out, ask them questions, or emulate their moves. In this sense, the smaller ciphers were like breakout groups or smaller units of students working within a particular classroom.

"Around 9 p.m. or so, the emcee will start bringing the crowd together by letting people know that the battle is going to begin," Lee said. "But he'll also start with some knowledge. He'll begin with a story."

"A story?"

"About the history and roots of hip-hop," she explained. "If the emcee is good, he'll use the history to frame the battle so people will know why hip-hop exists and what it means to be a part of it."

From Lee's description, one sees the event as a learning experience that engages a student on several levels. The emcee fills an authoritative role of a teacher by framing the moment with a narrative for listeners to debate and consider. The onstage battlers also teach through their moves while the emcee suggests what makes a particular bodily expression stronger than another. At the same time, the battlers are learning because they are in an onstage cipher conversing with opponents. Conversing with the battlers are the others watching as spectators or participating in ciphers.

I had stumbled into hip-hop in 2007, shortly after defending my doctoral dissertation while working in-between teaching jobs as an early morning coach at a local branch of the women's fitness center Curves. My coworker was Naj, who was Lee's elder sister and, like her, a competitive break dancer. Naj would arrive at work at 10 a.m. to relieve me, usually yawning. She spent most of her evenings at practices in churches and community centers, or dancing at after-hours clubs. She would show up at work carrying a bowl, a box of cereal, and a carton of almond milk. She would wish me good morning, confess to being tired because she had been dancing all night, and use the down time at the fitness center to study videos of dances of which she'd been a part or which she had been encouraged by her mentors to watch.

Interested in finding out more about how Naj and her community of break dancers had come together, I began to ask her questions, attend her performances, and bring her and Lee and other artists with whom they connected me into my classes. I learned through them that while many people saw hip-hop as "just music," they saw it as knowledge, self-discovery, and transformation of self. I didn't understand this point of view entirely, but I felt that it might resonate with my students and that we could then connect their statements to the readings on politics, society, and civic participation that I was asking them to do. I also wanted to learn more about their language and culture. Naj and Lee were optimistic that the world could be made better through education and they saw participation in hip-hop as education. Conscious of the gendered, racial, and economic stratifications of society, they seemed dedicated to creating through dance, art, and music a more environmentally sustainable and socially just world. I felt somehow that their stories might be transformative, not just for my students but also for me.

Their quest mirrored the battling, ciphering, and building that occurred in my Cornish class. When I allowed myself to profess ignorance and to invite guests or other students to participate in the learning process, I was engaging in hip-hop's Fifth Element in that I was allowing myself to gain knowledge in ways that democratized the classroom and valued the learning and experiences of others. Coming to Empire State College as my understanding of this view of knowledge was just burgeoning, I saw orientation materials offered to new mentors on process learning, prior learning assessments, the development and design of independent studies, and treating mentoring as an act of listening as other ways of understanding the art of ciphering.

But even if I did not realize it fully, I also was joining the College in an era of a changing institutional culture and, too, I held a less conventional role in the College because of my affiliation with CDL. The question that I faced was one of how to bring the intensely personal exchange of knowledge-building that characterized the hip-hop cipher and the intimacy of mentoring to my online classes. Could one create a cipher in a space where you never met your students face-to-face?

## THE CYBER CIPHER

Hip-hop events like the battle in Seattle open spaces where a skilled emcee is able to show through narrative how the activities of the immediate fit into a larger story. The online classroom depends often on preset curricula, where students are able – if they wish – to "read" the entire class from start to finish before a term starts. The structure is asynchronous, which means that while there are project deadlines and start and end dates for learning activities, the work needs only to be done by – not at – a particular date. This asynchronous structure makes learning more convenient for the busy adult, but it subdues spontaneity and erodes the possibility of the surprises that occur routinely in face-to-face interchanges. Such surprises create "teaching moments" that offer insights and ignite learning in ways that could not have been predicted by an instructor in advance.

Hip-hop educators often see such teaching moments as opportunities to freestyle, or to drop all inhibitions and speak frankly from the heart. These words from the heart comprise the knowledge-building that pursuit of the Fifth Element advocates, and, in many cases, change the tenor of what learning means. In one classroom at a high school in St. Paul, Minnesota, which is organized with a hip-hop pedagogical ethos, I watched such freestyling in action. Students were discussing their neighborhoods. One young man had grown up in Gary, Indiana. "If you don't know anyone in the city," the student said, "you're fucked. If you don't have a weapon to protect you, you're fucked. And you don't want to carry anything you don't actually need on your person." As other students began to titter over the student's use of obscenities, the teacher asked: "How many of you know where Gary is, what Gary is?" Silence fell and the teacher said, "It's a city that's been completely destroyed by urban decay."

"Yeah, 'Ghost Town Gary' was what we called it," the student said, quieter and more serious now.

"So when a town's industry leaves, when people move out, what remains?" the teacher asked.

Other students spoke up: "Guns. Violence. Drugs."

Incorporating that kind of give-and-take dialogue comes easily face-to-face. Shifting to the online, asynchronous format forces one, however, to consider differently what is of value in the knowledge that is co-created in conversations. After my first term of teaching at ESC's Center for Distance Learning, I began to believe that gaining knowledge through conversation, while a way of engaging students, also offered a way for instructors to evaluate a student's performance through a co-learning practice. Such a practice focused on students sharing and instructors listening to how students learned through an application of knowledge emerging in the activity and enhancing their prior knowledge. That knowledge may have come from lived experiences, from other classes, or from a text assigned in the class at hand. What mattered was not the source of the knowledge, as much as the meaning that students made of it. With an understanding of learning as a connecting of multiple dots of experience, I began to see how the cipher might be built in cyberspace so that knowledge-building was conceptualized as a lifelong learning practice that was not dependent on the immediacy of the face-to-face moment; and I also could see how that practice would continue ESC's mission of encouraging the education of adults by facilitating an integration of prior learning with present inquiry.[8]

I also quickly saw that such a cyber cipher need not occur synchronously and need not even be collective in its process. While the discussion forums that form the core of many CDL courses offer one vehicle for creating a cyber cipher, these forums are linear in format and rely on what are often formally written questions that tend to produce essay-type responses as opposed to freestyled discussions. In addition, the in-and-out presence of the instructor can have the effect of freezing a knowledge-building conversation-in-progress because when the instructor weighs in, students remember that they're in a course, receiving a grade, and that freestyling might make them look less studious.[9]

As a result, in my course, Hip-Hop America: The Evolution of a Cultural Movement, I sought to build a learning cyber cipher from the ground up. Instead of focusing on vehicles for dialogue, I shaped the course's entire structure around hip-hop's multiple modes of conversation-generated knowledge. Students study hip-hop history through several documentary films and three required texts. Several video interviews in which key hip-hop figures discuss the history, foundational elements, and knowledge-building practices of hip-hop also are embedded in the course. Learning activities include participation in five discussion forums, the writing of two papers, the completion of two creative projects, and the maintenance of a learning journal throughout the term. But the students do not just read and regurgitate their learning. They converse with each other about their own place in hip-hop history, and share with one another stories about their favorite songs. As they articulate their experience with their songs, they identify the meanings and reflect on the messages of the songs in relation to the histories they are gaining from the course, as well as from the lived experiences that their classmates share. I, too, participate in this sharing by talking to the students about my own experiences of encountering hip-hop as a woman in my 40s and about the connections I see between the music they share and socio-economic conditions of the past and present.

Students also work in a collaborative learning space known as a "wiki" to create both an historic timeline of significant hip-hop events and resource guides for hip-hop activities in the communities where they live. The information that students contribute to the wiki becomes part of a resource pool that they are able to tap to develop their creative projects: a mixtape of hip-hop history prepared in an artistic or academic genre of their choice, and an ethnographic project on a hip-hop activity in their communities. The knowledge that is built and shared in the wikis remains in the course template, with each contributor's name beside it, after the term ends. In this way, students not only help those in future classes but also contribute to the body of emergent work on hip-hop.

I first taught the class as a guided independent study with two ESC students. One was nearly 50 years old and had served as a deejay in her neighborhood in Queens, New York for more than three decades. The other was in her early 20s and was working at an afterschool program run by the Hirschhorn Museum in Washington D.C. called ARTLAB+. When the term opened, the students were hesitant. They told me they didn't "get" how they could study hip-hop as an academic topic because it was all about their lives. I asked them to start by talking about their experiences, and as they opened up, I began suggesting that they apply the work they were doing as deejays and with youth to their mixtapes and community projects. Since then, other students have submitted poetry books, drawings, musical pieces, and autobiographical essays that frame their understandings of their lived histories within the history and their awareness of and relationship to hip-hop. In the learning journals that they submit about once a month, they document their progress in the course in terms of their personal growth. The course continues to evolve as my relationship with hip-hop and Empire State College grows.

## CONCLUSION

Working through the processes of battling, ciphering, and building has helped me see how hip-hop's central components embody a pursuit of knowledge that requires a simultaneous engagement with dueling practices: speaking and listening, teaching and learning, breaking down concepts and rebuilding them anew. When applied to the adult learning relationships that Empire State College encourages its faculty to cultivate with students, the practices of battling, ciphering, and building can encourage an engagement with active learning through reminding faculty that a central goal of the College is to create an environment where students can take control of their learning and their lives' development in the process. These practices force faculty to step aside as disciplinary experts, and invite them to shrug off their credentials in order to do what one hip-hop pioneer, George Clinton (2011), advocates, which is "not to learn tricks" but "to learn how to be open to learning" in and of itself (p. viii).

Such practices, all components of hip-hop pedagogy, informed how I myself learned and taught as an adult who returned to graduate school in a midcareer shift. Even with the title of "professor," I have a difficult time understanding anyone who claims that her expertise is paramount. The challenge perhaps is promulgating that understanding of learning as a dynamic, ever-changing process in an era where both hip-hop and higher education are transmogrifying into powerful, profit-oriented corporate forces seemingly beyond one's control. Hip-hop nears its first half-century known less as a grassroots set of artistic and communal practices and more as a billion-dollar global music, video, and clothing industry – an industry that mass produces symbols of greed, gangsterism, and sexual misogyny.

Empire State College struggles to educate tens of thousands of working adults through technologies that can appear machine-like, inhuman, and demoralizing. Calls to increase student enrollments through an embrace of such things as massive open online courses (MOOCs) and pre-structured degree plans threaten to replace the individualized relationships between mentors and mentees, the co-learning that occurs, and the wonderfully localized characters of regional centers that gave the College its initial intellectual and cultural fervor. In this environment, it is only fair to ask, can the cipher survive? Can mentoring practices that were grounded in tenets that also informed hip-hop still be relevant? Can they be sustained in a political and social environment where debates about the meaning, value, and pursuit of higher education have grown increasingly contentious? Can they prosper in an era where tightening budgets, limited public resources, and a contracting economy are resulting in declining enrollments? Can they withstand increased challenges to colleges to base their success on collecting tuition by enrolling more students and not necessarily on how well the students are educated?

I do not know the answers to such questions. Yet, one recent encounter with a faculty member from another university gives me reason to believe that Empire State College still offers an example of success that should translate to hope. I was at the national conference of Imagining America, a Syracuse, New York-based consortium of higher education, arts, and community organizations with a mission of rekindling democratic revival through partnerships with each other. The faculty member and I were walking from one session to another, and she, upon learning that I was with Empire State College, began praising lavishly a student project she had visited the previous year at the Settlement House in Manhattan. The student had connected her work in the world with the learning experiences she had gained through the College in a way that the faculty member found inspiring.

Pressing me, she asked, "How do you teach? Who are your students? What are your classes like?"

I explained to her that I was at the Center for Distance Learning, and taught two online classes a term. I added that I usually worked with between five and 10 students in one-on-one studies that either centered on their degree planning or focused on studies that interested them. I also explained that my students were mostly from New York but also from other parts of the U.S. and that I worked with mentees and others abroad.

"How do you do it?" she asked. "Well, I mostly just try and listen to what the students tell me they want," I replied. "And then I suggest ways that they can study what interests them. A lot of time, I work with them myself because I'm pretty interdisciplinary in my approach and don't mind being stretched. But if their interests are too far out of my academic range, I try to find someone who can work with them."

"Is that the norm at your college?" she asked. "Or are you the radical fringe?"

I laughed, because I felt that it was the College mission that was radical. I was only marching to the beat it established. Yet, I also would not be writing this chapter if I did not believe that hip-hop as a way of thinking and being with the world might help keep that spirit of radicalism alive.

## NOTES

[1] I draw this understanding of hip-hop pedagogy from my ongoing work with the Hip-Hop Education Center at New York University as part of a nationwide taskforce to draft a document on articulations and practices of teaching and learning that are used by artists, community organizers, and educators at the K-12 and university level who self-identify with the arts and values that hip-hop culture advocates.

[2] Jackson, a longtime emcee and entrepreneur who shapes his personal and professional ethics around his engagement with hip-hop, describes the idea of building as being akin to a practice in academia of deconstruction, in which existing truths or prevailing views are broken down and taken apart in order that one might see the forces of race, gender, and economic hierarchizing that gave them the power of truth in order then to reconstruct new, more egalitarian views.

³  I did not understand the processes I refer to in a particularly intellectual way when I was first hired, which is perhaps typical of faculty joining the College new. I am just now beginning to gain an epistemological understanding of what it means to be both a teacher and a mentor at Empire State College through conversations with colleagues, readings in the in-house publication *All About Mentoring*, and the co-authored book *From Teaching to Mentoring* by Lee Herman and Alan Mandell (2004). This lack of an epistemological awareness of what Empire is about perhaps contributes to the crisis of meaning that the College community appears to be grappling with. Yet, when meaning is unclear, there are opportunities for dialogues within the mode of ciphering to flourish and for new understandings and knowledge practices to emerge.

⁴  By way of example, I appreciate the historical insights that Xenia Coulter and Wayne Willis offer in their essays, and thank co-editors Alan Mandell and Katherine Jelly for sharing them with me. At the same time, I question assertions made by both that new faculty are more focused on preset degree requirements, disciplinary expertise, and concerns that might be voiced by professors at more traditional colleges than the pioneering Empire State College mentors of the past.

⁵  I served as an evaluator in September 2012 for an Empire State College student requesting college credit through prior learning assessment for The Art of Hip-Hop. The student's ability to articulate in written and oral statements what was meant by sampling and mixing, and to demonstrate how he used these practices to create songs and music videos effectively showed mastery of these art forms at a college level.

⁶  Universal Zulu Nation, formed by early hip-hop figure Afrika Bambaataa in 1975, is perhaps the leading voice worldwide in perpetuating an understanding of hip-hop as a form of philosophy and knowledge creation. Bambaataa, who continues to be active in hip-hop, has defined the Fifth Element of hip-hop as the underlying core of the genre and articulates it as the binding source that brings not only the foundational elements of hip-hop but its wide-ranging practices globally together. Bambaataa was also an early member of a group known as the Five Percenters, as well as the radical black empowerment group the Black Panthers that called attention to racially demeaning practices inherent in westernized forms of Christianity and governmental public policies.

⁷  As earlier described, the "crew" in hip-hop is the group of people with which a dancer, artist, or writer most closely affiliates. The concept is derived from gangs who engaged in violent street fights before some members saw the arts as a peaceful alternative to voice grievances and assert selves. Many of my interviewees liken their crews to their families. For more, see Pabon (2012).

⁸  Much of my understanding of this iteration of knowledge through conversation came through workshops offered at Empire State College in January 2011 and October 2011 by Dan Apple of the Pacific Crest Institute on assessing student learning and course activity design.

⁹  I work around that dilemma by using a different space within the course to share my observations on the learning in discussion forums such as the course announcements or bulletin board. But, in doing so, I am conscious that I am not democratizing the learning space because I am separating myself – as the instructor – from the cipher.

## REFERENCES

Anderson, B. (1991). *Imagined communities: Reflections on the origin and spread of nationalism.* London, UK: Verso.

Clinton, G. (2011). Foreword. In S. Seidel (Ed.), *Hop hop genius: Remixing high school education* (pp. vii–ix). Lanham, MD: Rowman & Littlefield Education.

Forman, M. (2012). Represent: Race, space, and place in rap music. In M. Forman & M. A. Neal (Eds.), *That's the joint: The Hip-Hop studies reader* (2nd ed., pp. 247–269). New York, NY: Routledge

Herman, L., & Mandell, A. (2004). *From teaching to mentoring: Principle and practice, dialogue and life in adult education.* London, UK: Routledge.

Pabon, J. P. F. (2012). Physical graffiti: The history of hip-hop dance. In M. Forman & M. A. Neal (Eds.), *That's the joint: The Hip-Hop studies reader* (2nd ed., pp. 56–62). New York, NY: Routledge.

Pough, G. (2004). *Check it while I wreck it: Black womanhood, hip-hop culture, and the public sphere.* Boston, MA: Northeastern University Press.

Schapiro, S. A. (1999). Higher education for democracy: Renewing the mission of progressive education. In S. A. Schapiro (Ed.), *Higher education for democracy: Experiments in progressive pedagogy at Goddard College* (pp. 3–14). New York, NY: Peter Lang Publishers.

Schloss, J. (2009). *Foundation: B-boys, b-girls, and hip-hop culture in New York City*. New York, NY: Oxford University Press.

SECTION III

# LET 1,000 FLOWERS BLOOM

*Our Students and the Programs and Procedures That Support Them*

In Section III, authors from a range of programs and roles across the College first describe their particular practice and place in the institution, and then examine the issues and questions arising in their mentoring and teaching as they work toward ESC's mission and values. Each of these chapters, though focusing on disparate facets of the institution and highlighting their unique challenges in carrying out genuinely student-centered pedagogy, also speaks to a shared struggle to sustain ESC's progressive heritage and identity.

In Chapter 8, "'I Don't Write, I Work': Writing and Reading with Trade Union Apprentices," R. Fraser and S. Mavrogiannis, colleagues in The Harry Van Arsdale Jr. Center for Labor Studies, a unique program at ESC that serves trade union members, consider some of the creative tensions and contradictions arising when faculty are striving to develop genuinely student-centered pedagogy for students who are required by their unions to complete their degrees. In Chapter 9, "A Progressive Institution Takes on Academic Support, 21st Century Style," S. Logsdon and L. Guyette, both directors of academic support in a regional center, explore some of the questions involved in providing academic support for underprepared students in an alternative model of student-designed study. They argue that such support must be systematic, responsive to the individual student's academic needs, and well and effectively integrated into a student's ongoing learning experience. In Chapter 10, "On the Leading Edge: International Programs and Mentoring in Transnational Settings," D. Starr-Glass, a mentor in the College's International Programs based in Prague (the Czech Republic), discusses the complexities, demands and rewards of working in a student-centered model with those whose higher education experiences have been shaped by a culture of teaching and learning so different from the progressive tradition of Empire State College's pedagogy. And, in Chapter 11, "Inherent Tensions within the Practices of Prior Learning Assessment at SUNY Empire State College," N. Travers notes the enormous growth of PLA across the world today and examines the effects of abiding tensions in varying philosophical emphases and goals related to PLA, not just within Empire State College but in all institutions undertaking assessment of prior learning.

REBECCA FRASER AND SOPHIA MAVROGIANNIS

# 8. "I DON'T WRITE, I WORK"

*Writing and Reading with Trade Union Apprentices*

THE SHANTY, OR AN INTRODUCTION

"I'm sorry you had to read this. I don't write, I work." That was the closing sentence in an essay written by one of our students at orientation. We always knew that this apparent crisis of work versus writing – labor versus academics – existed for many of our students, but we'd never encountered a statement as poignant as this one. Many students question the purpose of a college degree (and especially a writing class!) in their apprenticeship programs, and still others have somehow come to believe that they are incapable of writing anything of merit, scholarship, or interest. However, this is a statement that goes beyond common insecurity and suggests a larger issue of identity. This student did not apologize for any one particular skill set; he apologized for the *action* of writing, as if to imply that he had no business writing in the first place because he is a worker. So then what does it mean to be a worker? And what does it mean to be a writer? This tension between work and writing, between labor and academics, is a significant underpinning of the curriculum we have developed for our College Writing and Critical Reading Strategies courses, courses that all associate degree-level students take during their first year at The Harry Van Arsdale Jr. Center for Labor Studies (HVACLS) of Empire State College.

From the outside, it might appear that HVACLS is the most traditional program at the very nontraditional Empire State College – after all, our program is classroom and semester-based, students meet in a conventional classroom setting, with desks, a whiteboard, and a teacher at the front of the room. However, this setup is not a blind following of tradition; rather, it comes at the request of the union leaders who created and sustain our program. Harry Van Arsdale Jr., former International Brotherhood of Electrical Workers (IBEW) Local 3 president and founder of our program, was insistent on a classroom setting for his apprentices: They work together on the job, they work together in their apprentice training classes, and he wanted them to work together in their college classes as well. Students in our classrooms participate in a great deal of group work and active learning exercises, and are required to meet with learning coaches each semester. The curriculum we have developed for them is meant *for* them in particular.

When we consider our students – trade union apprentices whose unions *require* them to attend college in a classroom setting, whose successful completion of college courses is directly related to their pay raises, and many of whom chose a trade as a means of avoiding school – it is evident that our program is, necessarily, nontraditional. That many students chose to go into a trade as a way to ensure that they wouldn't have to go to college is most salient, as these students identify themselves as workers, not writers, and as apprentices, not academics.

In this chapter, we describe the first-year curriculum we have developed to meet the educational experiences of these students – electrical and plumbing apprentices. We discuss how their backgrounds[1] have shaped their writing and reading; and we elucidate how our curriculum was designed to meet the very particular needs of students who do not consider themselves writers in any way.

Most importantly, though perhaps lurking in the background, we explore the tension inherent in creating a curriculum that meets the needs of both the individual and the group. This tension is present in most societies, groups and organizations, and is especially present in our classroom-based program situated in an institution that has historically focused on, and been committed to study based on, individual needs and interests. In recent years, the variety of teaching and learning forms at ESC has expanded, and at this time in the College's history, there are many so-called "study groups" – both in person and online – that are not fully "individualized." Still, the Van Arsdale program is unique in the size of its classes (often 20 or 22 students in a class) and its face-to-face models of teaching and learning. Remaining student-centered and attentive to individual needs and interests in a program where so much is group-based and required of all students requires *us* to seek out and create opportunities in which students can exercise individual agency over their education.

## THE CONTROL PANEL, OR CONTEXT AND BACKGROUND

From its inception 40 years ago, the Van Arsdale Center was unique in forging strong partnerships with various trade unions throughout New York City. In fact, the Van Arsdale Center of SUNY Empire State College has staked its claim in the fight against orthodox notions that "workers" and those in trade unions are nothing more than unintelligent "union thugs," that college is a place only for the already-privileged, and that there is no place for workers in higher education. At its core, the Van Arsdale center has long promoted, supported and advocated for opportunity, equity and a democratic society. This is echoed in our center's mission statement, that:

> The best possible society, from the perspective of labor studies, is one in which everyone who wants to work can, and everyone who does work is paid enough to live a good life as a respected member of the community. Learning how to ensure these desires, which are well expressed by the traditional labor

movement slogan, 'a fair day's wages for a fair day's work,' is the guiding purpose of a labor studies degree. (SUNY Empire State College, n.d., para. 2)

We use this mission statement throughout all our programs as an attempt to help our students to gain awareness of and examine for themselves their roles in the labor movement, the powers they have, and the greater power they can have in instigating change. Our politics are both overt and open for discussion. There is, for instance, no question where HVACLS stands when it comes to workers' rights. Central text choices communicate clearly our perspective, sometimes challenging students' ideas about the place of work and unions in society. Many of our assignments, then, are designed to encourage students to engage these issues and to make the connections to their own workplace and work circumstance.

The Associate in Science degree at HVACLS is made up of 64 credits, 32 of which come from a generic evaluation of a student's apprenticeship – a combination of theory courses and work in their field. We provide the other 32 credits in a pre-structured, liberal arts, labor-centric program. All students take the same eight 4-credit courses, one class per semester:[2] College Writing; Critical Reading; Literature and Society; U.S. History; Global Civilizations; Labor and the Economy; Class, Race and Gender; and Labor and Public Affairs. The first two courses students take are College Writing and Critical Reading; half take the writing course first and the other half take the reading course first.[3] These two courses are foundational to the remaining curriculum, which is both reading and writing intensive.

## THE TOOLBOX, OR SOME THEORY

Unlike many other learners, our students often show up for class with construction dust covering their boots and jeans, with what at least one student termed "hardhat hair." In these very concrete ways, our students bring their work into the classroom. An instructor would have to be most insensitive not to notice this presence of labor and understand the need to incorporate it into the activities of the day and of the semester. Since most students also have been awake since 4 or 5 a.m. and have been on a job site from 7 a.m. until 3 p.m., they have just enough time to grab a snack and maybe take a short nap on the subway or in the student lounge before class.

Engaging these tired, hungry students in academic work is challenging, as is getting them to invest emotionally, intellectually and physically[4] in the benefits of an education (even a *free* education!) when their motivation is powerfully external rather than internal. As Lytle (2001) argues, it requires us to:

> construct a rich conceptual framework for inquiring into the many facets of literacy development in adulthood, [one that] includes the cultural scripts adults bring to, and take from, learning; their family, school, and community histories, their specific and global intentions; their knowledge of the world; and, in particular, their tacit and shifting awareness of the forms and functions of written language, as experienced in the contexts of daily life. (p. 378)

To this end, we adopt a willingness to learn alongside our students, entering into their territory as much as we ask them to enter into ours because, as Denny (2010) describes it, our students "aren't looking to surrender their working-class identities" (p. 77). And, quite frankly, we don't want them to. Instead, we argue for a pedagogy and praxis of equity and inclusion, one that engages learners in their contexts and discourses, and in the worlds they inhabit both in and out of our classrooms, whatever these worlds may be. And it requires us to work actively to adopt a discourse that does more than simply give a nod to what we might call their "on-the-job speak." At least one of our instructors, early in the College Writing course, asks students to put up on the board as many job-specific terms as they can come up with – names for tools, work processes, and locations – terms that are often new to us.[5] Bringing this language into an academic setting lends credence to it, especially when instructors make use of it in class discussions and encourage students to use this discourse in the essays they write.

Wage workers and those in blue-collar professions are often seen as less intelligent and lacking basic literacy, whether because of the work they do or because of their completion of a vocational school, either of which can erroneously mark them as *deficient*. Language, literacy, and culture scholar Glynda Hull (2001) objects "to the tendency in current discussions to place too much faith in the power of literacy [defined in this context as the ability to read and write] and to put too little credence in people's abilities, particularly those of blue-collar and non-traditional workers" (p. 667). As our students are part of this social group, in order to design first-year courses that best serve their needs, we have to take into account the popular beliefs that exist about workers within our society, beliefs that our students have often internalized. This necessity creates an interesting and potentially creative tension in the classroom, as instructors assist students in confronting the ways in which they have adopted an image that does not necessarily fit them at all.

Unfortunately, one dominating representation of our students (and all members of trade unions) is that they are nothing more than "union thugs."[6] This name-calling has gone so far as to cause union members to turn the phrase on its head, taking on the moniker proudly. Some examples include the AFL-CIO setting up "Hug-a-Thug" booths (Tortora, 2012), and memes with headings like "I love union thugs" all over the internet depicting firefighters rescuing families from flood waters during Hurricane Sandy. However, even in the context of so many powerful and positive images of union workers, it is impossible to ignore or escape the overwhelming abundance of overweight, oaf-like, loudmouthed characters like Archie Bunker, Homer Simpson, Doug Heffernan and Peter Griffin – all popular television characters with blue-collar jobs: factory workers, truck drivers, etc. And, of course, all of these representations – all of these characters and *caricatures* – are of men. These stereotypes, we admit, sometimes permeate our classrooms as new instructors (who are acculturated to traditional college settings and students, and, therefore, often carry with them expectations and assumptions about our students) lament a general "lack of basic skills" among their class.

However, all of these ways of thinking about workers (and our students!) show a lack of understanding about the intelligence of work[7] and the "supplementary knowledge [that] is necessary" for workers to accomplish tasks and work through on-the-job obstacles, both social and labor (Hull, 2001, p. 672). To this extent, our students are quite literate in the discourse of their *secondary Discourse* (that is, the Discourse of their workplaces). Linguist James Paul Gee (2001) makes a distinction between *Discourse* and *discourse*, explaining that Discourse (with a capital D) is an "identity kit" that encompasses "ways of being in the world; [these ways of being] are forms of life which integrate words, acts, values, beliefs, attitudes, and social identities, as well as gestures, glances, body positions, and clothes" (p. 526). This identity kit encompasses a "secondary Discourse," the "non-home-based social institutions – institutions in the public sphere, beyond the family and immediate kin and peer groups" and our *primary Discourse,* which we are initially socialized into at home, and which we "first use to make sense of the world and interact with others" (p. 527). Thus, lowercase *discourse* differs from uppercase *Discourse* in that it refers to "connected stretches of language that make sense" (p. 526), meaning that various *discourses* are part of a given *Discourse.*

This sociolinguistic theory of D/discourse informed our design of the first-year reading and writing courses because "the focus of literacy studies or applied linguistics should not be language, or literacy, but social practices" (Gee, 2001, p. 525) since, after all, "learning to read is always learning some aspect of some discourse" (p. 540). Learning, however, differs from acquisition – a distinction Gee makes to further illustrate the tensions and complexities of how we develop literacy in D/discourses. In its simple form, *acquisition* is a subconscious act or process of acquiring knowledge and information by circumstance and exposure; conversely, *learning* is a conscious process, taking place through inquiry and analysis (p. 539). Most of what we know we have mastered with a balance of these two sources, the role of each shifting at different points and for different reasons. The same holds true for our students, so it seemed imperative that we design courses that embrace their *secondary Discourse* of work, and use it as a medium for enculturating them into an academic environment, which for many is yet another *secondary Discourse.*

## BENDING PIPE, OR DESIGNING CURRICULUM TO MEET STUDENT NEEDS

Eight years ago, College Writing was a writing course where most, if not all, of the writing was done in class by hand; there was an emphasis on grammar and writing in the rhetorical modes. Little or no reading was done. When Rebecca Fraser joined the faculty, she instigated a major shift. Today, the three cornerstones of the course are: that writing is a process, that to write is to discover, and that reflection on learning and language is a valuable practice. Reading about some form of work is assigned for discussion and for potential writing topics, as well as to provide students with the chance to reflect on their own, newly-minted, work lives. In addition, students are challenged by the amount of informal writing assigned and by the number of revisions expected of each paper. Eventually, in an effort to help students with those revisions, we decided to require all students to see a writing coach at the College for every paper they write. These writing sessions, which happen at least four times a semester, are one of the places where individual learning and development get addressed.

In many of these ways, our College Writing course is very much like many freshman composition courses offered across Empire State College and the country. What makes our course unique is what our particular students bring to the classroom. As described earlier, many students identify as workers rather than as writers, and they are not comfortable sitting at desks that often seem too small for them. All of this becomes a topic for discussion, writing and reflection. Not only are we acclimating these students to the college setting, but we also are providing them with the opportunity to talk about their discomfort, fears, and even past failures.

Four years ago, during one of our all-inclusive faculty development meetings (where adjuncts are invited to participate and are paid for their time), an adjunct called out the elephant in the room: the extent to which our students struggle with the reading required of them in their reading-intensive courses. The discussion was wide-ranging, with some instructors keen on blaming students for laziness and others questioning where the source of resistance to reading might come from. A few noted our students' well-known bias toward visual learning and wondered how that affected their reading abilities.

Certainly, many students also struggled with their writing, but there was a required writing course, as well as writing coaches to help them. But what kind of support were we providing for our students when they encountered difficulties with their reading? An invigorating discussion followed, with many instructors telling stories of students not reading assignments and not buying the required books, and noting the discouragement students expressed when assigned readings from, for example, Walt Whitman's *Leaves of Grass* or Jared Diamond's *Guns, Steel and Germs*. We decided that we needed to investigate this situation – to get more input from faculty and students about the struggles both parties were having with reading assignments so that we could support our students in their reading efforts.

And we began to dream about what a required, nonremedial reading course might look like within our program and how it might fit into our curriculum. At the top of our list were opportunities for individual student agency, which we hoped would create a sense of ownership of texts – that is, the chance to make their own reading selections and to select a group of classmates to work and read with all semester long. In addition, we wanted a common, and challenging, text on the topic of work that all students would work through together across the semester. More importantly, we wanted to bring to the surface early in our program students' resistance to reading, with the hope that they might resolve some of that resistance before studying Labor and Economics, a course in which they would face some tough reading on a topic with which they might not be familiar.

## THREADING PIPE, OR IMPLEMENTING A NEW CURRICULUM

The two main objectives we set out to meet in any curriculum design (or redesign) are: (1) to identify our students' individual and communal literacies and their access to discourses; and (2) to create pathways of agency for students by making use of their primary and secondary discourses – "their own language" (NCTE, 2008, Resolution section, para. 1) – in the midst of a "traditional" classroom. And we do all of this in the context of labor studies. By approaching curricular design with these objectives, we hope to become knowledgeable and aware of our students' world. Here, we attempt to follow the spirit of Freire's (1998) pedagogy, that we "need to know the universe of [our students'] dreams, the language with which they skillfully defend themselves from the aggressiveness of their world, what they know independently of the school, and how they know it" (pp. 72–73).

### THE SPECS

For both the College Writing and the College Reading courses, we use a common, shared syllabus. That is to say, each of the two course syllabi is laid out for participating instructors. There is room for instructors to put their imprint on the semester, to fit the syllabus to their particular group of students, as well as to their own teaching style. But, in general, all students in College Writing, for example, will write and revise four papers; each student will see a writing coach for each paper; these papers will be the same length across the board; but the assignments may differ from one section to the next (though suggestions are made for paper topics). Similarly, all sections of the Critical Reading Strategies course will read the same main text (Gabriel Thompson's *Working in the Shadows: A Year of the Doing Jobs (Most) Americans Won't Do*), and all students will read an additional nonfiction book, a novel, and some poetry of their choice. All students will also keep a reading journal and write a reader's autobiography. Each section of each course has an explicit and shared curriculum, and an explicit and shared pedagogy.

### *College Writing*

*Objective #1: Identifying our students' literacies and their access to various D/discourses.* Our students are nothing if not storytellers; in fact, their worksites are full of stories and storytellers. At a recent conference presentation, we discussed the important role storytelling (or, what our students call "shootin' the shit") plays in our work with students (Fraser & Mavrogiannis, 2012). For us, it is an essential component of our ability to acquire the cultural capital necessary to engage with them. It is not unusual for an instructor to enter a classroom where students are telling tales of the day's events: threading or bending pipe for the first time, getting a slip, taking two hours to fill a coffee order, a reaffirming "brotherhood" experience, or taking home some "mongo."[8] In these moments, it is not unusual for an impromptu story circle to emerge, with the instructor sharing and performing alongside students. Part of our job as instructors, we believe, is to begin to grasp the secondary Discourses of our students – honestly learning about things like BX, Mae Wests, Alimaks, pencil rods, shanties and channel locks. These are prime learning opportunities for instructors, as we listen to the Discourse spoken and acquire some new vocabulary ourselves.

Literacy Inventory Using Informal Assignment: On the first day, a story circle scene often lays the groundwork for the first piece of writing students will complete. In this low stakes, ungraded, informal homework assignment, called "Notes of Expectations," we encourage students to write about their hopes for and concerns about the course. We ask them to openly and honestly discuss five key items: (1) their definitions and perceptions of writing; (2) the ways in which they view themselves as writers; (3) their expectations of the course and the instructor (i.e., what they hope to learn, what they hope to read/write about, what they hope to achieve, how they hope to be engaged as learners, etc.); (4) their fears or concerns about taking a writing or reading course; and (5) the kinds of support they expect to have in and out of the classroom.

We hope students will lay all of this out so that, as a class, we can identify the ties that bind us: where we are, where we want to go, and how we are going to get there. However, a key component to the success of this assignment is getting students to trust instructors enough to speak candidly and openly. And, in our classrooms, the shortest distance between two strangers seems to be a great story. For this reason, it is important that instructors set a tone of openness and "relatability" from the very first day of class so that students feel comfortable speaking about what they are thinking and feeling. Additionally, keeping the assignment ungraded and low stakes lessens students' worry about "failing" or "not doing a good job" and allows them to focus their energy on saying the stuff that really matters to them. The insights instructors gather from this assignment about particular students and about the whole group are invaluable, as tensions between our assumptions about our students and their reality are often exposed. What comes to the surface in this assignment and the consequent discussion is relentlessly examined and negotiated throughout the semester, both with our students and among ourselves, as instructors.

*Objective #2: Creating pathways for students' use of "their own language" in College Writing.* Time and time again, writing, language and cultural scholars advocate for this kind of pedagogy, one that invites and includes students into educational landscapes as whole beings.[9] Nowhere do we see this more than in writing studies where scholars advocate often (and vehemently) for a pedagogy of inclusion – one that invites, embraces and encourages students' home languages within the context of the academy. If we consider that every part of language is tied with culture – that every phoneme, nuance of sound, etc. is tied with some cultural context[10] – then we begin to see how forcing any kind of discourse (standard English, middle-class conventions, etc.) onto students is the same as asking them to leave who they are at the curb before entering our hallways. Instead, we look to combine our world with theirs. More importantly, we look to move closer to where they are – to meet them halfway and on their turf, like in those story circles – and create within that shared space *hybrid discourses* that more accurately represent who our students are, who we are, and who we might all become through our exchanges.

Creating Pathways Using Formal Assignment: In College Writing, we make an explicit attempt to engage our students' storytelling – encouraging storytelling during a class session, and moving toward writing stories down for both informal and formal writing assignments. One of the first formal assignments in our writing course asks students to tell the story of how they got "here" – that is, into the union and consequently into our college program and their particular writing class. Over and over again, we hear a familiar story – the story of the child shadowing family members or neighbors who do their own house renovations or car repairs. The protagonist *acquires* a kind of work literacy, not through the reading of books, but by watching and doing, watching and doing.

This process is also seen in their apprenticeships, where journeymen take on apprentices to mentor them and show them how things are done. Though apprentices are also enrolled in what they call "theory" classes, where they learn through reading about electricity and its applications, most apprentices are comfortable learning on the job rather than in the classroom. As a result of this writing assignment, and many of the stories that get voiced, the notion of acquisition versus learning can be brought into course discussions where students can reflect on how they "get" the knowledge and information they need to succeed in college and on the job.

Creating Pathways Using Student Anthologies: One of the ways we help students consider themselves to be writers is through our annual student anthology *Labor Writes*,[11] which is a compilation of student writing from across the curriculum. *Labor Writes* is one of the central texts used in College Writing. As students read essays written by their fellow apprentices, especially their "How I Got Here" essay, they come to realize that their writing has value. Whether they realize it or not, our students are strong agents in designing our curriculum for the writing course. Not only are they encouraged to write in the discourse of their identity, but they are also writing the scripts for our first-year associate degree curriculum. In addition, we celebrate this publication with a public reading, where students read their essays to an audience of fellow students and family members. This is one of the most exciting components of our curriculum because the work included in these collections is exclusively student writing and art.

*Critical Reading Strategies*

*Objective #1: Identifying our students' literacies and their access to discourses.* Literacy Inventory Using Formal Assignment: In Critical Reading Strategies, one of our central assignments is a "reading autobiography." Here, students discuss what they remember about their early reading experiences, how their perception/experience of reading changed when they went to school, what they read now, and what they have learned over the course of the semester. While this is an assignment that comes later in the semester, they begin their writing on this piece in an informal, in-class writing assignment on the first day of class.

At its foundation, the purpose is similar to the "Note of Expectations" in the writing course: to help students gain reflective distance from some of their literacy experiences. In assignments like this, we are doing just as Lytle (2001) encourages us to do: constructing "a rich conceptual framework for inquiring into the many facets of literacy development in adulthood" (p. 378).

Once students pause to think about how much reading they do (though they often claim not to be readers), they begin to realize that they are reading all the time – and are quite adept at a variety of kinds of reading.

We bring this awareness of reading done outside of the classroom into the classroom by way of discussion and application. So, for example, students might be asked to explain to the class how they read a manual explaining how to repair their car engine; and, in all likelihood, they will touch on skills like skimming, as well as vocabulary and section titles. These same skills can then be applied to an assigned reading, either in the classroom itself or for homework. Building on students' direct, even practical, experience with language is an important part of what we do.

*Objective #2: Creating pathways for students' use of "their own language" in Critical Reading.* A cornerstone of the reading course is the amount of reading students do; it equals the amount of reading they will have to do in each of the courses they have not yet taken: four full-length books, a combination of both nonfiction and fiction. Students in the reading class are usually reading more than one book at a time, which is quite a feat for some students who have never actually read a book from cover to cover. Just as freewriting begets writing fluency, we believe that continuous reading begets reading fluency. Through this, we hope that students will begin to explore and hone their reading processes, and become conscious agents of their own reading. Essentially, we're looking to help students unpack the complexities that exist in the cognitive interaction between readers, texts and culture – as well as the interaction between a reader's primary Discourse, the discourse of a text, and the discourse community in which both the text and the reading are happening.

To eliminate some of the stigma students may still feel about their own reading, we designed the course to include reading groups as a place where students can share their thoughts, confusions, boredom, etc. about a text with members of their own discourse community: their fellow apprentices and classmates. Students create groups of four or five, which they will stay with for the duration of the semester. In this group, they will pick three of the four books they will read that semester. These reading groups are given time during each class session to discuss the book they are currently reading. Students who are further along in the book encourage students who are lagging behind in their reading, even talking them through plot difficulties and empathizing with the challenges fellow readers are facing. Eavesdropping on these conversations is revealing; having chosen the book on their own, they are engaged personally in completing the book. And, as a group without the instructor, they are more apt to fall back on their primary Discourse to discuss their reading experiences.

When they are finished with each of their books, the groups make a presentation to the class about the book. These reports are meant to go beyond "book report" territory and into reflections on the reading process. Students may talk about where they got stuck in a book and why, and they may explain how they got beyond that stuck point. After a good presentation, it is not unusual for fellow students to express interest in reading the book themselves. Here, the pathway for students to better understand their own reading process lies in their collaboration with one another, and in their challenging of one another. It is through the negotiation of questions created by their assumptions, uncertainties, interpretations and meanings in a *group* (and not merely in the subjective privacy of their own minds) that students have the opportunity to reflect on (or, to "read and reread," if you will) their own reading process, reading skills and acts of interpretation.

In addition, we take time in each class to read silently. This particular group activity functions on a number of levels: it is a literacy act that we do together, students and instructor alike; it is a chance for students to get ahead on an assignment; and it provides an opportunity for students to raise questions as they read, which often leads to a deeper discussion of the text. Week after week, for approximately 30 minutes, students sit quietly in the classroom, reading one of their books. It is a remarkable experience, especially from the perspective of an instructor looking at a room full of Carhartt jeans and Timberland boots, thick, sometimes sweaty necks, bent over a book, the only noise in the classroom being the turning of a page (or the occasional snore from a student who has succumbed to the long day's challenges). The very individual act of reading within the context of a group is an interesting place for our students to live into, embodying the tension between an individual and group identity.

In a sense, we are encouraging students to "learn" how to read again – for longer periods of time than a magazine or newspaper article may demand of them, and to engage with material that is not technical in its nature. The more they do it, the more engaged and skillful they become. It is not unusual for students to write in their final reading autobiography that they are amazed to have accomplished as much reading as they did during that semester.

## MONGO

As we continue to dream of better and more just societies with our students, as we work to help them become agents of change in their worlds, we understand that we need constantly to evaluate and reevaluate our curriculum. This means getting student responses to both writing and reading assignments. It means getting all instructors together twice a semester to discuss the materials of the course, our students' engagement with the material, and our own thoughts about how all of this comes together and where it hangs too loosely. For example, over the past few years, our students have become much more tech savvy; it is rarer that we encounter a student who has not had computer experience (which was not an unusual situation in the past). Our students – like so many others – are engaging in social media, and the discourses practiced in those places are evolving even as we write this article. So, too, "occupy" has become a household word; just a few years ago, when the movement was nascent, our students visited Zuccotti Park in New York City, interviewing protesters and having some of their assumptions about the protestors shattered. Thus, we need to be attentive to these and other changes in our ongoing development of pedagogy and curriculum.

Even while we have pinned down the "what and why" of our curriculum, we also understand that on any given day our students will move through a variety of discourse communities, sometimes with mastery and other times barely understanding. No one pedagogy then will ever be a "best fit" for the teaching and studying of literacy, because discourse, education and the acquisition of knowledge are not static; nor is literacy itself. More importantly, neither are our students or their experiences. As such, it is probably a good idea to stay open to improvising and/or renewing a literacy curriculum as necessary to meet the needs of each group of students. Much as we adjust our rhetoric for different situations, so too are we open to adjusting our literacy curriculum to suit the experiences, needs and expectations of our varying classroom communities.

Earlier in this chapter, we made note of the fact that our students meet in a classroom setting, which may appear traditional from the outside, precisely because their union leaders designed the program to be collaborative. Again, our students work together with other apprentices and journeymen on the job; to say that their lives depend on their ability to support one another is not an overstatement. Working in high rise buildings, often on open decks, on ladders, with electricity, is dangerous work. As noted earlier, Harry Van Arsdale Jr. envisioned his apprentices working together both on and off the job. And so it makes sense that we work with our students in a group setting, that is, in a classroom, with approximately 15 to 20 students.

This group setting is often in tension with the more individualized study that takes place at Empire State College, where the site of learning is in a mentor's office, between a mentor and one student. In individual study, student and mentor read and study and learn together, and while the mentor is more a master of the material at hand, it is also true that in these encounters the best mentors learn from their students as well. This individual study is often designed by the student in collaboration with a mentor, depending on how self-directed and motivated the student is. While students don't play a direct part in the design of our curriculum at HVACLS, it is true that we receive feedback from students at the end of each semester, feedback in which they comment on reading and writing assignments and discuss what worked or didn't work for them. This information is fed into our discussions of curriculum and recently brought about a change in the central texts used in both our reading and writing courses.

More importantly, perhaps, is the interactive, collaborative style of learning that is also a marker of many labor education programs, which are worker-centered. If one were to peek inside our classrooms, one would see groups or pairs working together, as well as a mentor traveling from group to group or pair to pair, conferring over the assigned task. In this setting, students are learning together, creating knowledge together, not only with the instructor, but with each other. While it is true that a mentor may enter a classroom with a lesson plan, it is also true that those lesson plans are ready to be ditched depending on what the students bring to the table on that particular day. Working this way, in small groups, with many oral presentations throughout the semester, provides mentors with an opportunity to get to know students as individuals. When it is discovered, for example, that a number of students are veterans, that fact will likely inform future class discussions as co-designed by the instructor and the students. In the College Writing class Rebecca Fraser recently taught, she had six graduates of NEW – Nontraditional Employment for Women, a construction skill, pre-apprenticeship program provided free for women interested in going into the trades. The presence of so many women in a program dominated by men has made a huge impact not only on the tenor but also on the content of those discussions. Though Rebecca could not have anticipated this student population in her class, she was happy to modify discussion topics accordingly. Once again, the tension between teaching an individual and teaching a group rises to the surface.

Just as a mentor and a single student will develop a relationship over the course of an individual study, so too do a mentor and a group of students develop a relationship across a semester. A class might begin with informal conversation about what happened on that day on the job site; a mentor may enter the classroom in the midst of a student telling a story about an incident at work – a fudged wire pull perhaps, or a successful, complicated pipe bend. Instructors and mentors learn where their students are working, perhaps at the World Trade Center, or underground in the subway system, at a sewage treatment plant or at Rikers Island. Their experiences, from doing a coffee run to shutting down a job site for the day, are integrated into course discussions and writing assignments, as we intentionally ask our students to make connections between what they do at their workplaces and what we are doing in the classroom. So while it is true that individualized mentoring is different from mentoring in a group setting, it is also true that mentoring in these two settings shares many of the same features: active learning, dialogue, relationship building, and independent learning.

As we look to the future of the college with changes in pedagogies already taking place, we believe it is important to recognize that individualized study and group study have much in common, and issues related to each can inform one another. There is creative tension between the two models of learning, though we do not see these modes at odds with each other; rather we view them as on a continuum. While there may be more room for self-direction in an individualized study, it is also true that self-directed learning can take place a group setting. At the core, dialogue occurs in both settings – in one place mostly between mentor and student, in the other place among students and between students and mentor/instructor.

We will continue to listen to and learn from our students about their worlds, picking up construction vocabulary, learning the ins and outs of what it means to be a trade union apprentice. We will continue to encounter challenges to our dreams for our students, as well as our dreams for a more equitable society. As we go about our work, we will keep in mind that many of our students don't identify themselves as writers or readers; however, we will aim to expand their identity kits to include such things as learners, readers, and yes, perhaps, even writers.

All of this is to say: Literacy is an act as much as it is a theory; as we wrote at the start of this chapter, literacy is also identity. As we help our students to expand their literacies, we also help them to expand their identities and to develop new ways of interacting with the world around them – whether it is written, read, observed or worked.

## NOTES

[1] As we set out to write about our students' "working-class background," we discovered that how we define working class – and, by extension, how we might (or might not) define our students as working class – is complicated, multidimensional and downright frustrating. Everything we read claimed some combination of economics, education and access to education as contributors to this definition. Other scholars posited that many people who do not fit those descriptors still consider themselves working class and that, perhaps, it is a sociocultural phenomenon – i.e., that those of us who do not meet the economic and education criteria to "count" as working class but still connect with that identity do so because of a historical context tied to our family or immediate communities.

A third of our students already hold two or four-year college degrees; the other two-thirds have completed some college or only high school. Economically, our student population is just as diverse – unless, of course, we consider only their current salaries as apprentices, in which case all of our students in the trade union programs could be considered "working class." However, we are weary of using such taxonomies because they do not accurately represent who our students are. Additionally, attempting to fit our students into a neatly packaged class box seems to create the very same walls, boundaries, road blocks, chasms (and whatever other metaphors one might choose to invoke) we want to avoid. For the purpose of this chapter, we choose not to set our discussion in the context of any particular theory of class, nor to assign our students to any social, economic or socioeconomic group. To us they are "our students" – electrical and plumber apprentices.

[2] Once in their second year of college study, students with a minimum GPA of 3.0 may opt to "double up" and take two college courses per semester. Those who do this complete the college portion of their apprenticeship early, but cannot earn their degree until they have successfully completed their electrical theory courses.

[3] These courses are non-sequential, and students are typically placed in their section randomly.

[4] When we say "emotionally, intellectually and physically," we mean exactly that. We are in no way implying that our students are lazy; quite simply they are very often literally physically tired, no different than any of us might feel after a grueling day of long meetings and consultations. The thought of more work (mental or physical) is itself exhausting and a burden.

[5] Take for instance the word "shanty," which sounds like an old-fashioned run-down cottage, but is in fact the job site locale for their union meetings and headquarters.

[6] Google "union thugs" to find a variety of right-wing blogs and articles about "union thugs."

7   Read *The Mind at Work: Valuing the Intelligence of the American Worker* by Mike Rose (2004) for more on this.
8   Mongo is the scrap metal that can be sold for cash; many companies let apprentices collect the mongo from the job site to earn a bit of extra money to compensate for their low wages.
9   Some strong pieces include Anyon's (1980) "Social Class and the Hidden Curriculum of Work"; Finn's (1999) *Literacy with an Attitude*; Ryden's (2005) "Conflicted Literacy: Frederick Douglass's Critical Model"; Smitherman's (2001) *Talkin' that Talk*; and Tonouchi's (2004) "Da State of Pidgin Address1."
10  The idea here is that there is meaning and value to sounds and words, but part of that meaning comes from the context in which those words and sounds are experienced and acquired (in the unconscious way that Gee [2001] discusses).
11  Online issues of *Labor Writes* can be accessed at http://www.esc.edu/news/magazines-journal/labor-writes/

## REFERENCES

Anyon, J. (1980). Social class and the hidden curriculum of work. *Journal of Education, 162*(1), 67–92.
Denny, H. C. (2010). *Facing the center: Toward an identity politics of one-to-one mentoring*. Logan, UT: Utah State University Press.
Finn, P. J. (1999). *Literacy with an attitude*. Albany, NY: State University of New York Press.
Fraser, R., & Mavrogiannis, S. (2012, April). *The importance of shootin' the shit and other lessons from a non-traditional writing center*. Roundtable discussion at the Northeast Writing Centers Association (NEWCA) 2012 Conference, Queens, NY.
Freire, P. (1998). *Teachers as cultural workers: Letters to those who dare teach* (D. Macedo, D. Koike, & A. Oliveira, Trans.). Boulder, CO: Westview Press.
Gee, J. P. (2001). Literacy, discourse, and linguistics: Introduction *and* what is literacy. In E. Cushman, E. R. Kintgen, B. M. Kroll, & M. Rose (Eds.), *Literacy: A critical sourcebook* (pp. 525–544). Boston, MA: Bedford/St. Martins.
Hull, G. (2001). Hearing other voices: A critical assessment of popular views on literacy and work. In E. Cushman, E. R. Kintgen, B. M. Kroll, & M. Rose (Eds.), *Literacy: A critical sourcebook* (pp. 660–683). Boston, MA: Bedford/St. Martins.
Lytle, S. L. (2001). Living literacy: Rethinking development in adulthood. In E. Cushman, E. R. Kintgen, B. M. Kroll, & M. Rose (Eds.), *Literacy: A critical sourcebook* (pp. 376–401). Boston, MA: Bedford/St. Martins.
NCTE (National Council of Teachers of English). (2008). *NCTE position statement: Resolution on the students' right to their own language*. Retrieved from www.ncte.org/positions/statements/righttoownlanguage
Rose, M. (2004). *The mind at work: Valuing the intelligence of the American worker*. New York, NY: Penguin.
Ryden, W. (2005). Conflicted literacy: Frederick Douglass's critical model. *Journal of Basic Writing (CUNY), 24*(1), 4–23.
Smitherman, G. (2001). *Talkin' that talk: Language, culture and education in African America*. New York, NY: Routledge.
SUNY Empire State College. (n.d.). *Welcome to the Van Arsdale center*. Retrieved from http://www.esc.edu/labor-studies-center/message-from-the-dean/message-from-the-dean.html
Tonouchi, L. A. (2004). Da state of pidgin address1. *College English, 67*(1), 75–82. Retrieved from http://search.proquest.com/docview/236963662?accountid=8067
Tortora, J. (2012, July 31). Hugs from union "thugs" [Web log post]. Retrieved from http://www.aflcio.org/Blog/In-The-States/Hugs-from-Union-Thugs

SEANA LOGSDON AND LINDA GUYETTE

# 9. A PROGRESSIVE INSTITUTION TAKES ON ACADEMIC SUPPORT, 21ST CENTURY STYLE

INTRODUCTION

Each semester, faculty and academic professionals in colleges and universities across the country encounter students who require academic support to be successful in their studies. These students oftentimes come reluctantly to that support. Typically, the student is singled out through various placement exams, or through diagnostic testing, or, after the semester is underway and the course instructor recognizes a problem with the student's performance. The student is then either diverted into remedial courses or encouraged – and in some cases required – to engage in academic support provided by the college or university's tutoring center. However, they arrive, or in whatever manner they engage, college students are increasingly finding themselves consigned to some type of academic support.

This trend has not gone without notice, and in May of 2012, the State University of New York formed a SUNY Remediation Task Force "to determine how a collaborative effort between SUNY and K-12 school districts across New York can best alleviate the need for remedial education at the college level" (SUNY, 2012). The SUNY system is not alone in its attention to this issue. Recent data collected across Connecticut's 12 community colleges, for example, show that approximately 70 percent of students enroll in at least one remedial course during their first year of college (Fain, 2012a, para. 3). And more than 50 percent of students entering Maine's community college system place into at least one remedial course (Lawrence, 2012). Nationally, 40 percent of all students entering college now require some kind of remedial course work, and 60 percent of students enrolling in community colleges require remediation (Complete College America, n.d.). Further, very recent data suggest that almost four out of 10 students who enroll in remedial course work fail to complete those remedial courses (Mangan, 2014, para. 1). These numbers are staggering, and voices in support of, and in opposition to, remedial, or developmental, education have begun to weigh in. The State University at San Marcos, Texas, for example, in response to this trend, has recently launched Ph.D. and Ed.D. programs to prepare the Developmental Education scholar and practitioner. On the other side of the issue are such groups as Complete College America, who argue that remediation in its current form is not effective and should be abolished. Indeed, there is data to support both sides of this provocative issue, depending on who's presenting it. Progressive institutions like Empire State College (ESC), that serve, in large part, the nontraditional student, face the same academic support challenges as traditional institutions and community colleges across the country. And those challenges are only growing, as adult learners increasingly decide to return to college to earn a degree.

According to the National Center for Educational Statistics (NCES), adult learners make up 39 percent of the undergraduate population in the U.S. (Plageman, 2011, para 1). The challenge of how best to serve our nontraditional students who need academic support is the focus of this chapter. While specific data on this special, but growing, group is hard to find, we know that our adult learners return to college after having been away from an academic setting, in most cases, for a number of years. Many of our adult learners arrive eager to earn the degree, but are ill equipped with the skills or the time that it takes to be successful in their course work. For a progressive institution like Empire State College with a nearly open admissions policy, the challenge has been to find ways to meet the diverse, and growing, needs of the nontraditional student, and to remain true to the college's mission of valuing and privileging individualized, self-directed learning that occurs in collaboration with a faculty mentor. Moreover, when the various modes of study for which the college is known are juxtaposed against the characteristics of its student population, a tension results that must be acknowledged.

Unlike a traditional setting where students meet with a faculty member two to three times a week with prescribed topics and classroom activities, nontraditional students in an independent learning model meet with faculty on a far less frequent basis. In many cases, there is a two to three-week period between meetings. While online courses at ESC may be more structured, often the same space exists between deadlines. Learning activities such as research, reading, paper development, interviews, applied learning, etc. are developed collaboratively with a faculty member and are designed to meet the student's learning goals. While there is guidance in the identification of these activities, the student is expected to work independently to develop a schedule and process for completing the activities. Formative evaluation, which might be rendered via e-mail or a phone conversation, often occurs every few weeks versus every few days. This model, praised for its attention to individualization and independence is refreshing for many nontraditional learners. It allows these students much more control over their own learning and the ability to move at a pace that best suits them.

However, the underlying assumption in this model is that all learners are equipped with the skills to operate independently. For example, a student who is asked to research a topic and write an eight to ten page paper needs to be able to develop a research question, adopt a research strategy that includes identifying and navigating appropriate research databases, draw upon higher order critical thinking skills to evaluate the research for its appropriateness to the topic, develop an organizational framework based on the research findings, integrate sources into the paper, and ultimately present a successful research project. Throughout the process, the student is assumed to have skills in academic research, critical thinking, college-level reading, college-level writing, and time management. Yet, as the statistics indicate, many students arrive with academic skills that suggest a need for remediation. And while much of the available data on remediation is largely focused on the community college learner, who may or may not be required to engage in a research project, these statistics nonetheless apply here at ESC. Indeed, nontraditional learners who make their way to community colleges are, in many cases, the same learners that progressive, four-year institutions like SUNY Empire State College serve. In other words, though most of the available data on college readiness focus on the community college learner, that learner is, in many cases, the very learner that nontraditional four-year institutions like ESC are engaged in serving. And those students who seek the bachelor's degree will be required to demonstrate competency in these higher order skills. Thus we increasingly find that one of the College's central goals – of supporting independent learning – is at odds with the very learner we serve: the learner who often arrives underprepared in reading, writing or math skills; the learner who comes with the challenge of learning disabilities; the learner burdened by the competing demands of career and child or elder care.

How then does an institution address these challenges while continuing to value self-directed learning that relies on the student's independence in his or her study? How does an institution like ESC take on academic support initiatives that support that student's learning and do not detract from the specialized mentoring relationship that happens here? How and where, when we have such a diverse group of learners in a distributed college environment, do we situate the learning, demonstrate the learning, and provide support for multiple modes of learning in relation to specified academic standards?

This chapter seeks to explore the inherent tensions and challenges of serving underprepared, nontraditional students and to answer these questions by examining the evolution and practice of an academic support initiative that removes many of the traditional barriers that students in other colleges and universities face. By bringing academic support to the student, to the syllabus and to the student's learning experience, this initiative, which we call Embedded Academic Support, takes on a unique form here at Empire State College, as it promotes collaboration between faculty and the academic support professional, can be applied across academic disciplines, and can be used to support various learners and various learning styles.

## A NEW FORMAL ACADEMIC SUPPORT ROLE

According to the most recent data, Empire State College serves just over 19,000 learners at 35 locations across New York state, online, and at eight international locations around the world. The average age of students is reported as 36, although academic support professionals have worked with students ranging from age 18 to 75. A little less than two-thirds of the students of the students are female. Nearly 35 percent of students identify as being minority or multi-racial status (SUNY Empire State College, 2014–2015).

While age, race and gender may provide a snapshot of the student population, these factors alone do not describe an adult or nontraditional learner. Choy (2002) defines a nontraditional learner as one who has any of the following characteristics: delayed enrollment in postsecondary education; part-time attendance; financial independence from parents; full-time work; having dependents other than a spouse; being a single parent having no high school diploma or GED. In most cases, the Empire State College student meets one or more of those criteria. According to recent data, part-time enrollment at Empire State College was approximately 60 percent of total enrollment. Financial aid grants were awarded to 20,725 students and 11,054 received loans suggesting both need and financial independence (SUNY Empire State College, 2014–2015). Marital and dependent status is more difficult to capture, and the only data collection is through financial aid applications, which record only those who choose to apply for aid. Empire State College's current admissions requirement mandates that students provide evidence of a completed high school diploma or GED. However, what is perhaps more interesting is the low number of students who arrive at Empire as first- time freshmen, defined as having no prior higher education experience. In 2014–15, first-time freshmen were only 1 percent of the ESC population, suggesting that most students may have previously attempted, and in some cases completed, some form of higher education (Student Achievement Measure, n.d.).

Yet, still, these characteristics do not fully describe the Empire State College learner. For a more apt description, one must turn to the faculty and staff who work with the students each day. Asked to describe the "typical learner" at Empire, the most likely response is "it depends." Each learner at the college is viewed as an individual with his or her own unique needs, circumstances and goals. A single parent with a modest income and two children, for example, may have limited academic skills, but may also have a substantive support network that will allow her to persist in her studies and eventually earn her degree. Another student may have strong academic skills, but no support network to step in when a child or elderly parent becomes ill, forcing the priorities of that adult learner to shift away from academic study, resulting in abandoned coursework. Yet another example might include a successful CEO who returns to college to complete a lifelong goal of earning a degree, but who is unfamiliar with academic writing. A refresher writing study is recommended but due to her perceived status – she is after all the head of her company – she chooses not to enroll in the writing study and becomes frustrated when her paper is returned with feedback on how to improve her writing skills. Meanwhile, in the next office, a student is working closely with his mentor. He simply wants to learn, and knows his writing skills need development. He participates in every academic support opportunity, meets regularly with his mentor and actively seeks out anything he can do to improve his ability to succeed in college. And, finally, there is the student who arrives at Empire, goal-driven, academically strong and with a solid support network. This student seeks an independent path, and the mentor acts as a guide, fostering opportunities for the student to independently demonstrate his learning.

All of these scenarios and more are possible at Empire State College. Although it is tempting to dismiss these scenarios as anecdotal, they are reflective of the core value of the College – that each learner deserves to be viewed as an individual, in terms of both needs and goals.

This core value of prioritizing the focus on the individual, central to Empire's mission, is admirable. Yet, support of this model has required significant resources. The student's mentor, described in previous chapters in this volume, is central to a student's experience and success. But despite the significance of the student-mentor relationship, it is tremendously challenging, and perhaps not even possible, for one person to meet all of the academic needs of each student. Therefore, in 2007, the College made a significant change to its staffing model and added seven Directors of Academic Support (DAS) to its ranks of professional employees. Located at each of the major centers in New York state, including the Center for Distance Learning (CDL), each Director was tasked with developing both local and statewide academic programming services to support the growing student needs at the college.

In a traditional college or university, this undertaking would be substantial, but there would be models to emulate. National organizations such as the College Reading and Learning Association (CRLA), the National Association of Developmental Education (NADE), and the National Tutoring Association (NTA) among others have large networks and large data banks of "best practices" when establishing a learning center and related programming. While the requisite challenges of establishing any new department would exist, there would also be a strong data set to which one could refer in arguing for support, in terms of both funding and programming format. At Empire State College, however, several unique conditions challenged this approach.

At many campus-based universities, there is a central learning center which provides traditional tutoring in core academic subjects. Tutoring may take on many forms such as individual, peer or group, but the learning center itself has a visible presence on campus. Increasingly, some tutoring has been integrated into specific academic departments, particularly those areas defined as high-risk. Again the services are campus-based with an identifiable presence, whether it be through signage, web-presence or printed materials. As simple as it sounds, the absence of a central location has created significant challenges to developing academic support initiatives at Empire State College. While separate regional locations shared the College's mission, policies and commitment to independent learning, each center had developed its own culture and interpretation of those policies. So, while the core practice might be the same – students designing their academic programs, pursuing studies and completing a degree – the process of how they did so was at times quite different among the various locations. Given the College's model of individual and independent learning, the diversity of approaches is not all that surprising. But for developing academic support initiatives, it created some challenges.

The first challenge was establishing the DAS role in each region. The answer seemed simple enough: support students with their academic development to provide them with the best opportunity for success. But how? While it was a collegewide initiative to hire a cohort of seven Directors of Academic Support, each regional center was responsible for hiring its own DAS, and that DAS reported to the dean at each individual center. The first cohort of DAS was comprised of six women and one man, with academic qualifications that ranged from Ph.D.s and an Ed.D. to an M.S., an M.A. and an MFA. Some members of the cohort had extensive experience in teaching, particularly in the areas of reading and writing, and some had more administrative experience, even at the dean's level. Hired as professional employees with concurrent academic rank, the position was defined as nonteaching faculty, yet the academic rank and responsibilities suggested some expectation of mentoring (and teaching) students. While administrative and instructional roles are frequently integrated in the academic support field, such an integration was not a typical practice at ESC, and was met with varying response.

As the first cohort of DAS began their positions, some were met with the suspicion that this new role would undermine, or usurp, the important student-mentor relationship. Others were met with sighs of relief that finally there was someone to deal with all of the "problem students." Still other DAS were welcomed as equal voices and immediately integrated into committee structures and academic decision-making roles. It was a delicate balancing act first to learn the culture of each center and then to gauge how quickly, or in some cases how slowly, to proceed. Quite simply, time was required to establish relationships and build trust with faculty and staff colleagues before a voice and role for academic support could be developed.

The first DAS cohort also faced the internal difficulty of creating good will and trust among members of the cohort, all the while working at a distance. Yet this group found a way to work closely and collaboratively, through bi-weekly conference calls and taking advantage of every opportunity to meet together, face-to-face. It might also be argued that the diversity of professional backgrounds and interests of each DAS actually contributed to the climate of good will and the sharing of resources. For example, expertise that one DAS might be lacking to respond to a particular need at her center could easily be requested of a fellow DAS at another center, sometimes hundreds of miles away.

However, the road to building collegewide academic support services was not entirely a smooth one. Initial efforts were less successful not just because of some of the challenges listed above, but also because each DAS had both a local direct reporting relationship with a regional dean and a dotted line reporting relationship with the collegewide Office of Academic Support. This model frequently resulted in competing priorities, with collegewide directives often conflicting with regional centers' priorities. It was clear that a change in the leadership model was necessary to realize the full-potential the college's investment in academic support. Therefore, in 2009, the Collegewide Office of Academic Support was replaced with a self-governing model whereby co-conveners were elected from the cohort. With this model, DAS collaborated to leverage the resources within the group, set collegewide priorities and identify implementation plans that accounted for regional differences. This shift in the leadership model created a sense of shared ownership and the group was able to successfully develop and implement a number of academic support initiatives, not least of which is the Embedded Academic Support initiative.

Assessing student need was yet another challenge. The individualized nature of study, combined with the vastly different environments of the regional centers, created varied learning environments across the state. For example, some regional centers were in largely metropolitan centers, others were in wealthy suburban areas and yet others were in extremely rural communities. And CDL presented an additional challenge as its environment was entirely online. Why does this variation matter? Depending on a given location, the majority of students may have graduated from underserved urban districts, while in another area the majority may have come from highly funded, high performing school districts. In one location, a single community college may be the only other higher education institution, while in another location, 12 colleges, including multiple community colleges, may be within an hour's drive. While one could argue that every college has a diversity of learners, the range of educational preparedness across the geographic regions was significant and at times meant that the emphasis for meeting the needs of a majority of learners varied greatly from one site to another. In fact, in some cases, these differences created competing demands for resources and focus between locations.

Because Empire State College students are all commuters, the frequency and availability of transportation cannot be ignored. Transportation has an impact on access, and opportunities for on-site academic support programming may be limited, at best. For urban students, it can mean hours on public transportation. For more rural students, it can require a significant investment in gas and a reliable vehicle. For those students who need additional support, added transportation requirements can often be an impediment to their success. These challenges are especially relevant for those students who continue to work while attending college. In addition, the high number of students who qualify for grant-funded aid suggests limited financial resources for many students. Lastly, in addition to the regional centers, CDL also had a unique set of challenges. While transportation issues may not affect these students, access to and familiarity with technology is a significant variable when assessing student need.

Therefore, unlike traditional academic support models where needs assessment may be broken down by cohort or by departmental boundaries, needs assessment at Empire State College had to be considered by geographic area. Student profiles, educational opportunity and access, and faculty and staff resources all needed to be evaluated locally before any college wide discussions could begin. The results – not surprisingly – suggested that to be successful, academic support needed to be nimble to adjust for major variations in educational preparedness, geographic locations, and students' resource and financial limitations. The development of programs and services has needed to have variations both in levels and points of access in order to be replicable across the state.

The next significant challenge – limited budget support – is perhaps not unique to Empire State College. While the College made an important financial investment in hiring its Directors of Academic Support, funding for additional programming was virtually nonexistent. Despite hopes for grant funding to expand the initiative, Empire State College's unique distributed learning model did not fit the requirements for many traditional funding streams, such as a Title III Student Support Services Grant. While some initial funds were allotted for professional development, program funding was restricted to an online tutorial service that served a small segment of the college's population. In the beginning, most Directors were asked to provide direct service while also developing local and statewide resources. In more recent years, minimal funding has been released for Learning Coaches, who provide direct tutoring service. However, these resources are very small in comparison to student need and demand. Peer tutoring programs are on the rise with established programs at two of the centers, but even those programs do not address the more complex needs of students who may be woefully underprepared, restricted in their ability to attend additional sessions, and insecure about their capabilities within their studies.

Each of these challenges – uncertainty about the role of academic support in a mentor-student learning model; differing educational preparedness of students; the geographic variable; and limited resources in terms of both finances and time – presented an environment which challenged the traditional role of academic support. And, one more important dynamic, although perhaps not unique to Empire, also emerged. There is often a variation among faculty regarding how to measure progression of student learning – especially in introductory level courses. For some faculty, a student's demonstration of learning is measured primarily by "content knowledge" regardless of how that information is presented. For example, if a student can describe his or her learning through oral discourse, then the ability to show this same content knowledge with a written document may be less important, especially early in a student's time with the college. Indeed, how far the student has progressed in her learning, or how facile she is in discussing the content of the course, has often mattered more to faculty than if that student has, for example, properly cited her sources and demonstrated the use of correct grammar and punctuation. For other faculty, demonstration of learning must include not only content knowledge, but also college-level academic skills, particularly in the area of writing. In this case, the ability to follow traditional conventions of college-level papers and the content of the paper may be given equal weight in assessment; in some cases, a poorly written paper may negate the value of any demonstrated content knowledge. The reasons for these varying perspectives are numerous and not the focus of this chapter, but the tensions related to this difference have existed and created yet another dimension that has had to be accounted for within academic support initiatives.

# A PROGRESSIVE INSTITUTION TAKES ON ACADEMIC SUPPORT, 21ST CENTURY STYLE

## RETHINKING THE ROLE OF REMEDIATION

Given the unique learners and the unique conditions outlined in this chapter, the Directors of Academic Support have explored some of the traditional approaches to serving the underprepared or nontraditional learner, including, for example, mandating that students sit for placement testing in writing and, in some cases, mathematics, and advising poor performing students to take remedial writing courses. This practice is typical in most postsecondary institutions. In fact, in 2011, the National Assessment Governing Board reported that in a survey of 1560 postsecondary institutions, 71 percent reported using some mathematics test and 53 percent reported using some reading test in evaluating student need for remediation in those two subject domains. The majority of postsecondary education institutions use student performance on tests in determining entering students' need for remedial courses in mathematics and reading (Fields & Parsad, 2011). However, the DAS were concerned about this practice, and placement tests continue to be challenged in terms of their accuracy and efficacy in predicting student success. In a recent study by the Community College Research Center, high school grades were found to be much better predictors of student success than placement tests. "Placement tests are associated with severe error rates; three out of every ten test takers is either assigned to developmental education, despite being predicted to get at least a B in college-level English, or assigned to college-level English, despite being predicted to fail the course. Again, these results are in stark contrast with those of high school GPA, which yields error rates half as big" (Belfield & Crosta, 2012, p. 39). Yet not only placement tests may be problematic; using high school records as a predictor of success has been problematic at Empire State College as well. Given that the average age of the Empire State College student is 36 and that the student is likely to have had some previous college experience, high school records were both distant and often less relevant as they were eclipsed by experience at other postsecondary institutions. Thus, an alternative to traditional placement testing needed to be explored.

In addition to the questions surrounding placement testing, the DAS uncovered data suggesting that the effectiveness of developmental education is unclear. Increasingly, remediation is being questioned by practitioners and theorists in the field. It's unclear if developmental courses improve student outcomes, and some longitudinal studies suggest that students who take traditional pre-college level courses are unlikely to complete college. In reviewing "Achieving the Dream" (a nongovernmental reform movement focused on community college student success), Bailey (2009) noted less than one-quarter of community college students who enroll in developmental education complete a degree or certificate within eight years of enrollment in college (p. 5).

Much of the literature around development education has argued that these outcomes can be explained as a result of poor preparation. But another way to analyze what's contributing to the failure of under-prepared students in developmental courses is to consider the typical conditions in the approach. Oftentimes the underprepared student is segregated from the mainstream student population and shuffled into noncredit-bearing studies that teach skills development in isolation from content-rich, credit-bearing courses. This approach sets up a number of barriers to success, starting first with the isolation of these students from other "good" and/or "smart" students, suggesting to them from the outset that they are not "college material." This approach is additionally problematic because we then leave it up to the under-prepared student to determine how to transfer the knowledge and skills learned in isolation to content rich, credit-bearing courses in subsequent semesters. And lastly, the skills addressed in many of these developmental courses are often focused on the most basic level and not necessarily on the understanding and skill needed for college and for readiness to undertake independent application. According to research by Grubb et al. (2011) developmental courses typically involve "drill and practice … on small sub-skills … that most students have been taught many times before, in decontextualized ways that fail to clarify to students the reasons for or the importance of these sub-skills" (pp. 20–21).

In a review of the literature, the DAS began to question if traditional remediation really contributes to successful degree completion or if, in fact, it might impede it. The one-size-fits-all approach to learning has never worked at an institution like Empire State College, and that fact has certainly been applicable to academic support. The models that the directors developed had to be flexible and individualized, both in terms of their delivery mode – online, face-to-face, peer tutors, professional learning coaches – and in terms of the studies they enhanced. Academic support had to be integrated into introductory and advanced level studies, across all academic disciplines, and in courses that students engaged in through independent study, and traditional classroom settings, as well as through the Center for Distance Learning. In addition, academic support models had to recognize that not all faculty prioritized academic skills development as part of the progression of student learning. Finally, academic support models also needed to support underprepared students in a largely unstructured environment.

Thus, a new model of academic support emerged and was supported by three important tenets. First, academic support would be provided in *partnership* with the student and faculty member. Second, the support would be *embedded* in, not added on to, existing learning experiences in a variety of courses and modes of study. Lastly, the embedded support would make use of existing resources because there was no expectation that those resources would increase. From these tenets, the concept of "Embedded Academic Support," which included collaboration with faculty to integrate academic support and skill building directly into their credit-bearing courses, was developed.

## EMBEDDED ACADEMIC SUPPORT

Academic Support can and should take many forms. It can include requiring students to make appointments at a tutoring center or, at Empire State College, with a learning coach. It can include having the student work with a peer tutor, which the literature might represent as Supplemental Instruction. It can also take the form of required attendance in academic support workshops or labs, which in some cases is referred to as the "split credit model," most often seen in science courses that require a linked, credit-bearing lab. And sometimes it can include requiring students to enroll in a noncredit course concurrent with the credit-bearing one, an approach sometimes referred to in the literature as the "Co-requisite Course Model" (Goudas & Boylan, 2012).

While some may argue that these elements exist at many institutions, the Empire State College approach is an *embedded* academic support model that includes all of the above, an initiative that has striven to be as diverse in its approach as the students and courses it supports. Instead of choosing one or two approaches and applying them broadly to multiple programs or departments, this model has allowed the faculty mentor, the academic support professional, and in some cases the student to select a model which best fits the individual learner.

Certainly there were challenges at first, most of which we detailed earlier in this chapter. Indeed, much of the early work of the DAS was centered around community building within the DAS group, and trust building with faculty mentors at the regional centers. The trust that the directors worked to build with faculty then needed to be deepened and expanded. True embedded academic support requires full integration of academic support into the content of the credit-bearing study. This meant that the directors had to work collaboratively with individual faculty as they designed their studies and drafted their learning contracts. Collaboration of this kind requires trust, and the investment of time at the beginning of the project. The first step was in identifying willing faculty partners, instead of studies, as good opportunities for embedded support. As the directors later discovered, employing the embedded support model in upper- and lower division courses worked for all learners at all levels across varied academic disciplines. But the earliest goal was in finding willing faculty with whom to collaborate.

For some directors, those partners were easily identified and persuaded to participate in the pilot. Other directors had to work more diligently to find faculty collaborators. Still other directors faced a skeptical faculty who wanted to wait and see how this effort worked at other centers around the college before they decided to make a commitment to the project. Yet it soon became clear that embedded academic support was working. Faculty who participated in the embedded academic support pilot reported both anecdotally and through local center surveys that the experience was beneficial to the student, beneficial to the course, and beneficial to faculty. Students also reported that having academic support as part of the study itself contributed to less anxiety about completing assignments and less need for revision of those assignments. In addition, they said that it was helpful to have an additional person to turn to. As these data was shared at the local level during monthly regional center meetings and collegewide during meetings at our coordinating center in Saratoga Springs, additional faculty agreed to come on board.

Still, the Embedded Academic Support initiative did not expand as rapidly as expected. While some of the skepticism around collaboration with the DAS to embed academic support has to do with trust, it also has to do with territory. Course and curriculum development is sacred faculty domain, and the faculty mentors at Empire State College extend that authority and autonomy to include the wide range of their mentees' needs. The relationship each mentor has with his or her students is an important part of mentoring and teaching at Empire. As Zachary (2005) defines it, mentoring the adult learner "is a reciprocal and collaborative learning responsibility between two or more individuals who share mutual responsibility and accountability for helping a mentee work toward achieving clear and mutually defined learning goals" (p. 3). Indeed, the mentor essentially functions as a facilitator of knowledge acquisition, guiding the student to discover and pursue his or her own learning. Early faculty collaborators in this embedded academic support project had to struggle to make space in this close working relationship for another voice, particularly the voice of the academic support professional who had come in on a wave of change at this institution.

There were changes occurring at the highest level of the SUNY system, changes in leadership at ESC, and changes driven by technology and a push to measure student learning. Suddenly there were discussions happening center- and collegewide about academic quality, standards and assessment, and these resulted in a creative tension between valuing mentors' ability to individualize a student's study design and focusing on the progress their students were making in this new landscape of measurement of academic skills development.

In addition, faculty were seeing their students struggle with many of the challenges outlined earlier. Their students had always had the competing demands of home and career, and the challenges of financing their education, but increasingly it became clear that students were also struggling with the academic demands of pursuing a college degree. Faculty wondered how they could function as a facilitator of learning in their field when many of the student's basic skills were lacking or missing altogether. Faculty lamented the time lost to addressing those skills, time that some felt could be more productively spent on teaching content and developing new studies.

On the other side of the equation was the student who had decided to return to college during a period of profound change in higher education in general, and specifically at ESC. Students had to make choices about the different ways to engage in learning – guided independent study; face-to-face study groups; and online learning, for example – and they had to engage an institutional context that was significantly driven by new academic technologies. Degree programs were planned online; supplemental materials, if not entire courses, were found online; there was no brick and mortar library, instead one located on the web; and the Bursar and Registrar were all online. Attitudes towards teaching and learning were changing, and technology was changing how and when our students engaged in their studies and with their mentor. Both student and mentor, even in the regional centers, were feeling a fundamental shift in how they interacted. If ever there was an opportunity to try something new, it was now.

Yet before the directors could try an embedded academic support approach, there was another valued practice at Empire State College to address, and that was the reluctance to make things mandatory or required of students. So much of the learning that happens at ESC is based on the primary tenet of adult learning theory – that adult learners are internally motivated and self-directed (Knowles, 1970, p. 10). However, what the early effort of this embedded support initiative showed was that most students did not engage in the embedded learning opportunities unless those activities were written into their learning contracts as *required* learning activities. While the reasons for student reluctance could well be explained by some of the competing demands for their time, and the fact that the student often had to make a choice between something pressing at home or at the office and something that was presented as optional in their courses, still early efforts showed that across the regional centers most students chose not to participate. This reluctance extended to courses across the disciplines at both the introductory and advanced levels. And that did not change until the directors and faculty changed their approach to how those learning opportunities were presented to students. Once again, a fundamental shift was occurring. Learning contracts in which academic support had been embedded now outlined not only the required texts, and the required reading and writing assignments, but also the required participation in specified learning activities that included academic support programming.

Part of the process of implementing the embedded academic support pilot was to think about how to assess it. A critical part of that assessment was for the academic support professional and the faculty partner to meet at the end of the term. This meeting included a discussion about what worked and what needed to be changed, and it provided an opportunity for the academic support professional to review examples of student work. In fact, during one pilot, a study in which academic support had been embedded required the student to submit her completed assignment – in this case an annotated bibliography – to the academic support professional for grading. The score was calculated based on a rubric provided by the faculty member. That score was then forwarded to the faculty member to be included in the calculation of the student's final grade. Each of the directors who participated in the early pilot relied on feedback from faculty on student performance, and feedback from students who had engaged in the support activities. As the pilot moved into the implementation phase, students and faculty collaborators completed an evaluation form developed by the DAS.

And thus the embedded academic support initiative took hold at several regional centers. In the western part of the state, for example, in locations that served a mix between urban and rural areas, embedded academic support was piloted in a number of different ways. First it took on the form of a split course model which is most closely connected with the academic support concept of "supplemental instruction." Traditionally, supplemental instruction employs students who have previously completed a course to lead study sessions where students who are currently taking the course "compare notes, discuss readings, develop organizational tools, and predict test items. Students learn how to integrate course content and study skills while working together" (UMKC International Center for Supplemental Instruction, n.d., What is Supplemental Instruction section, para. 1). The goal of supplemental instruction is most often better test preparation in high challenge courses. While tests are rarely used at Empire State College, the concept of developing or reinforcing other academic skills through supplemental sessions seemed promising.

This was attempted in two ways. At the Genesee Valley Center, a traditional four-credit statistics study was replaced with a faculty member mentoring three credits and a learning coach mentoring a one credit connected lab. Together, the faculty member and the learning coach identified the academic skills necessary to be successful in the statistics study. They each provided content, but within the lab, necessary academic skills development was either introduced or reinforced. Students who arrived with skill deficits and who may have struggled with the study were given more intensive support and, as a result, experienced success in the course. Those students who did not need remedial assistance were given opportunities to work with the mentor on more advanced concepts within the study during the lab time.

At the nearby Central New York Center, the DAS and a faculty member also partnered to work together on a statistics study. In their model, the students completed the traditional study, but the DAS also attended the study meetings and then held weekly recitation sessions where the learning was reinforced through additional explanations and practice models. In this model, the recitation sessions were not mandatory for all, but there was an expectation that if assistance was needed, the student would utilize this element of the study. While it is still early, initial indicators suggest a sharp increase in the completion rate for statistics studies in both these models.

The Hudson Valley Center, which is located just north of New York City and serves a diverse population, both racially and economically, took a different approach. Using the web-based Elluminate platform, the faculty and DAS embedded an online workshop that addressed information literacy and instruction on how to prepare the annotated bibliography. The results proved immediately positive. Students were required to participate in one of two scheduled online workshops that lasted 90 minutes. One workshop was scheduled for the noon hour on one day, and the next workshop was scheduled in the evening on a different day. Students chose the time that best met their work and family needs. During the online workshop, students were "taken" to the college's online library and shown how to find appropriate scholarly material to inform their research and to be included in the annotated bibliography. After that, students looked at sample annotated bibliographies on the OWL at Purdue and the Diana Hacker websites. The faculty partner reported a dramatic improvement in the quality of the completed assignments from those students who participated in the workshop. This immediately translated into less time that the faculty member had to spend evaluating, and correcting, the annotated bibliography assignment. Equally important was that students reported satisfaction with the workshop experience and an appreciation for being led through the process and given examples of the annotated bibliography to model. Students also reported satisfaction with having an extra person to go to for questions and additional support. One might argue as well that the positive experience that students reported with embedded academic support also has an impact on retention, but it is too early in the implementation phase to make that claim.

Because early efforts were so successful at the Hudson Valley Center, additional faculty partners were easily recruited and academic support efforts were expanded to include embedded workshops in a range of introductory and advanced level studies, including workshops on academic writing, APA and MLA citation styles, time management, developing the dual entry journal, writing the research paper and writing article abstracts. In this model, the faculty member worked in partnership with the Director of Academic Support to assess the appropriate workshop level for students in the study. In addition, the Center set up a center-wide Turnitin.com account for student use as a way for students to educate themselves about plagiarism and how to avoid it. Roughly half of the faculty at the Center now require students to use the Turnitin account, and currently most of the full-time faculty include some form of embedded academic support in their credit bearing studies.

Other Empire State College locations have also successfully integrated academic support into their studies. And they have taken slightly different approaches. In some study groups, a writing coach was involved from the start, which meant that students had ready access to support with their writing. The coach was also there to help scaffold skills as the students progressed through the term and took on more challenging assignments. Individual help was also provided as the need arose, while mini-workshops were created if more than one student had similar needs. This model was also used in online content studies where peer tutors were accessible through a link in the online study space. Other studies required mandatory participation in workshops held outside of regularly scheduled classroom time. Those workshops were offered as in-person activities, or via the new web-based platform, Collaborate. Still other studies required the use of Smarthinking, an online tutoring service to which the college subscribes; or the use of Turnitin.com.

What all of these studies had in common is that the support activities were embedded into the content of the study and were represented in the learning contract as required learning activities. Also important to remember is that embedded academic support allowed for assistance to the student at the time that it was needed and the student was ready to work on the new (or forgotten) skill. The literature supports this approach, commonly referred to as "just in time tutoring," as an effective way to enhance student learning (Fain, 2012b). This approach directly addressed student concerns about that assistance being an "extra" requirement, as it had immediate relevance to their success in the study.

When serving a diverse adult learner population, as Empire State College does, it is important to consider not only the obstacles referred to earlier in this chapter, but also the physical barriers that often impede access to academic support. At many colleges and universities, the tutoring center is located in a building separate from the one in which the students take their courses. This means that students must seek out and locate the space, navigate a directory of personnel different from those with whom they have previously engaged, and, perhaps most importantly, present himself as students "in need." This could be particularly problematic, for example, for the affronted CEO used as an example earlier in this chapter. In fact, while Empire State College serves a number of high level professionals who have been successful in their careers and whose pursuit of a degree is driven entirely through internal motivation, the College also serves people in middle management as well as blue collar workers and parents whose circumstance has kept them out of the work force and who may be enrolled in college out of necessity. What's important is that so many of these students have been successful in their careers and in their efforts to raise children and manage households. It is not hard to imagine what it must feel like to one of these students who has been singled out for academic support, who has been taken aside by a faculty member and told that she has a "problem." It is true that learners need to be made aware of their limitations and to address their deficiencies. But many students at ESC are successfully writing their professional reports and managing their business's bottom line, only to be told that they need help with writing or help with math once they get here. That is why supporting these learners through an embedded academic support model is so important. It removes the stigma and the barriers to getting that support. The successful CEO participates in the required workshop in academic writing, for example, or information literacy, along with everyone else with whom she is participating in the study. And as the successful CEO progresses through her degree program and into more advanced level studies, she will engage in higher level skill building with the other students, as the embedded support grows and adapts to the needs of the particular study and the learners involved.

## CONCLUSION: RE-ENVISIONING ACADEMIC SUPPORT

Academic support programming must be nimble in order to meet the demands of its incoming learners. A menu of options must be available so that support is customized to the student need. Scholarly articles, op-ed pieces and blogs are choked with voices bemoaning the failure of public schools to graduate students with the basic skills that prepare them for college. Other voices debate who in higher education – the community college or the four-year institution – is best equipped to provide remediation and support to these underprepared students, a debate that sometimes also includes English Language Learners (ELL) and students with learning disabilities. Then, of course, as this chapter has detailed, there is debate among academic support professionals about which approach best serves the record number of underprepared students arriving in our classrooms, eager to earn a degree.

And that national debate is intensified at Empire State College because its adult learner population has the added burden of the competing demands of child rearing and elder care, and, thanks in large part to the technological revolution, careers that increasingly require round the clock attention. Accompanying all these demands is the increased emphasis in higher education on measurement and assessment that has affected how a progressive institution like Empire State College serves its students.

To be truly nimble, to meet student need, and to maintain the core commitment to individualized learning, traditional academic support needs constantly to be re-envisioned. The seamless integration of academic support within a student's learning experience creates opportunities as opposed to barriers for success. Intentional partnering between students, faculty and academic support professionals is progressive simply because it removes the traditional boundaries created by separate learning centers and promotes student success as a shared goal. And, true to Empire State College's approach, these partnerships around embedded academic support are progressive because they signal a respect for all members in the learning community, regardless of academic preparedness. Each member arrives with individual expertise and experiences which are a respected and important part of the learning process, and all members of the learning community participate equally in the support services that are integrated into the curriculum.

For students, the integration of academic support within studies places the learning within the context of the course. The development of academic skills is not seen as an additional burden, but rather a central expectation for the study. Support for skills development is not an extra activity, nor does accessing resources require another call or appointment. In this integrated model, students naturally create relationships with academic support professionals, thereby eliminating the stigma typically associated with "extra help" or tutoring centers.

It could appear that this model is resource-heavy, but in fact, it is likely simply to shift where the resources are allotted. By shifting academic support into students' studies and out of stand-alone centers, assistance is provided early in a student's time at the college and across multiple learning experiences. This model also allows faculty and academic support professionals to pilot a variety of approaches. In addition, this model clarifies the role of academic support and encourages students to continually build their academic skills.

As Empire State College continues to move forward as an innovator in higher education, it is now joined by the new voice of academic support. Intellectual exchange regarding academic skills development takes place not by announcement, but rather through conversation about the design of learning experiences. As we engage in that conversation and work to broaden our embedded academic support initiative, we have begun to wonder about the impact of technology on skills building and on new opportunities for academic support. Does the technological revolution, for example, change the expected skill set of today's students? Does embedded academic support work as effectively when delivered solely in an online environment? How much more effective – if at all – is the synchronous delivery of online support over archived sessions that are individually, and perhaps even passively, engaged? How does academic support – embedded or otherwise – change to meet the needs of a busy global community that increasingly values and demands services that are "in and out"? These are just some of the questions that are emerging as students engage in studies not bound by a specific time, place or space in a physical building. In this rapidly changing environment, embedded academic support is responsive and innovative and therefore, a natural fit for Empire State College.

REFERENCES

Bailey, T. (2009, March). Challenge and opportunity: Rethinking the role and function of developmental education in community college. *New Directions for Community Colleges, 2009*(145), 11–30.
Belfield, C. R., & Crosta, P. M. (2012, February). *Predicting success in college: The importance of placement tests and high school transcripts*. Retrieved from http://ccrc.tc.columbia.edu/media/k2/attachments/predicting-success-placement-tests-transcripts.pdf
Choy, S. (2002, August). *Nontraditional undergraduates*. Retrieved from http://nces.ed.gov/pubs2002/2002012.pdf
Complete College America. (n.d.). *Transform remediation: The co-requisite course model*. Retrieved from http://www.completecollege.org/docs/CCA%20Co-Req%20Model%20-%20Transform%20Remediation%20for%20Chicago%20final%281%29.pdf
Fain, P. (2012a, April 4). How to end remediation. *Inside Higher Ed*. Retrieved from https://www.insidehighered.com/news/2012/04/04/connecticut-legislature-mulls-elimination-remedial-courses
Fain, P. (2012b, June 19). Overkill on remediation? *Inside Higher Ed*. Retrieved from https://www.insidehighered.com/news/2012/06/19/complete-college-america-declares-war-remediation
Fields, R., & Parsad, B. (2012, November). *Tests and cut scores used for student placement in postsecondary education: Fall 2011*. Retrieved from http://files.eric.ed.gov/fulltext/ED539918.pdf
Goudas, A. M., & Boylan, H. R. (2012). *Addressing flawed research in developmental education*. Retrieved from http://files.eric.ed.gov/fulltext/EJ1035669.pdf
Grubb, W. N., Boner, E., Frankel, K., Parker, L., Patterson, D., Gabriner, R., Hope, L., Schiorring, E., Smith, B., Taylor, R., Walton, I., & Wilson, S. (2011). *Working paper: Basic skills instruction in community colleges number 2: The dominance of remedial pedagogy*. Retrieved from http://edpolicyinca.org/sites/default/files/2011_WP_GRUBB_NO2.pdf
Knowles, M. S. (1970). *The modern practice of adult education: Andragogy versus pedagogy*. Chicago, IL: Follett Publishing Company.
Lawrence, J. (2012, August 6). *Remediation costing colleges and students millions*. Retrieved from http://www.educationnews.org/higher-education/remediation-costing-colleges-and-students-millions/
Mangan, K. (2014, March 17). Remedial educators contest reformers' 'rhetoric of failure.' *The Chronicle of Higher Education*.
Plageman, P. (2011). Educator, planner and advocate: Higher education for adults in the new millennium. *Adult Learning, 22*(2), 32–36.
Student Achievement Measure. (n.d.). SUNY Empire State College. Retrieved from http://studentachievementmeasure.org/participants/196264
SUNY. (2012, May 24). *SUNY forms task force on remedial education*. Retrieved from https://www.suny.edu/suny-news/press-releases/may-2012/5-24-12-remedial-task-force/suny-forms-task-force-on-remedial-education.html
SUNY Empire State College. (2014–2015). *Fact book 2014–2015*. Saratoga Springs, NY: Author.
UMKC International Center for Supplemental Instruction. (n.d.). *What is supplemental instruction?* Retrieved from http://info.umkc.edu/si/
Zachary, L. J. (2005). *Creating a mentoring culture: The organization's guide*. San Francisco, CA: Jossey-Bass.

DAVID STARR-GLASS

# 10. ON THE LEADING EDGE

*International Programs and Mentoring in Transnational Settings*

At first sight it might seem strange that the State University of New York's Empire State College (ESC) has an international presence and academic programs in countries such as the Czech Republic and Greece. It could certainly be reasoned that, as a state university, its efforts should be exclusively directed toward the local community and state residents. Of course, in an era of increased globalization and boundaryless online education, it might be expected that some ESC learners would be located throughout the world, but why should the College maintain a separate and active presence abroad?

The origins of ESC's International Programs lie in two fundamental institutional concepts. The first is that the College's mission is to provide innovative non-traditional educational opportunities for *all* learners and to explore visionary ways of engaging with these learners. This vision is a vital part of the College's *raison d'etre* and, like all powerful visions, it is constrained neither by difference, culture, nor physical location. Since its inception in 1971, the College has maintained an active international presence as part of its ongoing effort to encounter cultural diversity, to explore educational difference, and to better appreciate the needs of all learners irrespective of their physical location (Bonnabeau, 1996).

The second institutional concept at work is that of *community*. ESC understands itself to be a community of learning, a community of practice, and a community of scholars. A fundamental strength of communities is that they learn from their constituent members, reflect collectively on individual experiences, and integrate these into a richer and more robust communal understanding. Two factors are crucial for this community endeavor: (a) the richness and extent of variation available; and (b) an effective means through which difference encountered can be shared, compared, and reflected upon. Those who work with ESC's International Programs are involved with educational challenges, learning possibilities, and mentoring relationships that are significantly different from their state-side colleagues. By actively sharing these experiences, internationally located faculty can provide new perspectives and possibilities for the whole learning community. Rather than viewing ESC's International Programs as an exotic peripheral engagement, it is more accurate to see it as part of the community that is working on the leading edge of discovery and channeling its experiences back to the domestic College.

So what are these leading edge experiences?

At the outset it will be helpful to briefly set the scene. The ESC International Program in Prague is actually a *transnational* program – that is, one in which the College works with a foreign partner (a private Czech university) to provide educational opportunities for students abroad (Knight, 2010; van der Wende, 2003). Curriculum design, academic quality assurance, and the degree awarding process are all strictly controlled and monitored by ESC. To reduce institutional costs, the program uses a blended instructional model in which mentors meet their mentees in Prague at the beginning of each semester and then work with them at a distance for the remainder of the semester. The physical encounter with mentees is a critical advantage in the mentoring relationship, providing unique learning opportunities that cannot be replicated in purely online distance learning work. My mentoring involves working with mentees in the design, necessary research, and the production of their undergraduate capstone experience. The capstone experience takes the form of a dissertation that is planned and written during the student's final two semesters (Boyer Commission on Educating Undergraduates in the Research University, 1998, 2001).

This chapter considers international engagement as a significant way through which ESC fulfills its mission of building bridges and of cultivating humanity. The first section identifies the challenge of distance in the mentoring relationship. This is followed by three strategies for reducing relational distance and creating more effective mentoring relationships: liminality, strangerhood, and *bricolage*. These are approaches that I find important in my transnational mentoring; hopefully, they may have resonance with other mentors, instructors, and learners. It is important to note that this chapter reflects a personal approach to mentoring; it seeks neither to impose solutions nor to project an institutional response.

## FOUR DEGREES OF SEPARATION BETWEEN MENTEE AND MENTOR

As might be imagined, in Prague most of our students come from the Czech Republic and neighboring Slovakia. However, as the reputation of the program has grown, students increasingly migrate from further afield. To provide a snapshot of this increasing diversity, a recent cohort of mentees that I worked with came from Russia (12), Czech Republic (6), Kazakhstan (5), Slovakia (4), Korea (2), and single representatives from Albania, Bosnia-Herzegovina, Georgia, Poland, Serbia, and Vietnam.

My understanding of the transnational mentoring process has been acquired over the years by directly exploring the attitudes, feelings, and constructs of my mentees. Although all mentors develop their unique understandings of the mentoring process, it may be helpful to begin with a formal definition. The definition that resonates most strongly with what I do – and aspire to do – was proposed by Powell (1997), who understood mentoring as a one-on-one relationship between an experienced and less experienced person (the mentee, or protégé):

to improve [the mentee's] chances for achieving his or her goals by linking them to resources and support not otherwise available. The role of the mentor is to pass on knowledge, experience and judgment, and/or to provide guidance and support... [to offer] psychosocial support for changes in behavior, attitudes and ambitions... with the goals of reassuring innate worth, instilling values, guiding curiosity, and encouraging a positive youthful life. Distinguished from child rearing and friendship, the mentoring relationship is intended to be temporary, with the objective of helping the protégé reach independence and autonomy. (p. 4)

My mentees bring with them different national identities, cultural behaviors, and educational expectations even although they are temporarily situated within the social and cultural norms of an American institution in Central Europe. Part of their educational experience involves recognizing and adjusting, socially and culturally, to these new norms. The collaborative exploration of adjustments adds to the richness of cultural exchange for students, local and visiting faculty, partner institution, and ultimately for the whole ESC community. The rich national-culture mix provides significant opportunities, but it also presents challenges. In the mentoring process, my mentees and I are initially distanced in four senses.

- *Distanced from the learning institution.* Transnational mentees are culturally distanced from the values and perspectives of the American-based educational system within which they are enrolled. Many have completed their final high school year in America in anticipation of an international career. They have some understanding of American educational perspectives, but remain culturally and intellectually separated from the assumptions of American higher education and the core values articulated by ESC, which place value on a liberal arts perspective. ESC emphasizes breadth in learning, critical thinking, student self-direction, and interdisciplinary constructions of knowledge. This can be challenging for students familiar with narrower definitions of education, surface learning styles, and disciplinary isolation. This is particularly a problem with my mentees, who are Business Administration majors, and who generally favor a narrower, more pragmatic, and essentially utilitarian approach to knowledge acquisition.
- *Unfamiliar with the mentoring concept.* Mentoring is unfamiliar to my mentees and any notions that they might have about the mentor-mentee relationship have been shaped by prior educational experiences (real or vicarious) in their home countries. Mentoring is personal and reciprocal, guiding rather than instructing, and requires an appropriate match between mentor and mentee. As a process, it must negotiate individual difference, assumptions of social status, traditions of authority, and perceived differences in cultural group affiliation (Starr-Glass, 2014a, 2014b). Mentees in Prague take great pride in being assigned a mentor and look forward to the relationship. However, although enthusiastic, they have yet to appreciate the structure and process of the relationship. The mentor's task is to demonstrate how mentoring allows mentees to achieve their goals.

Mentoring across ethnic and national-culture difference requires trust, respectful inclusion, anticipatory awareness, and authentic empathy. Although mentoring is often represented from the mentor's perspective, the voice of the mentee is equally critical in creating and maintaining a productive mentoring relationship. Indeed, part of the successful mentoring process is to "unpack the ways in which mentoring is personally experienced and constructed by students… including students with different perspectives and backgrounds" (Crisp & Cruz, 2009, p. 540).

- *Skeptical about distance learning.* Creating a productive mentoring relationship – just like producing a productive online learning environment – is complicated by physical, social, cognitive, and relational distances (Olesova, Yang, & Richardson, 2011; Yang, Olesova, & Richardson, 2010). Extensive and timely communication, high social presence, and mentor displays of commitment all reduce these distances and contribute to more effective mentor-mentee engagements. I meet with mentees at the beginning of the relationship, but for most of the time our mentoring is done at a distance. This is usually the mentees' first encounter with distant learning and, given their traditional educational attitudes, they are anxious about its utility and skeptical about its value. Distanced mentoring always challenges the mentor to relate with mentee concerns, to reduce social and cognitive distance, and to establish empathetic connections (Starr-Glass, 2005).

- *Distanced by national culture.* Blake-Beard (2009) notes that "mentoring is always fraught with the concern of how to cross boundaries, how to bridge cultural differences to show yourself, and to accompany another on their journey" (p. 15). In America, the impact of gender and ethnicity on mentoring has received attention (Barker, 2007; Blake-Beard, Bayne, Crosby, & Muller, 2011). In transnational mentoring, however, the central issue is national culture. Hofstede (1980) identified dimensions in national cultures: power-distance, individualism versus collectivism, masculinity versus femininity, uncertainty avoidance, and short-term versus long-term orientation. These dimensions – and the positioning of a national culture along them – are best considered statistically: clusters of probabilities and anticipated tendencies. They *do* significantly impact the process of communication and sense-making, but they should never be used to label or to stereotype (Osland & Bird, 2000). For example, mentees coming from high power-distance cultures (which most of my students do) often find it difficult to understand the low power-distance and reduced attention to status in mentoring relationships (Pawson, 2004). The mentor has to appreciate and respect these cultural assumptions and attempt to negotiate them in ways that demonstrate awareness, sensitivity, and understanding.

These four boundaries of separation challenge effective relational mentoring. Of course, these degrees of separation are not unique to transnational mentoring. To some extent they are relevant to all mentoring work, but their magnitude and ramifications are seen more clearly from the vantage point of transnational work. Those involved in our mentoring process have little appreciation of American-centered educational values. They also come from traditional educational cultures where distance learning is considered, at best, as poor substitute for in-person instruction. Likewise, they have no experience of – and faith in – a relational mentoring process because their national cultures privilege and accentuate power-distance.

Because of these complexities of distance and separation, mentors in Prague are on the leading edge of mentoring and their shared experiences may provide new perspectives for American-based mentors confronted with the challenges of dealing with an increasingly diverse student population. In the following sections, I consider three theoretical approaches for mentoring across these boundaries of separation. These approaches emerge from theoretical considerations, but they provide practical ways of improving the learning experience and enriching the mentoring relationship.

## LIMINAL PRACTICE: MOVING ONTO THE BRIDGE

Liminality is a transient stage in a transformational journey that allows us to pause and recognize the transformation. It is the threshold (Latin: *limen*) between one state of being and another, a state of temporary suspension that van Gennep (1960) saw as "betwixt and between" and which Turner (1969) described as "a moment in and out of time ... [in which] a generalized social bond that has ceased to be and has simultaneously yet to be fragmented into a multiplicity of structural ties" (p. 96).

Mentoring partnerships have three phases: (a) an initial phase, in which it is recognized that previous cultural and social structures are about to change; (b) a liminal phase that is "a cultural realm that has few or none of the attributes of the past or coming state" (Turner, 1969, p. 94); and (c) a transformed phase, in which there is a mutual recognition of a mentoring relationship that has re-formulated rules, behavior, and responsibilities. These three phases are separate and sequential, but it is always unclear how long each will last. The critical phase is the liminal phase, which acts as a bridge between the initial encounter and the negotiated mentoring relationship. In the liminal phase the rules and assumptions of power, authority, and status are deliberately suspended, allowing both mentor and the mentee to consider constructing a new and unique relational bridge: "not simply reproduce traditional power dynamics, social practices, modes of participation, and fixed senses of self, but rather create spaces within which to question these" (Cook-Sather, 2006, p. 122).

I purposefully extend the liminal phase when mentoring transnational students, signaling that prior cultural and social assumptions are about to change, but without imposing a new and non-negotiated relationship. This allows mentees to consider the ways in which they want to create the mentoring relationship. My aim is to preserve liminality, defer premature imposition of structure, and to sustain ambiguity. This can be achieved in a number of ways:

- *Reorienting the directionality of teaching and learning.* I study and discuss the student's national history and cultural norms. When mentees realize that the mentor has taken the time, interest, and effort to study their national histories they have more confidence in building their own bridges. Learning at least some of the student's language – I have learned Czech and Croatian – demonstrates interest, recognition, and respect. These acts acknowledge that mentees are rooted in different national cultures, historical experiences, and linguistic traditions: they recognize the uniqueness of mentees. They also place the mentor in a situation of *being a learner* – purposefully vulnerable in speaking a new language, willing to learn, and welcoming new perspectives. Power structures and assumptions of authority are inverted: the assumed directionality of learning is changed.
- *Deferring product and recognizing process.* Mentees are usually too focused on the pragmatic concerns of completing their capstone dissertation. They are caught up with the *product* considerations, rather than with the *process* through which their dissertations will evolve. Mentees do not need to be slowed down or diverted from starting their dissertations, but they do need to explore process considerations in the liminal space that exists before they begin their work. In time, they will discover that they are completing two related journeys: one in the mentoring relationship, the other in completing the capstone dissertation. Mentees need reminding that these journeys are parallel and connected; academic success rest on effective mentoring relationships. Reciprocity is a hallmark of the mentoring relationship; mentors can suggest a fragmentary sense of purpose, but mentees themselves must identify their own aspirations and begin to think about the process that will realize these goals (Starr-Glass, 2010).
- *Accentuating the liquidity of the task.* Mentees engage with me in a guided voyage of discovery, in terms of exploring the mentoring relationship and of writing their capstone dissertations. I deliberately focus on process considerations – not product ones – and use learning modules to explore issues such as the nature of research, the attributes of scholarly writing, and the mentee assessment of the work of previous students. The "betwixt and between" state provides a place for innovative thought, creative considerations, and fluid imagination about the future project. Sustained liminality "offers less predictability, and appears to be a more 'liquid' space, simultaneously transforming and being transformed by the learner as he or she moves through it" (Meyer & Land, 2005, pp. 379–380).

This is my *threshold work* (Starr-Glass, 2013a). Recognizing, encouraging, and sustaining liminality at the outset of the mentoring relationship permit both mentor and mentee to articulate dialogues that might otherwise have been suppressed or avoided. Encouraging liminality in the early stages of the mentor-mentee relationship moves prior experience and individual personality from the center to the periphery. Once that has been done, there is space for novelty, creativity, and innovation. Sustaining liminality makes space for inclusion, suspends prior discourses, and appreciates diversity. Many of my students would agree with me that in moving through liminality we enter a different world – one that was not previously imagined or accessible (Conroy & de Ruyter, 2009).

STRANGERS AND OTHERS: ENCOUNTERS ON THE BRIDGE

Discussions of mentoring usually accentuate the closeness of those in the mentoring dyad. Strangerhood, then, may seem an alien concept, but it is not. In considering the sociology of space, Georg Simmel (1950) noted that "to be a stranger is naturally a very positive relation; it is a specific form of interaction" (p. 402). Simmelian strangers are simultaneously near and remote, and that duality creates a freedom which is unconstrained by the familiarity of previous interactions, or by speculations about future relationships.

Simmelian strangers are in the process of perpetual transition; neither permanently located in their origins, nor seeking incorporation in the places through which they pass. They accept social and cultural dislocation. They allow *the other* the opportunity to come to deeper understandings his or her fixity and preoccupation with integration. Škorić, Kišjuhas, and Škorić (2013), commenting on Simmel, argue that social life is never static "because spatial and temporal gaps indicate that man [sic] is always in the state of 'being in between.' Distance is always a double structure (di-stance) between two positions ... social action is always 'between' and never 'within'" (p. 592).

That double structure defines the stranger; it also defines the *mentor* and the *mentee* – two distinct positions in a social dyad. In my mentoring practice, I recognize that *we* are each Simmelian strangers. I enter a mentoring relationship not to define the other, any more than I use it to define myself. I recognize that "the relationship with the 'other' is not an external relationship, but structures one's identity from within. I am who I am only in relation to the Other, and this sense of difference prevents me from claiming that my existence is whole or complete" (Kostogriz & Doecke, 2007, p. 7). I also appreciate that this existential reality must always recognize and respect the mentee's distance, apartness, and strangerhood.

My mentees are usually expected to embrace the set of educational goals, aspirations, and values of the educational system in which they have enrolled. Sometimes they do, more often they do not. Some compare American educational values favorably with those of their home countries, appreciating the breadth and scope of the learning opportunities. However, a deeper questioning indicates that many reject a *distinctive American* approach to education. They are more likely to recognize pragmatic, rather than philosophical differences, based on the anticipated value of an American degree in the globalized marketplace. Their educational journeys are often complex and serendipitous. They have come from different countries to study in Prague, but they almost always insist that it is a temporary sojourn: they will return to their native countries, or seek postgraduate opportunities in more distanced ones. In their writings and reflective journals most of my mentees concede that strangerhood is ever-present, but they rarely communicate a sense of isolation or alienation (Starr-Glass, 2014c).

- *Recognizing the legitimacy of strangerhood.* Strangers meet as people, with origins and legitimacies not marginalized by place or past. Transnational mentees have opted for a degree of strangerhood when they engage with a different educational culture. When they migrated from their native country to Prague they have also assumed another dimension of strangerhood. Within the mentor-mentee engagement, and as members of a transitory educational community, mentees have ethical claims to be accepted as unique persons, neither as the *exotic other* nor as the incidental flotsam on the currents of globalized education (Kim, 2009).
- *Allowing mentees to value their strangerhood.* Simmelian strangers have real and intrinsic value. It is important for mentees to appreciate that value and it is important for the mentor to assist, rather than impede, that appreciation. The mentor must remain sensitive to transience, tolerant of ambiguity, and accepting of otherness. The mentor, as a helping guide, should also encourage the cultivation of that sensitivity, tolerance, and acceptance in mentees. Mentoring is a transient relationship and it ends when the mentee has been sufficiently empowered to no longer need the guidance that the mentor provides.
- *Avoiding "pedagogies of narcissism."* When one is working with mentees across national-culture borders, absolutist values need to be suspended; difference needs to be dignified. Recognizing or promoting a single agenda – whether in knowledge production, ethnicity, or cultural values – only results in narcissism. The locus of narcissism can be varied – centered on the personality of the mentor, on the nature of the College, or on a restrictive "American" view of education – but its result always compromises the mentoring alliance. In Ovid's *Metamorphoses*, the failing of Narcissus and Echo was not an exclusive concern for self, but rather their inability to recognize the "other." That is what Carol Hess (2003) alludes to in her discussion of the pedagogy of narcissism, where she contrasts it with the "pedagogy of conversation" and recognizes that in the closeness of the mentoring relationship "the ultimate role of the mentor is to help students articulate their particular voices. When the mentor is also able to receive from the voice she [sic] nurtures, conversational education takes place" (p. 136).

This is what I call my *bridge work* – recognizing the transitions that both mentor and mentee must make in their relationship. This requires that the bridges constructed during the liminal phase are subsequently used with confidence by both mentor and mentee to move to other places. Acknowledging strangerhood provides the opportunity for mentor and mentee to meet as fellow travelers, recognizing that their journeys – whether expressed in social, cultural, or educational terms – are valuable and empowering. For my mentees, strangerhood is an invitation to understand that knowledge is not *situated* in one a place, but remains with them on their journey.

Through the self-construction and internalization of knowledge, mentees come to realize that they can *detach* knowledge from the structures that shape it and possess it fully in their futures. They can more easily appreciate the value, possibility, and need for on-going life-long learning – and they can move forward, recognizing the natural and positive nature of the sojourner, to new destinations and to new bridges.

BRICOLEURS AND BOUNDARY-WORKERS: TRAFFIC ACROSS THE BRIDGE

The mentor needs to have broad disciplinary knowledge, the agility to recognize novel research directions, and a sense of enjoyment in undertaking creative challenges. Specifically, the concept of "subject matter expertise" needs reconsideration. In Prague, I am not so much a subject matter expert as a simple *bricoleur*.

The *bricoleur* is an eclectic collector and discerning improviser (Levi-Strauss, 1966). *Bricoleurs* are travelers and in their experiential journeys they acquire fragments of insight, possibilities, and connections. These are stored away because *bricoleurs* know that they will be useful at some future time. *Bricoleurs* are the hunter-gatherers in the academic landscapes of epistemology and ontology. Subject matter experts, by contrast, are the settled agrarians who cultivate their disciplinary plots and protecting them with disciplinary fences. *Bricoleurs* tend to be boundary workers: exploring the disciplinary boundaries, the interstices between disciplines, and the liminal spaces that have yet to be colonized. This was captured well by the late Joe Kincheloe (2005) when he wrote that "bricoleurs, acting on the complexity principle, understand that the identification of social structures is always problematic, always open to questions of contextual contingency" (p. 330).

My task in working with mentees who are writing their capstone dissertations is to help them recall prior knowledge and experience that can be used to select their dissertation topic. My task is to share with them the fragments and perspectives that I too have collected, and which might be useful in their novel constructions. In guiding them, I see myself not as a subject matter expert ground in a particular disciple – even although they may see me as such. They are Business Administration majors and will write on business or economic topics, but my task is to encourage them to explore inside and outside their chosen discipline, to seek out new areas of interest, and to sort through what they – as unwitting and unknowing *bricoleurs* – have collected throughout their undergraduate studies.

In writing this chapter, a central goal has been to demonstrate that ESC International Programs is on the leading edge of incursions into different learning systems and cultural contexts. This experience, however, remains with the individual mentor unless an effort is made to share it with others. It is this aspect of my *bricolage* work that I want to mention here.

- *Contributing to the disciplinary community.* The transnational mentor is in the best position to see different aspects of a discipline, or fragments that are often unrecognized. Certainly, engagement with hundreds of mentees in their exploration of business and economic topics encourages the mentor to adopt a *bricoleur's* perspective. These alternative aspects can be collected, brought across the bridge (as it were), and shared with disciplinary peers who have not had my opportunities. Whether that is in different ways to see Human Resource Management in small and medium-sized businesses in different countries (Starr-Glass, 2013b), the cultivation of cultural sensitivity in teaching Cross-cultural Management (Starr-Glass, 2014c), the marketing and non-profit ventures in the Czech Republic (Bulla & Starr-Glass, 2006), or enhancing business internship experience in Southeastern Europe (Starr-Glass, 2006), these *bricolage* works could not have come about without my international engagement and exposure to other-country experiences.

- *Contributing to the teaching-learning community.* Experience in multiple national culture environments, if shared, allows others to reconsider knowledge production and relevancy. It provides a better understanding of the transfer and the co-creation of knowledge across cultures, permitting a deeper appreciation of diversity and of our learners as they engage in lifelong knowledge growth. This can be shared with others engaged in teaching international business (Starr-Glass, 2009, 2011). Because my mentoring practice is carried out mostly at a distance, experienced gained and shared can also add to the knowledge base of instructional communities involved in online distance learning in multi-cultural settings (Starr-Glass, 2014d). Sometimes, sharing experiences of different national education structures and systems can help to clarify what our learners face (Starr-Glass & Ali, 2012).
- *Contributing to the collegiate community.* Working directly in locations where cultural issues are significant in the mentoring process provides knowledge that is unavailable in the domestic community of learning at ESC. The importation of that knowledge, shared and made public, can stimulate the College community to consider issues that they may otherwise only encounter in attenuated ways. For example, the growing diversity in the domestic-based ESC community presents mentoring challenges that are qualitatively similar to those encountered in ESC International Programs. Reports from the front line, as it were, can provide College-wide benefit. As a member of the extended ESC collegiate community, I contribute extensively to the College's publication, such as *All About Mentoring*. I also contribute to the publications of our private university partner in Prague, aiming to create and support collegiate bridges that provide mutual benefits to both communities of scholars and of practice.

*Bricolage* is an essential quality in confronting the different topics that my mentees will explore in writing their undergraduate dissertations. This is what I call my *bricolage work* – collecting fragments, bringing them across the bridge, sifting through them, assembling them in novel combinations, and then sharing the new assemblies with others. *Bricolage* provides benefits for those in the mentoring relationship, but it also provides benefit for others outside this relationship.

CONCLUSION

Transnational mentoring provides an opportunity for self-discovery, reconsideration, and humility. The mentor-mentee encounter is neither on an American campus nor on a foreign one, but on a bridge of greater understanding and of constructive engagement. The meeting place is on a cusp of difference, where new cultures and experiences collide. It may also be thought of as a boundary zone, with the familiar behind and the yet-to-be-experienced beyond. Boundaries can be places of demarcation, division, and separation – but they are also starting points for exploration, discovery, and transformative contact.

The International Programs of ESC provides the opportunity to refine our understanding of the diversity of learners and of different approaches for effective learning and mentoring in an increasingly inclusive and globalized educational environment. Those involved in such enterprises have the opportunity to share their experiences with others. However, I suggest that we not only have to ability to share, but that we have the *obligation* to share – particularly our ESC collegiate community.

In this chapter, I have set out some of the approaches that I use in working with my mentees. Liminality, strangerhood, and *bricolage* can be looked upon as pedagogic strategies, but they are also ways of making sense of transnational mentoring and of researching (literally "re-searching") our experience. With this in mind, it seems fitting to end with Joe Kincheloe's (2005) conclusion to his essay on *bricolage*. Although he was writing about research and methodology, it has always seemed to me that his words are particularly helpful in a more general sense, especially when thinking about what we do in ESC International Programs and about what I do in transnational mentoring. Much is possible.

> Understanding that research that fails to address the ontology of the human existential situation, with all of its pain, suffering, joy, and desire, is limited in its worth, bricoleurs search for better ways to connect with and illuminate this domain. In this context, much is possible. (p. 348)

ACKNOWLEDGEMENT

In writing this chapter, I would like to acknowledge the generous support, collegiate encouragement, and constructive feedback received from the editors Alan Mandell and Katherine Jelly. Their collective insights and thoughtfulness have been exceptionally valuable and any remaining deficiencies in this work are my own.

REFERENCES

Barker, M. J. (2007). Cross-cultural mentoring in institutional contexts. *The Negro Educational Review, 58*(1–2), 85–103.

Blake-Beard, S. (2009). Mentoring as a bridge to understanding cultural difference. *Adult Learning, 20*(1/2), 14–18.

Blake-Beard, S., Bayne, M. L., Crosby, F. J., & Muller, C. B. (2011). Matching by race and gender in mentoring relationships: Keeping our eyes on the prize. *Journal of Social Issues, 67*(3), 622–643.
Bonnabeau, R. F. (1996). *The promise continues: Empire State College – The first twenty-five years.* Virginia Beach, VA: The Donning Company Publishers.
Boyer Commission on Educating Undergraduates in the Research University. (1998). *Reinventing undergraduate education: A blueprint for America's research universities.* Stony Brook, NY: State University of New York.
Boyer Commission on Educating Undergraduates in the Research University. (2001). *Reinventing undergraduate education: Three years after the Boyer Report.* Stony Brook, NY: State University of New York.
Bulla, M., & Starr-Glass, D. (2006). Marketing and non-profit organizations in the Czech Republic. *European Journal of Marketing, 40*(1/2), 130–144.
Conroy, J. C., & de Ruyter, D. J. (2009). Contest, contradiction, and security: The moral possibilities of liminal education. *Journal of Educational Change, 10*(1), 1–12. Retrieved from http://dx.doi.org/10.1007/s10833-008-9072-z
Cook-Sather, A. (2006). Newly betwixt and between: Revising liminality in the context of a teacher preparation program. *Anthropology and Education Quarterly, 37*(2), 110–127.
Crisp, G., & Cruz, I. (2009). Mentoring college students: A critical review of literature between 1990 and 2007. *Research in Higher Education, 50*(6), 525–545.
Hess, C. L. (2003, July). Echo's lament: Teaching, mentoring, and the danger of narcissistic pedagogy. *Teaching Theology & Religion, 6*(3), 127–137.
Hofstede, G. (1980). *Culture's consequence: International differences in work-related values.* Newbury Park, CA: Sage.
Kim, T. (2009). Transnational academic mobility, internationalization, and interculturality in higher education. *Intercultural Education, 20*(5), 395–405.
Kincheloe, J. L. (2005, June). On to the next level: Continuing the conceptualization of bricolage. *Qualitative Inquiry, 11*(3), 323–350.
Knight, J. (2010). Higher education crossing borders: Programs and providers on the move. In D. B. Johnstone, M. B. D'Ambrosio, & P. J. Yakoboski (Eds.), *Higher education in a global society* (pp. 42–69). Cheltenham, UK: Edward Elgar Publishing.
Kostogriz, A., & Doecke, B. (2007). Encounters with 'strangers': Towards dialogical ethics in English language education. *Critical Inquiry in Language Studies, 4*(1), 1–24.
Levi-Strauss, C. (1966). *The savage mind.* Chicago, IL: University of Chicago Press.
Meyer, J. H. F., & Land, R. (2005). Threshold concepts and troublesome knowledge (2): Epistemological considerations and a conceptual framework for teaching and learning. *Higher Education, 49*(3), 373–388.
Olesova, L., Yang, D., & Richardson, J. C. (2011). Cross-cultural differences in undergraduate students' perceptions of online barriers. *Journal of Asynchronous Learning Networks, 15*(3), 68–80. Retrieved from http://files.eric.ed.gov/fulltext/EJ935586.pdf
Osland, J. S., & Bird, A. (2000). Beyond sophisticated stereotyping: Cultural sensemaking in context. *Academy of Management Perspectives, 14*(1), 65–77.
Pawson, R. (2004, October). *Mentoring relationships: An explanatory review.* (Working Paper No. 21). London, UK: ESRC UK Centre for Evidence Based Policy and Practice. Retrieved from http://www.kcl.ac.uk/sspp/departments/politicaleconomy/research/cep/pubs/papers/assets/wp21.pdf
Powell, M. A. (1997, October). *Academic tutoring and mentoring: A literature review.* Sacramento, CA: California Research Bureau, California State Library. Retrieved from http://www.library.ca.gov/crb/97/11/97011.pdf
Simmel, G. (1950). The stranger. In K. H. Wolff (Ed., & Trans.), *The sociology of Georg Simmel* (pp. 402–408). Glencoe, IL: The Free Press. (Original work published 1908)
Škorić, M., Kišjuhas, A., & Škorić, J. (2013). "Excursus on the Stranger" in the context of Simmel's sociology of space. *Sociológia, 45*(6), 589–502. Retrieved from http://www.sav.sk/journals/uploads/01091217Skoric%20OK.pdf

Starr-Glass, D. (2005). Tutorials at a distance: Reflection on the process. *New Horizons in Adult Education and Human Resource Development, 19*(3), 12–20. Retrieved from http://dx.doi.org/10.1002/nha3.10221

Starr-Glass, D. (2006). Enhancing the transformative potential of business internships. *Managing Global Transitions International Research Journal, 4*(4), 285–297. Retrieved from http://www.fm-kp.si/zalozba/ISSN/1581-6311/4_285-297.pdf

Starr-Glass, D. (2009). Teaching international business abroad: Paradigms suggested by metaphor theory. *Journal of Teaching International Business, 20*(3), 230–243.

Starr-Glass, D. (2010). Reconsidering the international business capstone: Capping, bridging, or both? *Journal of Teaching International Business, 21*(4), 329–345.

Starr-Glass, D. (2011). Between stereotype and authenticity: Using action research in a cross-cultural management course. *Journal of International Education in Business, 4*(2), 112–124.

Starr-Glass, D. (2013a). Threshold work: Sustaining liminality in mentoring international students. *International Journal for Mentoring and Coaching in Education, 2*(2), 109–121.

Starr-Glass, D. (2013b). The synergistic potential of human resource management in small and medium enterprises. In C. Machado & P. Melo (Eds.), *Effective human resources management in small and medium enterprises: Global perspectives* (pp. 74–95). Hershey, PA: IGI-Global.

Starr-Glass, D. (2014a). Three degrees of separation: Strategies for mentoring distanced transnational learners. In F. J. García-Peñalvo & A. M. Seoane-Pardo (Eds.), *Online tutor 2.0: Methodologies and case studies for successful learning* (pp. 176–200). Hershey, PA: IGI-Global.

Starr-Glass, D. (2014b). Servant mentors and transnational mentees. In R. Selladurai & S. Carraher (Eds.), *Servant leadership: Research and practice* (pp. 92–113). Hershey, PA: IGI-Global.

Starr-Glass, D. (2014c). Internalizing cross-cultural sensitivity: Reflective journals of migrant students. *Journal of International Education in Business, 7*(1), 31–46.

Starr-Glass, D. (2014d). Blending was not an option: Variation theory and reluctant international distance learners. *South African Journal of Higher Education, 27*(6), 1464–1478.

Starr-Glass, D., & Ali, T. (2012). Double standards: When an undergraduate dissertation becomes the object of two different assessment approaches. *Assessment & Evaluation in Higher Education, 37*(2), 179–192.

Turner, V. W. (1969). *The ritual process: Structure and anti-structure*. Chicago, IL: Aldine Publishing Company.

van der Wende, M. C. (2003, June). Globalisation and access to higher education. *Journal of Studies in International Education, 7*(2), 193–206.

van Gennep, A. (1960). *The rites of passage* (M. B. Vizedom & G. L. Caffee, Trans.). Chicago, IL: University of Chicago Press. (Original work published 1909)

Yang, D., Olesova, L., & Richardson, J. C. (2010, September). Impact of cultural differences on students' participation, communication, and learning in an online environment. *Journal of Educational Computing Research, 43*(2), 165–182.

NAN TRAVERS

# 11. INHERENT TENSIONS WITHIN THE PRACTICES OF PRIOR LEARNING ASSESSMENT AT SUNY EMPIRE STATE COLLEGE

Prior learning assessment (PLA)[1] in higher education has grown tremendously over the past decade and is reaching across multiple sectors worldwide (Colardyn & Bjornavold, 2004; Hawley, Otero, & Duchemin, 2010; Werquin, 2010). As part of the higher education degree completion agenda in the United States, PLA is increasingly accepted as a legitimate means to assess and credential university-level credits (Sherman, Klein-Collins, & Palmer, 2012). In a recent Gallup poll, the Lumina Foundation (2013) determined that:

> [87% of Americans] think students should be able to receive college credit for knowledge and skills acquired outside the classroom ... [and] 75% indicate[d] that they would be more likely to enroll in a higher education program if they could be evaluated and receive credit for what they already know. (p. 8)

In Europe, the Commission of the European Communities has made direct efforts to promote the recognition and validation of nonformal and informal learning as part of their lifelong learning policies (i.e., PLA). Colardyn and Bjornavold (2004) noted that PLA is "becoming a key aspect of lifelong learning policies" (p. 69) and mobility initiatives across European countries. Werquin (2012) indicated that the "'recognition of nonformal and informal learning' is at the top of the agenda everywhere because countries are faced with the same questions and issues about the labor market: bad demographics, high unemployment, unqualified labor force ..." (p. 2).

Latest developments in the open education movement have linked PLA to assessing emergent learning gained through online resources (Conrad, 2013; Friesen & Wihak, 2013). Movements in higher education to recognize open resources such as MOOCs (massive open online courses) have intensified the national focus on assessing and credentialing learning gained through nontraditional means. One means of recognition for example, which has gained prominence of late, is "badging." Badging allows institutions of higher education to concentrate on students' entry into, placement within, and award of credit for qualifications for advancement in the workplace and higher education (Harris & Wihak, 2011); and they focus on the role of PLA in decreasing time to degree completion and on lowering costs (Tate, 2013; Klein-Collins, 2010).

The approach to and acceptance of PLA as a viable educational strategy are grounded in the underlying philosophical positions of those involved. Travers (2013) re-examined data from the Hoffmann, Travers, Evans and Treadwell (2009) study of 34 institutional PLA policies and practices and determined that underlying each were key institutional philosophies. Van Kleef (2014) indicates that PLA quality differs across institutions based on philosophical perspectives. Examination of PLA literature spanning the past 40 years reveals positions that are rooted in a history of redress and access (Harris, 1999), lifelong learning promotion (Carless, Joughin, & Mok, 2006), and credentialing for workforce or higher education achievement (Moss, 2007).

Understanding differences across the principles underlying PLA is essential to understanding the disparity in practices and beliefs across an institution. Unexamined, perspectives regarding these principles can appear incongruent, and differences between practitioners may develop; through careful examination, differing attitudes and practices can be placed into relationship with one another and reconciled.

## PART 1: PHILOSOPHICAL APPROACHES TO PLA

The following analysis positions philosophical tenets underlying PLA in relation to the goals of redress, access, lifelong learning and credentialing in a framework in order to explore differences in approaches to and acceptance of PLA and their impact on policy and practice. This chapter uses these four different goals, or emphases, and possible inherent tensions that can arise between and within them in order to examine PLA policies and practices at SUNY Empire State College.

*Redress*

Cooper (2006) describes the origins of redress in South Africa in this way: "Against the background of the history of apartheid, RPL is viewed as a central mechanism with which to address past discriminations and disadvantage, and to bring about greater equity and redress" (p. 221). The basic philosophical tenet underlying redress is that by recognizing individuals and their knowledge, which has previously been disallowed under systems of domination, there can be a correction of wrongdoing (Michelson, 1997). Redress has enormous political ramifications as it challenges the status quo and questions established boundaries that have been well-fortified by authorities within the system within which the "outsider" wishes to be recognized and accepted.

Redress has a critical historical place within PLA philosophy and practice. It has led to essential questions about who has the power to determine which knowledge belongs in higher education, how that knowledge is organized, who can create new knowledge, and who determines how this new knowledge can be accepted and integrated into what already exists. Although redress also questions who can access higher education, the idea that a student can bring new knowledge into higher education is a fundamental assumption of redress. For that reason, this chapter defines the philosophy of redress as the acceptance of students' knowledge as a curricular change agent. In other words, PLA is a means to allow new knowledge, via the student, into higher education.

One way in which tensions surrounding redress are evident relates to the role of the faculty in curricular design and evaluation of learning. According to the Middle States Commission on Higher Education (2006) the "... faculty bear primary responsibility for promoting, facilitating, assuring, and evaluating student learning" (p. 37), and "... educational curricula [are] designed, maintained, and updated by faculty and other professionals who are academically prepared and qualified ..." (p. 38). This view can be interpreted to mean that the faculty totally "own" the curriculum or that the faculty can approve external knowledge, regardless of its source. Tensions can occur between those faculty who want to recognize student knowledge that sits outside the curriculum and those who wish to assess learning in relation to knowledge that already exists within the academy. Redress forces conventional knowledge to expand and include what previously was not known, unacceptable, or ignored, while the counter viewpoint helps preserve traditional curricular elements and beliefs.

Counter to the philosophy of redress is the concept that only preconceived, sanctioned knowledge can be part of higher education. From this viewpoint, the faculty not only "own" the curriculum, but their role is to protect it as well. In doing so, faculty imply that they must either know or at least be aware of the body of knowledge before it can be sanctioned. Such PLA approaches use careful matching systems to ensure that the accredited knowledge is equivalent to what already has been deemed acceptable, with no role for PLA to influence new developments in academic programming.

*Redress: Mentoring approaches.* Empire State College has philosophical underpinnings of redress in its mission and policies. As part of their educational experience, students are able to use PLA in their curriculum design and in planning their degree programs without matching to pre-existing courses. By self-designing their degrees, students can use PLA to recognize knowledge that isn't already taught in the College or at any other university, thus expanding what is considered acceptable knowledge in higher education.

A mentoring approach grounded in principles related to redress encourages a dialogical relationship between the student and the faculty mentor, which can bring to the surface hidden and/or disenfranchised knowledge. The PLA process encourages students to explore beyond any given curriculum to discover their own knowledge and legitimizes that knowledge as something that others can benefit from and learn more about. In this approach, the student's knowledge is recognized as having a place in higher education when it is shared, is seen as having value beyond the individual, and can be placed within a context of knowledge that has already been accepted. Within Empire State College, the learning revealed through PLA gains even more legitimacy when it is given a place within the individual student's degree plan or curriculum.

The PLA process expands beyond the single student engaged in the process. Faculty transform their own understanding of knowledge boundaries by expanding the community of understanding (Hamer, 2010; Naudé, 2013) and what is accepted as knowledge. At Empire State College, faculty frequently comment that mentoring students through the degree planning and PLA processes is an important element of their own professional development, indicating a willingness to recognize and gain new knowledge through the student. This type of engagement provides opportunities for redress philosophies to shape curriculum and knowledge development across the College.

There are some faculty at ESC who use existing courses to guide students in developing PLA requests and/or in evaluating student learning (Travers et al., 2008). This approach legitimizes knowledge through predefined criteria that anchor that knowledge in existing curricula. Policies and procedures within the institution do not make distinctions between these approaches and thus they exist concurrently, albeit sometimes in tension.

As Empire State College explores more structured curriculum choices for students, the question of how to include students' prior knowledge in predetermined curricula will necessarily become part of the discussion. This may be the first time in the College's history in which faculty may need to engage notions of matching learning to existing courses as a common practice. From a redress viewpoint, faculty are apt to struggle with this concept, while others will find it supportive of their own views and mentoring styles. In addition, as the College explores implementing competency-based programs, PLA becomes central to the concept of direct assessment of student learning. Since competency-based education doesn't use course matching, but rather assesses competencies, prior knowledge can easily shape the resulting program. These two newer approaches provide end points to a range of approaches to curriculum development and related assessment processes.

*Redress: Assessment approaches.* As the use of PLA to serve the purpose of redress asks us to examine the possibility of new knowledge being added to what already exists, current assessment strategies do not suffice. Rather, redress assessment approaches are exploratory, hermeneutic, and evolutionary as they take into account divergent perspectives. Assessing new knowledge requires existing knowledge to expand its boundaries to allow for new constructs within its assessment context.

Hamer (2010) studied the PLA evaluator-learner relationship and argues that assessing prior learning has "negotiated meaning," (p. 106) that "the learner and assessor together ... seek an exchange of stories regarding skilled, professional, competent, and ultimately, *qualified* practice ... and finally agree [from] their respective positions" (p. 108, emphasis in original). Naudé (2013) suggests that the PLA evaluator negotiates between traditional disciplinary standards and transdisciplinary aspects of knowledge to create an adjusted framework, which allows new meaning to be considered. Cronbach and Meehl (1955) argue that construct validity is dependent on the relationships across concepts, an approach that defines and expands the definition of any one construct and without which validity is lacking. The challenge is to find ways to evaluate the connected concepts and their relationships in order to understand what a student knows. In contrast, many summative assessment strategies recognize learning by comparing it to predetermined criteria, thus assessing what the learner knows against what is already expected. In these ways, then, assessment strategies reinforce the practices and policies derived from any given philosophical perspective.

*Access*

For some, access and redress are intertwined; the student and the knowledge come together. For others, access is about providing an opening into higher education and does not examine the impact of new knowledge on the current system. Access expands the pool of who has the knowledge, while redress expands what knowledge is accepted. By its very nature, access is somewhat less political; to accept new people into the circle is easier than to incorporate their beliefs and knowledge into that which already exists. The belief behind the philosophy of access is that barriers to higher education can be reduced and provision for access increased. Prior learning assessment has been endorsed to reduce barriers to students through lowering costs, decreasing time to completion, and increasing graduation rates (Klein-Collins, 2010). As a result, PLA is now seen as a mechanism to increase access to gaining degrees.

Access is also discussed in regard to PLA itself. Open PLA access is understood to mean that any student can have his/her learning assessed for college-level credits, that all types of prior learning assessments are available, and that the credits awarded can be used to meet any of the degree requirements. On the other hand, some institutions restrict use of PLA by using criteria as to who can participate, which credits can be included, and ways in which the credits can be applied within the degree. Along the continuum are institutions that partially restrict the use of PLA; for example, requiring a particular GPA or academic pre-requisites, such as English Composition, or only allowing PLA through some programs or to be counted only toward elective credits. At one end of the spectrum access means that anyone can use PLA credits, and at the other end, only some students can use PLA credits to meet some of the degree requirements.

At Empire State College, access to higher education through access to PLA opportunities is important, and College policy is more open than restrictive. No student is prevented from using PLA credits toward his or her undergraduate degree. Students are allowed to use PLA credits toward all degree requirements. The only restrictions are that students cannot use PLA credits toward residency requirements and must be matriculated into a degree program. Students are encouraged to seek out many different forms of PLA, from pre-evaluated learning (such as military credit evaluated through the American Council on Education) to individualized portfolio assessment. The College is also one of the earliest adopters in the U.S. to allow PLA credits to be used in a master's degree.

*Access: Mentoring approach.* A mentoring approach focused on access inspires students to try different PLA options and emphasizes ways that PLA can open up new opportunities and degree options. The goal is to help students frame their learning so that it can be included in a degree, thus including the student in constructing his or her own higher education. Mentoring strategies focus on helping students understand how their prior learning fits into different degrees and related policies and guidelines. Students are encouraged to explore different ways to identify and organize their knowledge for the purpose of discovering the possibilities for developing their individual plan for study.

Not all mentors at the College advise in such an open-ended spirit (Travers et al., 2008). Some mentors are hesitant to allow students to "fish around" and instead recommend that PLA requests be considered only once the degree is basically designed. In this context, PLA is used as a way to complete requirements toward that degree rather than as a way to explore how the student's prior knowledge can inform possible individual degree designs. Others use external course analogs to help frame the student's prior learning, which can restrict the knowledge that can be used and, thus, who can use knowledge that sits outside of the analog.

These differences in approaches can spur intense debate and even undermine trust among faculty at Empire State College, especially when some faculty believe that students should be recognized for all their college-level learning and should be encouraged to design degrees from this pool of knowledge, while others believe that only that learning that fits within a defined degree should be evaluated. These oppositions have different philosophical roots – to recognize and include all possible knowledge versus to recognize and validate only that which already fits.

*Access: Assessment approach.* Opening access to PLA includes the assessment of learning originating from various backgrounds, cultures, and preparation. Yet, current assessment structures are often built on classical psychometric criteria that are dependent on set and known outcomes. These can disadvantage groups that were intended to be included. Knowledge does not develop independently from experience (Sheckley, 2007); it is embedded in culture, context and history (Harris, 1999, 2006, 2013; Hill, 2004; Michelson, 1997, 2006, 2012; Shalem & Steinburg, 2006). Assessment is interpretive and biased (Diedrich, 2013; Naudé, 2013; Timma, 2005) and is dependent upon the background and approaches engaged by the evaluator. Boud and Falchikov (2006) propose that the assessment process be participatory and the focus of assessment activities emphasize the social construction and contextual nature of learning. In this philosophy related to access, assessment strategies must take into account situated contextual knowledge (however individualistic or communal) and relate its constructs to existing academic structures. Assessment thus requires a "negotiated fit" (instead of "negotiated meaning" as in a redress approach), regardless of whether or how the assessment system or types of supports provided to the learner have to change.

A counter view employs an approach that keeps specific students or a restricted pool of students who meet specified criteria in mind, and limits possible variance in measures to improve validity. However, as Knight (2006) explains, "assessment is a practice of judgment ... [and] reflect[s] the context in which the achievement arose and the circumstances in which the judges judged" (p. 435). Knight argues that assessments become contextualized within their own framework and only measure internalized judgments, rather than purported academic complexities. Thus by constraining membership while applying pre-constructed measures, generalizability becomes so localized that it is not trustworthy beyond that immediate environment. And thus, Knight argues, predefined assessment criteria restricted to membership-driven knowledge become insular and reproduce their own partialities.

*Lifelong Learning*

The promotion of lifelong learning has a very different philosophical undertone from advocacy for redress or access. The encouragement of lifelong learning opportunities stems from the belief that, provided the right opportunity, adults are continuous learners and can acquire new knowledge and perspectives. There is a plethora of stories in the adult learning literature describing transformational experiences as adults learn new information and discover fresh implications to what they know. Adult learning theorists (e.g., Cross, Brookfield, Kegan, Mezirow) for decades have described developmental changes and growth in the adult when stimulated by new ideas and challenging concepts, changes which can allow them to move from societally normed knowledge to new insights into themselves, their learning, and knowledge.

From the lifelong learning perspective, the actual process of learning is what is paramount, rather than achieving an end product. Prior learning assessment in this context focuses on the developmental and transformative processes of the individual, emphasizing the student's reflection as a way to gain perspective on what is already known and to generate new knowledge by focusing on and contextualizing evolving perspectives (Stevens, Gerber, & Hendra, 2010). This developmental perspective cultivates motivational and supportive practices to encourage adult learners to try out new experiences and improve their lives.

Counter to the assessment of prior learning as part of a developmental and transformative process is the underlying idea that PLA can help students to persist and achieve their degrees faster. In this, more pragmatic orientation philosophy, the focus is on PLA as a vehicle to achieve an end point. The process does not matter so much as reaching the end, whether of gaining particular knowledge or earning a given degree or credential.

*Lifelong learning: Mentoring approaches.* Mentoring toward lifelong learning from a developmental perspective encourages students to reflect analytically upon their experiences in order to discover emergent learning possibilities, and to contextualize and situate that learning within academic expectations. Critical reflection upon experience helps reinterpret the meaning of the experience and can result in new perspectives and understandings. In articulating this knowledge, the student makes tacit knowledge explicit (LeGrow, Sheckley, & Kehrhahn, 2002) and integrates new understanding, and sometimes new knowledge, with prior knowledge. This "converged learning" – of new and prior knowledge – is not an additive of the old plus new, but rather a new assemblage of constructs. The developmental aspect of the lifelong learning approach builds on the student's ability to reflect in order to help students transform their understanding and gain new insights into their knowledge.

Mentoring from the lifelong learning perspective encourages students to engage in the reflective process and situate their learning within a new academic context. By situating prior knowledge within education systems, the student not only becomes more aware of academic meanings, but also increases an understanding of his or her own knowledge and how it fits within the system. Empire State College mentor, Lambe (2011), writes that

> Prior Learning Assessment (PLA) brings students into active and reflective engagement with significant life experiences at the nexus of academic and non-academic cultures. When done successfully, PLA orients students to academic ways of thinking and writing while encouraging self-exploration. Often students feel a sense of empowerment and confidence as they come to realize that they accomplished significant college level learning outside of the academy. (p. 50)

Lambe describes the mentoring process as one of facilitating the bridging of the "experiential and the academic" (p. 51) and as a process that encourages students to engage in reflection and to develop an awareness of their knowledge and how it fits into academic settings. Popova-Gonci (2009) stresses that many students need to develop college-level skills and academic language, and the role of the mentor is to help students develop these as they pursue PLA. By focusing the developmental aspect of PLA engagement onto academic expectations, the mentor can help the student develop academic skills while also pursuing PLA.

Counter to this perspective would be a mentoring style that guides students to use PLA credits specifically to complete the degree. With sights on the endpoint, advising may support the student in using PLA options that are faster to complete, such as standardized exams, rather than a portfolio development process. Efficient routes to completion drive the conversations rather than personal exploration. The argument against a more transformative approach is that it is time consuming and more costly for the student, mentor, and institution, and can divert or slow down the student from accomplishing his or her path. In addition, some argue that students indicate that they just want to accomplish their goals and do not want to go through "a process"; that is, a process that takes considerably longer. Mentoring approaches grounded in this perspective tend to be more pragmatic, sticking to academic requirements and negotiating degree designs.

*Lifelong learning: Assessment approach.* In the lifelong learning assessment process, student reflections help to explore both their prior learning and their personal, educational and professional goals, to identify gaps in knowledge, and to determine how to address these gaps to meet their goals. The outcome of the assessment is more than just a credit recommendation; it includes an assessment of what the student has learned and what the next learning should be for that student. The assessment process also builds a lifetime skill and practice of reflection and self-assessment. The credit evaluation report plays a role in helping the student further the self-assessment with an outside expert's observations and recommendations.

The counterpoint to a lifelong learning philosophy uses a pragmatic assessment approach that is a means-end process. The evaluator is concerned with collecting, processing and interpreting multiple data sources on the student's learning in order to draw conclusions and make a credit recommendation. The evaluator's recommendation report is focused more on learning outcomes than on the learning process. The Travers et al. (2011) study found that some evaluators at Empire State College were sparse in their descriptions of students' learning and that they provided, instead of a detailed description of the learning process and its outcomes, an overall summation.

These two different approaches to assessment of prior learning at the College result in different evaluator practices as well, both in the ways in which students are interviewed and in how the learning outcomes are recorded.

*Credentialing*

The lens of credentialing learning – whether for workforce or higher education – through prior learning assessment relates to the philosophy that knowledge can be liberated, recognized and validated against "external requirements emanating from standards, curricular outcomes, or from more embedded understandings" (Harris, 2006, p. 54). The belief in this context is that learning acquired outside the formal system can be compared to and legitimized as learning which the formal system has declared essential to meet its requirements for particular credentials. From this perspective, the origin of the learning becomes less critical in determining its worth, while verifiability of the learning is essential.

Recently in the U.S.A., PLA has been encouraged as a means to support accelerated routes to degree completion. Other credentialing solutions, emphasizing the need for faster and more frequent recognition and validation methods, have also emerged (such as micro-credentials, including, e.g., badges), which have raised questions about traditional credentialing processes (Kamenetz, 2010). Micro-credentials that are "stackable" and that use PLA to validate academic learning are seen as promising models for integrating higher education and workplace development (Conrad, 2013; Friesen & Wihak, 2013; Benke, Davis, & Travers, 2012). In addition, the current focus on competency-based learning uses PLA as a form of direct assessment and encourages students to pursue PLA as a viable means to document learning and competency, and to gain credentials.

The credentialing approach extends beyond higher educational degrees to include all credentials, including, for example, industry certifications and licenses. The approach can open up possibilities for integrating knowledge gained through the workplace and academe, and for using this assessed knowledge to award credentials for learning in both sectors. The continuum in the credentialing arena ranges from using all forms of assessed learning to attain a given credential, to using well-defined criteria or standards against which the assessed learning must be matched and which therefore document the acquisition and demonstration of comparable knowledge. This approach can be important to some fields (for example, when the knowledge is essential to public safety and health); as a result, some accrediting bodies restrict or forbid the use of PLA.

*Credentialing: Mentoring approach.* A mentoring approach related to PLA as a means of credentialing concentrates on ways to use PLA credits to complete certifications, licenses and degrees. It also explores learning in a way that places it within different contexts and valuing systems in order to equate its worth to existing structures. In this context, institutional partnerships become important to give students direct pathways from the workplace into higher education and vice versa. The focus is on recognizing and validating the learning and competencies developed by the student and providing guidance on ways these competencies can be equated to credentialing requirements.

The counterpoint to using PLA to achieve credentials is an approach that restricts its use by requiring exact matching to well-defined standards. This approach can severely limit the ways PLA can be used toward gaining various credentials. A mentor in this context would encourage the student to focus on standardized exams and/or other normed processes for better applicability of the knowledge to the desired credential. The mentor is also likely to encourage the student to research the particular field in order to learn what prior learning would be relevant.

*Credentialing: Assessment approach.* Movements to use PLA as a credentialing assessment tool stem from demands to increase a qualified workforce and to provide alternative routes to certifications. PLA provides an experiential context that many credentialing assessments lack. The process can generate evidence of learning that can be used to verify workplace abilities in applied ways. From this perspective, assessment of prior learning focuses not just on knowledge acquisition but also on ways in which knowledge is used.

Using PLA for credentialing starts from the basic premise that learning can be objectified, measured, judged in relation to particular criteria, and documented to exist. The very act of credentialing in this approach implies that individual abilities have been compared to and validated against external criteria. Whether the knowledge is "new" to the academy or well recognized, when a credential is assumed to represent particular learning and capabilities and is accepted within a particular community, the act of acceptance imparts *construct validity* onto the credential (Cronbach & Meehl, 1955). Thus, the use of PLA for credentialing may use the assessment process to align to very specific requirements; the more specific the criteria, the less flexibility there is in these alternative assessments.

*Part 1 Summary*

Table 1 summarizes the philosophical viewpoints and counterpoints related to the lenses of redress, access, lifelong learning and credentialing in the assessment of prior learning, and notes their key foci and respective policy considerations. Each of these lenses, including a spectrum of perspectives on and approaches to PLA can be seen throughout higher education; Empire State College is no exception. The varying approaches can be in tension with one another. Typically, faculty at Empire State College blend the different philosophies and are not purists who would privilege any one over the others (Travers et al., 2008). The College's policies are also blended, creating the opening and support for multiple approaches. Understanding the characteristics of each approach can be helpful to examining current policy and practices and to determining where changes may need to be made. In the next section, these concepts are used to examine Empire State College PLA policy and its impact on practices.

Table 1. *Goals and emphases in PLA: Philosophical points and counterpoints and their implications for policy*

|  | Point | Counterpoint |
|---|---|---|
| Redress | All knowledge (beyond a secondary level) has the potential to be part of higher education. PLA allows for an expansion of accepted knowledge in higher education through the student's prior learning. | Only sanctioned knowledge can be accepted by institutions of higher education. Prior learning should be assessed against standards that reaffirm existing criteria for accepted knowledge. |
| Focus: Knowledge | Policy: Learning can be assessed for college-level credit regardless of when, where or how it was learned. | Policy: Assessed prior learning must match existing curricula. |

*(Continued)*

*Table 1. (Continued)*

| | Point | Counterpoint |
|---|---|---|
| Access | Higher education should be open to all. PLA is provided through all disciplines, can be applied toward all degree requirements, and can be used in admissions process and for placement within the system. | Only those people who meet specified criteria are accepted into higher education. PLA is restricted to only specific disciplines, degree requirements and/or student characteristics; not part of admissions or placement criteria. |
| Focus: Inclusion | Policy: PLA is open to all learners. | Policy: PLA is limited to students in a given discipline, with a particular GPA or according to other criteria. |
| Lifelong Learning | Higher education is developmental and transformative. PLA provides opportunities to explore personal, educational and professional goals and is considered part of the educational experience. PLA can surface new knowledge in relation to an individual's past learning. | Higher education is a means to an end. PLA provides a way to meet degree requirements or other certifications. Emergent learning is not considered in the assessment process. Focus is on the product not the process. |
| Focus: Development | Policy: Students are supported in their work toward PLA through various resources, workshops, courses and/or advisement. | Policy: PLA is used in a more limited context to support students in meeting degree requirements; only learning acquired prior to attending the institution can be assessed. |
| Credentialing | The purpose of higher education is to acquire credentials, especially for workforce development. PLA provides ways of validating and accrediting learning to advance standing toward certifications. Through PLA, individuals leverage existing knowledge and competencies to move into or progress within a field. | Criteria and standards are important and PLA is used in relation to these to credential. PLA is restricted to some pathways and may use only formal assessment methods, such as standardized exams. In some cases, PLA may be used only to meet noncore elements of the credential (e.g., electives). |
| Focus: Credential obtainment | Policy: PLA is connected to and built into degree and career pathways to complete requirements for credentials. | Policy: PLA is restricted based on discipline, particular credentials sought, types of assessments, or how the credits can be used. |

## PART 2: PLA PHILOSOPHICAL APPROACHES IN ACTION AT EMPIRE STATE COLLEGE

As noted above, these four philosophical themes within PLA practice exist across Empire State College in many forms. Faculty hold a range of philosophies; they employ a variety of approaches; and policies and procedures reflect these differences. At times these philosophies build upon each other, but at other times they contribute to different perspectives on what constitutes appropriate PLA practice. This second section looks at the College's mission, policies, procedures, and some commonly employed PLA practices in relation to these themes and explores some of the creative tensions they raise.

*Institutional Mission*

The mission of SUNY Empire State College (n.d.) reads:

> SUNY Empire State College's dedicated faculty and staff use innovative, alternative and flexible approaches to higher education that transform people and communities by providing rigorous programs that connect individuals' unique and diverse lives to their personal learning goals. (para. 1)

Dissecting this statement reveals all four philosophical themes to be in evidence. The phrase "transform people" draws on language used in discussion of lifelong learning, while "rigorous programs that connect ..." refers to a focus on credentialing. The wording "connect individuals' unique and diverse lives" is centered on recognizing the individual and his/her context, which relates to redress, while reference to individuals' "personal learning goals" suggests a notion of access and individuals' reasons for pursuing higher education. Thus multiple viewpoints can comfortably exist within an institution and in support of the same mission. And the creative tensions continue to play out as faculty can approach PLA from different assumptions, and sharply distinct perspectives and practices can arise.

*PLA Policies and Resources at ESC*

SUNY Empire State College has developed two policies and three practice guides to inform and support the implementation of PLA across the College. The "Advanced Standing: Policies and Procedures that Govern the Assessment of Prior Learning Policy" (2008a) and "Individualized Prior Learning Assessment Policy and Procedures" (2008b) provide the college with policy on how to conduct prior learning assessment, while internal resources such as "Resources and Criteria for Assessment and Program Review" give direction on how to put these policies into practice. In addition, the Student Degree Planning Guide (2015) and the Individualized Prior Learning Assessment (iPLA) Guide (2013) provide students with resources to help them to actualize these policies. Each of these documents purposefully approaches articulating PLA policy and practice in very general terms in order to allow for flexible interpretation that is based on individual student situations. Although this intentionally general articulation supports individualization, it also perpetuates varying and uneven practice arising from different philosophical perspectives.

For example, as seen in the Travers et al. (2008) study and as earlier noted here, one key difference in ESC faculty's PLA mentoring approaches is whether or not to use existing courses to shape the PLA request. Policy allows for an "open curriculum" process to develop PLA requests; that is, it neither requires nor prevents matching to existing courses in PLA requests. Therefore, the study found, practices of matching or nonmatching are based on mentors' philosophical positions and/or particular preferences related to their students' situations.

There are other examples of how policy and practice can be interpreted differently. The opening statement of the advanced standing policy begins:

> Since the degree program is central to the awarding of advanced standing at Empire State College, its development is a task on which students and mentors spend considerable time and thought. ... The degree program describes studies done at previous colleges, college level learning from life or work experiences and contracts to be undertaken at Empire State College. The emphasis on degree program planning provides students with an opportunity to design their program of study at Empire State College in light of both their long-range goals and their previous education. Another reason for the importance of degree program planning derives from the college's perspective on assessment. Each student's request for advanced standing is evaluated in the context of the student's goals and the nature of the whole degree program. This orientation precludes a piecemeal approach to the granting of advanced standing. (SUNY Empire State College, 2008a, Statements section, para. 1)

This statement consists of several philosophical underpinnings. First, the awarding of advanced standing is noted as being central to the degree planning process, which is indicative of the goal of credentialing; students may use prior learning to meet degree requirements to obtain a credential. The developmental perspective is clearly referred to in the description of the mentoring process, which emphasizes the need to "spend considerable time and thought" on the process. Consideration of access is also indicated by noting the opportunity to design a degree aligned to the student's goals and previous educational experiences.

This policy, however, by restricting PLA to the context of a degree plan, appears not to support all aspects of redress. Under this policy, the College assesses only that learning which will be used within the degree; assessed prior learning must fit within constraints set by the area of study guidelines and College policy. The guidelines can provide an opportunity to include new knowledge, but they can also restrict that opportunity; the determination is based on faculty interpretation. Clear tensions – in this case among and between individual faculty and committee members as well as their ideas – arise as they debate what learning can be included in a degree and how a student should meet the area of study guidelines.

In addition, the College does not support students' being assessed for learning not part of their degree; that is, PLA may not be used simply to validate and transcribe all possible college-level learning. Also the policy does not support a student's having prior learning assessed prior to engaging in his or her first enrollment. Thus the policy restricts both who can access PLA and, in many ways, what knowledge can be assessed. Interestingly, the statement in the individualized PLA policy, "Empire State College is committed to the idea that people should be awarded credit for verifiable college-level learning regardless of where or how it was acquired," implies that PLA should be able to be employed for all verifiable learning (SUNY Empire State College, 2008b, Purpose section, para. 1). But current practice seems to add to the policy a hidden clause that could read: "*as long as it fits into an acceptable degree program.*"

This hidden clause is actually found explicitly stated later in both policies, in slightly different wording. The first policy refers to all advanced standing credits and forms of prior learning; the second to individualized prior learning assessment only. The two policy statements read:

> Advanced Standing Policy: Each student's request for advanced standing is evaluated in the context of the student's goals and the nature of the whole degree program. (SUNY Empire State College, 2008a, Statements section, para. 1)

> Individualized PLA Policy: Empire State College … relies on the Empire State College faculty, acting through center portfolio-review committees, to approve the award of credit appropriate to the overall context of the student's degree. … Evaluators need to be able to see how the learning they are evaluating fits into the context of the student's proposed degree program in order to address questions of level of learning, potential redundancy with other degree components, etc. Therefore, the student should submit, along with a learning request, a draft degree plan reviewed by the mentor (and may sometimes include other materials such as the degree program rationale essay), so that the request can be placed in the context of a full degree program. (SUNY Empire State College, 2008a, Statements: Award of Credit section, para. 2)

The advanced standing policy situates PLA requests in the context of students' goals and the overall nature of their degree. The individualized PLA policy specifies that it is the responsibility of the faculty to approve the award of credit for prior learning after an evaluator has assessed that learning (and has addressed the level, whether introductory or advanced, and possible redundancy with other learning in the student's approved program of study). These two statements have strong impact on practice, especially in the ways in which they are interpreted.

- One difference in the ways that the two policies are interpreted is how pre-evaluated prior learning (prior learning evaluated for credit by entities outside of the College) and individualized prior learning assessment (an individual student's prior learning evaluated for credit through processes within the College) are treated. Except for individualized PLA, all other forms of advanced standing are evaluated against predetermined criteria set outside the College. Examples include transfer credits from regionally-accredited institutions or credits recommended by the American Council on Education (ACE) and other organizations that evaluate military and industry training and standardized exam results against pre-determined criteria. Typically, these kinds of learning and documentation are matched to existing courses taught at colleges and universities. Since these assessments involve academic and professional experts in the evaluation and recommendation of credit, the College has deemed these external assessment processes sufficient. During the faculty review of the degree plans, such pre-evaluated credits are not typically renegotiated; thus, by regularly accepting pre-evaluated credits without alteration, College practice reflects an unchallenged acceptance of pre-determined criteria.
- However, individualized prior learning assessment (iPLA) is held to different standards. These assessments are guided by Empire State College faculty and evaluated by internal faculty or the equivalent (i.e., evaluators qualified to assess the learning and hired by the College to do this evaluation). The iPLA goes through many reviews: 1) a faculty mentor reviews the student's request for its substance and relevance before submitting it to a local office of academic review; 2) professional staff review the request for compliance with policy requirements before it goes to a faculty evaluator and, upon its return, before it is included in the degree plan; 3) a faculty review committee reviews the evaluator's PLA recommendation and either accepts or suggests revision; and 4) a collegewide office of academic review then provides a policy evaluation of the degree program, including any learning credited through PLA. At any point, the request and recommendation can be modified, which often occurs at the faculty review stage. No other credits, from either external sources (e.g., transcripts) or internal studies (i.e., credit earned at ESC), undergo the level of review, or possible renegotiation, that iPLA credits do. In this way, it is clear that the College's faculty are more willing to reconsider and question credit earned through iPLA than any other learning included in a student's degree, a practice which serves to marginalize individualized PLA.
- Another difference in how these two policy statements are interpreted occurs when students are advised to engage in the PLA process. Some faculty interpret the policy to mean that the degree program needs to be drafted prior to students seeking PLA, so that there is a degree context within which to assess the prior learning. The Council for Adult Experiential Learning's fifth standard states: "Credit or other credentialing should be appropriate to the context in which it is awarded and accepted" (Fiddler, Marienau, & Whitaker, 2006, p. ix). Often this standard has been used to argue that the PLA credits need to be evaluated within

the context of the degree program. However, this standard could be understood to suggest that college credit, in itself, is an appropriate context.
- Others believe that the learning to be assessed through PLA can shape the degree program design; these faculty encourage students to engage in the PLA process early on, perhaps even to serve as a way to initiate the degree planning process. Still others argue that students should be assessed for verifiable college-level learning regardless of the degree pursued.
- All three perspectives have philosophical underpinnings: The first relates to credentialing: A degree program needs to exist first, within which prior learning can be credited. The second relates to redress: PLA can shape the knowledge captured within the degree. And the third is about access: PLA provides additional opportunities, beyond the degree, and, through recognizing and validating learning, can aid the student in reaching additional goals.
- These policies have also been interpreted differently in regard to who should seek credit through PLA. Mostly, the policies have been interpreted to mean that only degree-seeking students can have their prior learning evaluated. The original purpose of limiting PLA requests to matriculated students stemmed from a concern that the College could not afford to cover costs of PLA services if matriculated students had additional credits beyond the degree assessed or if non-matriculated students used PLA services. Now that PLA fees are based on a per credit-request scale, the original purpose to restrict PLA to matriculated students is less important from a business model perspective. Yet, while some now advocate for broader use of PLA to include non-matriculated students, many faculty, who interpret this policy to mean that prior learning must be evaluated within the context of a degree, argue that such a policy ensures the degree more integrity.
- Policy also prevents individualized PLA credits from being transcribed prior to the degree program being approved (in College parlance, "concurred"). These credits earned through PLA have been approved by College faculty through the mentoring process and through the College's academic review process, just as have other courses taken at Empire State College. If a student successfully completes a course, those credits are transcribed regardless of when the student took the course or where the student is in his/her degree program. But credits earned through individualized PLA are restricted to being transcribed only after the degree plan is concurred.[2] The implied message here is that individualized knowledge is valued only if contained within a degree; if it is not, the College does not recognize, verify or credit that learning – a view that is in direct opposition to the argument that all learning credited through PLA has inherent legitimacy. Thus, as it now stands, individually assessed credits are not useful to the student – at least not at ESC –unless or until the degree is concurred.

Another way in which current practices marginalize iPLA credits assessed by the College is that the practice of "fishing for PLA credits" is considered taboo, while experimenting with courses is considered a good developmental practice. Both help students understand their learning and articulate their goals, but they are not valued in the same way. Thus, again, while the College implies that credits earned through PLA are equal academically to credits earned through its own studies, and while it controls and validates the PLA process, nonetheless it treats credit earned through PLA differently, both in policy and in practice.

These differences in interpretation of policy regarding iPLA raise important questions for the College to consider:

- Why must individualized PLA credits go through an additional review, a step above and beyond that required for all other credits accepted by the College?
- Why are matriculated students, if they are willing to pay the necessary fees to cover the costs of the process, not permitted to engage in the PLA process for as many credits as they seek?
- Why are non-matriculated students, if willing to pay the fees, not eligible to engage in the PLA process?
- Why are credits earned through individualized PLA not recorded on a transcript before a degree program is concurred?

*Other PLA Practices Reflecting Tensions within the College*

The basic expectations of students seeking PLA are that that they will reflect upon, assess, articulate and document their learning, and engage in an assessment interview. The expectations of the institution, through its faculty, are to recognize, evaluate, validate and credential that learning. At Empire State College, there are three key practices to individualized prior learning assessment that often vary in the approaches used: ways in which students are mentored through the PLA process, what is required of students to articulate and document their learning (i.e., portfolio development), and ways in which evaluators assess and report on students' prior learning.

The policy guiding individualized PLA states:

> The student's mentor for educational planning (and/or the mentor/tutor who supervises the student's work on prior-learning requests) is responsible for helping the student to shape each prior-learning request to meet college expectations. (SUNY Empire State College, 2008b, Applicable Legislation ...: Prior Learning Request and Documentation section, para. 1)

The ways in which a mentor guides students through the PLA process is totally up to the individual faculty member, who acts in accord with his or her philosophical inclinations. The policy provides principles for the assessment of prior learning, but each faculty member must create his or her own mentoring style to assist students through the process. Variation in philosophical approaches can result in uneven student experiences across the College, including for example, the varying degree to which students are encouraged to seek credit for prior learning. At the same time, each approach accents different possibilities for the mentoring of the PLA process. Travers et al. (2008) found variety in mentoring styles ranging from an exploratory approach based on a developmental perspective to a more instrumental approach based on a credentialing perspective. The College is at a point where it needs to explore ways to be more intentional and explicit in its engagement of the tensions underlying PLA practice among mentors.

Policy describes the requirements for what is contained in a PLA request as such:

> The student's request includes a learning description and a list of relevant documents or other materials that s/he can provide to the evaluator to support the credit request. ...
>
> Guided by her/his research and consultation with the mentor, the student proposes a specific title for the learning component, the amount and level of credit, and liberal arts and sciences and/or SUNY general-education designations, if appropriate. In the request, the student makes a case for any of these elements, when needed. (SUNY Empire State College, 2008b, Applicable Legislation ...: Prior Learning Request and Documentation section, paras. 6, 3)

Even with what seemingly is a straightforward policy, differences in interpretation exist. The learning description is the first point of contention. From a redress point of view, the learning description may frame the learning in such a way as to support the recognition of new learning and its applicability to the degree. The access point of view would accept different formats of learning descriptions, including multimedia. (Typically the description is presented as a written essay, but other formats, such as video or concept maps, would provide greater access for some students.) The developmental orientation could encourage students to describe how they acquired their learning, the learning path that led them to this point, and how they have grown through this learning. And the credentialing viewpoint might ask the student to relate the learning to academic terminology and document equivalencies, such as learning outcomes or competencies.

Documentation also varies. The policy indicates that the student is to provide a "list of relevant documents or other materials" that can be given to the evaluator. "List" meant that the College didn't have to store quantities of items as part of the assessment process. As the College now provides technologies that support electronic evidence, different views regarding what is considered evidence have surfaced; and some faculty debate as to whether a list is still a valid way to document learning. (It would be interesting to explore the extent to which variations in what is now considered to be acceptable evidence are linked to the varying philosophical perspectives identified in this chapter.)

The third area of variation in PLA practices across the College concerns the criteria and strategies by which learning is assessed for credits. Effective mentoring and evaluation are dependent on the ability to understand assessment criteria and strategies; key is which criteria and strategies are chosen. Advising students through the process requires faculty to interpret the assessment criteria for the learner and to guide the learner to document knowledge in such a way that it can be evaluated. The evaluator is expected to interpret the criteria, to understand how to use them to review the evidence of learning, and to place that assessment within an academic context. Thus, here again, both moments in the assessment process – the advising moment and the evaluating moment – reflect underlying philosophical perspectives. And the extent to which the mentor and the evaluator share an underlying perspective can have significant impact on the assessment outcome.

Such issues related to the prior learning assessment process at ESC exist within a context of more general questions raised about lack of validity and reliability within PLA due to its individualization. The most common questions raised about prior learning assessment concern its lack of reliability and validity due to its individualization. Stenlund (2013) found poor interrater reliability across assessors. She notes a lack of shared criteria within the community and recommends that such sharing would increase reliability. However, the difficulty in sharing criteria is that these criteria originate from different philosophical perspectives.

Tigelaar, Dolmans, Wolfhagen and van der Vleuten (2005) suggest that standardizing criteria could "detract from the intended contributions of portfolios" (p. 601), which, by their very nature, are individualized. Weigel, Mulder and Collins (2007) concur and indicate that standardization distracts from the context, which provides much information about the learning. They also have argued that when a competency actually has been accomplished is very difficult to measure. Duvekot, et al. (2007) studied more than 200 cases of PLA practices across 11 European countries and found that

> 'Valuing learning' has two main paths, a summative one and a formative one. The summative approach aims at an overview of competencies, recognition and valuation. …When 'valuing learning' goes one step further and includes practical learning and/or personal competence-development, we call this the formative approach. … [It] is pro-active and aims at development. (p. 10)

Boud and Falchikov (2006) suggest that beyond the traditional purposes of assessment, the objective for assessment should also be to provide self-assessment skills, which are essential for the development of lifelong and workplace learning. They argue that traditional assessment approaches are based on the "metaphors of acquisition and judgement … [and] less … [on] the metaphor of participation that is being increasingly used to characterise workplace learning" (p. 406). These different perspectives on assessment criteria emphasize how important it is to understand the purpose behind the assessment strategy, the impact of the strategy on the outcome, and the way in which any assessment strategy is linked to the philosophical perspective of the assessor. The choice to use a summative approach versus a formative approach, for example, is clearly linked to the philosophical perspective of the assessor.

Travers et al. (2011) studied the language PLA evaluators used to write about learners' knowledge at Empire State College. Through a content analysis process, the study unveiled multiple approaches to describing learning. For example, in their reports, evaluators wrote to different audiences. Some provided lessons to the student (from a developmental perspective), while others provided justifications to peers or administration (reflecting a redress perspective). Some justifications used internal or external course matching (counter to redress); others used observations and thick descriptions (related to both redress and access); still others used their own knowledge (also counter to redress). The variety in these approaches appeared to reflect evaluators' philosophies regarding assessment and regarding their role as experts in that process.

## CONCLUSION

Thus, different viewpoints on mentoring and assessing within the PLA process are in evidence throughout Empire State College. When mentors, evaluators and faculty committees come from different perspectives in advising students and accepting learning for credit, tensions can arise between colleagues. And often, students can get caught in the middle. Yet the tensions that arise across the College result less from the fact that people employ different approaches, and more from not understanding the various philosophical underpinnings of both policies and practices.

The analysis of mentoring and evaluating styles presented in this chapter is not intended to imply that faculty should have singular emphases when mentoring students or evaluating PLA. Travers et al. (2008) found that many faculty blended their philosophical approaches, rather than relying upon one single approach. And Travers et al. (2011) found the same in evaluators' reports; often there was evidence of methods being blended. The purpose of presenting these four philosophical themes is to help understand different viewpoints and to recognize when and why they – and the ideas on which they are based – may be in tension. Importantly, the particular interaction of all these goals, policies, and practices – including the student's purpose in pursuing PLA, the mentor's perspective and practice, the evaluator's approach, the faculty committee's decisions, and the institution's philosophy and policy – can alter completely the individual student's experience. Understanding the array of advising and assessment approaches and the impact these have on students' success in completing PLA could help to improve mentoring and assessment practices across the College.

The irony of dissecting each of the philosophical themes as presented in this analysis – including the range of perspectives within each – is that such an analysis, while attempting a closer look at the underlying concepts, may actually reinforce the divisions. By contrasting various perspectives, the associated practices may be dichotomized, and thus result in a view that one or the other is *the way* to do PLA. Yet an augmented approach, one that adds together perspectives, could be more fully respectful of and helpful to the learner and could deepen and enrich his or her experience of this process.

In a discussion of higher education in a postmodern world, Strohl (2006) describes tensions that exist in higher education by noting those who view the university as "a service provider and knowledge producer, for the socio-economic benefit of the individual and society" (p. 135) and those who view the university as a social site, intended to foster deeper discussions and be a "centre of consciousness" (p. 145). He proposes that higher education be an "arbiter – rather than disseminator or guardian – of knowledge" (p. 144) and suggests that to reconcile these different perspectives, we should not place them on an either/or spectrum, but instead bring them together and join in a common effort – in this case, the valuing of student learning.

The question then is how seeming oppositions can be joined as an "and" rather than be contrasted as an "or"; that is, how they can be situated in *creative* rather than oppositional tension with one another. Such an "additive" approach would neither ignore nor negate different views, nor would it try to blend them; rather it would allow them to co-exist and benefit from each other's qualities. Like the mixing of a good olive oil with an excellent balsamic vinegar, each alone is fine and distinctive, but suspended together they achieve much more flavor and enjoyment. What would bringing together the inherent creative tensions in the practices of PLA look like?

Redress provides for the acceptance of new knowledge into the curriculum, with the student acting as an agent for the integration of that new knowledge. If we combined redress with an emphasis on access, the student could be recognized as a partner in higher education and could support an institution in remaining current with developments in industry and society. Adding lifelong learning perspectives, we could view students across a continuum of growth that benefits every student. Although higher education represents only a point in time for the student, it can play a powerful role in helping students develop lifelong learning abilities. Goal obtainment and credentialing provide recognition of this place in time, a summative marker that represents learning required for societal and employment demands. Thus bringing all of these approaches to bear on a student's education would give a fuller learning experience to the student.

What I have called counter perspectives within each of these themes can help us to see advantages of entertaining all points of view. For example, an emphasis on an outcomes orientation can provide a structure needed for credentials and employment; predefined knowledge can provide specific, recognized pathways to identified fields. Highly structured degrees can shorten time to completion for some students. They can provide a clear path and help students see what is needed of them. Pre-structured degrees (as opposed to those that are student-designed) may also be essential for certain areas, such as health care, where knowledge needs to be regulated. When one end of the continuum of possible approaches within a given goal is placed in relation to the other, students have more opportunities. What we need is to be clear about these processes in order to help students sort through which approaches best fit their goals and needs.

INHERENT TENSIONS WITHIN THE PRACTICES OF PRIOR LEARNING ASSESSMENT

Higher education helps individuals make sense of their knowledge and place that knowledge in an academic context. Prior learning assessment plays an important role in accomplishing just that. The future opportunities for the uses of PLA are vast. Understanding the philosophical differences underlying the implementation of PLA is important to seeing more fully how these can coexist and augment each other. And in order to begin to reformulate the ways in which knowledge is constructed, perceived, valued and credentialed, dialogues about PLA across divergent groups working with PLA are critical. By bringing the perspectives together, efforts to employ PLA thoughtfully and intentionally can help move higher education out of the quagmire of debate and in directions that work toward the good of the economy, society and the individual.

## NOTES

[1] Although the assessment of prior learning has various naming conventions and terminology associated with the concepts globally, in this chapter and at SUNY Empire State College, prior learning assessment is referred to as "PLA." The only time other terms are used is within direct quotes from cited authors.

[2] Interestingly, and most relevant to this discussion, as of May 16, 2014, the Empire State College Senate approved new policy that allows PLA credits to be transcribed outside of a concurred degree; however, both PLA policies still need to be revised to allow the transcription.

## REFERENCES

Benke, M., Davis, A., & Travers, N. L. (2012). SUNY Empire State College: A game changer in open learning. In D. G. Oblinger (Ed.), *Game changers: Education and information technologies* (pp. 145–158). Louisvile, CO: EDUCAUSE. Retrieved from http://net.educause.edu/ir/library/pdf/pub7203.pdf

Boud, D., & Falchikov, N. (2006). Aligning assessment with long-term learning. *Assessment and Evaluation, 31*(4), 399–413.

Carless, D., Joughin, G., & Mok, M. (2006). Editorial: Learning-oriented assessment: Principles and practice. *Assessment and Evaluation, 31*(4), 395–398.

Colardyn, D., & Bjornavold, J. (2004, March). Validation of formal, non-formal and informal learning: Policy and practices in EU member states. *European Journal of Education, 39*(1), 69–89.

Conrad, D. (2013). Pondering change and the relationship of prior learning assessment to MOOCs and knowledge in higher education. *Prior Learning Inside Out: An International Journal on Theory, Research and Practice in Prior Learning Assessment, 2*(1). Retrieved from http://www.plaio.org/index.php/home/article/view/51

Cooper, L. (2006). 'Tools of mediation': An historical-cultural approach to RPL. In P. Andersson & J. Harris (Eds.), *Re-theorising the recognition of prior learning* (pp. 221–240). Leicester, England: NIACE.

Cronbach, L. J., & Meehl, P. E. (1955). Construct validity in psychological tests. *Psychological Bulletin, 52*(4), 281–302.

Diedrich, A. (2013). 'Who's giving us the answers?' Interpreters and the validation of prior foreign learning. *International Journal of Lifelong Education, 32*(2), 230–246.

Duvekot, R., Scanlon, G., Charraud, A., Schuur, K., Coughlan, D., Nilsen-Mohn, T., Paulusse, J., & Klarus, R. (2007, September). Introduction: VPL is about empowerment, employability and lifelong learning. In R. Duvekot, G. Scanlon, A. Charraud, K. Schuur, D. Coughlan, T. Nilsen-Mohn, J. Paulusse, & R. Klarus (Eds.), *Managing European diversity in lifelong learning: The many perspectives of the valuation of prior learning in the European workplace* (pp. 9–26). Amsterdam: HAN University. Retrieved from http://www.iriv.net/pdf/VPL2.pdf

Fiddler, M., Marienau, C., & Whitaker, U./CAEL. (2006). *Assessing learning: Standards, principles, & procedures* (2nd ed.). Dubuque, IA: Kendall Hunt Publishing.

Friesen, N., & Wihak, C. (2013). From OER to PLAR: Credentialing for open education. *Open Praxis, 5*(1), 49–58. Retrieved from http://www.openpraxis.org/index.php/OpenPraxis/article/view/22/pdf

Hamer, J. (2010). Recognition of prior learning: Normative assessments or co-construction of preferred identities? *Australian Journal of Adult Learning, 50*(1), 100–115.

Harris, J. A. (1999). Ways of seeing the recognition of prior learning (RPL): What contribution can such practices make to social inclusion? *Studies in the Education of Adults, 31*(2), 124–139.

Harris, J. A. (2006). Questions of knowledge and curriculum in the recognition of prior learning. In P. Andersson & J. Harris (Eds.), *Re-theorising the recognition of prior learning* (pp. 51–76). Leicester, England: NIACE.

Harris, J. A. (2013). Reflection on "Ways of seeing the recognition of prior learning (RPL). *Prior Learning Inside Out: An International Journal on Theory, Research and Practice in Prior Learning Assessment, 2*(1). Retrieved from http://www.plaio.org/index.php/home/article/view/51

Harris, J. A., & Wihak, C. (2011). Introduction and overview of chapters. In J. A. Harris, M. Breier, & C. Wihak (Eds.), *Researching the recognition of prior learning: International perspectives* (pp. 1–13). Leicester, England, UK: National Institute of Adult Continuing Education.

Hawley, J., Otero, M. S., & Duchemin, C. (2010). *2010 update of the European inventory on validation of non-formal and informal learning: Executive summary of final report*. Retrieved from https://cumulus.cedefop.europa.eu/files/vetelib/2011/77641.pdf

Hill, D. (2004). The wholeness of life: A native North American approach to portfolio development at First Nations Technical Institute. In E. Michelson & A. Mandell (Eds.), *Portfolio development and the assessment of prior learning* (pp. 135–159). Sterling, VA: Stylus.

Hoffman, T., Travers, N. L., Evans, M., & Treadwell, A. (2009, September). Researching critical factors impacting PLA programs: A multi-institutional study on best practices. *CAEL Forum and News*.

Kamenetz, A. (2010). *DIYU: Edupunks, edupreneurs, and the coming transformation of higher education*. White River Junction, VT: Chelsea Green Publishing.

Klein-Collins, R. (2010, March). *Fueling the race to postsecondary success: A 48-institution study of prior learning assessment and adult student outcomes*. Chicago, IL: Council for Adult and Experiential Learning (CAEL). Retrieved from http://files.eric.ed.gov/fulltext/ED524753.pdf

Knight, P. (2006). The local practices of assessment. *Assessment and Evaluation in Higher Education, 31*(4), 435–452.

Lambe, J. P. (2011). Communicating college learning through noncourse matching: An approach to writing the prior learning assessment essay. *The Journal of Continuing Higher Education, 59*(1), 50–53.

LeGrow, M. R., Sheckley, B. G., & Kehrhahn, M. (2002). Comparison of problem-solving performance between adults receiving credit via assessment of prior learning and adults completing classroom courses. *The Journal of Continuing Higher Education, 50*(3), 2–13.

Lumina Foundation & Gallup. (2013). *America's call for higher education redesign: The 2012 Lumina Foundation study of the American public's opinion on higher education*. Retrieved from https://www.luminafoundation.org/files/resources/americas-call-for-higher-education-redesign.pdf

Michelson, E. (1997, Fall). Multicultural approaches to portfolio development. *New Directions for Adult and Continuing Education, 1997*(75), 41–53.

Michelson, E. (2006). Beyond Galileo's telescope: Situated knowledge and the recognition of prior learning. In P. Andersson & J. Harris (Eds.), *Re-theorising the recognition of prior learning* (pp. 141–162). Leicester, England, UK: NIACE.

Michelson, E. (2012). Inside/out: A meditation on cross-dressing and prior learning assessment. *Prior Learning Inside Out: An International Journal on Theory, Research and Practice in Prior Learning Assessment, 1*(1). Retrieved from http://www.plaio.org/index.php/home/article/view/15

Middle States Commission on Higher Education. (2006). *Characteristics of excellence in higher education: Requirements of affiliation and standards for accreditation*. Retrieved from https://www.msche.org/publications/CHX-2011-WEB.pdf

Moss, L. (2007, December). *Prior learning assessment and recognition (PLAR) and the impact of globalization: A Canadian case study* (Doctoral dissertation). McGill University, Montreal, Canada. Retrieved from http://search.proquest.com/docview/304372369?accountid=8067

Naudé, L. (2013). Boundaries between knowledges – Does recognition of prior learning assessment represent a third space? *International Journal of Continuing Education and Lifelong Learning, 5*(2), 57–69.

Popova-Gonci, V. (2009). All work and no PLA makes Jack a dull boy. *The Journal of Continuing Higher Education, 57*(1), 42–44.

Shalem, Y., & Steinberg, C. (2006). Portfolio-based assessment of prior learning: A cat and mouse chase after invisible criteria. In P. Andersson & J. Harris (Eds.), *Re-theorising the recognition of prior learning* (pp. 97–115). Leicester, England, UK: NIACE.

Sheckley, B. G. (2007). *Mental models of how the world works: A foundation of adult learning*. Presentation at the International CAEL conference, San Francisco, CA.

Sherman, A., Klein-Collins, B., & Palmer, I. (2012). *State policy approaches to support prior learning assessment: A resource guide for state leaders*. Chicago, IL: Council for Adult and Experiential Learning.

Stenlund, T. (2013). Agreement in assessment of prior learning related to higher education: An examination of interrater and intrarater reliability. *International Journal of Lifelong Education, 32*(4), 535–547.

Stevens, K., Gerber, D., & Hendra, R. (2010). Transformational learning through prior learning assessment. *Adult Education Quarterly, 60*(4), 377–404.

Strohl, N. M. (2006). The postmodern university revisited: Reframing higher education debates from the 'two cultures' to postmodernity. *London Review of Education, 4*(2), 133–148.

SUNY Empire State College. (n.d.). *College mission*. Retrieved from http://www.esc.edu/about-esc/college-mission/

SUNY Empire State College. (2008a). *Advanced standing: Policies and procedures that govern the assessment of prior learning policy*. Retrieved from http://www.esc.edu/policies/?search=cid%3D40463

SUNY Empire State College. (2008b). *Individualized prior learning assessment policy and procedures*. Retrieved from http://www.esc.edu/policies/?search=cid%3D36988

SUNY Empire State College. (2013). *Individualized prior learning assessment: A guide for students*. Retrieved from http://www.esc.edu/media/academic-affairs/ocar/2013-14/iPLA-2013-2014.pdf

SUNY Empire State College. (2015). *Student degree planning guide*. Retrieved from http://www.esc.edu/media/academic-affairs/ocar/2014-2015/SDPG2015-2016.pdf

Tate, P. J. (2013, July). *Keeping college within reach: Improving higher education through innovation* (Hearing before the Committee on Education and Workforce, U.S. House of Representatives, 113th Congress, first session). Washington, DC: Government Printing Office. Retrieved from https://www.gpo.gov/fdsys/pkg/CHRG-113hhrg81802/html/CHRG-113hhrg81802.htm

Timma, H. (2005). Assessor judgements and everyday work performance. *Australian Journal of Adult Learning, 45*(2), 155–171.

Tigelaar, D. E. H., Dolmans, D. H. J. M., Wolfhagen, I. H. A. P., & van der Vleuten, C. P. M. (2005, October). Quality issues in judging portfolios: Implications for organizing teaching portfolio assessment procedures. *Studies in Higher Education, 30*(5), 595–610.

Travers, N. L. (2013). PLA philosophy, policy, and practice implications: Revisiting the 2009 Hoffman, Travers, Evans, and Treadwell study. *The Journal of Continuing Higher Education, 61*(1), 54–58.

Travers, N. L., Smith, B., Ellis, L., Brady, T., Feldman, L., Hakim, K., Onta, B., Panayotou, M., Seamans, L., & Treadwell, A. (2011). Language of evaluation: How PLA evaluators write about student learning. *International Review of Research in Open and Distance Learning, 12*(1), 81–95. Retrieved from http://www.irrodl.org/index.php/irrodl/article/view/946

Travers, N. L., Smith, B., Johnsen, J., Alberti, P., Hakim, K., Onta, B., & Webber, E. (2008, Fall). Faculty voices: A Cinderella story at the PLA ball. *All About Mentoring, 34*, 60–64. Retrieved from http://www.esc.edu/media/ocgr/publications-presentations/all-about-mentoring/2007-8/Issue-34-AAM-Fall-2008-pgs83-91removed.pdf

Van Kleef, J. (2014). Quality in PLAR. In J. Harris, C. Wihak, & J. Van Kleef (Eds.), *Handbook of the recognition of prior learning: Research into practice* (pp. 206–232). Leicester, England, UK: National Institute of Adult Continuing Education.

Weigel, T. M., Mulder, M., & Collins, K. (2007). The concept of competence in the development of vocational education and training in selected EU member states. *Journal of Vocational Education & Training, 59*(1), 51–64.

Werquin, P. (2010, February). *Recognition of non-formal and informal learning: Country practices.* Retrieved from http://www.oecd.org/education/skills-beyond-school/44600408.pdf

Werquin, P. (2012). A second chance for qualification: An interview with Patrick Werquin [Interview by A. Mandell, & N. Travers]. *Prior Learning Assessment Inside Out: An International Journal on the Theory, Research and Practice of Prior Learning Assessment, 1*(2). Retrieved from http://www.plaio.org/index.php/home/article/view/35

SECTION IV

# ORGANIZATIONAL FRAMEWORKS

*Infrastructure, Culture, and Change*

The five chapters in Section IV seek to examine the complex institutional contexts in which teaching and learning at Empire State College take place. How does a particular organizational infrastructure affect efforts to support and echo across the College the core values of a progressive institution? And how can the institution sustain its organizational glue and its identity across disparate pedagogies and cultures while responding to pressures to grow and develop new and widely-varying programs?

In Chapter 12, "Organizational Complexity in a Progressive Educational Environment," L. Wiley raises key questions about the managerial challenges of a geographically dispersed and pedagogically disparate organization, and asks if such an institution can thrive. In Chapter, 13, "Technology Meets the Local: One Mentor's Reflections on Autonomy and Connection in a Dispersed Institution," C. Rounds addresses some of the challenges and tensions arising when a college championing access is located in multiple offices across the state of New York and so develops diverse procedures and cultures. He looks at the ways in which the College's evolving uses of technology in mentoring, teaching, and learning have served both to connect and to distance us and our cultures from one another; and he argues that we can and must be more creative in bridging that distance. In Chapter 14, "Family Feuds, Shotgun Weddings and a Dash of Couples Therapy: The Center for Distance Learning/ Metropolitan Center Blended Learning Initiative," the authors, S. Hertz, C. Leaker, R. Bonnano, and T. MacMillan (one of whom is a faculty member in a regional center working with students in person, and three of whom are faculty in ESC's Center for Distance Learning), relate their experience in combining distinct pedagogical models in order to give students learning opportunities that blend not only diverse pedagogies but also very different organizational cultures. In Chapter 15, "Growth and Its Discontents: Organizational Challenges to a Radical Vision," C. Conaway, based in the Center for Distance Learning and, C. Whann, based at a regional center, examine what they view to be the extraordinary pressures that growth in enrollment has placed on ESC's individualized education model, and question the sustainability of this model in a continually expanding institution. In Chapter 16, "At a Crossroad: The Shifting Landscape of Graduate Education," B. Eisenberg, a mentor in ESC's MBA program, describes a rapidly expanding ESC graduate school, with programs responding to demands for increasing vocationalization and professionalization in higher education, and to changes in technology that allow for greater educational access. Exploring the relationship of these programs to ESC's core values, he then examines the tensions arising and questions the sustainability of models reflecting these values.

LYNNE M. WILEY

# 12. ORGANIZATIONAL COMPLEXITY IN A PROGRESSIVE EDUCATIONAL ENVIRONMENT

Unlike most modern institutions of higher education, SUNY Empire State College (ESC) was not created with academic disciplines in mind, or faculty, or curricula. It was not established with the intention of instructing students in traditional courses by traditional methods, but to guide students in self-discovery. In general, its students do not study together, but alone; its faculty does not plan their studies together, but alone; its programs and divisions operate independently of one another; students enter and leave the college throughout the year; it has no single location; and its alumni are only loosely connected to the institution. The primary model of instruction upon which the college was founded – guided independent study – owes more to the universities of Oxford and Cambridge than to American higher education; although its philosophy of progressive education is very much an American construct.

In keeping with this philosophy, the administrative structures supporting the College's main instructional system emerged organically, as an outgrowth of student and faculty needs, rather than providing a framework from which the College grew. This makes it almost unique in the annals of late twentieth century higher education, a legacy of which founder Ernest Boyer was understandably proud: Boyer not only proclaimed Empire State College his greatest achievement as Chancellor of the State University of New York, but emphasized that his conception of "a new kind of college based on student learning … *around which all other arrangements would be organized*" [emphasis added] was an idea whose time had come (Bonnabeau, 1996, pp. 6–7).

Speaking in July 1981 at the 10-year anniversary of the College's founding, Boyer elaborated on this theme, noting that "My dream was a college … where the focus was not on buildings or bureaucracy or on rigid schedules – not on mindless regulations but on students and education. … My dream was a college located all across the state geared to serve the student, *not the institution or the process*" [emphasis added] (Bonnabeau, 1996, p. 106). In the early 1970's, when the College was conceived and brought into being in a matter of months, student radicals on campuses across the country were clamoring for relevance in higher education, criticizing the staid academy for its outmoded hierarchies and unwillingness to engage the critical issues of the day. In the midst of this turmoil, Boyer imagined an institution that would encourage the kind of personal and social transformation students seemed to want, one based in the progressive tradition of higher education.

Boyer's vision of Empire State College was explicitly non-authoritarian. It was also non-hierarchical, unstructured, and so loosely coupled (Weick, 1976) that in purely analytical terms, the college possessed few of the features theorists associate with organizations: rules, policies, plans, organizational charts, coordinated activity, boundaries, communication systems, self-regulation, interdependence, or predictable responses. As Bonnabeau (1996) observed, "Empire State College began enrolling students while it was constructing an academic program, somewhat akin to laying track fast enough to stay ahead of the locomotive" (p. 40). The College was chartered before it had an academic plan; the *Prospectus* (Boyer, 1971) around which it was organized was conceived in three months; and much within the *Prospectus*, such as the role of mentors and the structure by which the College would operate, was either "suggested" or not fully articulated.

## COMPLEXITIES OF THE PROGRESSIVE EDUCATIONAL ORGANIZATION

Clearly, the movement in higher education today is in the very direction Boyer envisioned. Years before "disruptive innovation" (Christensen & Eyring, 2011) became a byword in higher education, and before the "big three disruptions" of prior-learning assessment, competency-based learning, and efforts to issue credit for MOOC's were receiving attention, Ernest Boyer was enamored of a different educational disruption, one rooted in the work of John Dewey and his pedagogical forbearers. Progressive education is a uniquely American educational philosophy, part of the progressive movement that swept America at the turn of the twentieth century. Its educational principles are lofty: education is based on activity directed by the student; students learn best when they are involved in experiences in which they have a vital interest; individual differences are to be honored; methods, classroom practices, and curricula should be adapted or reorganized to meet student needs; formal, "authoritarian" procedures should be opposed; and ideally, studies should reflect and contribute to the life of society.

True to that spirit, Empire State College built itself around the students whom it intended to serve. Table 1 illustrates the connections between the principles of progressive education and the Empire State model.

Innovative in conception, many of these features are now being adopted by both traditional and non-traditional/for-profit institutions. However, important structural differences exist between SUNY Empire State College and most other academic institutions that relate directly to its progressive origins. Boyer alluded to the major difference, and the one most linked to organizational complexity, when in a 1996 preface to *The Promise Continues*, he admitted that looking back he was struck by "about just how difficult it was [and is] to create a college with no buildings, no traditions, and no procedures to guide people through the day" (Bonnabeau, 1996, p. 7).

Table 1. *Progressive principles embodied in Empire State College pedagogy and organization*

| Progressive education principle | Corresponding ESC education principle |
|---|---|
| Students learn best in those experiences in which they have a vital interest | ESC will be "a college based on student learning around which all other arrangements are organized." Students are responsible for directing their own learning. |
| Education should be a continuous reconstruction of experience based on activity directed by the student | Student interests determine study objectives. Student degree plans are developed individually by students, in consultation with a mentor and a degree planning committee. |
| Recognition of individual differences considered critical | Individualized learning contracts for every study. Credit given for prior learning in multiple domains. Students study at own pace. Accommodations made for differences in learning styles. |
| Opposed to formal authoritarian procedure | Steadfastly opposed to creating a college orthodoxy. No bylaws or operating procedures until after students enrolled. Mentors responsible for typical administrative duties. |
| Fostered a reorganization of classroom practices and curriculum | No fixed curriculum. No classrooms. Guidance rather than "teaching." Student academic interests replace curriculum committees. Independent study a main instructional mode. |
| School should reflect the life of the society | Students' personal and career goals determine academic needs. Social and personal transformation a stated objective. Institution willing and able to respond to changing contexts. |
| Adapt the method to the needs of the student | No seat requirement for successfully completing studies. Only one required course. Open evenings and weekends. Studies available in person, online, in blended formats, statewide. |

Progressive education is at its heart an unregulated, unplanned enterprise. Student needs and abilities determine all that follows. The *Prospectus'* statement that the College "… will rely on a process, rather than a structure, of education to shape and give it substance as well as purpose" (Boyer, 1971, p. 2) illustrates this point: not only was Boyer reflecting the progressive theory that education (i.e., the process) must be a *continuous* reconstruction of students' lived experience, and therefore not only individualized but incapable of being determined beforehand; but signifying that the College would begin with no pre-set structure in mind. Clearly, Boyer and his colleagues were thinking of conventional academic structure – required courses, set periods of time, residency requirements – when they referred to its purposeful absence. Nonetheless, the same principle logically extends to other forms of institutional structure if one begins with the idea that the institution exists "to create alternative models of education other than the classroom ... and to experiment with other models, keeping the student at the center" (Bonnabeau, 1996, p. 24).

When Boyer decided to form a college based on student learning "around which all other arrangements would be organized," the "arrangements" to which he was referring are the characteristics that most organizations use to coordinate and carry out their activities. At ESC, these elements have largely emerged as byproducts of learner issues rather than actions taken intentionally by the college to ensure that its systems are, for example, consistent, rational, or predictable. Hampered by its distributed, individualized model from systematically gathering data related to trends or patterns, leaders are often unable to identify issues as problems until they reach a tipping point – when systems become unusable, dissatisfaction becomes widespread, or disruptions in workflow become inimical to the effective functioning of the institution. The founders' desire to have the institution follow the process of students' learning – to pointedly *not* be concerned with such things as policies, procedures, lines of communication, or coordinating mechanisms – makes it distinct from most other institutions of higher education.

Seen in a different light, the organizing principles illustrated in Table 1 bring with them a set of tensions that complicate the Empire State model. Table 2 displays the progressive and historical foundations of the College in juxtaposition with the related outcomes that it holds in tension.

Each tension listed here, if properly balanced, provides an opportunity to strengthen the institution. As Boyer observed, though, it *was* "difficult" to start a college before an academic program was in place; to envision, propose, and get a new institution approved in a matter of months; to begin operations with no bylaws or operating procedures; and to eschew organizational arrangements that in most other institutions would be considered commonplace. The very features that make Empire State College distinctive have made it difficult to govern: In effect, the institution has backed into the creation of managerial and organizational structures that make leadership possible rather than conceiving of them at its start (as nearly all other organizations do). Further, its principled decision to remain true to its learner-centered vision as the College has grown larger and more complex has magnified the following set of organizational challenges.

## ORGANIZATIONAL CHALLENGES

### 1. Systems are Ambiguous and Unknown

Few processes for getting things done are transparent or predictable, or exist in common across the college, e.g., how mentors notify other mentors about student issues; how to determine needs for particular specializations within areas of study; what happens if an instructor of a group decides to cancel a class; what a new adjunct

*Table 2. Creative tensions associated with the Empire State Model*

| Characteristic/organizing principle | Tensions |
|---|---|
| Purposely created without structure (opposed to formal authoritarian procedures) | Tension between the lack of structural elements that restrict problem-solving, allowing mentors to respond to students as circumstances dictate; and the equity and stability associated with coordinated activities, common practices, and common understandings. |
| Student-driven (education should be based on activity directed by the student; student learns best in activities in which s/he has a vital interest) | Tension between putting the learner first and allowing studies, degree planning, and curriculum development to react; and possessing enough control to ensure that academic oversight informs the process. Between individualization and organizational complexity. |
| Mentors at center of institutional model (reorganization of classroom practices and curriculum) | Tension between the role of mentors as guides of student learning who embody ESC's philosophy of individualized attention; and the ability to know, understand, or plan in relation to one another's practices, specialties, philosophies, and capabilities. |
| Distributed | Tension between the ability to be locally-focused, and serve students statewide through multiple modes of learning; and the need to break down resource and information silos that, while promoting autonomy, lead to issues of integration, coordination, and control. |
| Recognition of individual differences considered critical | Tension between remaining open to the diversity of adult learners and first generation students; and responding effectively to their wide range of needs, preparation, learning styles, and personal circumstances. Between accepting differences and providing/envisioning a realistic chance for students to succeed. |
| Adapt the method to the needs of the student | Tension between the willingness to meet students where they are; and students perceiving their experience as a commodity exchange. Between self-selected modes of study and learning issues that could impede success. Between few requirements and the ability to assess and monitor students' progress. |
| Schools should reflect the life of the society | Tension between having the flexibility to modify systems, structures, programs and methods in response to external demands; and ensuring that the college's core values determine its direction. Between remaining competitive and remaining institutionally coherent. Between new program development and skills of the current workforce. |

faculty member can expect with regard to a sequence of interaction with the college once he or she is hired; identifying where students stand in the educational planning process. Major institutional functions appeared late in the college's history. Formal connections between subunits are weak. Solutions tend to follow problems, rather than being anticipated.

The College's progressive philosophy affords mentors and students great room for creativity and adaptation – something which the relative absence of systems facilitates. At the same time, organizational theorists have observed that as institutions grow larger, more diverse, and more highly differentiated (i.e., specialized), all of which has been the case at ESC in recent years, the greater the need for linkages, coordination, and sophisticated forms of control to keep things organized.

To be sure, academic institutions are far more loosely coupled than most organizations: colleges and universities typically have multiple goals, unclear boundaries, informal mechanisms for coordination, loose vertical and horizontal integration, high levels of autonomy, and few rules. Finding a way to balance the learner-driven, individually inspired ESC model with the needs of a complex organization is a creative challenge facing the College, though. Indeed, Bolman and Deal (1984) assert that "achieving a balance between differentiation and integration is one of the most fundamental issues of structural design" (p. 33). As tasks, functions, locations, and goals proliferate, people and subsystems become dependent on one another to get things done. In turn, increasing institutional diversity requires that special attention be paid to matters of integration among units and subsystems to avoid having organizations become "fragmented, fractionated, and ineffective" (p. 37).

Bonnabeau (1996) observed that ESC was "more chimera than substance" when approved by the SUNY Board of Trustees (p. 34), and that both Arthur Chickering, (its first vice president) and the faculty were comfortable with that ambiguity, wanting no part of anything that smacked of planfulness (p. 165). Finding a way to respond to "… the inevitable intellectual and practical evolution inherent in an increasingly fluid and unpredictable world" (Hancock as cited in Edelman, 2014, The Unique Experience section, para. 5) while maintaining the flexibility and openness that rests at the heart of the college is a key organizational issue.

## 2. Communication is Uneven and Difficult

Numerous problems exist due to: (a) the dispersed nature of the institution, (b) local practices, (c) centralized and decentralized decision-making in a single structure, (d) the independent, highly individualized work of mentors and students, and (e) the existence of silos based on location, modes of delivery, and competing conceptual frameworks. Appropriate people often are not informed about issues relevant to their work; it is difficult to know who should be informed; and linkages that are essential for positive and negative communication are hard to create or maintain.

Linkages, in particular, are the glue that holds most organizations together. In complex organizations, relationships among individuals and groups typically grow stronger as a result of increasing interdependence. If these relationships are not present, or less than effective, "specialized efforts do not get linked together, and various individuals and units may pursue their own goals while ignoring the larger mission of the institution" (Bolman & Deal, 1984, p. 37). At Empire State, linkages of these kinds are both more casual and less likely to happen as a result of formal coordination and control mechanisms than would be the case in other organizations.

The lack of hierarchical control carries certain advantages. Among others, it gives life to the principle that mentor/student interactions rest at the center of the institutional model, and that each mentor embodies the college in his/her interactions with students. The progressive philosophy of re-organizing classroom practices and curriculum to meet student needs manifests itself in mentors' individualized attention to students, as well as their freedom to adapt whatever methods or studies they think necessary to meet students' personal learning goals. Additionally, the relative absence of rules and guidelines means that the college has fewer barriers to overcome when encountering changing circumstances to which it must respond.

These advantages exist in tension with less desirable outcomes, however. The decentralized, mentor-as-college model restricts the flow of information about excellent practices and methods to peers statewide who could use it. Few good channels exist for "scaling up" promising ideas. It is difficult for mentors to keep abreast of colleagues' evolving interests and specializations. People are forced to reinvent existing practices when they don't have regular channels for hearing about and sharing information. In "open systems," especially, where the flow of information to and from various parts of the institution is dynamic and nonlinear, access to information is particularly critical. As Birnbaum (1988) observes, "[S]ystems can respond only to stimuli to which they are sensitive ... data for which no channels exist do not come to [people's] attention" (p. 188).

In order to avoid dysfunctional adaptations (Argyris, 1964), mechanisms need to be found to communicate important information to the right people, and useful information to peers, without adopting the kind of one-size-fits-all measure that compromises the integrity of the Colleges' locally focused, learner-driven model.

*3. Dissonance Exists between Centers and the Whole*

Regional locations of the college tend to function like mini-colleges rather than parts of a single system: micro-cultures, goals, and practices develop at diverse locations that often are only loosely linked to other locations or to the college as a whole. Regional cultures tend to be collegial, while the college's institutional model is bureaucratic. Envisioning one's center or unit as part of a whole runs counter to physical constraints as well as budgetary realities that, historically, create intra-organizational incentives to compete for resources. The difficulty of being heard or understood regardless of one's position in the system contributes to uncertainty and can foster discontent.

In effect, many of the organizing principles on which the college is based unintentionally create silos that, while functional in terms of promoting autonomy and inspiring allegiance among the members of dispersed groups, detract from the ability of the college to function as one college. Structural issues are part of the problem, as is the nature of college life itself.

An institution like ESC – spread across a state, operating in regional and remote locations, offering studies online, face-to-face, and in blended formats – clearly fits the definition of a complex organization. Horizontal forms of coordination like meetings and task forces are typically used to supplement vertical controls in such organizations (i.e., standard operating procedures, hierarchy, etc.). Their use in a dispersed environment like ESC tends to reinforce one's allegiance to center cultures and local mores, though. At units, which are so small that most employees interact with each other on a daily basis, local solutions to problems are both necessary and desirable.

Furthermore, while the managerial need to coordinate activities has grown in recent years, ESC still functions mainly as a collegium, in which members have equal status, decision-making is egalitarian and democratic, and thoroughness and deliberation are prized. Unfortunately, as Birnbaum (1988) notes, because collegial relations are based on the opportunity for regular face-to-face contact, "size ... limits the possibility of the development of collegiality on an institutional level to relatively small campuses" (p. 93). Two cultural systems are therefore in play and potentially at odds with one another as ESC grows larger and more complex: a locally-driven culture that builds community and encourages people to feel like working together – typical of loosely coupled systems in which "the elements of the system are responsive to each other, but ... [seek to] preserve their own identities and some logical separateness" (pp. 37–38); and a bureaucratic culture that, while less personal, facilitates decision-making, advances the college's statewide footprint, and ensures consistency and predictability in students' experience of the college.

Balancing the progressive impulse to respond locally to students' unique circumstances with system-wide issues of academic quality, curricular oversight, and the need to serve students equitably across all divisions of the college is another creative tension facing the college.

*4. Consistency in Instructional and Administrative Practices is Rare*

New employees learn that at ESC "there are no policies, only practices." In keeping with the learner-centered commitments of progressive, adult-serving institutions, responses to particular situations vary; exceptions are readily available; most curricula are governed by guidelines, rather than requirements; and most "rules" governing students' progress are advisory, e.g., when in their careers students should submit degree plans; which studies are essential to a particular degree; how late in a term a mentor may consider a student to have "attended"; what content should be covered in the College's one required course (Educational Planning). Student-centeredness often competes with academic integrity, equity, and reliability in decisions about enrollment, grading, and student service. In brief, there are few policies to guide people's work.

Flexibility in responding to student needs and interests is, of course, what the founders intended. The progressive focus on individual differences, student interests, and student-directed learning fosters a culture in which mentors and administrators are willing to go to some lengths to accommodate learner issues, an attitude encouraged by the lack of authoritative rules that one finds in most other higher education institutions. This focus parallels emerging trends in higher education (Benke, Davis, & Travers, 2012; Fain, 2012a, 2012b), as well as accrediting agencies (Pond, 2002), which are revisiting previously held assumptions about the nature of the educational experience and the resources required to ensure academic quality. In nearly all respects, the 'post-disruption' context for accreditation and quality assurance mirrors the Empire State model, emphasizing local, open, flexible, collaborative, dynamic, tailored, and learner-centered approaches to education.

"Student centeredness" is neither one-dimensional nor unidirectional, however. Creative tensions abound in the interstices between helping students achieve individual goals and ensuring that such goals are of high quality, capable of being assessed in relation to internal and external standards, and adaptive to the skills and learning needs of the students involved. Affording mentors great leeway in interpreting academic guidelines requires, conversely, some method for ensuring that those guidelines are regularly reviewed, discussed, revised based on evidence of students' learning success or lack thereof, and used as a source of inspiration for the development of student learning outcomes. Lack of consensus about what constitutes student progress or acceptable oversight of student work is a source of confusion for both students and mentors.

Remaining true to the College's organizing principles in the face of a growing need for some degree of orthodoxy suggests that the tension between serving students well and ensuring that those services lead to productive, meaningful outcomes receives sustained attention.

## 5. Visions Compete for Priority

The College is proud of its origins and points to its multiple delivery systems as a strength. The heated debates of Chickering and Baritz (its first provost for instructional resources) over the primacy of individualized vs. structured study still engage the college, however; as do concerns as ESC moves into a new age about the relative priority of online, group, and guided independent study. Faculty and programs associated with one mode of learning tend to see curriculum, policy, and culture in one way, while others may view it in another way. Similar differences occur between disciplines, and between newer faculty and those who have been with the institution for some years. Multiple and competing views can be held together, but they can also be a source of intransigence, discord, and confusion.

Because the college is relatively new (having celebrated its 40th anniversary in 2011), and its founding saga so compelling, its organizational history is well-known by most employees. New arrivals are advised to read Bonnabeau's (1996) excellent *The Promise Continues: Empire State College – The First Twenty-Five Years*; and a fair number of employees hired within the first five years of the college's existence still remain. In an institution in which symbols, myths, and significant events provide a backdrop for current discussions about the college's direction, this history plays a substantial role.

Institutional culture can both facilitate and inhibit institutional effectiveness. Organizations with strong cultures, often founded during times of dramatic change, help employees cope with uncertainty, reconcile contradictions, and resolve dilemmas (Bolman & Deal, 1984, p. 151). They provide a sense of clarity when organizational processes are substantially ambiguous or unclear, offering explanations for otherwise perplexing events. As Birnbaum (1988) notes, culture "induces purpose, commitment, and order; provides meaning and social cohesion; and clarifies and explains behavioral expectations" (p. 72).

On the other hand, institutional myths can be stubbornly resistant to change, even when internal or external circumstances alter considerably. At present, the College is facing challenges to its institutional vision on three fronts: (a) it is among the leaders in the national conversation about college completion – which privileges those parts of the college that can provide low-cost, scalable study alternatives; (b) traditional colleges are now moving into the same markets, forcing the College to find new sources of students – often those with professional goals or employers seeking structured learning opportunities; and (c) the College's size and complexity compel its administrative and budgetary models to become more bureaucratic.

Empire State is, therefore, at a crossroads requiring both practical and symbolic change. How well it adapts its vision to accommodate these changes will determine whether it "re-emerge[s] ... stronger, more agile, more creative and poised" to withstand and address the current challenges confronting it (Hancock as cited in Edelman, 2014, The Unique Experience section, para. 5).

## LOOKING TOWARD THE FUTURE

As discussed above, the college's founding philosophy carries with it a set of organizational tensions that it strives to keep in balance. These tensions are creative, in that they offer opportunities to resolve longstanding structural issues while retaining values and features that have informed the College's work since its inception. Many of the principles now being cited as "disruptive innovation" have long been in place at ESC: Rosen (2013) predicts, for example, that 25 years from now higher education will be more mobile, personalized, focused on learning outcomes, disaggregated, accessible, global, and "cooler." To a significant extent, Empire State College has embraced these qualities for years, a true testament to Boyer's vision.

A critical distinction exists between the principles underlying the formation of the College and those of the new paradigm, however. The forces driving the current national conversation are about access, degree completion, reducing costs, finding new sources of revenue, employing business models to increase the efficient production of outcomes, and customizing and packaging educational 'products' for students. The radical, student-centered vision that prompted the founding of Empire State College, on the other hand, took its inspiration from the idea that the experience itself, rather than the outcome of graduating, was paramount. The organizational schizophrenia occasioned by the clash of goals is significant. As the College moves forward it will be important to bring the two models more closely together to advance understanding and organizational coherence. In turn, re-envisioning the College's progressive foundations in light of the changing environments in which it is now operating will allow the College to affirm its distinctive character while addressing many of the systemic issues discussed above.

First among them is the opportunity to create better systems to help people carry out their work. Intellectual and educational policy agendas have converged on a set of changes that many see as irreversible, including changes to disciplinary boundaries, pathways to degree completion, and options for delivering instruction (Ward, 2013). Finding ways to reduce the uncertainty caused by transformative change in the external environment is both critical and challenging for an institution like Empire State College. Developing systems that enable people to communicate more effectively, coordinate their activity, process information, anticipate problems, clarify expectations, and better support student learning will require attention to the interdependent nature of college functions.

Second, the College has an opportunity to validate the quality of the student learning that mentors individually judge is taking place. By finding workable methods to extrapolate what mentors know and see to the institutional level, the information can be used to increase learning outcomes, inform the way that mentors plan and deliver studies, contribute to the College's ability to respond to local needs, and allow local administrators to be more proactive in anticipating student demand and mentor capacity. Better data will also foster innovation, providing a platform for faculty to experiment with creative methods for organizing studies within and across programs, centers, and AOS's. More robust academic program review processes will enhance quality by facilitating regular discussion of the review findings.

Third is the opportunity to ensure that Empire State stays true to its mission and progressive heritage by continuing to serve society. A key incentive for Ernest Boyer, today's leaders have recognized that "… combinations of multiple pathways with multiple delivery options [are] necessary if we are to fulfill the expectations of mass higher education" (Ward, 2013, p. 16). SUNY Chancellor Zimpher's stated goal of enrolling 100,000 new adult students in online programs during the next several years foreshadows increases in structured and online programs, modular short courses, certificates, and graduate degrees. Retaining key ESC features at their core is not only essential for student success and institutional integrity, but will help bridge the gap between present circumstances and those that animated the college at its founding.

Fourth, perhaps most importantly, the College has an opportunity to reaffirm one of its most enduring values by promoting and enhancing individuality in learning. At a time when higher education is in the process of discarding an old paradigm – a teacher-centered, static, prescriptive, model grounded in the concept of time as constant/learning as variable (Pond, 2002) in favor of ESC's learner-centered, dynamic, flexible, and tailored model – these laudable student-centered features no longer set the College apart. What does distinguish Empire State College from other institutions, though, is its continuing focus on individual learners, and on the quality of the educational experience made possible through the interaction of mentors and students. The depth and significance of this relationship, which at its best inspires personal and social transformation, is the realization in practice of Boyer's vision of "a new kind of college based on student learning." As the college continues to strengthen and adapt its systems to meet the demands of a new age, it is this central fact that gives ESC purpose and to which it must remain attached.

## REFERENCES

Argyris, C. (1964). *Integrating the individual and the organization*. New York, NY: Wiley.

Benke, M., Davis, A., & Travers, N. L. (2012). SUNY Empire State College: A game changer in open learning. In D. G. Oblinger (Ed.), *Game changers: Education and information technologies* (pp. 145–157). Washington, DC: EDUCAUSE. Retrieved from https://net.educause.edu/ir/library/pdf/pub7203.pdf

Birnbaum, R. (1988). *How colleges work: The cybernetics of academic organization and leadership*. San Francisco, CA: Jossey-Bass.

Bolman, L. G., & Deal, T. E. (1984). *Modern approaches to understanding and managing organizations*. San Francisco, CA: Jossey-Bass.

Bonnabeau, R. F. (1996). *The promise continues: Empire State College – The first twenty-five years*. Virginia Beach, VA: The Donning Company Publishers.

Boyer, E. L. (1971, February 8). *A prospectus for a new university college: Objectives, process, structure, and establishment. Draft*. Albany, NY: State University of New York.

Christensen, C. M., & Eyring, H. J. (2011). *The innovative university: Changing the DNA of higher education from the inside out*. San Francisco, CA: Jossey-Bass.

Edelman, H. (2014, Fall). ESC 2.0. Leading the future of higher education. *Connections. The Empire State College Magazine*. Retrieved from http://www.esc.edu/connections/fall-2014/esc-20.html

Fain, P. (2012a, November 12). New momentum for an old idea. *Inside Higher Ed*. Retrieved from https://www.insidehighered.com/news/2012/11/12/lawmakers-and-foundations-push-prior-learning-assessment

Fain, P. (2012b, November 19). Another push on prior learning. *Inside Higher Ed*. Retrieved from https://www.insidehighered.com/news/2012/11/19/catholic-colleges-completion-coaching-prior-learning-credits

Pond, W. K. (2002, Summer). Distributed education in the 21st century: Implications for quality assurance. *Online Journal of Distance Learning Administration, 5*(2), 1–7.

Rosen, A. S. (2013). *Change.edu: Rebooting for the new talent economy*. New York, NY: Kaplan.

Ward, D. (2013, July/August). Sustaining strategic transitions in higher education. *EDUCAUSE Review, 48*(4), 13–22. Retrieved from http://er.educause.edu/articles/2013/8/sustaining-strategic-transitions-in-higher-education

Weick, K. E. (1976, March). Educational organizations as loosely coupled systems. *Administrative Science Quarterly, 21*(1), 1–19.

CHRIS ROUNDS

# 13. TECHNOLOGY MEETS THE LOCAL

*One Mentor's Reflections on Autonomy and Connection
in a Dispersed Institution*

Empire State College (ESC), a statewide organization, has eleven operating centers, most of which have several smaller units attached, thus allowing the institution to increase access and serve students locally across the state of New York. Drawing on my 35-year experience at ESC, in this essay I will explore the role that these regionally dispersed centers and their units have played in the evolution of a progressive college and the impacts that increasingly available technologies have had on the institution's organization, on our autonomy and connection, and on our service to students. I will begin by analyzing the key role that local units played in the college's early decades, before the Center for Distance Learning (CDL) emerged as a viable alternative for all students within the state of New York. Next, I will explore some of the ways in which an array of technological changes has transformed our organization and our approaches to teaching/mentoring over the past 15 years. Finally, I will consider both possible pitfalls and potential benefits in our uses of technology to support our organization as one college that offers many avenues of access and many possibilities for study. It is this tension between collegewide connection and local autonomy that I want to elucidate in these pages.

THE CENTER/UNIT MODEL IN EMPIRE STATE COLLEGE'S FORMATIVE YEARS

In 1977, the center at Buffalo, where I began my ESC career, was organized as several others across the state were, with a relatively large center and several outlying units. This pattern responded well to the college's commitment to reaching out to communities across the state, putting mentors within an hour's drive of most students, and serving underserved audiences in less densely populated parts of New York. Before the introduction of the desktop computer, the printer and even the home answering machine, physical closeness to adult students made a difference. Meeting every two weeks or so, exchanging assignments by mail, and talking occasionally on the phone were the order of the day.

Such a commitment to access for underserved populations provided an institutional justification for this unit model. Other benefits emerged only as our experience with the model evolved. As I was to discover in my later incarnation as an associate dean at what was called the Center for Statewide Programs, in order to survive, unit faculty, who needed to support students in fields outside their area of academic expertise, evolved into interdisciplinary problem-solvers. Whatever their academic discipline, unit faculty learned to be generalists because the success of their students depended on it. While many of our faculty were trained, for example, in the humanities, they might find themselves working with students interested in business or human services. And, within the unit, there was not necessarily an expert down the hall in a student's chosen field; so we learned to be *mentors* – question-askers rather than answer-providers.

In addition, few of us on the faculty had any training in education or any formal exposure to the more theoretical underpinnings of progressive education or adult learning. And without formal training in mentoring, we learned from our colleagues and from our students what collaborative learning entailed. We became reflective practitioners in the mentoring trade.

Unit mentoring incorporated several distinct elements. We were teachers in the sense that we supported individual students in designing and carrying out studies within our fields of academic expertise. We were advisers in the sense that we consulted with them as they planned both each term of study and their overall academic program. We also served as academic entrepreneurs and recruiters, always on the lookout for new students and new organizations from which to recruit. We were administrators coordinating our efforts with colleagues, working with unit staff, and identifying and hiring specialists from local colleges and organizations to support our students' studies. For many of us, this broadly conceived mentoring role was a new career path, which existed, to some extent, across the College, but most purely in the units.

I found the unit model, in this early incarnation, to be quite a wondrous thing. By its very nature, the model rewarded well targeted recruitment and punished poorly thought out strategies. Successful recruitment and orientation methods rewarded units with strong enrollments and students who spread the word. Less well thought out or inappropriately targeted recruitment efforts resulted in the enrollment of students ill prepared to succeed in our particular college environment and the creation of a huge and unrewarding workload, as mentors struggled to respond to audiences we were not equipped to serve. Perhaps most importantly, we learned that, to the extent that we supported our students in becoming effective independent learners, we helped them to thrive while helping ourselves by reducing attrition and the need constantly to recruit new students. We learned that the best measure of success as a unit was not the enrollment count but the number of students who stayed with us, successfully completed an individualized plan for their degree, and went on to graduate from Empire State College.

Thus, as long as members of the unit team paid attention to what was going on in their units and communities, they were well positioned to respond quickly and effectively to changes in their local communities. They were free to experiment with new approaches to recruitment, orientation and helping students plan their programs of study. They could adapt the studies designed in response to the changing needs and interests of students; and every successful adaptation made their jobs easier and their students happier.

While the college has come to rely increasingly on enrollments as a measure of faculty workload, unit mentors quickly discovered that substantial time and effort needed to be devoted to other elements of the job. Thus, for example, early conversations with prospective students, whether in group sessions or individual meetings, were crucial to long-term student success. In these meetings, students began to understand what a "mentor" was and how he or she might be helpful. They were alerted to some of the important differences between college study in their previous experiences and college study at ESC. They were, at the very least, given an initial sense of our expectations for their becoming independent learners. At the Binghamton Unit, located in a small city about three hours northwest of New York City, where I spent the last 22 years of my ESC career, we thought of this as "expectation management." Our objective was not to enroll every prospect who showed up at our door, but to help each of those who did to make a well-informed decision regarding whether our college could meet their needs and whether they could meet our expectations.

In the years before the college's Center for Distance Learning went online (as distinct from corresponding with students through postal mail), unit mentors also devoted time to nurturing relationships with people in the community who could serve as tutors (faculty working one-on-one or in small groups with students) and evaluators of students' prior experiential learning. Whether teachers in local colleges or professionals in non-profit agencies or private firms, these people played vital roles as expert tutors, as consultants in the educational planning process, and as recruiters of future students. They got to know, through direct experience, what it took for a student to succeed in the College and were well positioned to advise their employees and students when the fit with ESC seemed good. Many of the College's units also developed very close working relationships with the state's community colleges. Indeed, most of our students were their graduates and many of our tutors were their faculty. We learned to complement rather than compete with one another. As I will discuss below, having come to rely more heavily on CDL as a resource for our students, we have allowed this crucial linkage with community resources to atrophy.

Getting to know more of the whole student through the process of recruitment and orientation positioned unit mentors to provide effective advisement in the most challenging aspect of mentoring: Educational Planning. That process actually had begun for students when they initiated their search for an institution like Empire State College. At the Binghamton Unit, many of them already had two-year degrees and/or years of experience in the corporate world, in human services agencies, and/or in raising families. They had come to realize that completing a bachelor's degree would be a key element, even a necessity, in their personal/professional growth. Though they knew they wanted the degree, and often could identify specific content areas they needed to master, typically they had little idea how to get from point 'a' to point 'b.' And, not infrequently, they had decided to undertake something completely new; for example, though having little background or interest in math, they might have decided still to go into computer programming or accounting, where they had heard jobs were available. Through Educational Planning, a credit-bearing study required of all students at ESC, they took their thinking, planning, and learning about their chosen field further.

Another dimension of Educational Planning that proved challenging to our students was our policy of acknowledging and offering potential credit for their prior college-level learning. For the majority of our prospective and incoming students, receiving credit for learning gained through experience was mysterious and suspicious. Could this potential credit be taken seriously? Would future employers or graduate schools accept it as legitimate credit? It was incumbent upon the mentor to help the student to see the legitimacy of this process of identifying and documenting past learning and acquisition of skills, the validity of its possible outcomes, and its relevance to their overall education.

Through Educational Planning, orientation, and ongoing advising, unit mentors were in the business of helping prospective students become independent learners. This was a learning process for mentors as well that took time and effort in order to gain the necessary expertise. Success in this pre- and early enrollment aspect of mentoring made a significant difference between a student's persisting and a student's floundering and perhaps even disappearing through the initial weeks of his/her studies. Students not succeeding cost both the College and the student – in regard to the investment we had made in them and in regard to the hope they held for themselves for completion of their college degree. And these failures also cost the College in our reputation within the communities upon which we relied; for, no matter how hard we had worked, many of those unsuccessful students explained that failure, to anyone who would listen, as our responsibility.

Recruitment was integral to the unit mentoring role. No one did it for us, and no advertising money was available. Our recruitment took several forms. First, it relied on currently enrolled students and alumni. By being responsive to their needs, our expectation was that they would be pleased with their experience and proud of their college. Their word of mouth marketing was better than anything we could pay for. Second, our recruitment relied on our contacts in the private and public sectors – ESC graduates in corporate and non-profit management positions who thought highly of the College, human resources professionals whose respect we had earned, and community college faculty and staff looking for next steps for their students and graduates who fit our profile: mature, self-motivated and disciplined people looking for an institution that would accept their community college credits and acknowledge their learning acquired outside the classroom.

Once a student applied and was accepted to ESC, another key moment in the process, we came to realize, was the decisive role that well placed and interrelated questions played at the time of the student's initial enrollment: Was the student prepared to devote the time and energy crucial to success in the College? Did the student have financial aid or alternative funding in place? If the answers to these questions were positive, then attention shifted to what studies should be pursued, what mode of study made the most sense, and what course load seemed viable. We once had an extended debate about whether we were playing a parental role with our students regarding these decisions. Why not respect students' individual autonomy and let them make their own decisions? From painful experience, we had learned that many students came to us insufficiently informed to make these choices without assistance. Many assumed that their often dated experience in community college could effectively inform their decision-making in this new context. Too often, they were tempted to choose studies based on the appeal of brief descriptions rather than on an understanding of the foundational studies needed for success. Perhaps most fundamentally, new students were ill-prepared to appreciate the distinctions among modes of study at ESC: How different could these modes be – a small group study, an individual tutorial, a distance learning course – as long as the topic and amount of credit were the same? Our mentoring experience taught us that investing heavily with students in this early decision-making process paid dividends in the long run.

All of this is not to suggest, of course, that the units existed in perfect isolation. Unit mentors were members of a regional center faculty, attending monthly meetings and participating in center committee work. We were also involved at the college level in governance and other service. In addition, learning contracts for individual studies and plans for degree programs designed by unit mentors and students were subject to review and approval at the center level; and unit mentors were reviewed by their center peers and administration, as well as at the college level. So while, for many of us, most of the time, the unit was home, and the rules of the larger institution were open to local interpretation, our work was always subject to review and to the evolving policies and procedures of the mother ship.

## THE MIDDLE YEARS: THE GOLDEN AGE OF THE UNITS

I think of the years between 1990 and the early 2000s as peak years for the unit/center model. The diversity and quality of learning resources available to students were growing. Relationships between units and local communities were vibrant and reliance was mutual. Center for Distance Learning courses contributed to this mix; yet CDL had not emerged as a serious competitor to our regional centers in local markets. Within such a context, we, at the Binghamton unit, felt in control of our fate. We maintained a strong positive reputation by attending to the needs of our students and establishing good relationships with employers in both the public and private sectors. Though having no advertising budgets, we kept enrollments strong by relying on the word of mouth of our students and alumni and keeping channels of communication open with community college faculty, who, as noted above, both directed their students to us and served as tutors and evaluators of the prior learning of our students. Across the college, units had a good reputation both for sustaining enrollments and for the retention of students through graduation.

In these years, our academic year started in late August, with a focus on completing the orientation of students with whom we had already been in contact, and on making sure that returning students were appropriately enrolled for the fall. Long before the college mandated a term enrollment system (which replaced a system allowing for enrollment at many times during any given year), the Binghamton unit effectively worked on that term model. Many students, especially those with family commitments and vacations planned, opted to take the summer off, returning to their studies in September. For those with outstanding incompletes, the summer also provided an opportunity to finish previously neglected work, especially in relation to Educational Planning, the single study most likely to require more time than could be devoted to it during a single term. September set the pattern for the remainder of the year. Students who missed that deadline, or whose applications were received in September and October, often opted to begin their studies in November, while the bulk of our students planned to enroll for the first time or re-enroll in January. The March term offered a second opportunity to enroll for those who had missed January deadlines. May provided another light-enrollment opportunity. Thus the year's workload was not evenly distributed, with heavy workloads between September and May, and a much lighter load during the summer months – a model that seemed to serve our students well. We never turned anyone away at any time in the year, and most students seemed very content with a calendar that was strictly of local creation. Light enrollments in the summer allowed not only student but mentors to catch up on those aspects of the workload that had become lower priorities during the high enrollment months, and allowed everyone to recharge their batteries before the new year began in August.

The vitality of this model depended on a series of interlocking feedback loops. Our daily engagement with both prospective and current students kept unit faculty fully aware of changes occurring in their communities. Discussions over lunch kept each of us engaged in the reflective practice of sharing and examining our work with students. We focused many of those conversations on our failures – students who did not seem to be thriving in our environment and those who opted not to re-enroll though they seemed to be doing well. Recognizing that several dimensions of attrition were beyond our control, we knew that students who left because we, or the College, had not served them well represented a failure on our part. We discussed what had gone wrong, what we might have done differently, and how these failures might be avoided in the future. We valued the reputation we enjoyed in the community, and saw every student who felt badly served as a threat to that reputation. Engagements with colleagues at other units and centers, facilitated by our growing reliance on the internet and by our active engagement with both center and collegewide governance, kept us informed about shifts in college policy and the impact of changes at the level of The State University of New York (SUNY), of which we are a part, and beyond. While our decision-making at the unit remained relatively autonomous, we were free to seek help and advice from administrators at regional and collegewide levels. Supported technologically and academically by administrative and collegial structures, we were free to experiment both with constant adaptations of the topics of the studies we offered and with the ways in which we offered them.

Over the decades, as records were digitized and computer systems evolved, and as the College's ability to track enrollments and student progress improved, the degree of autonomy available to the units shrank. These changes were paralleled by the evolution of institutional rules, driven in part by pressure from external entities such as the state legislature, the State University, and accrediting bodies, and in part by administrative efforts to make sense of an institution that, in its early years, had let 'a thousand flowers bloom.' Students now had to enroll for 16 week terms at either a half-time or full-time rate (policy which would later again be changed). Students actually had to pay their tuition before we could work with them. They had to make progress determined by more stringent rules toward the completion of their degrees. And they were now required to have learning contracts for their studies in place much earlier in the enrollment term than when mentor and student dialogue might have shaped the contract over time. Degree programs needed to reflect the expectations of faculty specialists as codified in the College's Area of Study Guidelines. The good news was that, even with these kinds of changes, Empire State College evolved and survived while many other innovative institutions failed. The bad news was, at least in the eyes of some old hands, that things were no longer what they had been in the "good old days" and that certain kinds of flexibility allowing for responsiveness to our students were gone. From this perspective, the Golden Age had definitely passed.

## THE TRANSFORMATION OF THE UNIT/CENTER MODEL: NEW TECHNOLOGIES, THE CENTER FOR DISTANCE LEARNING AND PEDAGOGICAL CHANGE

*Technologies Lead the Way*

During the past 15 years, the pace of change at Empire State College has dramatically increased. In particular, the arrival of new technologies has had significant impact on the College. Among many other innovations, those with the most direct impact on the units were the answering machine, the desktop computer and the internet, especially the College's increasing reliance on its website. In addition, adopting new technologies for mentoring, teaching and learning resulted in the dramatic growth of the Center for Distance Learning, which has reflected and encouraged many of these changes.

The answering machine might seem to have been a modest change, but in the lives of unit and center faculty its impact was substantial. Over a number of years, as more and more people adopted answering machines both within and outside of the College, the quality and speed of our communications with each other and with students improved dramatically. It might be hard to remember now, but previously phone communication had been exceedingly problematic. With our students working, the likelihood of their answering the phone either at home or work was low. And their return calls were often missed by faculty. That obliged us to rely all but exclusively on the mail and face-to-face meetings. The answering machine transformed that experience, and enhanced the role of the phone in our work with both students and colleagues. In many instances, it also improved the lives of unit support staff, who, over time, were able to abandon the familiar secretarial role of taking and forwarding messages and making appointments. They were freed to play additional roles in the units. The answering machine also enabled us to leave more detailed messages for students. (Trying to explain to a spouse or child our concerns about a student assignment had been challenging!) Now we could have reasonable confidence that the message would be clearly received. While in recent years, e-mail, smart phones and texting have left the answering machine in the dust, during a transitional period, it played a key role.

The desktop computer and the internet also transformed all of our lives, largely for the better. When I became an associate dean in 1982, one of the perks was getting an IBM Correcting Selectric – a marvel, about the size and weight of a sewing machine. And by the early 1990s, most mentors and all support staff had desktop computers. Over the next few years, the evolution of both the computer and the internet allowed each of us to produce, save, and send documents, both within the College and to a growing percentage of our students. On the positive side, this capability resulted in more rapid and clearer communication with students and colleagues, and it made working with colleagues and recruiting tutors to work with our students much easier. Such changes have also greatly facilitated our ability to work with each other's students, at first within the regional center to which each unit is administratively attached and then, very gradually, in other centers and programs across the College. Greater ease of working with colleagues' students also meant that I could ask them to work with one of my mentees, knowing that I could, in the future, reciprocate. Thus each mentor's expertise could be utilized by colleagues and their students, as this suite of technologies enabled each of us to develop and offer studies within our areas of knowledge and research for students across the State of New York and beyond.

At some level, Empire State had always been 'one college.' But during the first 20 years or so that was truer in theory than in practice. Working with each other's students was extraordinarily difficult, and learning from one another's practice took real effort. The advent of digitization, though, has made working across centers and programs possible and has meant that we have the potential to make full use of the broad range of expertise represented by our faculty. Sadly, these new capacities have also brought to light the barriers to achieving that potential of which we had previously been only vaguely aware (about which, more below).

These technologies have dramatically changed the experience of prospective students as well. When I joined the college in 1977, Empire State was quite literally the only option available to most of our students. Residential alternatives were simply not in play. Rigid program and attendance requirements and the inability to integrate experiential learning into their programs of study meant, for many prospective students, that traditional colleges were not an option. The internet, however, has facilitated the proliferation of academic alternatives easily available to anyone with an internet connection. And this increase in possible modes of study allowing students to work from home – which has occurred not just within ESC but across higher education – has meant that, in order to remain competitive, Empire State College must continuously innovate and strengthen both its programs and its modes of delivery.

The creation of the ESC website and prospective students' increasing reliance on it as their 'window' on the college as a whole has, I believe, played a central role in our institutional evolution over the past decade. Simply discovering that ESC exists has always been a bit of a challenge for prospective students. There's no local campus to drive by. There's no football team to root for. There aren't even any school colors, for goodness' sake. So the advent of the internet seemed to us at ESC to be a godsend in letting folks know of our existence. All that a prospective applicant would need to do was a key word search and, presto, there Empire State College would be. How wonderful!

But a key question quickly arose: Exactly *which* Empire State College would prospective applicants find? Would they encounter us in all of our statewide diversity? Would prospects be asked to enter their zip code and be directed instantly to the nearest college location? Would the website showcase highly qualified and creative faculty? Short answer: No. Instead, prospective students, along with all other visitors to the site, were confronted with a welter of choices that seemed intended to offer everything to everybody and that too often ended in discouragement and confusion. For those prospects who actually found their way to an application site, the very first question they were asked, and the one that essentially defined their experience of the College, was: "Do you want to study onsite or online?" Absent any real understanding of what "onsite" might mean at ESC, and given the increasing public awareness of "online" as a promising alternative for adult learners, it should have been easy to anticipate the consequences of this approach (which I will discuss more below).

For prospects who did make their way to the regional centers and units (that is, to the physical locations of ESC across the state) and did enroll, the benefits of the computer and internet were readily apparent. They could produce and transmit documents readily, receive feedback from faculty much more quickly than in the past, and have a much wider array of learning resources available to them – from spell and grammar checks to our own online libraries, with librarians willing to field questions from students and mentors. Importantly, as a result of these kinds of changes, students could become more independent learners. Indeed, I would argue that the very definition of an "independent learner," what I have always thought of as an overall goal of our mentoring and teaching for our students, has changed. Students can now be more independent than ever. Especially for our most isolated learners, the internet has had the potential to be transformative.

## The Center for Distance Learning: Its Growth and Impacts on the Units and Pedagogy

Yet, while these and other technological innovations changed all of our work lives, there seems little doubt that the greatest impact was experienced by the Center for Distance Learning, which was transformed by the evolution of the internet. At CDL, the move from print-based to online courses was sudden and dramatic. Instead of receiving a printed course guide in the mail and communicating with tutors by mail and phone, students in CDL could now complete assignments online, communicate with tutors easily and quickly on the web – a substantial improvement over the previous "snail mail" model – and perhaps most significantly, communicate online with other students enrolled in the study. Students' isolation from one another had always seemed a regrettable yet inevitable by-product of our commitment to individualization. Web-based courses, however, eliminated that obstacle with a keystroke. Now, students who had always been isolated from one another had opportunities to interact within the context of CDL courses.

That benefit is dramatically illustrated in the following student comment offered in a CDL course with a focus on responding to disasters: "Those people have the most amazing experience! Some had been at ground zero, while others were involved with Katrina in New Orleans. And here we are, with no experience at all. Just listening to their conversations is awesome!" On one level, the distance learning course was beginning to resemble the conventional classroom, a questionable direction for some faculty. Nonetheless, for the well-prepared student, the active participation and engagement that these CDL courses could provide for had great potential.

And while CDL had grown substantially in its paper-based incarnation, the move to online courses dramatically improved its ability to deliver studies to remote students. The College's investment in course development and delivery, which has involved instructional designers as well as faculty, has radically improved its appeal, both to prospective CDL students and to regional center and unit-based students who enroll in CDL courses as part of their overall study plans.

Students with strong internet connections had the potential to benefit substantially from access to a wide range of CDL courses; but to enjoy the full range of benefits, they also needed to possess a specific set of skills, which local mentors were in a position to help them acquire or enhance. And, to take advantage of these new learning resources, our students needed to be strongly motivated, self-disciplined and confident in their writing and analytical abilities. They also needed to make realistic decisions about which courses to take, how many to take, and in what sequence to take them. Effective, proactive mentoring was, in short, central to our students' effective use of CDL and to their success in CDL courses. One could say that even in what seemed to be a post-mentoring world, mentoring became that much more vital to our students' success.

In the Binghamton unit, we developed a group study, "Independent Learning Strategies," specifically designed to prepare newly enrolled students to succeed in an independent, distance-learning environment. This study was developed in response to two things I had begun to learn when I earlier served as an associate dean. The first was that most of our students who failed did so during their first enrollment. The second was that their failure reflected their lack of success in adapting to the particular expectations of the college and/or of distance learning, rather than their lack of academic ability. Most students, working with most mentors, devoted their initial studies to topics within their concentration (their "major"), often at the advanced level. When they failed, I concluded, it was more often because they were not effective independent learners than because they didn't have the ability to do the work required.

"Independent Learning Strategies" focused on the process of learning, rather than on the content. It began with a discussion of several keys to survival in the independent learning environment: creating study space, managing time, attending to the development and nurturing of a supportive personal community, and honing critical skills as a reader, writer and thinker. It also introduced students to web-based learning resources and research methods. The group-study format, with bi-weekly meetings, encouraged strong mutual support among students and facilitated a high level of engagement and completion during a student's initial enrollment in the College. In every meeting, we took time to talk about challenges students were facing in their other studies, and about whatever was on students' minds, whether it was the Educational Planning course or responding to family crises. Students discovered that they were not alone, that others shared their worries, and that being an independent learner did not mean never needing to ask for help. Our hope and experience was that this study would build student confidence and capacity, preparing them to engage successfully both in Educational Planning, which required that they take ownership of their studies, and in a wide array of learning modes, whether offered through CDL or highly individualized studies done face-to-face, or simply independent studies carried out at a distance. By marketing this "Independent Learning Strategies" study at information sessions and orientations, and relying on those who had already engaged in the study to promote it to new students as the best investment they could make in their own academic success, we at the Binghamton unit sustained enrollments in the study over a period of 10 years, until various institutional changes (such as SUNY's General Education requirements) crowded out this and other elective studies.

Through our many communications with prospective as well as current students, we strove to manage student expectations around each mode of learning that we offered. The vast majority of our new students had been exposed only to classroom-based learning, mostly at the community college level. For them, that experience defined college study. The alternatives we offered them represented a range of quite distinct approaches, every one differing from what they were used to. Without doubt, every approach to learning has its strengths and weaknesses, just as each imposes its own expectations on students. Yet, as we never tired of saying to each other and wanted to communicate to our students, to the extent that students are aware of and prepared for these expectations, they can anticipate and prepare for each study in each mode.

At the unit, we described the Center for Distance Learning as an important resource that every prospective student should seriously consider, along with the independent studies, group studies and distance tutorials readily available to all students through both their own and other regional centers. We characterized CDL courses as highly structured and relatively time-sensitive, requiring consistent student engagement within a week-long time frame, and thus potentially attractive to students who might have difficulty in scheduling their own engagement in a less structured study. We acknowledged that CDL courses, precisely because of their high level of structure, were less adaptable to particular student needs and interests than independent and/or individualized tutorials. And we alerted students to the fact that CDL tutors, like adjunct instructors throughout academe, might vary some in regard to both degree and kind of engagement with students. We told our students that they could thrive in the CDL environment as long as they had the discipline required to respond to CDL course expectations for a set schedule of participation. If they were searching for deeper, more individual engagement with faculty, or for a study specifically tailored to their particular interests and needs, we encouraged them to rely more heavily on guided independent studies. In sum, we in the Binghamton unit found the online CDL courses to be a great help for many of our students. They enhanced our ability to respond to a diverse student body with a broader range of learning opportunities. As long as we, as mentors, were in a position to guide students through their choice, pace and sequencing of studies, our unit's capacity and effectiveness in responding to student needs were strengthened.

The distinctiveness of unit and center cultures was quite apparent here. Other units and centers across the college, depending on their views of CDL's approaches and of the potential of online learning, responded differently to the opportunities presented by CDL. Some welcomed these new learning opportunities; others questioned their appropriateness for their students. What has been most striking to me is how the choices available have been explained by mentors with less enthusiasm about the CDL option. The most frequent response I've heard is: "My students don't want to take distance learning courses. They want to meet with their tutors." Other mentors, in more geographically isolated units, have offered a more pragmatic explanation: "My rural students don't have access to high-speed internet; so taking CDL courses isn't a realistic option." In Binghamton, we've wondered if student attitudes toward distance learning studies, or any other learning option, are strongly influenced by the ways in which those options are presented to them – or not presented at all.

A similar pattern can be seen in regard to offering group studies. In ESC's early years, even suggesting group settings for students' study caused consternation. "Everyone knew," the argument went, "that adult learners had had enough of classroom-based learning; they preferred studying on their own." Additionally, the argument continued: "It was well known that busy adults would find it impossible to shoehorn group studies into their busy schedules." Beyond these learner-focused reasons, our administration was concerned that offering study groups would make Empire State College look like every other college, and put our hard earned exemption from Carnegie unit rules (related to contact hours per credit) at risk. Institutionally, it took us years to recognize, to rediscover, that adult learners were glad to do things together in groups. In many regional centers, study groups became a staple, sometimes taking on many of the characteristics of traditional classes. Even in the smaller units, where recruiting enough students to constitute a study group presented challenges, we learned to adapt the group model in ways that responded to the constraints on our students' time. When thoughtfully constructed, we realized, study groups can serve as a helpful supplement to independent study, rather than as a substitute. Occasional meetings allow students to share their experiences with each other and, it is important to note, did not have to become an opportunity for a mentor to lecture. Still, in some units, study groups continue not to be offered, with one typical explanation being something in the spirit of: "Our students can't do group studies."

In the Binghamton unit, our experience has been mixed. "Independent Learning Strategies" was a popular group study, offered in the fall and spring, with enrollments between five and 10 students every term over a period of 10 years. We also offered, for a similar period of time with equally positive results, a group study designed to meet the General Education requirement in foreign language. In each of these cases, we found that the study group format tended to improve retention. The more structured format, coupled with peer pressure to come prepared for each meeting, appeared to support new students through the transition to independent learning. (Interestingly, when General Education requirements were relaxed, demand for the language study evaporated.) We concluded that carefully designed group studies, developed in response to students' perceived needs, are not only possible but academically desirable, even in the small units.

In an ideal world, students and mentors together would make decisions regarding what to study and how to study it based exclusively on the needs and interests of the student. While this ideal was probably never perfectly achieved at Empire State College, the degree to which mentors and students have approached it has been noteworthy. Although a more difficult task as the college has grown, most mentors are aware of the range and quality of collegewide learning resources available to their students, guiding them toward the selection of studies and methods of delivery that are realistic in terms of their students' interests, abilities and constraints. In my experience, new students want, more than anything else, to be successful. And they look to their mentors for guidance in choosing their studies. Of course, that is not always the case. There will, I suppose, always be students who insist on enrolling as full-time students for 16 credits in their first enrollment, just as there will always be those who reject the argument that advanced level studies may indeed require prerequisites. Almost as often, though, a student will prove me wrong, by thriving in a study for which I considered him/her ill-prepared, or failing in a study which seemed a perfect fit. The norm, however is that most students, most of the time, are happy to be guided in their selection of topics and methods of delivery. Students, after all, expect their mentors to be experts and to have their best interests at heart. Indeed, mentors face a greater challenge when they persist in asking students to make decisions for themselves than when they offer them a limited array of options from which to choose. In sum, mentors at ESC have long walked a tightrope, highlighting the rich and creative tension between supporting students' independence and guiding them in helpful ways.

## CLIMATE CHANGE AT ESC: CHANGES IN FUNDING AND THE NEED TO GROW

The past decade has, I believe, witnessed a series of crucially important changes in the College. The impact of these changes at the unit level has been strong. The model that had worked so well for us previously, involving local connections and word-of-mouth student reports on their studies at ESC, has been superseded by one capitalizing on web-based recruitment and enrollment. Enrollment growth, which had not been an objective in the unit model, has become the coin of the realm. And even as the centers and units have continued to generate the majority of graduates, recently much of the college's creative energy and administrative attention has been devoted to programs promising growing enrollments through investment in distance learning course development and delivery.

Focusing on enrollments was easy to understand. With ESC's state funds shrinking, sustaining the college's drive for innovation and its reputation as a leader in non-traditional higher education seemed to require increasing enrollments. Yet, the centers and units had always focused on serving students; they were not really designed to foster continuing growth. The mentoring model was simply not 'scalable,' to use the economists' term and one more and more present in higher education today. To serve more students, we needed more mentors, but faculty lines were a scarce and expensive commodity. The Center for Distance Learning, by contrast, was designed from the outset to be scalable. More enrollments could be accommodated by increasing the number of sections available during a given term. And while more sections required more instructors, these adjunct faculty could be hired on an as-needed basis at costs well below that of full-time faculty.

The Center for Distance Learning has also benefitted from the college's shift to online application and enrollment processes. As noted earlier, prospective students, when they approach the college through its website, are asked if they wish to pursue their studies online or on site. Without a thorough understanding of the differences between these alternatives, most prospects have opted to study online. Why would they want to go to a college location to study when they could study at home? Many are not even aware that they live close to a center or unit, and none are likely to appreciate the benefits inherent in being able to meet, face-to-face with a mentor.

On a somewhat more abstract level, the increasing digitization of the College has driven a process of standardization, including for example, the term calendar and faculty-developed courses offered college-wide, a standardization that has imposed limits on mentors' ability to adapt the College's rules to local realities and our students' needs. The growing ESC presence online has provided leverage for the central administration's long-held desire to achieve more uniformity across the institution. Yet, while this desire is entirely understandable, it threatens the diversity which, I would argue, is the key to ESC's long-term survival in turbulent academic, economic and political times, and reminds us of the ongoing tensions between autonomy and connection that drive so much of our institutional lives.

In retrospect, one of the perverse consequences of our growing reliance on web-based access to the college involves recruitment. When recruitment was tethered to the center and unit, the drive to recruit new students was tempered by the awareness that those new students would have to be served. In the case of the units, recruitment was a responsibility of mentors, who would have to provide that service. In this environment it was relatively easy to resist the urge to promise more than we could deliver; it was reasonable to pose questions of applicants whose needs might not match well the College's offerings or approaches. Local mentors and staff, who understood both the College's strengths and its weaknesses at their location, could responsibly advise each prospect in his or her search for a college that could meet his/her needs.

Recruitment in the online environment, however, took on quite a different tone. It looked a good deal more like marketing. The number of 'hits' on the website and the numbers of expressions of vague interest that resulted in applications completed were the key measures. How effective the fit was between the student and the program was harder to measure and was, in any event, not the recruiter's problem. And while the traditional centers and units confronted a limited geography and demography, the web was accessible to prospective students from literally anywhere. As a consequence, while people recruiting at centers and units were keenly aware of the potential costs of poorly informed enrollment decisions within delimited communities, recruitment online, which included an infinite universe of prospective students, was entirely insensitive to these costs.

During a period of enrollment growth, these new systemic stresses were not particularly apparent. With the college's enrollments growing at about 5 percent per year, the centers and units could continue to meet their targets while CDL enrollments boomed. Good times generate good feelings. But with the massive economic recession beginning in 2008, the context (and mood) changed. SUNY budgets had been and continued to be cut, and, as the recession spread, prospective students found it increasingly difficult to justify devoting their scarce resources to pursuing the dream of a college education. Many employers, who had historically provided reimbursement for education expenses to their employees, reduced these and other benefits in response to hard times. And gradually, as state funding decreased and enrollment growth slowed, the college's 'rainy day' funds were exhausted, hiring freezes were imposed, and the search for cost-saving measures was on.

In this challenging environment, the real costs of the College's long term budgeting model became apparent. In that model, our academic centers, which included their units, had actually been, in some small way, in competition with one another. Centers where enrollments were growing were fed resources while those that lagged behind saw their budgets trimmed. And within the centers, units, and programs, the pattern was the same: The weak were sacrificed so that the strong could grow. As long as the centers in question were fundamentally comparable, this model made some sense; and in its implementation, central administration and center deans could adapt it to the College's commitment to the communities it serves and the social role it plays.

As state funding is significantly diminished and the reliance on tuition to meet our budgetary needs increases, the struggle for scarce resources has taken on a more destructive role. In these circumstances, decision-making may be informed more by the goal of increasing enrollments than the goal of meeting the needs of the academic program or even of carrying out the College's social mission. Could it be that we are reaching a point at which whether students are succeeding – as measured by their successful completion of studies, by approval of their degree program designs, and by their graduation – becomes less a sign of the College's success than enrollment generation?

Had the web-based marketing been truly national in its scope, its impact at the center and unit level might have been negligible. But that was not the case. Even though the Center for Distance Learning was designed to serve national and international students, the vast majority of its students have been residents of New York. As a result, units like Binghamton gradually became aware that they were in direct competition for students —more than had been the case among regional centers, whose marketing had been local and whose demographics varied – with another branch of *their own college*. And here again the issue of what prospective students knew or did not know was crucial. Prospective students from the southern tier who indicated, when they began the application process, their interest in studying online, were typically unaware of the existence of units located close to them. And the units themselves have never been provided with information regarding CDL students located in their communities. Only those CDL students who happened to hear about the units and centers from friends or acquaintances, or who searched diligently, discovered that they might meet with an advisor locally and find guidance in the academic planning process from mentors with deep experience in that area. Thus the College has, through its incomplete marketing, which has placed CDL in direct competition with regional centers, effectively deprived its students of access to the broad array of learning resources that should have been available to them. Once again we see the tension between the potential benefits of one college that the use of new technologies has enabled and the advantages of multiple locations of a dispersed institution.

### A GLIMPSE OF ONE FUTURE: THE NEXT FEW YEARS

The next few years promise a bumpy ride. Declining state support seems to be a given. Increasing competition from other institutions in the distance learning arena seems assured. And continued reliance on enrollment growth as a measure of success within the College looks increasingly like an addiction. How we deal with these external and internal challenges will be key to the College's future. If Empire State College is to thrive, it must embrace its complexity, integrate its disparate elements, and celebrate its uniqueness as an institution offering a rare mix of individual attention, responsiveness to the particular needs of every student, distance learning, and programmatic diversity. We must also become truly one college – a college with diverse modes of study and program offerings, but one college – a college that is driven by a commitment to provide not just a hodgepodge of courses, but coherent, thoughtfully designed degree programs, and a college that is both anchored in communities across the state and able to respond to distance learners around the world. To accomplish these goals, we will have to abandon bickering amongst ourselves, to present one, multi-faceted but coherent identity to external audiences, and to nurture a faculty that combines the best aspects of both individualized and more structured programs and of both face-to-face and online mentoring and teaching.

Through its budgeting, marketing, and enrollment management systems, ESC has created a series of barriers that unnecessarily narrow the range of academic options available to its students and inhibit centers from working together. These unfortunate results of our policies and procedures could have been and could still be avoided. A few straight-forward and doable changes could have transformative institutional impact, increasing the array of options available to students and challenging mentors and administrators to respond creatively and collaboratively to a new pattern of demand within New York state.

For example, if prospective students were asked simply to enter their zip codes as the first step in a single application process, they could be put in direct touch with the ESC center or program nearest them. Their orientation could then introduce them to the full array of study options available to them, and guide them through the design of a degree program that was responsive to their particular needs in terms of both content of study and delivery mode. In this approach, the Center for Distance Learning would continue to provide orientation and support students' degree program design, to provide services for students outside New York, and to continue course development and delivery within the state. Centers and units, with a commitment to employing all study options, as appropriate to each student, would continue to provide orientation and support degree program development to students in their area, while also focusing on the full range of study options available to all, as they work with an increasing body of students. Thus, in order to assure that all students would be well positioned to make informed choices regarding what they study, when they study it, and how they study it, online, blended, and face-to-face modes of study, as well as individualized and pre-structured programs, would all be included in orientation and available in planning.

With this modest change, in my view, Empire State College could, even within our current challenging context, regain its competitive advantage as a leader in nontraditional adult learning, offering every student the opportunity to work with a richly qualified faculty and professional staff in the design of a degree program that is responsive to his or her academic and professional interests, and that is specifically tailored to his/her needs and preferences regarding modes of study. Thus, we could respond to tensions between the pressures and demands upon us and our intention to remain genuinely student-centered. We could work with tensions between ongoing change - including technological and budgetary change – and sustaining our progressive identity. And we could be one college, with units, regional centers, and the Center for Distance Learning all working together to meet the needs of our students.

SARAH HERTZ, CATHY LEAKER, REBECCA BONANNO AND
THALIA MACMILLAN

## 14. FAMILY FEUDS, SHOTGUN WEDDINGS AND A DASH OF COUPLES THERAPY

*The Center for Distance Learning/Metropolitan Center
Blended Learning Initiative*

Almost from its inception in 1971, Empire State College has offered students and faculty opportunities to work in different learning modes, including the foundational face-to-face teaching and learning model at regional centers and distance learning through the Saratoga Springs-based Center for Distance Learning (CDL). As of the early 2000s, all distance learning (that began at ESC in correspondence course fashion) has been provided through electronically mediated instruction. While some faculty members have taught in both modes, by and large, mentors and students working face-to-face and at a distance have existed on parallel, rather than intersecting, tracks.

In 2011, the college instituted an experiment by locating distance learning faculty at the regional Metropolitan Center in New York City, a center in which most of the teaching and learning occurs face-to-face (in one-on-one tutorials or in small seminar-like "study groups"). This experiment provided multiple opportunities for students and faculty members to learn and collaborate. Students at the Metropolitan Center (Metro) were provided with a more scaffolded introduction to online learning through a blended approach to learning, one that combined face-to-face and online instruction within a given study. Regional and distance learning faculty were able to bring their respective expertise to this blended learning initiative by working together to develop five blended courses in multiple areas of study, all of which were offered to students at Metro and CDL, and one of which was co-taught by a faculty member from Metro and a faculty member from CDL. In this chapter, we describe how the seemingly uncomplicated endeavor to blend online and face-to-face learning became very complicated indeed.

In early 2012, with the full support of the deans of the Metropolitan Center and CDL, the three New York City-based CDL mentors (Rebecca Bonanno, Sarah Hertz, and Thalia MacMillan) met with Associate Dean Cathy Leaker of the Metropolitan Center to plan a blended learning initiative. We recruited faculty mentors from the Metropolitan Center to work with us and, together, we selected five courses to be offered in blended format for the September 2012 term. This apparently seamless collaboration between the Metropolitan Center and CDL slowly began to feel more like a shotgun wedding, with all the challenges and complications that such a wedding may involve.

In a 2012 white paper, *Blended Learning Technology: Navigating the Challenges of Large-Scale Adoption*, Greenberg (2012) noted that successfully integrating technology into educational contexts involves not only procedural and academic challenges, but cultural challenges as well. This insight partially explains the complications we were experiencing in our relatively small-scale project. We frequently found ourselves up against not only procedural barriers (e.g., how we would list and market the courses), but also more basic questions about what course (terminology used in CDL) or group study (terminology used in regional centers) development and delivery meant in each of the centers and how language and other pedagogical assumptions reflected the centers' different cultures. Indeed, it gradually became apparent that, by necessity and preference, each of the centers had developed its own philosophy about, and procedures for, teaching and learning within the larger context of Empire State College as a nontraditional institution of higher education.

While there was undoubtedly overlap between our approaches, the discrepancies we encountered were substantive enough to constitute a tangible binary. In full recognition of the reductive risk inherent in any such schematic framework, we tentatively posit the following characterization of the binary as it became increasingly evident in the course of our work together: Metropolitan Center faculty were initially guided by a "contractual paradigm" in their approach to their blended studies, while CDL faculty's approach initially stemmed from an "instructional design paradigm." According to the ideal of the contractual paradigm operative at the Metropolitan Center, mentors are encouraged to promote learner-centeredness through developing with students individualized studies guided by student goals and interests. By contrast, CDL's instructional design paradigm operationalizes this same value but by offering students a wide variety of more structured, faculty-developed courses that meet the needs of many adult learners in a competitive labor market; in these courses, teaching and learning activities are set by faculty and are enhanced by principles of instructional design. These distinctions were not absolute, nor were they new; rather, they are contingent and somewhat fungible products of a longstanding cultural division within the college that, over time, resulted in two distinct paradigms for teaching and learning. Ultimately, we found that we needed to have the ability and willingness to acknowledge and engage openly and honestly with the cultural dissonance generated by these paradigms. By doing so, we were able to move the project forward in a way that maximized cooperation and minimized conflict.

## I. STAR CROSSED PEDAGOGIES: A BRIEF HISTORY OF A FAMILY FEUD

ESC faculty and staff are justifiably proud of our historic mission, the college's role within the State University of New York (SUNY), and, more broadly, within the ever-growing field of adult higher education. With that said, we have a mistaken tendency to assume the college grew from a singular origin and is sustained by a singular tradition. Yet, as college historian, Richard Bonnabeau (1996), pointed out, ESC was conceived, designed and developed within a context of two competing models of alternative higher education. According to Bonnabeau's account, when SUNY Chancellor Ernest Boyer developed the prospectus for ESC in 1971, he and his team were guided by two successful, contemporary models of alternative adult education: Goddard College – a small liberal arts college in Vermont, and the British Open University (BOU). Goddard College, guided by the ideas of seminal theorists like John Dewey (1938) and William H. Kilpatrick (1951), and shaped, in part, by Arthur Chickering's pioneering research on student identity, embraced a model of individualized learning as operationalized in the learning contract, a document that articulates the agreed upon goals, focus, and activities of a particular student's study. Within this model, even group studies were co-conceived and developed by students and faculty in relation to the students' particular goals. The BOU, in contrast, was built around a model of the widest possible access to expertly conceptualized and mass produced courses. While Boyer's decision to hire Chickering as ESC's first academic vice-president suggested a conscious preference for the Goddard model at the college's inception, the rejection of the BOU model was never absolute. As the college grew and changed, the BOU approach remained an increasingly powerful countervailing force to Chickering's model. Indeed, what we in 2011 encountered as the contractual paradigm and the instructional design paradigm were arguably the theoretical and pedagogical legacies of Chickering and the BOU, respectively. And while the separate development of these paradigms may not have engendered the violence of more famous family feuds and shotgun weddings, it certainly provoked some tension, disagreement, conflict and competition.

Many of the assumptions the Metropolitan Center team brought to the blended project emerged from practices established during Chickering's tenure as the college's first academic vice-president. Perhaps foremost among these was the individualized learning contract. Chickering's belief in the individualized learning contract as the fundamental instrument for actualizing student centered practice was based on his conviction, shared with other adult educational theorists like Malcolm Knowles (1986) and Allen Tough (1979), and grounded in progressive theorists like John Dewey (1938) and William H. Kilpatrick (1951), that true learning is best facilitated by a system of mutual commitments between student and faculty member rather than of entrenched hierarchy, with faculty stipulating the content and processes of a given study. For these theorists, authentic learning emerged from an individual's unique desire and curiosity, not from imposed, predetermined curricula. This theoretical perspective had an enormous influence on the early workings of ESC. As the 1971 *Empire State College Bulletin* explained to its potential students, the learning contract is "an agreement between student and Mentor to a series of activities and responsibilities which *both agree* [emphasis added] have merit and value" and "must, therefore, be drawn to *take account of the realities which characterize both parties*" [emphasis added] (p. 36).

Although the vision of the learning contract expressed in the 1971 bulletin has been subjected to regional variation, the core assumption that all learning starts within a faculty mentor/student dyad and not within a larger organizational framework remains the defining feature of the contractual paradigm. It exerts considerable influence on the assumptions and practices at the Metropolitan Center and is palpable at a number of levels:

- Language: In order to emphasize the role of student agency in learning initiatives, the preferred Metropolitan Center terminology is "studies" rather than "courses."
- Curriculum: Study offerings emerge organically from discrete dialogic encounters of student need on the one hand, and faculty expertise, on the other. Accordingly, studies change frequently and are not tied to set standards or predetermined objectives; faculty, and, theoretically, student autonomy are privileged above institutional curricular expectations and administrative oversight.
- Teaching and learning: Facilitated by full and part-time faculty, teaching and learning occur in small groups or one-to-one independent studies; adjuncts both design and deliver approximately 15 percent of group instruction.

Given the cultural dominance of the contractual paradigm at the Metropolitan Center, the Metropolitan Center team approached the blended initiative with a number of tacit assumptions, which only gradually became apparent. As these assumptions began to surface, members of the Metropolitan Center team were surprised to discover that these ideas were not only not fully shared by their CDL colleagues, but also seemed baffling to them.

The ambivalent reaction of CDL colleagues to the contractual paradigm can in part be attributed to the history and development of CDL within the college and to the culture that emerged as a result. Equally committed to the founding mission of access and progressive education, CDL was established with a mandate to create a series of replicable, free-standing courses that would support students working at a distance and, in its inception, maintaining communication primarily through telephone and postal service. Although this directive might seem a departure from the individualized contractual practice nurtured by Chickering and others, the college's founders had always recognized that many students would need and want faculty developed courses, marked by careful design, which would provide clear structure in addition to, and sometimes even instead of, personalized learning experiences. In its first two years, under the leadership of the early Chickering adversary and ESC provost for instructional resources, Loren Baritz, the college had supported the design and delivery of expertly constructed "learning modules" that could be incorporated into learning contracts. Founding President James Hall conceptualized these ideas on a more programmatic level, arguing that as valuable as individualized education could be at its best, an educational program that offered "reasonably structured though not wholly prescriptive" learning opportunities would be especially beneficial to those students who lacked academic preparation and/or confidence and those who could not take advantage of the face-to-face mentoring that was a necessary supplement to individualized learning (Bonnabeau, 1996, p. 80).

When CDL was formally established, its charge to support students' learning at a distance provided a rationale for a broader, more systematic implementation of Baritz's structured learning resource modules. It was posited that because they could not meet regularly with a mentor, distance learning students would presumably need a more structured and predictable delivery of defined content. As its own learning center, moreover, CDL could design an entire course for its enrolled students, rather than simply create an array of resources that regional faculty and students might or might not include in a given learning contract. While some regional faculty remained suspicious of the new model (significantly around issues such as equitable distribution of limited resources), CDL could now move forward with its commitment to developing student-centered courses outside the terms of the contractual paradigm.

In addition to the influence of the BOU and of Baritz, the growing instructional design movement influenced course development practices and would gain even greater ascendance with the explosion of online learning in the '90s and CDL's transformation into a preeminent provider of online public higher education. The instructional design approach began to take hold in the '50s and '60s, but really flourished as the potential for delivering education over the Internet became more apparent. Initially drawing from the theories of behaviorist B.F. Skinner and bolstered by early practical successes in the military, instructional design emphasized the value of clearly defined learning objectives and of assessment targeted to those objectives. Gaining legitimacy to the degree to which they could schematize effective teaching, instructional design precepts dovetailed with the philosophy, encapsulated in the BOU, that outstanding teaching could be "packaged" (and replicated for mass audiences). For CDL, instructional design promised an approach to the needs of adult learners that was simultaneously innovative and systematic. It should also be noted that since advocates of instructional design, such as BOU and CDL, had historically invested in cutting-edge instructional media to deliver their packaged content, they were well positioned to take advantage of the Internet's possibilities in the late 1990s and early 2000s. Indeed, the revolutionary impact of the Internet introduced a new actor to the development process: the professional instructional designer, whose expertise in educational technology, learning theory, and instructional design could support effective sharing of faculty expertise in online environments (Clark & Mayer, 2011; Thach, 1994). All these elements contributed to the explosive growth of CDL since 2002 and the particular processes by which the center managed that growth. By 2010–2011, CDL accounted for 46 percent of total Empire State College enrollments, a remarkable jump over a mere seven-year period from the 26.7 percent of total enrollments CDL posted between 2002 and 2003. In 2012, over 500 courses were offered online. (Important to note is that while the number of CDL's full time faculty has more than tripled since 2002, approximately 75 percent of its courses are taught by adjuncts.)

Fortunately, the CDL model and the instructional design practices that facilitate it are expressly suited to manage such growth. At CDL, the process of course development is by necessity more carefully structured than it is at regional centers. Each course is developed through a multi-step process involving faculty mentors and specialists in online curriculum design. Faculty with content area expertise develop course goals and learning objectives, as well as select up-to-date learning materials and activities. Instructional designers help faculty design the course employing effective practices in online pedagogy, including ADA (Americans with Disabilities Act) and copyright compliance. Once designed, a committee of mentors reviews each course for content clarity and cohesion, as well as determination of appropriate course designations (liberal or non-liberal, advanced or lower level). This rigorous process provides an official approval of the course before it becomes available to students and usually results in courses that are highly structured. Students are provided with an entire term's content laid out in the online learning management system, with content organized into modules and assignments with specific deadlines. So as to provide students with course content that is academically rigorous, accessible, and consistent across instructors, all sections of a particular course use the same learning goals and objectives, materials, and activities. Still, students are often given freedom to individualize learning by choosing their own topics for projects and assignments. Optimally, instructors are in close contact with students to help each one get the greatest benefit from his or her particular experience in the course. Given the course development process at CDL, it is clear that the differences between the two learning paradigms are cultural as well procedural – the one involving student designed, the other involving faculty designed study; the one open to modification as the term progresses, the other laid out from the start.

Not surprisingly, before discussing in more detail the impact of these distinctive legacies on the joint CDL/Metro blended project, it is worth noting that our initiative was not by any means the first college attempt to blend face-to-face and online learning modalities. Perhaps the most innovative and certainly the college's most successful blended model is the residency model, in which intensive face-to-face learning experiences (often over the course of a weekend) are supplemented with ongoing and, after 2000, online interaction between a mentor and a group of students. This model has been successfully implemented in our regional centers (but not in the Center for Distance Learning), in our graduate school, in the Forum program, which until recently served business students in Albany and Buffalo, and in a host of specialized learning opportunities that focus on a special theme, such as the Civil War residency and the Environmental Studies residency. Part of the success of these blended efforts is that, by and large, the blend was limited to a blend of modalities and not ideologies. Rather than surfacing a clash of paradigms, the blended residencies have, both in terms of personnel and approach, typically been developed under the aegis of one prevailing paradigm; for example, regional center-based residencies like the Civil War History Residency and the Adirondack Environmental Studies Residency have been developed and delivered according to the precepts of the contractual paradigm, while graduate residencies have tended to adhere to the assumptions of the design paradigm. Within the past two years, a workshop series supporting faculty development in blended learning brought to the surface some of the challenges we found ourselves facing. Even though immediate curricular decisions were not dependent upon resolving those challenges, experiences with the workshop caused the investigators to conclude that any effort to support blended learning at the college would function most effectively in the context of a larger attention to organizational change and support (Hayes, Jelly, & Whann, 2011).

## II. GETTING TO THE ALTAR: DEVELOPING OUR BLENDS

The Blended Task Force, led by Associate Dean Cathy Leaker (Metro), represented both ESC paradigms with faculty from CDL and all three units of the Metropolitan Center (Manhattan, Brooklyn, and Staten Island). The original group was comprised of Rebecca Bonanno (CDL), Sarah Hertz (CDL), Thalia MacMillan (CDL), Amanda Sisselman (Metro), and Christopher Whann (Metro) and eventually grew to include Kimberly Roff (Metro) and Gina Torino (Metro). In our initial meetings, we explored the distinct cultures of the regional centers and CDL and how the differing assumptions of faculty members would be reflected in course design. Discussions on assessment of the course material, for example, demonstrated the vast divide between ESC's two cultures. Through these meetings, we realized that the processes enabling course blends are just as important, if not more so, as the blended courses themselves. This recognition led to a series of strategies, some of which we based on the literature and some of which emerged only as we made missteps and needed to regroup. More often than not, the mismatch between design decision and procedural imperative was a function of our respective ideological assumptions, assumptions we needed to address critically as a team.

As the conclusions of Hayes et al. (2011) indicated, however grounded in shared ideals and however contingently they evolved, the different historical development of CDL and the regional centers led to distinct approaches to learning that increasingly acquired a cultural as well as a procedural dimension. Broadly speaking, regional center mentors take pride in the flexibility of their studies and in their ability to adapt to meet their students' needs. They believe that this approach is integral to Empire State College's mission to "use innovative, alternative and flexible approaches" (Empire State College, n.d.). Some CDL mentors, however, perceive studies at the regional centers as too loosely structured, with unspecified performance expectations and somewhat arbitrary grading practices. They view the high degree of flexibility that regional center mentors offer their students as less rigorous and less efficient than CDL's course offerings. To regional center mentors, however, CDL's higher degree of structure seems limiting and inflexible, especially for students who have intentionally sought out a nontraditional higher education environment at Empire State College.

As a result of our varying socializations into distinct cultures of practice, Metropolitan Center mentors and CDL mentors came to the development stage of blended project with differing, and as it turned out, clashing expectations. For the Metro team, the blended project represented a series of new opportunities for both faculty and students; they approached the study development process with a sense of freedom and possibility, constrained only by disciplinary expertise, technological fluency (or lack thereof), understanding of students and their needs, and their own convictions as experienced practitioners. The Metro team was certainly committed to careful planning, but that commitment was balanced by a collective embrace of spontaneity, creativity and open-endedness, ensuring that, in effect, studies would always be developing. Moreover, while Metro faculty valued collaboration and consultation, they knew themselves to be the ultimate arbiters of the quality of the studies they would individually both develop *and* deliver, with student input and response itself being a necessary phase of the study development. In practical terms, this meant that as Metro Center faculty began to imagine adding online elements to what were face-to-face outlines, in that model, no previously articulated learning objectives or activities were so sacrosanct that they couldn't (theoretically at least) be modified or even jettisoned altogether, and at any moment, if it meant creating a better and more integrated learning experience for students. For all their excitement about innovation, the Metro team faculty engaged the development process in the spirit of the contractual paradigm: with a premium on responsiveness, autonomy, individuality and adaptability.

Given CDL's history and the set of curricular processes engendered by that history, the CDL members of the blended team approached the project with a vastly different set of assumptions from those held by the Metro team. Rather than imagining they were embarking on an entirely new development process, these colleagues understood their proposed course offerings in relation to courses that already existed. Because they were proposing to blend existing CDL courses, their questions were not so much "What can and should we do?" but "How much can and should we change?" More importantly, they did not expect, as their Metro colleagues did, that they could simply answer these questions according to their own professional judgment, but that they would have to resolve them through a necessarily complex consultative process. Because CDL colleagues valued careful design and transparent structure, and because both design and structure had curricular implications beyond individual course sections (blended or otherwise), the CDL faculty understood that any change made to the existing template needed to have a substantive rationale. They were not, in other words, independent actors on an isolated stage, but contributing and valued members of an orchestrated team, working together to support student learning according to the best design practices. As such these faculty were acutely aware that any decision to make wholesale changes to a course structure would potentially impact not only the small number of students who enrolled for their particular sections, but also the broader group of faculty and instructional design colleagues who developed courses and the still broader group of CDL students who enrolled in them.

Procedurally, only after talking through these quite basic differences were we able to create blended courses with a coherent underlying pedagogical strategy as a group. We felt it was important to formulate an agreed upon definition of blended learning that would clearly communicate the parameters for our project and that, at some later date, might serve to establish a common expectation for the entire college. However, this "agreement" could neither be overly restrictive or prescriptive, nor the opposite – so loosely articulated as to have no definition whatsoever. Ultimately, we created a flexible, adaptive definition that we hoped would communicate our objectives, but still provide enough flexibility to serve other faculty with different ideas about how and what to blend. We settled on a balance of roughly 60 percent online and 40 percent face-to-face instruction. The face-to-face component would occur at any time throughout the course term, depending on how the specific course material was to be best presented.

Our regular team meetings next focused on incorporating the research on blending courses into course (re)design to create effective interactivity between the two modes within the courses. The echoing mantra of our mission was: "successful hybridity – however that may be defined – requires bringing the two dissimilar parts together so that they work in concert and may produce a third result" (Sands, 2002). We spent a great deal of time on course development, both individually and as a group, to make sure that the courses would be a success. Our group studied and examined "best" practices (drawn from the literature and other ESC faculty members) for balancing and managing the blended (or hybrid) course environment to ensure that students would receive the best learning experience. According to Aycock, Garnham and Kaleta (2002), students do not readily grasp the blended reality. Since the blended model is new to them, its use needs to be clearly rationalized. The group decided that as we were striving to blend not only courses but also the disparate cultures of CDL and regional centers, we needed to be that much more deliberate in how we explain this model to students.

As noted by Aycock et al. (2002), any course redesign needs to be taken seriously in order to maximize student and faculty interaction and engagement. It is imperative to recognize that a face-to-face course cannot simply be switched to a blended course, and the same holds for an online course. Serious thought about what would work best face-to-face and best online needs to occur, as does consideration of the content flow in order to maximize engagement with the material (Garrison & Kanuka, 2004). As noted above, the challenge for the Metro and CDL mentors was determining what aspects of a course would best translate into each mode of learning. As the team was working through this question, we realized that this process of deciding which material would be best suited to each mode could not be rushed, particularly since our decisions would inevitably be affected in unexpected ways by our many taken-for-granted center and college-wide processes. Thus, we came to see that a key element of the redesign process is time: an instructor needs a great deal of time to work on the new blended course design, and our centers needed time to consider the implications and to adjust local processes to fit those design choices, or, in some instances, vice versa. In traditional institutions, research suggests that time allowances of six months to a year are warranted (Aycock et al., 2002). Since we were in many ways operating within two sets of institutional/cultural norms, it became increasingly apparent that we would need at least a year, if not more, just to complete the development phase.

Throughout the course development process, we were mindful of all the research that we had gathered on blended learning with a focus in the literature on best practices for balancing and managing face-to-face and online instruction. Most importantly, we strove to ensure that the courses were seamlessly integrated between the face-to-face and online components. Research indicates that the key to successful hybridity is that the online work must be relevant to the in-class activities. As mentioned previously, proper integration of the face-to-face and online components is key to success for both the student and instructor. Research has also shown that there is always the threat or presence of a discordant blend that will frustrate both students and the instructor (Osguthorpe & Graham, 2003). It is imperative that courses selected for blending be fully redesigned to integrate properly and seamlessly the two modes of instruction. We formulated several key questions to be kept in mind when designing the blended course:

- What are my objectives? What do I want to achieve with this blend?
- What is the best sequence of learning activities?
- How much weight should be given to each activity (reading, reflection, other learning activities)?
- How do we assess student progress through the study?

Our group of CDL and Metro Center mentors dedicated both our individual and collective resources toward ensuring optimum integration of the courses' modes. Utilizing tools from the University of Central Florida and American Association of State Colleges and Universities' (n.d.) online BlendKit course, we engaged in various exercises to map out the course designs and create unique course materials for a blended course.

Another component of the (re)design of courses was to infuse academic skill development into the instructional model. Given that the skill sets for regional students and instructors differed from those of CDL students and instructors, we needed to be aware of the strengths and limitations of the audience. For regional students and instructors, areas that needed development included: developing online skills, particularly in discussion; extending planning timeline; learning to make the tacit explicit; budgeting out-of-class time to incorporate designed learning activities. For CDL instructors and students, areas that needed development included: sharing synchronous learning spaces; developing strategies for adapting the studies to students' questions and interests; budgeting in-class time.

Although at times we felt impatient with the slow progress we were making, the delays we experienced were ultimately beneficial. As Singh and Reed (2001) argue, there are distinct benefits to an incremental and deliberate roll out of any blended initiative. From early on, we advocated among ourselves and to our administrators for a scaffolded "roll out" of the blended courses; we realized that if our initiative was to effect a cultural as well as a modal shift, we needed the development of the materials and the outreach to students and other faculty to be a gradual and recursive process. That process began with ourselves, specifically our willingness to approach our blended courses as a necessary occasion for professional development.

As noted throughout this discussion, blending a course is more than just taking an existing course and splitting the presentation – half online and half face-to-face. In order to ensure that the blended course is conducive to learning, faculty members need ample time and information on how to blend a course effectively. In initial attempts at blending, it has been found that faculty may overestimate what can be done in a blended course and, as a result, overburden both the students and themselves (Aycock et al., 2002). We recognized the need to approach these questions collectively. As noted by Sands (2002), ideas about blending need to be shared with the blended learning faculty members. From the beginning of this initiative, Metro and CDL faculty worked together to attend and present in webinars and at conferences on the topic of blending, as well as to create shared learning spaces.

*The Wedding Album: Scenes from a Marriage*

The initial course offerings were done with courses that we felt were especially amenable to blending: Introduction to Human Services, Disabled in America, Survey of Social Science Research Methods, Corporate Finance, and Introduction to College Writing. The majority of the studies were offered at the main Metropolitan Center location in Manhattan, with one section of Introduction to Human Services offered at the Staten Island unit location. These specific courses were chosen since, we felt, they both supported the two largest areas of study within the college (Community and Human Services, and Business, Management and Economics) and lent themselves particularly well to diverse learning modes. Each contained a component that is ideally learned face-to-face and another component that might more easily be grasped in the flexibility of an online environment. Despite what we took to be these attractive features, all courses (with the exception of the one offered in Staten Island) had low enrollments, which may have been the result of a lack of publicity or the very novelty of such a modality.

*Introduction to human services.* Each term, in order to meet the demand of students pursuing degrees in Community and Human Services, the Metropolitan Center offers several studies in this area. Likewise, CDL offers a large number of similar courses for online students. Mentors Rebecca Bonanno from CDL and Amanda Sisselman from the Staten Island Unit of the Metropolitan Center decided to pool their knowledge of the subject matter, the student population, and course design to develop a blended course called Introduction to Human Services. Rebecca and Amanda hoped to take the concept of blending a step further by bringing together students in two geographic locations in order to offer all of the students a wider scope of interaction and discussion. The initial idea was to connect two groups of students, one in Manhattan and one in Staten Island, in a single online course shell and to link in-person class sessions through videoconferencing technology.

Rebecca and Amanda planned the course carefully and gave great thought to scheduling face-to-face sessions and online activities around subject matter that would be best presented in a particular modality. For example, the history of social welfare could be presented online in a relatively simple and engaging way, with students reading content, watching videos, and participating in online discussion; however, the mentors believed that basic counseling skills could best be taught in-person, using role plays and getting immediate feedback from peers and the instructors. In an attempt to provide continuity throughout the term, online discussion boards connected each course topic.

A few contingencies – some major and some minor – made it difficult to carry out the plan for maximum connectivity across the two geographic locations. First, because of scheduling and space restrictions, the two groups could not be held simultaneously, making it impossible for the student groups in Staten Island and Manhattan to interact synchronously. Though students were still united in the online portion of the course, they did not have access to the real-time discussion and interaction that the mentors had hoped to provide.

Second, Hurricane Sandy hit the area midway through the term. While ESC students throughout New York City and Long Island were affected, Staten Island was hit especially hard. The Staten Island Unit was forced to close for the remainder of the term and classes were temporarily held in a nearby high school. Many students were displaced and suffered significant losses due to the storm. It became more difficult for Staten Island students to travel to in-person classes and, therefore, Amanda Sisselman (the mentor for this group) was forced to rely on the online element of the course to a much greater degree than originally planned. When faced with cancelled sessions, she moved much of the course content online so that students could continue to learn. In Manhattan, Rebecca Bonnano and her students missed two sessions of face-to-face contact, but the disruption was relatively minor.

At the beginning of the term, the students in both groups were not very active in the online discussion groups. Most had not taken fully online or blended courses before and were not in the habit of working regularly in a learning management system (LMS). The mentors encouraged, cajoled, and prodded their students until they reached an acceptable level of online participation; yet some students struggled with this element throughout the term. The course also included two online tests which were especially daunting for some students, who reported discomfort reading and answering questions on a computer screen. In response, Rebecca emphasized that computerized test-taking is an important skill for students to develop, as many state certification exams in a variety of professions are now administered on computer only. Despite these difficulties, in the end, most of the students in this blended version of Introduction to Human Services reported that they appreciated the flexibility the course offered and would participate in a blended study again.

*Disabled in America and survey of social science research methods.* In preparation for teaching, CDL mentor Thalia MacMillan had a discussion with the Community and Human Services (CHS) faculty at the Metropolitan Center regarding the types of courses that students might be interested in with respect to topic and/or career developmental need. Given her own interests, Thalia inquired about the topics of disabilities and research; the Metro faculty suggested that both were topics, in particular disabilities, in which many students had interest and which were not currently offered in any Metro study groups. In the past, Thalia had found that several aspects of research are easier to learn about in person. For example, as each student's individual project can be discussed with respect to the particular topic of that week, the material can be more engaging. In addition, the topic of disabilities would benefit from face-to-face sessions that would allow for visits to agencies and museums that focused on disabilities and offered ways to engage students and connect them to potential professional communities.

Given these assumptions, Thalia created blended versions of two CDL courses that she had taught previously, namely, Disabled in America and Survey of Social Science Research Methods. The same materials and learning objectives that she had used before were included in both courses; however, the learning activities and the presentation of course content evolved to be more user-friendly and engaging than in the distance learning-only form. For both of these course offerings, presentation of content was organized around a set of key topics. A review and discussion of the material began in the face-to-face sessions, and then continued online. Similarly, activities to enhance that learning were carried out in the face-to-face setting and additional online resources were highlighted and utilized to bolster learning and engagement.

From the outset, students in the Disabled in America course actively participated in both the online and face-to-face sessions; for those students who were lacking in participation online, several students became class "champions" to ensure that all students participated in all aspects of the course. Indeed, due to student interests, additional topics were added to the course over the progression of the semester. Given that in the first class the students were free to talk about their backgrounds, questions, and reasons for taking the course, the students developed a great bond and camaraderie that they shared throughout the semester. Many came together to attend offsite events, such as going to a museum. All of the students stated that they appreciated the freedom and accessibility of the blended course and would definitely register for another.

However, in the Survey of Social Science Research Methods course, a different story prevailed. Both online and face-to-face participation was problematic, as students did not actively engage in the material in either modality from the outset. After consultation with other members of the taskforce, Thalia chose to alter her design and to change several of the course assignments to adapt to students' needs. In many ways, in order to support the possibility of student success in the course, she ended up changing what had been constructed as a blended group study into multiple online individual independent studies.

*Corporate finance.* The Corporate Finance course, taught by CDL mentor Sarah Hertz, aimed to develop a strong conceptual framework for the understanding and application of the theories of managerial finance. The study was well structured and followed a topical module organization using *Principles of Managerial Finance* by Lawrence J. Gittman and Chad J. Zutter, the textbook used in the CDL course. The course began with an orientation to the LMS in the context of blended courses, in which students participated in hands-on activities that would be used for the online portion of the course. Content was divided into seven modules based on the textbook sections, with two or three chapters of text covered in each module. As an experienced instructor in both face-to-face and online courses, Sarah was committed to ensuring that students understood key concepts so that they would be able to further their financial knowledge through various day-to-day applications. Textbook and background reading and participation in discussion boards occurred online prior to each module's face-to-face session. In-class time was primarily used for presentation of the quantitative topics, and for hands-on application of concepts and formulas. Sarah presented quantitative material by showing a number of different ways to compute the problems: mathematically, using Excel, and using a financial calculator. Concepts were reinforced with problem sets posted and solutions submitted online, extensive feedback given to students, and follow-up questions posed in a subsequent class.

Course content was similar to Corporate Finance courses that Sarah has taught both face-to-face in other institutions and online for CDL. However, the quality of the interactions in the blended course was, in Sarah's view, far superior to an online-only setting. Due to the give-and-take of a conventional classroom, questions were answered immediately, and students were able to grasp the material more readily and to gain more thorough understanding of the concepts. In fact, Sarah noted that for students who did not do the background reading and/or who did not participate in online discussion prior to the in-class meeting, more face-to-face contact would have enhanced the learning experience. In their evaluations of the blended mode, both students and instructor had mixed assessments of its success. While Sarah appreciated being able to walk students through problems step-by-step in person, to explain concepts with which they had difficulty, and to try to alleviate their confusions early on, she did find it challenging to deal with the lack of consistency of the online interaction.

Periodic student feedback indicated that the CDL students especially valued the face-to-face contact, while the Metro students felt there was too much independent online work. Much of the difficulty that students (whether from CDL or the Metropolitan Center) experienced may have been due to the advanced nature of the course. Satisfaction with the blended mode varied among students, as did the likelihood that they would recommend a blended study to a friend or take another blended course. As was reported in regard to the two CHS courses, all students seemed to appreciate the flexibility of accessing online content anytime and the convenience of not being expected to attend weekly face-to-face meetings.

*Introduction to college writing.* The College Writing study was designed to help students achieve a set of outcomes that the Metropolitan Center writing faculty had agreed the previous year should form the core of any college writing study at the center. Chief among these was the ability to engage with other written texts in writing, which in turn demanded that students be able both to summarize and to respond to a series of texts, as well as to use appropriate documentation in order to indicate clearly the terms of that engagement. As an experienced writing instructor, Cathy Leaker was committed to common practices in composition instruction like drafting, revising and peer review. Strategically, then, the course was designed to move learning resources (for example assigned texts) online while establishing community activities like peer review and drafting strategies in the face-to-face setting. Built into the overall design of the study was the hope that as students became familiar and comfortable with an activity like peer review, that activity could effectively migrate to the online environment so that face-to-face meetings could be devoted to instruction in increasingly sophisticated rhetorical strategies.

In their evaluations of this experiment in Introduction to College Writing via the blended mode, both students and instructor had mixed assessments of its success. Cathy appreciated the time devoted to a preset design and felt that, as a result, the study was as tightly constructed as anything she had offered at ESC. In particular, she noted that the range and kind of learning resources she incorporated into the study lent themselves very well to the particular assignment sequence that she had developed without necessarily distracting from the close scrutiny of student writing that was the appropriate focus of the study.

Yet even as she valued the materials she had both found and created to support the study's learning objectives, Cathy was less sanguine about what she ultimately concluded was a premature effort to organize time and space in order to best facilitate those same objectives. In particular, because of space constraints at the Manhattan location, and because she had taken to heart the imperative to fully integrate online and face-to-face activities, Cathy had carefully planned a balanced structure of alternating face-to-face and online meetings, but had done so well in advance of meeting the students, gauging their skills, and assessing the dynamics of the group as an emergent learning community. While in her regular fully face-to-face studies, Cathy felt free to slow down or accelerate learning activities based on student progress, she found the blended structure less amenable to "on the fly" revisions. Thus, for example, Cathy's decision to delay peer review for a week, in order to give students more time to complete first drafts, meant that an activity – peer review – specifically designed for a for face-to-face session suddenly needed to be introduced in an online environment.

Student feedback about the blended College Writing study was equally mixed; while students varied in terms of their satisfaction with the mode and in terms of their likelihood of taking another blended study, students across the board reported similar assessments of the overall strengths and weaknesses of a blended approach to College Writing. Specifically, almost all students valued the flexibility of the alternating schedule, noting that fewer face-to-face meetings made it easier to manage both their work schedule and the demands of their other studies. At the same time, students almost without exception were disappointed with the limited opportunities to interact with their classmates and reported that they wished they'd had more time to get to know their fellow writers.

Given that all the students in the blended College Writing group study were Metropolitan center students and that none of them had yet taken a CDL class, these two sets of responses are not as self-contradictory as they might initially appear. It was noteworthy that students liked the flexibility of the schedule not because they had class face-to-face one week and online the next, but because "I only had class every other week." We might conclude from this that, despite Cathy's intentions when designing the study, the College Writing students perceived the face-to-face meetings as the "real study" – and certainly as the sole occasion for interaction – and the online activities as supplemental at best. Hence, most did not feel compelled to be fully present in online activities, while the few that did were discouraged by the lack of online community and reported feeling detached during the weeks devoted exclusively to online learning. This lack of commitment to the online portion of the study was exacerbated by the concerns Cathy had about managing time and space in accordance with a predetermined schedule; that is, when forced to use the online mode for activities that she felt were better served in a face-to-face setting, Cathy became almost as disaffected with the online component of the blend as were the students. Increasingly, she found herself "deferring" complex learning tasks to the face-to-face settings, thereby minimizing either the imperative or the overall rationale for maintaining online presence.

*Joint Thoughts*

As with any new initiative, continuous reflection is fundamental. At the close of the term, we formally surveyed both students and faculty to gauge success of the undertaking/project and to pinpoint where improvement is needed. The detailed questions focused both on overall course design – especially in regard to the integration of online and face-to-face elements – and on specific learning activities, whether face-to-face or online. Responses indicated that in spite of the incorporation of the strategies gleaned from our extensive research on blended teaching and learning models, the results were far from perfect. While the courses on a whole were successful, much more work is necessary to improve the student and faculty blended experience. Though we had hoped that these blended courses would be an opportunity for Metro and CDL students to come together in one academic setting, most of the enrolled students were Metro students with little online experience. They seemed unprepared for the online component of the course. Though most noted that they enjoyed the scheduling flexibility, the lack of consistency of interaction was widespread in all the courses. Student satisfaction varied by the type of course; the "topical" courses (i.e. corporate finance, disabled in America) seemed to proceed more smoothly than the "process" courses (i.e. research, writing).

Despite the problems encountered, all of the faculty hope to take what they have learned from the blended experience and to continue to rethink their courses (past, current, and future) accordingly. Specifically, all noted that the clustering of the face-to-face meetings needs to be examined. For example, Thalia found success in having the first two face-to-face meetings back-to-back as this allowed students and the instructor to become engaged and break the ice on the blended learning concept; other instructors, such as Cathy, noted this as well. Similarly, additional time may be needed to build the online community. It is possible that a series of online icebreaker activities would be beneficial to continue the positive level of engagement that was found in the face-to-face meetings. Additional research into building more effective transition between the face-to-face and the online environments is needed. Ultimately the goal of fostering learning in *both* modes, deemed of equal importance by all of the faculty participants in these pilots, would be advantageous. Finally, each instructor should consider the notion of instructor presence, availability, and influence within both modalities. While this presence may be easily established in the face-to-face classroom, the same strategies cannot necessarily be used online; nor are successful on-line strategies necessarily equally effective in face-to-face contexts. The team would like to imagine and try out other strategies that can be developed to create a lasting connection among the students and between faculty and students.

*Advice to the Lovelorn: Finding the Elusive ESC Blend*

The initial five "pilot" courses of the January 2013 term will influence future blended learning opportunities. Certainly we learned a good deal from the pilot both at the level of particular pedagogical strategies for blended learning and at the level of integrating the two broad and historically contingent cultures that had emerged at our institution over more than four decades. While all participating faculty were pleased with the content offered in the courses, we recognized the need to integrate more effectively our approaches to teaching and learning, specifically, the need to restructure the pace and relationship of face-to-face and online activities. We also plan to develop a more extensive introduction for students to the LMS, both with regard to basic navigational skills and with regard to students' facility and confidence with online interaction.

Beyond the adjustments noted above, however, we realize that we need to encourage a broader dialogue about the future of blended learning at ESC. From our experiences, we can imagine at least two broad institutional strategies for perfecting the ESC blend:

1. Promoting a wide mix of online and face-to-face learning environments without attempting to characterize blended learning as a distinct mode.
2. Establishing an institutional definition of blended learning as a distinct learning mode with its own set of parameters, pedagogies and technologies.

We note that these two options can be loosely aligned with our characterizations of the "contractual paradigm" and the "design paradigm." Thus for example, the contractual paradigm would seem to dictate a "just in time blend" with faculty members adjusting the balance of face-to-face and online learning based on an immediate and ongoing assessment of the needs and interests of enrolled students. On the other hand, the design paradigm would demand an approach to blended learning that stipulates in advance *a* structuring of online and face-to-face modalities and the relationship between them.

We might easily argue that a truly distinctive ESC blend can emerge only in relation to the first strategy cited above, if only because a more expansive definition of blended learning, while not *precluding* attention to design, would at the same time not *prescribe* a particular vision of design by, for example, determining in advance the exact ratio – or even the acceptable range – of face-to-face and online learning. Because such a loose definition apparently accommodates the flexibility so often needed (and, commented upon) by adult learners, it is tempting to conclude with an exhortation to let a thousand blended blossoms bloom. And yet to do so would be to ignore the literature on blended learning as well the lessons gleaned from our pilot, both of which point to blended learning as a distinctive learning modality with distinctive advantages for students, faculty and entire institutions. Moreover, the most recent research indicates that those advantages are most reliably leveraged in the context of a clear – if reasonably variable – set of institutional expectations for blended learning.

Three studies are especially illuminating in this regard. In 2010, the U.S. Department of Education's Office of Planning, Evaluation and Policy Development conducted a meta-analysis of 99 experimental and quasi-experimental studies published between 1996 and 2008. The report issued two findings to justify the effort required to design and implement blended approaches. The first is their conclusion that online learning is *as effective* as face-to-face instruction, but *not more so* (Means, Toyama, Murphy, Bakia, & Jones, 2010). The second is that blended learning is *more effective* than face-to-face learning (Means et al., 2010). It is important to note here that these conclusions were issued with some caution because there were so many variables in the studies under analysis that the report could only speculate as to the precise conditions under which students in the blended learning modes perform better than students in exclusively online or face-to-face modes.

The second study proposes at least two conditions for improved learning outcomes in blended learning modes. Building on the work of Bliuc, Ellis, Goodyear and Piggott (2010), which correlated positive academic outcomes in blended learning with students' perception of the integration of modes, and drawing upon her own extensive interviews with students in an adult liberal arts degree completion program, McDonald (2014) concluded that students valued blended learning more when they could easily make sense of the relationship between online and face-to-face activities. This finding in turn suggested that blended studies should be designed so as to promote awareness of the intersection between components, activities and interactions for the learner. Beyond the value of their awareness of the relationship between modes, McDonald (2014) also discovered that students were more successful when they were aware of blended learning as itself a distinct mode with distinct expectations. While conceding that further research could better explain her results, McDonald suggested that awareness of blended learning as a mode was fostered both by careful design and by repeated experience in blended environments.

Together these recent studies echo our own assessment of the blended learning pilot at the Metropolitan Center and suggest to us that ESC students and faculty, whatever their preferred mode of study, would be best served by the college explicitly designating "blended" courses or studies that meet distinct criteria as such. In terms of the relative proportions of online and face-to-face activity, we propose that the college embrace the Sloan Consortium's definition of blended learning, simply because by characterizing blended courses as those that have a range from 30 percent to 79 percent online content, the Sloan-C definition offers faculty and students appropriately wide flexibility (Allen, Seaman, & Garrett, 2007). Beyond stipulating a minimum and maximum blend, and in part because of the degree of flexibility within that stipulation, we also suggest that courses petitioning for the blend designation demonstrate the following:

- An integrated balance of face-to-face meetings and online activities delivered over a full term of study.
- Carefully designed learning contracts that reflect a blended (face-to-face and online, synchronous and asynchronous) approach to achieving learning objectives, to the learning activities, and to the formative and summative assessment strategies.
- Deliberate attention to using online and face-to-face modes according to their distinctive pedagogical affordances.
- An aspirational and institutional commitment to online and digital learning resources that support digital and new media literacies.

For us, these four criteria are important because they promote an awareness of integrated modalities and a meta-awareness of blending as itself a modality that is neither mostly face-to-face nor mostly online, but rather is the distinct offspring, the love child if you will, of the two. Awareness at the institutional, pedagogical, and procedural levels is needed in order for faculty and students to realize the demonstrable advantages of blended study as a learning mode. More specifically, we believe that setting clear parameters for blended learning will, over time, allow for the growth of an expanded community of practice around blended learning design. We also anticipate that a distinct and recognizable blended modality will, again over time, promote a higher level of student engagement in blended courses. Ultimately, our goal, our shared "family" value, is to promote student-centered learning whereby students, fully aware of their options, can become informed agents of their own learning blend.

*Happily Ever After? Toward One Big Blended Family*

We launched the blended learning project in order to expand modes of instruction, to take advantage of faculty expertise in both subject matter and delivery mode, and to offer enhanced student-centered learning opportunities. While our initial flirtation quickly (d)evolved into a thornier and more contentious relationship, those tensions proved to be more productive than otherwise, particularly because they forced us to confront and work within our differences rather than simply ignoring or minimizing them in the service of expediency or surface collegiality. As a result, the blended courses we delivered, and continue to develop, represent more than a combination of the best features of online and face-to-face groups; they offer an entirely new mode of delivery with its own distinct set of advantages and affordances.

As in any marriage, however, the institutional environments in which we contracted our union refused to stay cooperatively stable, but instead shifted and shook even as we cemented our relationship. Much of our experience, and thus the structure of this paper, was predicated on a long-standing and seemingly intractable distinction between regional and online cultures at ESC. Those distinctions arguably will and must become less pronounced as the college moves toward a new structure organized by academic disciplines rather than by locations or modes. But if our experience in the blended pilot taught us anything, it taught us that blending is seldom a simple matter of cohabitation, enforced or otherwise. Blending, in other words, doesn't just happen. Whether we are blending delivery modes, pedagogical paradigms, or learning cultures, whether we initiate blending or have blending thrust upon us, successful blends require work, patience, creativity and dialogue. In this sense, the relatively small pedagogical initiative jointly developed by the Metropolitan Center and the Center for Distance Learning might serve as a kind of nuptial trial balloon for a far more fraught, complicated, but ultimately fruitful marriage than we could have imagined.

## REFERENCES

Allen, I. E., Seaman, J., & Garrett, R. (2007, March). *Blending in: The extent and promise of blended education in the United States.* Retrieved from http://sloanconsortium.org/publications/survey/blended06

Aycock, A., Garnham, C., & Kaleta, R. (2002, March 20). Lessons learned from the hybrid course project. *Teaching with Technology Today.* Retrieved from https://hccelearning.files.wordpress.com/2010/09/lessons-learned-from-the-hybrid-course-project.pdf

Bliuc, A-M., Ellis, R. A., Goodyear, P., & Piggott, L. (2010). A blended learning approach to teaching foreign policy: Student experiences of learning through face-to-face and online discussion and their relationship to academic performance. *Computers & Education, 56*(2011), 856–864. Retrieved from https://www.researchgate.net/profile/Ana-Maria_Bliuc/publication/220140476_A_ blended_learning_Approach_to_teaching_foreign_policy_Student_experiences_of_learning_ through_face-to-face_and_online_discussion_and_their_relationship_to_academic_performance/ links/0046353213f2e54a4d000000.pdf

Bonnabeau, R. F. (1996). *The promise continues: Empire State College – The first twenty-five years.* Virginia Beach, VA: The Donning Company Publishers.

Clark, R. C., & Mayer, R. E. (2011). *E-learning and the science of instruction: Proven guidelines for consumers and designers of multimedia learning* (3rd ed.). San Francisco, CA: Pfeiffer Publishing.

Dewey, J. (1938). *Experience and education.* New York, NY: Collier.

Empire State College. (1971). *Empire State College bulletin.* Saratoga Springs, NY: Author.

Empire State College. (n.d.). *College mission.* Retrieved from http://www.esc.edu/about-esc/college-mission/

Garrison, D. R., & Kanuka, H. (2004). Blended learning: Uncovering its transformative potential in higher education. *The Internet and Higher Education, 7*(2), 95–105.

Greenberg, A. (2012, March). *Wainhouse Research white paper: Blended learning technology: Navigating the challenges of large-scale adoption.* Retrieved from http://www.wainhouse.com/files/papers/wr-blended-learn-tech-adoption.pdf

Hayes, S., Jelly, K., & Whann, C. (2011, Winter) As strong as the weakest link: Organizational development models and supporting blended learning. *All About Mentoring, 40,* 64–67. Retrieved from http://www.esc.edu/media/ocgr/2011/Issue-40-AAM-Winter-2011.pdf

Kilpatrick, W. H. (1951). *Philosophy of education.* New York, NY: Macmillan.

Knowles, M. S. (1986). *Using learning contracts.* San Francisco, CA: Jossey-Bass.

McDonald, P. L. (2014). Variation in adult learners' experiences of blended learning in higher education. In A. Picciano, C. D. Dziuban, & C. R. Graham (Eds.), *Blended learning research perspectives* (Vol. 2, pp. 215–234). New York, NY: Routledge.

Means, B., Toyama, Y., Murphy, R., Bakia M., & Jones, K. (2010, September). *Evaluation of evidence-based practices in online learning: A meta-analysis and review of online learning studies.* Retrieved from http://www2.ed.gov/rschstat/eval/tech/evidence-based-practices/finalreport.pdf

Osguthorpe, R. T., & Graham, C. R. (2003, Fall). Blended learning environments: Definitions and directions. *Quarterly Review of Distance Education, 4*(3), 227–233.

Sands, P. (2002, March 20). Inside outside, upside downside: Strategies for connecting online and face-to-face instruction in hybrid courses. *Teaching with Technology Today, 8*(6). Retrieved from https://www.wisconsin.edu/systemwide-it/teaching-with-technology-today/

Singh, H., & Reed, C. (2001). *A white paper: Achieving success with blended learning.* Retrieved from http://maken.wikiwijs.nl/userfiles/f7d0e4f0bd466199841ede3eea221261.pdf

Thach, E. C. (1994). *Perceptions of distance education experts regarding the roles, outputs, and competencies needed in the field of distance education* (Doctoral dissertation). Texas A & M University, College Station, TX. Retrieved from UMI Dissertation Services.

Tough, A. (1979). *The adult's learning projects: A fresh approach to theory and practice in adult learning* (2nd ed.). Toronto, Canada: The Ontario Institute for Studies in Education.

University of Central Florida & American Association of State Colleges and Universities. (n.d.). *BlendKit course.* Retrieved from https://blended.online.ucf.edu/blendkit-course/

CINDY CONAWAY AND CHRISTOPHER WHANN

# 15. GROWTH AND ITS DISCONTENTS

*Organizational Challenges to a Radical Vision*

Empire State College (ESC) founders and its early faculty developed and shared innovative ideas about higher education. As a small and nimble institution under the umbrella of a large public university system, in some ways ESC had more flexibility than other non-traditional institutions; at the same time, the College was more beholden to the bureaucratic structures of a large system than some small schools (see, for example, Gross, 1976; Skidmore College, 2011; Ryan, 1988). This tension between its identity as a small non-traditional institution and its place in a larger traditional system has challenged Empire State College since its earliest days. New York state has changed a great deal since 1971, and, recently, the College has been challenged to grow, while maintaining its core values. There are new students; there is a large State University of New York (SUNY) system; and there are statewide needs that ESC did not so directly have to respond to and serve when it was founded. The challenges and tensions surrounding whether it can even try to serve significantly larger numbers of students in the particular way it has been structured for more than four decades are the focus of this chapter.

Can Empire State College now, 45 years since its founding, effectively respond to the external pressures and internal conflicts it faces? From the outside, the College is confronted with: unfavorable demographics in large swaths of New York state, which is losing population in its northern and western parts; federal and state government expectations for increased assessment and for systematic evaluation of higher education services and outcomes; and SUNY expectations that the college continue to grow and serve its constituents across the state. Internally, there is evidence of increasingly disparate patterns of growth within the college and an organizational structure that may no longer be adequate to meet changing needs of students and faculty mentors. The confluence of these pressures from outside and in has spurred us, Cindy Conaway, a faculty member in the Center for Distance Learning (CDL), based at the Metropolitan Center in New York City, and Christopher Whann, interim associate dean at the Metropolitan Center, to consider the notion of "growth and its discontents" as this growth challenges ESC.

Both of us are enthusiastic about possibilities for the College. ESC can continue to provide meaningful opportunities for students who are looking both for experimental approaches to study and for the chance to succeed when they have the talents to do so but have been ill-served by other higher education institutions. And we are excited about the prospect of change, so that the goals that we and our students hope for can be fully realized. Yet, as the college grows beyond the model that has – to a great extent – worked for the last 45 years, we are also concerned that some of the processes and patterns currently in effect might clash with the need for an organizational design and for college-wide academic and administrative processes that would be sustainable over the long run.

## OUR CHANGING ROLES AND CONTEXT

Having served as faculty members and in administration at different centers in ESC, together we have experienced Empire State College from a range of vantage points. Cindy, a mentor in Cultural Studies at the Center for Distance Learning, ESC's online arm, teaches media studies and manages courses in media and communications. Located for several years in Saratoga Springs, where CDL is based, she now works out of the Metropolitan Center's Manhattan office. Chris, as of this writing serving as Interim Associate Dean of the Metropolitan Center, the largest of ESC's regional centers, teaches in the area of Business, Management and Economics. He previously served as the "unit coordinator" of the Metropolitan location's Brooklyn Unit, and also was a full-time faculty member in the College's International Programs, now a part of CDL. For much of the 2013–14 academic year, Chris served as the Metropolitan Center's acting Director of Academic Review, the office responsible for preparing individualized student degree plans for faculty assessment of quality and consistency.

Without doubt, however, our individual professional shifts and perspectives on the College are small factors in a larger swirl of events, as ESC has been going through a period of significant change since each of us arrived. Recently, the College has been through the departure of President Alan Davis in 2012, the brief tenure of an acting president, Meg Benke, who served for about a year; we are now, as of July, 2013, being led by a new president, Merodie Hancock, who defines her presidency as one of change. And, over the past several years, we have seen much turnover in the Provost's position as well.

Now with a new president, a new provost, and ongoing discussions about and multiple plans for changing internal organizational arrangements, writing this chapter is akin to shooting at a target that is not only moving, but moving in multiple directions at the same time. While some of our opinions are just those, opinions, they reflect Chris' familiarity with organizational theory and strategic management, about which he teaches in many of his business, management, and public affairs courses. He brings background to the challenges any rapidly growing organization faces and to the ways in which restructuring, whether in theory or in practice, often accompanies these challenges when old ways of doing business may not suffice to address a changing context and growth.

In our respective roles, we see internal organizational tensions stemming from the need to maintain the core values and mission of ESC in the midst of a changing context; students' expectations for clarity, predictability, and transparency in an institution with widely varying procedures across the centers; and bureaucratic imperatives that drive the management of growth and the direction of the College. Moreover, since Cindy teaches primarily in online environments and Chris teaches primarily face-to-face study groups and guided independent studies, we work with ESC students in different contexts.

## EXPERIENCE, DATA AND THEORY

Our experiences at the College lead us to approach this chapter using a variety of methods. First and foremost, we are *participant observers.* Like anthropologists coming to a new community, we are a part of it and, at the same time, we are studying it. We have full-time responsibilities for teaching, mentoring, service, research, and administration on a day-to-day basis, but we do try regularly to step back and reflect on why and how we do what we do. As such, this chapter can also be read as commentary, including our insights and our occasional frustrations about getting our work done in a rational way.

We also will use some *quantitative data* to illustrate our points and to support some of the positions we take about changes we see and about others we might recommend. The College has been collecting data for its annual *Fact Book* since 2003. The Office of Decision Support (previously known as the Office of Institutional Research) also provides some information through the College's intranet. At the same time, more information can be found online or derived from databases available to the college community as a whole. While some information that could be helpful is not systematically available, still, the numbers we have access to sustain elements of our argument, especially for the years before mid-2007 when Cindy came to the College.

Since Chris has taught and written about organization theory and strategy, he also brings additional insight to the issues that the college faces. Thus, for example, he has been attentive to the changing and increasingly competitive environment in which ESC operates, which includes the explosion of non-profit and for-profit schools that serve adult students in evening divisions and in asynchronous online environments. For-profit institutions, such as the University of Phoenix and the American Public University System, and other private institutions, such as Southern New Hampshire University and Western Governors University, drive costs down, promote new educational approaches, and threaten to undermine ESC's early dominance of the degree-seeking adult market. And the organizational strains that ESC experiences as a result of aggressive growth continuously threaten to overwhelm the College's efforts to maintain the mission of individualized degree planning and study, early hallmarks of Empire State College.

## VALUES AND EVOLVING STRUCTURES

Richard Bonnabeau, Empire State College's historian, has written elsewhere about the fierce debates concerning how ESC's mentors and staff would translate the institution's core values into practical service to actual students. Because the deepest commitment is to a radically student-centered, mentor-student collaborative model of education, many early administrators and faculty concentrated on the one-to-one, face-to-face relationship between mentor and student. This approach was a far cry from the more traditional bureaucratic universities that were growing in the post-World War II period and that had become the target of many dissatisfied faculty and students during the 1960s and the Vietnam era (Bonnabeau, 1996; Lemann, 1999).

When the college opened in 1971, ESC was small (552 full-time students, with part-timers resulting in a "head count" of 745), a true experiment for the State University of New York (SUNY) system, which itself was founded in 1948 (Bonnabeau, 1996; SUNY Empire State College, 2010–2011). A primary difference between ESC and traditional colleges is the mentoring model itself. Although we officially have traditional academic titles such as assistant, associate, or full professor, all faculty are also called "mentors." The faculty mentor role combines teaching (sometimes in face to face groups, frequently as independent studies, more often, now, on-line) with advising, which goes well beyond the traditional meaning of that function. In the College's "high touch" model of advising, each mentor and student discuss the student's personal, professional and academic goals at length, and the student develops an individualized degree program that both meets that student's needs and responds to a broad set of academic guidelines put in place by the faculty. Mentors shepherd students and their programs through an assessment process that includes the creation of an individualized degree program plan (in effect, a personal curriculum), the writing of a "rationale essay" justifying that student's study choices, the submission of these materials to the assessment office, and the review of this portfolio by a faculty committee. The mentor has long been considered the student's "first contact" at the College, and although there is now an array of professional staff dedicated to helping students (a kind of academic and student support infrastructure that did not exist in the College's early years), mentors are generally consulted on many issues on which faculty in more traditional institutions would not be.

## EMPIRE STATE COLLEGE'S ORGANIZATION: SOME ADVANTAGES AND WEAKNESSES

From the perspective of organization theory, it appears that some of ESC's management design elements were made quite consciously; others evolved as a matter of necessity. Improvisation is not unusual in organizations, but it helps to have an underlying strategic impulse to guide it. There are many different descriptive models that shape the way one sees an organization, for example: machines, organisms, brains, cultures, political organizations, and even (psychic) prisons (see Morgan, 1999/2007). As has been acknowledged for some time, while organizations can adapt and change, they can also be mechanisms for domination (Morgan, 1999/2007).

There is little doubt that ESC as an organization has changed from its founding in 1971. The question is whether it has done so in a way that is both deliberate and forward-looking. Thus, Chris has described ESC in the last few years as a "mom and pop store on steroids," a reflection of the early choices made amidst slow growth, but also of the way in which the results of those choices have morphed into what could be considered large sub-organizations (for example, the so-called "regional learning center") that have taken on a life of their own in periods of more rapid growth.

It is important to acknowledge that at its opening in 1971, ESC was not the only such experimental institution of higher education, and not the only small program. For example, the Ford Foundation funded a consortium of "university without walls" programs at 29 different schools (Gross, 1976). Chris spent 16 years at one of these, the (now-defunct) Skidmore College University Without Walls, an early adopter of this radically student-centered educational model (Lynn, 2000).

Still, ESC as an organization had many advantages over some other experimenting institutions. First, unlike most university without walls programs, it was a freestanding institution, not a program in an existing college. Second, it had the branding advantage of SUNY, the largest public university system in the United States. Third, it had the full support of the SUNY Chancellor, Ernest Boyer. Fourth, it had a young and energetic founding president, James Hall, who had not been a president before he came to ESC and was not wedded to old models of administration. Finally, it had locations all over New York state, which offered the opportunity for political support from various state legislators who had ESC locations in their state assembly and state senate districts.

One additional advantage, in theory, was that ESC was not dedicated to an organizational model used by existing universities. It could be adaptable, flexible, and innovative when students and mentors needed it to be. Administrators and mentors could solve problems on the fly, without the cumbersome bureaucracy that often limits the possible solutions that faculty, staff and students are able to explore together.

To facilitate ease of management, ESC's organizational structure looks more like a solar system than a traditional pyramid. The Coordinating Center, located in Saratoga Springs (less than 40 miles north of Albany, the state capital, but quite purposefully *not in* Albany), contains most of the senior administrative functions connected to the President's and Provost's offices, including vice presidents, assistant vice presidents and directors. The regional centers, located around the state, revolve much like planets around the Coordinating Center "sun." Smaller unit locations function like moons in the orbit of centers and stretch from far western New York to Long Island, and from the Canadian border to Staten Island. Centers and units include their own faculty mentors, professional employees, and support staff. For the most part, centers have equal representation on college committees and the college senate, and, in theory, have an equal voice in most college decisions, regardless of the number of students served, or the number of full-time faculty and staff at each center.

There are clear advantages but also obvious weaknesses to this configuration. The dispersed nature of the centers is simultaneously a political strength and an organizational weakness. ESC has statewide support from its legislators, but the centers can become power bases unto themselves. At traditional colleges, departmental authority determines the distribution of resources and drives the organizational structure. Although currently contested, it has been the centers, rather than the areas of study (AOS) (statewide, loosely knit groupings of faculty in related disciplines or interdisciplinary fields), that have hired faculty, assigned students to mentors, and administered studies. Each center, historically, has had at least one faculty member from each AOS, regardless of center size, and each center determines its own study offerings. In many cases, the mentor, in consultation with that center's dean, is the primary "decider" of the configuration of her or his own workload and study delivery. This practice has led to imbalances among offerings at the centers and in mentor loads. Seen as an entire statewide institution, ESC ends up with redundant offerings and with considerable expertise in some academic areas and obvious gaps in others.

## AREAS OF STUDY AND CONCENTRATIONS AS AN ACADEMIC ORGANIZATION

A critical difference between ESC and other institutions is the presence of Areas of Study, created as a deliberate alternative to academic departments; another is the replacement of majors with what the college describes as "concentrations." In planning their curricula, students use appropriate areas of study "guidelines." ESC's innovative idea is that students should not have to fulfill specific requirements, but rather should follow guidelines that provide them (and their mentors) with flexibility to include appropriate studies according to their goals and experience. In more traditional institutions, curriculum committees and departments review the structure of majors to ensure consistency and academic quality. At ESC, faculty assessment committees (historically made up of faculty based at the student's home center) review students' individually designed degree programs and the rationale essays that justify their educational choices, both created in consultation with their mentors.

As a conscious choice, this AOS model of organization has some distinct advantages over departments. For example, it allows mentors with broad and changing interests to relocate their intellectual home when their interests change. The notion of a narrowly defined academic discipline, accompanied by rules that bind one to it and by professional punishment for those straying outside it, is anathema to many at the College. The AOS model also allows students to explore their questions and concerns more openly and gives them permission to cross what, in other higher education organizations, may be rather fixed academic boundaries.

It is important to recognize, however, that as a coordinating tool for a large organization, an AOS-centric system carries with it some challenges. For some mentors who are less steeped in the core values of the College, the AOS model is harder to navigate than a department/disciplinary structure. While more traditional systems may have their drawbacks for both students and faculty, for many faculty, traditional structures are easier to see and are more predictable. Thus, for example, for students who already struggle with too much flexibility (many are thrown when we do not tell them exactly what studies to take or how to plan out a whole curriculum in a single phone call; and many lack the background, the academic capital, to "know what they don't know"), the problem with the AOS structure can be insufficient clarity and little predictability. For mentors, especially "generalist" mentors who are guiding students far outside of their own academic fields (which is often the case when mentors are located in smaller units with few local colleagues), similar gaps in clarity and predictability occur. In order to advise and guide students in *any* discipline, and to give feedback on student degree programs at the locally-based assessment committee meeting, such mentors need to be prepared to work outside of their area of expertise.

As acting Director of Academic Review, Chris saw hundreds of student degree plans and rationale essays submitted over the course of a given year. Cindy, like all mentors, has served on many assessment committees. Both Cindy and Chris have guided many students through the process. What we have both witnessed is a lack of clarity and consistency in the interpretation of the area of study guidelines. What a mentor who has worked with the student in the planning process judges to be an appropriate curriculum, an assessment committee may have concerns about, or even reject completely. Thus, what might be seen by some as the core of academic flexibility can lead to student and faculty uncertainty and frustration. Mentors' and students' interpretations of guidelines vary considerably—even those guidelines that appear to be relatively clear-cut. While such ambiguities can occur, though differently, in more traditional academic structures, ESC has its own distinctive brand of varying interpretations.

We also are aware that at individual centers (in which distinctive cultures of practice have developed over decades), there are conventions (some explicit, some hidden) about which studies meet which guidelines, even if those are not clearly set out in the AOS official guideline statements. Thus, unlike traditional departments, where a student knows which numbered courses are required, which are optional, and which permit some choice for degrees in particular majors, the AOS model celebrates openness, flexibility and choice. Hidden expectations or multiple interpretations of what a "guideline" is and how much like a "requirement" it is taken to be can pose problems for a student who has to navigate these uncharted waters of curriculum planning, sometimes with a mentor who is not necessarily an expert in that particular field. So while the lack of constraint can be helpful, it can also be challenging.

It is in this way that the individualization of degree program planning and the organizational framework that supports it create the risk that students with similar plans, similar tracks of study, and similar professional backgrounds might have very different educational experiences at Empire State College. These experiences can depend on the mentor to whom they are assigned, the instructors and type of instruction they receive, the evaluators of prior experiential learning they encounter, the leanings and/or quality of the coaching and advising available to them, and the particular assessment processes at work in their home location. Consistency is difficult to attain; the challenges to students and to faculty are great.

Of course, though the "stripe" may differ, no institutions of higher education are immune from such on-going ambiguities and challenges. But, as we will argue below, these kinds of issues, when occurring in an institution that prides itself on attention to the individual and to flexibility, are intensified and made that much more problematic in a context of growth.

## INSTITUTIONAL SIZE AND THE STUDENT EXPERIENCE

From its founding, when ESC was much smaller and more nimble, the College not only consciously avoided establishing "majors" but, too, sought to avoid articulating explicit ladders of study— in particular, from introductory to advanced level. So, it has been challenging to question or even to prevent students from pursuing their own interests in the order they encounter them. Here again, the existing organizational structures create problems. In many situations, the opportunity for serendipity is helpful: Students are free to explore learning as it excites them. Nonetheless, in most fields, it is essential to have some building blocks. Few would argue that taking calculus before algebra is a good idea; few would argue that taking finance before accounting is reasonable; and few would argue that taking German literature before gaining a foundation in the German language makes any sense. Yet, aside from gentle nudging from a mentor, all these decisions are possible at ESC, and students in some cases choose to enroll for *advanced* media or *advanced* business studies before taking the foundational ones, a phenomenon that has become more frequent as the College has grown and mentor loads have increased.

Without the time and patience a mentor needs to spend with a specific student – to raise questions, offer suggestions, interrogate the logic of a particular plan, and evaluate choices – a student's decisions may be less than well considered. With a small load of mentees (for example, 20 or 30), it should be very possible for a faculty mentor to find the time to serve a student well and help with the choices that ESC's academic organization calls on a student to make, assuming the student makes the time as well. But with a load well above 100 – not unusual in some college locations today – that task is much harder, if not impossible.

Empire State College's admissions policies and strategic commitment to growth, both central to its organizational core, can result in admitting students who are not fully prepared for college-level work, an issue shared by many institutions of higher education today. In addition, most of ESC's adult students work, often full-time, which contributes to the challenges they face. The objective conditions related to their work and family responsibilities make it harder for them to attend groups, meet deadlines, and handle a rigorous academic workload. Students generally register for several two- or four-credit courses each term (students on financial aid must take 12–16 credits for full-time status). Both students who are not fully prepared and students who have demanding daily lives can suffer when mentors and academic support staff, who carry heavy student loads, have less time to monitor student progress and provide the guidance that these students need.

## GROWTH: THE BIG PICTURE

Organizations can rest on a more top-down or on a more bottom-up approach to decision-making. So long as an organization performs its basic functions – communication and coordination – relatively effectively and consistently, the balance of these two approaches and their relationship to one another will probably work itself out. However, if there is lack of clarity about which approach applies, and when, in each of these areas, those functions can be undermined; and if decisions seem less predictable, especially if external forces overwhelm the ability of the organization to adjust and make necessary change, problems can result.

One could argue that in a small organization, or in one that faces few external threats, these kinds of issues, related to communication, coordination and consistent implementation, might never rise to the level of crises, or might be addressed in a patient, thoughtful way. But when faced with an increasing pace and disparate patterns of growth, the need for greater clarity regarding when and where decisions are top-down and when and where bottom-up is critical: More attention must be paid to this key question.

In the early 2000s, for example, the size of regional locations was relatively similar (between 1,100 and 1,500 headcount) (SUNY Empire State College, 2015b). CDL had already been growing significantly larger than other centers, and CDL continued its very rapid growth through 2012 at which time it accounted for more than 40 percent of the total undergraduate headcount (SUNY Empire State College, 2015b). But recently the picture has shifted. For example, in 2010–2011, while overall college credits increased, differences in size among the regional centers also increased.

For example, between the 1999–2000 academic year and the 2011–2012 academic year, credits in the college overall grew by more than 120,000, a prodigious increase of about 75 percent (SUNY Empire State College, 2015a). The growth, however, was uneven; it occurred in three places: CDL, the Metropolitan Center, and the School for Graduate Studies. (International Programs [IP] has also been up and down, but its programs are ostensibly self-supporting, are built on partnerships with non-U.S. universities, and have a different impact on overall college programming.) In other centers, growth was steady or in slight decline. (The Harry Van Arsdale Jr. Center for Labor Studies has experienced some steeper declines, but, somewhat similar to International Programs, it has a distinct budgetary arrangement through partnership programs tied to labor unions in the New York City area.)

The data suggest a variety of possible explanations. One could argue that the demographic shifts in New York state are an obvious cause. Population stasis or decline in upstate New York limits the pool of new students, which has been especially true in the region from Syracuse to the western border of the state. Conversely, the downstate population, especially in the New York City metropolitan area, has been growing much faster. These data alone would explain much of the disparity in the size of regional centers statewide. Along with population changes, online learning has become a much more widely accepted mode of study for both students and employers, and has gained new legitimacy in graduate education. This change in the environment—even with a much more competitive higher education landscape in online and distance learning—would explain much of CDL's growth.

Such external forces provide reasonable explanations for disparities in growth. The internal forces involved are, however, somewhat more complicated and harder to pinpoint.

## GROWTH: SUNY AND ESC FORCES

At its founding, SUNY Empire State College (2010) declared its commitment to broadening access to higher education, which has meant that growth has been an institutional imperative. Since 2010, growth seems to have been deemed even more central to the institution's mission. There are many reasons for this, which we suspect come not just from ESC's goal of access but from SUNY and from New York state budgetary pressures. Every year in recent memory, a smaller proportion of the ESC budget has come from direct state subvention. (New York is not the only state where this is true, to be sure.) Among other factors, the statewide tax base suffers from a relative movement of population from New York to the rapidly growing U.S. South and West.

The state's fiscal situation means that for SUNY to be successful, overall enrollment must go up. Many SUNY schools have soft or hard enrollment limits, partly because of structural capacity; and schools that are tied to communities and physical plants are typically slow to change. ESC leases much of its space; it does not have dorms, gyms, dining halls, physical libraries, or the other buildings to serve students of residential colleges; it has no sports teams, or recreation facilities for co-curricular organizations, which traditional-aged students increasingly expect of a college. Thus, that ESC's enrollment is not limited by its physical plant is part of the reason the college has been a significant source of potential growth within SUNY. In fact, ESC has now become the largest SUNY college by enrollment, with about 20,000 students.

Given this requirement for growth, as mentioned above, three parts of ESC seem to have the most potential: the School for Graduate Studies, the downstate regional centers, and the Center for Distance Learning. Graduate programs throughout the country, especially in tight job markets, are attracting more and more students. The demography of New York state suggests that the greatest growth nodes are in the lower Hudson Valley, the New York City Metro Area (Brooklyn alone has a population nearly the size of Chicago), and Long Island. In addition, online learning has been the fastest source of growth in all of higher education. And ESC's Center for Distance Learning is no exception.

For many years, CDL benefited from the shift away from paper-based correspondence-type courses to online platforms, as well as from limited competition in the distance learning mode. ESC enrollment reports demonstrate the rapid absolute and relative growth of CDL, which employs a disproportionately large component of the faculty, and delivers about half the total credits of the entire College. In spite of greater competition, CDL's enrollment numbers continued to climb (until recently, about which more below). CDL is now ESC's largest center by a wide margin, nearly four times the size of the Metropolitan Center (which is, by far, the largest regional center).

While there is no doubt several factors involved in CDL's enrollment plateau, there are two that we would mention here: First, the College started charging out-of-state tuition to CDL students who are not New York residents, which made it a less attractive option for them. Second, innovative educational models like massive open online courses (MOOCs) offer a low cost alternative for students who are not degree seekers or who can use these courses for credit at a variety of institutions. While MOOCs are a very different learning experience from the small sections with high levels of faculty attention that the CDL model offers, still they appear to be enrolling hundreds of thousands of students nationwide; and though at this stage, few of these participants complete these courses (the completion rate is below 15 percent [Jordan, 2015]), MOOCs and other online opportunities signify more and more competition with ESC's offerings.

## GROWTH AND ONLINE LEARNING AT ESC

CDL faces its own additional challenges connected to growth. To better manage large-scale processes as it has grown, it has adapted its structure, its teaching and administrative practices, and its delivery of student supports. At CDL, most studies are delivered as online courses through a course management system (CMS), which was Angel in the mid-2000s, is now Moodle, and is expected to change again to a new system in 2017. Most sections of CDL courses have a cap of 20–25 students. Each course is managed by an Area Coordinator (AC)—a full-time faculty mentor who manages a group of courses, a role which includes recruiting and working with full- or part-time colleagues from within the college, and with adjunct instructors. Supervising the development, revision, and maintenance of each course, ACs are usually subject-matter experts, who also teach, mentor students, and participate in service and research much like faculty in other centers. Until 2011, all full-time faculty members at CDL were also ACs, but there is now a second "mentoring model" where newer faculty are expected to carry a heavier teaching and mentoring load, but do not coordinate an area.

CDL's organizational structures are different from the regional centers. Course creation is a case in point. Unlike in other centers, where faculty are relatively free to create and offer the studies they choose, CDL faculty obtain approval for each new course from local faculty teams, from a CDL curriculum committee, and from SUNY, if General Education credit will be granted. (The latter review is not required at other centers where each faculty member determines if a particular study adheres to general education guidelines.) ACs then work with a Curriculum Instructional Designer (CID) on staff and with the mentor who develops the contract, that is, who plans the syllabus, chooses readings, and creates instructional material—including discussion prompts and assignments. This organizational model can be frustrating: CMSs are not always easy to work with; developers are often in different physical locations from ACs and CIDs (most communication is done by phone or email); and developers with an already heavy teaching and mentoring load may need to make course development a lower priority than it is for ACs.

As described earlier in this essay, in keeping with both the vision of ESC and its academic values, rather than beginning with a conventional "major" and developing courses based on traditional requirements as part of a pre-set curriculum, most courses in CDL have been developed "bottom up," meaning that a faculty member has had an idea he or she thought would be useful or interesting to students and would fulfill one of the college's area of study guidelines in some way. With growth, however, faculty at CDL are less able now to give priority to timely course development and revision.

And here again, the organization of academic decision-making is implicated in the everyday academic realities of the college. In many cases, the course development and revision process creates a de facto curriculum. Although the college guidelines mention "depth" and "breadth" of study, as noted earlier, student-mentor deliberation and mentor guidance are central to the college's model, but with mentors carrying more students, there is less time for individual consultation with the result that CDL students may choose courses less knowledgably or look to the courses that are available, rather than those that reflect their personal, academic and professional aims.

There are many facets of CDL's growth that have placed even greater strain on its academic-mentoring model. First, because CDL students in the past typically brought to ESC a significant number of transfer credits (especially from courses at the first and second year levels), and therefore many more CDL courses were advanced-level, this academic organization worked well. Now, however, with the number of credits having increased exponentially from 16,000 to 110,000, and the catalog of on-line courses having ballooned to around 420 across the 11 areas of study, our academic organization may no longer be sustainable. Second, with more and more students preparing for new jobs, the need for knowledgeable individual consultation is even greater. And third, with more younger students having little or no college experience and with more academically underprepared students, together accounting for a significant portion of CDL's overall growth, our lack of traditional academic structure necessitates highly individualized and supportive mentoring that our growing numbers make less possible.

## CONSISTENCY AND CREATIVE TENSIONS

In our experience, students want clarity, predictability, stability, and consistency. This is true in regard to the feedback they get, the grades they earn, and the eventual outcomes of their degree paths. To what extent does ESC offer these as it grows larger, while remaining true to its core educational philosophy? For example, is there a *creative* tension between the goals of individualized degree planning and some consistency of course content, course delivery, and assessment of outcomes, or is it just plain tension? And, if it is creative, will ESC be able to sustain this balance between consistency and individualization as faculty's mentoring loads increase?

Students may once have come to Empire State College because they wanted "a different kind of education" and because they wanted an opportunity to design their own programs. These days, while some wish for that, many, especially at CDL, tell us they come to us because they perceive our type of education as something they can do faster, more cheaply, and more easily. They are often surprised and overwhelmed by the amount of work, research, and time required for their studies. Some are unready for the creativity and effort needed to complete independent studies, develop their own degree plans, write their own rationale essays, apply for prior learning credit (if appropriate to their circumstances), and get their portfolios approved by a faculty assessment committee. Students are used to catalogs, rules, and course sequences that lead to greater depth and sophistication in a "major." Thus, for example, when they come to us, many are baffled by hard-to-comprehend guidelines in the *Student Degree Planning Guide*. They find these and the lack of prescribed sequence challenging. Students' first question is nearly always: "What should I take?" and they are surprised when mentors choose not to tell them what will be important for them to determine for themselves. Yet many are concerned about finishing as quickly as possible, spending or borrowing as little as possible, and not losing any transfer credits; and so the "tensions" for them may be enormous and may not feel very "creative" at all.

If the fastest growing parts of ESC are finding themselves needing to be more traditional structurally than what the college's core values called for and expected (and many online and graduate courses and entire degrees do look more traditional), what does this mean for sustaining these values? And if the most non-traditional approaches of the College in this period of growth and ever-increasing faculty loads result in inconsistent processes and disparate outcomes, what does this mean for ensuring the predictability and consistency to which students are entitled?

## TECHNOLOGIES IN USE AND GROWTH

Chris and Cindy have both taught in other ESC centers and have been struck by how much our basic electronic administrative tools vary, and how difficult it is to get access to needed technological supports, a difficulty that makes it harder to focus on the mentoring so essential to our daily jobs and a difficulty that becomes much more stark as growth becomes the overriding goal.

For example, when it comes to mentoring students, because various technology programs and tools used for student administration do not "talk" to each other, it is often very difficult to respond promptly to student questions or to give clear advice. It is frustrating that a mentor's toolbox still often involves a printer, highlighting pens, and a calculator simply to answer the typical student question: "How many credits do I still need?" The mentors' work as it is now supported less than helpfully by technology is not "scalable." And while the college is working on implementing other types of software for these functions, because of our unique model, any off-the-shelf software requires significant and expensive customization to meet our needs. These needs also differ across the areas of study and across the state.

In addition, faculty's need for communication across the College and within the Areas of Study – essential to ongoing examination and strengthening of academic quality in any institution – is undermined by our inadequate technology systems. With our geographical and organizational dispersion, effective technologies are essential to collegial conversation. Even with improved communications technology, such as wireless broadband or video chatting equipment and online conferencing software (the availability of which varies across the College), careful and systematic communication with our colleagues at other locations and in our areas of study is too rare. Too much time is spent fixing technical issues. And cross-center meetings too often involve parsing an array of vocabularies and systems. A major question remains: Can new technologies effectively support student learning, an increased faculty work load and the exigencies of an administrative infrastructure in a growing college?

## GROWTH AND SUSTAINABILITY: IDEAS FOR THE FUTURE

The organizational model and the administrative and academic processes that were developed during the early days of ESC and that have evolved since grew out of the college's core values and mission grounded in individualized study that required attentive mentoring. They were in the service of students and of their learning. In a then small institution, it was possible to work within, and around, whatever processes were in place without too much trouble. However, for a college that now has so many locations, and with more students than any other SUNY institution, in our view, these processes are unsustainable.

With its many layers of administration related to its dispersed institution, ESC is "over-bureaucratized" in many ways, and runs the risk of becoming what Ginsberg calls the "all-administrative university" (Ginsberg, 2011). Yet, ESC's dizzying array of ways to do what all colleges must do means it is "under-bureaucratized" in other ways. In our view, the lack of predictability – of both processes and outcomes – is reaching crisis proportions. As we all try to do more with less in the face of scarce resources, we spend too much time covering the same administrative ground, too much time on redundant clerical work, and too much time repeating past discussions and trying to understand one another's different vocabulary for equivalent things. All of this wasted effort leaves us with too little time to focus on our students, who expect us to provide the kind of education that our advertising and marketing – and our core values – say we do and that we want to do.

How do we protect our institution's core values and ESC's commitment to progressive education in this time of increasing growth? No doubt it will be hard. We do not want ESC to become the sort of traditional institution that our founders railed against, that is, to retreat without clear rationale and intention to pedagogies that fail to respond to students' learning goals and needs. But, as Cindy has said, just because other colleges endorse a particular practice, does not automatically make that practice unhelpful. Consistent administrative and technical connections between processes and outcomes would be a good start. Access to administrative tools that look the same throughout ESC no matter where one works, and that interact with each other, would be helpful. Making sure to examine the value of what we do and making sure not to assume that "the way we've always done it" yields the greatest value would also be beneficial.

We do not have a magic formula for future success, but we do have some ideas about what might work as ESC's leaders try to navigate the rapid pace of growth while sustaining our mission and values and renewing approaches that serve students and mentors better. For example:

Many students want, even beg for, direction. As noted above, the first question each asks, almost invariably, is "What should I take?" In our view, faculty can continue to be progressive and creative in their approach to curriculum *and* give students the direction they seek. It serves no one well to deny students, in the name of the core values, the experience and knowledge faculty have in their academic fields. A recent initiative to develop registered degree plans with required courses is a good start, but the College will need to address questions related to varying faculty expertise in required areas.

We should identify our most helpful, effective practices and procedures and move toward employing these across the College. Criteria for identifying such practices should include: consistency, predictability, reliability – enough that students and mentors can have confidence that their degree plans and studies will serve students well in their academic quests and in their plans after they graduate. We can apply those practices in our mentoring and teaching, our uses of technology, and in our organization. In light of our dispersed locations, we have a special obligation to do so.

There is nothing special or magical or even, often, especially useful about the structures we now have. A diverse committee of mentors recently drafted an AOS Futures Report to balance the best ideas of the past with necessary changes for the future in relation to our Areas of Study. The President, in conjunction with constituencies across the College, is undertaking conversations about structural reorganization to overcome some of the locally driven inconsistencies that undermine mentors' ability to serve students well and make it harder for students to navigate our systems. We should consider reorganizing the structures we have when that makes sense. We have done so before in our history, and we should not be afraid of doing it now. In fact, as we write this, the College is in the process of moving away from this regionally organized structure to one based on a more conventional divisional model.

One way to maintain the experimental ethos on which the College was founded would be to create a Center for Innovation, a sort of intellectual "skunkworks," as management people call it. The Center could investigate things like blended learning, mobile learning, ELL/ESL student success, and other possible initiatives and questions. Depending on outcomes of these initiatives, it could then develop and distribute these new tools and approaches to other parts of the College. Such a center would serve as a "mini-ESC," and be creative in the same ways that ESC was innovative in 1971. To do so, it must have its own separate setup, just as ESC was a freestanding institution within the larger SUNY system. Staff, faculty, students and administrators could rotate in and out of it frequently (a few years should be the limit), to keep this new center fresh and vibrant and stop it from ossifying, as organizations so often do. While there is much creative energy throughout ESC now, it is always going to be limited by the demands of the existing organization model that, innovation experts tell us, can ultimately be a recipe for failure.

We should remember to listen to and respect the voices of our students—both current and prospective. The demographics of New York state are shifting, and the needs of its citizens and our students are shifting, too. If we truly believe in individualized learning and student-centeredness, we must respond to the people we claim to serve now and know we need to serve in the future. And we should also hear the voices of people who have elected not to attend ESC.

Clearly, these initial suggestions are not intended as an exhaustive list of things we might try to do differently to help us manage growth while maintaining our core mission. Many in the College might disagree with what we have offered. Indeed, we don't always agree with each other. And, of course, some of these suggestions would be much easier to implement than others. But as long as we respect our students and invite them to learn at a college that treats them as partners in their own learning, maybe the hard changes won't look so hard after all.

## REFERENCES

Bonnabeau, R. F. (1996). *The promise continues: Empire State College – The first twenty-five years.* Virginia Beach, VA: The Donning Company Publishers.

Ginsberg, B. (2011). *The fall of the faculty: The rise of the all-administrative university and why it matters.* New York, NY: Oxford University Press.

Gross, R. (1976, June). *Higher/wider/education: A report on open learning.* New York, NY: Ford Foundation. Retrieved from http://files.eric.ed.gov/fulltext/ED127933.pdf

Jordan, K. (2015, June 12). *MOOC completion rates: The data.* Retrieved from http://www.katyjordan.com/MOOCproject.html

Lemann, N. (1999). *The big test: The secret history of American meritocracy.* New York, NY: Farrar, Strauss and Giroux.
Lynn, M. (2000). *Make no small plans.* Saratoga Springs, NY: Skidmore College.
Morgan, G. (1999/2007). *Images of organizations.* San Francisco, CA: Berrett-Koehler Publishers, Inc.
Ryan, D. P. (1988). *About the Union Institute.* Retrieved from http://community.plu.edu/~ryandp/Union.html
Skidmore College. (2011). *Commemorative book of reflections, University Without Walls 1971–2011.* Retrieved from http://www.skidmore.edu/odsp/documents/UWWReflections.pdf
SUNY Empire State College. (2010, May). *Vision 2015: Strategic plan for 2010–2015.* Retrieved from http://www.esc.edu/media/president/president-office/2010-15-Vision-5-24-10.pdf
SUNY Empire State College. (2010–2011). *Fact book 2010–2011.* Saratoga Springs, NY: Author.
SUNY Empire State College. (2012–2013). *Fact book 2012–2013.* Saratoga Springs, NY: Author.
SUNY Empire State College. (2015a, July). *Credits by center/program/school: 1999–2000 to 2014–2015.* Saratoga Springs, NY: Author.
SUNY Empire State College. (2015b, July). *Headcount by center/program/school: 1999–2000 to 2014–2015.* Saratoga Springs, NY: Author.

BARRY EISENBERG

# 16. AT A CROSSROAD

*The Shifting Landscape of Graduate Education*

INTRODUCTION

"... [T]he competitiveness of the United States and our nation's capacity for innovation hinge fundamentally on a strong system of graduate education." So begins *The Path Forward: The Future of Graduate Education in the United States* (Wendler et al., 2010). But the same report suggests that our system of graduate education is facing what are perhaps unprecedented challenges that could go a long way toward revealing and, likely, exacerbating vulnerabilities. Changing demographics, coupled with ever-evolving societal needs, will certainly influence patterns of enrollment and, conceivably, the very role of graduate education; rapidly emerging technologies are altering the way students engage educational institutions and their relationships with them; and given unprecedented levels of debt associated with tuition and the tightening of subsidies for graduate education, finding novel ways of managing the costs of delivering educational programs, including through partnerships among institutions of higher education, is likely to take on heightened importance.

As the next generation of graduate education unfolds, where will the student fit in? What are the obligations of the college or university relative to the student? How can a graduate program honor the individuality of the student while responding to the volume-driven pressures viewed as inextricably linked to institutional viability? How can institutions resolve the tensions that arise when seeking to personalize the learner's experience in increasingly structured programs that lack interdisciplinary opportunity and, by virtue of new technologies, take place in learning environments that are more and more remote?

In response to these kinds of questions, and in the context of significant change, this chapter focuses on the role and mission of graduate education, and in particular graduate education at Empire State College of the State University of New York (ESC). As more and more professional fields seek employees with graduate level education, and as distance technologies expand access to higher education, obtaining a graduate degree is becoming both more essential and more convenient (if not always affordable). Thus, schools such as ESC are increasingly compelled to examine where and how graduate programs fit into their mission and where and how to best offer these programs so as to stay true to that mission and, at the same time, to remain competitive.

The goal of this chapter is twofold: first, to advocate for the notion of the "student-citizen" as an organizing principle for a meaningful and productive graduate-level education; and second, using the experience of ESC, to identify key issues, creative tensions, and operational necessities for progressive institutions of higher education that seek to sustain their nontraditional models and to embrace principles of student-citizenship. To do this, I will draw on the experience of ESC graduate programs, which provides insight into a progressive approach for meeting the challenges that lie ahead while offering a valuable glimpse into the difficulties and dilemmas facing higher education today. And, as a faculty member in ESC's MBA program with a background in health care management, I will draw on the experience of the health care industry, which has been forced to make far-reaching adjustments over the past few decades, and which has developed strategies that have been successfully employed and hold considerable potential value for higher education, particularly for graduate education.[1]

In this chapter, I will first say more about the current context of higher education; second, I will outline issues and tensions inherent in graduate education and which are especially prominent at ESC today; and lastly, I will propose what, in my view, would be the most efficacious ways of balancing these tensions within our current context – all toward the goal of supporting the development of well informed, skilled, thoughtful student-citizens who can contribute to our society and the common good.

## HIGHER EDUCATION IN A CHANGING CONTEXT

To look at the changes and challenges confronting higher education today, I want first to note some developments in the health care industry in the last 30 years. Looking at this comparison between health care and higher education can shed light on some of the challenges and tensions that progressive institutions of higher education, like ESC, are experiencing.

I joined the health care industry as a hospital manager in the early 1980s, and have remained professionally involved in health care since – as a health care executive, consultant, and faculty member in a graduate program. I vividly recall a conversation I had with a senior administrator when I joined the industry. He advised me that I was entering the field during a period of unprecedented and profound change, and he spoke of trends that, as he put it, would redefine much about the industry: clinical challenges created by an aging population; tighter and less predictable revenue streams; higher costs due to increased regulation; changes in how information would be stored, managed, and exchanged due to rapidly advancing technologies; changes in access to health care due to new legislation affecting insurance; pressures on employers to contain the rate of cost escalation of premiums; redirecting of patients away from traditional hospital settings due to new ways of providing care; and more aggressive attention to the satisfaction of the consumer. Health care tomorrow, the administrator concluded, would look significantly different from health care today.

Fast forward more than three decades and the challenges appear much the same, although many of the forces mentioned above have intensified. For example, technological advances are now occurring more swiftly, profoundly influencing how care is provided and how institutions gather and use patient data; the Affordable Care Act has broad potential to expand coverage as well as influence the national economy; the consumer's experience of care and services is increasingly important; and the number of mergers and acquisitions is reaching new heights. Not all hospitals have succeeded in responding to all these changes. In 1975, there were approximately 7,200 hospitals in the United States; by 2009 there were 5,800, a decline of almost 20 percent. During the same period, the number of hospital beds decreased at an even more dramatic rate of over 30 percent.[2] And yet, all this took place while the population was both growing and aging. It is safe to say that the forces of change have had a transformational influence on the landscape of the industry (Eisenberg, Belasen, & Huppertz, 2013).

It is also safe to say that many of the winds of change that health care has been confronting are blowing fiercely in the direction of higher education. For example, emerging and swiftly expanding technologies are altering how students engage their educational institutions and, coupled with the expense associated with obtaining a college education, may enable consumers to exercise even more discrimination in their selection of colleges.

The shifting landscape in higher education will undoubtedly prove disruptive to the status quo. As noted, new tensions are emerging. For example: How can the student's experience maintain an individualized character as he or she engages the academic institution on increasingly distant bases? What categorizations of students will replace labels – such as "conventional," "nontraditional," and "adult-learner" – that once contributed significantly to a college's identity, programmatic direction, and pedagogical orientation, but which appear prone to lose relevance? How can a college maintain and even strengthen an identity if pressures to assimilate into collaborative networks prevail, much as has occurred in health care? How can graduate education honor the late Chancellor of the State University of New York Ernest Boyer's call to encourage students to examine their place in society while colleges experience pressure to arm increasing numbers of students with competencies for success in the job market (1990)? How can colleges feel confident that their systems of pedagogy enable them to fulfill a broad mandate that not only includes skill and knowledge development, but also encourages critical inquiry and an enduring love of learning? How can curricula reconcile what could be construed as competing interests in which structure and flexibility are pitted against one another? And finally, how can resources in an institution function more collaboratively and efficiently without compromising disciplinary integrity?

Ultimately, how well any college positions itself in a changing world itself may be a function of how it defines and resolves the great tensions of the day. And this may be a question, at least in part, of reframing. Debates over how much curricular flexibility is appropriate in an adult-centered learning environment may prove worn and, worse, distracting. Simply, some programs cannot be sanctioned and fully serviceable to a student if the curriculum is not considerably structured. There are things a learner must learn to perform effectively in his or her chosen field, and the college must demonstrate that it has taught those things, and the learner must demonstrate mastery. This is not to suggest we refrain from doing our best to ensure that the student can carve out some space for his or her particular interests to be satisfied through such vehicles as electives, independent studies, internship opportunities, or individualized guided research. But the question is, can we provide these kinds of opportunities for student design of study along with and within required areas of inquiry? And, as we strive for both integration and balance, can we keep the student's needs and purposes at the center?

A college – or any organization for that matter – that does not plan for its future runs the risk of having its future defined by others or by the circumstances of the moment. If other colleges, both within and outside of the State University of New York system, implement distance learning systems, ESC risks losing students who perceive, rightly or wrongly, that other colleges can provide a more relevant or qualitatively superior educational experience. If so, what identity will ESC proudly present to the world? If adult learners' needs can be satisfied by other colleges, what can ESC claim as its mantel of distinction? Returning to its roots and focusing on the student's role in and obligations to society should prove instrumental in reaffirming its identity.

## SERVING THE NEEDS OF ADULT LEARNERS: STUDENT-CENTEREDNESS

SUNY Empire State College was founded to serve the needs of nontraditional learners (Bonnabeau, 1996) and, most particularly, of those who, by virtue of being rooted in careers, communities and families, elected not to relocate to obtain a college education. Instead, ESC brings the academic experience into the communities of its students, first through its 35 centers and units in New York State and then, to strengthen its capacity to reach students in their communities, through online technologies. Both approaches – regional and electronic – have promoted the centrality of the student in the learning process. And both have further supported that focus on student-centeredness through the development of curricular plans that incorporate the student's prior experience and academic achievements into a sequence of studies and/or courses organized around individual students' specific learning goals.

Originally an undergraduate institution, in 1982 ESC's commitment to student-centeredness extended to those seeking graduate education, which, not unexpectedly, has involved the development of programs that are more structured than exist at the undergraduate level at ESC. Pre-established educational plans, particularly for students in programs oriented toward professional pursuits, enable students to acquire an education with coursework that is duly recognized by accrediting organizations, professional associations, and licensing bodies, and which is tailored to the specific challenges students face and the responsibilities they assume in their professional capacities. Thus, tensions such as between pre-structured and student-directed studies, between individuals' goals and external requirements, and between professional and liberal study are particularly salient in graduate education.

However, while adherence to such requirements may constrain flexibility in some ways, it is not the extent of those constraints which determines the degree of student-centeredness of a given program. Rather, the degree to which a program is student-centered may be more fully determined by the extent to which the following three questions can be answered in the affirmative: First, within the curricular parameters imposed by external organizations or by professional standards, does the student have opportunities for customizing some portion of the academic experience to his or own interests, professional goals, and educational needs? Evidence of such tailoring should be present at the course level as well as in the overall program curriculum. Second, is the dignity of each student honored and supported by the institution? Signs include opportunities for a student's prior experience – both professional and educational – to be incorporated into the degree plan, as well as the respectful and collaborative approach of the advising function. As discussed below, the more the student's life and professional experience are integrated into the educational plan, and the more interdisciplinary the academic experience, the greater the need for a mentoring presence that supports the student in reaching his/her learning goals. Third, does the program have a mission that extends beyond strengthening cognition and competency and into the realm of the student's place in society? That is, does the program support critical inquiry and students' sense of their responsibilities in relation to the public good?

## THE STUDENT-CITIZEN

As the demands of society become increasingly complex and the knowledge requirements for professional advancement strengthen, graduate education is growing in importance. More and more, industries and professions have been modifying selection criteria for key jobs to include a graduate degree. For example, in the health care industry, according to the Bureau of Labor Statistics, "A master's degree in one of a number of fields is the standard credential for most generalist positions as a medical or health care manager" (USDOL, 2008, p. 71), a claim echoed by the American College of Healthcare Executives: "[Many] positions that previously required only a bachelor's degree now require a master's degree."[3]

We may ask: Is preparing a student to apply a specific skill-set in a work environment a sufficient goal for a graduate program? Each college or university may determine its response to this question in light of its history, tradition, values, and purpose. Notwithstanding, many believe that graduate education must go further. As I will argue below, while supporting students' professional development constitutes a core purpose of graduate education, its role should be defined more expansively: Graduate education must also strengthen students' acumen for critical and intellectual inquiry, promote an aptitude for conducting research, enrich expertise in a given discipline, and support students' understanding of their role in society. Most importantly, these are not discrete functions but, rather, significantly interrelated.

Here again the health care parallel is useful. Until recently, the combination of pressures and incentives in health care made it difficult for providers to exercise a more individualized and patient-centered approach to caregiving. Many economic, regulatory, and policy incentives promoted the notion of a volume-driven model, inhibiting, many contend, a focus on comprehensive individualized approaches to patient care (Sultz & Young, 2011; Martin, Williams, Haskard, & DiMatteo, 2005; Lighter, 2011; Landro, 2013). Moreover, health care organizations are highly rule-governed and commit a significant portion of resources to ensuring compliance with a vast number of standards, which, coupled with the compulsion to practice medicine defensively, can detract from a focus on the consumer as an individual (Eisenberg, 1997).

But trends related to technology, economics, legislation, accreditation, and epidemiology have been coming together to support progress in understanding the patient in the wider context of his or her life, including before and even well after care is rendered. Providers are encouraged to become better positioned to see the patient as a human being and to place the person at the center of the caregiving experience. And, importantly, a patient-centered approach provides a basis for the patient to take a more active and knowledgeable role in his or her care management. Such an approach reframes the health care experience from one in which the patient functions as a passive recipient, abiding by a directive, to one in which he/she becomes a partner in the process.

The variable most central to a patient-centered approach is not the extent to which the patient defines the treatment plan options but rather, the nature of the relationship established by the participants in the process and the context which defines their respective roles. The more the patient is encouraged to understand the diagnosis and treatment alternatives (including all the benefits and risks), and is granted decision-making latitude about courses of treatment, the more we can say a *patient-centered* context has been established. Whether multiple treatment options or just a few or even just one treatment option may be available, it is not the range of options that determines patient-centeredness, but the extent to which the patient's perspective occupies a respected place in the provider-patient relationship.

Here, I could share a personal example. In a routine visit to her primary care physician a few years ago, my mother was told she should not drive a car any longer. At the time, my mother was 87 years old, but was in good health and had an excellent driving record. She lived alone and cherished her mobility and independence. Stunned and frightened by the physician's instruction, which was tossed off in a casual manner as she was departing his office, my mother asked if I would contact him to hear his reasoning. The physician informed me that he tells all his elderly patients to stop driving. He acknowledged that this practice enables him to avoid "getting into trouble" in the event the patient experiences a driving mishap. The physician then indicated that since my mother had not suffered any impairment of health, judgment, or reflexes, she could continue to drive. In this example, the physician was motivated principally by self-protection and, in so doing, treated a patient as a member of a group rather than as an individual. Never mind that the consequence of this action would have been to deprive an able person from continuing an activity that would allow her to maintain a life free of dependency on others for transportation. At some point my mother would surely have to give up driving. But that day was clearly not it.

By honoring her aptitude – not to mention her right – to participate in decisions about her life, my mother would be more able to understand the potential consequences of her health and lifestyle choices. In this respect, individualizing the patient's health care experience actually asks *more* of the patient, not less. A patient-centered approach does not relieve patients of responsibility or make it easier on them. Quite the contrary, it imposes a sense of responsibility. And in the case of my mother, for example, this responsibility takes into account not only her welfare, but that of other drivers and pedestrians in her proximity. By personalizing the caregiving experience, the patient's obligations to self and others are made clearer and the responsibilities for engaging in behavior that contributes to the public good are more well-defined. Thus, by focusing on the patient as an individual, the caregiver is promoting *citizenship* – respectful and responsible conduct which supports and sustains the well-being of one's community as well as oneself.

## OPERATIONALIZING A STUDENT-CITIZEN VISION

Establishing – and, more particularly, sustaining – a student-centered model is enormously challenging. Organizational dynamics coupled with externally imposed demands and environmental trends can present powerful obstacles. The years ahead will undoubtedly demand far more adaptation than has been necessary over the past several generations. Specifically, the future is likely to hold more promise for institutions that are able to: (1) overcome the tendency toward disciplinary and organizational fragmentation and strengthen internal collaboration; (2) embrace and exploit emerging technologies as a creative force in student-centered pedagogy; and (3) implement collaborative arrangements with other institutions. These three areas of focus, when taken together, offer a template of opportunity for operationalizing a student-citizen model. Below, I will look at how each area can help graduate education respond to the challenges – both internal and external – that we confront, and how we can continue to work toward providing the student with the richest, most coherent, purposeful education possible.

Ultimately (as discussed in a section that will follow a description of these three points), it is imperative – perhaps as never before in light of the challenges higher education faces – that colleges and universities ensure alignment among core values, purpose and mission, aspirations, and strategic direction.

*1. Toward an Integrated Academic Environment: Interdisciplinary Inquiry and Liberal and Professional Study*

In recent years, by virtue of necessity, health care has made significant – but by no means sufficient – strides toward building a patient-centered model. A brief examination, along with a review of the SUNY Empire State College graduate program, will shed light on how a student-centered approach in support of student citizenship may be sustained.

When I first joined the field of health care, one of the more astonishing revelations to me was the extent to which health care organizations felt more like collections of small businesses than coherent, highly integrated entities. From the outside, each hospital had the appearance of being a fixed entity, a building housing a well-oiled operation with various functions interweaving in a coordinated manner to provide care to patients. But a careful look inside revealed this to be illusory. Each profession and each department tended to work far more independently than interdependently, often exceedingly so. Professionals from different fields came to the institution with very distinct and, often, very dissimilar training. Much about how the work was organized, including all the daily routines of attending to the needs of patients and the institution, legitimized such separateness. And the failure to synchronize such activities is not without cost: if it adds even a small increment to the average length of stay by patients in the hospital, the annual cost to the hospital can be in the millions of dollars.

A lack of integration has also meant that resources could not be easily shared. In fragmented health care environments, employees are deprived of opportunities to gain insights into a patient's experience in other parts of the organization and less able to understand the full range of a patient's experience in the hospital. Thus, fragmentation has made it difficult for hospitals to hold a truly patient-centered perspective. And it has also meant that employees would have restricted opportunities for professional development. In such an environment, interdisciplinary or multidisciplinary activities are more difficult to define and pursue.

Developments in health policy, accreditation, clinical progress, and health economics have come together in recent years to turn the tide on fragmentation. For example, accreditation criteria have evolved from a predominantly disciplinary orientation and have begun to encourage caregiving processes that cut across a range of diagnostic and clinical functions that contribute to the patient's experience (Belasen, Eisenberg, & Huppertz, 2015). Accordingly, the fragmented model is quickly losing capacity to be serviceable in health care environments. Hospitals still have a long way to go to function on a significantly integrated basis, but they have little choice but to strive toward this integration in the face of new incentive structures that reward efficiency and punish wastefulness.

Similarly, higher education is in a period of major adjustment to comparable environmental trends. As has occurred in health care, colleges are increasingly obliged to reflect on how they provide meaningful and enriching experiences to those they serve, and, in particular, how they can reduce academically unhelpful and administratively wasteful fragmentation in their organization. Developments in national and state policy, emerging technologies, demographic fluctuations, economic ups and downs, evolving employer demands, globalization, and changes in skill and knowledge needed in the labor pool have pushed institutions of higher education to review and, where necessary, not only to adjust their curricula, learning environments, and pedagogical approaches, but also to reconsider how they assemble and deploy resources. Despite aspirations toward more integrated approaches to inquiry (about which, more below), many colleges suffer from the barriers posed by academic and organizational fragmentation, barriers which result in redundancy and waste and in systems that fail to work together to provide the best possible service to the student – and thus, ultimately, undermine the student's academic experience.

The complexities of our current environment place a particular burden in this regard on graduate programs. Students who enroll typically live and work in a world increasingly characterized by technological advancements that seem to arrive at a bewildering pace, globalization and rapidly changing work processes, and ever more complicated social demands, including, for example, the need to care for aging relatives. All these can stymie efforts to balance work and all the other dimensions of a student's life. A student-centered approach must include both an understanding of a learner's needs and interests and effective organization of programs and resources to support the satisfaction of those needs.

Of course, this does not mean turning a blind eye to the necessities of a given program, including responsiveness to accreditation criteria, learning goals, and other academic requirements, such as for licensure. But it does mean searching for ways to ensure that the student's specific interests are properly served. The art student may seek some business courses to explore how his passion can translate into professional opportunity. The business student may seek an appreciation of multiculturalism from a sociological perspective as it may increase her understanding of and sensitivity to the consumer market. The health care management student may desire an understanding of the role of gender in a workforce. The teacher-in-training may seek an in-depth understanding of the role of the political, economic and social context for educational practice. The more fragmented the environment, the less possible any of this becomes. Fragmented environments tend to be program-centric rather than student-centered.

So, like the health care industry and like most institutions of higher education, graduate education at ESC, if it is to keep the student at the center and to support development of the student-citizen, should pay focused and proactive attention to integrating its academic offerings, organizational structures and administrative systems.

Much like health care institutions, college environments are generally segmented along disciplinary lines. And differing programmatic emphases among academic fields can, in highly fragmented environments, stir up anxieties about unfair distribution of resources or excessively pious protectionism of epistemological purity. But the achievement of enhanced interconnectedness does not have to entail abandonment of disciplinary integrity. Just as cardiology and orthopedics can preserve their disciplinary character while seeking common ground, so can literature and history; productive working relationships among disciplines and departments can strengthen quality and breadth of service.

And while distinctions among disciplines can inspire intellectual curiosity and nurture scholarly development, when the environment encourages creative integration, students and faculty can imagine possibilities that would otherwise be impossible. At ESC, new or planned graduate certificates in fields such as Medical Humanities, Women and Leadership, Community Development, Global Brand Marketing, to name just a few, could not occur without some shedding of disciplinary parochialism. Therefore, an environment grounded in a multi-disciplinary ethic, if managed properly and supported by an effective mentoring foundation, can provide the student a better-rounded, student-centered educational experience, while at the same time serving the institution's needs for greater operational efficiency.

Not unrelated to disciplinary insularity and the need to bring together the varied lenses and inquiry that the disciplines provide, there may be a tendency to limit the objective of graduate education to the acquisition of proficiencies associated with specific career pursuits. This pressure to emphasize such competencies would not be unexpected in a period in which the graduate degree is more and more becoming the educational standard for professionals in many fields. Indeed, it could compound the loss of a more balanced approach that stimulates intellectual curiosity and critical inquiry, obliges us to consider ethical implications of our professional conduct and motivates us to build productive and rewarding relationships. That is, much like with health care prior to some of the more recent trends, it might be difficult to resist the pressure to limit the scope of responsibility of the educational institution toward its students. Moreover, as will be discussed more fully below, as technology continues to establish a firm foothold in mediating the relationship between educator and learner, the barriers to a more comprehensive approach to education could actually increase.

An exclusive focus on professional advancement may prepare the graduate student to exercise requisite skills in the work place. However, separating this purpose from critical inquiry – a key element of citizen education – may deprive students of a related and essential responsibility: to appreciate the impact of their work on society. In discussing the documentary on transformational education, *Most Likely to Succeed*,[4] *New York Times* columnist David Brooks (2015) claims, "The better approach [to education], the film argues, is to take content off center stage and to emphasize the relational skills future workers will actually need: being able to motivate, collaborate, persevere and navigate ..." (para. 4). Ernest Boyer spoke passionately about the vital interconnectedness between application, inquiry, and understanding of one's contribution to the public good:

> In its current climate, graduate study is, all too often, a period of withdrawal – a time when many students are almost totally preoccupied with academic work and regulatory hurdles. In such a climate, doctoral candidates rarely are encouraged or given the opportunity to see connections between thought and action. To counter such isolation, would it be possible for graduate students to participate in a practicum experience and, in so doing, be challenged to see the larger consequence of their work and help reconnect the academy to society[?]. ... [F]uture scholars should be asked to think about the usefulness of knowledge, to reflect on the social consequences of their work, and in so doing gain understanding of how their own study relates to the world beyond the campus. (Boyer, 1990, p. 69)

ESC's commitment to operationalizing Boyer's student-citizen vision is reflected in the work of its graduate curriculum. Notwithstanding the more structured nature of some of its graduate programs, explicit attention to student-centeredness and to an integration of liberal and professional study permeates its programs. Consider that all graduate programs, which span Adult Learning, Business, Liberal Studies, Policy, and Teaching: (1) promote an understanding of ethical and social responsibility; (2) include provisions for prior experiential learning to be incorporated into curricular plans; (3) place an emphasis on responsibilities of *citizenship*, whether applied to one's community, work environment, or profession; (4) offer multiple opportunities in coursework for students to adapt theories and principles to their professional work and aspirations; and (5) provide a capstone experience for students – often of an interdisciplinary nature – organized around a student's particular interests and career objectives. While these graduate programs may vary with respect to degree of curricular flexibility – from the relatively student-directed studies of the Master of Arts in Liberal Studies Program to the necessarily more structured licensure courses of study in the Master of Arts in Teaching Program—all programs are dedicated to the proposition that some balance of structure and customization is essential. Further, to effectively serve the needs of students, all programs encourage, where appropriate, some degree of interdisciplinarity and the integration of liberal and professional study.

By way of example, ESC began the development and implementation of advanced graduate certificates in 2009. Since then, approximately 20 certificates have been available to graduate students (and several other such specialized certificates are in various stages of proposal development); these programs, consisting generally of four to six courses, are "... designed to provide focused study to support a particular career interest."[5] Curricula are infused with opportunities for students to explore the relationships among engaging in critical inquiry, gaining functional knowledge, and examining obligations to the communities served by the student's professional practice. The certificate in Veteran Services, for example, includes studies in Military and Veteran Culture, Veteran Programs and Benefits, Veteran Services and Public Policy. These kinds of studies and programmatic learning goals reflect the obligation felt by Empire State College to support student citizenship through professional *and* liberal inquiry. Thus, the student pursuing an accounting specialty will also be exposed to principles of business ethics, and that student also will be encouraged to examine and reflect on how such principles relate to his or her role as a professional. In so doing, ESC broadens its commitment to the student by asking the student to conceive of his or her professional role not as confined to knowledge and skill acquisition, but also to how these may be employed in the service of supporting others and contributing to society. Graduate education may become increasingly pressured to provide predominantly skill-based curricular programs; yet, as students graduate and move ahead with their lives, those programs which challenge them to consider their role in society and to respect the world around them will be stronger and are likely to be held in more esteem than those which fail that test.

## 2. Emerging Technologies and Pedagogical Possibilities

In virtually every facet of diagnostic and clinical activity in health care, technology has had an increasing presence. And it mediates, more and more, the interactions between practitioner and patient. No one would dispute the extraordinary benefits that technology brings to the health care environment. But what we are less sure of is its influence on the social and interpersonal dimensions of caregiving. We may intuit that some technologies can impede communication effectiveness by virtue, simply, of being there – a machine standing between the interactants – depriving them, perhaps, of some essential aspect of "human connection." The body of research on the matter is inconclusive (Chen, 2010; Doyle et al., 2012; Fonville, Choe, Oldham, & Kientz, 2010; DuPre, 2010; Smith, 2013; Stack, 2013; Topol, 2012). There is still a long way to go to gain a comprehensive understanding of the impact of technology on the patient's ability to participate in and trust the medical context, develop confidence in the person providing care, and comprehend and make well-reasoned decisions about diagnostic and treatment options.

What is the future of higher education with respect to increasing reliance on electronic technologies in teaching and learning? Unquestionably, these technologies have introduced wonderful benefits into learning environments, bringing a universe of information and a burgeoning repertoire of tools for learning and discovery directly into the hands of the student. Such distance modalities may hold particular benefits for graduate students who can expect their degree programs to focus extensively and directly on the relationship of their studies to their professional activities and career pursuits. For graduate students, whose academic and work experience are interrelated and who seek to apply the work of one to the other, distance learning opportunities can be quite helpful. By permitting the student to remain in his or her community and tending to be flexible in how and when the learning environment is accessed (for example, through asynchronous participation), graduate programs grounded in distance formats, like those at ESC, can directly support students in integrating the professional and academic parts of their lives.

The growth of online education has been considerable. According to Allen and Seaman (2013), 1.6 million students took an online course in 2002; ten years later, the number jumped to 6.7 million. Expansion is projected to continue at a rapid rate, and the implications are many. The distinction between adult learners and more conventional learners should blur as colleges develop a capability to provide education that does not require the learner to leave his or her community or significantly rearrange his or her lifestyle. Coupled with the increasing emphasis on graduate education as a condition of employment in key sectors of the economy, the flexibility afforded by online programs could stimulate accelerated growth in online graduate study. The growth of online programs should provide prospective students with more choice; freed from having to consider where a college is located, students will be able to focus on other criteria in their selection of institution, and colleges will likely need to market themselves in new ways to distinguish themselves from competitors.

As all this unfolds, the practice of awarding college credit for learning from prior professional or life experience is likely to increase. Online options will encourage greater participation from nontraditional students who may include in their evaluation of programs the extent to which institutions honor and factor professional experience and prior learning into a student's degree plans. As colleges seek a competitive advantage in this regard, the systems for evaluating the educational value and relevance of prior learning and professional and life experience should improve. Doing all this and doing it well and economically are two different things. Acting with urgency to satisfy anticipated demand could render an institution unprepared to ensure that students will have a good quality educational experience; acting with complacency could put an institution at a competitive disadvantage.[6]

Colleges have evolved as relatively independent entities. In the model that has prevailed for centuries, students pick themselves up, enroll in a particular college, select an academic concentration, and embark on a course of study. But we are in the early stage of what may be a paradigm shift: With the very technology that enables the student to bring the college into his or her world, the student can scan the environment for options that will permit the educational experience to be customized. Educators can help bring definition to those possibilities and help students sort out those which are more relevant to the student's learning goals. Technology and economics are coming together in a way that will make this occur far more fully than exists today – similar, perhaps, to what has occurred in health care. In this regard, mentoring – from the start a cornerstone of ESC practice, guiding a student through the creative processes of organizing a relevant curriculum and helping the student achieve curricular goals – could become even more essential in the days ahead.

ESC also has a tradition built on the notion of bringing the College into the communities of its students. The majority of its graduate programs have employed an online foundation for many years. This has served an adult learner population quite well. Students have become accustomed to assimilating their academic experience into their lives, enabling a swift and comprehensive application of principles and theory to their professional activity. Faculty employ a host of tools to promote a responsive learning environment, and many programs augment the online experience with residencies in which students have face-to-face learning opportunities.[7]

So we have two fields – health care and higher education – caught in the push and pull of seeking to individualize the consumer's experience while employing more and more technology which, despite all its benefits, can also function as a barrier to that goal.[8] Given that technological advancement is inevitable, the higher education community may look to the experience of colleges that have implemented successful online programs, as well as that of the health care industry, which has been contending with the increasing role of technology for a long time, to gain insight into how to minimize the barriers associated with the introduction of new technologies and to maximize the opportunities they afford.

SUNY Empire State College instituted a distance education program not separate from but, rather, as an extension of the core value of placing the learner's experience and needs at the center of educational planning. While it is tempting to view these two phenomena – distance education and personalizing the learner's experience – as mutually exclusive, throughout its history, ESC has employed the notion of the student-citizen as a vehicle for transcending this seeming incompatibility and thereby of unifying *distance learning* and *student-centeredness*. This effort has required ongoing reflection on founding principles and examination of their application to evolving environmental, societal, and technological conditions. And in so doing, as discussed above, ESC has continued to provide an educational experience for the student that goes beyond the acquisition of competencies; in myriad ways, students are encouraged to consider societal commitments associated with such competencies.

The experience of ESC in the uses of technology to support students' study may not be universally generalizable. Similarly, the application to higher education of health care's experience in this realm could be dismissed as comparing apples and oranges. But four principles are worth noting: First, developing an online capability while remaining faithful to core institutional values is a vital condition for program success. Those values constitute the common ground that will serve the institution well as it seeks to mobilize support for its programs among a full range of stakeholders. Second, engaging learners in the design of their studies will not only produce a better program, but will encourage students to commit more fully to it. Third, establishing meaningful feedback and evaluation systems will enable the institution to learn how the online program is functioning and how it can continue to improve. Fourth, and perhaps most critically, committing to ongoing study of the effectiveness of distance learning technologies and contexts is crucial to our understanding of how to make them better. We may understand that various modes of distance learning can facilitate cognitive and skill development. But do we know enough about how to employ these technologies so that participation can instill in students the sense of social responsibility demanded by the student-citizen model? Those institutions that embrace the technology have an obligation to acquire an understanding of its effectiveness across a comprehensive range of student learning goals. In so doing – in accepting the responsibility for researching how our work helps students not only to learn, but to become better citizens – we will be serving as a role model for our students, asking from them no more than we ask of ourselves.

Finally, it should be noted that emerging technologies can serve as a basis for imagining possibilities for the design and use of "classroom space." Traditional models of education focused on such things as number of students and patterns of engagement among the learners and the instructor. Will technologies that are on the horizon allow for more creative definitions of a "classroom," reconciling in ways yet to be determined how we maximize student participation even in the presence of larger numbers of students? How might the MOOC model[9] be more broadly and effectively applied, particularly so that those who benefit from more intimate educational settings do not experience compromise? How can a college with a particular academic specialty reach a significantly broader segment of the target market while economizing resources as well as – and this is critical – strengthening quality of the educational experience? Can a classroom with 20 students maintain – and even increase – the richness of the educational experience if the number of students expands to 100? 200? 500? Colleges with a significant history of technologically-mediated study have an obligation to consider such questions, and should pursue a leadership role in gaining insight into how pedagogy and technology relate to one another in the spirit of advancing student-centeredness.

## 3. Collaboration among Institutions

Thirty years ago, most hospitals functioned as independent entities. Today, most are affiliated with other hospitals and health care systems. In 2011, for example, a staggering $231 billion of merger, acquisition and takeover activity occurred in the health sector market.[10] Health policy, economics, technology, and the increasing focus on the needs of the consumer of health care have come together such that functioning independently could render an institution vulnerable.

Partnerships of all sorts are taking shape, from the more formal and legal mergers to looser confederations or alliances, in which organizations with independent management structures implement any of a variety of collaborative models to achieve common goals. Horizontal systems consist principally of like-organizations, particularly hospitals.[11] Vertical systems, in which complementary services are provided – for example, ambulatory care, primary care, acute care, rehabilitation therapy, and geriatric services – are growing in response to mounting pressure to expand access, promote continuity of care, and facilitate patient movement from one health care venue to the next. The need to demonstrate value-added care following a patient's visit demands a level of coordination among providers never before required, and new advances in information technology, particularly electronic medical records, are making partnership arrangements easier to implement and manage.

Even if differences between the health care and higher education fields are such that it is unlikely that the same trend of broad-based consolidation will occur in higher education, it is hard to ignore three important parallels that are likely to generate higher levels of integration and collaboration among colleges.

First, tuition increases, which are accompanied by diminished public support for colleges, are not likely to expand to compensate for the anticipated flattening of enrollments in the coming years. According to The College Board, "Average published tuition and fees at public four-year colleges and universities increased by 13 percent in 2015 dollars over the five years from 2010–11 to 2015–16, following a 24 percent increase between 2005–06 and 2010–11."[12] These rates of increase are comparable to rates of cost and premium increase in health care in the several years leading up to the initial flurry of mergers in the 1990s.

The mountain of debt accrued by college students may also constitute a factor in slowing enrollment. MSNBC recently reported that "Americans now owe more on their student loans than they do on their credit cards. ... [S]tudent loan debt is growing at a rate of $2,853.88 per second. ... It [surpassed] $1 trillion in 2012."[13] Consumers can tolerate just so much cost escalation before they start reconsidering the necessity of the service or product or their ability to purchase it. So revenue stream constriction, whether due to decreased public funding or decreased enrollment, to the extent that it occurs, will certainly have some impact on higher education. How it manifests may not be fully known. But as organizations strive for prudence in financial management, economy of scale and collaborative models become increasingly attractive options.

Second, as discussed earlier, the increasing presence of technologies which have become so central to the provider-consumer relationship may dramatically redefine methods of student engagement. To the extent that students have the option to attend "campus-less" colleges, will it be possible for students to develop something of an "a la carte" approach to education, seeking out courses in different institutions which suit their needs? This, of course, is done now, though to a limited degree; for example, a student at home for the summer may take a course at a local college that will be transferred to the college in which the student is matriculated. But absent a need to make such choices on the basis of geography, students may, over time, exercise such an option more comfortably and frequently. As this occurs, the economic benefit – for both students and institutions – of developing systems and/or consortia should stimulate colleges to consider ways of working together.

Third, just as the health care system has had to reorient itself to accommodate a rapidly expanding older population, so too is education gearing up to support an expanded base of learners who are older than previous generations of college students. Health care has had to make considerable adjustments over the past 20 years in this regard. To address the particular health needs of an older population, disciplines have come to depend on one another to provide more holistic care. And while the need for an ongoing caregiver presence tends to be more acute with an older population, resource coordination across all segments of the patient population has proven beneficial for the health and well-being of all patient groups.

With the 35+ age group projected to expand at a rate faster than any other age group attending college, and with students more and more able to select colleges with less regard for their physical location, prevailing systems of categorizing students may become obsolete, and the distinction between the "traditional" and "nontraditional" learner is likely to continue to blur, perhaps even become anachronistic. This may be particularly true for graduate education. Similarly, as the retirement age drifts up, larger numbers of older people are likely to pursue continuing education to keep current in their fields and compete with a younger generation. In such a scenario, enrollments in advanced study could appreciably expand as would the age range of the graduate learner population. As these broad shifts occur, might colleges benefit from partnering with others to ascertain the best way of meeting emerging needs? Such partnerships might not only support goals related to operational soundness and efficiencies; they might also allow educational institutions more readily to serve student needs and satisfy their expectations.

Moreover, as noted above, as the age of students increases so too will students' demand for clearer connections between their studies and careers. Thus, much as in health care, partnerships may emerge not only on horizontal bases, but on vertical bases as well. The former provide opportunities for colleges to offer supplementary coursework as well as opportunities for complementary learning environment options (e.g., online and face-to-face); the latter, in which colleges partner with corporations, civic organizations, government agencies, NGOs, professional associations, and so on, provide limitless opportunities for students to apply what they have learned. In addition, apprenticeships, internships and other career development opportunities not only serve students' professional development interests, but also allow employees at partnership institutions to observe first-hand the benefit to these students of their educational experience. As such, these kinds of partnerships also constitute a marketing tool.

The SUNY Empire State College MBA in Healthcare Leadership is a case in point. During their participation in the program, students will be provided with opportunities to gain administrative experience in health care facilities, e.g., through internship arrangements. Collaborative models such as these enable students to draw on expertise from a wider range of programmatic options and allow students to apply and practice what they learn more readily. Partnerships – vertical and horizontal – will prove particularly important in an era in which graduate programs become an increasingly vital component of a college's offerings.

Yet, the development of and participation in collaborative arrangements are not without challenge. These efforts demand that leaders work with their organizations to adapt to a larger system and to frame their organizations' missions, values, and academic emphases in broader organizational contexts. Maintaining an institutional identity while integrating into a larger system constitutes a delicate balancing act. College leaders capable of moving their institutions into systems in which program complementarity prevails over needlessly excessive program redundancy – and of organizing their academic plans in accordance with a well-developed understanding of their segment of the student market – will be more assured of their institutions' success.

Existing multi-unit organizations, such as the State University of New York, have an advantage by virtue of already having a common management structure. For example, recently, SUNY Empire State College collaborated with SUNY College of Optometry to develop a graduate certificate in Optometry Business Management. The six-course program is designed to prepare optometry students for the rigors of managing a health care practice. Students take courses in financial management, operations management, inter-professional relations, leadership, and public health. Principles of business ethics are included in the curriculum. This joint effort in the service of optometry students is the first of its kind in the United States. Such collaborations are particularly valuable on the graduate level as they enable professional goals to be defined and satisfied in more comprehensive ways.[14] The more educators team up, the more they can provide a rich and meaningful range of options.

Yet while large systems have a built-in potential for collaborative engagements, like smaller colleges, they too should be mindful of the difficulties. For example, because of their size, organizational complexity, and expectations for public accountability, implementing complementary approaches to program development could prove unwieldy and cumbersome. The challenge for such systems involves transitioning from a loose confederation of relatively independent operating centers to a more structurally integrated environment while helping the individual colleges preserve and affirm their distinctive identities.

Providers in the health care industry have had to become adept at differentiating themselves as well as functioning as part of a system. Might we be on the verge of seeing this, to some degree, in higher education? If so, the experience of health care can be quite instructive. Organizations that begin by taking stock of what they do well, how such assets serve the public good while ensuring institutional viability, who their consumers are, who they want them to be and why—all such organizations will have a distinct advantage. But they must be careful in how they approach this critical phase of strategic planning, for it is easy to get derailed. If their analysis is guided by hubris, distraction or inflexibility, or if the leadership cannot bring the organization together to take an honest accounting, the analysis will serve the institution poorly. On the other hand, if the analysis provides a point of departure for reflecting on how the organization can position itself to adapt to changing circumstances and for participating in collaborative frameworks, a focus on what it does well may prove priceless. Mobilizing an effective approach demands nothing less than very talented leadership.

## INSTITUTIONAL IDENTITY: CORE VALUES AND COMMITMENTS

An institution's identity provides the basis or rationale for which programs and academic themes to emphasize, which students to seek and how, which pedagogical strategies to employ, and which partners to engage. A college cannot define itself effectively if it cannot link its core academic areas with its purpose, values and commitments to its students. It will become increasingly imperative for a college – for every college – to let the world know what it teaches and why particular prospective students will benefit from studying in a given area at this particular institution.

The concepts of student-citizen and student-centeredness can be instrumental in reframing vital tensions – such as between liberal and professional study – not as mutually exclusive, but as an opportunity to bridge the college's core values with its aspirations and to provide definition for institutional identity. These concepts enable SUNY Empire State College to declare that it will prepare students for careers and jobs while also helping them to think about their role in society, a commitment which emanates from a liberal arts and social justice tradition. And this commitment is of particular value at the graduate level, for it is there that students may seek a more defined relationship between their studies and livelihoods. Employers seek people with such well-rounded educational backgrounds. Consider the views of Laszlo Bock, senior vice president, responsible for recruitment and hiring at Google, who said in response to *New York Times* columnist Thomas Friedman's question, "Are the liberal arts still important?"

> [They are] phenomenally important. … Ten years ago behavioral economics was rarely referenced. But [then] you apply social science to economics and suddenly there's this whole new field. I think a lot about how the most interesting things are happening at the intersection of two fields. To pursue that, you need expertise in both fields. You have to understand economics and psychology or statistics and physics [and] bring them together. You need some people who are holistic thinkers and have liberal arts backgrounds and some who are deep functional experts. Building that balance is hard, but that's where you end up building great societies, great organizations. (Friedman, 2014, para. 12)

Similarly, the notion of student-centeredness, that is, the placement of the student's interests at the center of study and program design and planning, provides the impetus for disciplines to be brought together to contribute to the student's inquiry, for liberal and professional studies to support one another, for technologies to provide the access and the tools that students need, and for programs and institutions to work collaboratively. Student-centeredness, when it is employed genuinely, is institutionally humbling, for it places the student's needs before a program's or an institution's interests. And it is this student-centeredness that should be the organizing principle for all our efforts at both the undergraduate and graduate levels.

Like many colleges and universities, SUNY's Empire State College will be tested. The climate in the years ahead may be largely unforgiving and there is little room for error – for institutions of higher education in general and for progressive institutions of higher education in particular. But as a progressive institution, ESC has a long and proud history of partnering with the student in the development of a compact, an agreement developed by a mentor and student called a "learning contract." And so, as a progressive institution, ESC has an astounding opportunity to thrive if it undertakes a rigorous and comprehensive examination of how that history can intersect favorably with both the opportunities and the challenges of the future. In so doing, its identity, as well as its goal of supporting the development of the student citizen, will be strengthened and understood by all stakeholders, and its ability to continue to serve the public good will be enhanced.

## EPILOGUE

Recently, I was consulting on a project that brought me to a health care system in the Midwest. I spent the day at one of the member hospitals and, at about 9:00 PM, was preparing to leave. I stopped in the lobby and sat on a couch to gather my papers before heading back to my hotel. Sitting next to me was a woman who appeared to be in her 70s. Dressed nicely and sitting quietly, she sat with her hands folded in her lap. After a moment, she leaned toward me and asked if I had been visiting a patient. I replied I was there on business.

"And you?" I asked. "Are you here to visit someone?"

She sighed, shifted her gaze to the floor, and then looked back at me. "My sister has been here for three days. She has cancer. They told her today she has about three months."

I looked in her eyes and could see a trace of redness. Otherwise, her face did not reveal her sadness. Maybe she was still in some shock. I expressed how sorry I was, and asked if I could help her with anything. At that moment, a young woman wearing a hospital ID badge approached the woman sitting next to me. She put her hand on the woman's shoulder and said, "Mrs. Sullivan, we can meet now. Let's go to my office."

Mrs. Sullivan introduced me to the young woman, a social worker who was going to help Mrs. Sullivan get support for the difficult time that lay ahead. As she stood, she shook my hand, thanked me for offering to help, and then said, "I'm in good hands here."

I have worked in health care for many years, most of them in health care management. I made it a point to visit patients regularly, to ask how their stay was going. I made sure our employees did as well. But at this moment, all I could think about was that I had walked through hospital lobbies thousands of times, and now I wondered how many Mrs. Sullivans had I passed by – people suffering quiet moments of powerful sadness; or having exhilarating moments following the birth of a child; or feeling anxiety over the expense of all this care; or experiencing confusion because they did not feel capable of navigating through a complex organization. How many people have I passed by, never knowing how their time in that place may have changed their lives? How many people felt as though we did not do enough for them, or that we botched something, or that we did not care enough? How many people felt that a pressing need for an answer to a question went unmet?

I looked down at the folders in my lap. They were filled with charts and graphs about admission patterns and target markets, revenue streams and aggregate labor costs. Juxtaposed against the difficult days ahead for the Sullivan family, this stuff can feel awfully sterile. But in the grand scheme of things, maybe not. Health care is a gigantic business, a behemoth industry. Yet, at the same time, it is a million very human encounters, people helping people, touching their lives in the most extraordinary way. One perspective is neither more important nor more correct than the other. The challenge is to bring both perspectives together, to help all the people who devote themselves to the organization to view these perspectives as compatible, necessary, and as pieces of the larger picture. Leadership must set the tone for that. When it successfully integrates seemingly competing or conflicting perspectives, it has done its job. Steering an organization toward a common purpose – one that motivates and unites all sectors of an organization – may be the most fundamental test of an organization's leadership. It is not likely to succeed if it allows any part of the organization to glance away from those it serves. If that happens, the different parts of the organization can develop an outsized sense of their own value. They become less humble. They can come to believe they are more important than those they serve.

Organizations that have worked diligently to stay focused on the consumer embrace change positively and constructively. They are far more likely to see changes in the world around them as wonderful opportunities – not necessarily to start fresh, but to employ their history, traditions and values as the basis of renewal. This can be exciting, rejuvenating, reinvigorating.

Just as higher education in general, and graduate education in particular, can learn from health care, health care can learn from higher education. For one thing, health care would benefit from an examination of the concept of "shared governance" as a means of considering how the decision-making environment can become more democratized. But most important, the two fields will always be joined by the commitment to serve others. Higher education bears an enormous burden for helping people grow, to challenge themselves and to take responsibility for approaching the world more knowledgeably, more skillfully, and with a greater sense of commitment to contribute to the common good. Health care would be wise to study how higher education approaches this mission, and particularly how students' personal responsibility is nurtured. As both fields strive to find ways to do this better, the citizen in every one of us – student *and* teacher, patient *and* caregiver – will have that much more opportunity to flourish.

## NOTES

[1] It must be noted that, of course, learning is best viewed as a two-way street. As such, health care would benefit just as much from an examination of how higher education approaches its charge of serving the public good. Moreover, health care and higher education share vital characteristics. Both are essential

to the well-being and the advancement of society and both touch the lives of every person in the country in one fashion or another. Health care and higher education are giant fields, cutting across the private and public domains of our economy. When they work as they should, they make our lives better, more productive, healthy, enriched, and fulfilling.

2. http://www.cdc.gov/nchs/data/hus/2011/116.pdf
3. http://www.ache.org/carsvcs/ycareer.cfm
4. http://mltsfilm.org/
5. http://www.esc.edu/degrees-programs/graduate-certificates/
6. See Fain (2012) for a useful discussion about potential problems associated with awarding credit for prior learning.
7. http://www.esc.edu/graduate-studies/graduate-student-center/residency-information/general-residency-information/
8. Surely, there are other barriers that conspire with technology to make the goal of consumer-centeredness that much more difficult to achieve. For example, consider that the solo practitioner is virtually gone, replaced by multi-specialty groups which themselves may be part of larger health care conglomerates (Harris, 2011); thus, the likelihood is diminishing that patients will see the same physician during routine visits to a medical practice. Analogously, perhaps, is the trend in higher education of deploying non-tenured and part-time faculty (up from 34.3 percent in 1975 to 56.2 percent in 2009) and decreasing use of full-time tenured or tenure-track professors (down from 45.1 percent in 1975 to 24.4 percent in 2009) (American Association of University Professors, 2011).
9. Massive online open courses. See http://www.theatlantic.com/education/archive/2015/06/the-secret-power-of-moocs/396608/.
10. http://www.businesswire.com/news/home/20130121005788/en/Health-Care-MA-Spending-Falls-40-2012. It should be noted that these figures cover the entire health sector of which hospitals are a part.
11. The largest is the Veterans Administration system which operates 158 hospitals, followed by Universal Health Services (157 hospitals) and HCA, Inc. (140 hospitals) See http://www.billianshealthdata.com/news/vitals/InFocus/10_Largest_Health_Systems_by_Hospital_Ownership.
12. https://trends.collegeboard.org/college-pricing/figures-tables/tuition-and-fees-and-room-and-board-over-time-1975-76-2015-16-selected-years
13. http://www.cnbc.com/id/41511601
14. While system expansion and integration hold the potential for providing a broader range of options for consumers, as well as increased access, it is important to remain mindful of the risks. As systems enlarge, the possibility of monopolistic conduct grows concomitantly. Already there is concern that the incentives for system growth among hospitals are becoming too strong, creating the potential for systems to control – and raise – prices (Creswell & Abelson, 2013; Rosenthal, 2013). To the extent this occurs, access could become limited. Similarly, absent competition, steadfast attention to quality could diminish. A key objective for expansion is to ensure that the incentive structure is organized with consumer needs in mind, that is, sufficient to encourage provider collaboration and competition but not collusion.

## REFERENCES

Allen, I. E., & Seaman, J. (2013, January). *Changing course: Ten years of tracking online education in the United States.* Retrieved from http://www.onlinelearningsurvey.com/reports/changingcourse.pdf

American Association of University Professors. (2011). *It's not over yet: The annual report on the economic status of the profession, 2010–11.* Retrieved from http://www.aaup.org/reports-publications/2010-11salarysurvey

Belasen, A., Eisenberg, B., & Huppertz, J. (2015). *Mastering leadership: A vital resource for health care organizations.* Sudbury, MA: Jones and Bartlett.

Bonnabeau, R. (1996). *The promise continues: Empire State College – The first twenty-five years.* Virginia, Beach, VA: The Donning Company Publishers.

Boyer, E. (1990). *Scholarship reconsidered: Priorities of the professoriate.* San Francisco, CA: Jossey-Bass.

Brooks, D. (2015, October 16). Schools for wisdom. *The New York Times*. Retrieved from http://www.nytimes.com/2015/10/16/opinion/schools-for-wisdom.html?_r=0

Chen, P. (2010, April 22). *An unforeseen complication of electronic medical records*. Retrieved from http://www.nytimes.com/2010/04/22/health/22chen.html?pagewanted=all

Creswell, J., & Abelson, R. (2013, August 12). *New laws and rising costs create a surge of supersizing hospitals*. Retrieved from http://www.nytimes.com/2013/08/13/business/bigger-hospitals-may-lead-to-bigger-bills-for-patients.html

Doyle, R. J., Wang, N., Anthony, D., Borkan, J., Shield, R. R., & Goldman, R. E. (2012, October). Computers in the examination room and the electronic health record: Physicians' perceived impact on clinical encounters before and after full installation and implementation. *Family Practice, 29*(5), 601–608.

DuPre, A. (2010). *Communicating about health: Current issues and perspectives* (3rd ed.). New York, NY: Oxford University Press.

Eisenberg, B. (1997, Spring). Customer service in healthcare: A new era. *Hospital & Health Services Administration, 42*(1), 17–31.

Eisenberg, B., Belasen, A., & Huppertz, J. (2013). *The "ambidextrous leader": An integrated model of healthcare management for the future*. Paper presented at the annual conference of the Association of University Programs in Healthcare Management, Monterey, CA.

Fain, P. (2012, May 7). College credit without college. *Inside Higher Ed*. Retrieved from https://www.insidehighered.com/news/2012/05/07/prior-learning-assessment-catches-quietly

Fonville, A., Choe, E. K., Oldham, S., & Kientz, J. A. (2010, November). Exploring the use of technology in healthcare spaces and its impact on empathic communication. In T. Veinot (Ed.), *Proceedings of the 1st ACM International Health Informatics Symposium* (pp. 497–501). New York, NY: ACM.

Friedman, T. L. (2014, April 19). How to get a job at Google, part 2. *The New York Times*. Retrieved from http://www.nytimes.com/2014/04/20/opinion/sunday/friedman-how-to-get-a-job-at-google-part-2.html

Harris, G. (2011, April 23). Family physician can't give away solo practice. *The New York Times*. Retrieved from http://www.nytimes.com/2011/04/23/health/23doctor.html

Landro, L. (2013, April 8). The talking cure for health care: Improving the ways doctors communicate with their patients can lead to better care – and lower costs. *The Wall Street Journal*. Retrieved from http://online.wsj.com/news/articles/SB10001424127887323628804578346223960774296

Lighter, D. E. (2011). *Advanced performance improvement in health care: Principles and methods*. Sudbury, MA: Jones and Bartlett.

Martin, L. R., Williams, S. L., Haskard, K. B., & DiMatteo, M. R. (2005, September). The challenge of patient adherence. *Therapeutics and Clinical Risk Management, 1*(3), 189–199.

Rosenthal, E. (2013, December 2). As hospital prices soar, a stitch tops $500. *The New York Times*. Retrieved from http://www.nytimes.com/2013/12/03/health/as-hospital-costs-soar-single-stitch-tops-500.html?pagewanted=all

Smith, C. W. (2013, October 23). Is the EMR enhancing or hindering patient-provider interactions? *Journal of Participatory Medicine*. Retrieved from http://www.jopm.org/opinion/editorials/2013/10/23/is-the-emr-enhancing-or-hindering-patient-provider-interactions/

Stack, S. (2013). *Report of the board of trustees of the American Medical Association: Exam room computing & patient-physician interactions*. Chicago, IL: American Medical Association.

Sultz, H. A., & Young, K. M. (2011). *Health care USA: Understanding its organization and delivery* (7th ed.). Sudbury, MA: Jones & Bartlett Learning.

Topol, E. (2012). *The creative destruction of medicine: How the digital revolution will create better health care*. New York, NY: Basic Books.

USDOL (United States Department of Labor). (2008). *Occupational outlook handbook, 2009*. New York, NY: Skyhorse Publishing.

Wendler, C., Bridgeman, B., Cline, F., Millett, C., Rock, J., Bell, N., & McAllister, P. (2010). *The path forward: The future of graduate education in the United States: Executive summary*. Retrieved from http://www.fgereport.org/rsc/pdf/ExecSum_PathForward.pdf

SECTION V

# EMPIRE STATE COLLEGE IN A BROADER CONTEXT

*The Impacts of External Forces*

In Section V, authors look at three important aspects of ESC's wider environment that affect directly the College's financial situation, administrative functioning, academic programs, and modes of study. Taking up questions related to the larger, more traditional bureaucracy within which the College sits, to continuously expanding and changing uses of technology in education, and to increasing emphasis on accountability and its impacts on assessment, these essays bear relevance not just to nontraditional institutions but to traditional institutions as well, as they strive to meet the challenges of a rapidly changing context for higher education.

In Chapter 17, "Empire State College: Exceptionalism and Organizational Change in the SUNY System," E. Warzala takes a step back and helps us to see the possibilities and complexities of an experimenting college seeking to find its place within a large public university system that often understands neither ESC's progressive heritage nor its academic models. In her essay, "Current Technologies and Their Uses at Empire State College: Benefits, Costs, and Possibilities," B. Hurley examines some of the creative tensions arising in ESC's evolving uses of technology in teaching, mentoring, and learning. Using three lenses – related to modes of interaction, modes of pedagogy and inquiry, and organizational communication – to look at the history of the College's uses of technology, she argues that the potential is great for technologies, if used thoughtfully and intentionally, to continue to support individualized study and enhanced connection across the College. Finally, in this section, J. Elliott, in Chapter 19, "Implications of Emergent Content, Experimentation, and Resources for Outcomes Assessment at Empire State College," first notes that the validity of prescribed and emergent content has always been contested terrain at ESC. Concluding that to carry out meaningful assessment practices, ESC, like all institutions of higher education, needs adequate resources, she also argues, emphatically, that defining consistent learning outcomes across unique learning experiences, and conducting systematic research on an experimenting institution are not only possible but consistent with the mission, values, and identity of the College.

EDWARD WARZALA

# 17. EMPIRE STATE COLLEGE

*Exceptionalism and Organizational Change in the SUNY System*

The State University of New York has so many assets, but there is not one greater than our 'systemness.' Beyond the individual strengths that each of our 64 campuses possess, there is a powerful and unmatched capacity to reach our most ambitious goals together and to realize our highest achievements. In 2012 and beyond, SUNY will tap into that power of 'systemness' to create a more affordable, productive, and accessible university, while doing its part to generate economic development, create jobs, and prepare the workforce of tomorrow for New York State.[1]

Nancy L. Zimpher

SETTING THE STAGE: ESC WITHIN THE SUNY SYSTEM AND WITHIN A CHANGING HIGHER EDUCATION CONTEXT

Public university systems like SUNY are dynamic, interactive complexes consisting of numerous constituent campuses and system-level organizations. The approach adopted in this chapter assumes that the parts, 64 SUNY campuses, are tethered to the system headquarters through legislation, which defines the system's budgetary and personnel authority. The parts of any system are understood relationally and that interrelatedness is centrally important to a systems approach. College presidents in the system are accountable to system demands, and universitywide programmatic influences originate at the systems level. Annual budget allocations and supervisory reporting channels are controlling linkages between campuses and SUNY System Administration. SUNY System Administration (SUNY Plaza) is located in Albany, the capital city of New York, within eyesight of the State Capitol Building.

The SUNY Chancellor is beholden to the state legislature and the governor for annual budget allocations. The system has the authority to reward and punish primarily through its control of campus budgets, budgets that may be "adjusted" during any particular budgetary year. Campus presidents serve at the pleasure of the chancellor and SUNY Board of Trustees. From this perspective, the behavior of a campus president is fully understandable only in relationship with the system from which campuses obtain the resources necessary for their survival and fulfillment of their campus mission.

*K. Jelly & A. Mandell (Eds.), Principles, Practices, and Creative Tensions in Progressive Higher Education, 339–356.*
*© 2017 Sense Publishers. All rights reserved.*

This analysis views Empire State College (ESC) as one particular instance of the SUNY University Colleges Sector within the SUNY system and assumes that the defining developments in the history of any single SUNY campus stem from its relationship with and linkages to the SUNY system. Further, in the current higher education climate, System authority and control is increasing due to emerging trends and forces in economics and politics. This understanding is often difficult for campus communities to see due to the internal, campus-centered developments and initiatives and the everyday functions and circumstances of the individual campuses. As these external pressures mount, I believe that it is important for campuses in their own planning to recognize the shifts in the broader environment within which they operate and hope to prosper. An abiding issue is that campus presidents and provosts are far more sensitive to system demands than are the faculties of the system campuses.

Public higher education is currently at a critical, if not revolutionary, juncture, and the SUNY system, like all public university systems, is adapting to changes coming at it through strategic planning initiatives led by system leaders and driven by external pressures. Colleges in the system are being challenged to adapt to lower levels of state funding, and calls for efficiency are changing the ways public higher education delivers and assesses essential services. Increasing demands from government for accountability and competition from for-profit institutions have created a challenging and uncertain operational environment. The uncertainty today for American public higher education stems ultimately from the country's relative economic decline vis-à-vis global economic competitors. It stems equally from educational competition from newly industrializing countries, whose educational systems are producing at higher rates than are American universities graduates with skill sets demanded by the global economy of the 21st century. "The overall picture is clear: employment opportunities and incomes are high, and rising, for the highly educated people at the upper end of the tradable sector of the U.S. economy, but they are diminishing at the lower end" (Spence, 2011, p. 32). American public higher education is not producing enough qualified graduates for certain growth sectors of the economy and not enough college graduates to meet national strategic objectives. Governmental demands for efficiency and a greater contribution from public higher education in preparing the workforce of the 21st century challenge the Post WWII liberal arts orientation of public systems. State legislatures are increasingly demanding tangible results in terms of immediate employment for college graduates in exchange for declining, but still essential levels of public funding. It is unclear whether American public higher education, steeped in the liberal arts tradition, can deliver the educational attainment necessary for American workers in the coming decades.

Increasing demands by government for efficiency and accountability are understandable when one recognizes the economic impact of SUNY within New York state. The minimum annual economic impact of SUNY in New York is $19.8 billion, supporting 173,000 jobs and generating $460 million in state and local taxes (Rockefeller Institute of Government UA & UB Regional Institute, 2011). "The 64 campus SUNY system, including 463,000 students, 83,800 faculty and staff, and a budget over $11 billion, is a powerful source of economic activity in New York State" (p. 4). These numbers explain in part the demands for efficiency and the corporate orientation of university initiatives and of the leaders who formulate them. They also help to explain the appointment as campus presidents of CEOs or others with business management acumen.

The response by public universities to political and economic pressures has been to pursue efficiencies through both academic and operational management principles led by managers and business-minded college presidents with the guidance of management consulting firms whose primary focus is economic efficiency. At considerable expense to the SUNY system, the services of McKinsey & Company, a leading global management consulting firm, were employed in two major SUNY initiatives in 2012–2013: The Open SUNY proposal (which was intended to grow enrollments and revenues through the expansion of online and open learning), and the Shared Services strategic sourcing initiative (which was supposed to economize procurement across the 64 campus system). Each initiative was an attempt to achieve efficiency through organizing and managing the scale of systemwide online academic opportunities and procurement activities (SUNY, n.d.-b).

In such a context, the SUNY system's decades of organizational weakness, which evolved into a system in which individual campuses have grown more autonomous, played into the hands of those seeking efficiencies through centralization and new management models. The new tone set by SUNY Chancellor Zimpher can be discovered in the conference themes of the annual SUNYCON Critical Issues in Higher Education Conference, which Zimpher established in 2011. The theme of the first SUNY Critical Issues Conference, "Universities as Economic Drivers: Measuring Success," and the theme of the 2015 summit, "Building a New Business Model for the Academy: Partnerships, Affiliations, Mergers & Acquisitions," help to illustrate the ideology and organizational culture of SUNY System Administration under Chancellor Nancy Zimpher, who in 2009 became the 12th chancellor of the SUNY system. And trustees and governing boards, typically composed of successful business leaders, and against the backdrop of political and economic pressures, appoint system and campus leaders, who like themselves, see the university as a business. "Governing boards favor administrative candidates who want to change the college or university into something it isn't. That desire can often be a wonderful thing, particularly when an institution's survival is threatened. Too often, however, it means that new presidents want to change their institution in ways that diminish what made them great in the first place" (Buller, 2013, para. 3).

Yet, SUNY campuses have resisted the growing authority of the central system as it has impinged on their hard-earned autonomy and independent decision-making, and their faculties have resisted what they perceive to be the corporatization of the university. That is, from the perspective of these faculties, as well as of faculty unions and professional organizations, the trends are disturbing and are perceived as threatening academic quality and faculty control of the academic program. The faculty tend to reject the "University of the Customer Model" (Sams, 2010) that identifies colleges and universities as "businesses" and students as "customers." Faculty are often unaware of the fiscal and budgetary pressures on local administrators and perceive administrative initiatives to secure the finances of a college as insensitive to faculty roles and the faculty obligation to oversee the academic program. Conversely, administrators often see the faculty and its commitment to the academic mission and shared governance as intransigence and obstructionism. It is ironic that trustees, chancellors, systems, campuses, presidents, and the faculty, all united in the quest to deliver high quality education for society's learners, so often perceive their respective interests as contradictory and threatening.

More than ever before, the college-system relationship will shape the future direction of Empire State College in fundamental ways. SUNY Chancellor Zimpher's Open SUNY initiative of "The Power of SUNY" strategic plan places high expectations on Empire State College and its president. The ESC president will need to translate and articulate for the ESC community, SUNY's strategic vision, a challenge for ESC's leadership because SUNY's vision for the college and the historical mission of the college are misaligned (about which more below). From this perspective, leadership at SUNY makes a difference, leadership at the college makes a difference, and most importantly, campus-system relations are likely to be the defining difference for Empire State College in the second decade of the 21st century.

For example, decisions made by Empire State College will determine whether the college assumes a commanding leadership role in Open SUNY, or whether Open SUNY progresses separately and in competition with Empire State College. So far, the SUNY system has pursued the latter approach and has treated Empire State College as just one of the many SUNY campuses that can deliver online learning for the larger system. ESC leadership has acquiesced in this "one among many" role in Open SUNY. The leadership of the system-controlled SUNY Learning Network (SLN), a fee-for-service provider of online technology support and faculty development for online users on the individual SUNY campuses, has used Open SUNY to expand and enhance its role and budget within System Administration. To date, the Open SUNY initiative has developed as a fee-for-service provider model for campuses in the system and SLN has elected to distribute its services systemwide, rather than to support and invest in one or more of the more highly developed online campuses. The approach pursued by SUNY has served the immediate interests of SLN; it remains to be seen how well it will serve the system's students and how competitive SUNY will become in the online sector of higher education where it lags behind competitors. A major conceptual and practical problem for SUNY is that the SUNY system is not itself authorized to award college degrees. Only the respective campuses have statutory authority to do so. For this reason, I and others, including then ESC President Alan Davis, argued that Open SUNY needed a home campus and that one SUNY campus should be funded to operate and manage SUNY's online capacity (SUNY Empire State College, 2012). The logical choice to objective observers would be to have Empire State College, with its robust online capacity, serve in this coordinating role.

## EMPIRE EXCEPTIONALISM: IT'S NOT ALWAYS GOOD TO BE SPECIAL!

One of the principal challenges for ESC's leadership will be the Empire State College mythology of "exceptionalism," which in many ways and over many decades has disguised the college's linkages to the SUNY system and outside higher education world. Exceptionalism informs the college's great tradition and it is instilled in new faculty and administrators through focused orientation trainings and socialization processes that take place at the coordinating center in Saratoga Springs and at every college location across the state of New York, 35 in all. The college expends considerable effort and resources in faculty development directly related to its mentoring model and the delivery of individualized education for its students. The same identity and culture of education inform the college's online division. Serving adult learners and accommodating the special needs of adults is central to the ESC identity. This identity and the ideology that accompanies it is certainly unique among SUNY campuses and is rare within American higher education in general. The ESC Center for Mentoring and Learning and its predecessor, the Mentoring Institute, have helped to inculcate the values of mentoring, individualization and self-directed learning into the educational culture of decades of academic employees. And this institutional self-consciousness at Empire State College is often striking to individuals who join the college from other, more traditional institutions of higher learning. Taken together, these values constitute what is termed here as Empire State College "exceptionalism."

The conventional interpretation of the College's founding, copiously documented by Richard Bonnabeau (1996), traces the idea for Empire State College directly to then SUNY Chancellor Ernest Boyer and the radical experimentation of the 1960's, but in doing so, the ESC-SUNY relationship is "personified" rather than framed in terms of the system. And the inward-looking culture at ESC goes back to the founding of the college and the 27-year presidency of James Hall. Not enough can be said about the impact of President Hall's extended 27-year leadership of ESC, especially in light of the Association of Governing Board's finding of an 8.5-year average term for presidents (Cook & Kim, 2012). Under Hall, the ideology of the founding became deeply embedded in the organizational culture and values of the institution. This culture of exceptionalism has since been reified and reproduced for generations of faculty and professional staff. But Boyer and Hall, who brought the college into being, were essential to creating the institution's mythology and organizational culture.

Yet this culture of exceptionalism, celebrated internally and taken for granted by the college community – more so at Empire than at most colleges – is often misunderstood or misperceived on other SUNY campuses and at system administration. No chancellor after Boyer could have understood or respected Empire State College to the same degree as the extraordinary founding chancellor. In sum, what is celebrated and esteemed in the college is often confusing to and disdained by those with more traditional views about higher education, including those in other parts of the SUNY system. So, while after Boyer, the system tolerated Empire State College's exceptionalism, it never embraced the alternative pathways to higher education that defined the college's internal mission.

When Chancellor Boyer left SUNY in 1977, Empire State College was well along in its development. By this time, the college was funded primarily by tuition and budget allocations from the state through annual budgeting processes at SUNY. ESC had merged into the massive SUNY bureaucracy and was left to its own devices to develop its internal practices and ethos.

From the perspective of SUNY System Administration, the college had many characteristics of other sector campuses, and for budgetary purposes, it existed alongside the traditional residential SUNY colleges located around the state of New York. ESC was always treated differently, however, in budget negotiations, due to its distributed nature, which meant for the system, the absence of a physical campus in the traditional sense. With no library, gymnasium, dining hall or athletic fields, the system economized in setting the Empire State budget allocations.

One device used by the system to account for ESC's nontraditional campus was what was called the "negative mission adjustment," which remained in effect until 2013. No other college in the system received a "negative adjustment" to its budget; in fact, many campuses received "positive" mission adjustments to fund special programs. By the late 1970's, from the SUNY perspective, Empire State appeared as another annual budget line item within the University College sector balance sheet, except for the penalty, the "negative adjustment," imposed each year for *not* having a physical campus. Otherwise, Empire State College's exceptionalism, by this time, was strictly an internal matter, except when it came to budget matters, when the college was indeed treated exceptionally.

In the absence of a personal commitment by a SUNY chancellor, it was inevitable that Empire State College would recede to some extent into the massive SUNY bureaucracy. It thus was both natural and safe for the college to turn inward to attend to its own development, with all of the philosophical and pedagogical debates of the early years playing out among internal stakeholders while President Hall both guided astutely the college-system relationship for decades and focused on the internal development of a geographically distributed and progressive learning environment. In some ways, Hall guided the college below the radar of System Administration, while strengthening and solidifying the internal workings of an unusual model of higher education. ESC's relative isolation helps explain how its exceptionalism became so deeply entrenched. It also helps explain why change has been so gradual and minimal over four decades.

## EMPIRE STATE COLLEGE'S PLACE IN THE SYSTEM

President Joseph Moore, the college's second president, came to Empire State College with a significant background in university system administration that was instrumental in shaping his perceptions of SUNY and university systems in general. Moore never had to deal with an energetic, activist chancellor like Zimpher, who is a national leader in higher education and whose change agenda for the system is unprecedented in the history of the system. Moore served as Director of Planning and Academic Affairs in the Office of the Chancellor of the Vermont State College system. His experiences in a system office defined his thinking about system-campus relations and provided him with relevant experience in dealing with SUNY. According to Moore in speaking about his Vermont experience: "In New York the legislature is larger and the dollars have more zeros in them, but the dynamics remain the same" (Warzala, 2013, p. 51). Aside from having a background in administration, as president, Moore enjoyed relatively robust budgets that came from enrollment growth during his tenure with the college. Much of this growth resulted from the expansion of the online program, which grew significantly during Moore's term as president. The online program at Empire State currently produces approximately 45 percent all undergraduate credits delivered by the college (SUNY Empire State College, 2012–2013). SUNY budgets during the Moore years were stable and tuition revenues were growing. The college enjoyed significant financial reserves when Moore left the college. On systems in general, according to Moore:

> ... I think people consistently overrate systems. ... Systems are constantly seeking affirmation of their presence and seeking meaning, whereas, at the institutions, the meaning is right in front of you, if you can see it. That is where students and faculty meet and engage in intellectual work. So, systems have to figure out what their role is, whether that is SUNY Central or the Coordinating Center in Saratoga Springs. I would say SUNY was trying to figure out what its role was; certain roles were pretty clear, and certain roles were not clear at all. I would bet that is still the case and that systems are always trying to find their identity. (Warzala, 2013, p. 51)

The circumstances of Moore's presidency and at SUNY System allowed ESC greater autonomy and independence of action. Leadership at SUNY during the Moore administration was characterized by benign neglect when compared to the aggressive movement for change under Zimpher. Moore did not believe that he could significantly advance the interests of the college by petitioning SUNY for a larger share of the university's resources. It was determined that there were few opportunities for gaining increases in the operating budget from the system. This fostered the Moore administration's legislative agenda. During Moore's presidency, the college remained one of SUNY's best kept secrets. He apparently saw few opportunities in his interaction with the system and so elected to focus directly on the legislature and some key contacts in the governor's office. As a budget line item, and from the perspective of the budget back-offices at SUNY, the legacy of being a college "without walls" had been an impediment to obtaining a fair share of the university budget. This reality forced President Moore to seek capital resources for the college by direct appeal to high-ranking elected officials, while essentially bypassing the SUNY capital budget process. While giving SUNY its due, Moore went outside of the SUNY system in his pursuit of capital funding and successfully broke the closed circle of facilities funding for the college. Given the changes in state politics and at SUNY, it is doubtful that this type of approach could succeed today (Warzala, 2013, 2013–2014).

The SUNY system is divided into sectors, which include research universities, liberal arts colleges, colleges of technology, and academic medical centers. Empire State College is one of 13 campuses designated as a "university college," even though it has little in common with the other campuses found within its sector, which consists of traditional residential campuses distributed across New York state, from Old Westbury on Long Island to Fredonia in Western New York. No degree beyond the Master's level is offered by the sector. Except for ESC, with its 35 locations, the university colleges have the look and feel of a traditional college campus and serve the typical 18–24 –year old student. The four SUNY university centers, Ph.D. granting institutions, and colleges of technology are traditional residential campuses. Though people at ESC rarely, if ever, think of the college as a "campus," the same is not the case across the system or at System Administration, where the focus and working assumptions about ESC are of it as an overwhelmingly traditional campus.

As noted earlier, faculty and staff across the system campuses and at System Administration are generally unfamiliar with the policies and practices of Empire State College. The organizational structure of the college and the unique practices of mentoring and adult pedagogy are typically mysterious and of little concern to the traditional campuses, making ESC until recently a little known outlier within the massive SUNY system. Another segment of the external audience, i.e., external to SUNY, has come to understand Empire State as the "online" SUNY College. With the growth in online learning at ESC since the mid-1990s, and the growing enrollments in ESC's Center for Distance Learning, many SUNY people now incorrectly identify Empire as a strictly online college. And the online program has attracted the attention of System Administration because it assumes that it is scalable.

The absence of clarity about what the college does and how it does it has led some across SUNY to imagine that the college will play a prominent role in the revolutionary and rapid changes taking place in higher education and within the SUNY system. The confluence of the college's alternative and online capabilities and the revolution in higher education have placed Empire State College in the center of the Open SUNY conversation. But so far, there has been more conversation and little action in terms of funding ESC's online division. In some measure, this is so because the college's mission and culture of individualization are not scalable.

The new assertiveness of SUNY System Administration under Chancellor Zimpher and the chancellor's emphasis on "systemness" and shared services suggest a more centralized SUNY system, and with that, much less autonomy for the campuses, including Empire State College. The potential impact of changes both in higher education, including for example, standardization, on-line education, emphasis on efficiency, and a decline of funding for public institutions, and in SUNY cannot be overstated. Navigating the near future will challenge campus administrations as it will challenge the System Administration. Creative and visionary leadership will be essential at every level, but the building economic and political pressures previously noted will undoubtedly bring increased expectations and scrutiny of ESC executive leadership. The restructuring currently underway at ESC, labeled ESC 2.0, which would create a more centralized academic and administrative structure, seems to reflect the preferences of the SUNY system.

Generally speaking, in the conventional lexicon at the SUNY System Administration, the unique structure, culture, and mission of Empire State are relevant only in their quirkiness and in the misperception of ESC as an online college. There is lack of understanding and/or disrespect and disdain for the individual degree design requirement of the four-credit Educational Planning course for each student. Individualization, a core pillar of the ESC mission, is perceived as highly inefficient, if not bizarre, cruel, and unusual; it is certainly seen as unscalable. Executive level officials in SUNY do not even understand or appreciate the value of the college's 35 locations across the state. Rents and leases are seen by system administrators as wasteful and redundant. There are those who misperceive hallmarks of ESC, such as mentoring, one-to-one guided independent study, and courses offered only once (and without course numbers or predetermined curricula and learning objectives), as academically unsound and as luxuries that can no longer be afforded in the era of accountability. Since few administrators at the system level were at SUNY in the 1970's when Empire State was founded, remarkably little is known about the college among high level decision-makers in SUNY. Educated overwhelmingly at elite, traditional colleges, system administrators do not easily identify with the special mission of Empire State College.

Quietly, and sometimes out of ignorance, some are suspicious of the college's unconventional practices and overall academic quality. Being ignorant of Prior Learning Assessment (PLA), tailored degree programs, adult pedagogy, and even online learning, some from traditional campuses express reservations about the academic offerings of the college. Once again we see the college's sense of exceptionalism and all that it entails is limited mostly to itself. And ESC's strong mythology of exceptionalism in the college is in conflict with the political and economic forces currently at work in the system and in higher education generally.

At the same time, changes in higher education and Open SUNY are drawing attention to the college in unprecedented ways. The college's online capabilities and its experience with PLA, however, have attracted the attention of the SUNY leadership. The national expansion in online learning, experimentation with course delivery methods like MOOCs, competition from for-profit colleges and political and economic pressures on public higher education position ESC potentially to play a lead role in future SUNY strategic planning, but exactly how ESC's unique role in SUNY plays out will depend completely on what System wants from the college and what the ESC leadership and faculty will deliver. At this time, it is unclear what, if any, role ESC's regional centers and the traditional mentoring model and individualized degree study can play in the future.

The Open SUNY proposal potentially draws on ESC's online program as a remedy for a deficiency in online delivery capabilities of the larger system. The problem for ESC is that SUNY's main interest is in online learning and not the unique identity of the college and all of its various programs and learning opportunities. Until the Open SUNY initiative was enacted, SUNY had no systemwide online capability; it had only its separate campus-based online offerings, with ESC's being the most developed and robust. Unlike numerous other large state university systems including Massachusetts, Pennsylvania, California, Arizona, Georgia and Maryland, SUNY is relatively backward in the coordination of its online programming.

The colleges in the University College sector, with the exception of Empire State, are traditional, four-year, residential campuses. Despite the extensive network of centers and units and the rapidly expanding physical presence of the Coordinating Center in Saratoga Springs, the founding principle of a limited physical infrastructure, i.e., of no campus as such for ESC, actually presented a clear opportunity for a more prominent role in SUNY for the College. Indeed, the college's Open SUNY proposal, submitted by the administration of ESC President Alan Davis to SUNY, was devised to elevate the profile of Empire State College within the system and to secure its fiscal future by assuming a systemwide role as New York's Open University. Open SUNY was also in part designed to capture the attention of SUNY and its campuses and to make public the exceptional character and potential of Empire State College, against the backdrop of the revolution in higher education. Davis thought he could generate revenue with Open SUNY and use the proceeds to fund and subsidize more expensive and less efficient land-based centers and units.

Empire's alternative, progressive nature has not been seen as particularly advantageous to the system until recently and in parallel with the expansion of online and open learning and the proliferation of for-profit institutions. Stanford's spinoff, Coursera, and Harvard and MIT's, edX threatened and challenged public higher education to innovate and plan strategically for what may prove to be a paradigm shift in higher education. Now Empire State is SUNY's closest approximation to the changes in higher education. No SUNY campus is as well-equipped as Empire State to provide the missing systemic capability in online and open learning. But ESC's mission of individualization makes even the online program of ESC's Center for Distance Learning (CDL) unscalable and resistant to growth and systemwide expansion.

Yet, regardless of the exact role that ESC is asked to play in Open SUNY, and though it is unknown whether ESC, with a new role to play, will be able to sustain its alternative approaches to pedagogy, including in its online programs, we do know that ESC's future will be emphatically shaped by decisions made by the Chancellor and the SUNY system administration. As noted above, planning at SUNY typically begins with the initiative of a chancellor and members of the upper level staff and cabinet. And, like Boyer, Chancellor Zimpher moved quickly early in her administration to establish a dramatic change agenda via The Power of SUNY plan (SUNY, n.d.-c). In addition, in recent years, the governor has used the SUNY budget to influence the system to serve the state's economic development efforts. Now more than ever, any understanding of the future of Empire State College must consider its role within the larger university system and its dependence on SUNY for a share of the state budget. And, to strengthen further SUNY's control over the campuses, a new performance-based budget allocation model, SUNY Excels (SUNY, n.d.-a), will be implemented in the 2016–2017 academic year. In sum, as SUNY goes, so goes Empire State College; the days of campus autonomy and a benign SUNY system have passed.

## SYSTEM LEADERSHIP AND BUDGETARY INSTABILITY

President Alan Davis and Chancellor Zimpher were greeted by New York state and SUNY with three consecutive years of debilitating budget cuts. Systemic budgetary pressures, amounting to cuts over 10 percent annually for three years, forced the Davis administration to choose between abandoning its strategic vision for the college or expending cash reserves that had been accumulated over the course of decades. The Davis administration opted to maintain most of its strategic initiatives by spending those reserves and devised the Open SUNY proposal, which was, as mentioned above, intended to expand online and open learning in an effort to position the college for an uncertain financial future and at the same time secure a more prominent position for the college within the SUNY system.

Open SUNY was a prosperity maintenance strategy from its inception. The Davis proposition to SUNY coincided with the global revolution in higher education and the goal of "systemness" at SUNY. As noted earlier, Zimpher is an activist chancellor and the influence of her administration on the SUNY campuses is considerable compared to that of her predecessors. Past ESC President Davis and current President Merodie Hancock are Zimpher-era presidents and both have had to negotiate the college's relationship with a new, activist SUNY System Administration, during a tumultuous time for public higher education. As Hancock so directly put it: "Empire State College, like all SUNY campuses and public higher education institutions (HEIs) throughout the nation, has to respond to students' needs and to the demands of the state and its citizens. It is within this context that the college and SUNY will continue to assess what we do, how we do it, and the relevance we have to the current and future needs of our learners and the state" (M. Hancock, personal communication, January 8, 2016).

The disinvestment in higher education by New York State has contributed to uneven and irregular leadership of the SUNY system and this in turn has weakened the system and resulted in a large, but comparatively undistinguished university system. The NY 2020[2] legislation and "rational tuition policy" notwithstanding, unpredictable budgets have stifled innovation and planning since the 1970's. The state legislature's control of SUNY budgets, and more importantly, control over tuition rates, have frustrated SUNY chancellors and limited their ability to make strategic investments. It is likely that the individual campuses in the system will become increasingly dependent on tuition revenue and will be driven to respond to the demands of the higher education market for financial security and survival. Still, unlike the more traditional University Colleges, Empire State is uniquely positioned to meet the challenges of changing demographics and decreases in state support. It remains to be seen if the college can meet these challenges and if it can adapt to change and preserve its mission and core values.

Founding president James Hall, in his 27-year presidency, served under eight SUNY chancellors, some of whom were interim or acting. President Joseph Moore, in seven years, served under two chancellors, and Alan Davis in four years served under an Officer in Charge, an Interim Chancellor, and finally, Chancellor Zimpher, under whom President Merodie Hancock now serves. Leadership changes at the university level and at colleges are accompanied by lags in innovation and development. Transitions for academic CEOs take approximately two years when conditions are favorable. This does not take into account failed searches and extended interim leadership appointments, so leadership changes at SUNY have contributed to idiosyncratic planning and development at the system level. The best strategic plans are subject to devolution when executive leadership changes occur during the implementation of any plan. Should the leadership of SUNY change in the near future, and this is always a possibility, policy implementation could stall or take a different direction under a new leadership team. So ESC, like the other individual SUNY campuses, will continue to need to adjust as it rides the waves of broader SUNY change.

## SYSTEM INFLUENCES AND ON-LINE LEARNING

The relationship of Empire State College with SUNY accounts for critical formative initiatives that have driven the evolution and current organizational change of the college. As influential as individuals can be, one would be remiss to discount the systems perspective in any effort to understand the organizational development of an institution. After the founding itself, and the recent years of budget instability and personnel changes, the most dramatic development in the history of ESC came as the result of a SUNY System initiative in online learning. Open SUNY, originating initially at Empire State and adopted by the system is a parallel case in organizational change. The online learning program at Empire State was launched in the 1995–1996 academic year, and would not have occurred in 1995 without SUNY system leadership and funding. As ESC colleagues Lefor, Benke and Ting (2001) described it:

> If examined from the perspective of program development, Empire State College, as well as other institutions engaged in developing online academic programs, required an extensive investment to actually implement such

programs. The College's development was subsidized by grant funding, through the State University of New York. SUNY as a system has supported the expansion of online course development for interested members of the system. ESC's successes in this area would not have been possible had funding been restricted to the annual budget of the College. (p. 13)

Since 1994, SUNY led and funded the development of online learning and invested heavily in synchronous audio-video and televised lecture-based courses (Lefor, Benke, & Ting, 2001). The SUNY Learning Network (SLN) reached across the SUNY system. Funding from SUNY and grants supported these systemwide efforts because no individual campus could possibly have afforded the technological infrastructure and staffing needs of a statewide delivery system. As Lefor, Benke and Ting (2001) further noted: "By 1994, the potential of technology in instruction had exploded onto the higher education scene. After 15 years of experience in print-based distance learning, Empire State College began to work with others in the State University of New York to initiate online educational delivery" (p. 3).

The establishment of online learning at the college was stimulated by SUNY to meet perceived systemic needs; SUNY will similarly promote Open SUNY to meet the systemic needs of the current context. The system is woefully behind in online and open learning and Open SUNY is the system response to the revolution in higher education and competition for students. SUNY's agreement with Coursera, announced in the spring of 2013, the system-led goal of devising a three-year fast track to degree completion, systemwide PLA, and an emphasis on workforce development - all a part of a future Open SUNY – are likely to filter down through the system to individual campuses. As was the case when the SLN was created under system leadership in the 1990s, Open SUNY is now an initiative larger than any single campus.

If, as expressed by the chancellor and as found in The Power of SUNY strategic plan, Empire State College earns a leadership position in Open SUNY, it is likely that the college will experience yet another fundamental adjustment to its mission and core values. These proposed initiatives, like those in online learning in the 1990's, will challenge Empire State's founding pedagogical model of mentored one-to-one guided independent study. If Empire State does not play a leadership role in Open SUNY, the college will experience the effects of competition from SUNY itself, along with the rising competition for adult learners from for-profit institutions. The latter outcome could be devastating to the future prosperity of the college and to its unique role within the SUNY system. Collectively, these forces will certainly influence strongly the decisions of the ESC leadership for the foreseeable future.

President Hall's leadership, dating back to the Boyer-appointed ESC planning committee at SUNY in 1970, was a driving force in the promotion of all forms of learning technology at the college. Hall's appointment to a cabinet level position at System Administration in 1993 came at a critical juncture in the history of learning technologies and at a critical juncture in the history of the college. "In 1993,

Chancellor Johnstone recognized Hall's leadership in educational technology, both within Empire State College and within the SUNY system, by appointing him to a two-year term as Vice Chancellor for Educational Technology" (Bonnabeau, 1996, p. 120). Aside from Hall's career-spanning support for and promotion of using learning technologies in pedagogy by serving this joint appointment, Empire State College and SUNY were joined through the persona and administrative responsibilities of President and SUNY Vice Chancellor James W. Hall. Whether President Hancock or another Empire State College academic leader will find herself in a similar position remains to be seen. Without doubt, the college's authorship of the initial Open SUNY proposal did not guarantee a leadership role in the initiative. The 2014 launch of Open SUNY suggests an alternative model for the immediate future and one that may or may not include a leadership role within SUNY for Empire State College.

## FUTURE SYSTEM INFLUENCES ON EMPIRE STATE COLLEGE

SUNY Chancellor Zimpher's coinage of the term "systemness," and some specific policy shifts now in the implementation stage are designed to strengthen the linkages between the system and the campuses. The campuses can expect significant restructuring efforts by the system, and generally, more centralized control by the university over the campuses. This is evidenced in the "SUNY Shared Services" initiative (SUNY, n.d.-b) and in the introduction of a "performance-based resource allocation model" (SUNY, n.d.-a), which when fully implemented, will shift system resources away from inefficient campuses and toward more efficient ones, with efficiency defined in part as growth in enrollments, student retention, and degree completion. Unless Empire State College assumes a leadership role in Open SUNY, and thereby realizes gradual increases in its enrollments, the proposed resource allocation model will further reduce state support for the college. If Empire State and CDL are forced to compete with Open SUNY, if Open SUNY results at some future time in the creation of a 65th SUNY campus, dedicated to open and online learning, competition for online students will increase and will threaten the college's ability to sustain its tuition-based revenue streams.

SUNY recognizes Empire State as the system leader in online and open learning, PLA, and online academic support services and is likely to rely on the college to coordinate some aspects of the Open SUNY proposal. The precise role for Empire State College in Open SUNY and how SUNY intends to support that role, though not yet known, are likely to contribute to another critical turn in the evolution of the college. The relative autonomy of the college in the early 2000s may be replaced with interdependencies that will exert pressure on the college and its traditional policies and practices. It is this larger context that Chancellor Zimpher emphasized in her 2009 "The Power of SUNY Strategic Plan":

> Building on SUNY's current open and online initiatives, OPEN SUNY has the potential to be America's most extensive distance learning environment. It

will provide students with affordable, innovative, and flexible education in a full range of instructional formats, both online and on site. OPEN SUNY will network students with faculty and peers from across the state and throughout the world through social and emerging technologies and link them to the best in open educational resources. OPEN SUNY will provide an online portal for thousands of people worldwide. ... (SUNY, 2009, p. 19)

We would do well here to remember the history of ESC's role thus far in the development of Open SUNY and to pay attention to the potential hazards that ESC will inevitably encounter as it identifies and navigates its future role in SUNY.

The college's third president, Alan R. Davis (2009–2012), was heavily influenced by the SUNY strategic planning process initiated by system administration. Upon arrival, Chancellor Zimpher energized the system through this process, which resulted in "The Power of SUNY Strategic Plan." Zimpher visited Empire State College in her first months with the university and met with President Davis. In 2009, Davis introduced the concept of Open SUNY to Zimpher, who had challenged SUNY campus presidents to come up with "BHAGs" (Big, Hairy, Audacious Goals) and Open SUNY was Empire State College's BHAG. Through discussions with the SUNY Chancellor in her first year with SUNY, the Davis Administration directly influenced the Power of SUNY strategic plan, which includes specific references to Open SUNY (Zimpher, 2012). The proposal, and structural changes in higher education brought on by the proliferation of for-profit colleges, forced the university to think in terms of the system's capacity to deliver an online program. But Open SUNY, like the inception of online learning and the creation of SLN in the mid '90s, is larger than any single campus. The problem for Empire State may be the competition for online students that emerges if Open SUNY targets New York's adult learners, a segment of learners that has historically sustained the prosperity of Empire State College.

It is also important to remember that, in response to the chancellor, no other University College submitted to SUNY anything as "hairy" and "audacious" as ESC's Open SUNY proposal; it is evident that the proposal attracted the attention of the chancellor and SUNY provost. And, during Zimpher's administration, no University College has influenced the system or gained as much recognition through creative program design as Empire State College. In submitting the college's Open SUNY proposal, the Davis Administration was responding to system demands, structural changes in American higher education, and years of budget cuts from the state and from SUNY. Davis' administration believed, following its own strategic plan, that telling the college's story to SUNY would be essential in the effort to garner a larger share of system resources. In part, Davis set out to market the college to SUNY through the Open SUNY proposal. Recognizing the current highly competitive context in which SUNY finds itself and seeing ESC's unique position to support SUNY's initiative in online education, Davis was attempting precisely the navigation necessary, of those potential hazards mentioned above in the ongoing relationship between ESC and SUNY.

ESC'S FUTURE: SYSTEM INFLUENCES AND POSSIBLE DIRECTION

It remains to be seen what specific form Open SUNY will take by the end of the decade and specifically what role Empire State College will play in the grand scheme formulated by the System. At the outset, Chancellor Zimpher elected to chair The Chancellor's Online Advisory Group, which was designed to brainstorm on how Open SUNY might be implemented across the system and how the initiative might be funded. Representatives from Empire State were among others from the University on the advisory group. The chancellor's self-appointment to chair the group suggests that online learning in SUNY is among her highest priorities for the system. How Open SUNY is implemented and what role the college will play will depend on the administration of ESC's fourth president, Dr. Merodie Hancock, who possesses an extensive background in online learning and business process improvement. The recommendation of Hancock for the Empire State presidency by Chancellor Zimpher, along with the support of SUNY Board of Trustees Chair, Carl McCall, and Hancock's relevant experience in online learning (at both the University of Maryland University College and at the University of Central Michigan World Campus), suggest a significant, but yet to be defined role for the college in Open SUNY. Hancock will find herself firmly lodged between a college community somewhat reluctant to change and an external environment that demands it.

As was the case with the implementation of the online program, the SUNY Learning Network, in the 1990s, SUNY's influence via Open SUNY is likely to change significantly the structures, functions, and internal dynamics of Empire State College. President Hancock will need to engage the college community in discussions about the future of the college, its mission and its core values. She also will need to be responsive to the external environment and SUNY in particular. Due to the general disinvestment in higher education by New York state, the days of relative campus autonomy in SUNY have ended. In addition, budgets will continue to decline, making each SUNY campus responsible for its own survival and prosperity.

SUNY began implementation of Open SUNY in 2014 and Empire State College has committed itself to the initiative and has become a significant contributor. The chancellor in typical fashion has established a high bar for the key system initiative in her 2012 "State of the University Address":

> We will also work to ensure access by developing a truly open path to accessing SUNY. Hatched as part of our Big Idea around SUNY and the World, Open SUNY means great access to the best of SUNY, online, from anywhere, here and abroad. ... It will provide innovative and flexible education. It will network students with faculty and peers from across the state and throughout the world and link them to the best in open educational resources. ... We'll do this through a combination of online courses, an expanded YouTube channel, and a newly created presence on iTunes U. And we'll look to our campuses already

deeply invested in on-line learning; to an expansion of the SUNY Learning Network; and to the role Empire State College can play in certifying prior work and learning experience to create SUNY's on-line university. (Zimpher, 2012, Opening the Door section, paras. 1, 2, 5)

The System perspective on Open SUNY and the centrality of Empire State in the online sector are quite clear, though not yet fully articulated. Whether over time SUNY will allocate significant resources, and with resources, significant demands on the college, can only be speculated about at this time. If the college is asked by SUNY to coordinate online learning, degree completion across the system, prior learning assessment, open educational resources, and teaching and learning functions, the college will inevitably enter a new and unprecedented phase in its development. Meeting system demands will require additional resources from SUNY and the college may need to reallocate resources within the college itself to meet the expectations of SUNY and the demands of New York state. Whether the college's exceptionalist tradition and the mentoring model can coexist with Open SUNY is a fascinating organizational question that cannot be answered at this time. The manner in which policy is implemented over time will determine what Empire State College will look like and how it will act for decades to come.

Looking back at the founding of the college from a systems perspective, the SUNY planning group that created Empire State College consisted of senior SUNY administrative officials who were charged by an activist chancellor to design and establish a "new University College" (Bonnabeau, 1996). Four decades later, another activist chancellor has committed the system to establishing a new, open and online capability and has set a system target of 100,000 new online students. Empire State College will be asked to change once again, as it did with the inception of online learning in the mid-1990s. How much time, effort, and resources the system is willing to commit will determine whether the vision of Empire's Open SUNY proposal will ever come to fruition or whether it will wither away and be lost in the layers of special interest bureaucracies of the system.

Over the course of its 45 years, SUNY has permitted Empire State College to continue on its path, but has not always shared completely Boyer's vision and enthusiasm for open, flexible, alternative learning. The Power of SUNY strategic plan, introduced by Chancellor Nancy L. Zimpher in 2010, suggests that Empire State College will be called upon by the system to fulfill an increasingly important and specialized role in SUNY's future. From the start, each ESC administration has struggled on various levels to stay true to the original mission, to sustain the college's academic legitimacy in the eyes of SUNY, and to receive an equitable share of the state university's resources. It has done so while fiercely maintaining its exceptionalism and independence of philosophical perspective. The challenges now facing ESC are unprecedented in its history. Those committed to the great tradition of Empire State College will struggle to preserve what is indeed exceptional, what is so dear, to generations of students and educators.

## NOTES

[1] Statement by SUNY Chancellor Nancy L. Zimpher in a press release following the "2012 State of the University Address: Getting Down to Business," January 9, 2012. Accessible at https://www.suny.edu/suny-news/press-releases/january-2012/1-9-12-sou-release/suny-chancellor-nancy-zimpher-systemness-to-drive-success-in-2012.html

[2] NY2020 is a SUNY and Office of the Governor partnership "to establish the NYSUNY 2020 Challenge Grant Program; an initiative that has spurred economic growth across the state and strengthened the academic programs of New York's public universities and colleges" (SUNY, 2011). The challenge grant program is designed to provide incentives for capital and economic development on SUNY campuses.

## REFERENCES

Bonnabeau, R. F. (1996). *The promise continues: Empire State College – The first twenty-five years*. Virginia Beach, VA: The Donning Company Publishers.

Buller, J. L. (2013, May–June). Academic leadership 2.0. *American Association of University Professors*. Retrieved from http://www.aaup.org/article/academic-leadership-20

Cook, B., & Kim, Y. (2012). *The American college president 2012*. Washington, DC: American Council on Education.

Lefor, P. J, Benke, M., & Ting, E. (2001, January). Empire State College: The development of online learning. *The International Review of Research in Open and Distance Learning, 1*(2), 1–13. Retrieved from http://www.irrodl.org/index.php/irrodl/article/view/22

Rockefeller Institute of Government UA & UB Regional Institute (The Nelson A. Rockefeller Institute of Government of the University at Albany & The University at Buffalo Regional Institute). (2011, June). *How SUNY matters: Economic impacts of the State University of New York*. Retrieved from http://www.rockinst.org/pdf/education/2011-06-01-How_SUNY_Matters.pdf

Sams, B. (2010, October 22). The university of the customer. *The Chronicle Review*, p. B9.

Spence, M. (2011). The impact of globalization on income and unemployment: The downside of integrating markets. *Foreign Affairs, 90*(4), 28–41.

SUNY. (2009). *The Power of SUNY: Strategic plan 2010 & beyond*. Retrieved from https://issuu.com/generationsuny/docs/powerofsuny?mode=embed&layout=http%3A%2F%2Fskin.issuu.com%2Fv%2Flight%2Flayout.xml&showFlipBtn=true

SUNY. (2011). *NYSUNY 2020 challenge grants*. Retrieved from https://www.suny.edu/impact/business/nysuny-2020/

SUNY. (n.d.-a). *SUNY excels*. Retrieved from https://www.suny.edu/excels/

SUNY. (n.d.-b). *SUNY shared services*. Retrieved from http://www.suny.edu/sharedservices/

SUNY. (n.d.-c). *The power of SUNY*. Retrieved from https://www.suny.edu/powerofsuny/

SUNY Empire State College. (2012, April). *Open SUNY*. Saratoga Springs, NY: Author.

SUNY Empire State College. (2012–2013). *Fact book 2012–2013*. Saratoga Springs, NY: Author.

Warzala, E. (2013, Summer). Declaring adulthood: A conversation with Joseph B. Moore, part I. *All About Mentoring, 43*. Retrieved from http://www.esc.edu/media/ocgr/publications-presentations/all-about-mentoring/2013/Issue-43-AAM-Summer-2013.pdf

Warzala, E. (2013–2014, Winter). Declaring adulthood: A conversation with Joseph B. Moore, part II. *All About Mentoring, 44*. Retrieved from http://www.esc.edu/media/ocgr/publications-presentations/all-about-mentoring/2013/Issue-44-AAM-Winter-2013.pdf

Zimpher, N. L. (2012). *2012 State of the university address: "Getting down to business."* Retrieved from https://www.suny.edu/about/leadership/chancellor-nancy-zimpher/speeches/2012-sou/

BETTY HURLEY

# 18. CURRENT TECHNOLOGIES AND THEIR USES AT EMPIRE STATE COLLEGE

*Benefits, Costs, and Possibilities*

Science and technology revolutionize our lives, but memory, tradition and myth frame our response.

Arthur M. Schlesinger Jr.

Capturing in one essay not only the uses of various electronic technologies in mentoring, teaching and learning at Empire State College (ESC), but also what they have yielded – for students, faculty and staff – is a daunting task. The technologies used – and by whom and how – all vary tremendously across the College. First, ESC's geographical dispersal across the state of New York, with centers having differing student demographics, cultures, and pedagogical models emphasized at those centers, greatly influences an individual's use of technology. For example, faculty and staff at the Center for Distance Learning (CDL) use more electronic media in their mentoring and teaching than many faculty and staff at ESC's regional centers, where meeting in person with students has been both possible and more the norm. But, not unusually, practices differ across and within the regional centers as well. The technological terrain is complex.

In addition, discussion about technology can be emotion-laden, since technology systems employed at ESC have affected people's use of time, work with students, and work life satisfaction in interesting ways. Although technologies in and of themselves may be neutral, various uses of technology can help or hinder mentoring, teaching and learning. And people – including faculty, students, and staff – can have strong feelings about the technologies they are provided, such as particular learning management systems, tools for conferencing, or administrative software. So statements such as, "Technology is my friend," or "I hate my computer!" are not unusual. With these kinds of reactions not uncommon, I was tempted to title this chapter, "Technologies at ESC: Friend or Foe?" It is of course neither. At times, it can seem to be a "friend," as it helps us to achieve our academic and administrative goals, or it can feel more like a "foe," as it sometimes appears to present obstacles to us in reaching those goals. I will say more about this question in the conclusion of this essay.

Given the important effects of one's own context upon one's experience with technology at the college, I begin this essay with some background about my experience at ESC. I joined the college as a regional center mentor (in Rochester, NY) in 1982. My area of study is Science, Math and Technology, and I mentor students primarily in the math and technology areas, although I have mentored students pursuing degrees in other areas as well. In 1992, I took a reassignment with the College's Center for Learning and Technology (focusing on faculty development in the technology area) and then moved to what was then called The Center for College-wide Programs, where I was a mentor with the Forum East, a business-related program, and with CDL. I have been full-time with CDL since 1998, and so I have had the opportunity to experiment with a wide array of electronic media in my mentoring and teaching.

In this chapter, I will introduce some of the creative tensions that arise with the use of various technologies in our mentoring, teaching and learning and will consider these in relation to ESC's core values. And I will offer an historical perspective as needed throughout the chapter, since technologies available and our uses of them have changed considerably over time. But, my primary framework for examining our uses of technology will be three lenses: (1) "Modes of Interaction and Learning: Face-to-face, Online, and Blended; One-to-One and Group," (2) "Modes of Pedagogy and Inquiry: Student and Faculty Designed; Individualized and Pre-Structured," and (3) "Organizational and Administrative Communication."

The first lens, related to interaction, will focus on our academic conversations, primarily between mentor and student, but also between and among all learners. The second lens, not unrelated but focused more on pedagogical modes, will look at how development of the "learning contract," the blueprint for any given study at ESC, has evolved over time, and how technology has affected that evolution. Finally, the third lens will focus on wider communications of and within the College, such as communication related to registration, or to systems for tracking student degree programs, or to committees and other group communication. The chapter will conclude with some of my thoughts about what the future may hold. For each of these lenses, I will address the topic through my experience, as well as my sense of the experience of others. While necessarily this chapter will be far from comprehensive, my hope is that it will raise questions for further conversation.

It will be important to consider the uses of technology by the college in relation to the institution's core values. Therefore, these are summarized below and will be referred to throughout the chapter.

## THE CORE VALUES

The introduction to the core values of the college states:

> The core values of SUNY Empire State College reflect the commitments of a dynamic, participatory and experimenting institution accessible and dedicated to the needs of a richly diverse adult student body. These values are woven into the decisions we make about what we choose to do, how we carry out our work

in all parts of the institution, and how we judge the outcome of our individual and collective efforts. More than a claim about what we have already attained, the core values support our continuing inquiry about what learning means and how it occurs. (SUNY Empire State College, 2005, para. 1)

These core values include building on learners' experience and on their existing knowledge and skills; fostering critical exploration of that knowledge and experience; and fostering self-direction, questioning and reflective inquiry through a community that respects and treats every member of the community as a learner. And, as is so evident in these core values, dialogue between mentor and student and collaboration with other members of the community are expected to be key to the ESC experience.

Through the lenses employed below, I will explore how various electronic media and tools can either support or undermine our ability to act fully in accord with our core values. A number of critical questions follow: For example, do our uses of technology support active student participation in their study design or do they facilitate passivity? Do they serve to enhance creativity or to promote conformity? Do these tools and technologies support a climate for creative thinking and questioning, or do they tend more to dampen that creativity?

## MODES OF INTERACTION AND LEARNING: FACE-TO-FACE, ONLINE, AND BLENDED; ONE-TO-ONE AND GROUP

During the first decade of the College (1971–1981), interaction between mentor and student was primarily in person, with some interaction via phone calls. The face" of the college for the student was very much his/her mentor. There were some group meetings, including, for many, a group orientation. And, for some students, there were single group learning sessions or workshops (for developing writing skills, for example), and some group studies, which were understood then to be independent studies with group components. But, the individual mentor-student interaction was the core of a student's experience.

Over time, although the mentor-student relationship has remained central to any ESC student's experience, many students began to engage with a wider range of the college community. For example, the number of group study offerings increased, providing students (especially at particular locations around the state) an opportunity to work with a group of students and perhaps with a faculty member other than one's mentor. Though one-to-one work with a mentor or tutor remained the major mode of learning, any ESC student could register for group study offered by other faculty.

In 1979, the Center for Distance Learning began offering what could be considered correspondence courses, adding another option for interaction between students and faculty. For most of the '80s, connections between faculty and students and among students were still primarily through face-to-face individual and group meetings, phone conversations, and mailings. But, around 1986, the College began to provide email accounts for all members of the college community, including students. And in the late 1980s, I began using computer conferencing (with a text-based system called CAUCUS) with some of my computer science mentees. This conferencing provided an excellent opportunity and a convenient way for my mentees who shared a common interest in computers to interact with and learn from each other. Though only text-based and therefore not visually appealing, we were learning about ways of connecting online.

With the introduction of the World Wide Web in the '90s, more significant changes began to occur. The impact of these new technologies increased with the offering of the first five online courses (in business) by CDL in 1996. Initially, there were only a few interested students, and the College actually had to pay students to try out this option. The number of available online courses grew slowly over the first few years, but reached over 350 by the time the college moved to a new delivery system, ANGEL, in 2006. In 2013, over 500 courses were available.

Online courses provided "distance learning" students with a radically different environment for learning. Instead of depending on a few phone calls and "snail mail" for interaction, as with the earlier correspondence courses, students now had access to a community of learners through online discussion boards. They also could contact their instructor more easily and thus get more immediate feedback on their work.

Online courses also have provided the opportunity for collaboration among students, quite in keeping with one of the college's core values. Through activities in an online course, learners can share experiences, as in discussion boards, and work together toward a common goal, as in a group assignment. For example, in "Exploring the Disciplines: Thinking Mathematically," an on-line course that I developed, students engage in a group problem-solving exercise. The assigned problem is complex and benefits from different perspectives and talents. In other courses, students might take on different roles in a role-playing exercise. As new technologies are invented and tried out, and as we learn how to use them more effectively and imaginatively, there are more and more opportunities for student connection and collaboration.

Realizing that students often needed more support for their online learning, the college, through the efforts of several faculty, developed an online "Writers' Complex" with a collection of tutorials, as well as access to an online writing tutor. The online tutor was available asynchronously and provided personal feedback on student papers. To further strengthen such on-line student support, over the past few years, the College has moved toward the use of online tutors through "Smarthinking," an outsourced online tutorial service available to all of our Empire State College students.

Over time, electronically mediated learning resources have played an increasing role for many students, especially for quantitatively-based studies; these resources have increased in their interactive aspects. Many textbooks now come with extensive web-based resources, and some publishers include their own online tutorial services, including online problem sets, animation and videos of instructors working through problems. With the increasing sophistication of some of these services, and their ability to provide meaningful and timely responses to individual questions and assignments, the difference between an in-person tutorial interaction and one that is electronically mediated has surely blurred.

Still, these extensive resources, more and more available through technology, have raised a question regarding the quality of the student's learning experience. Often, for example, assessments provided on these websites focus on the relatively low "remembering" level of Bloom's taxonomy. Of course, activities addressing higher levels of learning and thinking (applying, analyzing, evaluating and creating) are wrapped around these lower-level activities, but because they are usually easier to measure, there may at times be too much focus on these lower level skills. And, too, with online exercises that are sometimes assigned, students are spending more time online "alone" with the assessment, rather than interacting with their peers in discussions and group projects. Thus, while technology can enable interaction with content, it can also isolate learners; such isolation may undermine the reflective inquiry and critical thinking that working with others can encourage and support.

Currently, many online resources provide for interaction between the user and a given computer program. For example, students in a math course may view a math video and then answer questions for which the program gives them feedback. The use of online resources allows for self-pacing, which can be helpful to individual learners. But in this case, the learner is not in a dialogue with another person or group of people about the math concept. And so, though students may get the technique right, they may have touched only the surface. Will they be able to apply this skill to a related problem? If all they have is human/computer interaction, without the give and take and shared exploration with others, the probability of the ability to then transfer and use that knowledge in another context is relatively low.

But, as these resources become richer, this kind of concern may lessen. For example, at the Khan Academy[1] a learner can register on the site with a coach, a role which I have filled for over 20 learners. A coach can drill down and see much detail about the interaction a learner has had with the computer. The coach can see how much time the learner has spent on a problem, how many tries she has made, what answers she has given, and how often she has requested a "hint." From that data, a coach is often able to identify a conceptual error, which then can serve as the basis for beginning a dialogue with that learner about that concept. This integration of human-computer interaction with human-human interaction has real potential for facilitating deeper learning. But without this interaction, a learner might "succeed" with these materials (by trying again and again) though without achieving full comprehension or the important ability to apply what he/she has learned.

Online courses often focus on asynchronous activities such as individually completing online exercises, submitting files of work and engaging in discussion boards, but synchronous interaction can also occur. For example, some instructors have "live" office hours, where they are available for questions from students. And instructors can use web-based conferencing systems, such as Blackboard/

Collaborate, which allow for a live online session to review difficult concepts. Students can also use these online spaces for collaborative work. Such modes of interaction have become more regular features of many Empire State College online courses.

Interaction and modes of learning during a term for students enrolled in regional centers across the State of New York have also changed over time. In place of some (or many) of the face-to-face studies previously carried out between individual faculty mentors and individual students, during any particular enrollment term, many students now enroll for at least one CDL course, in effect, a group study carried out from a distance. In addition, for studies completed at their center location, students often email their work and receive feedback through email as well, thus reducing the number of face-to-face meetings throughout the term. Many faculty have online webpages and even course sites (formally in ANGEL and now in Moodle) where they send students for resources and interaction with other students. And, of course, web-based resources connected with textbooks are being used by students collegewide.

Adding to the enrichment of this on-line resource base, a few faculty have begun to develop and offer MOOCs, or Massive Open Online Courses, which, though typically traditional in format (they are, in most cases, faculty-designed and often provide faculty videos as the basis of instruction), do provide for interaction within networks of human and non-human resources as the locus of learning. Artificial intelligence may be used to surface the most common questions from discussion boards in courses that often have thousands of registrants. Another kind of MOOC, sometimes labeled a cMOOC, is based on connectivist theory,[2] where learning is focused on connections among and between areas of knowledge and resources and among and between learners as constructors of knowledge (Downes, 2006). That is, it is through the interaction with MOOC resources (of which one main source is the blogs written by participants themselves) that most learning occurs. For example, participants in a cMOOC might engage in a synchronous discussion using twitter about a topic of interest. Possible uses of, as well as questions about the quality of learning achieved through, MOOCs will be discussed further below.

Other tools used around the college have continued to blur the lines between face-to-face and online interaction. For example, faculty are using Skype (which allows for video connection) to interact with individual students within individualized studies, thus bringing the interaction closer to a face-to-face experience. Similarly, through a Google "hangout," in which up to 10 participants can be seen (through cameras on laptop and desktop computers), a group can easily share resources and engage in a conversation about a topic of interest. With this live visual component, one can see facial expressions and some body language. And having the visual connection can encourage fuller attention, in contrast to the multi-tasking that often occurs when the visual dimension is not present. Disadvantages, however, relate to the efficacy of the technology itself. Participants may lose connection with the audio and/or video, and either can be of poor quality, which is distracting and frustrating.

Recently, the college has begun integrating an e-portfolio system collegewide. Within Mahara, all members of the college community can connect with each other through profile pages and groups. In addition, through their pages, students can keep reflective journals, as well as share artifacts from their learning. Although there are over 22,000 Mahara accounts on the ESC system as of fall 2015, usage is still spotty, with still a small number of profile pages developed by college community members. But the potential is there to support collaborative dimensions of learning, as well as reflection, which, as noted above, are key to ESC's core values (Catalyst for Learning, n.d.).

Without doubt, these uses of technology have allowed for more interaction between faculty and student. But this ease of connection has also raised questions. While mentors have always wrestled in some ways with maintaining a professional relationship with their mentees as they work with the "whole student" and strive to integrate the personal into a given learning moment, the social networking that technology has made possible may serve to further complicate these relationships. Thus, for example, faculty must remain mindful of the benefits and pitfalls to sharing aspects of one's personal life. How much should a student share about his/her personal life on a Mahara profile page? What does "friendship" mean in Mahara? Some faculty using social networking tools such as Facebook and LinkedIn continue to face similar questions.

A safe route could be for mentors not to share any aspect of their personal life through a social network. But then, does this safe path also reduce the potential for mentor and student to connect as fellow learners experiencing similar struggles? Thinking of transformative learning theory, we might ask: Can we facilitate a transformative environment if we hold back our own personal explorations? Clearly, a delicate balance exists between sharing about oneself and making one's own journey the focus of the conversation. And faculty must support an appropriate balance for the student as well. Each learner needs to address these questions to identify what balance works for him or her. And, in this connected environment, we all need to consider the wider audience of our personal posts. In my view, as sharing of oneself can facilitate transformative environments, and as the risk may be worth the rewards, we need to work not to eliminate all personal reference, but rather to support integration of the personal and the academic (or professional) where that can broaden or deepen the learning.

A related question is whether there are differences between technology-mediated relationships and face-to-face ones. From my experience, a fully online relationship can be quite rich, especially if both correspondents are good communicators in writing. An online relationship in which there has been some face-to-face interaction can be especially rich. One which includes some visual connection (through Skype, for example) can have characteristics very similar to a relationship that is based on face-to-face interaction.

Certainly, over time, the use of new technologies has moved faculty at ESC from primarily one-to-one interactions to one-to-many and many-to-many environments.

While these environments can enrich our students' learning through the opportunity to interact with a wide range of students and faculty who are experts in their field, they can also, as noted earlier, contribute to a superficiality in their learning and reduce the potential guidance or influence of the mentor, who may have less opportunity to work with the learner to create a cohesive learning experience. That is, while various electronic media – through increased potential for connection and individualized pace of study – can enrich a learning experience, they can also, through lessened contact with faculty, result in a learner's proceeding on a disjointed learning journey.

This potential for disjointedness, existing not only in educational environments but in many aspects of 21st century living, presents a tension that is not new, but that is perhaps brought to a different level in our uses of technology. One sees so many people now with cell phones in hand, many even texting someone at a distance while speaking with someone present. We are so "connected" to those outside our physical space that we may be less connected with those in our presence. And we may be less able to live in the moment. If we cannot be fully mindful of what is around us physically, but are instead interacting on our phone with someone elsewhere or making plans for the next event or looking at photos of a past event, we reduce the opportunity to be fully in and learn from that present moment. Such a distracted mode reduces our ability to gain deeper understanding. And as our attention span may be reduced, for many the ability to explore one idea or inquiry for an extensive period of time and/or to delve more deeply has also lessened.

Before the days of extensive use of the electronic technologies that have been taken for granted over the last decades and that were not tools to which mentors and students could turn in the earlier years of the college, these distractions were fewer, and a mentor had more opportunity to gain a learner's focused and sustained attention. And, too, from more extensive and penetrating dialogue, the mentor was able to develop a good sense of the learner's strengths and areas in need of improvement and thus could better direct the learner to helpful resources. Now, learners may be too distracted by the volume of available interactions to focus for any length of time on a particular question or on what their mentors can contribute to their growth. Learners may be less inclined to spend significant blocks of uninterrupted time on their reading, inquiry and reflection. And mentors, too, may be distracted by the barrage of communication and material coming at them.

## MODES OF PEDAGOGY AND STUDY: STUDENT- AND FACULTY-DESIGNED; INDIVIDUALIZED AND PRE-STRUCTURED

The first three areas (goals, processes, modes) of the college's core values form the underlying principles behind our use of learning contracts. Rather than identify blocks of content (courses) from which learners can choose, the learning contract begins with the student's goals (in the *Purpose* section of the document) and then lays out a plan for the learner (through *Learning Outcomes*, *Activities* and *Methods and Criteria for Evaluation*), using a range of learning processes and modes, to meet these stated goals.

Although individualization in student degree plans (that is, at the curricular level) is still a prominent practice at ESC, the individualization of learning contracts for studies has decreased. First, the growth of the college and faculty's increased student load have necessitated some "standardization" of learning contracts. Second, the change in the calendar from having fifty possible student enrollment dates to having only five per year has had a significant impact: Faculty can no longer develop individual learning contracts for all students within each enrollment window. Over the years, each faculty member has developed a file of "standard" learning contracts, to be used by any student for whom they are appropriate. For example, I have developed and offered a learning contract for College Algebra. Third, the use of various technologies and tools for online teaching and learning has influenced our learning contract development. On the one hand, these technologies have permitted faculty to take a "generic" contract, such as for College Algebra, and easily revise it to meet an individual student's goals. (With typewritten learning contracts, one had to literally pencil in revisions for the student and then retype the whole learning contract to submit.) On the other hand, the ability to post studies available in any given term online has enabled the development of our "Learning Opportunities Inventory" (LOI), which students may access at any time. Some have come to see the LOI as an electronic college catalog of faculty-designed courses, which results in students simply selecting from a menu and thus diminishing their creative design of their own courses and degree programs.

The LOI presents another example of a creative tension at ESC. On one hand, it provides learners around the college access to a wider range of studies. However, because the faculty member offering a study through the LOI rarely has the opportunity to communicate at any length with a particular learner about his/her goals for the study or its place in the student's degree program, the study may not address the learner's particular interests and purposes. And, if a degree program is composed primarily of faculty-designed CDL courses and/or LOI-offered studies, the degree plan may lack the coherence it could have had with more mentor consultation. That is, the degree program may have more "generic" ESC studies that do not build as well on the learner's background. Importantly, too, these studies may be more instructor-centered than learner-centered, thus undercutting the spirit of the college's core values.

Related to the discussion above on modes of interaction and learning, a review of the elements of the LOI demonstrates how the modes of learning in the college have changed as a result of increased reliance on particular electronic technologies. There are hundreds of learning opportunities available at a distance. The communication in these cases ranges from email to interaction through a website. And, for many of those that are restricted to a particular location, the descriptions often indicate that the mode of learning is "blended," with in-person group meetings as well as work in an electronic Learning Management System or at least via email.

New technologies are being used in many different blended options provided around the college. As mentioned earlier, some mentors are using webpages as resource pages for independent studies. Many mentors use publisher-provided online resources as supplementary materials for a study. Several CDL faculty who are situated at regional centers are combining face-to-face meetings with the use of online resources.

And, of course, there is the extensive catalog of faculty-designed courses available now from CDL. Although the Learning Management System has changed (from Lotus Notes to ANGEL to Moodle), the components of the online courses at CDL have remained quite consistent. Courses are divided into modules. Within each module, there are content files, discussion boards, and activities, all designed by faculty, with the support of curriculum instructional designers.

A range of approaches exists within this standard framework, however. These include:

- *Blend of asynchronous with synchronous,* in which faculty include some online synchronous meetings with students, including online office hours and meetings through Blackboard/Collaborate. This blended approach can allow for both an individualized pace and faculty led discussion.
- *Collaborative Projects*, in which CDL learners can be assigned online "spaces" to work together and then come back to the large group to share their results. Some of this group work can happen synchronously through Blackboard/Collaborate or Google Hangouts. These studies bring together both the collaborative dimension of small group work and the interaction with faculty and other students.
- *Mobile Learning*, in which some students access their courses through their mobile phones, according to their desired schedule and their own location. As the use of smartphones increases, so will the possibilities for engaging with learners through these mobile devices.
- *MOOCs.* Much of course could be written about the possible benefits and limitations of MOOCs (Massive Open Online Courses.) One version of a MOOC, earlier described as a connectivist MOOC, (cMOOC) focuses on the ability of technology to connect learners in a way that the focus is really on development as a learner, rather than as an absorber of particular provided content. A learner in a cMOOC environment literally develops his/her own path, identifying through shared blogs the directions he/she will take. Of course, the challenges noted earlier, such as possible superficiality and disjointedness, exist for the cMOOC.

The cMOOC environment provides another helpful example of the creative tension between self-directed and faculty-directed studies discussed in this chapter. Some learners who are self-directed have found the environment to be transformative, providing them with the opportunity to engage with other learners and create rich artifacts of their learning that they can then share with others. But learners who are more used to being guided through their studies have sometimes found this environment to be confusing and frustrating. We've not yet identified good strategies to facilitate these learners' development from dependency on external directions to feeling empowered to design their own learning path.

The faculty-designed structure of a CDL course provides both advantages and disadvantages for students. For learners preferring more structure, the benefits of pre-set activities, a calendar for completion, and criteria for evaluation are clear. And a CDL course may be a good starting point for some of our learners. But, with a pre-structured CDL course, there is the challenge of addressing the wide range of backgrounds of learners, another core value of the college, within a particular course offering. Many courses include a project where learners can build on their previous background and develop projects related to their own learning goals. But, for some students, a given course may duplicate previous experience and/or not address their particular interests or needs. In addition, it is important that CDL students work closely with their mentor to prevent redundancy between a request for credit for prior learning and a CDL course.

The tension between structure and individualization in an online course at CDL may now be less "creative" than it could be. That is, the tension exists mostly because our current online course management systems are too linear. In most cases, each learner is led through the same learning steps, no matter how well he or she does on a previous step. So-called "adaptive learning techniques" will provide opportunity for branching learners along different paths, depending on their responses. Over the next few years, as more adaptive learning approaches become available, courses may strike a more helpful, "creative" balance between pre-determined structure and flexibility.

Over the past few years, discussion of "Personal Learning Environments" (PLEs) – electronic environments constructed by the learner, who has access to vast resources via the internet – has increased (Dabbagh & Kitsantas, 2012). Resources are extensive and include online dictionaries, eBooks, and full-text journal articles, open education resources (OERs), and access to experts in their fields, often through their blogs, to name just a few. Recently, free online resources that look much like online courses have become available. For example, Coursera and Udacity provide free courses in many areas. The Peer 2 Peer University (P2PU) connects learners to experts. The Saylor Foundation has funded collections of courses in "typical" majors such as math, psychology, business and history. As the student selects from among these resources, he or she is creating his/her own learning environment, which is in this way could be termed "individualized." However, most of the courses accessed are faculty designed and not necessarily adaptable to an individual student's interests and goals – a concern to be addressed as the college continues to experiment with PLEs.

In addition to content resources, learners can connect with experts and other learners globally. Google has tools that facilitate such interaction. Through Google, one can form and join "circles," loosely defined communities that share a common interest. These circles can connect via Google Hangouts, mentioned earlier, which are synchronous meetings that provide video as well as audio connection for participants and which allow participants to share resources, such as YouTube videos or links and notes through a text box with one another. Skype for Business, which the college recently acquired as part of a move to Microsoft Outlook, also provides a space for groups to interact and share online sources synchronously. Using these tools, students can create and administer their own groups.

These learners, however, are sometimes missing mentors to help them organize their learning in meaningful ways. While many developers of Personal Learning Environments (or Spaces) have already been successful in a more traditional learning environment, learners unused to directing their own studies will need help navigating this new educational landscape.

Often OERs are key components of Personal Learning Environments. But finding high quality and appropriate OERs and incorporating them in meaningful ways into one's PLE is central to effective learning. One needs a guide to help in navigating this terrain of resources. UNESCO and the Commonwealth of Learning have been working on this challenge, drawing on the ideas of Jim Taylor from the University of South Queensland, where he connects the learners using OERs with academic volunteers who then facilitate the learning from these OERs.[3] Thus students are developing their own environments but with faculty support, a direction quite in keeping with ESC's vision of learning.

A look again at the College's core values shows a clear parallel between the PLE and the learning environment that has always existed for Empire State College students. While over the past few years, as discussed above, some technologies have served to foster a move away from individualization, with improved technology, the college could actually more systematically return to a more individualized approach. Thus, for example, our move to the use of an e-portfolio system could facilitate a reinvigoration of quality individualization. Through a shared e-portfolio page or collection of pages, a student could, with his/her mentor's support, document his/her learning journey. While increased faculty workload, use of the LOI, and the availability of more faculty designed, pre-structured learning contracts have led to less integration of studies and sometimes less thoughtfully planned degrees, use of an e-portfolio system to document a student's journey could bring us back to more integration by the student of his/her studies overall. So, too, could these e-portfolios (about which, more below) provide ways to reflect on and document learning, both within a study and across a full degree program. Thus, while individualized study, designed by students in consultation with a mentor, has waned at the College, various technologies with which we are now experimenting could help ESC to restore a creative, helpful balance between student-designed and faculty-designed studies and between emergent and more pre-structured curricula.

## ORGANIZATIONAL AND ADMINISTRATIVE COMMUNICATION

While organizational communication intersects significantly with modes of interaction and of pedagogy, certain dimensions of the impacts of new technologies on this realm should be noted. As mentioned earlier, ESC has moved from primarily one-to-one communication in person and via mail and phone to an extensive electronic communication network. Members of the college community, including students, faculty and staff, are connected through an email system, which one could say has become the life blood of our college's communication. Students and mentors work out registration through an online registration space. Today, more and more of the college's committee work now happens through web conferencing and, increasingly, through videoconferencing. Such means of communication, of course, both enable greater connectivity and present limitations that, as they may supplant face-to-face communication, can undermine collegewide connections.

The online registration area presents several of the advantages and challenges mentioned earlier regarding our online environment. In that space, any student can see hundreds of study options, from individualized study to group studies to residencies. And students can actually register without any communication with their mentor. Thus while the ability to access resources from around the college can be an advantage for students, this autonomy and lack of consultation can also lead to a degree program that lacks cohesion, an unintended and unfortunate consequence of students having this particular control.

It should also be noted that the LOI as currently conceived is incomplete in that it does not list all possible studies; rather, it includes only those studies that faculty choose to publicize and offer collegewide. Thus, while technology should be making our use of faculty resources across the College seamless, whereby a student needing a particular study can connect with a faculty member in the College who can do that study, the LOI has never accomplished this seamlessness. Students can find studies that faculty have designated as available collegewide; but if a mentor wants to connect a student with a mentor who is not listed for that area in the LOI, the process is complicated and frustrating. And because physical locations often still function as competitors for enrollment within the College, there is little motivation for a mentor to work with students outside his/her center. In this way, the electronically supported LOI has not yet achieved our goal of providing students collegewide access to all studies.

Our uses of new tools have fallen short in other ways as well. New systems for submitting grades electronically have proven clunky, especially for mentors facilitating many individualized studies. And the ability now to calculate and to see online any mentor's workload has not yet eliminated confusion about formulas or concerns about inequities, which no given technology is equipped easily to fix.

Over time, mentors have gotten better online access to information about their students. In the mentor space, mentors can access all the enrollments for a mentee, view academic progress, and get contact information. In addition, mentors and students work on the degree program development in a college-developed online tool called DP Planner, which allows for revision and dialogue between mentor and mentee. And students submit applications for prior learning assessment in PLA Planner, another college-developed online program. Evaluators of these applications for credit for prior learning can access the materials through PLA Planner as well. Unfortunately, PLA Planner does not yet provide very helpful reports for the offices of Academic Review to track PLA submission and review. And mentors can check only student by student; they cannot generate reports of all their mentees for easy review. So, most mentors have to keep personal lists for summarizing – another way in which our uses of available technologies lag behind our needs.

An area less explored, but also important is the relationship of students to each other and alumni, a key population within our organization, to students and faculty. Our new e-portfolio system, Mahara, makes feasible connecting of ESC learners, alumni and faculty in many different ways. Communicating through the Mahara message system, students in a group can work on a group page. Mentors can introduce students of similar interests to each other and can form groups of their mentees. Because their Mahara space is with them throughout their time with the college (and possibly beyond as alums), and because any page they create has its own URL and can be publically shared, students can use their Mahara account to create an ongoing online presence. How the forming of online student groups will affect student-student connections is a question, as is the potential for alumni connection – to one another and to students and to faculty.

## TECHNOLOGIES TO WATCH, ISSUES TO ADDRESS: WHAT SHOULD THE FUTURE BRING?

Innovations in technology occur rapidly, making predictions challenging, but we can imagine and be thoughtful and intentional about the not-too-distant future.

The development of online educational resources over the past few years has been impressive, and the richness of these resources keeps increasing. Yet the difficulty of finding appropriate resources and of assessing their quality remains. Therefore, it will be important to support our students becoming "critical consumers" and effective users of these resources. Our learners need to develop skills in research and evaluation. And, as we move forward, we should probably focus much less on content that we provide and much more on facilitating our students' finding, organizing, evaluating, and using the content they discover.

This distinction between content and process introduces another creative tension for our college. As the tools for connecting become easier to use (e.g., the relative ease of creating a webpage to share information about oneself and one's work), faculty must help students not just to develop but also to critically assess both what they access and what they develop, and to create and organize thoughtfully their own Personal Learning Environments (or spaces) that respond to their particular ideas, directions and professional/academic plans.

It is also important to recognize that although asynchronous interaction is convenient, real-time interaction can be still richer. With smartphones, the ability to have a visual connection with another person is becoming easier, and Google

Hangouts make group interaction via video possible. Electronic technologies can also make face-to-face meetings easier to plan; Coursera and Udacity are using meetup.com to facilitate informal meetings of learners taking MOOCs.

At ESC, we use technology to facilitate blended learning experiences for our students. We could, and need, to do much more in this arena, which would enhance students' connection and enrich their learning, as the online and face-to-face modes support and fuel one another.

Adaptive learning, rather than posing the same questions to every learner, can alter the questions depending on each student's responses, an approach which holds great potential for reducing frustration and boredom in online learning. Adaptive learning would reduce the linearity of our current online courses and would make more individualization possible. An experiment is underway now with adaptive learning in one of our online introductory psychology courses. Again, though, the tension between instructor-controlled and learner-controlled learning is apparent. The issue here would be one of balance – using adaptive learning to assist with the more "factual" aspects of a study while giving the learner responsibility and opportunities for the more creative aspects.

Gamification may be a trend to watch as well (NMC, 2013). While the College has done very little with games, there is a large population of adults playing games on a daily basis (Campbell, 2015). And game creators can teach us a lot about motivation for learning and collaboration. We should consider ways of incorporating games into our learning activities.

While there has been much discussion at ESC about Learning Management Systems (LMSs) over the past year as we have changed from ANGEL to Moodle, both the literature and conversations and presentations at conferences suggest that we will be moving away from LMSs. Controlled primarily by course designers and instructors, LMSs load course content and activities and put questions on discussion boards. Yet, learners today are gaining skills (as they should) in finding their own content. For example, only 50 percent of students now purchase the assigned textbook. Some may be depending on the "lecture," but an increasing number have figured out how to find the resources they need online. The proliferation of shared videos and images on Facebook, YouTube and SlideShare indicates that there is a shift to finding one's own content rather than simply reading and summarizing content provided by the instructor.

The theme of learners' control, i.e., of learners developing studies in relation to their own purposes and interests, has been prominent in this discussion. And review of ESC's core values points clearly to the College's early appreciation for learner-generated and designed inquiry. My hope is that we will improve our uses of the technologies available to us to continue to facilitate the individualization that inspired our early days as a college. At ESC, we have always valued the learner's viewpoint and contribution to study design. And more than ever, it seems that we now have the technologies that can support us in acting in accord with these values. Over the next few years, I expect to see an increased focus on learner-generated learning environments, such as websites, online art galleries, apps for mobile devices and digital stories – all in the spirit of Empire State College's core values.

Thus, in the near future, we may well see more technology-enabled DIY ("do-it-yourself") degrees. That is, even with efforts, such as the Bill & Melinda Gates Foundation project, that seek to greatly reduce the cost of the first two years of college, learners who find higher education at many institutions far too expensive will be seeking other routes to achieving their goals. OERu, for example, a project led by Wayne Mackintosh of WikiEducator that brings together OERs, volunteer academic guides and credentialing by academic members of OERu, provides one potential DIY model for global learners and, without doubt, in the coming years, there will be other models too.

For years, colleagues at ESC have discussed a student portal, which would provide an individualized entryway to a comprehensive electronic learning environment for each student. On this completely individualized page, each student would have access to his/her degree program, to college resources and to his/her e-portfolio. Announcements would populate students' individual portal page only to the extent that they concerned them. And students could further customize their portal page, for example adding their own calendar and organizing items in a way that is most useful to them.

In keeping with the student portal, as mentioned above, the addition of an e-portfolio system provides an opportunity for us to embrace our core value of genuinely student-centered study through students' development of Personal Learning Spaces (or Personal Learning Environments). With each new student being given an initial space in an electronic platform such as Mahara, each learning contract could be documented there. Learners could keep an ongoing journal about their journey and get feedback on that journal from their mentor or instructor. They could join online groups and engage in group projects facilitated by experts in their field of interest. Their degree program could be developed within the e-portfolio and shared with others – both students and faculty – for feedback. When ready, this degree program would be submitted to a faculty committee, again within their portfolio. And students and faculty could use public pages to share their work outside the ESC community.

The student portal model (which we could adopt for all members of the college community, including faculty and staff), coupled with the e-portfolio system, could facilitate a radical shift for our learning organization. Very much in keeping with the heart of the college, through a portal, learners could control their learning spaces and we would have created the structure for an environment that could be truly learner- and learning-centered. Through e-portfolios, learners could reflect on their learning experience and engage in dialog with their mentors as they document their journey. And e-portfolios would support meaningful assessment as well, as faculty would be able to access artifacts of learning; viewing these artifacts, they could assess how well students are achieving both their own learning goals and learning outcomes set by the College.

Unfortunately, it could also be the case that we at the College will use technologies available to us to facilitate sameness. Without clear intention to develop genuinely student-driven learning environments and activities, online courses could remain primarily linear and instructor-led, with little opportunity for learners to establish and meet their more specific goals. And defining "interaction" as mostly responding to imposed questions rather than finding creative ways to support learners in pursuing their own questions would also work against the practice of individualized study. Such studies, would inevitably not only fail to live up to our core values, but also, over time, become less attractive to learners. To avoid this mediocrity and, eventually, the loss of ESC's non-traditional approaches and progressive identity, ESC must continue to look critically and intentionally at its uses of electronic technologies, both to support students' learning and development and to strengthen our institution as a connected learning community.

## CONCLUSION

In the introduction to this chapter, I asked a question about whether various electronic technologies and our uses of them are more friend or foe to Empire State College and to our core values. Overall, if we examine what our uses of these technologies have yielded, we see much that has been a help to us in supporting our students' learning and development: These technologies have helped us to improve communication – whether between faculty and student or among students or among faculty and staff across the College; they have given us and our students access to greatly expanded resources and to new ways of working with these resources; and they have provided increased learning options, new modes of mentoring, teaching and learning, as they have allowed us to connect with our students and each other in wonderful ways.

But this discussion also has identified some challenges that current technologies – and our uses of them – present. Without thoughtful, intentional use of LMSs, for example, studies can remain more faculty driven and less individualized in relation to each student's goals and interests. Without intentional support of deep reflection and creative use of learning platforms to encourage that reflection, today's hectic and distracted uses of electronic connection can lead to increased superficiality and lack of clarity in our inquiry. And flitting from one site, one resource to another can serve to increase the disjointedness many, students as well as faculty, already experience. In sum, without critical, intentional use of technologies that become available, without keen awareness of the possible pitfalls, depth of learning will suffer.

To maintain our innovative approaches, risks will need to be taken. There will surely be failures along the way. But if we remain focused on our core values and evaluate whatever technologies we have in relation to those values, we will continue to serve the changing needs of our, now global, learners.

## NOTES

[1] See the Khan Academy website at https://www.khanacademy.org/
[2] More information on connectivist theory can be found in George Siemens' seminal essay at http://www.itdl.org/journal/jan_05/article01.htm
[3] See for example, mention of Jim Taylor's work at the OpenCourseWare Consortium Global Conference at http://archive.is/UxVRA

## REFERENCES

Bill & Melinda Gates Foundation. (n.d.). *What we do: Postsecondary success: Strategy overview*. Retrieved from http://www.gatesfoundation.org/What-We-Do/US-Program/Postsecondary-Success

Campbell, C. (2015, April 14). *Here's how many people are playing games in America*. Retrieved from http://www.polygon.com/2015/4/14/8415611/gaming-stats-2015

Catalyst for Learning. (n.d.). *Pedagogy*. Retrieved from http://c21.mcnrc.org/pedagogy/

Dabbagh, N., & Kitsantas, A. (2012, January). Personal learning environments, social media, and self-regulated learning: A natural formula for connecting formal and informal learning. *Internet and Higher Education, 15*(1), 3–8.

Downes, S. (2006, October 16). *Learning networks and connective knowledge*. Retrieved from http://itforum.coe.uga.edu/paper92/paper92.html

NMC. (2013). *NMC Horizon report: 2014 higher education preview*. Retrieved from http://www.nmc.org/pdf/2014-horizon-he-preview.pdf

Schlesinger Jr., A. M. (n.d.). Retrieved from http://www.brainyquote.com/quotes/quotes/a/arthurmsc109503.html

SUNY Empire State College. (2005). *Empire State College core values*. Retrieved from http://www.esc.edu/academic-affairs/provost-office/esc-core-values/

JOYCE E. ELLIOTT

# 19. IMPLICATIONS OF EMERGENT CONTENT, EXPERIMENTATION, AND RESOURCES FOR OUTCOMES ASSESSMENT AT EMPIRE STATE COLLEGE

In this essay, I consider Empire State College's progress and prospects in institutional assessment of student learning. I argue that the validity of prescribed content in contrast to emergent content has always been contested ground within the college and that assessing learning outcomes necessarily means grappling with what I call below the content question. I also argue that authentic assessment of student learning outcomes for the purpose of improving academic quality is entirely consistent with the college's mission, values and identity as an experimenting institution. Indeed, assessment undertaken as a collective faculty project is one key to sustaining the progressive nature and quality of the college's academic program. Finally, I argue that to sustain its progressive vision, the college must devote dramatically greater resources to both the faculty and the assessment function.

The college has always protected space for emergent learning and experimentation. And, there have always been internal and external forces seeking to limit that space. The broader higher education context, coupled with particulars at Empire State College (e.g., enrollment growth, organizational structures, student profile, delivery models, funding), has influenced the content question, prospects for continuing academic experimentation and the robustness of faculty resources, which in turn have affected the nature of outcomes assessment at this institution.

On the content question, one common view – within and beyond the college – is that pre-defining the "content" to be learned is central to outcomes assessment. Yet while to some emergent curricula may seem entirely incompatible with outcomes assessment, in my view they are not. And, though a move toward more prescribed curricula might seem an obvious solution, I would argue that making that move does not really simplify the project. On the experimentation question, one common view is that embracing outcomes assessment inevitably means the end of experimentation in teaching and learning. Yet, in my view, the assessment cycle actually affords faculty creative and collegial opportunities to experiment with practice toward improving student learning. On the resource question, sustaining the college's experimental, progressive vision requires substantial increases in the number of full-time faculty and support for faculty professional development and assessment-based academic quality improvement projects.

## UNDERGRADUATE DEGREE STUDIES AT EMPIRE STATE COLLEGE

A brief description of key elements of the college's undergraduate program provides context for this discussion, which necessarily focuses on the primary historical model rather than on what may unfold in the future. Since the mid-1970s, the curricular core of Empire State College has been "registered Areas of Study" (AOSs) which serve as umbrellas under which students can design associate or bachelor's degrees. The New York State Education Department (NYSED) registers the AOSs as the titles under which ESC has authority to award degrees. The degree awarded is the AOS title (e.g., Business, Management and Economics; Cultural Studies; the Arts). In the context of curricular guidelines established for each AOS, the student works with a faculty mentor to individually design the overall degree program and a concentration (e.g., Small Business Management, Spanish Language and Literature, Women in the Arts). The student's program is subject to approval by a faculty committee and a technical review by the Office of Academic Affairs.

The State University of New York's system-wide general education requirements, established by the Trustees in the late 1990s, also shape individualized program design. The college adopted the SUNY requirements verbatim and has taken a rather inclusive approach to designating studies and courses as meeting one or more general education requirements. Direct assessments of student learning outcomes focus on the AOS guidelines and general education requirements.

The academic program has also featured tremendous experimentation with delivery models, teaching and learning methods, and academic policies, underpinned by the principle of sustaining close mentor-student relationships. The college offers student-friendly transfer credit policies and extensive use (indeed, pioneering) of prior learning assessment (PLA). Delivery models have included independent study, study groups, satellite video, intensive residencies, courses and various hybrids. Within those formats, faculty have developed face-to face, distance and online learning methods, and various combinations of these. Taken together with the college's historically open curriculum, these innovations have enabled the college to become one of the most successful and interesting institutions serving adults in the country. And the varied methodologies for teaching and learning also present unique opportunities for assessing learning outcomes.

## THE DEBATE OVER EMERGENT AND PRESCRIBED CURRICULA

Since its founding, Empire State College has grappled with the relative value and validity of emergent and prescribed learning. Should we define common study content and curricula for students (and sometimes faculty) to use or follow, or encourage study content and program design to emerge from the evolving needs and interests of individual students? Responses to the question have implications for how we work with students, assess what students learn, and improve learning experiences and outcomes – all core concerns of the student learning outcomes assessment movement.

Positions on this question reflect contrasting perspectives on educational theory and practice, student needs and preferences, the value of generalist and specialist faculty expertise, and prospects for sustainable faculty work lives. Opposition to prescribed content is rooted in progressive educational theory and practice and in intellectual and political challenges to the traditional canon. Support of prescribed content has roots in many of the disciplines and professions, views of student preferences and career needs and concerns about external understanding of the college. Both camps, and those who straddle the two, also reference faculty workload and academic quality concerns.

The content question centers on what is to be learned, for what purpose, and who decides that. Should the content of a degree or a particular study be defined by the canon, the profession, the marketplace, the faculty as a body, the mentor or the student? Is the purpose of a college education to foster personal and intellectual growth, to foster the critical knowledge and skills needed to participate in democratic institutions, to prepare graduates for careers and/or to meet whatever goals the student individually defines? And who is responsible for answering these questions – the faculty or the student? The college's answers to these questions have several origins.

*Progressive Education, the Founders and the Regulators*

Empire State College has obvious roots in the progressive education movement. Central commitments of the movement and the college include experiential, constructivist, emergent, student-centered, personalized, problem-oriented, community-based and lifelong learning. John Dewey's work has arguably had the broadest influence on the college's educational model, as is evident in the college *Prospectus* and the work of the first college leaders.

College historian and archivist Richard Bonnabeau chronicles how key founding players and external stakeholders shaped the college's early development. Chancellor Ernest Boyer's planning team, led by founding president James Hall, considered three alternative models for the new college: a low-residency liberal arts program based on one at SUNY Brockport, the British Open University model with its distributed organization and highly structured curriculum, and a mentor/tutor model for working with individual students (Bonnabeau, 1996, pp. 16–18). The planners chose individualized curricula over more prescriptive models. The founding charter, *A Prospectus for a New University College,* set a progressive agenda calling for faculty to work with students inductively to design programs of study that fit the individual student's experience and purposes (Boyer, 1971, pp. 16–19).

In *Education and Identity*, published just before the creation of Empire State College, founding academic Vice President Arthur Chickering (1969) explored how different institutional arrangements may influence progressive educational outcomes such as developing competence, autonomy, identity and "freeing interpersonal relationships." Anticipating the open, individualized approach envisioned in the college *Prospectus,* he saw the least content-driven models as the most capable of supporting these outcomes.

Founding President Jim Hall also advocated vigorously for curricular openness and progressive education. Writing in the early 1980s, Hall argued that a single common curriculum may result in superficial knowledge, cannot address the needs and purposes of the diverse student populations we now serve, and cannot create the shared community values that many educators and policymakers claim to foster:

> Such an educational approach and such a curriculum are sorely deficient. The ultimate purpose of education ... is neither socialization nor indoctrination into a community value system, but is instead to gain the capabilities by which one ultimately makes good judgments ... The ultimate purpose of education is to give students the capacities to distinguish between what is good and less good, between what is better in one situation than something else in equal circumstances. (Hall & Kevles, 1982, pp. 36–37)

The appointment of Loren Baritz as Provost for Instructional Resources provided dramatic contrast. Baritz was also committed to creating student-centered alternatives to traditional higher education, but he did not believe that meant constructing individualized degrees and learning contracts. For him, student-centered, non-traditional education meant developing creative, challenging, structured curricula and learning resources designed to meet students' intellectual needs, more than creating individualized curricula and studies responsive to students' backgrounds and goals (Bonnabeau, 1996, p. 24). From the beginning, this conflict between Chickering and Baritz over content worked its way into the fabric of the institution.

During the 1970s, the New York State Education Department (NYSED) pressed the college to "normalize" the curriculum. In response, the faculty defined nine areas of study that represented "loose confederations of related fields of interest" and developed guidelines for degrees in each area (Bonnabeau, 1996). Though the Middle States Commission on Higher Education also pressed for more content definition early on, accreditation focuses more now on continuous improvement of the academic program, regardless of its content or format. In my view, that is a welcome shift.

Empire State College faculty members have always debated whether the AOS guidelines are prescriptive. Officially, they are not. Though in practice the guidelines are sometimes (often) treated as prescriptions, the introduction to the guidelines still states:

> The guidelines have authority but they are not a fixed set of course requirements. They are open to interpretation; many of the studies can be undertaken in a wide variety of ways, and they encourage concentrations that may differ from traditional majors. The principle which governs degree program planning is individualization: Empire State College students design programs which, within very broad parameters, meet their own needs and

interests. Many students' needs and interests are best met by concentration in one of the conventional academic disciplines ... others use the guidelines as a point of departure in defining their distinctive approaches to their studies. (SUNY Empire State College, 2014, Statements section, para. 2)

As this debate continues, faculty are presently reframing AOS guidelines in terms of learning outcomes, even as more prescribed curricula are also moving to center stage.

*PLA Principles and Practice: Recognizing Unconventional Content*

The content question is also rooted in the college's approach to prior learning assessment. As the following excerpt from the prior learning assessment policy demonstrates, the college explicitly recognizes learning that extends beyond the standard content found in college course catalogs:

5. ... [Empire State College] recognizes emergent knowledge areas and perspectives, as well as experience-based learning by adults, which may not be represented in standard college curricula. Other institutions may limit prior-learning credit requests to course equivalents. Empire State College does not use course equivalents to automatically allow or exclude consideration of a request for prior-learning credit. ... (SUNY Empire State College, 2007, Scope of Learning section, para. 1)

At various points since the college's founding faculty would have been hard pressed, for example, to find course equivalents at other colleges for learning in African American history, women's studies, global energy policy, computer science, nanoscience, brain and behavior or equine therapy for the disabled. At one time or another, such studies did not exist. They do now, and Empire State College students continue to present college-level learning in fields that have not yet found their way into mainstream curricula. In principle, policy and practice, the college still recognizes learning in emerging fields that does not yet fall within conventional knowledge domains.

*Social Change and the Critique of the Canon*

The movements for social change that emerged in the U.S. in the '60s and '70s framed the founding of the college and also contributed to ESC's content debate. A college conference in 2009 addressed the theme "Celebrating our Creativity and Innovation: Re-imagining the Areas of Study at Empire State College." Speaking to the gathering as then-Provost, I noted that the college's founding in 1971 as a progressive, experimenting institution coincided with the civil rights and anti-Vietnam-War movements and pre-dated the challenges to the traditional canon that emerged from the civil rights, women's, LGBTQ and international liberation movements.

By profoundly questioning the societal status quo, movements for social change underscored the fundamentally political, provisional and experiential nature of knowledge. Knowledge depends on the knower's position in society, on the material conditions of our lives and on the organization of social systems. The disciplines and professions and the "canon," so taken for granted by the academy and the general public, are human creations. The college's areas of study themselves were born of regulatory mandates; the critiques of bodies of knowledge that became available in the 1970s; views of what serves students educationally and professionally; the college's ability to sustain a faculty who have the necessary breadth, depth and currency to serve students; and the disciplinary and professional identities of the faculty. They necessarily reflect the experience and perspectives of those in a position to define what counts as knowledge.

Over time, the faculty have modified the Areas of Study established over 40 years ago, reflecting changes in the disciplines and professions, societal demands and student interests. And they have struggled with deeper questions about the structure of knowledge and how it has changed over time. What might we actually wish to prescribe? What content ought we to protect? What are the implications for recognizing knowledge that does not yet exist? The emergence of new fields (women's studies, environmental studies, biopsychology) and the complex, cross-disciplinary nature of the real global problems we face today call into question whether our current knowledge frameworks are sufficient and enduring. Certainly, there is reason to resist time- and place-bound notions of what knowledge and skills should be recognized by the academy.

*Researching an Experimenting Institution*

Empire State College's early institutional research efforts reflected a need to demonstrate the value of this educational experiment to interested stakeholders, such as the legislature, the State University of New York, NYSED, Middle States, national higher education organizations and early funders such as Ford and the Fund for the Improvement of Postsecondary Education (FIPSE). The first decade of research was a rich mix of qualitative and quantitative studies of student pathways through the college and of outcomes ranging from academic learning to personal development (T. Lehmann, personal communication, December 4, 2013).[1] But by the end of the first decade, the external funding that had jump-started research at the college had ended. With that, and with state funding challenges that emerged just as the college was being built and have only worsened over time, the early research infrastructure proved to be unsustainable.

By the early 1980s, most of the Office of Research and Evaluation (ORE) was disbanded. During the '80s and '90s, ORE continued some research projects and helped to establish the National Center on Adult Learning (NCAL), formed in 1988 to support research into the theory and practice of adult education (T. Lehmann, personal communication, December 4, 2013). The Office of Program Review and

Assessment (OPRA) reported regularly to the college on transfer, prior learning and ESC credits and degrees awarded, by academic center and area of study. The college also met external reporting requirements, produced management reports on academic documentation, and initiated periodic reviews in each area of study (AOSR). And, Vice President for Academic Affairs Jane Altes initiated participation in the SUNY Student Opinion Survey (SOS), the results of which have consistently placed the college at or near the top of SUNY institutions in terms of numerous indicators of student satisfaction.

By 2000, the college's dedicated institutional research infrastructure consisted of one individual who also served as registrar and director of OPRA. Over the next few years, the college once again built a modest Office of Assessment and Institutional Research (OAIR) within academic affairs. OAIR continued student surveys, added the national Higher Education Research Institute (HERI) surveys on faculty climate and the National Survey of Student Engagement (NSSE), prepared an annual college *Fact Book*, conducted a variety of surveys for planning purposes, implemented regular student assessments of learning experiences and worked with faculty to implement learning outcomes assessments based on authentic examples of student work in the "major" and general education.

## HIGHER EDUCATION DEVELOPMENTS

Over the years, broad higher education developments have intensified the college's internal tensions and challenges. Massive disinvestment in public higher education nationally and in New York has weakened the infrastructure undergirding the college's student-centered model. The college has embraced and led the way in adopting emerging learning technologies that have vast potential to support both more standardized and less standardized educational models. Yet those technologies are expensive, have a steep learning curve and must be carefully adapted to the college's mentoring and learning models. Dramatic growth in enrollment, while responsive to student demand, has also been driven by the need to replace public funding with tuition as the primary revenue source. With enrollment growth come challenges related to scalability, quality, workload and sustainability of practice.

In addition, the conservative ascendance building since the Reagan years has redefined even *public* higher education as a private rather than a public good. This shift has coincided with a decreased emphasis on education for citizenship or for a life well lived and more concern for the immediate employability of graduates and the role of higher education itself as an economic driver. Increasingly, the public, students, and higher education leaders accept career training as the purpose of a college degree. And, in my observation, a more instrumental view of degree studies comes with more prescriptive curricula and reduced space for emergent learning. Taken together, these external trends challenge the sustainability and validity of a student-centered, individualized, experimental model of education.

In regard to certain key policies affecting adults within higher education, very little has changed since the college's founding. For state and national policy makers and higher education leadership, adult learners remain just plain invisible despite the fact that they now make up roughly half of the college-going population. Federal and state financial aid policies are *still* designed for first-time, full-time, residential students. Such policies set up an obstacle course for adults that actively promotes failure. A student who works full time while raising a family, and who would be best served academically by taking one course at a time, is not permitted to do so while receiving financial aid. The inevitable results for these students are incomplete and failed studies and low rates of degree completion.

Highly-structured curricula with elaborate course sequencing and unfriendly transfer policies also create barriers for adults, who may attend several institutions over a span of 20 years. Empire State College has successfully served adult learners through friendly transfer and prior learning assessment policies, multiple modes of study that are not time- or place-bound, individually-tailored program design, support for emergent, student-defined learning purposes and faculty mentoring. Yet, such an experimental, adult-learner friendly model just does not make sense to many policymakers and educational leaders.

## OUTCOMES ASSESSMENT IN HIGHER EDUCATION

Current models for outcomes assessment tend to emphasize predefined rather than emergent outcomes and also tend to ignore the educational experiences and pathways of adult learners and the innovative ways some institutions serve them. A well regarded example is the Lumina Foundation's Degree Qualifications Profile (DQP), which establishes learning outcomes at the associate, bachelor's and master's degree levels. In a recent essay on promising models for assessing the DQP outcomes, Peter Ewell (2013) presumed that the defined outcomes are achieved through highly-structured curricula with tight course sequencing: "... courses constituting the curriculum should be intentional and cumulative. ... Course sequencing, therefore, is critical – to ensure that the series of courses a given student takes includes successive benchmark assessments that build toward culminating demonstrations of mastery (p. 17).

As noted above, such curricular arrangements do not fit the pathways and needs of part-time, transfer and adult students. Learners who attend multiple institutions over a long time span are not in a position to achieve the specified outcomes in the specified order. Indeed, a reverse educational pathway is fairly common, with specialized knowledge first acquired in work and community settings, and breadth and context later acquired through upper division studies.

The contemporary U.S. outcomes assessment movement views defining intended learning outcomes as a prerequisite for assessing learning. But the tensions surrounding content and emergent curricula at Empire State College appear to complicate this essential step. Additional content-related assessment challenges for adult-learner-friendly-institutions (ALFIs) are the sequencing of learning described above and the question of whether and how to assess college learning outcomes achieved through work and life experience or through study at other institutions.

At the same time, however, the outcomes assessment movement has evolved over the past few decades to embrace a continuous cycle of improvement that includes defining outcomes, designing learning experiences to support them, assessing student learning, reflecting on the results and making improvements to academic programs. This model is ideally suited to the experimental nature of Empire State College.

## OUTCOMES ASSESSMENT, OPEN CONTENT AND EXPERIMENTATION: PROSPECTS FOR EMPIRE STATE COLLEGE

The Middle States Commission on Higher Education (MSCHE) describes outcomes assessment as a cycle of continuous improvement that includes:

- "Developing clearly articulated written statements ... of key learning outcomes: the knowledge, skills, and competencies that students are expected to exhibit upon successful completion of a course, academic program, co-curricular program, general education requirement, or other specific set of experiences.
- Designing courses, programs, and experiences that provide intentional opportunities for students to achieve those learning outcomes.
- Assessing student achievement of those key learning outcomes.
- Using the results of those assessments to improve teaching and learning" (MSCHE, 2006, p. 63).

Thus, assessment asks us to examine systematically whether and to what extent we have enabled students to meet intended learning goals and how we might make improvements. Key to this effort is that the examination occurs at the institutional or collective faculty level, rather than only at the level of individual practice.

*1. Defining Learning Outcomes*

Much of the college's recent work on assessment centers on the first element of the Middle States continuous improvement model: defining outcomes. For example, in 2011 the college adopted college-level learning goals for undergraduates (active learning, breadth and depth of knowledge, social responsibility communication, critical thinking and problem solving, quantitative literacy, and information and digital media literacy). Since 2013, faculty have been re-framing area of study and concentration guidelines as learning outcomes. The purpose of this initiative is to improve the clarity and transparency of the guidelines for students and mentors, to facilitate outcomes assessment, and ultimately to improve student learning. Another effort involves aligning student learning outcomes across college, program (AOS and general education) and study/course levels. As faculty reframe guidelines as learning outcomes, they are also mapping them to the college-level learning goals. The most important aspect of alignment is to explicitly integrate expected learning outcomes into studies and courses, which falls under the second element of the assessment cycle, designing learning experiences.

It is in relation to defining learning outcomes that tensions between emergent and prescribed content come to the fore. Many faculty, here and elsewhere, interpret the drive to make intended learning outcomes explicit and transparent to students and faculty as an unwelcome mandate to pre-define standardized "chunks of content" that must be mastered by all. Whether revising the historically broad AOS guidelines to include more specifically articulated outcomes, or seeking to establish more traditionally prescribed curricula, it is important to recognize that a number of Empire State College faculty and administrators favor just such an approach.

An alternative that, in my view, readily embraces emergent content is to define learning outcomes in terms of academic and professional skills/values/habits of mind, while allowing and expecting the content to vary according to the student's interests and goals. To a significant degree, the college learning goals adopted in 2011 take this approach. And, by way of example, during their 2014 assessment project, Historical Studies faculty explored this approach with considerable creativity and excitement.

> The team ... recognized that students have various purposes in pursuing a degree. ... Some are history buffs, some have professional goals that require a professional master's degree (e.g., as archivists, librarians, museum staff, teachers) and some hope to go on for advanced degrees in history. ... [The team explored the] ... minimum threshold for skills and knowledge expected of a history graduate, regardless of what the learner plans to do later with the degree.
>
> There was a consensus that the *essential elements* include at least (1) literacy skills (intellectual, research, communication), (2) recognition that history involves contested narratives rather than a single agreed-upon narrative, (3) some depth of knowledge of "something" in the field (including fluency with the relevant vocabulary), and (4) some understanding of how that knowledge fits within larger contexts or narrative(s). (Elliott & Ostroot, 2014b, p. 9)

Following the 2014 assessment in Social Science, a faculty team has been revising the guidelines in a similar fashion, influenced in part by the Historical Studies faculty discussions and rubrics that they developed. The current draft identifies seven areas of learning: broad social science perspective, historical and comparative perspective, theoretical perspectives, social science research methods, skills of analysis, information literacy in the social sciences, and presentation skills.

For several of these elements, the phrase "In relation to their chosen topics, questions or problems" precedes specific learning outcomes. This signifies that the *content* around which students develop their knowledge, skills, vocabulary, etc. will vary by discipline or topics of study. The learning outcomes themselves address the student's capacity to work effectively with whatever content is relevant to her/his purposes and falls reasonably under the Social Science AOS umbrella. Table 1 provides two examples.

*Table 1. Examples from draft social science guidelines (Elliott et al., 2015, pp. 4, 9)*

| Elements | Learning Outcomes |
|---|---|
| Broad social science perspective | • Students identify questions and topics that social scientists typically pursue.<br>• Students recognize how social scientists look at those topics, as compared to the explanatory lenses used in other fields.<br>• Students build a social science vocabulary relevant to their concentrations.<br>• Students examine relationships among different elements of social life (e.g., human behavior, cultural values and social structures).<br>• Students identify how the social sciences may provide solutions to social issues. |
| Information literacy in the social sciences | • In relation to their chosen topics, questions or problems:<br>• Students access and use a range of relevant academic sources.<br>• Students effectively conduct electronic searches.<br>• Students distinguish scholarly sources from other kinds of sources.<br>• Students recognize the possible biases or limitations of their sources. |

The Social Science Area of Study happens to be especially broad. As the preamble to the draft revised guidelines states:

> Among the best known social science disciplines are anthropology, economics, political science, sociology and social psychology. Many other concentrations are also possible, including but not limited to: African-American studies, communications, community organization or development, criminology, environmental studies, ethnic studies, family studies. … (J. Elliott and colleagues, personal communication, June 2015)

If the task were to define learning outcomes for a single discipline or field (e.g., political science, gerontology), would this team still use an emergent approach? Yes. As the preamble to the draft states, "at the core of this area of study is learning to think like a social scientist." The difficult task is to define the kinds of knowledge, skills, vocabulary, etc. (learning outcomes) that add up to being able to think like a social scientist in any relevant field of study.

Can this be done outside of social science? Sure. What does it mean to think like an historian? Are the essential elements similar for concentrations in U.S. Labor

History, History of the Roman Empire and Modern European History, even though the content of study varies widely? What does it mean to think like a natural scientist? Are the key learning outcomes parallel for concentrations in biology and geology, though the subject matter is divergent? These are the kinds of questions that we need to and can answer as we develop outcomes that specify skills and knowledge while leaving particular content open.

Can an emergent approach be taken to professional fields? Yes. The Community and Human Services AOS, which encompasses a variety of concentrations, has worked extensively on AOS guidelines and assessment rubrics since 2013. Taken together, the elements of the guidelines define what it means to be an effective helping professional, with the expectation that those learning outcomes be achieved in relation to the student's chosen field of professional practice (Elliott & Ostroot, 2014a).

Is it easier to define learning outcomes for pre-structured degrees (or studies/ courses) than to define them for emergent programs of study? In regard to the implications of the content debate at Empire State College as it relates to the outcomes assessment project, this is a critical question.

And my answer is: There is no real difference. Defining learning outcomes is both critical and difficult whether faculty take a more prescriptive or emergent approach to content. Both approaches require the intellectual and collegial discipline to establish common ground regarding the purposes of a program (or study) and the learning outcomes it is intended to engender. Done well, the work is painstaking, whether it begins with a set of course requirements or with more open curricular arrangements. Either way, the work of identifying intended learning outcomes is both hard and essential.

I would argue that the second, third and fourth elements of the Middle States continuous improvement cycle – designing learning experiences that support intended learning outcomes, assessing their impact, and revising them accordingly – are an absolutely natural fit with Empire State College's history and identity as an experimenting institution. The three elements together simply call for experimentation. The college's faculty have historically taken great pride in such an experimental approach in their everyday practice.

*2. Designing Learning Experiences*

As Suskie (2009) noted regarding the second element in the assessment cycle: "There's no point in assessing something that students don't have an opportunity to learn ..." (p. 98). In recent outcomes assessments at Empire State College, a persistent finding has been that learning experiences (studies, courses) thought to foster certain learning outcomes may not actually provide opportunities for students to learn related to the expected outcome (e.g., Elliott & Riley, 2013; Elliott & Ostroot, 2014c, 2014d).

Designing a learning experience to foster certain learning outcomes requires us to be intentional. That means explicitly stating intended learning outcomes in a learning contract or course outline, which makes the outcomes themselves part of the learning environment. In regard to the third element of the assessment cycle, sharing directly with students the rubrics we create to assess learning also adds to the learning experience. Being intentional also means intentionally designing one or more relevant assignments to enable students both to learn and to demonstrate their learning. Are studies that explicitly state learning outcomes and include relevant assignments more likely actually to result in those outcomes? That is the question, and it is researchable.

The second element of the assessment cycle, assessing learning activities' impact, offers a rich opportunity for creativity, collegiality and scholarship among faculty dedicated to teaching and learning. There are many ways to design assignments to elicit relevant learning, which faculty can then assess. And, any given study or course may incorporate not just collectively defined learning outcomes, but also other important learning outcomes established by the mentor and student.

*3. Assessing Outcomes*

Outcomes assessments need to provide a basis for drawing reasonable conclusions about how students are performing and for creating action plans to improve student learning outcomes. This is action research for improving programs:

> Assessment, like any other form of action research ... uses many of the methodologies of traditional research ... [and] aim[s] to keep the benefits of assessment in proportion to the time and resources devoted to them. ... (Suskie, 2009, p. 13)
>
> We must ... strive to make assessment sufficiently truthful that we will have reasonable confidence in our findings and can use them with enough assurance to make decisions about goals, curricula and teaching strategies. (Suskie, 2009, p. 38)

In light of its educational models, the college determined early on that faculty review of examples of student work was the most fitting methodology for directly assessing student learning outcomes at this institution. Two of the college's three assessment methods (Assessment in the Major and the General Education Assessment Review) involve direct assessment of student learning using rubrics developed by the faculty.

As faculty conduct periodic assessments of student work for the purpose of outcomes assessment, they revise or replace rubrics used in past assessments, depending on the extent of changes in the guidelines. Of course, unless intended learning outcomes are clearly defined, it is not possible to devise ways to assess their achievement. In 2014, the Community and Human Services team found that the process of improving the assessment rubrics led to important refinements of AOS guidelines, even though they had recently been revised and approved. Thus, the task of defining learning outcomes (guidelines) and the task of designing and testing measurement tools (rubrics, in this case) intersect with one another. And, as noted above, clearly written rubrics that are directly available to students can become an important part of the learning experience.

*4. Using Results to Improve Teaching and Learning*

The phrase "closing the loop" refers to the fourth step in the cycle of continuous improvement: reflecting on and using the results of the assessment to improve teaching and learning. Common closing the loop initiatives include refining learning outcomes (i.e., returning to part 1 in the cycle), improving the design of learning experiences to achieve those outcomes (part 2 in the cycle) and refining assessment methodologies such as rubrics (part 3 in the cycle).

The *Comprehensive Review* of institutional learning outcomes completed in 2013 identified closing the loop as arguably "the weakest link in assessment at Empire State College" (Elliott & Riley, 2013, p. 31). While this is probably true for most institutions, the college's academic organization makes this particularly difficult. Responsibility for academic delivery rests with academic centers which are dispersed geographically and/or emphasize different modes of study and/or audiences. Responsibility for defining expected learning outcomes generally rests with the Areas of Study which assemble faculty into loose interdisciplinary groupings. These organizational and academic structures of the college are not aligned and this poses challenges for assessment and academic quality.

While this essay focuses on the collective faculty work of assessing learning outcomes at the institutional level, it is worth noting that there are obvious parallels and much potential for cross-fertilization between institutional outcomes assessment and faculty assessment of student learning within a study or course. We assess learning outcomes at the institutional level using a wide range of methodologies in order to see how our students are doing and to create ways to improve student learning in the aggregate. We assess an individual student's learning in a specific study – in myriad ways – to monitor the student's progress, to provide feedback to the student to support greater success in that study and beyond, to reflect on whether we might re-design elements of the study to better support future students' learning, and of course to serve as a basis for evaluating quality and awarding credit.

These activities are almost exactly parallel and they richly inform one another. In every institutional outcomes assessment I have been a part of, participants have contributed creative ideas about possible ways to think about outcomes and conduct institutional assessments. These ideas are informed by their everyday practice with students. And, they have brought back to their individual practice wonderful insights into new ways of designing learning experiences and assessing student work.

RESOURCES AND SUSTAINABILITY

In the previous sections, I have explored the tensions around the college's open orientation to academic content and concluded that fluid content is no barrier to effective institutional outcomes assessment. I have also examined the continuous improvement process used in our outcomes assessment and concluded that the model is completely compatible with the college's identity as an experimenting institution, and with faculty commitments to their work with individual students and to the quality of the overall academic program.

The final issue that must be addressed is the resource base for and the sustainability of the work. Outcomes assessment has important implications for institutional resource allocation. As Suskie (2009) argued, "assessment results ... [need to be used] to improve teaching and learning and [must] inform important planning and budgeting decisions" (pp. 83–84).

Each element of outcomes assessment is core faculty work, from defining intended learning outcomes, to designing and conducting institutional outcomes assessments, to closing the loop on the findings. Each element, done well and yielding worthwhile results, is very labor intensive. As an institutional-level project, the work requires the collective effort of faculty and academic administrators, and that makes it even more labor intensive. In my view, Empire State College needs to identify and support closing the loop in outcomes assessment as central to the collective and individual work of the faculty and academic administration.

During my own time as provost, we did not succeed in establishing institutional outcomes assessment as essential faculty work that has enormous implications for academic quality and requires substantial resources. And we are not there yet. Neither are most other colleges and universities. This college is far from alone in under-valuing and under-resourcing outcomes assessment. After years of disinvestment in public higher education, very few institutions have what they need to do this work well. Still, as an experimenting, progressive institution we have even more at stake than most.

To sustain a robust assessment program, and in turn to sustain academic quality in our own terms, the college needs to take four steps. First, the college needs to articulate the central place of outcomes assessment in supporting student learning; and this should occur not once a year, but every time an academic leader – faculty or administrative – has the opportunity. Second, the college needs to have enough full-time faculty to do this labor intensive work and bring it home. That means filling more positions (not fewer). It also means building assessment into faculty responsibilities and recognizing this work in the faculty review process. Third, the college needs to expand greatly its faculty development program. The Center for Mentoring and Learning (CML) is a critical resource for faculty development and, properly resourced, has the potential to support collective faculty work across organizational and academic structures, closing the loop projects and innovation in mentoring, teaching and learning. Fourth, the college needs to staff fully and fund the outcomes assessment function itself.

In my judgment, Empire State College has made significant progress in understanding what it actually takes to do this work on assessment well, and in that sense we have a leadership role to play. In having more to do, we are in the good company of many other institutions.

## CLOSING

This essay explores the implications for learning outcomes assessment of Empire State College's curricular openness and experimentation in teaching and learning, as well as the resources needed for an effective assessment program. Assessment of learning outcomes entails defining learning purposes, designing learning experiences, assessing how well students are doing and making changes based on the results. I have argued that these efforts are compatible with a broadly progressive vision and the college's core values. Further, outcomes assessment for emergent curricula is no more nor less challenging than for prescribed content. I have also argued that the assessment cycle (e.g., the Middle States model) naturally coincides with and supports experimentation with teaching and learning at the college. Thus the mandate to carry out outcomes assessment can support rather than undermine our model. Finally, I have outlined resources needed to sustain both the academic program and assessment of student learning.

Though Empire State College is evidently shifting now toward more pre-defined degree study, its historical role in emergent education positions the institution to provide tremendous leadership in outcomes assessment for open educational arrangements. It would be a loss to the broader higher education community to set that legacy aside.

What does outcomes assessment add to our history of openness and experimentation in individual practice? First, it asks us to make our own individual efforts more explicit, more transparent to ourselves. What are we and our students striving for in terms of what is to be learned? How have we gone about it? How do we know in what ways our designs have led to the hoped-for learning? What changes could we make in our practice based on what we learn? Posing these kinds of questions helps us to achieve our goals and fulfill our promise.

Second, outcomes assessment makes our practice public rather than private, thus opening the door to collegial sharing and questioning of insights and results. Just as we expect scholarly work to be informed by and contribute to a body of work and to be informed by the responses of scholarly peers, so teaching practice benefits from collegial discussion and analysis (Boyer, 1990; Banta & Associates, 2002). With adequate resources and an intentional approach to assessing our students' learning, ESC is well situated to make use of outcomes assessment to support our ongoing experimentation and innovation – all toward strengthening our academic program and enhancing our students' learning. This is, indeed, the collective work of the faculty.

## NOTE

[1] The Office of Research and Evaluation of Empire State College published a "Research Series" that included "bullets," research reports, monographs and handbooks.

## REFERENCES

Banta, T. W., & Associates. (2002). *Building a scholarship of assessment.* San Francisco, CA: Jossey-Bass.

Bonnabeau, R. F. (1996). *The promise continues: Empire State College – The first twenty-five years.* Virginia Beach, VA: The Donning Company Publishers.

Boyer, E. L. (1971, February 8). *A prospectus for a new university college.* Albany, NY: State University of New York.

Boyer, E. L. (1990). *Scholarship reconsidered: Priorities of the professoriate.* Princeton, NJ: The Carnegie Foundation for the Advancement of Teaching.

Chickering, A. W. (1969). *Education and identity.* San Francisco, CA: Jossey-Bass.

Elliott, J. E., & Ostroot, K. (2014a). *Assessment in the major: Community and human services.* Saratoga Springs, NY: SUNY Empire State College.

Elliott, J. E., & Ostroot, K. (2014b). *Assessment in the major: Historical studies.* Saratoga Springs, NY: SUNY Empire State College.

Elliott, J. E., & Ostroot, K. (2014c). *Assessment in the major: Social science.* Saratoga Springs, NY: SUNY Empire State College.

Elliott, J. E., & Ostroot, K. (2014d). *General education assessment review: Basic communication.* Saratoga Springs, NY: SUNY Empire State College.

Elliott, J., & Riley, D. (2013). *Institutional learning outcomes assessment: Comprehensive review of methodologies and results 2006–2012.* Saratoga Springs, NY: Author.

Ewell, P. T. (2013, January). *The Lumina Degree Qualifications Profile (DQP): Implications for assessment* (Occasional Paper #16). Champaign, IL: National Institute for Learning Outcomes Assessment. Retrieved from http://www.learningoutcomesassessment.org/documents/EwellDQPop1.pdf

Hall, J. W., & Kevles, B. L. (Eds.). (1982). *In opposition to core curriculum: Alternative models for undergraduate education.* Westport, CT: Greenwood Press.

MSCHE (Middle States Commission on Higher Education). (2006). *Characteristics of excellence in higher education: Requirements of affiliation and standards for accreditation.* Philadelphia, PA: MSCHE. Retrieved from https://www.msche.org/publications/CHX-2011-WEB.pdf

SUNY Empire State College. (2007). *Individualized prior learning assessment policy and procedures.* Retrieved from http://www.esc.edu/policies/?search=cid%3D36988

SUNY Empire State College. (2014). *Area of study guidelines: An introduction to the area of study guidelines policy.* Retrieved from http://www.esc.edu/policies/?search=cid%3D36241

Suskie, L. (2009). *Assessing student learning: A common sense guide* (2nd ed.). San Francisco, CA: John Wiley & Sons, Inc.

ALAN MANDELL AND KATHERINE JELLY

# AFTERWORD

*Living the Questions to Sustain the Vision*

We have wanted in this volume, not to presume to answer, but to pose the questions that in our view need to be addressed, to sharpen awareness of the issues and challenges that institutions of higher education are facing, and to present as clearly as we can what is at stake in deciding how to meet those challenges. The questions that we have raised throughout – about the philosophical underpinnings, the students we serve, the pedagogies we use, the organizational structures we put in place, and the broader context within which our work takes place – are, we should emphasize again, perennial questions in education; they are questions that continue, and that must continually be addressed. Institutions of higher education – both so-called traditional and alternative – are always dealing with these questions, whether implicitly or explicitly, and are always making choices, whether as a part of their day-to-day planning and implementation or as part of their envisioning and developing new programs or procedures or policies. Empire State College is no different. And this case study bears relevance to all institutions.

In traditional as well as nontraditional institutions change occurs. Institutions are constantly trying new forms, responding to new ideas and pressures of all kinds, and dealing with changing systems of influence and power; they are not static. Rather, institutions of higher education, like all social institutions, are continually in flux – or should be – if they are, in an ongoing way, critically examining their structures, programs, and processes in order to improve. And, it is important to remember, the ways in which an institution grapples with the questions at hand and the "answers" an institution decides upon are never neutral. The decisions made are value-laden and reflect, whether intentionally or not, an institution's purposes and priorities. Thus, it is essential that colleges and universities be keenly aware of the questions they are addressing, of the criteria by which they make judgments, and of the implications of their choices.

Progressive institutions in particular, acting from strong emphases both on experimentation and on positive social change, have a commitment to intentional innovation – whether in regard to pedagogy, curriculum, institutional organization, or academic and administrative processes. Innovation in practice and ongoing evaluation of those experiments are part of their charge and of their responsibility as institutions operating in accord with the tenets of progressive education.

In keeping with this conceptualization of the perennial nature of the questions we have framed, we want to emphasize that the case study we have provided offers only a snapshot in time. At Empire State College, since we began soliciting essays for this volume, largely in response to external pressures, as well as in response to the internal workings of the institution, dramatic change has occurred: Key policies have undergone (and continue to undergo) significant revision. Faculty, for example, no longer write a narrative evaluation of each student's study; they must now assign a grade. Areas of study have been reconfigured as departments to reflect more closely conventional academic disciplines. Program development, which has included more pre-structured programs, has taken the College in new directions. In response to increased demands for accountability, the College is placing more emphasis on institutional assessment that makes public the results of its programs and activities. The College is now developing a collegewide course catalog, which demonstrates a turn to more predesigned study. New organizational structures have reduced the relative autonomy of the regional centers and, in so doing, have altered significantly the processes through which the College administers its programs. And, related to all of these changes, the role of faculty has been closely examined; the very definition of mentoring is under scrutiny; and many faculty have felt it necessary to modify their approaches to mentoring and teaching often in response to growing numbers of students. Over the last few years – precisely during the process of writing and editing this book – Empire State College has been in an especially intense process of re-examination and change.

Yet still, even with the myriad changes taking place, the creative tensions that we have highlighted throughout the book do not go away. Still we must, for example, decide on the appropriate balance between student-designed and faculty-designed study, must work to honor our adult students' independence while offering them guidance, must walk the tightrope between liberal and professional education, must support flexibility in administrative procedures across the College while also maintaining consistency and clarity for students, and for faculty and staff as well. Still we must respond to market realities while also maintaining our mission. Buffeted by external demands and constraints, challenged by internal dynamics and unease, still these creative tensions and the rich questions to which they give rise must be attended to. They remain – for ESC and for all institutions of higher education. Key is to be utterly intentional, as a progressive institution, in how we choose to address these ongoing questions, in how we choose to navigate what are indeed *creative* tensions.

As we have noted elsewhere in this volume, whether it is within a given study, within a program, across different programs, or within the organization of the institution as a whole, a genuinely creative tension can be mined for all the learning and understanding that it can yield. And acknowledging and working with creative tensions is crucial to an institution's existence. Such tensions can be a source of new ideas, new directions and the kinds of debates that can spur us to re-examine what we are doing and to take up new ways of working.

Essays in this book have presented many instances of how these varied, complex creative tensions are alive and valuable.

In regard to underlying philosophical principles, a tension between sometimes competing emphases on access and on individualization, both of which aim to meet student needs, is evident in any number of the essays contained here. As W. Willis lays out this tension in his discussion of the "conflicted legacy" within progressive education itself, he points to the ongoing, and only imperfectly met at ESC, challenge of satisfying both of these goals. And R. Bonnabeau, examining the same tension in his history of the College, outlines the parameters of a debate – in this particular case between faculty-designed, electronically-mediated study, as modeled by the British Open University, and student-directed, face-to-face learning as exemplified by Goddard College – highlighting a tension that in discussions, for example, about new program development and pedagogies, has continued to this day.

Additionally, ongoing debates about how "student-centeredness" is defined and played out in practice and how it can coexist with a wide range of external expectations reflect a key creative tension. As S. Oaks' essay makes clear, the history of educational planning in the College has made us aware of the thin line between meaningful planning in relation to faculty-driven programs of study, and giving attention to the academic, personal and professional goals of our students. So, too, D. Starr-Glass' analysis shows how difficult – but how possible – it is to be appreciative of students' often more conventional academic ways and expectations by posing questions focusing on their particular goals and purposes that had been left unasked in their previous university experiences. And the essay by R. Fraser and S. Mavrogiannis reminds us that even within the classroom format that students take for granted, they can become active participants in their own learning while faculty can gain insight into and respond to their students' lives in imaginative ways.

And in regard to analyzing its place as an alternative institution answering to the requirements of deeply-rooted conventional contexts, a creative tension experienced by many institutions, examples of navigating this challenge abound. As the E. Warzala essay on ESC's place within the State University of New York (SUNY) outlines some of the tensions involved in this challenge, the College must continue both to comply and to experiment: It will need to, and can, work within SUNY's academic requirements while it also finds new ways to sustain for students the flexibility and opportunity for individualization so important to the ESC model. Or, as J. Elliott's essay on assessment looks at the very same tension but in the broader context of accountability to accrediting agencies and the public, first, the College needs to continue to articulate student learning outcomes in ways that both support students in designing their own unique studies and meet external demands for clear indication of the learning to be gained; and, second, we must continue to develop assessment practices that give to students meaningful evaluation of their work while also providing clear demonstration to outside audiences of the quality and learning outcomes of that work.

Yet it is important to recognize that rich creative tensions such as these can also lose their vitality and surrender their creative force. Often without notice, such tensions can slide into divisions – often deep ones – that become solidified into rigid camps of understanding and of practice. In response to a changing context, to the strains and challenges of living with ongoing questions, and to pressures to let progressive principles fade away, some voices, discouraged and impatient with what they perceive as the wasteful slog of addressing the same questions time and time again, descend into distance, disinterest, and cynicism. And such cynicism often succumbs to an acceptance of what is more familiar and to a kind of capitulation to more conventional academic ways, ways that seem so safe and sound – precisely the ways that progressive institutions have sought to question and to re-form.

At Empire State College, for example, broadly framed, conflicts have erupted between those who claim to understand and speak for the need to be practical in the face of grave threats to institutional viability and those who are deemed "idealists" – members of the community who, in the "pragmatists'" eyes refuse to acknowledge the need for compromise of first principles. Such divisions, which can gain a life of their own, make it difficult to carry on constructive conversation and can harden what ought to be *creative* tensions into another kind of tension altogether.

We have seen any number of particular examples of what could be creative tensions sliding into these broadly-framed camps. While those who see themselves, for example, as responding to market realities have argued that we must meet student demand for pre-structured programs and for professional preparation, those who see themselves as maintaining the College's mission have advocated for sustaining our emphasis on individualized degrees and for reaffirming our liberal, critical core. Along similar lines of debate, many have argued that given current realities of public funding, which only exacerbate the dependence on tuition dollars, the College must grow; and if enrollment increases, we must alter our mentoring model in response to those realities. Yet others have maintained that the mentoring model as currently conceived is central to the institution's identity and values. Sadly, rather than considering creatively and collaboratively the changes that might satisfy market realities and, at the same time, allow the College to sustain and renew its mission, debates surrounding key questions such as these have often slipped into precisely the defensive and/or hardened stances we warned against earlier. And when that has happened, when colleagues have succumbed to either/or thinking, the discussions have lost their creative potential; they have lost the opportunity for "living the questions" so necessary to meeting the challenges we face and to advancing the important work of alternative institutions.

How essential it is to be mindful of those points when creative tensions fail to inform ongoing reflection and lose their creativity. Such oppositional thinking dampens imaginative practice, wastes energy, and creates distrust and division among faculty, yes; but more importantly, it diminishes students' learning and education, to say nothing of the outcomes our society so desperately needs: thoughtful, critical, knowledgeable, and skilled citizens and workers.

It is true that it can be particularly difficult for nontraditional institutions to stay the course and to live and grapple with the ongoing and demanding questions they inevitably face. Yet while any of the challenges we are confronting have the potential to undermine, at ESC and other nontraditional institutions, our progressive vision, if mindfully and creatively addressed, they also present us with opportunities for re-examination and experimentation in keeping with our philosophical underpinnings and with our mission and values.

Such mindfulness entails identifying what we need to change and what we need to sustain, a distinction which, we would argue, must be guided by our awareness of and attention to our underlying principles. To neglect the principles or to imagine a kind of pragmatism that claims that any consideration of principles is an unnecessary effort – a distraction from attending to what are taken to be the demands of the moment – is to fall into a sloppy embrace of the whims of the time and to surrender to the huge pressures (economic, political and ideological) that have sometimes pulled academic institutions away from the progressive missions that guided them from the start. The danger here is great.

A set of core values has guided Empire State College and shaped the ongoing debates about institutional direction and pedagogical ways through the inevitable ups and downs of an experimenting public institution within a large state university system. Responsiveness to student purposes; careful listening to the interests and questions of the individual; access to those who have been denied higher education; attention to the melding of past, present and future student experiences; commitment to working outside of conventional disciplinary boundaries; the desire to innovate and experiment; and an ongoing critical responsiveness to the society within which we live and work, which helps to develop capacities to act – these are principles that have animated Empire State College's history. And it is our argument that they should – and can – continue to do so.

We are very aware of the challenging context within which Empire State College, other experimenting and progressive institutions, and, we believe, all of higher education exists right now. There are, as we have said, diminished resources, demands for accountability from multiple sources (from the state, from accrediting agencies, and from the public), and significant competition among colleges and universities (sometimes for the same "nontraditional" students in whom institutions had shown no interest only a decade ago). And there is the prevalent view that only by returning to so-called traditional ways can academic quality be salvaged; as well, there are the myriad cultural tugs to reduce all of higher education to the thinnest versions of workforce training. For some institutions, even surviving such an onslaught is considered a victory; and in many contexts, it seems to be.

It is our argument that despite these constraints, pressures, and challenges, we can sustain a progressive vision and practice. The future of Empire State College and many other institutions committed to an alternative vision of teaching and learning, and to an alternative understanding of the role of higher education in society, is at stake. With full awareness of what often seem to be debilitating impediments, we are arguing that an institution can renew its vision and its commitments if, as we have tried to show in the contributions to this volume, it directly addresses the creative tensions at hand and if change, so vital to any institution, is guided by its core principles.

We should emphasize that the goal here is not to champion a naïve romanticism about some ideal of progressivism; nor is it to construct simplistic dichotomies that might help us stand on ceremony but would shield us from the hard work ahead. Rather, our goal must be to create new forms of communication, community and governance that can thoughtfully and critically engage rich, abiding tensions and imaginatively respond to changing realities, as we work together to sustain and renew a progressive vision of education. In the end, what this takes, for us all, is persistence and an enduring hope amidst so much that might beat us down.

# ABOUT THE CONTRIBUTORS

EDITORS

**Katherine Jelly** recently retired from SUNY Empire State College, where she served as director of the Center for Mentoring and Learning at from 2008–2015. Prior to joining Empire State College, she served as core faculty in education at Goddard College and as director of the Master of Education program at Vermont College, Union Institute & University. She holds a B.A. in history from Yale University, an M.A.T. in English from Harvard University, and an Ed.D. in education from Boston University. Active at the local, state and national levels in education reform and school improvement efforts, Jelly has served on the boards of the Adult Higher Education Alliance; the Vermont Council of Teacher Educators (where she was co-chair, 1999–2001); the Vermont Deans, Directors, and Chairs of Education Group; the Vermont Commission on Educator Quality; the North Dakota Study Group; and the Vermont Standards Board for Professional Educators. Having taught and served as an administrator in progressive higher education for 30 years, she has presented at national and international conferences (including the American Association for Adult and Continuing Education, the Adult Higher Education Alliance, the National School Reform Faculty Research Forum, and the Sloan-C [now the Online Learning Consortium] Blended Learning Conference) on topics related to professional development, adult learning, reflective practice, learning communities, and faculty development in the uses of technology in teaching. She is the author of "Between Individual and Society: An Essential Dialectic in Progressive Education," in S. Schapiro (Ed.), *Higher Education for Democracy* (1999, Peter Lang Publishers). And she has authored: "The Scholarship of Mentoring and Teaching: Mining our Practice and Sharing our Learning" (2012), "Animating Transformation: Progressive Higher Education for Adults at Mid-Life" (with S. Schapiro, 2009), and "As Strong as the Weakest Link: Organizational Development Models and Supporting Blended Learning" (with S. Hayes and C. Whann, 2011). She is currently working on a book, *Layers of Learning*.

**Alan Mandell** is college professor of adult learning and mentoring at SUNY Empire State College. In his more than four decades at the College, he has served as administrator, mentor in the Social Science area and director of the College's Mentoring Institute. Mandell edits the College's journal, *All About Mentoring* and co-edits (with colleague Nan Travers) the first scholarly online journal entirely devoted to the recognition of prior experiential learning, *Prior Learning Assessment Inside Out: An International Journal on Theory, Research and Practice in Prior Learning Assessment* (www.plaio.org). Mandell regularly makes presentations at conferences; facilitates workshops; and serves as a consultant/reviewer on many projects on adult learning, mentoring and experiential learning. With Elana

ABOUT THE CONTRIBUTORS

Michelson, he is the author of *Portfolio Development and the Assessment of Prior Learning* (2nd ed., 2004, Stylus Publishing). With Lee Herman, he has written many essays and book chapters, and has co-authored the book, *From Teaching to Mentoring: Principle and Practice, Dialogue and Life in Adult Education* (2004, RoutledgeFalmer). Over the last several years, Mandell and colleague Xenia Coulter have regularly published on the state of adult learning today, including a chapter, "Academic Mentoring as Precarious Practice" in the edited volume, *Mentoring in Formal and Informal Contexts* (2016, Information Age Publishing). Recognition of his work includes the Eugene Sullivan Award for Leadership given by the Adult Higher Education Alliance (2009), the SUNY Chancellor's Award for Excellence in Teaching (2001) and for Professional Service (1991), and the Empire State College Foundation Award for Excellence in Mentoring (2000). Mandell held the first Susan H. Turben Chair in Adult Learning and Mentoring (2008–2009).

CONTRIBUTORS

**Rebecca Bonanno** is an assistant professor in Community and Human Services at SUNY Empire State College. She has an M.S.W. and a Ph.D. in social welfare from Stony Brook University (SUNY). Bonanno's research and teaching interests include topics related to children and families. She has recently completed a study of human services students' experiences with blended learning at the College.

**Richard F. Bonnabeau** is an associate professor emeritus at SUNY Empire State College. He is currently a visiting professor in its International Programs. He holds his Ph.D. and a master's degree from Indiana University. Bonnabeau joined ESC in 1974 and since that time has been at the College in four different programs, three as a founding faculty member, and has served in various administrative capacities. His history of the college, *The Promise Continues*, was published in 1996 (The Donning Company Publishers) on the occasion of ESC's 25th anniversary. More recently, he has co-authored two chapters on Turkey as part of major global scholarly initiatives: one on ethnopolitcal conflict and the other on gender.

**Cindy Conaway** teaches media studies and communications at SUNY Empire State College's Center for Distance Learning. She earned her Ph.D. in American culture studies from Bowling Green State University and has degrees from Florida State University and the University of Chicago. She writes most about gender and television. Her book in progress is *Girls Who (Don't) Wear Glasses: Brainy, Talented, and Connected Girls on Teen Television*.

**Xenia Coulter**, professor emeritus at SUNY Empire State College, has scholarly interests in psychology and education. With Alan Mandell, she has published many articles, book reviews, and chapters, most recently, "Rediscovering the North American Legacy of Self-Initiated Learning in Prior Learning Assessments," in S. Reushle, A. Antonio, & M. Keppell (Eds), *Open Learning and Formal Credentialing in Higher Education* (2015, IGI Global), and "Academic Mentoring as Precarious Practice," in K. Peno, E. M. Silva Mangiante, & R. A. Kenahan (Eds.), *Mentoring in Formal and Informal Contexts* (2016, Information Age Publishing).

**Barry Eisenberg**, Ph.D. (organizational communication, Temple University), is associate professor in the School for Graduate Studies at SUNY Empire State College and directs the College's M.B.A in Healthcare Leadership program. He also consults with health care organizations on strategic planning, governance, and market development. Eisenberg is a former hospital executive and co-author of *Mastering Leadership: A Vital Resource for Health Care Organizations* (2016, Jones & Bartlett Learning).

**Joyce E. Elliott** joined SUNY Empire State College in 1988 as associate dean (and later served as dean) of the Northeast New York Region. She then served as provost/academic vice president of the College for nine years (including a period as interim president of the College). Before retiring in 2014, she joined the Center for Distance Learning as a mentor in Social Science and women's studies and also served as director of outcomes assessment. Elliott continues to draw on her academic and administrative background in work with community organizations and currently chairs the Planned Parenthood Mohawk Hudson board of directors.

**Rebecca Fraser** is an associate professor at the Harry Van Arsdale Jr. Center for Labor Studies of SUNY Empire State College; she coordinates writing and reading courses. Recently, she contributed a chapter to *Class in the Composition Classroom*, titled "Telling Our Story: 'College Writing' for Trade Unionists," forthcoming from the University of Colorado Press. She is at work on a biography of her grandmother, a pioneer in special education and music therapy.

**Himanee Gupta-Carlson**, a mentor at SUNY Empire State College, develops curricula and does scholarly and community-based research related to hip-hop. She has published several book chapters and articles on hip-hop and developed the online course Hip-Hop America: The Evolution of a Cultural Movement. Her current work extends hip-hop philosophies and practices to rural projects centered on small-scale farming, community outreach via local farmers markets, and a farm-to-fork nutritional education and food sampling program and community garden at a Saratoga Springs, New York food pantry.

**Linda Guyette** was the director of academic support at the Hartsdale location/Hudson Valley Region of SUNY Empire State College from 2007–2014. Guyette has a B.A. in English from the University at Albany (SUNY) and an M.F.A. from Brooklyn College. She has held faculty and administrative positions in higher education for many years. Her areas of interest include Virginia Woolf and women's literature, creative writing, and academic and student support.

**Lee Herman** is a longtime mentor, an educator in humanities, at SUNY Empire State College. His Ph.D. is from The Committee on Social Thought, the University of Chicago. With Alan Mandell, he co-authored *From Teaching to Mentoring: Principle and Practice, Dialogue and Life in Adult Education* (Routledge, 2004). Currently, he is writing a book of philosophy, *Dialogue as the Form of the Good*, and learning to be a fine arts photographer.

**Sarah Hertz** is an assistant professor and mentor at SUNY Empire State College. She has a Ph.D. in finance with a minor in economics from Rutgers University. Her research focuses on pension fund accounting and its implications for disclosure versus recognition and for ethics in business leadership.

**Betty Hurley** is a professor and mentor at SUNY Empire State College. She has a doctorate in mathematics education from the University of Rochester. As a mentor of students studying mathematics and technology, she is particularly interested in how technology can be used as a tool to enhance deeper, collaborative learning. Her current interests include the use of e-portfolios and of open educational resources such as MOOCs (massive open online courses).

**Lorraine A. Lander** is an associate professor at SUNY Empire State College. She holds a B.S. in nursing, an M.A. in applied psychology, and a Ph.D. in human development in educational contexts. She has been a faculty member at ESC for 13 years. Lander's research interests are interdisciplinary and focus on interactions between cognition and motivation in educational settings. Projects have examined achievement motivation, self-directed learning, wisdom as the culmination of cognitive development, and applications of this work to sustainability education.

**Cathy Leaker** is currently the interim executive director for enrollment and retention at SUNY Empire Stare College, having previously served as both faculty mentor and associate dean. She earned her Ph.D. in English from the University of Rochester and has spent much of her career in the field of composition and rhetoric. As a faculty member and administrator, she is committed to ensuring access to public education for underserved populations and has published on equitable practice in prior learning.

**Seana Logsdon** is a director of academic support at SUNY Empire State College and has a B.A. in psychology from SUNY at Geneseo and an M.S. in student personnel administration from SUNY College at Buffalo. She has held both faculty and administrative positions within higher education for over 25 years. She has presented at numerous national conferences such as the College Reading & Learning

Association, National Resource Center First-Year Experience and Students in Transition, American Association for Adult and Continuing Education and more. Her areas of interest include research in interdisciplinary education, academic skills development and motivation.

**Thalia MacMillan** is an assistant professor at SUNY Empire State College, Center for Distance Learning. Her academic background began with a bachelor's degree in human services and psychology, and a master's degree and doctorate in social work from Fordham University. MacMillan's interests and publications are in the areas of coping with life changes, mental health outcomes, gerontology, spirituality, and online learning.

**Sophia Mavrogiannis** is the director of academic support at the Harry Van Arsdale Jr. Center for Labor Studies of SUNY Empire State College. Her research interests include writing center theory, writing across the disciplines/writing in the disciplines theory, sociolinguistics, and class affect. She has presented at national and regional conferences on a variety of topics related to learning support, writing and curriculum design.

**Susan Oaks** is a mentor and coordinator of courses in writing and literature at SUNY Empire State College's Center for Distance Learning. She has a Ph.D. from New York University, an M.A. from the University at Albany (SUNY), and a B.A. from Elmira College. She is interested in the teaching of writing, teaching in online environments, mentoring students, and using e-portfolios as learning tools. In 2015, she presented on "Self-Assessment and Formative Assessment Using Rubrics in an e-portfolio Environment" at the Association for the Advancement of Computing in Education (AACE) Global Learn conference, and in 2013 published a chapter on "Individualized Undergraduate Curricula at Empire State College" in *The College Curriculum* (Peter Lang Publishers).

**Chris Rounds** joined SUNY Empire State College in 1977 as an Eli Lilly Foundation Fellow. He has a Ph.D. in Latin American history from Stony Brook University (SUNY). He served ESC in a number of capacities, including assistant dean for assessment in the Niagara Frontier Region, associate dean for statewide programs, and mentor at the Binghamton location of the Central New York Region. He retired in 2012. Since retiring, he has been active in local organizations and has continued his travels in Mexico. He is currently involved in the creation of a retirement community in the greater Binghamton area.

**David Starr-Glass** is a mentor with International Programs (Prague Program) of SUNY Empire State College and a research fellow at the University of New York in Prague (UNYP), Czech Republic. He has earned master's degrees in business administration, organizational psychology, and education. Starr-Glass has written more than 30 book chapters and 60 peer-reviewed articles, focusing mainly on mentoring, learning, and intercultural education. When not in Prague, he lives in Jerusalem, Israel where he also teaches with a number of local colleges.

**Nan Travers**, Ph.D., director of the Center for Leadership in Credentialing Learning at SUNY Empire State College, has concentrated her research on the policies and practices of adult learning and prior learning assessment, and has published nationally and internationally in these fields. She led the development of the Global Learning Qualifications Framework (GLQF) to assess learning acquired outside of the traditional academic setting. She serves on the board of the Prior Learning International Research Consortium and is a member of the Connecting Credentials Team. Travers is a founding co-editor of *Prior Learning Assessment Inside Out: An International Journal on Theory, Research and Practice in Prior Learning Assessment* (www.plaio.org). She has held a variety of administrative positions at community colleges in Vermont and New Hampshire.

**Edward Warzala** has been a faculty member at SUNY Empire State College since 2002. He earned his Ph.D. in political science at the Rockefeller Graduate School of Public Affairs and Policy, University at Albany (SUNY); a master's degree from New York University; and a B.A. from the SUNY at New Paltz. He served as coordinator of the Batavia Unit of ESC, and is currently teaching in the Public and Social Policy program in the College's School for Graduate Studies and the Center for Distance Learning. Warzala represented ESC on the SUNY University Faculty Senate from 2010 to 2016, during which time he also served on the SUNY Provost's Open SUNY Advisory Committee and the SUNY Shared Services Steering Committee. Warzala's current research examines organizational change in public higher education and the ways in which open and online learning are changing the higher education landscape.

**Christopher Whann** is currently interim executive director for the downstate region of SUNY Empire State College. He previously served at ESC as an associate dean in the Metropolitan New York Region and is an associate professor of Business, Management and Economics. His teaching and research are in business and public and international affairs. His current research is for a textbook (with colleague Renata Kochut) titled *Essentials of Global Business*.

**Lynne M. Wiley** is visiting professor in the School for Graduate Studies of SUNY Empire State College and previously served as associate dean in the College's Genesee Valley Region. She earned her Ph.D. from the University of California at Berkeley specializing in the history and philosophy of higher education, leadership and administration, and moral philosophy. Wiley's academic interests concern ethics and higher education leadership, moral disagreement, and justice as fairness. Her most recent publication is "Bridging Learning Activism and Critical Adult Education" in ESC's occasional paper series, *Explorations in Adult Higher Education* (2016).

ABOUT THE CONTRIBUTORS

**Wayne Carr Willis** is professor emeritus at SUNY Empire State College, where he mentored students in the humanities and social sciences for 37 years. A recipient of ESC's Foundation Award for Excellence in Mentoring, he was a faculty leader in the development of M.A. programs in Policy Studies and Liberal Studies. He holds a Ph.D. in history of American civilization from Brandeis University. He has done research on a wide range of topics in modern American cultural history and has presented at many national and international conferences.

# INDEX

**A**

Academic planning (degree program planning, educational planning), 10, 23, 36, 91, 96, 102, 111–131, 135, 140, 228, 232, 248, 250, 257, 258, 260, 265, 270, 298, 301, 326, 347, 378, 395
  credit-bearing study, 119, 124, 192, 193, 197, 258
  ongoing process, 1, 4, 6, 390
Academic Support, 22, 24, 165, 183–200, 352
  credit-bearing, 78, 115, 119, 124–126, 193, 197, 258
  embedded, 185, 189, 192–200
Access (to higher education), 133, 219, 304, 313, 372
Accountability, 1, 2, 22, 23, 25, 38, 40, 44, 106, 115, 124, 194, 330, 337, 340, 347, 394, 395, 397
Accreditation, 41, 251, 318, 320, 321, 378
Active learning, 113, 122, 133, 134, 160, 167, 179, 383
Adaptive learning, 62, 128–130, 251, 367, 371
Administrative structures, 15, 243, 347
Adult education, 4, 6–15, 30, 46, 67, 76, 133, 134, 275, 380
Adult learning and development, 60, 150
*All About Mentoring*, 36, 41, 66, 72, 162n3, 210
Andragogy, 113
Antioch College, 4, 46
*A Prospectus for a New University College*, 47, 48, 62, 113, 377

Areas of study, 12, 18, 25, 37, 57, 77, 115, 122, 135, 140, 142, 246, 273, 283, 300–302, 306, 308, 309, 376, 378–380, 388, 394
Assessment (outcomes assessment, assessment of student learning), 1, 2, 10, 19, 24, 25, 38, 51, 54, 76, 102, 112, 117, 119, 120, 126, 127, 137–139, 157, 162n5, 165, 189, 190, 194, 195, 199, 206, 215–237, 244, 277, 279, 286–288, 290, 291, 295, 296, 298, 300–302, 307, 337, 347, 355, 361, 369, 372, 375–390
Asynchronous learning, 44, 58, 63, 155, 157, 158, 291, 297, 324, 360, 361, 366
Authority (locus of), 17

**B**

Baritz, Loren, 15, 49–54, 56, 59, 251, 276, 277, 378
Bennington College, 45
Blended learning, 12, 15, 143, 202, 225, 235, 245, 250, 271, 273–292, 310, 358–365, 371
Bonnabeau, Richard, *The Promise Continues*, 244, 252
Boyer, Ernest, 9, 13, 24, 34, 43, 46–49, 53, 62, 63, 82, 113, 134, 138, 146, 202, 243–246, 252–254, 275, 299, 315, 322, 323, 343, 344, 348, 351, 355, 377, 390
Bricolage, 202, 209–211
British Open University, 9, 23, 27, 43–63, 275, 277, 377, 395
Brookfield, Stephen, 4, 7, 221

INDEX

**C**

Center for Distance Learning, 14, 35, 36, 54–60, 87n23, 119, 127, 142, 153–155, 157, 158, 161, 187, 189, 192, 241, 255, 257, 259, 261–268, 270–292, 295, 296, 303–307, 346, 348, 352, 357–360, 362, 365–367
Center for Mentoring and Learning, 36, 343, 389
Certificates, 37, 191, 253, 322–324, 330
Chickering, Arthur, 15, 34, 36, 43–47, 49–52, 54, 56, 58, 59, 115, 134, 138, 146, 248, 251, 275, 276, 377, 378
Civil Rights Movement, 9, 44, 133
Collaborative inquiry, 91
College level learning, 10, 11, 39, 69, 116, 220, 222, 228, 229, 231, 258, 379, 383, 384
Community (in progressive education theory), 4, 5, 49, 377
Connectivism, 125
Conscientization, 7
Constructed knowledge, 10, 17, 65–88
Constructivism in education, 5, 7
Core values (of Empire State College), 9, 11, 15, 36, 62, 91, 128, 152, 155, 187, 203, 241, 242, 247, 295–298, 300, 307–309, 326, 331, 332, 350, 351, 354, 358–360, 363–365, 367, 368, 371–373, 390, 397
Counts, George, 32
Cranton, Patricia, 7
Creative tensions (defined), 1–25, 247, 307, 394
Credentialing, 215, 216, 223–228, 230, 231, 233, 236, 372
Cremin, Lawrence, *The Transformation of the School*, 29
Critical reflection, 6, 7, 222
Critical theory, 7, 8

Critical thinking, 80, 81, 116, 120, 184, 203, 361, 383
Critical writing, 119
Curriculum, 1, 10–12, 14, 17, 19, 24, 31, 45, 50, 67, 73, 75, 80, 81, 86, 88n23, 98, 100, 111, 115, 138, 145, 167–169, 171–173, 175, 177, 178, 194, 199, 202, 217, 218, 228, 236, 245, 247, 249, 251, 276, 278, 298, 300, 301, 306, 309, 316, 317, 323, 325, 330, 366, 376–378, 382, 393
 emergent, 14, 19, 375–390
 pre-set, 30
 pre-structured, 15, 35, 36, 364–368

**D**

Daloz, Laurent, 71, 72, 86n1, 113, 114
Davis, Alan, 36, 59, 61, 224, 251, 296, 342, 348–350, 353
Davis, Forest, 43, 46, 51
Democracy and education, 5, 32, 45
Democratic education, 11, 31, 33, 49, 75, 76
Developmental education, 183, 191
Dewey, John, 4, 5, 7–10, 23, 27, 29–33, 43–45, 65–88, 115, 133, 244, 275, 377
Dialogical inquiry, dialogical teaching and learning, 99, 103, 106, 107
Discipline-based study, 78
Dispersed institutions, 255–272, 308
"Disruptive innovation," 244, 252
Distance learning (online learning), 12, 22, 40, 54–62, 155, 194, 202, 204, 205, 210, 259, 265, 266, 268, 270–292, 304–306, 316, 324, 326, 342, 346–348, 350–355, 360, 371, 376
Diversity, 2, 5, 18–20, 39, 81, 187–189, 201, 202, 206, 210, 211, 247, 248, 259, 263, 269, 271
Downes, Stephen, 125, 129, 362

## E

Emancipatory education, 6, 113
Emergent learning (for credit, outside the academy), 215, 222, 226, 287, 375, 376, 381, 382
*Empire State College Bulletin (1971)*, 32, 96
E-Portfolios, 118, 121, 122, 363, 368, 370, 372
Equity in education, 17, 124, 126
Evaluation of student work, 5
  narrative evaluation, 31, 36, 37, 45, 57, 394
  self-evaluation, 5
Exceptionalism ("Empire exceptionalism" within SUNY), 339–356
Experiential learning, 10, 22, 31, 38, 97, 112, 125, 153, 257, 301, 323
Experimentation in education, 4–9, 11, 15, 20, 41, 62, 347, 375–390
External degree programs, 13

## F

Freire, Paulo, 4, 7, 8, 173
Funding of public education, 1, 22, 268–270, 328, 340, 347, 381, 396

## G

Gamification, 371
Gee, James Paul, 171, 181n10
General education (SUNY general education requirements), 37, 233, 265, 306, 376
Ginsberg, Benjamin, *The Fall of the Faculty: The Rise of the All-Administrative University and Why It Matters*, 308
Globalization of education, 1, 201
Goddard College, 2, 23, 27, 43–63, 275, 395
Gould, Samuel, 46, 47, 63

Governance, higher education, 103, 104
Graduate education and graduate programs at Empire State College, 313, 314
Groups in teaching and learning, group study at Empire State College, 11, 14, 266, 267, 281, 359

## H

Hall, James, 48, 79, 86n3, 88n24, 276, 299, 343, 350, 377
Hancock, Merodie, 34, 248, 252, 296, 349, 350, 352, 354
Harry Van Arsdale Jr. Center for Labor Studies, 11, 12, 14, 24, 165, 167, 178, 303
Health care and higher education institutions, parallels, 314, 326, 328, 333n1, 334n1
Herman, Lee and Mandell, Alan, *From Teaching to Mentoring: Principles and Practice, Dialogue and Life in Adult Education*, 36, 39, 162n3
Hip-hop, 149–162
  battling, 150–152, 157, 160
  cipher, 149–162
  fifth element, 150–152, 155, 157, 158, 162n6
  mixing, 154, 155, 162n5
  sampling, 154, 155, 162n5
Holistic education, 329

## I

Inclusivity in education, 13
"Independent learning strategies," 264, 265, 267
Independent study, 20, 34, 35, 44, 45, 50, 52, 54–56, 58, 67, 72, 82, 85, 100, 119, 133, 138, 140, 144, 157, 159, 192, 194, 243, 245, 251, 265–267, 276, 286, 297, 298, 307, 316, 347, 351, 359, 366, 376

INDEX

Individualized learning, 10, 12, 15, 31, 33, 34, 36, 37, 40, 44, 54, 56, 57, 59, 72, 133, 150, 153, 199, 245, 275, 277, 310
Instructional design, 2, 264, 274, 275, 277, 278, 281, 306, 366
Integration of theory and practice, 5, 6, 8
Interdisciplinary education, 24, 91, 133–146
International education (transnational education, cross-cultural education), 201–211
International programs at Empire State College, 24, 201–211, 296

**J**
Jacobson, John, 52, 54, 55, 58, 94, 115

**K**
Keep-Mills Symposium on Ways of Knowing, 143
Khan Academy, 361
Kilpatrick, William Heard, 4, 43, 45, 275
Knowledge-building, 154, 155, 157–159
Knowles, Malcolm, 4, 67, 113, 195, 275

**L**
Labor education, 178
Labor studies, 12, 168, 169, 173
Learning coaches, 125, 167, 190, 192, 196
Learning contracts, 10, 11, 34, 35, 37, 40, 49, 50, 52, 54, 55, 57, 78, 79, 96, 102, 133, 142, 145, 193, 195, 197, 245, 259, 261, 275–277, 291, 332, 358, 364, 365, 368, 372, 378, 387
Liberal arts education, 96, 119

Lifelong learning, 99, 119, 158, 215, 216, 221–223, 225–227, 234, 236, 377
Light, Richard, 125, 126
Liminal practice, 205–208
Lindeman, Eduard, 4, 74
"Living the questions," 393–398

**M**
Mackintosh, Wayne, 372
MBA program (at Empire State College), 241, 314
Meaning perspectives, 6
Mentoring at Empire State College, 2, 3, 5, 11, 14, 16, 25, 36, 59, 60, 62, 66, 68, 79, 84, 91, 93, 94, 100, 105, 112, 115, 125, 128, 153, 154, 157, 185, 188, 194, 201–205, 217, 218, 220, 222–224, 228, 231, 235, 241, 255, 258, 259, 261, 263, 264, 268, 271, 298, 305–309, 322, 325, 337, 343, 346–348, 355, 357, 358, 373, 382, 394, 396
  definition of, 86n1, 123
  role of, 86n3, 114
Mezirow, Jack, 4, 6, 7, 67, 113, 221
Middle States Commission on Higher Education (MSCHE), 136, 217, 378, 383
MOOCs, cMOOCs, 60, 160, 215, 244, 305, 327, 347, 362, 366, 371
Moore, Joseph, 36, 37, 59, 344–346, 350
Multi-disciplinary education, 84

**N**
National Center on Adult Learning (NCAL), 87n13, 380
New University College, 47–49, 355
Nonformal learning (informal learning), 10, 215

## O

Open education, 215, 353–355
Open SUNY, 59, 61–63, 341, 342, 346–355
Organizational change, 279, 337, 339–356
Organizational development, 350

## P

Participatory decision-making, 5, 8
Perry, Walter, 49, 56, 58, 81
Personal learning environments, 128, 129, 367, 368, 370, 372
Pitkin, Royce, 43–49, 60
Portfolio, 220, 222, 229, 232, 234, 298, 307, 372
Prior learning assessment (PLA, iPLA), 10, 24, 54, 76, 102, 117, 126–128, 157, 162n5, 165, 215–237, 244, 347, 351, 352, 355, 369, 370, 376, 379, 382
Problem-focused education 137
Professionalization in education, 241, 242
Professional study, 15, 20, 74, 320–324, 331
Progressive education, basic tenets, 4
Project-based education, 137

## R

Rationale essay, 57, 111–113, 115, 119–121, 229, 298, 300, 301, 307
Redress, education as redress, 216–219, 221, 225, 227, 228, 231, 235, 236
Reflection, 6, 7, 12, 48, 70, 80, 84, 112, 119, 120, 129, 153–155, 171, 172, 177, 221–223, 255–272, 282, 288, 299, 326, 363, 364, 373, 396
Reflective practice, 8, 260
Remedial education, 183, 191, 196
Rilke, Rainer Maria, 16

## S

Scalability of mentoring model, 268
Schön, Donald, 7, 70
Siemens, George, 125, 374n2
Social justice, 2, 5, 39, 331
Social reconstruction, 5–8, 23
Standardization in education, 1, 2, 22, 24, 72, 137, 138, 268, 269, 346, 365
State University of New York (SUNY), ix, 9, 13, 21, 22, 25, 33, 34, 37, 39, 43, 46–50, 53–56, 58, 59, 61–63, 76, 77, 82, 87n21, 97, 103, 115, 123, 133, 136, 137, 165, 168, 169, 183, 185, 186, 194, 201, 215–237, 243, 244, 248, 253, 260, 265, 269, 274, 275, 295, 298, 299, 303–306, 308, 310, 313, 315, 316, 320, 326, 329–331, 337, 339–356, 358, 359, 376, 377, 379–381, 395
Student-centered pedagogy (student-centered learning), 2, 9, 10, 12, 16, 23, 31, 33, 69, 73, 88, 91, 165, 319
Student citizen, 314, 317–332
Student-directed learning, 251, 317, 323, 395
Students, underprepared, 13, 24, 165, 192, 198, 306
SUNY Learning Network, 59, 61, 342, 351, 354, 355
Supplemental instruction, 193, 195, 196
Systemness, 61, 63, 339, 346, 349, 352

## T

Technologies, uses of in education, 1, 12, 22, 44, 58, 59, 61, 62, 107, 189, 194, 199, 233, 241, 242, 255–272, 307–309, 357–374
Tough, Allen, *The Adult's Learning Projects*, 275

INDEX

Transformative learning, 7, 8, 113, 363
Transmission of knowledge in teaching and learning, 91, 99

**U**
Universities "without walls," 13, 46, 47, 299

**V**
Vocationalization in education, 1, 22, 241, 242

**Z**
Zimpher, Nancy, 47, 61, 63, 253, 339, 341, 342, 345, 346, 348–350, 352–355, 356n1